I0896836

The Mitigation of Marine Plastic Pollution in International Law

World Trade Institute Advanced Studies

Thomas Cottier (World Trade Institute and University of Ottawa)

Editorial Board

Marc Bungenberg (Saarland University/University of Lausanne)
Mira Burri (World Trade Institute and University of Lucerne)
Manfred Elsig (World Trade Institute)
Ilaria Espa (Università della Svizzera italiana)
Joseph Francois (World Trade Institute)
Henning Grosse Ruse-Khan (King's College – University of Cambridge)
Michael Hahn (World Trade Institute)
Markus Krajewski (University of Erlangen-Nuremberg)
Rosa Lastra (Queen Mary University of London)
Luca Rubini (Burmingham University)
Debra Steger (University of Ottawa)
Peter van den Bossche (World Trade Institute)

VOLUME 8

The titles published in this series are listed at *brill.com/wtia*

The Mitigation of Marine Plastic Pollution in International Law

Facts, Policy and Legal Implications

By

Judith Schäli

BRILL
NIJHOFF

LEIDEN | BOSTON

This is an open access title distributed under the terms of the CC BY-NC 4.0 license, which permits any non-commercial use, distribution, and reproduction in any medium, provided the original author(s) and source are credited. Further information and the complete license text can be found at https://creativecommons.org/licenses/by-nc/4.0/

The terms of the CC license apply only to the original material. The use of material from other sources (indicated by a reference) such as diagrams, illustrations, photos and text samples may require further permission from the respective copyright holder.

Open access publication of this book has been made possible by the Swiss National Science Foundation.

The Library of Congress Cataloging-in-Publication Data is available online at https://catalog.loc.gov
LC record available at https://lccn.loc.gov/2022933536

Typeface for the Latin, Greek, and Cyrillic scripts: "Brill". See and download: brill.com/brill-typeface.

ISSN 2405-9331
ISBN 978-90-04-50860-6 (hardback)
ISBN 978-90-04-50861-3 (e-book)

Copyright 2022 by Judith Schäli. Published by Koninklijke Brill nv, Leiden, The Netherlands.
Koninklijke Brill NV incorporates the imprints Brill, Brill Nijhoff, Brill Hotei, Brill Schöningh, Brill Fink, Brill mentis, Vandenhoeck & Ruprecht, Böhlau and V&R unipress.
Koninklijke Brill NV reserves the right to protect this publication against unauthorized use. Requests for re-use and/or translations must be addressed to Koninklijke Brill NV via brill.com or copyright.com.

This book is printed on acid-free paper and produced in a sustainable manner.

Contents

Acknowledgements

This book is based on a doctoral thesis submitted in fulfilment of the requirements for the degree of Doctor iuris at the Faculty of Law of the University of Bern.

The faculty accepted this work as a doctoral thesis on 28 May 2020 at the request of the two reviewers, Prof. Emer. Thomas Cottier and Prof. Emer. Alan Boyle.

I express my deepest gratitude to my husband for his loving attention and inexhaustible patience, as well as my parents, whole family and close friends for their continued support and care. I owe particular gratitude to my supervisors Thomas Cottier and Alan Boyle, who guided, advised and inspired me during my dissertation. I would also like to thank my esteemed colleagues at the Universities of Zurich and Berne and especially at the World Trade Institute for the enriching academic and social exchange, as well as the staff for their support and encouragement. Particular thanks go to Zaker Ahmad, Iryna Bogdanova, Lucia Satragno, Alexander Beyleveld, Rosa Maria Losada, Elisabeth Bürgi Bonanomi, Joëlle de Sépibus, †Rachel Liechti-McKee, Isabel Kölliker, Gabriela Thut-Wermelinger, Rosemarie Coeppicus, Yvonne Peter, Margrit Vetter, Monika Scherler, Sandra Joseph, Melanie Mettler, Susan Kaplan, Morven McLean, Susan Plattner, Dannie Jost, Christian Haeberli, Chrisitan Steiger, Wulfhard Stahl, Franz Perrez, Jin Millea, Christine Kreis, Shaheeza Lalani, Karolis Gudas, Hojjat Khademi, Beatrice Nybert, Clarence Sibiza, Tilman Dralle, Maria Anna Corvaglia, Laura Marschner, Christine Kaufmann, Ilaria Espa, Rodrigo Polanco, Fitzgerald Temmerman, Kateryna Holzer, Sascha Finger, Simona Weber, Sebastien Duyck, Brigitta Imeli, Andrea Schläpfer and Christiane Erkoreka-Fürst. I would like to thank Peter Tobias Stoll, Krista Nadakavukaren Schefer, Duncan French and Oisin Suttle for their valuable feedback.

Further thanks go to Edinburgh Law School, especially James Harrison, Jürg De Pietro from the Plastics Training and Technology Center KATZ, and also Christian Rytka from the Institute of Polymer Engineering at the University of Applied Sciences and Arts Northwestern Switzerland. I am also grateful for the thematic exchange within the UN Environment Advisory Group on Marine Litter and the Massive Open Online Course on Marine Litter. Harald Reichenbach, Chris Jordan, Ferdi Rizkiyanto and many other artists deserve my thanks for the inspiration they have given me through their artistic engagement with marine plastic pollution.

The finalization of this thesis would not have been possible without the support of the Swiss National Science Foundation and my team and superiors at the Federal Office for the Environment. Finally, my thanks go to Hugh Jackson for the professional editing of the text and to Brill/Nijhoff, especially Marie Sheldon, Kelley Baylis and Wai Min Kan for their kind support and the uncomplicated publication process.

I dedicate this work to Ronijah, Iri, Johnny and Kalif, who are my strictest and yet mildest teachers, who made me work on myself more than anyone else, who were first and foremost entitled to the time I invested in this book, who opened up a world to me.

Figures and Tables

Figures

Tables

Abbreviations

ABS	Acrylonitrile-butadiene-styrene
ACC	American Chemical Council
AFS	(International Convention on the Control of Harmful) Anti-fouling Systems on Ships
AHEG	Ad Hoc Open-Ended Expert Group on Marine Litter and Microplastics
ALDFG	Abandoned, lost or otherwise discarded fishing gear
APEC	Asia-Pacific Economic Cooperation
ASEAN	Association of Southeast Asian Nations
ASTM	American Society for Testing and Materials
BAT	Best available technique
BBNJ	(Global instrument on) biodiversity beyond national jurisdiction
BBP	Butyl benzyl phthalate
BC	Basel Convention on the Control of Transboundary Movements of Hazardous Wastes and Their Disposal
BEP	Best environmental practice
BIR	Bureau of International Recycling
BMP	Best management practices
BPA	Bisphenol A (2,2-bis[4-hydroxyphenyl]propane)
BSC	Black Sea Commission
CAMLR	Convention for the Conservation of Antarctic Marine Living Resources
CBD	UN Convention on Biological Diversity
CBDR	Common but differentiated responsibilities
CCAMLR	Commission for the Conservation of Antarctic Marine Living Resources
CEN	European Committee for Standardization
CEP	Caspian Environment Programme
CIEL	Center for International Environmental Law
CISDL	Centre for International Sustainable Development Law
CITES	Convention on International Trade in Endangered Species of Wild Fauna and Flora
CLC	International Convention on Civil Liability for Oil Pollution Damage
CMS	Convention on the Conservation of Migratory Species of Wild Animals
COBSEA	Coordinating Body on the Seas of East Asia
COP	Conference of the Parties
CPPS	Permanent Commission for the South Pacific
CSD	Commission on Sustainable Development
CTE	WTO Committee on Trade and Environment
DBP	Di-n-butyl phthalate

DDE	Dichlorodiphenyldichloroethylene
DEHP	Di(2-ethylhexyl) phthalate
DSB	WTO Dispute Settlement Body
DSU	WTO Dispute Settlement Understanding
EAS	East Asian Seas
EC	European Community
ECEBD	Eastern and Central European Business Development Ltd.
ECOSOC	UN Economic and Social Council
ed./eds.	Editor(s)
EEC	European Economic Community
EEIOA	Environmentally extended input–output analysis
EEZ	Exclusive economic zone
EIA	Environmental impact assessment
EIF	Entry into force
EOP	End-of-pipe
EPA	US Environmental Protection Agency
EPS	Expanded polystyrene
EQO	Environmental Quality Objective
EQS	Environmental Quality Standard
ETS	European Treaty Series
EU	European Union
FAO	UN Food and Agriculture Organization
GATT	General Agreement on Tariffs and Trade
GDP	Gross domestic product
GEF	Global Environmental Facility
GESAMP	Joint Group of Experts on the Scientific Aspects of Marine Environmental Protection
GPA	Global Programme of Action for the Protection of the Marine Environment from Land-Based Activities
GPA	WTO Agreement on Government Procurement
GPML	Global Partnership on Marine Litter
HCH	Hexachlorocyclohexane
HDPE	High density polyethylene
HIPS	High-impact polystyrene
HLPF	High-Level Political Forum on Sustainable Development
HNS	Hazardous and Noxious Substances
HS	Harmonized Commodity Description and Coding System
ICCM	International Conference on Chemicals Management
ICJ	International Court of Justice

ICP	UN Open-Ended Informal Consultative Process on Oceans and the Law of the Sea
ICRW	International Convention for the Regulation of Whaling
ICZM	Integrated Coastal Zone Management
IEEP	Institute for European Environmental Policy
IISD	International Institute for Sustainable Development
ILA	International Law Association
ILC	International Law Commission
ILM	International Legal Materials
IMAP	Integrated Monitoring and Assessment Programme
IMDC	International Marine Debris Conference
IMO	International Maritime Organization
IOC	Intergovernmental Oceanographic Commission
IPCC	Intergovernmental Panel on Climate Change
IPRC	International Pacific Research Center
IR	Polyisoprene
ISA	International Seabed Authority
ISEE	International Society of Environmental Epidemiology
ISO	International Organization for Standardization
ISO/TC	ISO Technical Committee
ISWA	International Solid Waste Association
ITLOS	International Tribunal for the Law of the Sea
IUCN	International Union for Conservation of Nature and Natural Resources
IUPAC	International Union of Pure and Applied Chemistry
IWC	International Whaling Commission
JIS	Japanese Standards Association
LBS	Land-based sources of marine pollution
LCA	Life-cycle assessment
LCSA	Life-cycle sustainability assessment
LDPE	Low-density polyethylene
LLDPE	Linear low-density polyethylene
LME	Large Marine Ecosystem
MAP	Mediterranean Action Plan
MARPOL	International Convention for the Prevention of Pollution from Ships (and the Convention's 1978 Protocol)
MBI	Market-based instrument
MCSD	Mediterranean Commission on Sustainable Development
MED POL	Mediterranean Pollution Assessment and Control Programme
MEDU	Mediterranean Action Plan Coordinating Unit

MEPC	IMO Marine Environment Protection Committee
MFN	Most favoured nation principle
MoP	Meeting of the Parties
MoU	Memorandum of understanding
MPA	Marine Protected Area
MSFD	EU Marine Strategy Framework Directive
n.i.f.	Not in force
NGO	Non-governmental organization
NOAA	US National Oceanic and Atmospheric Administration
NOAEL	No observed adverse effect level
NOWPAP	Action Plan for the Protection, Management and Development of the Marine and Coastal Environment of the Northwest Pacific Region
NPA	National programme of action
OECD	Organisation for Economic Co-operation and Development
OEWG	Basel Convention Open-Ended Working Group
OILPOL	International Convention for the Prevention of Pollution of the Sea by Oil
OJ	Official Journal of the European Union
OPRC	International Convention on Oil Pollution Preparedness, Response and Co-operation
PAH	Polyaromatic hydrocarbon
PAME	Working Group of the Arctic Council on the Protection of the Arctic Marine Environment
para	Paragraph
PBDE	Polybrominated diphenyl ether
PBS	Polybutylene succinate
PC	Polycarbonate
PCA	Permanent Court of Arbitration
PCB	Polychlorinated biphenyl
PCDDs	Polychlorinated dibenzodioxins
PCDFs	Polychlorinated dibenzofurans
PCL	Polycarpolactone
PE	Polyethylene
PEEK	Polyether ether ketone
PEI	Polyetherimide
PEK	Polyetherketone
PEMSEA	Partnerships in Environmental Management for the Seas of East Asia
PERSGA	Regional Organization for the Conservation of the Environment of the Red Sea and Gulf of Aden
PES	Polyethersulfone
PET	Polyethylene terephthalate

PHA	Polyhydroxyalkanoate
PIC	Prior informed consent
PLA	Polylactic acid
PLASTICS	US Plastics Industry Association, former SPI
PMMA	Polymethyl methacrylate
POM	Polyoxymethylene
POP	Persistant organic pollutant
PP	Polypropylene
PPM	Processes and production method
PPS	Polyphenylene sulfide
PRO	Packaging Recovery Organisation
PS	Polystyrene
PSU	Polysulfone
PTFE	Polytetrafluoroethylene
PUR	Polyurethane
PVA	Polyvinylalcohol
PVC	Polyvinylchloride
PVOH	Polyvinylalcohol
RAP	Regional action plan
RAP/ML	Regional action plan on marine litter
RCU	Regional cooperating unit
REACH	(Regulation [EC] No 1907/2006 Concerning the) Registration, Evaluation, Authorisation and Restriction of Chemicals
Res	Resolution
RIC	Resin Identification Code
ROPME	Regional Organization for the Protection of the Marine Environment (of the Persian/Arabian Gulf and Gulf of Oman)
SACEP	South Asia Co-operative Environment Programme
SAICM	Strategic Approach to International Chemicals Management
SBSTTA	CBD Subsidiary Body on Scientific, Technical and Technological Advice
SCM	WTO Agreement on Subsidies and Countervailing Measures
SDG	Sustainable Development Goal
SEA	Strategic Environmental Assessment
SIB	CBD Subsidiary Body on Implementation
SPI	Plastics Industry Association, formerly Society of the Plastics Industry, Inc.
SPREP	Secretariat of the Pacific Regional Environment Programme
SPS	WTO Agreement on the Application of Sanitary and Phytosanitary Measures
STAP	GEF Scientific and Technical Advisory Panel

TBT	WTO Agreement on Technical Barriers to Trade
TFEU	Treaty on the Functioning of the European Union
TPP	Trans-Pacific Partnership Agreement
TRIPS	WTO Agreement on Trade-Related Aspects of Intellectual Property Rights
TTIP	Transatlantic Trade and Investment Partnership
UK	United Kingdom of Great Britain and Northern Ireland
UN	United Nations
UNCC	UN Compensation Commission
UNCCD	UN Convention to Combat Desertification
UNCED	UN Conference on Environment and Development (1992 Rio Conference)
UNCLOS	UN Convention on the Law of the Sea
UNCSD	UN Conference on Sustainable Development (Rio+20)
UNDP	UN Development Programme
UNEA	UN Environment Assembly
UNECE	UN Economic Commission for Europe
UNEP	UN Environment Programme, also referred to as UN Environment
UNESCO	UN Educational, Scientific and Cultural Organization
UNFCCC	UN Framework Convention on Climate Change
UNGA	UN General Assembly
UNOPS	UN Office for Project Services
UNSC	UN Security Council
UNTS	UN Treaty Series
US/USA	United States of America
USMCA	Agreement between the United States of America, the United Mexican States, and Canada of 30 November 2018
UV	Ultraviolet (spectrum of solar radiation)
VCLT	Vienna Convention on the Law of Treaties
VLDPE	Very low-density polythylene
WACAF	West and Central Africa Region
WCED	World Commission on Environment and Development
WCO	World Customs Organization
WHO	World Health Organization
WSSD	World Summit on Sustainable Development
WTO	World Trade Organization
WWF	World Wide Fund For Nature

Table of Cases

Aegean Sea Continental Shelf, Judgment [1978] ICJ Rep 1978 3

Application of the Convention on the Prevention and Punishment of the Crime of Genocide, Preliminary Objections, Judgment [1996] ICJ Rep 1996 595

Australia – Measures Affecting Importation of Salmon (*Australia Salmon*) [1998] Appellate Body Report WT/DS18/AB/R

Australia – Certain Measures Concerning Trademarks, Geographical Indications and Other Plain Packaging Requirements Applicable to Tobacco Products and Packaging (*Australia Plain Packaging*) [2018] Panel Report WT/DS467/R, WT/DS467/R/Add.1 and WT/DS467/R/Suppl.1

Award between the United States and the United Kingdom relating to the rights of jurisdiction of United States in the Bering's sea and the preservation of fur seals (1893) XXVIII Rep Int Arbitr Awards 263

Barcelona Traction, Light and Power Company, Limited (*Belgium v Spain*) *Judgment* [1970] ICJ Rep 1970 3

Brazil – Measures Affecting Imports of Retreaded Tyres (*Brazil Retreaded Tyres*) [2007] Appellate Body Report WT/DS332/AB/R

Canada – Certain Measures Affecting the Automotive Industry (*Canada Autos*) [2000] WTO Panel Report WT/DS139/R, WT/DS142/R

Canada – Certain Measures Concerning Periodicals (*Canada Periodicals*) [1997] Appellate Body Report WT/DS31/AB/R

Canada – Continued Suspension of Obligations in the EC – Hormones Dispute (*Canada Continued Suspension*) [2008] Appellate Body Report WT/DS321/AB/R

Canada – Import, Distribution and Sale of Certain Alcoholic Drinks by Provincial Marketing Agencies [1992] GATT Panel Report DS17/R, BISD 39S/27

Case Concerning Land Reclamation by Singapore in and Around the Straits of Johor (*Malaysia v, Singapore*), *Provisional Measures* [2003] ITLOS case No. 12

Case Concerning Oil Platforms (*Islamic republic of Iran v United States of America*), *Judgment* [2003] ICJ Rep 2003 161

Certain Activities Carried Out by Nicaragua in the Border Area (*Costa Rica v Nicaragua*) *and Construction of a Road in Costa Rica Along the San Juan River* (*Nicaragua v Costa Rica*) [2015] ICJ General List Nos 150 and 152

Chagos Marine Protected Area Arbitration (*Mauritius v United Kingdom*) [2015] PCA (Arbitral Tribunal 2015)

China – Measures Affecting Imports of Automobile Parts (*China Auto Parts*) [2009] Appellate Body Report WT/DS339/AB/R, WT/DS340/AB/R, WT/DS342/AB/R

Commission v Federal Republic of Germany [2004] European Court of Justice C-463/01, 2004 I-11705 Rep Cases

Conservation and Sustainable Exploitation of Swordfish Stocks in the South-Eastern Pacific Ocean (Chile v European Union) [2000] ITLOS case No. 7

Dominican Republic – Measures Affecting the Importation and Internal Sale of Cigarettes (Dominican Republic Cigarettes) [2005] Appellate Body Report WT/DS302/AB/R

East Timor (Portugal v Australia) [1995] ICJ Rep 1995 90

EEC – Measures on Animal Feed Proteins (EEC Animal Feed) [1978] GATT Panel Report BISD 25S/49

European Communities – Measures Affecting Asbestos and Asbestos-Containing Products (EC Asbestos) [2001] Appellate Body Report WT/DS135/AB/R

European Communities – Measures Affecting the Approval and Marketing of Biotech Products (EC Biotech) [2006] WTO Panel Report WT/DS291/R, WT/DS292/R, WT/DS293/R

European Communities – Measures Concerning Meat and Meat Products (Hormones) (EC Hormones) [1998] Appellate Body Report WT/DS26/AB/R

European Communities – Measures Prohibiting the Importation and Marketing of Seal Products (EC Seals Products) [2014] Appellate Body Report WT/DS400/AB/R, WT/DS401/AB/R

European Communities – Regime for the Importation, Sale and Distribution of Bananas (EC Bananas III) [1997] Appellate Body Report WT/DS27/AB/R

European Communities – Trade Description of Sardines (EC Sardines) [2002] Appellate Body Report WT/DS231/AB/R

Gabčíkovo-Nagymaros Project (Hungary v Slovakia), Judgment [1997] ICJ Rep 1997 7

Gabčíkovo-Nagymaros Project (Hungary v Slovakia), Separate Opinion of Vice-President Weeramantry [1997] ICJ Rep 1997 88

Georges Pinson Case (France v United Mexican States) [1928] Arbitral Award 5 RIAA 327

India – Measures Affecting the Automotive Sector (India Autos) [2002] WTO Panel Report WT/DS146/R, WT/DS175/R and Corrigendum

Indus Waters Kishenganga Arbitration (Pakistan v India), Final Award [2013] PCA (Arbitral Tribunal 2015)

Island of Palmas case (Netherlands v USA) [1928] 2 UN Rep Int'l Arb Awards 829

Japan – Customs Duties, Taxes and Labelling Practices on Imported Wines and Alcoholic Beverages (Japan Alcoholic Beverages I) [1987] GATT Panel Report L/6216, BISD 34S/83

Japan – Taxes on Alcoholic Beverages (Japan Alcoholic Beverages II) [1996] Appellate Body Report WT/DS8/AB/R, WT/DS10/AB/R, WT/DS11/AB/R

Korea – Measures Affecting Government Procurement (*Korea Procurement*) [2000] WTO Panel Report WT/DS163/R

Korea – Measures Affecting Imports of Fresh, Chilled and Frozen Beef (*Korea Beef*) [2000] Appellate Body Report WT/DS161/AB/R, WT/DS169/AB/R

Korea – Taxes on Alcoholic Beverages (*Korea Alcoholic Beverages*) [1999] Appellate Body Report WT/DS75/AB/R, WT/DS84/AB/R

Lac Lanoux Arbitration (*Spain v France*) (1957) 7 UN Rep Int'l Arb Awards 281

Legal Consequences for States of the Continued Presence of South Africa in Namibia (*South West Africa*) *Notwithstanding Security Council Resolution 276 (1970), Advirory Opinion* [1971] ICJ Rep 1971 16

Legality of the Threat or Use of Nuclear Weapons in Armed Conflict, Advisory Opinion [1996] ICJ Rep 1996 226

North Sea Continental Shelf, Judgment [1969] ICJ Rep 1969 3

Nuclear Tests (*Australia v France*)*, Dissenting opinion of Judge de Castro* ICJ Rep 1974 372

Nuclear Tests (*Australia v France*)*, Joint dissenting opinion of Judges Onyeama, Dillard, Jiménez de Aréchaga and Sir Humphrey Waldock* ICJ Rep 1974 312

Nuclear Tests case (*New Zealand v France*) *Dissenting opinion of Judge Weeramantry* ICJ Rep 1995 317

Philippines – Taxes on Distilled Spirits (*Philippines Distilled Spirits*) [2011] Appellate Body Report WT/DS396/AB/R, WT/DS403/AB/R

Pulp Mills on the River Uruguay (*Argentina v Uruguay*)*, Judgment* [2010] ICJ Rep 2010 14

Pulp Mills on the River Uruguay (*Argentina v Uruguay*)*, Provisional Measures, Order of 13 July 2006* [2006] ICJ Rep 2006 113

Radlberger and Spitz v Land Baden-Württemberg [2004] European Court of Justice C-309/02, 2004 I-11763 Rep Cases

Request for an Advisory Opinion Submitted by the Sub-regional Fisheries Commission, Advisory Opinion [2015] ITLOS case No. 21

Request for an Examination of the Situation, Dissenting Opinion of Judge Weeramantry [1995] ICJ Rep 1995 312

Request for an Examination of the Situation in Accordance with Paragraph 63 of the Court's Judgment of 20 December 1974 in the Nuclear Tests (*New Zealand v France*) *Case* [1995] ICJ Rep 1995 288

Responsibilities and Obligations of States Sponsoring Persons and Entities with Respect to Activities in the Area (*Advisory Opinion*) [2011] ITLOS (Seabed Disputes Chamber) case No. 17

South China Sea Arbitration (*the Philippines v China*) [2016] Arbitral Tribunal 2016 Case No 2013-19, PCA

Southern Bluefin Tuna Cases (New Zealand v Japan; Australia v Japan), Provisional Measures [1999] ITLOS cases Nos. 3 and 4

Thailand – Restrictions on Importation of and Internal Taxes on Cigarettes (*Thailand Cigarettes*) [1990] GATT Panel Report DS10/R, BISD 37S/200

The Iron Rhine Arbitration (*Belgium v the Netherlands*) [2005] 27 UN Rep Int'l Arb Awards 35

The MOX Plant Case (*Ireland v United Kingdom*), *Provisional Measures* [2001] ITLOS case No. 10

The M/V 'Saiga' Case (*Saint Vincent and the Grenadines v Guinea*) [1999] ITLOS case No. 2

The Rhine Chlorides Arbitration Concerning the Auditing of Accounts (*Netherlands–France*) *Award* PCA 2004

The Trail Smelter Arbitration (*United States v Canada*) [1941] 3 UN Rep Int'l Arb Awards 1905

United States – Import Prohibition of Certain Shrimp and Shrimp Products, Recourse to Article 21.5 of the DSU by Malaysia [2001] Appellate Body Report WT/DS58/AB/RW

United States – Import Prohibition of Certain Shrimp and Shrimp Products (*US Shrimp*) [1998] Appellate Body Report WT/DS58/AB/R

United States – Measures Affecting Alcoholic and Malt Beverages [1992] GATT Panel Report DS23/R, BISD 39S/206

United States – Measures Concerning the Importation, Marketing and Sale of Tuna and Tuna Products (*Tuna II* (*Mexico*)) [2012] Appellate Body Report WT/DS381/AB/R

United States – Restrictions on Imports of Tuna (*US Tuna I*) [1991] GATT Panel Report (unadopted) DS21/R, BISD 39S/55

United States – Restrictions on Imports of Tuna (*US Tuna II* (*EEC*)) [1994] GATT Panel Report (unadopted) DS29/R

United States – Standards for Reformulated and Conventional Gasoline (*US Gasoline*) [1996] Appellate Body Report WT/DS2/AB/R

United States – Taxes on Automobiles [1994] GATT Panel Report DS44/R, BISD 41S/131

Whaling in the Antarctic (*Australia v Japan: New Zealand intervening*), *Judgment* [2014] ICJ Rep 2014 226

Table of International Law Instruments

Additional Protocol to the Abidjan Convention Concerning Cooperation in the Protection and Development of Marine and Coastal Environment from Land-Based Sources and Activities in the Western, Central and Southern African Region (2012 Abidjan Protocol) (adopted on 22 June 2012, not yet in force)

Agreement Between Canada and the United States of America on Great Lakes Water Quality (adopted and entered into force on 22 November 1978) 1153 UNTS 187

Agreement between the United States of America, the United Mexican States, and Canada (USMCA) (signed on 30 November 2018, entered into force on 1 July 2020)

Agreement Establishing the World Trade Organization (Marrakesh Agreement) (adopted on 15 April 1994, entered into force on 1 January 1995) 1867 UNTS 154, 33 ILM 1144 (1994)

Agreement on Subsidies and Countervailing Measures (SCM) Marrakesh Agreement Establishing the World Trade Organization, Annex 1A, 1869 UNTS 14

Agreement on Technical Barriers to Trade (TBT) Marrakesh Agreement Establishing the World Trade Organization, Annex 1A, 1868 UNTS 120

Agreement on the Application of Sanitary and Phytosanitary Measures (SPS) Marrakesh Agreement Establishing the World Trade Organization, Annex 1A, 1867 UNTS 493

Agreement on Trade-Related Aspects of Intellectual Property Rights (TRIPS) Marrakesh Agreement Establishing the World Trade Organization, Annex 1C, as amended on 23 January 2017, 1869 UNTS 299, 33 ILM 1197 (1994)

Agreement Relating to the Implementation of Part XI of the United Nations Convention on the Law of the Sea of 10 December 1982 (Implementing Agreement) (adopted on 28 July 1994, entered into force on 28 July 1996) 33 ILM 1309 (1994)

Amended Nairobi Convention for the Protection, Management and Development of the Marine and Coastal Environment of the Western Indian Ocean (2010 Nairobi Convention) (adopted on 31 March 2010, not yet in force)

Antarctic Treaty (adopted on 1 December 1959, entered into force on 23 June 1961) 402 UNTS 71, 19 ILM 860 (1980)

Basel Convention on the Control of Transboundary Movements of Hazardous Wastes and Their Disposal (1989 Basel Convention) (adopted on 22 March 1989, entered into force on 5 May 1992) 1673 UNTS 126, 28 ILM 657 (1989)

Cartagena Protocol on Biosafety to the Convention on Biological Diversity (Cartagena Protocol) (adopted on 29 January 2000, entered into force on 11 September 2003) 2226 UNTS 208, 39 ILM 1027 (2000)

Consolidated Version of the Treaty on the Functioning of the European Union (TFEU), 2016 OJ C202/1

Convention Concerning the Protection of the World Cultural and Natural Heritage (World Heritage Convention) (adopted on 23 November 19, entered into force on 15 December 1975) 1037 UNTS 151, 11 ILM 1358 (1972)

Convention for Co-operation in the Protection and Development of the Marine and Coastal Environment of the West and Central African Region (1981 Abidjan Convention) (adopted in March 1981, entered into force on 5 August 1984)

Convention for Cooperation in the Protection and Sustainable Development of the Marine and Coastal Environment of The Northeast Pacific (2002 Antigua Convention) (adopted on 18 February 2002, not yet in force)

Convention for the Conservation of Antarctic Marine Living Resources (1980 CAMLR Convention) (adopted on 20 May 1980, entered into force on 7 April 1982) 1329 UNTS 48, 19 ILM 841 (1980)

Convention for the Prevention of Marine Pollution by Dumping from Ships and Aircraft (1972 Oslo Convention) (adopted on 15 February 1972, entered into force on 7 April 1974, later replaced by the 1992 OSPAR Convention) 932 UNTS 3, 11 ILM 262 (1972)

Convention for the Prevention of Marine Pollution from Land-Based Sources (1974 Paris Convention) (adopted on 4 June 1974, entered into force on 6 May 1978, later replaced by the 1992 OSPAR Convention)

Convention for the Protection and Development of the Marine Environment of the Wider Caribbean Region (1983 Cartagena Convention) (adopted on 24 March 1983, entered into force on 11 October 1986) 1506 UNTS 157, TIAS 11085

Convention for the Protection, Management and Development of the Marine and Coastal Environment of the Eastern African Region (1985 Nairobi Convention) (adopted on 21 June 1985, entered into force on 30 May 1996, to be replaced by the 2010 Nairobi Convention)

Convention for the Protection of the Marine Environment and Coastal Area of the South-East Pacific (1981 Lima Convention) (adopted on 12 November 1981, entered into force on 19 May 1986)

Convention for the Protection of the Marine Environment of the North-East Atlantic (1992 OSPAR Convention) (adopted on 22 September 1992, entered into force on 25 March 1998, text last updated on 18 May 2006) 2354 UNTS 67, 32 ILM 1069 (1993)

Convention for the Protection of the Mediterranean Sea against Pollution (1995 Barcelona Convention) (opened for signature on 16 February 1976, entered into force on 12 February 1978, amended on 10 June 1995, amended version entered into force on 9 July 2004) 1102 UNTS 44, 15 ILM 290 (1976)

Convention for the Protection of the Natural Resources and Environment of the South Pacific Region (1986 Noumea Convention) (adopted on 24 November 1986, entered into force on 22 August 1990)

Convention for the Protection of the Rhine Against Chemical Pollution (adopted on 3 December 1976, entered into force on 1 February 1979) 1124 UNTS 375

Convention on Access to Information, Public Participation in Decision-Making and Access to Justice in Environmental Matters (1998 Aarhus Convention) (adopted on 25 June 1998, entered into force on 30 October 2001) 2162 UNTS 447, 38 ILM 517 (1999)

Convention on Civil Liability for Damage Resulting from Activities Dangerous to the Environment (1993 Lugano Convention) (adopted by the Council of Europe on 21 June 1993, not yet in force) 32 ILM 1228, CETS 150

Convention on Environmental Impact Assessment in a Transboundary Context (1991 Espoo Convention) (adopted on 25 February 1991, entered into force on 10 September 1997) 1989 UNTS 309, 30 ILM 802 (1991)

Convention on International Trade in Endangered Species of Wild Fauna and Flora (CITES) (adopted on 3 March 1973, entered into force on 1 July 1975, as amended in 1979 and 1983) 993 UNTS 243

Convention on the Conservation of Migratory Species of Wild Animals (CMS) (adopted on 23 June 1979, entered into force on 1 November 1983) 1651 UNTS 333, 19 ILM 15 (1980)

Convention on the High Seas (entered into force on 30 September 1962) 450 UNTS 11

Convention on the Prevention of Marine Pollution by Dumping of Wastes and Other Matter (1972 London Dumping Convention) (adopted on 13 November 1972, entered into force on 40 August 1975)

Convention on the Protection and Use of Transboundary Watercourses and International Lakes (1992 UNECE Water Convention) (adopted on 17 March 1992, entered into force on 6 October 1996) 1936 UNTS 269, 31 ILM 1312 (1992)

Convention on the Protection and Use of Transboundary Watercourses and International Lakes (UNECE Water Convention) (adopted on 17 March 1992, entered into force on 6 October 1996, as amended in 1999 by the Protocol on Water and Health) 1936 UNTS 269, 31 ILM 1312 (1992)

Convention on the Protection of the Black Sea Against Pollution (1992 Bucharest Convention) (adopted on 21 April 1992, entered into force on 15 January 1994)

Convention on the Protection of the Marine Environment of the Baltic Sea Area (1974 Helsinki Convention) (adopted on 24 March 1974, entered into force on 3 May 1980, later replaced by the 1992 Helsinki Convention)

Convention on the Protection of the Marine Environment of the Baltic Sea Area (1992 Helsinki Convention) (adopted in 1992, entered into force on 17 January 2000)

Convention on Wetlands of International Importance especially as Waterfowl Habitat (1971 Ramsar Convention) (adopted on 2 February 1971, entered into force on 21 December 1975, as last amended on 28 May 1987) 996 UNTS 245, 11 ILM 963 (1972)

Framework Agreement for the Conservation of the Living Marine Resources of the High Seas of the South Pacific (Galapagos Agreement) (adopted on 14 August 2000)

General Agreement on Tariffs and Trade (GATT 1947) (entered into force on 1 January 1948) 55 UNTS 194 1947

General Agreement on Tariffs and Trade (GATT 1994) Marrakesh Agreement Establishing the World Trade Organization, Annex 1A, 1867 UNTS 190, 33 ILM 1153 (1994)

General Agreement on Trade in Services (GATS) Marrakesh Agreement Establishing the World Trade Organization, Annex 1B, 1869 UNTS 183, 33 ILM 1167 (1994)

International Convention for the Prevention of Pollution from Ships (signed on 2 November 1973) 1340 UNTS 184, 12 ILM 1319 (1973) and Protocol Relating to the International Convention for the Prevention of Pollution from Ships (adopted on 17 February 1978) 1340 UNTS 61, 17 ILM 546 (1978), both entered into force on 2 October 1983 (1973/78 MARPOL)

International Convention for the Prevention of Pollution of the Sea by Oil (1954 OILPOL) (opened for signature on 12 May 1954, entered into force on 26 July 1958) 327 UNTS 3

International Convention for the Regulation of Whaling (1946 ICRW) (adopted on 2 December 1946, entered into force on 10 November 1948) 161 UNTS 72

International Convention on Civil Liability for Oil Pollution Damage (1969/92 CLC) (adopted on 29 November 1969, entered into force on 19 June 1975), as replaced by 1992 Protocol (adopted on 27 November 1992, entered into force on 30 May 1996)

International Convention on Liability and Compensation for Damage in Connection with the Carriage of Hazardous and Noxious Substances by Sea

(HNS) (adopted on 3 May 1996, not in force) superseded by its 2010 Protocol (adopted on 30 April 2010, not yet in force)

International Convention on Oil Pollution Preparedness, Response and Co-operation (1990 OPRC) (adopted on 30 November 1990, entered into force on 13 May 1995) 1891 UNTS 51, 30 ILM 735 (1990)

International Convention on the Control of Harmful Anti-fouling Systems on Ships (2001 AFS) (adopted on 5 October 2001, entered into force on 17 September 2008)

International Convention on the Establishment of an International Fund for Compensation for Oil Pollution Damage (adopted on 18 December 1971, entered into force on 16 October 1978, ceased to be in force from 24 May 2002), superseded by its 1992 Protocol (1992 FUND) (adopted on 27 November 1992, entered into force on 30 May 1996)

International Convention Relating to Intervention on the High Seas in Cases of Oil Pollution Casualties (1969 INTERVENTION) (adopted on 29 November 1969, entered into force on 6 May 1975) and Protocol Relating to Intervention on the High Seas in Cases of Pollution by Substances other than Oil (adopted on 2 November 1973)

Kuwait Regional Convention for Cooperation on the Protection of the Marine Environment from Pollution (1978 Kuwait Convention) (adopted on 24 April 1978, entered into force on 1 July 1979)

Kyoto Protocol to the United Nations Framework Convention on Climate Change (Kyoto Protocol) (adopted on 11 December 1997, entered into force on 16 February 2005) UN Doc FCCC/CP/1997/7/Add.1, 2303 UNTS 148, 37 ILM 22 (1998)

Minamata Convention on Mercury (adopted on 10 October 2013, entered into force on 16 August 2017)

Montreal Protocol on Substances that Deplete the Ozone Layer (1987 Montreal Protocol) (adopted on 16 September 1987, entered into force on 1 January 1989, last amended in 1999) 1522 UNTS 3, 26 ILM 1550 (1987)

Nagoya Protocol on Access to Genetic Resources and the Fair and Equitable Sharing of Benefits Arising from their Utilization to the Convention on Biological Diversity (2010 Nagoya Protocol) (adopted on 29 October 2010, entered into force on 12 October 1914)

Paris Agreement (adopted by UNFCCC COP decision on 12 December 2015, entered into force on 4 November 2016) in Report of the COP 21, FCCC/CP/2015/10/Add.1, Annex

Protocol Concerning Pollution from Land-Based Sources and Activities to the Convention for the Protection and Development of the Marine Environment of the Wider Caribbean Region (1999 Aruba Protocol) (adopted on 6 October 1999, entered into force on 13 August 2010)

Protocol concerning the Protection of the Marine Environment from Land-Based Activities in the Red Sea and Gulf of Aden (2005 Jeddah Protocol) (adopted on 25 September 2005, not yet in force)

Protocol for the Protection of the Caspian Sea Against Pollution from Land-Based Sources and Activities to the 2003 Tehran Convention (2012 Moscow Protocol) (adopted on 12 December 2012, not yet in force)

Protocol for the Protection of the Marine and Coastal Environment of the Western Indian Ocean from Land-Based Sources and Activities (2010 Nairobi Protocol) (adopted on 31 March 2010; not yet in force)

Protocol for the Protection of the Marine Environment against Pollution from Land-Based Sources (1990 Kuwait Protocol) (adopted in 1990, entered into force on 2 January 1993)

Protocol for the Protection of the Mediterranean Sea against Pollution from Land-Based Sources (1980 Athens Protocol) (signed on 17 May 1980, entered into force on 17 June 1983) 19 ILM 869 (1980)

Protocol for the Protection of the Mediterranean Sea against Pollution from Land-Based Sources and Activities (1996 Syracuse Protocol) (originally adopted in 1980 in Athens, amended on 7 March 1996, entered into force on 11 May 2008)

Protocol for the Protection of the South-East Pacific against Pollution from Land-based Sources (1983 Quito Protocol) (signed on 22 July 1983, entered into force in 1986)

Protocol on Liability and Compensation for Damage Resulting from Transboundary Movements of Hazardous Wastes and Their Disposal (1999 Basel Protocol) (adopted on 10 December 1999, not yet in force) UN Doc. UNEP/CHW.1/WG/1/9/2

Protocol on Preparedness, Response and Co-operation to Pollution Incidents by Hazardous and Noxious Substances (2000 OPRC-HNS Protocol) (adopted on 15 March 2000, entered into force on 14 June 2007)

Protocol on Protection of the Black Sea Marine Environment Against Pollution from Land Based Sources (1992 Bucharest Protocol) (adopted on 21 April 1992, entered into force on 15 January 1994) 32 ILM 1122 (1993)

Protocol on Strategic Environmental Assessment to the 1991 Espoo Convention (SEA) (adopted on 21 May 2003, entered into force 11 July 2010) Doc. ECE/MP.EIA/2003/2

Protocol on the Protection of the Marine Environment of the Black Sea from Land-Based Sources and Activities (2009 Sofia Protocol) (originally adopted in Bucharest in 1992, fully revised in 2009, revised version not yet in force)

Protocol to the 1972 London Convention on the Prevention of Marine Pollution by Dumping of Wastes and Other Matter (1996 London Protocol) (adopted on 7 November 1996, entered into force on 24 March 2006) 36 ILM 1 (1997)

Regional Convention for the Conservation of the Red Sea and Gulf of Aden Environment (1982 Jeddah Convention) (adopted in February 1982, entered into force on 20 August 1985)

Rotterdam Convention on the Prior Informed Consent Procedure for Certain Hazardous Chemicals and Pesticides in International Trade (Rotterdam PIC Convention) (adopted on 10 September 1998, entered into force on 24 February 2004, last revised on 10 May 2013) 2244 UNTS 393, 38 ILM 1 (1999)

Stockholm Convention on Persistent Organic Pollutants (Stockholm POPs Convention) (adopted on 22 May 2001, entered into force on 17 May 2004, last amended in 2015) 2256 UNTS 119, 40 ILM 532 (2001)

Understanding on Rules and Procedures Governing the Settlement of Disputes (DSU) Marrakesh Agreement Establishing the World Trade Organization, Annex 2, 1869 UNTS 401, 33 ILM 1226 (1994)

United Nations Agreement for the Implementation of the Provisions of the United Nations Convention on the Law of the Sea of 10 December 1982 Relating to the Conservation and Management of Straddling Fish Stocks and Highly Migratory Fish Stocks (adopted on 4 August 1995, entered into force on 11 December 2001) 2167 UNTS 88, 34 ILM 1542 (1995)

United Nations Convention on Biological Diversity (CBD) (opened for signature on 5 June 1992, entered into force on 29 December 1993) 1760 UNTS 79

United Nations Convention on the Law of the Non-navigational Uses of International Watercourses (1997 Watercourse Convention) (adopted on 21 May 1997, entered into force on 17 August 2014) 36 ILM 700 (1997), UN Doc A/RES/51/229 (1997)

United Nations Convention on the Law of the Sea (UNCLOS) (opened for signature on 10 December 1982, entered into force on 16 November 1994) 1833 UNTS 397, 21 ILM 1261 (1982)

United Nations Convention to Combat Desertification in Countries Experiencing Serious Drought and/or Desertification, Particularly in Africa (UNCCD) (opened for signature on 17 June 1994, entered into force on 26 December 1996) 1954 UNTS 3, 33 ILM 1328 (1994)

United Nations Framework Convention on Climate Change (UNFCCC) (opened for signature on 9 May 1992, entered into force on 21 March 1994) 1771 UNTS 107

Vienna Convention for the Protection of the Ozone Layer (1985 Vienna Convention) (adopted on 22 March 1985, entered into force on 22 September 1988) 1513 UNTS 323, 26 ILM 1529 (1987)

Vienna Convention on the Law of Treaties (1969 VCLT) (adopted on 23 May 1969, entered into force on 27 January 1980) 1155 UNTS 331, 8 ILM 679 (1969)

Introduction

A brief survey of the history of plastics reveals that the beginning of what now is often called the plastic age – the point in human history when plastic materials began to permeate our lives – is not as far back in the past as one would possibly think. While my grandparents barely knew synthetic materials in their younger days at all, today's children barely know anything truly free from plastics or their additives: not the gadgets in their hands, not their food, not their bodies, not the landscapes they grow up in or they might visit in their leisure time, not the oceans. And yet, few of our children, and few of us, are truly aware of plastic materials; we are oblivious to their constant presence, to their proximity, their ubiquity, their penetrative power. Or, as it has been said, plastic 'serves so many functions, assumes so many guises, satisfies so many desires, and so quickly recedes into relative invisibility as long as it does its job well'.[1]

Leo Hendrik A. Baekeland (1863–1944), a Belgian-born American chemist, is usually given the credit for inventing the first fully synthetic plastic in 1907.[2] He did probably not imagine what legacy his product would entail. In 1976, the American Chemical Council identified plastics as 'the most used material in the world'.[3] In 2019, annual world plastic production reached about 370 million tonnes or more.[4] Today, plastics are ubiquitous. They not only constitute a major component of our cars, clothes, home appliances and other everyday items, but can be found in our bodies, in beer, honey or sea salt, the gastro-intestinal tract of a broad range of animal species, and in every region of the natural environment, including remote regions such as the Antarctic, or the deep seabed. Of course, Baekeland is but one out of many actors who have been playing their part in this development – a piece of the puzzle that gets in your hands when you embark on the journey towards understanding the phenomenon of the plastic age.

---

1 Jeffrey L Meikle, *American Plastic: A Cultural History* (Rutgers University Press 1995) xiii.

2 See Leo H Baekeland, 'Method of Making Insoluble Products of Phenol and Formaldehyde', US Patent No 942699 (1909).

3 As cited by Charles Moore and Cassandra Phillips, *Plastic Ocean: How a Sea Captain's Chance Discovery Launched a Determined Quest to Save the Oceans* (Avery Trade 2011) 41.

4 Excluding rubbers and synthetic fibres: see PlasticsEurope, 'Plastics – the Facts 2020: An Analysis of European Plastics Production, Demand and Waste Data' (2020) 16. Production of rubbers and fibres amounted to 15 million tonnes and 65 million tonnes, respectively, in 2016: see Julien Boucher and Guillaume Billard, 'The Challenges of Measuring Plastic Pollution' [2019] Field Actions Science Reports 68.

© JUDITH SCHÄLI, 2022 | DOI:10.1163/9789004508613_002
This is an open access chapter distributed under the terms of the CC BY-NC 4.0 license.

The broader history of plastics reveals that their development has been driven by the desire of a number of entrepreneurial spirits to create the perfect material designed for human needs, a substitute to natural materials with enhanced qualities with regard to their designated use. This desire was fuelled by the scarcity of certain natural resources in view of the rapid technological progress during industrialization, and further nourished by advancement in polymer science, the development of the petroleum industry and military needs during wartime. Plastics came along with promises of comfort, safety, joy and prosperity. In many respects, they kept these promises and fulfilled their tasks well. Maybe this is why it took us so long to ask for the price.

Today, plastics can almost perfectly imitate the physical properties, that is to say, the general appearance, the texture, structure, colour, function etc., of other materials such as wood, metal, glass, stone, natural fibres, leather, hair, horn or even human tissue. What is perceived as something made of a specific substance often turns out to be a synthetic imitation. In the production of goods, plastics more and more displace natural materials, either because the former present certain physical or chemical properties the latter do not have (for instance because they are lighter, smoother, transparent, breathable, waterproof or heat resistant) or just because plastics are more abundant and, thus, cheaper. It is precisely these properties of plastics (i.e. the broad range of chemical and physical properties they can have, their versatility, their abundance and their affordability[5]) that have been crucial to their success. A further factor in the success story of plastic materials is the shift towards predominant, consumption-based economic models, which considerably amplified the range of application of plastics: while the materials were once designed to fill a need, their purpose is now to create one.[6] Plastics thus strongly influenced our consumption patterns, our economies and societies. And they changed our planet.

With plastics, many things have become possible that were, at our grandparents' time, inconceivable, and have yet become indispensable to our current way of life. With our new jets, we fly around the globe, just to spend our holidays in distant places. Our gadgets allow us to have group chats about

5 The fact that plastic goods often are available at relatively low prices does not necessarily mean that they entail low costs. When taking into account the externalities of a plastic product (that is to say, the costs imposed on other people and the environment by the production, consumption and disposal of the product), its real costs as paid by the society and the environment have yet to be established.

6 Jon Sterngass and Matthew Kachur, *Great Inventions: Plastics* (World Almanac Library 2006) 17.

ordinary banalities with colleagues, friends and family members across countries and continents. We have, if lucky enough, warm houses, clean toilets and the opportunity to choose between ten different types of yoghurt or vegetables, or convenience food, all kept fresh and clean in plastic films, cups or boxes. Our communication, our mobility, our accommodation and sanitation, our health care system, food supply, professional life and leisure activities all heavily depend on the availability of synthetic materials. Plastics are also a key factor of globalization. With the plastic evolution, many opportunities and amenities of life, goods and services that were once reserved to the upper class or did not exist at all, found their way through all social layers and through so many cultures in the world to the man and woman in the street.

The downside of this development, however, is as far-reaching as its benefits. With the man and woman in the street having cheap plastic products at their disposal, consumption levels rise at an ever-increasing rate. This of course includes the consumption not only of the materials themselves, but also of the resources needed to produce them (and dispose of them), including petroleum or natural gas, clean air, land, water and energy. And then there is the long and durable afterlife of these products. Since many of them are 'destined to break, become obsolete, get used up or become unfashionable'[7] in a very short period of time, the man and woman in the street have no choice but to dispose of what they acquired, to get rid of it, throw it away. Yet, not all our countries, cities, facilities and households are well equipped for the huge amount of trash that is entailed to the raising consumption rates. Overflowing dumping sites have become a regular feature in many townscapes. Streets are full of garbage. And worse still, litter found its way to the natural environment: to the rivers and shores, and from there, to the deep seabed, the Arctic and Antarctic regions and to the wide oceans in-between. In the form of plastic debris of all sizes, palpable or invisibly small, it travels across the oceans, round and round, up and down, and, unless it is consumed by marine wildlife, retained by the depths of the deep sea or cleaned up by a human technology yet to be developed, it will do so for many centuries to come.

One hundred and eleven years passed after Baekeland's famous invention before the former president of the United States of America, Donald Trump, signed a bipartisan bill to save the seas in November 2018[8] and found that: 'a vast, tremendous, unthinkable amount of garbage is floating right into our coast [...]. And we're charged with removing it, which is a very unfair situation.

7 Edward Humes, *Garbology: Our Dirty Love Affair with Trash* (Reprint, Avery 2012) 5.
8 US, Save Our Seas Act of 2018, S.3508, 115th Cong.

It comes from other countries very far away'. He, of course, referred to marine *plastic* garbage in particular, and noted that it is 'also unbelievably bad for the oceans'.[9] While the then acting American president was not primarily known for his interest in environmental issues (and his statement does not illuminate in detail the role of the US in relation to this pollution), it does, in a sense, strike at the heart of the matter: marine plastic pollution is a large-scale problem, vast, tremendous, unthinkable. It is global in scope, transboundary in nature and involves equity concerns. It poses a threat to marine life and human health[10] and entails important economic costs. Under the auspices of the UN, it has been identified as one of the greatest environmental concerns of our time, requiring urgent action.[11]

In a time of elusive global issues such as climate change, biodiversity loss and global migration, one might wonder how something as trivial, familiar and palpable as plastics could become the cause of a global catastrophe. Widespread plastic pollution is the combined effect of these persistent materials and a consumption-based, growth-oriented, linear economic system that needs constant input and generates constant output in the form of emissions and wastes. Projections suggest that, by 2050, about 12 billion tonnes of plastic wastes will be in landfills or the natural environment.[12] Oceans are a major sink of uncollected plastic wastes and unrecoverable microplastic particles as used in products throughout the world. In the 1970s, biologists found the first signs of this type of pollution in the guts of sea birds, such as fulmars. In the 1990s, accumulation zones of floating plastics have been observed in remote areas. Today, it is believed that oceans will contain more plastics than fish (by weight) by 2050 in a business-as-usual scenario.[13] Plastics and microplastics accumulate

9 'Remarks by President Trump at Signing of S. 3508, the "Save Our Seas Act of 2018"' (*The White House*) <https://trumpwhitehouse.archives.gov/briefings-statements/remarks-president-trump-signing-s-3508-save-seas-act-2018/> accessed 19 February 2022.

10 A 2019 study on health-related costs of plastics concludes that: 'Individually, each stage of the plastic lifecycle poses significant risks to human health. Together, the lifecycle impacts of plastic paint an unequivocally toxic picture: plastic threatens human health on a global scale': CIEL, 'Plastic & Health: The Hidden Costs of a Plastic Planet' (2019) 1.

11 See UNGA, 'Report on the Work of the United Nations Open-Ended Informal Consultative Process on Oceans and the Law of the Sea at Its Seventeenth Meeting' (2016) para 12; UNGA Res 72/73 (2017), 'Oceans and the Law of the Sea' para 188; UNEA Resolution 4/6 (2019), 'Marine Plastic Litter and Microplastics' UNEP/EA.4/Res.6 Preamble.

12 Roland Geyer, Jenna R Jambeck and Kara Lavender Law, 'Production, Use, and Fate of All Plastics Ever Made' (2017) 3 Science Advances e1700782.

13 World Economic Forum, 'The New Plastics Economy: Rethinking the Future of Plastics' (2016) 7 <http://www3.weforum.org/docs/WEF_The_New_Plastics_Economy.pdf> accessed 19 February 2022.

in all different media, including soil, fresh water and air. Accumulation in the marine environment, however, has attracted our attention in a special way. The reasons for this special attention may be manifold:

First, marine plastic pollution is visible in its own way, not in the form of a floating plastic island, as it is sometimes portrayed, but through the polluted beaches of holiday destinations of tourists, and in the form of images of deeply symbolic animals such as albatross chicks or baby seals crammed with or perished by plastic garbage. Such images are perceived as disturbing, spread quickly, and have great media effect, which greatly facilitated awareness-raising processes. Second, marine industry sectors and tourism are bothered by the direct economic costs of pollution. Third, the fate of our species is irrevocably linked to the fate of the oceans and their regenerative power. Oceans cover about 70 per cent of the Earth's surface and constitute about 99 per cent of the living space on Earth.[14] They hold an incredible variety of living species and unique ecosystems, most of which have not yet been discovered or explored.[15] For the broad range of ecosystem services they provide,[16] oceans have been referred to as the 'life-support system' of our planet.[17]

Oceans are also the place where life began. As Captain Charles Moore, one of the discoverers of a high-accumulation zone of plastics in the North Pacific Ocean, explained, '[p]lastic flotsam is the end product of an eons-long chain of transformations beginning with the planet's earliest life-forms in the oceans [...] planktonic creatures and algae living and dying over billions of years [transforming into petroleum, the raw material for plastics]. In a sense, our plasticized ocean represents recycling at its most epic, and worst'.[18]

What is the role of law, and especially of international law, in this threefold relationship of plastics, oceans and human behaviour? Since marine

---

14 See Ted Danson, *Oceana: Our Endangered Oceans and What We Can Do to Save Them* (Rodale Books 2011) 2; Sylvia A Earle, *The World Is Blue: How Our Fate and the Ocean's Are One* (Reprint, National Geographic 2010) 127.

15 See Michelle Allsopp and others, *World Watch Report 174: Oceans in Peril: Protecting Marine Biodiversity* (Worldwatch Institute 2007) 7; Earle (n 14) 131–32.

16 Oceans provide an important source of food and generate more than half of the atmosphere's oxygen. They play an important role in climate change mitigation, regulate climate and temperature and degrade pollutants. They include some of the most important transportation routes for world trade and are an important source of income, medicine, energy, water and mineral resources: see Judith Schäli, 'Intergenerational Justice and the Concept of Common Concern in Marine Resource Allocation and Ocean Governance' in Thomas Cottier, Shaheeza Lalani and Clarence Sibiza (eds), *Intergenerational Equity: Environmental and Cultural Concerns* (Brill Nijhoff 2019) 70–72, with references.

17 Astronaut Joe Allen, as cited by Earle (n 14) 265.

18 Moore and Phillips (n 3) 24–25.

plastic pollution is a relatively recent phenomenon that has developed into a global challenge in a short period of time, its reception in the law of nations – a process that is still in full swing – is particularly interesting. It is the aim of this book to illustrate this process as an example of how new complex global challenges can be dealt with under international law. This book is based on the thesis that problems of a global and complex nature, whether environmental or not, can only be tackled effectively in a coherent system and through close cooperation between the actors involved, including the states and relevant bodies of international law, and at all levels of governance.

The example of marine plastic pollution specifically shows that with a growing awareness of the severity of a problem, the political willingness for close cooperation and further development of the legal system also grows. Of course, perception and knowledge with regard to marine plastic pollution have constantly changed within the global political arena during the last couple of years, and so has the political will to address the problem at all levels of governance. While at the start of this project in 2012, existing state obligations had barely been tested against the specific problem of marine plastic pollution, especially from land-based sources, the need for action is no longer questioned, and the idea of an international binding convention dealing with precisely this issue is not as fanciful as it used to be. Against this backdrop, the book shows the central elements of international law relevant to marine plastic pollution from land-based sources, the foundations of the current 'regime', with the regime's various elements and their interplay.

The principal global legally binding instrument dealing with the protection of the seas, i.e. the United Nations Convention on the Law of the Sea (UNCLOS), was concluded prior to public awareness of the scale and impact of plastic pollution. UNCLOS nevertheless contains a number of core provisions which are of fundamental importance for the topic at hand. In fact, UNCLOS has laid the foundations for commitments to protect and preserve the marine environment and its biological diversity. UNCLOS is, therefore, at the core of the legal analysis in this book. This work examines the state obligations that derive from this framework with regard to plastic pollution mitigation from land-based sources when interpreted and applied in the light of contemporary international environmental law.

On the one hand, such a contemporary interpretation takes into account the increasing emergence of global problems, the resolution of which requires close cooperation at different levels of governance, including international. Current global challenges transcend national borders and include collective action problems.[19] Their consideration underscores shared responsibilities and bolsters relevant provisions that call for common, coordinated responses and the creation of global public goods.[20] On the other hand, a contemporary interpretation is based on the objective of a coherent legal system in which individual instruments are interpreted in relation to each other, in a mutually supportive way. Obligations as defined in UNCLOS have evolved in scope and must be interpreted in coherence with other relevant instruments. As the issue of plastic pollution touches on very different areas of international law, both environmental and other, the work also examines the interplay among the main specific instruments, and the role of UNCLOS in the creation of a coherent legal system. Coherence involves in this context the seamless interaction among the various environmental instruments on the basis of mutual support and the interaction with other relevant legal fields such as international trade regulation.

The legal part of this book thus provides a snapshot inventory of the most important obligations and legal instruments in international law in the field of marine plastic pollution mitigation from land-based sources. It also outlines main developments in global policy and the main underlying principles of the regime (2.1). In order to properly evaluate the strengths and shortcomings of the regime, the analysis of international conventions is complemented by an overview of regional frameworks and commitments (2.2). The regional frameworks are an important component of the system, as they serve as testing grounds for different mitigation strategies and approaches, which can potentially be transferred to the global level if need be. The regional schemes also point out some of the regime's main weaknesses in a conspicuous way, especially in geographical terms. The legal part finally contains a chapter on subregional and national implementation (2.3). The chapter illuminates the

---

19 Collective action problems related to the depletion of natural resources often relate to a phenomenon described by Hardin as the 'tragedy of the commons': Garrett Hardin, 'The Tragedy of the Commons' (1968) 162 Science 1243. Hardin uses the picture of a pasture open to all to explain the phenomenon of resource depletion in a system based on the freedom of the commons:

> It is to be expected that each herdsman will try to keep as many cattle as possible on the commons [… and seek] to maximize his gain. […] Each man is locked into a system that compels him to increase his herd without limit – in a world that is limited. Ruin is the destination toward which all men rush, each pursuing his own best interest in a society that believes in the freedom of the commons. Freedom in a commons brings ruin to all.

20 For more information, see Judith Schäli, 'Marine Plastic Pollution as a Common Concern of Humankind' in Thomas Cottier and Zaker Ahmad (eds), *The Prospects of Common Concern of Humankind in International Law* (Cambridge University Press 2021) 153.

coherence issue from a trade law angle and also shows very dynamic, prolific and promising developments at the subregional and national scales.

The legal part is preceded and informed by a fact-based part on plastic materials and wastes (1.1) and plastic pollution in the seas (1.2). The fact-based part provides the necessary basics to understand the policy and legal contexts. With the growing outcry regarding plastic pollution, there has been a proliferation of studies on sources, pathways, distribution and impacts of marine plastics and microplastics in recent years.[21] This paper captures the main findings up to September 2021.

As outlined above, the book also shows how the issue has gained momentum in international fora and has become a priority on the international political agenda. A concluding chapter will wrap up the main findings with regard to the general development of cooperative schemes, their coherence and their effectiveness, and add an outlook in a *de lege ferenda* perspective.

---

21 See UNEP, 'Consolidated Background Paper of the Discussion Papers Presented at the First Meeting of the Ad Hoc Open-Ended Expert Group on Marine Litter and Microplastics, Held in Nairobi from 29 to 31 May 2018' (2018) UNEP/AHEG/2018/2/2 para 18.

PART 1

Plastics and the Marine Environment

Plastics are the materials that mark our age. To meet the legal challenges related to plastics, we need to apprehend their value and difficulties from a social, economic and environmental perspective. We need to take into consideration the impacts they have – on us and our environment in general, and on marine life and ecosystems in particular. This first part of the book is fully dedicated to plastic materials (1) and marine plastic litter (2).

1 About Plastic Materials

In Section A, I will shed light on different aspects of the nature of plastics. Section B takes a close look at the end-of-life stage of plastics and shows whether and to what degree plastics have the ability to biodegrade. The section also deals with waste, which corresponds to the most hazardous and costly life-cycle stage of plastics. Section C deals with life-cycle analysis and impact assessment. Overall, this chapter aims at providing the necessary background knowledge for the legal discussion.

A *The Nature of Plastics*

A basic understanding of the chemical make-up and properties of plastic materials seems to me essential for any discussion on their sustainable use. This includes an idea on challenges related to biopolymers (i) and plastic additives (ii), some of which are of a major concern in the (marine) environment. I will also discuss the economic background and spirit in which plastics have been developed, and explain the main industry sectors in which the materials are used (iii).

i Terms and Definitions

Plastics are made of large molecules, known as polymers. Polymers are chemical substances consisting of long chains or networks of smaller molecules.[22] With the help of heat or specific chemical reactions, a high number of small

22 See Don V Rosato, Marlene G Rosato and Nick R Schott, *Plastics Technology Handbook Volume 1* (Momentum Press 2010) 10. cf Dietrich Braun, *Kleine Geschichte der Kunststoffe* (Carl Hanser Verlag 2013) 5 and 12.

© JUDITH SCHÄLI, 2022 | DOI:10.1163/9789004508613_003
This is an open access chapter distributed under the terms of the CC BY-NC 4.0 license.

molecules are linked together in repeat units, either in the form of long (straight or branched) chains or in the form of networks.[23] It is through this process of polymerization that the individual constituent molecules, which are called monomers,[24] join together to become very large molecules, or macromolecules, as the polymers may be called as well.[25] Both the Greek prefix *poly* (many) and the Latin term *macro* (long, large), allude to the repeat units in the polymers, the resulting length of the molecular structure and their relatively high molecular weight.

Owing to their chemical structure, plastics exhibit special qualities and useful properties. These properties are reflected in their name: the word 'plastic' comes from the old Greek word *plastikos*, which referred to something capable of being moulded or shaped. With the emergence of synthetic materials in the early twentieth century, the plural form 'plastics' came into use, indicating a 'commercial […] class of substances […] worked into shape for use by molding or pressing when in a plastic condition'.[26] Today, when speaking of plastics, we generally refer to polymeric organic materials, most often synthetic, that can be processed by flow during their manufacturing, but become solid in their final stage. When referring to plastics in a narrow sense, materials such as fibres, adhesives and paints – and sometimes also rubbers – are often excluded, even if they mainly meet the definition.[27] In a broader sense, however, these materials are also covered by the term.[28] The term 'resin' is sometimes used as a synonym for plastics or plastic feedstocks.[29]

---

23 Braun (n 22) 29.

24 The words poly- and monomer are derived from the Greek *polys*, meaning 'many', *monos*, 'one', and *meros*, 'part' or 'unit': see 'Polymers', University of Chicago (ed), *Encyclopaedia Britannica*, vol 14 (15th edn, 1977) 764.

25 Rosato, Rosato and Schott (n 22) 10 and 22. The number of monomers within a polymer is highly variable. Some synthetic polymers have hundreds of thousands of repeat units: see Donald L Burdick and William L Leffler, *Petrochemicals in Nontechnical Language* (4th edn, Pennwell Books 2010) 13. The polymerization of different monomers (that is to say, the linking of molecules with different chemical structures to a single sort of macromolecules) is generally referred to as co-polymerization: Braun (n 22) 29.

26 Meikle (n 1) 5.

27 'Plastic', in Jan W Gooch (ed), *Encyclopedic Dictionary of Polymers* (Springer New York 2011) 540–41.

28 See Braun (n 22) 32.

29 In a broad sense, the term is used to 'designate any polymer that is a basic material for plastics': 'Resin', in Gooch (n 27) 624. The term may, however, also refer to 'any of various solid or semisolid amorphous fusible flammable natural organic substances that are […] formed especially in plant secretions, are soluble in organic solvents (as ether) but not in water, [and] are electrical nonconductors': Merriam-Webster Online Encyclopaedia, 'Resin' (2019) <http://www.merriam-webster.com/dictionary/resin> accessed 19 February

Plastics are organic substances, which means that carbon is a main constituent in their chemical structure. Because of its tendency to link up with other atoms and, more importantly, with itself,[30] the carbon atom is predestined to form substances of extremely high molecular weight.[31] This being the case, carbon is the basic constituent of living matter. Organic polymers are thus ubiquitous in nature. There are, however, some differences in the chemical structure of natural organic polymers and the average plastic material. These differences have a fundamental impact on the properties of respective materials, including with regard to their biodegradability.[32]

Natural organic polymers can be found in a vast number of materials, including plant and animal tissue. They are typically synthesized within cells by complex metabolic processes. Some of the most prominent natural polymers are proteins and cellulose, but also lignin, starch, chitin and natural rubber.[33] In contrast, the basic building blocks of *synthetic polymers* are not, as such, taken from nature but are derived from petrochemicals or other substances and are then reacted into a new substance. Natural gas, crude oil and coal are the main

---

2022. Examples for natural resins include amber and shellac, both of which have properties comparable to the ones of synthetic plastics.

30 Each element can (and wants to) link with a fixed number of other atoms of the same or another kind. This specific number is called valence. Carbon has a valence of 4, generally binding itself to four other atoms. In methane (CH_4), the carbon atom is linked to four hydrogen atoms. In ethane (C_2H_6), the two carbon atoms are linked to each other and to three hydrogen atoms each, which amounts to a valence of four. In cases where a carbon atom cannot bind itself to four other atoms, it will form double, or even triple bonds in order to satisfy its valence of four (such as in ethene ($H_2C{=}CH_2$) or acetylene ($H{-}C{\equiv}C{-}H$)). Compounds in which there are only single bonds are called saturated. Compounds with double or triple bounds are unsaturated. They are, as a general rule, more reactive than saturated compounds, since double and triple bonds are weaker than single bonds: see Burdick and Leffler (n 25) 4; Hans Domininghaus, *Die Kunststoffe und ihre Eigenschaften* (Peter Elsner, Peter Eyerer and Thomas Hirth eds, Springer 2005) 22.

31 The molecular weight of a substance corresponds to the sum of the atomic weights of all the atoms in a molecule. For more information, see Walter Gratzer, *Giant Molecules: From Nylon to Nanotubes* (Oxford University Press 2009) ch 1.

32 See Section 1.1.B.i below.

33 *Rubber*, as occurring in nature, mainly consists of long chains of isoprene (also called 2-methyl-1,3-butadiene) and water. It can be found in (or produced of) the juice of specific sorts of trees. Rubber trees exude a milky liquid when their tissue gets hurt. When exposed to air, the liquid, or latex, partially coagulates and gets rubbery. Coagulation of latex can be enhanced by adding certain substances such as formic acid, which is usually done in modern rubber plantations: see Harry Linn Fisher, *Rubber and Its Use* (Chemical Publishing 1941) 25–31. The most common form of polymerized isoprene is *cis*-1,4-polyisoprene: see Jerry Bush and others, 'Synthetic Polyisoprene (IR)', *The Vanderbilt Rubber Handbook* (14th edn, RT Vanderbilt 2010) 57–67.

raw materials which synthetic polymers are currently derived from.[34] Through distillation, cracking or solvent extraction, intermediate products, such as ethylene, are derived from these raw materials.[35] The intermediate products serve as basic ingredients for plastics. The polymerized petrochemicals, together with a broad range of additives, form the feedstock of plastic granules, resins and pellets, which in turn are converted into all different kinds of products.[36]

Natural polymers often are highly complex in their molecular architecture, usually involving oxygen and other elements. By contrast, synthetic polymers, for instance as used in commodity plastics, are typically simple and uniform. This can easily be illustrated by the example of polyethylene, one of the most common plastics. Polyethylene consists of chains of an indefinitely large number of carbon atoms, each linked to two hydrogen atoms (see Figure 1).[37] Importantly, plastic materials consist of much larger (and often more densely packed) polymers than average natural organic materials.[38]

Plastic materials are often classified according to their thermal behaviour.[39] *Thermoplastics* mainly consist of linear chains or of string-like molecules,

---

34 About 90 per cent of all chemicals used in the chemicals industry are derived from petroleum. The produced substances have an extremely broad range of applications. The share of petroleum used in plastics amounts to about 5 per cent of global petroleum consumption: see Maurice Reyne, *Plastic Forming Processes* (John Wiley & Sons 2013) 2.

35 See Rosato, Rosato and Schott (n 22) 22.

36 For more information about the production of synthetic polymers and plastic feedstock, see Burdick and Leffler (n 25) ch 2; Mohamed A Fahim, Taher A Al-Sahhaf and Amal Elkilani, *Fundamentals of Petroleum Refining* (Elsevier 2009); James H Gary and Glenn E Handwerk, *Petroleum Refining* (CRC Press 2001); Moore and Phillips (n 3) 25; Reyne (n 34); Paul R Robinson, 'Petroleum Processing Overview' in Chang S Hsu and Paul R Robinson (eds), *Practical Advances in Petroleum Processing* (Springer New York 2006).

37 The monomer of polyethylene is called ethene or ethylene, which can be derived from ethane. It belongs to the hydrocarbons, a group of carbon molecules consisting of just carbon and hydrogen. The prefix *eth–* indicates that the longest carbon chain counts two carbon atoms. The suffix *–ane* is used when there are just single bonds between the individual atoms. Other members of this group of hydrocarbons are methane (CH_4) (*meth–* referring to one carbon atom), and, accordingly, *prop*ane (C_3H_8), *but*ane (C_4H_{10}), *pent*ane (C_5H_{12}), *hex*ane (C_6H_{14}) and so on. The structural formula of these compounds is very similar, except for the increasing number of carbon atoms in the backbone chain. Because they have just single bonds, methane, ethane, propane etc. belong to the family of *alkanes*, which are also called paraffins, or saturated hydrocarbons. The general formula of alkanes/paraffins is CnH_2n_{+2}. By contrast, the suffix *–ene* is used when there is at least one double-bond within a chain. *Alkenes*, such as ethene, propene, butene, pentene etc., are also known as olefins. Polyethylene, which is made from polymerized ethene, thus belongs to the family of polyolefins: see Gratzer (n 31) ch 2; Burdick and Leffler (n 25) 3.

38 See JA Brydson, *Plastics Materials* (7th edn, Butterworth-Heinemann 1999) 19.

39 See Braun (n 22) 30–32.

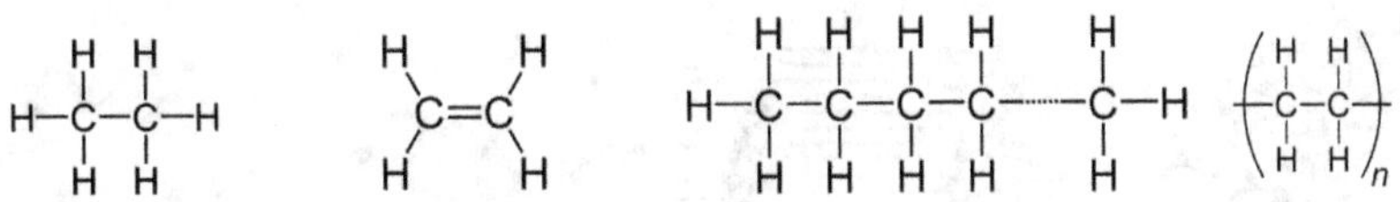

Structural formula of ethane. The dashes represent covalent bonds.

Structural formula of ethene, which is used in the production of polyethylene.

Polyethylene with an indefinite number of carbon atoms in the backbone chain.

Structural formula of polyethylene.

FIGURE 1 Structural formula of ethane, ethene and polyethylene

sometimes with branches on one or the other side of the chain, or on both sides. They are either amorphous, which means that the molecules are not organized in a specific lattice pattern, or semi-crystalline, which means that the molecules are organized in such patterns in some areas but not in others. Some plastics have a fairly high degree of crystallinity, which means that their chain molecules are well ordered to a large extent. Above a certain temperature, the molecules have enough energy to overcome the intermolecular attractions and start to slide past each other. As a result, the material starts to flow.[40] Thermoplastic materials, whether amorphous or crystalline, may therefore be deformed after heating, and remain in shape once they have cooled and become solid again. This process can be repeated for various times. Thermoplastics are the most important class of plastic materials that are commercially available today and include high- and low-density polyethylene (PE), polypropylene (PP), polystyrene (PS), polyvinylchloride (PVC) and many more.

By contrast, *thermosets* consist of three-dimensionally interlinked, close-meshed networks of molecules (see Figure 2). The chemical crosslinks within these networks inhibit the individual molecules from sliding apart and prevent the substance from melting or softening. Only with relatively high temperatures do the molecules chemically decompose.[41] As a result, the material chars. In addition to their heat resistance, thermosets are often quite resistant to solvents such as gasoline, oils or cleaning fluids, and stand out due to their mechanical and physical strength. Thermosetting materials include epoxy resins, phenolic resins, amino resins and polyester resins.

Polymers with wide-meshed networks and chemical crosslinks are called *elastomers* (elastic polymers). The term *rubber* is sometimes used as a synonym of elastomer, but may also refer to a substance that is obtained by coagulating the milky juice of certain plants (the substance is also known as caoutchouc, India rubber or polyisoprene and is, unless processed into hard rubber, one of

40 See Brydson (n 38) 23.

41 See Braun (n 22) 31.

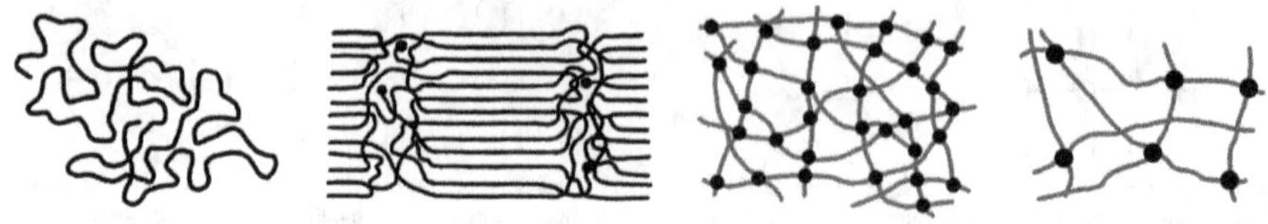

FIGURE 2 Order and arrangement within different types of polymers
ADAPTED BY PERMISSION FROM SPRINGER NATURE CUSTOMER SERVICE CENTRE GMBH: HANS DOMININGHAUS, *DIE KUNSTSTOFFE UND IHRE EIGENSCHAFTEN* BY PETER ELSNER, PETER EYERER AND THOMAS HIRTH EDS, © 2005 SPRINGER

the most important representatives of the elastomers). At room temperature, elastomers are relatively elastic when compared to the close-meshed thermosets. They may be stretched to great extent, and regain their original shape once the stress is released. The degree of elasticity depends on the chemical structure of the chain sections, the number of bonds and crosslinks between the chains, as well as the density of the networks and the respective size of network meshes.[42]

Plastics can also be classified according to their performance. The cheapest and most widely used plastic materials are commonly referred to as *commodity plastics*. Everyday objects, including single-use items and plastic packaging, are usually made from this kind of materials.

The term *engineering plastics* refers to plastics 'that have mechanical, chemical, electrical, and/or thermal properties suitable for industrial applications'. It has been defined as thermoplastic or thermosetting polymers 'that maintain their dimensional stability and major mechanical properties in the temperature range 0–100°C'.[43] Engineering plastics are more expensive than commodity plastics, and are thus produced in lower quantities and preferably used in very specific or high-quality applications.

At the very top of the performance (and price) scale are *high-performance plastics*, which have an extraordinary thermal and/or chemical stability and

42 ibid 32.

43 'Engineering Plastic', in Gooch (n 27) 269. Polyamides and polycarbonates belong to the most important groups of engineering plastics. Ultra-high-molecular-weight polyethylene, acrylonitrile-butadiene-styrene (ABS), polytetrafluoroethylene (PTFE, better known under its commercial name Teflon) and polyoxymethylene (POM), as well as many different kinds of (glass-) fibre reinforced or otherwise enhanced plastics also belong to this group.

may also differ from other plastics in their mechanical properties.[44] Their development, which mostly took place in the 1960s and 1970s, goes hand in hand with contemporary progress in new technologies, especially in the aerospace and nuclear industries, but also in medicine. Because of their premium price and complex processing requirements, there are comparably low quantities of these materials.

While in total there are thousands of different types of plastics, about 85 per cent of the world's plastic materials belong to a group of five different kinds of plastics: PE, PP, PVC, PS and PET.[45] These are the main commodity plastics of today. All of them are typically used in the form of thermoplastics. Ethene, propene, vinyl chloride and styrene are the respective monomers the former four plastics are produced with.[46] As a common denominator, they are usually low-priced and used in huge quantities, including for disposable products and packaging. With very few exceptions, they are made from petrochemicals and do not or badly biodegrade.[47]

---

44 The term high-performance plastics exclusively refers to thermoplastic materials, such as polyphenylene sulphide (PPS), polyethersulfone (PES), polysulfone (PSU), polyether ether ketone (PEEK), polyetherketone (PEK) and polyetherimide (PEI). Some of these materials are obtained by dubbing unreinforced engineering plastics: see 'Engineering Plastic', in ibid 269. See also 'Advanced Resin', in ibid 21.

45 See Anthony L Andrady and Mike A Neal, 'Applications and Societal Benefits of Plastics' (2009) 364 Philosophical Transactions of the Royal Society B: Biological Sciences 1977, 1977; Martin F Lemann, *Waste Management* (Peter Lang 2008) 106; Donald V Rosato, MG Rosato and Dominick V Rosato (eds), *Concise Encyclopedia of Plastics* (Springer Science & Business Media 2000) 415. Besides their traditional names, polymers usually have a structure-based and a source-based name. For the purpose of this book, the traditional names are preferred to the more technical ones. They do not necessarily correspond to the ones as recommended by the International Union of Pure and Applied Chemistry (IUPAC), an international scientific body that is largely recognized as an authority on chemical nomenclature and terminology: see International Union of Pure and Applied Chemistry, *Compendium of Polymer Terminology and Nomenclature: IUPAC Recommendations, 2008* (RSC Pub: IUPAC 2009) 259–60. The abbreviations PE, PP, PVC, PS and PET are based on the 2001 International Standard ISO 1043-1:2001.

46 They have a common chemical structure of CH_2=CH–R, where R stands for a hydrogen atom (ethene), a methyl group CH_3 (propene), a chlorine (vinyl chloride) or a phenyl group (styrene): Burdick and Leffler (n 25) 277; Domininghaus (n 30) 26. For the vinyl group (CH_2=CH–) as a common structure in their monomers, the corresponding polymers (PE, PP, PVC and PS) belong to the so-called vinyl plastics. In plastics literature, however, the term is most often used in reference to polyvinylchloride and its copolymers only: see Gooch (n 27) 795–96. PET is made from ethylene glycol and either dimethyl terephthalate or terephthalic acid.

47 See Section 1.1.B.i below.

In order to facilitate recycling of these materials, the US Society of the Plastics Industry (SPI), rebranded in 2016 as the Plastics Industry Association (PLASTICS), introduced the Resin Identification Code (RIC) system in 1988. The system assigns specific symbols (consisting of numbers from one to seven surrounded by an equilateral triangle) to the different resin types. The five above-mentioned plastic resins are assigned a number from one to six. All other types of resins fall under number seven. The system is broadly used across the world today (see Table 1).[48]

Both the fact that plastics are usually made from non-renewable resources and the fact that the majority of them do not biodegrade raised a call for more sustainable plastic materials. Since the early 1990s, these environmental challenges have been increasingly addressed by both scientists and manufacturers. On the one hand, they promoted plastics from renewable resources such as starch (so-called bio-based plastics).[49] On the other hand, they developed plastics that are, in contrast to conventional synthetic polymers, biodegradable.[50] The term *biopolymers* is sometimes used for both these groups of plastics and may, therefore, cause confusion. In fact, both polymers made from fossil fuel resources and from renewable resources may be biodegradable or not. With regard to the raw material they are produced from and their degradability, polymers can, as a consequence, be assigned to four different groups: non-biodegradable polymers made from non-renewable resources (generally referred to as conventional plastics), biodegradable polymers made from non-renewable resources, and both biodegradable and non-biodegradable polymers made from renewable resources.[51]

48 See ASTM D7611/D7611M-21, 'Standard Practice for Coding Plastic Manufactured Articles for Resin Identification' (2021).

49 See, for instance, Michael Tolinski, *Plastics and Sustainability: Towards a Peaceful Coexistence between Bio-Based and Fossil Fuel-Based Plastics* (John Wiley & Sons 2011); Troy A Hottle, Melissa M Bilec and Amy E Landis, 'Sustainability Assessments of Bio-Based Polymers' (2013) 98 Polymer Degradation and Stability 1898.

50 For a discussion on (bio-)degradability of plastic materials, see Section 1.1.B.i below. See also Madeleine R Yates and Claire Y Barlow, 'Life Cycle Assessments of Biodegradable, Commercial Biopolymers – A Critical Review' (2013) 78 Resources, Conservation and Recycling 54.

51 See Hans-Josef Enders and others, 'Biopolymers as a Source of Energy' (2010) 8 Kunststoffe 83, 83; UNEP, *Biodegradable Plastics & Marine Litter: Misconceptions, Concerns and Impacts on Marine Environments* (UNEP 2015) 16.

TABLE 1 Overview on main commodity plastics

Polyethylene

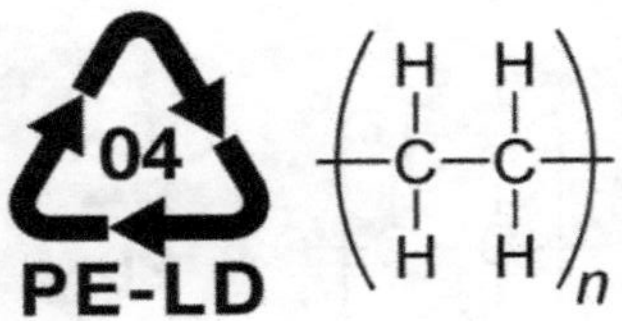

PE, with the recycling codes no. 2 for high-density polyethylene (HDPE) and 4 for low-density polyethylene (LDPE), is the most commonly used plastic of today. It has several benefits, including its extremely low price, excellent electrical insulation properties, chemical resistance, good processability, toughness, flexibility and transparency. Ethene, the main 'raw material' for PE production, was once obtained as by-product from the sugar industry but is now generally derived from ethane and propane, two petrochemical substances. Applications include sacks, carrier bags and other packaging materials, as well as films used in the building sector and for agricultural purposes, toys, containers, cases, buckets and many more items. PE is also often used in personal toiletries, including toothpastes and shower gels.

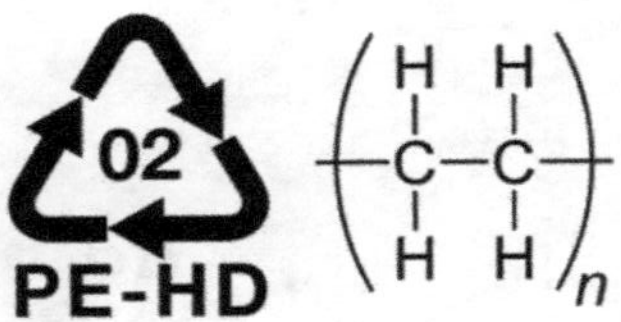

LDPE was discovered by two British chemists in 1933. It is obtained under high pressure and high temperatures. It has a relatively low density and a semi-crystalline, highly branched structure and softens at about 100–110°C. HDPE was developed at the beginning of the 1950s. It is harder than LDPE and has fewer branches, which allows the carbon chains to arrange themselves more closely in crystalline patterns. HDPE has a higher chemical and heat resistance. Further PE materials include linear low-density PE (LLDPE) and very low-density PE (VLDPE).

After the Second World War PE conquered private households, for istance through the famous Tupperware parties in the US, where housewives sold PE food containers among each other and generated their own income. In that, PE played its part in the emancipation of women from the 1950s.

TABLE 1 Overview on main commodity plastics (*cont.*)

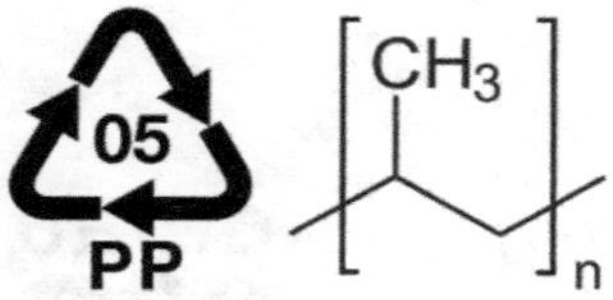

Polypropylene

PP is made from propene, an alkene with the formula C_3H_6. It is identified with recycling code no. 5. Commercial exploitation of PP began in 1957. Today, the plastic is widely used in packaging, medical applications (including underbody applications) and automobile interiors, as well as in mouldings for boxes and cases, luggage and water bottles. PP is moreover used for bottle caps and drinking straws, and as fibres in carpets and other textiles. When exhibiting a high degree of crystallinity, PP is similar to HDPE in its properties, especially with regard to its chemical and electrical resistance, but has a higher melting temperature of at least 160°C. It is moreover stiffer and has high impact strength. Finally, PP is semitranslucent and, therefore, easily colourable. PP with a lower degree of crystallinity is often used in conjunction with bitumen as coating compounds in roofing materials and road construction.

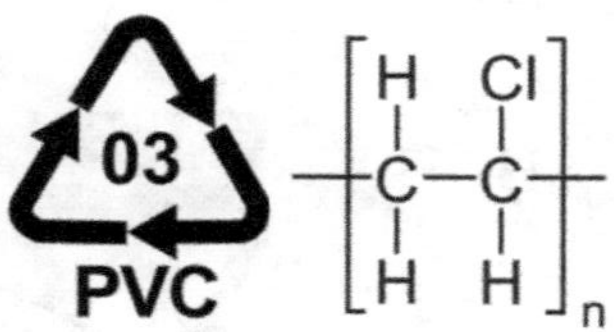

Polyvinylchloride

PVC is made from the monomer vinyl chloride (C_2H_3Cl) and has recycling code no. 3. In 1931, the first commercially available vinyl long-playing record was launched by RCA Victor. In the Second World War, plasticized PVC was used as a substitute for rubber in cable insulation and other applications. After the war, unplasticized PVC was increasingly used in the construction sector. The production of PVC was a welcomed opportunity to make use of the chlorine, an unpleasant by-product of the chemicals industries.

PVC is after PE and PP the third most widely used synthetic polymer. With the help of additives, the material's properties can be tailored to an extremely broad range of applications, including pipes in drinking and waste water systems, insulation of electrical cables, vinyl floor coverings, window profiles, blood bags, toys and clothes.

TABLE 1 Overview on main commodity plastics (*cont.*)

The proportion of stabilizing agents, plasticizers and other additives may be substantial or even predominant in PVC applications. Some of these chemicals are carcinogens or interfere with the human hormone system (as so-called endocrine disruptors) when consumed. Since the vinyl chloride monomer was also found to have toxic effects,[a] regulations on its use (especially in food-contact materials) are common.[b]

Incineration of PVC is highly problematic, since it produces irritant, corrosive and toxic products, especially dioxins and furanes. Mechanical recycling of PVC as a hybrid of inorganic and organic substances and relatively high chlorine content also poses some challenges. In 2000, the European PVC industry established Vinyl2010, a ten-year commitment to improve the environmental performance of PVC. After expiration of the campaign, VinylPlus was launched in 2011 as a follow-up programme with the aim to tackle the sustainability challenges for PVC.

Polystyrene

06 PS

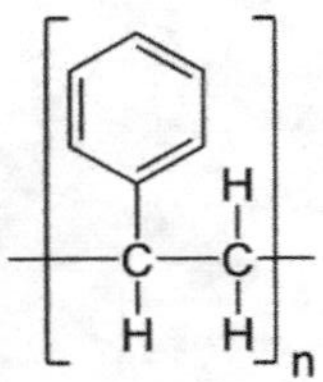

PS is made from styrene (C_8H_8) and has recycling code no. 6. It is a low-cost, easily mouldable, generally transparent, rigid thermoplastic which is broadly in use today. It can be processed into nearly all different kinds of daily objects, including furniture, packaging and toys. It is also common in electronic applications. Since PS is hard and brittle in its pure stage, it is often copolymerized with other monomers. An important example in this regard is the copolymer acrylonitrile-butadiene-styrene (ABS), discovered in 1948. Foamed PS, or expanded PS (EPS), was developed in the 1950s and is often used as a foam in packaging materials and building insulation, as well as in disposable cups and plates. High-impact polystyrene (HIPS) is a more resistant and flexible material often used as a substitute for natural rubber.

TABLE 1 Overview on main commodity plastics (*cont.*)

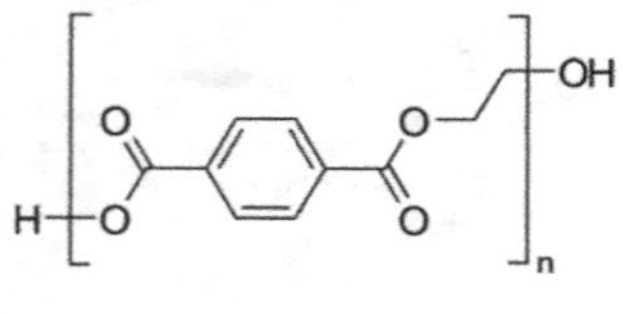

Polyethylene terephthalate

PET, with resin identification code no. 1, is one of the most common members of the family of polyesters. Injection-moulded PET is transparent and amorphous. At room temperature, it is relatively rigid, strong and scratch-resistant, but sensitive to hot water and alkaline solutions. When heated above 80°C, it may shrink and change colour.

PET was first patented in the UK in 1941. Disposable PET beverage bottles were first marketed in 1977 and soon became one of the most important applications of PET. PET is also of great importance in the production of fibres and films. PET films are widely used in food packaging because of their tensile strength, chemical resistance, light weight and elasticity. PET played a pioneering role in the recycling industries.

Further developments

A broad range of engineering plastics has been developed along with the commodity plastics. Applications range from security glass, commonly known as Plexiglas, made from polymethyl methacrylate (PMMA) to nylon stockings, polytetrafluoroethylene (PTFE) pot coatings, marine fisheries made from thermosetting polyurethanes (PURS) and CDS made from polycarbonate.

To this day, the sector is characterised by constant change and an ever faster pace of development. Many new plastics have been invented, and processing improved. Important developments have taken place in the fields of engineering plastics and high-performance plastics. Overall, today's plastics are amazingly versatile.

TABLE 1 Overview on main commodity plastics (*cont.*)

	In 1988, SPI introduced triangular resin identification codes for different plastic materials, in order to facilitate recycling. In the 1980s and early 1990s, the first biodegradable plastics were developed. In 1990, the first light-emitting polymers were discovered at Cambridge University. New, biocompatible synthetic polymers are broadly used in medical applications, including in implantable drug delivery systems, tissue transplants or bone fixation devices.[c] *Since the 2000s, synthetic nanomaterials have been on the advance and are increasingly used in commercial applications. More recently, the development of shape-memory-polymers (SMP), that is, of polymers that are able to return from a deformed state to their original shape, has stimulated research for self-repairing and intelligent materials.*[d] *As for processing methods, 3D printing (also called additional manufacturing) is one of the sensations of today.*[e]

a See Hermann M Bolt, 'Vinyl Chloride – a Classical Industrial Toxicant of New Interest' (2005) 35 Critical Reviews in Toxicology 307, passim; Brydson (n 38) 312; Braun (n 22) 219.

b See, for instance, Council Directive 78/142/EEC of 30 January 1978 on the approximation of the laws of the Member States relating to materials and articles which contain vinyl chloride monomer and are intended to come into contact with foodstuffs [1978] OJ L44/15.

c Severian Dumitriu, 'Preface' in Severian Dumitriu (ed), *Polymeric Biomaterials* (2nd edn, CRC Press 2001) v. See also S Sershen and J West, 'Implantable, Polymeric Systems for Modulated Drug Delivery' (2002) 54 Advanced Drug Delivery Reviews 1225, 1225; Jeffery A Williams and others, 'Synthetic, Implantable Polymers for Local Delivery of IUdR to Experimental Human Malignant Glioma' (1998) 42 International Journal of Radiation Oncology*Biology*Physics 631, 631.

d Andreas Lendlein and Steffen Kelch, 'Shape-Memory Polymers' (2002) 41 Angewandte Chemie International Edition 2034.

e See, for instance, Bettina Wendel and others, 'Additive Processing of Polymers' (2008) 293 Macromolecular Materials and Engineering 799.

ii Additives

Only very few synthetic polymers are suitable for commercial uses in solid products in their pure state. Most of them need the addition of adjuvants or auxiliary substances in order to meet the technological requirements in specific applications. With the same type of monomers (for instance vinyl chloride) but different modifiers or additives, a great variety of plastic products can be produced (e.g. rigid pipes, soft cable coats or foam plastic).[52]

Additives and other auxiliary ingredients may have the form of solids, rubbers, liquids or gases. They do not appreciably alter the chemical structure of the parent polymer. Yet, they alter the mechanical, electrical or chemical properties of the latter, and either facilitate processing or improve the final product's qualities and appearance. They work, for instance, as fillers, plasticizers and softeners, UV or heat stabilizers, blowing agents, reinforcing agents, nucleating agents, cross-linking agents, lubricants, antistatics, antimicrobials, antioxidants, flame retardants, colourants or optical brighteners, impact modifiers, initiators or catalysts. In the form of heat and light stabilizers or antioxidants they delay chemical ageing. The substances may be added to the plastic feedstock at different production stages, both by plastic producers and converters.[53]

There is an extremely broad range of substances that are used as additives in plastics production. The list includes a high number of organic substances, such as phthalates,[54] that are derived from petrochemicals and other materials by the chemical industry. Moreover, asbestos and other inorganic compounds can be found among the additives, including chlorine- and bromine-based flame retardants, barium, cadmium, lead or zinc compounds. The exact recipe for the production of a specific plastic is often a trade secret and remains unknown to the customers of the converting industry. While processing the materials into final products, converters may again add adjuvants to their feedstock.

Different sorts of additives as used in the industry have relevance beyond the mere processability of the resins they are used in or the performance and

---

52 See Brydson (n 38) 124.

53 See Hans-Georg Elias, *Makromoleküle: Band 4: Anwendungen von Polymeren* (4th edn, John Wiley & Sons 2003) 17; Gordon L Robertson, *Food Packaging: Principles and Practice* (3rd edn, CRC Press 2013) 44. For detailed information about different types of additives, see Brydson (n 38) 126–157; Robertson 44–47.

54 Phthalates are used as plasticizers. Different types include Di(2-ethylhexyl) phthalate (DEHP), Butyl benzyl phthalate (BBP) and Di-n-butyl phthalate (DBP).

appearance of the final good, especially for their (alleged) environmental and human health impacts. Some additives are not or only weakly bonded to the polymer and may be released into the air or leach out of the plastic material into whatever material surrounds it, be it the ground or groundwater in landfills or the ocean.[55] Migration of phthalates such as DEHP from PVC blood bags into stored human blood and their accumulation in biological systems, including humans, was first discovered in the 1970s.[56] Further studies revealed that no blood transfusions were necessary for phthalates to accumulate in human bodies; simple contact with everyday plastic goods would suffice for most people to have detectable amounts of phthalates in their bodies.[57] Human exposure is, for instance, due to inhalation of contaminated house dust (or, more general, indoor air) and dermal absorption of lipophilic phthalates, as well as to the use of personal care products (skin and sun creams, shampoos etc.).[58] Ingestion of contaminated food products is another route of exposure: when used in food packaging materials, additives can migrate into the food and be

55 US Environmental Protection Agency, T Randall Curlee and Sujit Das, *Plastic Wastes: Management, Control, Recycling, and Disposal – Pollution Technology Review No. 201* (Noyes Data Corp 1991) 159; Matthias Wormuth and others, 'What Are the Sources of Exposure to Eight Frequently Used Phthalic Acid Esters in Europeans?' (2006) 26 Risk Analysis 803, 803.

56 See Rudolph J Jaeger and Robert J Rubin, 'Plasticizers from Plastic Devices: Extraction, Metabolism, and Accumulation by Biological Systems' (1970) 170 Science 460; 'Migration of a Phthalate Ester Plasticizer from Polyvinyl Chloride Blood Bags into Stored Human Blood and Its Localization in Human Tissues' (1972) 287 New England Journal of Medicine 1114; WH Lawrence and others, 'A Toxicological Investigation of Some Acute, Short-Term, and Chronic Effects of Administering Di-2-Ethylhexyl Phthalate (DEHP) and Other Phthalate Esters' (1975) 9 Environmental Research 1. See also Ronald Green and others, 'Use of Di(2-Ethylhexyl) Phthalate-Containing Medical Products and Urinary Levels of Mono(2-Ethylhexyl) Phthalate in Neonatal Intensive Care Unit Infants' (2005) 113 Environmental Health Perspectives 1222.

57 A study found that most of the 500 plastic products sampled leached chemicals that had estrogenic activity: see Chun Z Yang and others, 'Most Plastic Products Release Estrogenic Chemicals: A Potential Health Problem That Can Be Solved' (2011) 119 Environmental Health Perspectives 989.

58 See Jennifer J Adibi and others, 'Prenatal Exposures to Phthalates among Women in New York City and Krakow, Poland' (2003) 111 Environmental Health Perspectives 1719, 1719; Ursel Heudorf, Volker Mersch-Sundermann and Jürgen Angerer, 'Phthalates: Toxicology and Exposure' (2007) 210 International Journal of Hygiene and Environmental Health 623, 623–64; John D Meeker, Sheela Sathyanarayana and Shanna H Swan, 'Phthalates and Other Additives in Plastics: Human Exposure and Associated Health Outcomes' (2009) 364 Philosophical Transactions of the Royal Society B: Biological Sciences 2097, 2098; Wormuth and others (n 55) 805.

directly consumed by humans.[59] Widespread contamination of bottled mineral water was demonstrated by a study in 2008.[60]

Phthalates and other chemicals used in the manufacturing of plastics, including bisphenol A (BPA),[61] are released into the environment throughout their life cycle, including production, use and disposal.[62] In the past few decades, they have become ubiquitous in the environment, where they persist.[63] They are absorbed by animals and humans and can have a wide range of effects on their health, development and reproducibility. Minimal exposure level and doses required to cause harmful effects are highly controversial.

The Swiss physician and father of toxicology, Paracelsus (1493–1541), once found that the dose makes the poison. This means that, at a certain level of concentration, any substance has toxic effects, but at concentration levels sufficiently low, it remains harmless. Based on this presumption, modern toxicologists have generally assumed that, for any substance, there is a level of exposure for below which no effect can be observed. This level is generally referred to as *no observed adverse effect level*, or NOAEL.[64] In order to determine the NOAEL of a chemical substance, a number of animal toxicity tests are

59 See Adibi and others (n 58) 1719; CIEL, 'Plastic & Health' (n 10) 35; Robertson (n 58) ch 22; Wormuth and others (n 55) 805–08.

60 Martin Wagner and Jörg Oehlmann, 'Endocrine Disruptors in Bottled Mineral Water: Total Estrogenic Burden and Migration from Plastic Bottles' (2009) 16 Environmental Science and Pollution Research 278.

61 BPA, or 2,2-bis(4-hydroxyphenyl)propane, is a high-production volume chemical which is mainly used in epoxy resins, polycarbonate plastics or polyester-styrene. It is used in impact-resistant safety equipment, baby bottles, food cans and containers, dental fillings, pipes and water storage tanks, as well as in protective coatings, adhesives and flame retardants. When BPA degrades into its monomeric form, it can leach out from the material into food and other contact materials: see Antonia M Calafat and others, 'Exposure to Bisphenol A and Other Phenols in Neonatal Intensive Care Unit Premature Infants' (2009) 117 Environmental Health Perspectives 639, 639; Meeker, Sathyanarayana and Swan (n 58) 2106.

62 See, in general, CIEL, 'Plastic & Health' (n 10).

63 See Adibi and others (n 58) 1719; Gerald Ankley and others, 'Overview of a Workshop on Screening Methods for Detecting Potential (Anti-) Estrogenic/Androgenic Chemicals in Wildlife' (1998) 17 Environmental Toxicology and Chemistry 68, 68; Calafat and others (n 61) 639; T Colborn, FS vom Saal and AM Soto, 'Developmental Effects of Endocrine-Disrupting Chemicals in Wildlife and Humans'. (1993) 101 Environmental Health Perspectives 378, 378; Meeker, Sathyanarayana and Swan (n 58) 2097; Robertson (n 58) 624; Wormuth and others (n 55) 803.

64 See Anderson JM Andrade and others, 'A Dose-Response Study Following in Utero and Lactational Exposure to Di-(2-Ethylhexyl)-Phthalate (DEHP): Non-Monotonic Dose-Response and Low Dose Effects on Rat Brain Aromatase Activity' (2006) 227 Toxicology 185, 185, including references.

usually carried out. In the tests, the substance is used on animals (such as rats or chimpanzees) in different, relatively high doses, until no adverse effects can be observed. To account for intra- and inter-species variations, a number of uncertainty factors are taken into account in the determination of acceptable human exposure levels, which are extrapolated from the NOAEL.[65] As long as environmental exposure (caused by the production, use or disposal of plastic goods) is far below the so defined threshold, no precautionary measures are usually postulated.

This way of proceeding is increasingly criticized by scientists, who have found evidence for a broad range of low-dose effects by different substances. Based on their observations, they have questioned the traditional (monotonic) dose–response concepts. In particular, substances that interact with the hormone system (endocrine system) of an organism (so-called endocrine disruptors[66]) supposedly have non-monotonic dose–response relationships, with maximum effects both at high and low doses,[67] contrary to what Paracelsus's statement suggests. Evidence indicates that they can be biologically active at concentrations far below the defined thresholds, including at doses within the range of current exposures in wildlife and humans.[68]

There is a broad range of studies on human and wildlife exposure to phthalates and BPA.[69] Studies on health effects both in wildlife and humans are

65 See ibid 185–86.

66 Endocrine-disrupting chemicals can be defined as 'exogenous agents that interfere with the production, release, transport, metabolism, binding, action, or elimination of the natural hormones in the body responsible for the maintenance of homeostasis and the regulation of developmental processes' or 'an exogenous substance that causes adverse health effects in an intact organism, or its progeny, secondary to changes in endocrine function': Ankley and others (n 63) 68.

67 See Laura N Vandenberg and others, 'Hormones and Endocrine-Disrupting Chemicals: Low-Dose Effects and Nonmonotonic Dose Responses' (2012) 33 Endocrine Reviews 378, 404.

68 See Andrade and others (n 64) 186; Ankley and others (n 63) 70; Wade V Welshons and others, 'Large Effects from Small Exposures. I. Mechanisms for Endocrine-Disrupting Chemicals with Estrogenic Activity'. (2003) 111 Environmental Health Perspectives 994, 994; Frederick S vom Saal and Wade V Welshons, 'Large Effects from Small Exposures. II. The Importance of Positive Controls in Low-Dose Research on Bisphenol A' (2006) 100 Environmental Research 50; Vandenberg and others (n 67).

69 See, for instance, Adibi and others (n 58); Ankley and others (n 63); Calafat and others (n 61); Green and others (n 56); Meeker, Sathyanarayana and Swan (n 58); Jennifer David Peck and others, 'Intra- and Inter-Individual Variability of Urinary Phthalate Metabolite Concentrations in Hmong Women of Reproductive Age' (2009) 20 Journal of Exposure Science and Environmental Epidemiology 90; RA Rudel and others, 'Correlations Between Urinary Phthalate Metabolites and Phthalates, Estrogenic Compounds 4-Butyl Phenol

more complex and tend to be limited in scope.[70] Adverse effects of endocrine-disrupting chemicals have been observed in birds, fish, shellfish and mammals, particularly humans.[71] Phthalates were reported to have potential disturbing effects on the development and function of sexual organs, decrease reproduction levels and fertility, delay sexual maturity and cause morphologic abnormalities and malformations in the external genitalia, as well as increase the risk of endocrine-related cancer.[72] Some data supports the hypothesis that exposure to endocrine disruptors at environmentally relevant concentrations can have transgenerational effects, which become apparent in the child- or adulthood of the next generation only.[73] Foetal or childhood exposure may lead to altered sex differentiation, effects on neurological and reproductive development and increased risk of cancer.[74] High concentrations of phthalates were also reported to increase asthma risk, rhinitis and eczema in

---

and o-Phenyl Phenol, and Some Pesticides in Home Indoor Air and House Dust' (2008) 19 Epidemiology ISEE 2008 Conference Abstracts Supplement; Sheela Sathyanarayana and others, 'Baby Care Products: Possible Sources of Infant Phthalate Exposure' (2008) 121 Pediatrics e260; Laura N Vandenberg and others, 'Human Exposure to Bisphenol A (BPA)' (2007) 24 Reproductive Toxicology 139; Wormuth and others (n 55). According to a WHO study of 2019, leaching of additives from microplastics in freshwater and drinking water is negligible. However, if microplastics are ingested through drinking-water, the relative potential for the additives to leach from microplastics in the gastrointestinal tract is also poorly understood and needs further research: WHO, *Microplastics in Drinking-Water* (2019) ix.

70 For a critical overview on BPA-related studies, see Vandenberg and others (n 69).

71 See T Colborn and C Clement, 'Chemically-Induced Alterations in Sexual and Functional Development: The Wildlife/Human Connection' [1992] Advances in Modern Environmental Toxicology (USA); Colborn, vom Saal and Soto (n 63); Eun-Joo Kim, Jung-Wk Kim and Sung-Kyu Lee, 'Inhibition of Oocyte Development in Japanese Medaka (Oryzias Latipes) Exposed to Di-2-Ethylhexyl Phthalate' (2002) 28 Environment International 359. For an overview of tests on mammalian, fish, reptilian, amphibian, avian, and invertebrate models, see, in general, Ankley and others (n 63).

72 See Adibi and others (n 58) 1719, including references; Andrade and others (n 64) 189–90; Meeker, Sathyanarayana and Swan (n 58) 2097, including references. See also Sathyanarayana and others (n 69) e260–61; Shanna H Swan, 'Environmental Phthalate Exposure in Relation to Reproductive Outcomes and Other Health Endpoints in Humans' (2008) 108 Environmental Research 177.

73 See Shanna H Swan and others, 'Decrease in Anogenital Distance among Male Infants with Prenatal Phthalate Exposure' (2005) 113 Environmental Health Perspectives 1056, 1056. Adverse effects of phthalates and bisphenol A have also been demonstrated at environmentally relevant concentrations: see, for instance, D Andrew Crain and others, 'An Ecological Assessment of Bisphenol-A: Evidence from Comparative Biology' (2007) 24 Reproductive Toxicology (Elmsford, N.Y.) 225.

74 See Meeker, Sathyanarayana and Swan (n 58) 2097–98, including references.

children.[75] Moreover, it has been discussed whether exposure to endocrine disruptors could be a possible cause for or contributing factor of widespread increase in obesity, as some animal experiments suggest,[76] or neurodevelopmental disorders.[77] Prenatal exposure to BPA was reported to cause changes in mammary and prostate gland development, with several effects on the children's later development and health.[78] Higher BPA concentrations in human blood were also associated with cardiovascular diagnoses and diabetes or recurrent miscarriages.[79]

Because of the observed effects, traditional dose–response concepts are claimed to be invalid for substances that imitate hormones or otherwise interact with the endocrine system. This might be explained by the very nature and functionality of the endocrine system, which is tuned to respond to very low doses of hormones.[80] Also, conventional methods of determining acceptable exposure levels usually neglect possible impacts of the prolonged timing of exposure (given that human and wildlife exposure is constant or increasing throughout the years and effects on exposed individuals and populations may only become apparent in adulthood or offspring). Traditional methods furthermore neglect the fact that simultaneous exposure to a multitude of endocrine-disrupting agents might bear additional and widely unpredictable health risks, which are not taken into account in tests which involve single substances only.[81]

Regulations on the use and declaration of additives in plastic products vary widely around the world. Additives, including phthalates and BPA, do not always have to be declared in the final product. Measures such as bans and declaration requirements usually require a high degree of scientific certainty regarding the harmful effects of a substance on human health or the environment. For example, the European Union banned the use of six phthalate softeners in PVC children toys designed to be placed in the mouth by small

75 See Wormuth and others (n 55) 804.

76 See Jerrold J Heindel and Frederick S vom Saal, 'Role of Nutrition and Environmental Endocrine Disrupting Chemicals during the Perinatal Period on the Aetiology of Obesity' (2009) 304 Molecular and Cellular Endocrinology 90, 90 and 93.

77 See Theo Colborn, 'Neurodevelopment and Endocrine Disruption' (2004) 112 Environmental Health Perspectives 944.

78 See Calafat and others (n 56) 639, including references.

79 See IA Lang and others, 'Association of Urinary Bisphenol a Concentration with Medical Disorders and Laboratory Abnormalities in Adults' (2008) 300 JAMA 1303, 1305–06; Meeker, Sathyanarayana and Swan (n 58) 2106; Vandenberg and others (n 69) 147.

80 See Vandenberg and others (n 67) 383.

81 See Swan (n 72) 183.

children.[82] Sensitive products also include food packaging materials, medical devices and baby bottles.

iii Economic and Social Considerations

The development of plastic materials is intertwined with the development of our economic models, lifestyles and social perceptions, and the history of war. Given the importance of plastics to our lives, it seems surprising that the first fully synthetic materials were developed just over a century ago. Their appearance at the beginning of the twentieth century heralded a new era of economic and social development. The development of plastics was boosted by new insights in polymer science, the shift from plant sources and coal to petroleum as a raw material in their production, the rapid growth of the petroleum industry[83] and the development of new processing machines, such as the extruder and injection moulding machines.[84] At the very basis of these developments, however, was the constant need for new materials with specific properties, such as insulating properties for cables. This need was driven by technological progress in the automotive, electronic, telephony, aircraft and cinematic industries and the two world wars. When plastic demand threatened to collapse after the wars, plastic manufacturers started to target the private sector. Advertising campaigns were launched to bring plastic products

---

82 European Parliament and Council Regulation (EC) No 1907/2006 of 18 December 2006 concerning the Registration, Evaluation, Authorisation and Restriction of Chemicals (REACH) [2006] OJ L396/1 Annex XVII.

83 See CIEL, 'Fueling Plastics: Fossils, Plastics, & Petrochemical Feedstocks' (2017); 'Fueling Plastics: How Fracked Gas, Cheap Oil, and Unburnable Coal Are Driving the Plastics Boom' (2017).

84 Injection moulding and extrusion are two of the most common methods for primary shaping of plastics. The *injection moulding machine* consists of an injection unit (which melts the plastic and conveys it to a mould) and a clamping unit, which holds the mould in a closed position during injection (until the heated plastic has filled the mould cavity and cooled in the appropriate shape) and then opens to eject the plastic part from the mould. In the machine, the material is plasticized by heating and grinding. As soon as the molten plastic enters the cavities of the mould whose shape corresponds to the shape of the final object, it cools and solidifies. The solid plastic object is then ejected from the mould, the mould is closed and the process cycle, which lasts only a few seconds, starts again. An *extruder* looks similar to an injection moulding machine, but is used to produce continuous materials rather than pre-sized moulded articles. Typical products of plastic extrusion are tubes and pipes, profiles such as angles (e.g. for window frames), sheets and plates, flexible films (for bags and packaging) or wiring insulation. For more information, see Domininghaus (n 30) 243–65; Charles A Harper, *Handbook of Plastic Processes* (John Wiley & Sons 2006).

into private households. The product range was adjusted and now included products from all different sectors, including toys, cars, housing and clothing.

Important backing was provided by the governments: John M. Keynes (1883–1946) had revolutionized macroeconomic thinking by suggesting that economic growth depended highly on average demand. Many well-known economists followed the Keynesian line and advised governments to artificially stimulate private consumption. An often-cited article by Victor Lebow from 1955 brings the post-war economic dogma of the big economies and start of modern consumerism to the point:

> Our enormously productive economy demands that we make consumption our way of life, that we convert the buying and use of goods into rituals, that we seek our spiritual satisfactions, our ego satisfactions, in consumption. The measure of social status, of social acceptance, of prestige, is now to be found in our consumptive patterns. The very meaning and significance of our lives today expressed in consumptive terms. The greater the pressures upon the individual to conform to safe and accepted social standards, the more does he tend to express his aspirations and his individuality in terms of what he wears, drives, eats – his home, his car, his pattern of food serving, his hobbies.
>
> These commodities and services must be offered to the consumer with a special urgency. We require not only 'forced draft' consumption, but 'expensive' consumption as well. We need things consumed, burned up, worn out, replaced, and discarded at an ever increasing pace. We need to have people eat, drink, dress, ride, live, with ever more complicated and, therefore, constantly more expensive consumption.[85]

Plastics suited the purpose perfectly well. A broad range of items were designed, and consumers were tempted to buy them. Where a material once was designed to fill a need, its purpose was now to create one.[86] The 1950s saw the rise of a range of plastic toys and other items, including the famous Barbie doll, which were distributed based on sophisticated marketing strategies. Plastics also rang in the 'Machine Age' in the average Western household: the age of radios, cars, electric washing machines and telephones.[87] The wide proliferation of plastics started with consumer goods, intended to be durable, but more and more included disposable goods and packaging. In 1976,

85 Victor Lebow, 'Price Competition in 1955' (1955) 31 Journal of Retailing 5, 7–8.

86 See Sterngass and Kachur (n 6) 17.

87 See ibid 19.

the American Chemical Council identified plastic as 'the most used material in the world'.[88] It has been so ever since. About 370 million tonnes of plastics were produced in 2019 – a tendency that is rapidly increasing.[89]

The global plastics industry had an estimated annual revenue of 1,722 billion Euro in 2015, which correspond to about 3 per cent of the total world economy in 2015. The majority of plastics are produced in China (28 per cent), North America (19 per cent) and Western Europe (19 per cent). The major plastics consuming regions are also China (20 per cent), North America (21 per cent) and Western Europe (18 per cent).[90] According to recent estimates, exports of primary, intermediate and final forms of plastics amounted to more than US$1 trillion in 2018, or 5 per cent of the total value of global trade.[91]

Thanks to their exceptional versatility, both with regard to their physical and chemical properties and with regard to their appearance, plastic materials can be tailored to the specific needs of various industries. The biggest market for plastics is the packaging industry: about 40 per cent of all plastic materials are consumed by it.[92] Packaging is one of the main sources of macroplastics found in the marine environment.[93] According to recent estimates, one to five trillion plastic bags are consumed worldwide each year. This corresponds to almost ten million plastic bags a minute.[94] Further markets include building and construction, and consumer goods (including home appliances and furniture, as well as sport, health and safety utensils). The automotive, electrical/ electronic and agricultural sectors are also important customers of the plastics industry (see Figure 3).

The reasons for the success of plastic materials in the packaging sector are manifold. Usually, plastic packaging is less expensive for the retailer to purchase than paper, metal or other alternatives. Second, it is light and takes less space than other materials (including on disposal). Third, plastic packaging

---

88 As cited in Moore and Phillips (n 3) 41.

89 Excluding synthetic fibres: see PlasticsEurope (n 4) 16. Production of rubbers and fibres amounted to 15 million tonnes and 65 million tonnes, respectively, in 2016: see Boucher and Billard (n 4). See also Geyer, Jambeck and Law (n 12).

90 UNEP, 'Mapping of Global Plastics Value Chain and and Plastics Losses to the Environment (with a Particular Focus on Marine Environment)' (2018) 24–30.

91 Diana Barrowclough, Carolyn Deere Birkbeck and Julien Christen, 'Global Trade in Plastics: Insights from the First Life-Cycle Trade Database' UNCTAD Research Paper No 53 UNCTAD/SER.RP/2020/12 1.

92 See PlasticsEurope (n 4) 24.

93 UNEP, 'Mapping of Global Plastics Value Chain' (n 90) 12.

94 If tied together, they would go around the world seven times every hour: see UNEP, *Single-Use Plastics: A Roadmap for Sustainability* (2018) 12.

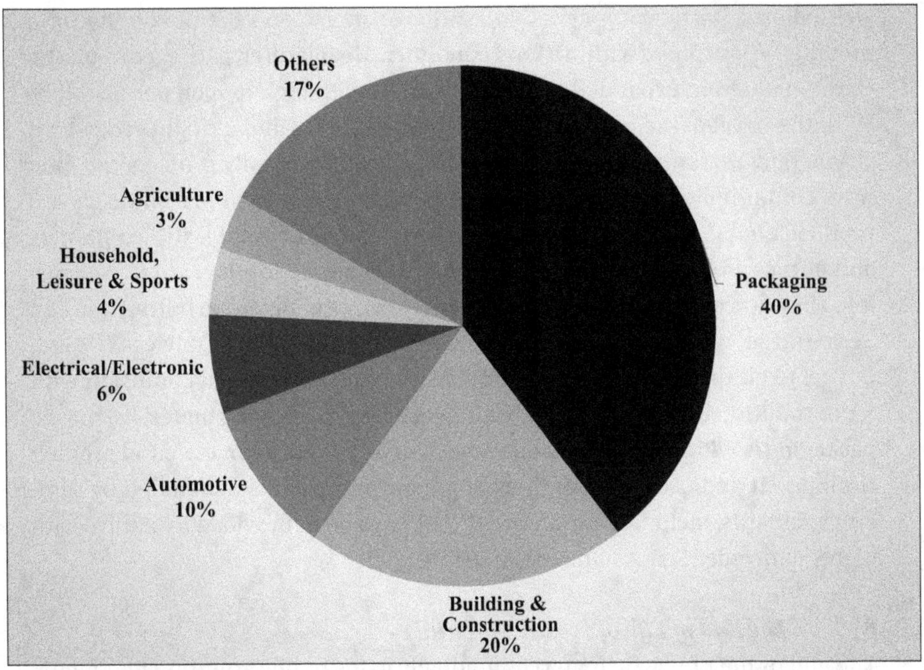

FIGURE 3 European plastics demand by segment (2020)
'PLASTICS – THE FACTS 2020: AN ANALYSIS OF EUROPEAN PLASTICS PRODUCTION, DEMAND AND WASTE DATA' © 2020 PLASTICSEUROPE.

often offers improved functionality to both retailers and consumers.[95] Plastic packaging may, for instance, provide an extended shelf life to food, protect against infections and contribute to the reduction of food waste,[96] all due to

95 The functions of packaging include containment, protection, utility and communication: packaging allows the transportation of liquids or granules and makes it possible to handle a number of goods in units (containment). It protects the product against contamination, damage from microorganisms or other environmental influences, impact, abrasion, corrosion etc. It might also protect humans or the environment from exposure to the product (protection). It facilitates stacking and storing of items, as well as their use (utility). Finally, packaging usually contains messages to those who interact with the products. The types of such massages range from basic consumer information, including identification of the product and its manufacturer, to bar codes (which are used to transmit price information or for tracking goods during distribution). They most often also include subtle advertisement in words, colour and shape: see Susan EM Selke, 'Plastics in Packaging' in AL Andrady (ed), *Plastics and the Environment* (Wiley Interscience 2003) 142–43.

96 See Peter Kershaw and others, 'Plastic Debris in the Ocean', *UNEP Year Book 2011: Emerging Issues in Our Global Environment* (UNEP 2011) 21.

well-tailored barrier properties, moisture resistance and the possibility for a modified atmosphere within a food container. Meat is often packaged in plastic trays (made from expanded PS) and PVC films with high oxygen permeability. With the oxygen, the meat changes its purple colour into a bright red, which is generally preferred by consumers. The film thus not only protects the food from contamination and moisture loss but is also transparent and displays a product quality corresponding to consumer preferences. Plastic containers and bottles are relatively flexible and can be squeezed for the ease of dispensing. They don't easily break when they fall down (e.g. shampoo bottle) and can be sterilized, which is important for medical instruments and devices.[97]

Due to all these benefits, and possibly also due to potential confusion with more traditional and more readily biodegradable packaging materials, plastic packaging is widely accepted as normal. It is perceived as an essential product component and used in quantities much beyond what is demanded by sanitary standards, including for products that have been provided by nature with highly convenient packaging (e.g. bananas).

B *The End of Life of Plastic Materials*

The end of life of plastic materials gradually gains public attention and media coverage, especially because of plastics' high visibility within the waste stream. Also, there is growing awareness with regard to the biological inertness of most plastics and related potential ecological impacts. This section sheds light on the end-of-life stage of plastics. It explores their degradability (i) and discusses (plastic) waste management, as a lack of proper waste management is an important contributing factor to marine plastic pollution (ii).

i Degradation of Plastic Materials

Until recent years, degradability was generally seen as an undesirable characteristic of a material. In order to guarantee for durability and a long service lifespan of products, material degradation was to be avoided. This very aim has been a driving factor in the development of plastic materials. With the increasing use of throwaway products and the tremendous accumulation of plastic wastes both in waste treatment facilities and in nature, however, the positive effect of the longevity of plastics is queried. Instead, biodegradability is more and more perceived as a positive attribute of materials, especially when used in non-durable products with a supposedly limited service life.[98]

---

97 See Selke (n 95) 144–45.

98 See Andrej Krzan and others, 'Standardization and Certification in the Area of Environmentally Degradable Plastics' (2006) 91 Polymer Degradation and Stability 2819,

To date, the field of application of biodegradable plastics is still limited. Products have been launched in the fields of agricultural films, food packaging and shopping bags. Major obstacles for increasing their market share include their high production cost (which are especially due to small production volumes and expensive investments in research and development), the lack of policy incentives for environmentally sound materials and limited public awareness and acceptance.[99] Label confusion is an aggravating factor in this regard: the biodegradability of plastics is not always easy to establish and much depends on specific environmental conditions. Sometimes plastics are labelled as biodegradable while they cannot biodegrade under prevailing disposal conditions. A consequence of such deceptive labelling may be that consumers directly dispose of their (supposedly biodegradable) products in the environment, where they fragmentize, disperse and persist. The use of biodegradable plastics has therefore been subject to widespread criticism.[100] On the other hand, the future of real biodegradable plastics is regarded as promising, especially in medical applications and single-use products.[101] The following subsections are dedicated to the degradation process of biodegradable and non-biodegradable plastic materials. Subsection 4) contains supplementary information on standards related to the degradability, biodegradability and compostability of plastic materials.

1) *Degradation, Biodegradation and Composting*

The degradability of an object depends on environmental conditions and other factors, including the form and composition of the degrading object. Degradation is induced by the presence of heat, sunlight, chemical substances (especially oxygen or water) and external stresses (abiotic degradation) or by the work of living organisms and enzymes (biotic degradation).[102] Under

2819; R Mohee and others, 'Biodegradability of Biodegradable/Degradable Plastic Materials under Aerobic and Anaerobic Conditions' (2008) 28 Waste Management 1624, 1624.

99 See Krzan and others (n 98) 2820.

100 See, in general, UNEP, *Biodegradable Plastics & Marine Litter: Misconceptions, Concerns and Impacts on Marine Environments* (n 51).

101 See Krzan and others (n 98) 2820.

102 For deteilaed information on photolysis or on thermal, mechanical or chemical degradation (including oxidation and hydrolysis), see Jort Hammer, Michiel HS Kraak and John R Parsons, 'Plastics in the Marine Environment: The Dark Side of a Modern Gift' in David M Whitacre (ed), *Reviews of Environmental Contamination and Toxicology*, vol 220 (Springer New York 2012) 11–12; Nathalie Lucas and others, 'Polymer Biodegradation: Mechanisms and Estimation Techniques – A Review' (2008) 73 Chemosphere 429, 431–33; Stephen P McCarthy, 'Biodegradable Polymers' in AL Andrady (ed), *Plastics and the Environment*

atmospheric conditions, most of the degradation mechanisms involve chemical absorption of oxygen atoms in the polymer chain.[103] Degradation affects the chemical bonds between the atoms of the polymer backbone. In doing so, it leads to an irreversible 'change in the structure of a material, typically characterized by a loss of properties (e.g. integrity, molecular weight or structure, mechanical strength) and/or fragmentation'.[104] It often also implies appearance changes, including loss of gloss, chalking, yellowing, or fading of colour. With progressing degradation, the material may get cracks on the surface and starts to get brittle.[105] Visible signs of degradation are often referred to as *weathering*.[106]

Abiotic transformation processes of organic compounds often only lead to partial (or primary) degradation, fragmentation and cross-linking of polymers. For the fragments and residues to go through the final degradation phase and be mineralized, they need to be consumed by living organisms, most often microorganisms, as food and source of energy (secondary degradation). The breakdown of an organic chemical compound by microorganisms to carbon dioxide, water (or methane), mineral salts and new biomass is generally referred to as *biodegradation*.[107] In the absence of suitable microorganisms, the fragments deteriorate into bio-stable microscopic parts susceptible to persist in the environment over an unpredictably long period of time.[108] Biotic

(Wiley Interscience 2003) 313–19; Aamer Ali Shah and others, 'Biological Degradation of Plastics: A Comprehensive Review' (2008) 26 Biotechnology Advances 246, 249.

103 See Boyan Slat and others, *How the Oceans Can Clean Themselves: A Feasibility Study* (2.0, The Ocean Cleanup 2014) 411.

104 Udo Pagga, 'Biodegradability and Compostability of Polymeric Materials in the Context of the European Packaging Regulation' (1998) 59 Polymer Degradation and Stability 371, 372; Krzan and others (n 98) 2832. The definition corresponds to the definitions used by most standard-setting organizations in this field.

105 See McCarthy (n 102) 320; Shah and others (n 102) 251; Slat and others (n 103) 411.

106 See McCarthy (n 102) 313.

107 See Pagga (n 104) 372. The breakdown of a substance to carbon dioxide, biomass, water and other inorganic substances is often referred to as *ultimate biodegradation*. In contrast, *ready biodegradability* means the 'biodegradability of a substance achievable in a short period of time after being exposed to the most common environment'. *Inherent biodegradability* refers to the 'biodegradability of a substance achievable in the most favorable (for degradation) environment': Krzan and others (n 98) 2832. See also ISO 472:2013; OECD, 'Revised Introduction to the OECD Guidelines for Testing of Chemicals, Section 3', *OECD Guidelines for the Testing of Chemicals, Section 3: Degradation and Accumulation* (OECD Publishing 2006) 2 fn 1; J Duffus, 'Glossary for Chemists of Terms Used in Toxicology (IUPAC Recommendations 1993)' (1993) 65 Pure and Applied Chemistry 2003, 2020; Jan P Eubeler, Marco Bernhard and Thomas P Knepper, 'Environmental Biodegradation of Synthetic Polymers II. Biodegradation of Different Polymer Groups' (2010) 29 TrAC Trends in Analytical Chemistry 84, 98; Lucas and others (n 102) 430; Shah and others (n 102) 250.

108 See Krzan and others (n 98) 2821; Mohee and others (n 98) 1626.

transformation processes are thus essential for ultimate degradation.[109] This is especially true for aquatic systems, including the marine environment, where there is limited exposure to sunlight.[110]

Not every degradable material is considered biodegradable. Owing to solar radiation, heat, cold or other factors, a specific material may lose its properties or break down into smaller pieces up to a certain point. This does not, however, necessarily mean that the material can be decomposed by any kind of living organisms present in the respective environment and reconverted into metabolically useful chemical products in a useful period of time.[111] Non-biodegradable materials thus fall out of the natural materials cycles. In the form of microscopic pieces or compounds, they persist in the environment and may cause harm to living organisms and ecosystems or pose a threat to human health.

The biodegradability of a material is not to be confused with *compostability*, which is defined much more narrowly. Compostability is the property of a material to biodegrade in a composting process. This implies that under the specific conditions of a composting system and within a given period of time (corresponding to a compost cycle), the material is biodegraded into an end product that meets the relevant compost quality criteria.[112] These criteria include, for instance, the requirement that composted material does not leave any ecotoxic traces.[113] Not every biodegradable material is compostable, and not every material that can be composted readily biodegrades in other environments.

Biodegradable plastics often are, but do not have to be, *bio-based*. Bio-based plastics are made from renewable materials.[114] Possible raw materials for the production of bio-based plastics include corn or potato starch, tapioca, sugarcane, rice, wheat or cellulose, but can also be derived from vegetable oils, such as palm seed, linseed or soybean. Fermentation products, like polylactic acid, are also commonly used.[115] Biodegradable plastics may be derived from petrochemical or renewable resources, and plastics that are made from renewable

---

109 See R Chandra and Renu Rustgi, 'Biodegradable Polymers' (1998) 23 Progress in Polymer Science 1273, 1274.

110 OECD, 'Revised Introduction to the OECD Guidelines for Testing of Chemicals, Section 3' (n 107) 11.

111 See Ewa Rudnik, *Compostable Polymer Materials* (Elsevier 2008) 12–13.

112 See Pagga (n 104) 372. Compost is defined as 'an organic soil conditioner obtained by biodegradation of a mixture consisting principally of various vegetable residues, occasionally with other organic material and having limited mineral content': ISO 472:2013, 'Plastics – Vocabulary'.

113 See Rudnik (n 111) 13.

114 See Joseph P Greene, *Sustainable Plastics: Environmental Assessments of Biobased, Biodegradable, and Recycled Plastics* (John Wiley & Sons 2014) 71.

115 ibid 73.

(bio-based) resources are not necessarily biodegradable.[116] As a matter of fact, however, the two features (bio-based and biodegradable plastics) often come together, and are, as a consequence, easily confused.

2) *Degradation Process of Plastic Materials*

a) Conventional Petroleum-based Non-biodegradable Plastics

Many of the conventional plastics, including the big five (PE, PP, PVC, PS and PET), most commonly share the property that they do not biodegrade. Especially when they enter the marine environment as floating or submerged debris, they show extremely low rates of degradation.[117] This is mainly due to the their morphology and high molecular weight:

- *Morphology:* In contrast to most natural polymers, conventional plastics often have regular configurations with short repeating units – a fact that allows the polymer chains to arrange in a very compact, crystalline order. High degrees of crystallinity make it difficult for living organisms to access the inside of polymer chains. Such polymers can hence only be attacked on their very surface, which is relatively small. By contrast, natural polymers, such as proteins, often have complex morphologies, which inhibit crystallization. The inaccessibility of crystalline parts for microorganisms and their extracellular catalytic agents is also the reason why in semi-crystalline polymers, amorphous parts are generally degraded first: the less-ordered packing of amorphous regions can be accessed more easily by enzymes than crystalline regions. The rate of degradation increases until the amorphous parts of a polymer are consumed. The cross-linked parts of a polymer are degraded at a slower rate.[118]
- *Molecular weight:* Proteins and other natural polymers can be converted into low-molecular-weight components by enzyme reactions which occur outside the microbial cell. By contrast, conventional synthetic plastics are not easily – or not at all – degraded by microorganisms in an extracellular environment. Apparently, there are no such mechanisms tailored by nature to most synthetic plastics.[119] As a consequence, plastic objects are relatively

116 See Rudnik (n 111) 13; Eddie F Gómez and Frederick C Michel, 'Biodegradability of Conventional and Bio-Based Plastics and Natural Fiber Composites during Composting, Anaerobic Digestion and Long-Term Soil Incubation' (2013) 98 Polymer Degradation and Stability 2583, 2584.

117 See Slat and others (n 103) 414–15.

118 See Chandra and Rustgi (n 109) 1290–91.

119 According to Shah and others, '[p]lastics are resistant against microbial attack, since during their short time of presence in nature evolution could not design new enzyme structures capable of degrading synthetic polymers': Shah and others (n 102) 247. According

immune to microbial attack as long as their molecular weight remains high. Only low-molecular-weight hydrocarbons can be degraded by microbes, as they can enter the cells and be converted into cellular metabolites *inside* the cells. In general, the more advanced degradation of a material is, the lower is the material's relative molecular weight and the easier it gets for the micro-organisms to access it.[120]

Conventional synthetic polymers such as PE, PP, PS and PET are considered highly bioinert and have to be degraded by abiotic mechanisms to the point that microbial attack can take place. However, even abiotic degradation of these polymers can be problematic. Most vinyl polymers are not susceptible to hydrolysis. High degrees of crystallinity and the use of antioxidants often also impede oxidation. In highly crystalline polymers, both H_2O and O_2 cannot diffuse easily.[121] This being the case, degradation of these polymers is extremely slow, as the average length of, for instance, a low-density PE (LDPE) polymer chain exceeds the maximal length considered to be biodegradable by a factor of 400.[122] Once the polymers have been broken down into low-molecular-weight components, microbes with the ability to decompose their specific chemical composition are needed to complete the degradation process. Yet, many microorganisms seem to lack the necessary genetic information for dealing with synthetic polymers and are unable to degrade them. Total assimilation of conventional polyolefins by microorganisms has not been proved yet.[123]

b) Petroleum-based Plastics with Enhanced Degradability

Non-biodegradable polymers are sometimes modified in such a way as to facilitate and accelerate degradation. Modifications include the addition of catalysts to promote oxidation or photo-oxidation, or the incorporation of easily oxidizable, hydrolysable or photosensitive functional groups into the polymer

to Gómez and Michel, most plastics are xenobiotic: 'That is, they were not present in the environment until very recently so that the evolution of metabolic pathways necessary for their biodegradation, a process that takes millions of years, has yet to occur': Gómez and Michel (n 116) 2584.

120 See Chandra and Rustgi (n 109) 1293; Shah and others (n 102) 250–56.

121 See Chandra and Rustgi (n 109) 1288–90; Lucas and others (n 102) 433. See also Jan P Eubeler and others, 'Environmental Biodegradation of Synthetic Polymers I. Test Methodologies and Procedures' (2009) 28 TrAC Trends in Analytical Chemistry 1057, 1058.

122 Chandra and Rustgi estimate LDPE with a molecular weight average of Mw = 150,000 to contain about 11,000 carbon atoms, while degradation rates are extremely slow when 'the length of the polymer chain exceeds 24–30 carbon atoms': Chandra and Rustgi (n 109) 1293.

123 See Lucas and others (n 102) 430. cf Shah and others (n 102) 256–57. See also Eubeler and others (n 121) 1065; Eubeler, Bernhard and Knepper (n 107) 87.

chain. Modified polymers are supposedly more susceptible to be attacked by heat, sunlight or other degradation mechanisms.[124] While some evidences of degradation have been observed in modified PE, biodegradation of such materials is highly controversial. A counterproductive effect is assumed in that modification may result in more rapid fragmentation, increasing the rate of microplastic formation.[125]

c) Conventional Bio-based Non-biodegradable Plastics

Conventional commodity plastics such as PE and PET can also be produced from renewable resources. PE, for instance, can be made from agricultural products such as sugarcane or corn, as it was done in the early days of history of the material, before petroleum-based plastics gained traction. For the production of bio-based PE, ethanol is fermented from sugars as contained in agricultural products, and converted to ethene by the use of catalysts. Once polymerized, it has the same composition and properties (including biological inertness) as petroleum-based PE. Similarly, PP and PET can (partially) be produced from plant resources.[126]

d) Biodegradable Plastics from Petroleum-based or Renewable Resources

Polymers are considered biodegradable (or compostable) if they meet the respective standards as described in Subsection 4) below. Yet, as most of the standards refer to composting, plastics that meet the standards do not necessarily readily degrade in other environments, such as landfills or the marine environment.

Examples for bio-based biodegradable polymers include bagasse-based polymers,[127] polyhydroxyalkanoates (PHAs), polylactic acid (PLA) and starch-based polymers. PHAs are polyesters produced in the cells of bacteria by the fermentation of different substances, including lipids and sugar. The fermentation of sugars, most often from corn starches, also yields lactic acid, which can be polymerized to PLA. Petroleum-based biodegradable polymers most often belong to the polyester family and include aliphatic polyesters such as polybutylene succinate (PBS) or polycarpolactone (PCL), as well as polyvinyl alcohol

124 See Chandra and Rustgi (n 109) 1288; Hammer, Kraak and Parsons (n 102) 12; Krzan and others (n 98) 2821; Shah and others (n 102) 256.

125 See UNEP, *Biodegradable Plastics & Marine Litter: Misconceptions, Concerns and Impacts on Marine Environments* (n 51) 22. See also Gómez and Michel (n 116) 2590; Greene (n 114) 120–21; Selke (n 95) 158–59.

126 Greene (n 114) 107–13.

127 Bagasse is a fibre-pulp product from the sugarcane stalk: ibid 75.

(PVOH/PVA). Biodegradable plastics can be used for packaging, food containers, bottles, bags, agricultural pots and films or ground coverings.[128]

The first biodegradable plastics were developed in the 1980s. In the last couple of years, several biodegradable plastics have been introduced into the market. However, biodegradable plastics only hold a very small share of today's plastic market.[129] This might be due to elevated production prices and longer production processes for many of these plastics when compared to conventional plastics, as well as to a limited field of application. For many applications, the properties of most biodegradable plastics do not match the ones of conventional plastics.[130] There is, however, an increasing interest in biodegradable materials, by both consumers and policymakers. Technological innovations and new developments can be expected in this field, which allow conventional plastics to be increasingly replaced by biodegradable ones.[131]

Biodegradable plastics are most usually non-recyclable. The need to separate biodegradable plastics from the non-biodegradable in the waste streams has been identified as a possible disadvantage of the widespread use of biodegradable plastics. Social misconceptions and a greater inclination to litter on the part of the public are further possible side effects that would seem most unwelcome.[132]

3) *Degradation of Plastics in Marine Environments*

Unlike plastics on land, floating debris cannot build up heat from the absorption of infrared radiation in sunlight, since ocean waters act as an efficient heat sink. Degradation of floating plastic debris is, thus, slower when compared to plastics exposed on land. This is even more true for submerged debris, since ultraviolet wavelengths in sunlight are readily absorbed by water. Moreover, marine debris is often susceptible to biofouling. The fouling coverage on the surface additionally shields the material from exposure to sunlight. While the degradation time for plastics in the marine environment is widely unknown, it is likely to be greatly increased at depth where oxygen concentrations are low

---

128 See ibid 71–97; McCarthy (n 102) 361–68; Rudnik (n 111) 14–36; Shah and others (n 102) 249.

129 See Shah and others (n 102) 248; CIEL, 'Fueling Plastics: Untested Assumptions and Unanswered Questions in the Plastics Boom' (2017) 10.

130 cf Hottle, Bilec and Landis (n 49) 1899.

131 See, for instance, Ge-Xia Wang and others, 'Seawater-Degradable Polymers – Fighting the Marine Plastic Pollution' (2021) 8 Advanced Science 2001121.

132 See UNEP, *Biodegradable Plastics & Marine Litter: Misconceptions, Concerns and Impacts on Marine Environments* (n 51) 3.

and light is absent. Marine plastics thus degrade at a significantly slower rate than they do on land.[133]

4) *Biodegradability Standards and Labels*

There are considerable differences in the time materials take to break down or decompose under specific environmental conditions. In particular, the extent to which materials can be mineralized in a given period of time varies greatly. As a consequence, there is a need to agree on common standards that distinguish readily degradable materials from environmentally stable ones. Where the specific line is drawn is a question of threshold values.

Standards related to the biodegradability of plastics or their bio-based content have been developed by major standardization organizations, whether national, regional or international in character, and increasingly harmonized in recent years. Respective organizations include the International Organization for Standardization (ISO), the American Society for Testing and Materials (ASTM), the Japanese Standards Association (JIS) and the European Committee for Standardization (CEN), an umbrella organization of the national standardization bodies of 34 European countries. Standardization bodies have adopted a large number of standards on plastics and could play an important role in a global approach to plastics. The ISO technical committee 61 (ISO/TC 61) works on plastics. Its subcommittee 14 was created in 2017 and works on environmental aspects in particluar. It has so far developed twenty-seven standards and has thirteen standards under development. The ISO technical committee 122 (ISO/TC 122) works on packaging, with its subcommittee 4 being dedicated to environmental aspects. ISO/TC 323 was created in 2019 for standardization in the field of Circular Economy.[134]

Most standards as developed so far refer either to aerobic or anaerobic biodegradation or compostability performance of plastic materials under specific

133 See David KA Barnes and others, 'Accumulation and Fragmentation of Plastic Debris in Global Environments' (2009) 364 Philosophical Transactions of the Royal Society B: Biological Sciences 1985, 390–92; Eubeler, Bernhard and Knepper (n 107) 87; Murray R Gregory and Anthony L Andrady, 'Plastics in the Marine Environment' in AL Andrady (ed), *Plastics and the Environment* (Wiley Interscience 2003) 1985–93; Hammer, Kraak and Parsons (n 102) 11; Karen K Leonas and Robert W Gorden, 'An Accelerated Laboratory Study Evaluating the Disintegration Rates of Plastic Films in Simulated Aquatic Environments' (1993) 1 Journal of Environmental Polymer Degradation 45.

134 See Carolyn Deere Birkbeck and others, 'A Review of Trade Policies and Measures Relevant to Trade in Plastics and Plastic Pollution' (2021) 16 Global Trade and Customs Journal 303, 315–17.

environmental conditions (and/or corresponding testing methods), or to the determination of bio-based content in plastic materials.

Biodegradation standards always refer to specific common disposal environments, including compost, marine, anaerobic digestion, soil and landfill.[135] They determine to what extent a material has to undergo degradation in these environments within a given period of time in order to be qualified as biodegradable. In this sense, the qualification of an object as 'biodegradable' refers not necessarily to its property to completely biodegrade but to its ability to decompose to an environmentally acceptable level within a given time frame.[136]

Most performance specification standards refer to the compostability of products in industrial composting facilities. For plastic products, including packaging materials, to be labelled as compostable in such facilities, most standards require the product to demonstrate three characteristics:

1. *Disintegration:* When sieved in a 2-mm screen, no more than 10 per cent of the original dry weight of the plastic material must remain after 84 days/12 weeks/3 months of exposure to industrial composting conditions.
2. *Biodegradation:* At least 90 per cent of the organic carbon in the original plastic sample must be converted into CO_2 after a period of 180 days/6 months of exposure to industrial composting conditions.
3. *No ecotoxicity:* The resulting compost soil must support plant growth (no measurable phytotoxicity). Heavy metals concentrations in the compost soil must not exceed a certain level.[137]

Industrial composting conditions mostly include temperatures of at least 58°C and 50 per cent moisture. Cellulose, a material that is considered fully biodegradable, serves as a reference material.[138] Some of the standards have been criticized for presupposing optimal composting conditions with regard

135 Greene (n 114) 188. See also Mohee and others (n 98) 1624; Shah and others (n 102) 250.

136 Krzan and others (n 98) 2828.

137 See ASTM D6400-19, 'Standard Specification for Labeling of Plastics Designed to Be Aerobically Composted in Municipal or Industrial Facilities' (ASTM International, 2019); EN 13432:2000, 'Packaging – Requirements for Packaging Recoverable through Composting and Biodegradation – Test Scheme and Evaluation Criteria for the Final Acceptance of Packaging'; ISO 17088:2012, 'Specifications for Compostable Plastics'. See also Greene (n 114) 193–204; Rudnik (n 111) 99–102. EN 13432:2000 is linked to European Parliament and Council Directive 94/62/EC of 20 December 1994 on packaging and packaging waste (Packaging and Packaging Waste Directive) [1994] OJ L365/10.

138 The mineralization level of cellulose is considered as the maximum mineralization achievable under the test conditions: Francesco Degli Innocenti, 'Biodegradability and Compostability' in Emo Chiellini and Roberto Solaro (eds), *Biodegradable Polymers and Plastics* (Springer Science & Business Media 2003) 39.

to temperatures, water availability, aeration and duration, which are not easily met in real composting processes. It has been argued that as a result, even when a plastic product passes the tests, polymer biodegradation could be limited under real conditions and compost full of residues.[139]

Along with minimum biodegradation *performance specifications*, standards often specify *testing methods* for simulating the intended environment and measuring biodegradation of the samples.[140] For some common disposal environments only test schemes are defined, while performance specifications are still missing.[141]

There are a few standards describing testing procedures to simulate the marine environment and methods to measure biodegradation. An ASTM performance specification standard referring to the biodegradation of plastic materials in marine environments was withdrawn in 2014.[142] Requirements within the specification included criteria for the degree of plastic disintegration in marine environments, biodegradation rates and ecotoxicological testing. ISO published two related standards in 2020, one defining the evaluation method for biodegradability in the ocean, the other specifying the method for evaluating the degree of disintegration in the ocean.[143] Since these standards are not specifically aimed at assessing the biodegradability of plastics within anaerobic marine habitats, saltmarshes and deep-sea environments, it has been assumed that test methods and specifications can significantly underestimate the durations required for polymer biodegradation within natural marine ecosystems.[144]

Standards referring to the determination of bio-based content in a product usually provide test methods to measure such content and establish procedures, equipment, materials and conditions for the tests.[145] A possible method to determine bio-based content consists of measuring the content of the

139 See ibid 40.

140 Greene (n 114) 188; Pagga (n 104) 372; Krzan and others (n 98) 2819. Such methods are, for instance, defined and described by OECD, 'Revised Introduction to the OECD Guidelines for Testing of Chemicals, Section 3' (n 107).

141 Greene (n 114) 188–89.

142 ASTM D7081-05, 'Specification for Non-Floating Biodegradable Plastics in the Marine Environment (Withdrawn 2014)' (ASTM International, 2005).

143 ISO 22403:2020, 'Plastics – Assessment of the Intrinsic Biodegradability of Materials Exposed to Marine Inocula under Mesophilic Aerobic Laboratory Conditions – Test Methods and Requirements'; ISO 22766:2020, 'Plastics – Determination of the Degree of Disintegration of Plastic Materials in Marine Habitats under Real Field Conditions'.

144 Jesse P Harrison and others, 'Biodegradability Standards for Carrier Bags and Plastic Films in Aquatic Environments: A Critical Review' 5 Royal Society Open Science 171792.

145 Greene (n 114) 72.

^{14}C isotope in the plastic sample through radiocarbon analysis.[146] Some standards require a minimum content of bio-based carbon in plastics as high as 99 per cent.[147] The use of bio-based plastics may reduce the consumption of fossil-based resources and CO_2 footprint of a product.

Based on the standards, a number of certification programmes were developed. Products are tested by independent organizations and issued a certificate if they meet the requirements specified in a particular standard. The certificates often come with a label. According to the different sorts of standards, there are two major groups of labels. The first group proves that a product is biodegradable under specific conditions, for instance industrial or home composting or anaerobic digestion. The second group of labels indicates that the product contains a significant (minimum) percentage of renewable (bio-based) content. Labels can be awarded to finished products only (including packaging) and not to materials or ingredients as such. The validity period of certificates is limited, and testing is repeated in sporadic intervals.[148]

The Belgian certification agency Vinçotte International developed a conformity mark based on the withdrawn ASTM standard for products described as biodegradable in seawater (see Figure 4). Accepted products are required to exhibit a biodegradation rate of 90 per cent following six months of exposure.

ii Plastic Wastes

When a plastic object comes to the end of its service life and is to be disposed, it enters –after production and use – the third major stage of its existence: the stage of waste. Waste is generally not regarded as a desirable stage of a product. The generation of waste implies a loss of materials and energy and entails

146 From the three isotopes of the carbon atom that can be found in nature, ^{14}C accounts for the smallest portion. In contrast to its counterparts ^{12}C and ^{13}C, the ^{14}C isotope is instable and undergoes radioactive decay. ^{14}C concentration in living organisms and the environment is almost equal and close to constant. After decease, an organism can no longer absorb new ^{14}C from the environment (through briefing), which is why the concentration of the ^{14}C isotope in the death matter starts to decrease. The concentration of ^{14}C in a (non-living) material halves in 5,700 years. In 50,000 years, proportions are too small to be measured. For this reason, ^{14}C concentrations in fossil resources are close to zero. The measuring of the radioactivity of ^{14}C in plastic materials therefore allows the determination of organic content from renewable resources, as ^{14}C concentrations in fossil resources are negligible.

147 E.g. ASTM D6866-18, 'Test Methods for Determining the Biobased Content of Solid, Liquid, and Gaseous Samples Using Radiocarbon Analysis' (2018). See Greene (n 114) 72.

148 For more information, see Petra Horvat and Andrej Kržan, 'Certification of Bioplastics' (Innovative Value Chain Development for Sustainable Plastics in Central Europe (PLASTiCE) 2012).

FIGURE 4
Certification scheme for products described as biodegradable in seawater
VINÇOTTE, 2015, ACQUIRED BY TÜV AUSTRIA IN 2017. REPRINTED WITH PERMISSION BY TÜV AUSTRIA.

environmental, social and economic costs. For this reason, there are efforts to minimize waste generation and keep the waste stage of a product as short as possible, by reintroducing the materials as used in the product into either the natural or socio-economic materials cycle. This not only allows resource and energy recovery and savings, but also leaves less waste to be stored and taken care of.

A sound waste management tries to keep waste, and plastic wastes in particular, out of wild nature and within a system managed and surveyed by humans. Waste management options within such a system include storage in a landfill (where degradability remains an issue), thermal treatment (including incineration) but also composting or anaerobic digestion, as well as different forms of recycling.[149] Each of these disposal options handles the negative impacts of waste differently, and contributes to waste-reduction efforts in a more or less efficient way. Each of the options bears, however, its own environmental, social and economic costs. Trade-offs are, therefore, inherent to waste management policies, and require careful assessment and decisions.

The current subsection first briefly analyses how and in what quantities waste, and plastic waste in particular, is generated throughout the world (1). It then discusses some environmental, social and economic impacts of waste and waste disposal (2).

1) *Waste Generation*

Wastes can be defined as 'substances or objects which are disposed of or are intended to be disposed of or are required to be disposed of by the provisions of national law'.[150] It can be inferred from this definition that an object's quality as waste alternatively depends on a factual element (effective

149 See Paul T Williams, *Waste Treatment and Disposal* (2nd edn, John Wiley & Sons 2005) 49–51.

150 Basel Convention on the Control of Transboundary Movements of Hazardous Wastes and Their Disposal (1989 Basel Convention) (adopted on 22 March 1989, entered into force on 5 May 1992) 1673 UNTS 126, 28 ILM 657 (1989) art 2.1. A very similar definition

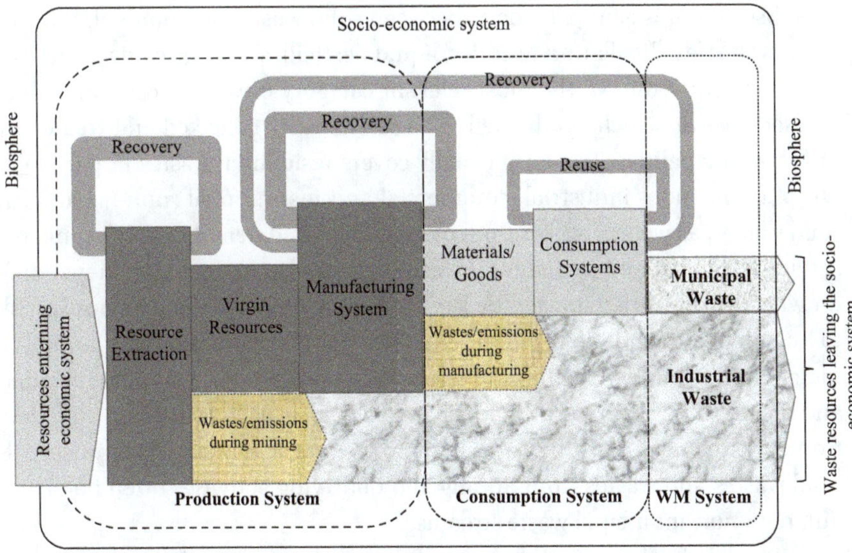

FIGURE 5 From resource extraction to waste disposal in a mainly linear system *Source:* Jagdeep Singh and others, 'Progress and Challenges to the Global Waste Management System' (2014) 32 Waste Management & Research 800, 801. © 2014 SAGE PUBLICATIONS. REPRINTED BY PERMISSION OF SAGE PUBLICATIONS.

disposal, including unintentional), a subjective element (the holder's intention of disposal) or legal requirements, respectively. Plastic waste is potentially generated in the pre-production stage of a product (e.g. pellet loss), during production (e.g. plastic residues and other industrial wastes), during transportation (e.g. packaging, container spills) and after use (in the form of litter, dumped wastes or municipal solid waste). In this sense, wastes are by-products or end products of the production and consumption processes, respectively.[151] In the case of by-products of the production process, we speak of industrial wastes. End products of consumption generally fall under the term of municipal wastes. The two categories can mingle and may have some overlaps (see Figure 5).

---

of waste is contained in European Parliament and Council Directive 2008/98/EC of 19 November 2008 on Waste and Repealing Certain Directives (Waste Framework Directive) [2008] OJ L312/3, as well as in ISO 14040:2006, 'Environmental Management – Life Cycle Assessment – Principles and Framework'.

151 See Jagdeep Singh and others, 'Progress and Challenges to the Global Waste Management System' (2014) 32 Waste Management & Research 800, 800.

A distinction is generally made between solid wastes and non-solid wastes such as slurries, distillation residues, liquid pesticides, sewage sludges etc. In a plastic-specific context, the most relevant category of waste is that of *municipal solid waste*, which can be defined as solid waste collected and treated by or for municipalities. The term usually covers residential wastes in particular but often includes industrial, commercial and institutional (non-hazardous) solid wastes, as well as wastes from construction and demolition or municipal services. Medical and agricultural wastes might also be included, depending on whether they are managed by the municipality.[152] Wastes that pose a risk to human health and the environment when composted, stored in a landfill or incinerated fall under the term of hazardous wastes and need to be recorded and disposed of separately. End-of-life vehicles, as well as electric and electronic wastes might also be collected and treated separately. Finally, agricultural wastes and wastes from mining and quarrying activities often belong to different, non-municipal waste streams.[153]

Solid waste has been regarded as the 'most visible and pernicious by-product of a resource-intensive, consumer-based economic lifestyle'.[154] Even 20 years ago, it was reported by the American National Academy of Sciences that '94 per cent of the substances that are pulled out of the earth enter the waste stream within months'.[155] Production and consumption patterns are, therefore, highly relevant for any discussion on waste generation, being the main drivers in in this regard. Plastic materials cannot be exempted here, as they are widely associated with short-lived consumption and throwaway lifestyles.

a) Disposal Behaviour

The decision of a holder to dispose of a substance or an object may have different reasons. A plastic object may reach the end of its service life because it has fulfilled its purpose (e.g. packaging), because it breaks and repair is not considered a feasible option or worthwhile (e.g. tools and other basic commodities, sport equipment, kitchen utensils, tents, technical equipment and devices) or because it becomes otherwise useless, for example when its contents are consumed and the plastic container is not supposed to be refilled (e.g.

152 See Daniel Hoornweg and Perinaz Bhada-Tata, 'What a Waste: A Global Review of Solid Waste Management' (World Bank 2012) No. 15 7; Lemann (n 45) 32; Anne Scheinberg, David C Wilson and Ljiljana Rodic, *Solid Waste Management in the World's Cities: Water and Sanitation in the World's Cities 2010* (Earthscan for UN-HABITAT 2010) 6–7.

153 See Scheinberg, Wilson and Rodic (n 147) 7.

154 Hoornweg and Bhada-Tata (n 152) 3.

155 G Bylinsky, 'Manufacturing for Reuse' (1995) 131 Fortune 102; Singh and others (n 151) 800.

packaging, disposable lighters, pens, tubes, ink cartridges etc.) or when it was designed for single use (e.g. disposable contact lenses, disposable nappies and other sanitary articles). Plastic objects are also frequently taken out of service and discarded because they no longer look new and lose their attractiveness (e.g. clothes, furniture, toys), do not meet new safety standards or sanitary regulations (e.g. in the case of new regulations with respect to food-contact materials or medical equipment), do not represent the state-of-the-art technology (e.g. cell phones and other electronic devices) or have become, for any reason, unfashionable (e.g. furniture, clothes, but also cars). As indivisible parts of bigger objects (e.g. houses and other constructions), their usefulness may come to an end whenever the latter are disposed of, demolished or discarded for any reason.

The lifespan of plastic products depends on many factors and differs significantly between different categories of products. Depending on whether they are designed as durable or disposable products, the average lifespan of plastic goods for usage varies from a few minutes (e.g. disposable dishes, straws, shopping bags) to several decades (e.g. aircraft windows, building floors or facades). In anti-consumerist circles, however, plastics, and commodity plastics in particular, are especially associated with disposables: as commodity plastics are cheap, many disposable objects are made from plastics (and vice versa: objects made from plastics are treated as disposables, since replacement is easily affordable). The list of such objects ranges from consumer goods that are relatively new to society (e.g. a broad range of toys, cosmetics, personal care items), to articles that were once designed as durables but are more and more perceived (and designed) as disposable objects, since they are easier to replace than to be stored and reused (e.g. packaging, containers, bags) or to be repaired when broken (e.g. home appliances). Boxes, dishes, bags and nappies were not usually disposed after a single use at times when they were made from more expensive materials such as wood, metal, ceramics or processed natural fibres. This is even more true for more complex goods, such as cameras or radios. While impetus for higher turnover rates and, with it, a higher throughput of resources in Western economies came from economic advisors and the media in the 1950s[156] (that is, before the breakthrough of commodity plastics), and although early plastic products were designed to last long (e.g.

156 See Lebow (n 85) 7–8. Shortly after Lebow's call for a 'constantly more expensive consumption', on 1st August 1955, an article published in LIFE, one of the United States' leading magazines, celebrated the new, modern, throw-away lifestyle, which was supposed to liberate housewives from arduous housekeeping tasks: 'Throwaway Living: Disposable Items Cut Down Household Chores' [1955] *LIFE* 49. The cover picture shows a happy

Bakelite radios and telephones), plastic often serves, in public discourse, as a symbol for a wasteful society.

A critical issue of plastic disposables (especially when made from conventional plastics) is the obvious disproportion between the lifespan or service life of the product and the durability of the respective material used in the product. While the product is discarded rapidly, the raw material (that is, petroleum) has taken millions of years to be formed, and the product or its fragments will possibly persist in the environment for an indefinable period of time,[157] in which it might have a series of harmful effects on humans, animals and entire ecosystems. The period of use is, thus, negligible in the product's entire life cycle.

Durability of plastic materials has, hence, environmental, social and economic implications, and might be more or less reasonable, depending on the use and disposal of a product. While highly durable plastics pose a series of difficulties, readily degradable materials seem to be unsuitable for certain long-term applications, may not meet consumer expectations and are difficult to recycle (material recovery). The optimal lifespan of consumer goods was little discussed in the literature until recently.[158] Today, however, the high ecological footprint of disposable products is well known.[159]

The phenomena of *planned obsolescence* and *perceived obsolescence* have received some more attention in literature, both academic and non-academic. In the first case, an object becomes obsolete because it was destined to break after a certain period of time or after it has been used for a certain number of times (e.g. light bulb, electronic devices). Software or hardware updates which are incompatible with previous versions and other programs or components, as well as a technical make-up which hinders repair or substitution of weak components, including batteries, often also fall under this term, as they push

---

family in the middle of numerous flying disposable objects, which do not have to be cleaned after use any longer but can now easily be discarded.

157 Studies suggest that plastic products can take up to thousands of years to decompose in the natural environment: see UNEP, *Single-Use Plastics: A Roadmap for Sustainability* (n 94) 12.

158 See, in general, Tim Cooper and C Kieren Mayers, *Prospects for Household Appliances* (Urban Mines 2000); Tim Cooper, 'Slower Consumption Reflections on Product Life Spans and the "Throwaway Society"' (2005) 9 Journal of Industrial Ecology 51; Michel Kostecki (ed), *The Durable Use of Consumer Products: New Options for Business and Consumption* (Springer US 1998); John J Heim, 'Consumer Demand for Durable Goods, Nondurable Goods and Services' (2009) 2 Proceedings of the New York State Economics Association 22.

159 UNEP, *Addressing Single-Use Plastic Products Pollution Using a Life Cycle Approach* (2021) 5.

the consumer to upgrade across the board, including parts which are still working. In the second case, the holder of an object feels that it is outdated and should be renewed, for instance because it has become unfashionable or does not represent the state-of-the-art technology. Objects are then discarded and replaced by newer ones long before they are worn out. Both phenomena are said to be caused and controlled by the industry, either directly by the use of specific techniques to artificially limit the durability of a manufactured good or indirectly by influencing consumer perceptions through commercials and advertisement, suggesting that a model is outdated and should be replaced by a newer version.[160]

Literature critically reflecting on consumption (as a main driver for waste generation) and economic growth is broad and comes from several disciplines, such as psychology, sociology, ethology, economics and medical science. Topics include *conspicuous consumption*, a term that was first used by the economist and sociologist Thorstein Veblen in 1899 and refers to the widespread phenomenon of people purchasing goods, including luxury, for pure show-off and not to satisfy real needs.[161] '*Keeping up with the Joneses*' is a related phenomenon, which also includes the accumulation of material goods and status symbols in a constant status competition with the neighbours and struggle for social recognition which is based on material wealth.[162] Several contributions focus

---

160 See, in general, Vance Packard, *The Waste Makers* (Reprint edn, Ig Publishing 1960); Peter L Swan, 'Optimum Durability, Second-Hand Markets, and Planned Obsolescence' (1972) 80 Journal of Political Economy 575; Jeremy Bulow, 'An Economic Theory of Planned Obsolescence' (1986) 101 The Quarterly Journal of Economics 729; Michael Waldman, 'A New Perspective on Planned Obsolescence' (1993) 108 The Quarterly Journal of Economics 273; Atsuo Utaka, 'Planned Obsolescence and Marketing Strategy' (2000) 21 Managerial and Decision Economics 339; Giles Slade, *Made to Break: Technology and Obsolescence in America* (Harvard University Press 2007); Joseph Guiltinan, 'Creative Destruction and Destructive Creations: Environmental Ethics and Planned Obsolescence' (2008) 89 Journal of Business Ethics 19.

161 Thorstein Veblen, 'The Theory of the Leisure Class' [1899] New York: The New American Library. See also Laurie Simon Bagwell and B Douglas Bernheim, 'Veblen Effects in a Theory of Conspicuous Consumption' (1996) 86 The American Economic Review 349; Aron O'Cass and Hmily McEwen, 'Exploring Consumer Status and Conspicuous Consumption' (2004) 4 Journal of Consumer Behaviour 25; Andrew B Trigg, 'Veblen, Bourdieu, and Conspicuous Consumption' (2001) 35 Journal of Economic Issues 99.

162 See, for instance, Richard C Barnett, Joydeep Bhattacharya and Helle Bunzel, 'Choosing to Keep Up with the Joneses and Income Inequality' (2009) 45 Economic Theory 469; Markus Christen and Ruskin M Morgan, 'Keeping Up With the Joneses: Analyzing the Effect of Income Inequality on Consumer Borrowing' (2005) 3 Quantitative Marketing and Economics 145; Jordi Galí, 'Keeping up with the Joneses: Consumption Externalities, Portfolio Choice, and Asset Prices' (1994) 26 Journal of Money, Credit and Banking 1;

on the question on how income and consumption levels influence our level of happiness. They describe and discuss human tendency to quickly return to a relatively stable level of happiness, even after positive stimulation through consumption.[163] *Hedonic adaptation*, as the phenomenon is often referred to, is the reason for the fact that a rising level of consumption does usually not entail a general rise in subjective well-being, as one might expect. The constant (and mostly unsuccessful) attempt to push the level of happiness through consumption is associated with a *treadmill*: in order to satisfy raising aspirations with regard to their status, income level and consumption, people need to gain more and more and work harder, while subjective well-being rapidly falls back to its normal level. Pathological accumulation of obsolete items and the inability to discard them is known as a *hoarding disorder*.[164] Differentiation between pathological hoarding and normal consumption behaviours is not always obvious. Furthermore, there is a range of literature examining new economic models, either suggesting a decoupling of economic growth and resource consumption or calling for economic *degrowth*.[165] Finally, there are several

---

Michael Rauscher, 'Keeping up with the Joneses: Chaotic Patterns in a Status Game' (1992) 40 Economics Letters 287.

163 See Daniel Kahneman and others, 'Would You Be Happier If You Were Richer? A Focusing Illusion' (2006) 312 Science 1908; John Knight and Ramani Gunatilaka, 'Income, Aspirations and the Hedonic Treadmill in a Poor Society' (2012) 82 Journal of Economic Behavior & Organization 67; Sonja Lyubomirsky, 'Hedonic Adaptation to Positive and Negative Experiences' in Susan Folkman (ed), *The Oxford Handbook of Stress, Health, and Coping* (Oxford University Press, USA 2010); Alois Stutzer, 'The Role of Income Aspirations in Individual Happiness' (2004) 54 Journal of Economic Behavior & Organization 89.

164 See Hélène Cherrier and Tresa Ponnor, 'A Study of Hoarding Behavior and Attachment to Material Possessions' (2010) 13 Qualitative Market Research: An International Journal 8; Ashley E Nordsletten and David Mataix-Cols, 'Hoarding versus Collecting: Where Does Pathology Diverge from Play?' (2012) 32 Clinical Psychology Review 165.

165 See Samuel Alexander, 'Planned Economic Contraction: The Emerging Case for Degrowth' (2012) 21 Environmental Politics 349; Giorgos Kallis, Christian Kerschner and Joan Martinez-Alier, 'The Economics of Degrowth' (2012) 84 Ecological Economics 172; Giorgos Kallis, 'In Defence of Degrowth' (2011) 70 Ecological Economics 873; Christian Kerschner, 'Economic De-Growth vs. Steady-State Economy' (2010) 18 Journal of Cleaner Production 544; Serge Latouche, *Le pari de la décroissance* (Fayard 2006); *Vers une société d'abondance frugale: Contresens et controverses de la décroissance* (Fayard/Mille et une nuits 2011); Joan Martínez-Alier and others, 'Sustainable De-Growth: Mapping the Context, Criticisms and Future Prospects of an Emergent Paradigm' (2010) 69 Ecological Economics 1741; Joan Martínez-Alier, 'Environmental Justice and Economic Degrowth: An Alliance between Two Movements' (2012) 23 Capitalism Nature Socialism 51; François Schneider, Giorgos Kallis and Joan Martinez-Alier, 'Crisis or Opportunity? Economic Degrowth for Social Equity and Ecological Sustainability' (2010) 18 Journal of Cleaner Production 511; Peter A Victor, 'Growth, Degrowth and Climate Change: A Scenario Analysis' (2012) 84 Ecological Economics 206.

contributions focusing on 'sustainable' or 'green' consumption, and the gap between green consumers' values and their consumption behaviour, which often does not properly reflect the consumers' ecologically oriented values.[166]

b) Sources, Quantities and Composition of Wastes

According to estimations of the World Bank, 2.01 billion tonnes of municipal solid waste were generated worldwide in 2016. This corresponds to 0.74 kg per capita per day, with considerable differences in waste generation rates between and within countries.[167] In absolute terms, the East Asia and Pacific region is generating most of the world's waste. North America produces the highest average amount of waste per capita, at 2.21 kg per day (see Table 2). Generation rates (per capita) of solid waste tend to be higher in high-income countries than in low-income countries, and in cities than in rural regions.[168] The US is the largest generator of plastic packaging waste on a per capita basis, followed by Japan and the EU.[169]

Global annual waste generation is expected to grow to 3.40 billion tonnes by 2050. Daily per capita waste generation increases all over the world. It is projected to increase by 40 per cent or more in low- and middle-income countries by 2050, compared to a projected increase of 19 per cent in high-income countries. The fastest growing regions are Sub-Saharan Africa, South Asia, the Middle East and North Africa. In Sub-Saharan Africa, waste generation is expected to nearly triple by 2050. In these regions, more than half of the waste is currently openly dumped.

---

166 See William Young and others, 'Sustainable Consumption: Green Consumer Behaviour When Purchasing Products' (2010) 18 Sustainable Development 20. See also Andrew Gilg, Stewart Barr and Nicholas Ford, 'Green Consumption or Sustainable Lifestyles? Identifying the Sustainable Consumer' (2005) 37 Futures 481; Stephanie D Preston, 'Toward an Interdisciplinary Science of Consumption' (2011) 1236 Annals of the New York Academy of Sciences 1; Gill Seyfang, *The New Economics of Sustainable Consumption: Seeds of Change* (1st edn, Palgrave Macmillan 2009); Gert Spaargaren, 'Sustainable Consumption: A Theoretical and Environmental Policy Perspective' (2003) 16 Society & Natural Resources 687.

167 National waste generation rates fluctuate from 0.11 to 4.54 kg per capita per day: Slipa Kaza and others, *What a Waste 2.0: A Global Snapshot of Solid Waste Management to 2050* (World Bank Group 2018) 18.

168 See Hoornweg and Bhada-Tata (n 152) 1; Azni Idris, Bulent Inanc and Mohd Nassir Hassan, 'Overview of Waste Disposal and Landfills/Dumps in Asian Countries' (2004) 6 Journal of Material Cycles and Waste Management 104, 104.

169 See UNEP, *Single-Use Plastics: A Roadmap for Sustainability* (n 94) 5. On per capita plastic waste generation rates, see also GRID-Arendal, 'The Trade in Plastic Waste' (April 2017) <https://grid-arendal.maps.arcgis.com/apps/Cascade/index.html?appid=002738ffb185488l8a61cc88161ac464> accessed 19 February 2022.

Table 2 and Figure 6 provide an overview of latest data collection and estimations by the World Bank, as published in 2018. They refer to municipal solid waste only.[170]

Important waste producing sectors include construction and demolition, mining and quarrying, the manufacturing industry, municipal solid wastes, waste and wastewater management, energy production and agriculture and forestry.[171] Owing to incomplete and heterogeneous data, industrial waste generation rates are largely unknown. Available data suggests, however, that wastes from mining and production activities are considerably higher in mass when compared with wastes leaving the consumption system. This implies that for every kilo of household waste, up to seventeen kilos of industrial waste are generated in order to produce the discarded goods.[172] Strictly speaking, the personal 'waste footprint' of individuals thus includes not only the waste discarded in person, but a multiple thereof, including industrial wastes generated along the production chain of the discarded goods.

Waste is extremely heterogeneous and its composition can greatly vary on a daily basis, between seasons and from one region to another. Geographical location, climate, culture and economic wealth are factors which greatly influence the composition of waste.[173] Waste components can be categorized in different ways, for instance into (putrescible) organic, paper, plastic, glass, metal and other wastes. According to a recent study by the World Bank, consumption of plastics, paper and metals (including aluminium) increases

170 Accurate data of waste arisings are difficult to collect and compare due to divergent definitions, inconsistent categorization and different collection, quantification and reporting methods. Data is, moreover, often incomplete and does not capture system losses. Waste-reduction strategies thus generally include as a key element the availability of accurate and comparable data on waste generation and composition: see Williams (n 149) 64. For detailed data on waste generation in the United States, see US Environmental Protection Agency, *Municipal Solid Waste Generation, Recycling, and Disposal in the United States: Tables and Figures for 2012* (2014). For data on waste generation in OECD countries, see OECD, 'Municipal Waste (Indicator)' (2022) <https://data.oecd.org/waste/municipal-waste.htm> accessed 19 February 2022.

171 See European Environment Agency, 'Total Waste Generation by Sector, 2004' (2009) <http://www.eea.europa.eu/data-and-maps/figures/total-waste-generation-by-sector-2004> accessed 19 February 2022; Eurostat, 'Archive: Waste Statistics' (*Statistics Explained*, 2011) <http://ec.europa.eu/eurostat/statistics-explained/index.php/Archive:Waste_statistics> accessed 19 February 2022; OECD, 'Generation of Primary Waste by Sector' (2018) <https://stats.oecd.org/Index.aspx?DataSetCode=WSECTOR> accessed 19 February 2022.

172 According to estimations of the World Bank, average daily per capita generation of industrial waste is at 12.73 kg, more than 17 times higher than for municipal solid waste: Kaza and others (n 167) 36. See also Singh and others (n 151) 801–02.

173 See Williams (n 149) 68.

TABLE 2 Present and projected municipal waste generation according to region

Region	Total waste generation 2016 (mio tonnes/year)	Total projected waste generation 2015 (mio tonnes/year)	Waste generation per capita per day 2016 (kg/capita/day)	Waste generation per capita per day 2050 (kg/capita/day)
Middle East & North Africa	129	255	0.81	1.06
Sub-Saharan Africa	174	516	0.46	0.63
Latin America & the Caribbean	131	369	0.99	1.30
North America	289	396	2.21	2.50
South Asia	334	661	0.52	0.79
Europe & Central Asia	392	490	1.18	1.45
East Asia & Pacific	468	417	0.56	0.81

DATA SOURCE: SLIPA KAZA AND OTHERS, *WHAT A WASTE 2.0: A GLOBAL SNAPSHOT OF SOLID WASTE MANAGEMENT TO 2050* (WORLD BANK GROUP 2018) DOI:10.1596/978-1-4648-1329-0, P. 28. LICENSE: CREATIVE COMMONS ATTRIBUTION CC BY 3.0 IGO.

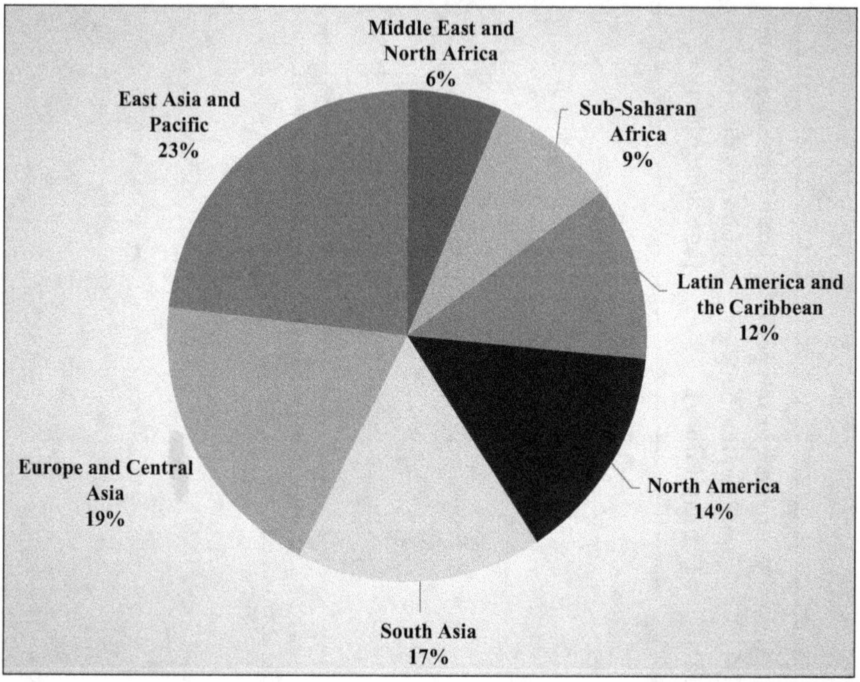

FIGURE 6 Municipal waste generation by region
SLIPA KAZA AND OTHERS, *WHAT A WASTE 2.0: A GLOBAL SNAPSHOT OF SOLID WASTE MANAGEMENT TO 2050* (WORLD BANK GROUP 2018) DOI:10.1596/978-1-4648-1329-0, P. 19. LICENSE: CREATIVE COMMONS ATTRIBUTION CC BY 3.0 IGO.

with progressive urbanization and economic development. While all types of wastes tend to increase with higher (disposable) income, putrescible wastes (such as food and yard waste or wood) increase at a slower rate than plastic, paper and metal wastes. Accordingly, the share of plastics, paper and metals in municipal solid waste grows, while the fraction of putrescible organic wastes decreases.[174]

Globally, 12 per cent of all municipal solid waste is plastic waste, that is 242 million tonnes in 2016 (see Figure 7). Since plastic materials are, on average, considerably lighter than other materials, they represent much more than 12 per cent of the waste volume and, accordingly, occupy more space in landfills and as litter in the streets.[175] The category usually includes bottles,

174 Hoornweg and Bhada-Tata (n 152) 17; Idris, Inanc and Hassan (n 168) 104; Kaza and others (n 167) 29 ff.

175 See Selke (n 95) 140–41.

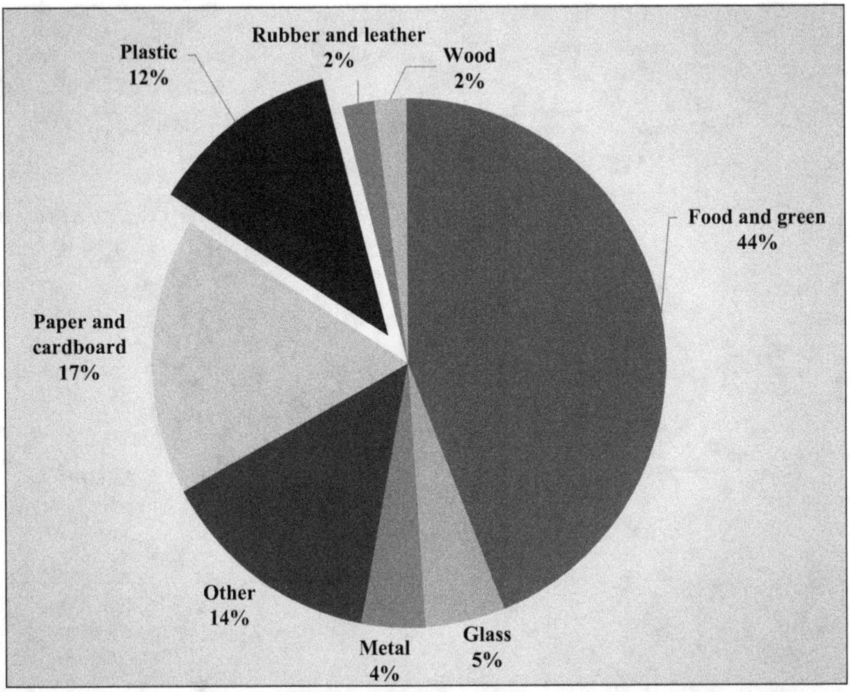

FIGURE 7 Global solid waste composition
SLIPA KAZA AND OTHERS, *WHAT A WASTE 2.0: A GLOBAL SNAPSHOT OF SOLID WASTE MANAGEMENT TO 2050* (WORLD BANK GROUP 2018) DOI:10.1596/978-1-4648-1329-0, P. 29. LICENSE: CREATIVE COMMONS ATTRIBUTION CC BY 3.0 IGO.

packaging, containers, bags and small plastic items, but often excludes rubbers and synthetic textile fibres, which are counted separately, as well as plastics used in construction materials, paper coatings, electric and electronic wastes, bulky wastes and household goods.[176]

At least a third of global municipal waste is openly dumped. In low-income countries, 93 per cent of waste is dumped, compared to 2 per cent in high-income countries. Some 37 per cent of global waste is disposed of in some form of a landfill, 8 per cent of which is disposed of in sanitary landfills with landfill gas collection systems. Incineration is used primarily in high-capacity,

176 See Hoornweg and Bhada-Tata (n 152) 16. About 21 per cent of an estimated amount of worldwide 20–50 million tonnes of wastes from electrical or electronic equipment are plastics. This corresponded in 2012 to a maximum of about 10.5 million tonnes – tendency increasing: Jef R Peeters and others, 'Closed Loop Recycling of Plastics Containing Flame Retardants' (2014) 84 Resources, Conservation and Recycling 35, 35.

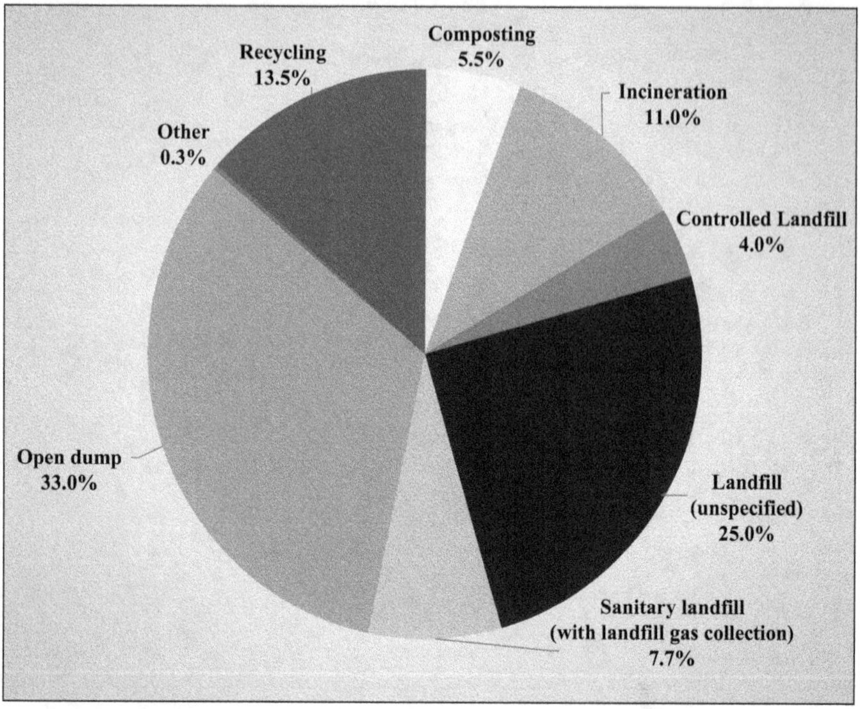

FIGURE 8 Global waste treatment and disposal
SLIPA KAZA AND OTHERS, *WHAT A WASTE 2.0: A GLOBAL SNAPSHOT OF SOLID WASTE MANAGEMENT TO 2050* (WORLD BANK GROUP 2018) DOI:10.1596/978-1-4648-1329-0, P. 29. LICENSE: CREATIVE COMMONS ATTRIBUTION CC BY 3.0 IGO.

high-income, and land-constrained countries. Globally, it accounts for 11 per cent of municipal solid wastes. Only 19 per cent is recovered through recycling and composting (see Figure 8).[177]

According to a study, approximately 6.3 billion tonnes of plastic wastes had been generated as of 2015, almost 80 per cent of which was accumulated in landfills or the natural environment. Three hundred million tonnes of plastic waste were generated alone in the year 2015. Without significant changes in production and waste management trends, about 12 billion tonnes of plastic wastes will be in landfills or the natural environment by the year 2050.[178]

177 Kaza and others (n 167) 4–6.

178 Geyer, Jambeck and Law (n 12); UNEP, *Single-Use Plastics: A Roadmap for Sustainability* (n 94) 5.

c) Recycling

Recycling is commonly seen as an important tool for waste minimisation. While degradable materials are returned to the agricultural value chain through the process of composting, recycling allows non-degradable materials to be returned to the industrial value chain. In a narrow sense, the term most usually refers to mechanical recycling, that is, material recovery in a proper sense.[179] There are also other ways of reintroducing wastes into the value chain and consumption cycle, including through the reuse of an object *per se*, fuel recovery (chemical or feedstock recycling) or energy recovery (thermal recycling).[180]

Recycling is motivated by the revalorization of resources and the 'sink value' of the waste absorption capacity offered by recycling activities.[181] Globally, less than 15 per cent of municipal solid waste is recycled (excluding energy recovery). In low-income countries, recycling rates tend to be high, while the biggest share of recycling activities can be attributed to the informal sector. Recycling markets are poorly regulated. By contrast, recycling in high-income countries is dominated by sophisticated collection services, high technology sorting and processing facilities, and effective regulation. Municipal recycling is promoted, with leading recycling cities achieving recycling rates of up to 70 per cent.[182]

Pre- and post-consumer thermoplastic polymers are sorted, washed, shredded and processed into 'new' polymers. The materials are upgraded, traded and fed into industrial supply chains. The purer the recyclate in resin types and colour, the more of the polymers' original properties can be retained and the higher the quality of yielded goods. Usually, the recyclability of plastic materials is limited to about six return cycles. Recycling with inherent quality loss of the material is sometimes termed *downcycling*. Accordingly, *upcycling* refers to recycling processes in which value is added to the original product, for instance because of an improvement in economic and environmental performance, or because the new product is suitable for a broader range of applications.[183]

---

179 Material recovery is referred to as primary recycling (if the end product has characteristics similar to the ones of the original product) or secondary recycling (if the end product has characteristics different from those of the original product). For more information about the process, see Michael M Fisher, 'Plastics Recycling' in AL Andrady (ed), *Plastics and the Environment* (Wiley Interscience 2003) 583–617; Greene (n 114) 114–17.

180 Fisher (n 179) 565.

181 Scheinberg, Wilson and Rodic (n 152) 126.

182 Hoornweg and Bhada-Tata (n 152) 5; Scheinberg, Wilson and Rodic (n 152) 128. See also Karin Blumenthal, 'Generation and Treatment of Municipal Waste' (Eurostats 2011) 31/2011 passim; Fisher (n 179) 569–73; 'Waste Atlas – Interactive Map with Visualized Waste Management Data' <http://www.atlas.d-waste.com> accessed 19 February 2022.

183 For instance, chemical recycling of waste polymers into carbon nanomaterials has been referred to as upcycling: Vilas Ganpat Pol, 'Upcycling: Converting Waste Plastics into

Durable goods are either collected by retailers, remanufacturers or kerbside collection services, or have to be dropped off.[184] Many objects, such as vehicles, are not designed to be disassembled and recycled. Disassembly costs most usually are not contained in the product price. Both industrial and municipal solid wastes often also contain composite materials, the mechanical recycling of which is generally problematic.[185] Adaptation of the product design to improve recyclability will take several years to show any impacts in recycling rates.[186]

The use of recycled plastics in food-contact materials is sometimes prohibited. Food containers made from recycled plastics therefore often include internal and external layers of virgin plastics in order to avoid contact between the recycled polymer and both the consumer and the food content.[187]

2) *Costs and Impacts of Waste and Disposal*

Integrated solid waste management addresses several issues: effective waste collection services help to maintain healthy conditions in cities, while careful waste treatment and safe disposal are necessary to reduce pollution and prevent waste-related environmental disasters.[188] Moreover, sound waste management plays a central role in broader resource management, for it can allow the reintroduction of valuable secondary resources into the production cycle, while mitigating resource depletion. This being the case, solid waste management belongs to the key responsibilities of local governments and is often their single largest budget item.[189] Full or nearly full cost recovery has so far only been achieved by high-income countries. While municipalities in high-income countries mainly invest in waste disposal, city governments in low-income countries spend most of their waste management budget on waste collection.

Paramagnetic, Conducting, Solid, Pure Carbon Microspheres' (2010) 44 Environmental Science & Technology 4753; Chuanwei Zhuo and Yiannis A Levendis, 'Upcycling Waste Plastics into Carbon Nanomaterials: A Review' (2014) 131 Journal of Applied Polymer Science 39931 (1). The production of biogas from wastes has also been associated with upcycling: Michael Martin and Amin Parsapour, 'Upcycling Wastes with Biogas Production: An Exergy and Economic Analysis', *Venice 2012: International Symposium on Energy from Biomass and Waste* (2012).

184 Fisher (n 179) 581.

185 Domininghaus (n 30) 2.

186 Ashwani K Gupta and David G Lilley, 'Thermal Destruction of Wastes and Plastics' in AL Andrady (ed), *Plastics and the Environment* (Wiley Interscience 2003) 635.

187 José Aguado and David P Serrano, *Feedstock Recycling of Plastic Wastes* (Royal Society of Chemistry 1999) 20.

188 See Scheinberg, Wilson and Rodic (n 152) xx.

189 Hoornweg and Bhada-Tata (n 152) 1.

Yet, collection rates in low-income countries tend to be lower, as collection is less efficient.[190] About 3.5 billion people lack access even to the most elementary waste management services.[191] As a result, uncontrolled waste disposal is still widespread.

Gradually, countries and cities move to more controlled forms of waste disposal. As a further step, they start now to move from mere end-of-pipe solutions to more sustainable and system-oriented forms of waste and resource management, which focus on waste prevention in the first place and allow for a circular economy, in which only small amounts of non-renewable resources have to be fed in and only small amounts of wastes are produced, as the bulk of the materials can be constantly renewed and reused.[192]

From the moment an object loses its usefulness and value to the holder, costs start to arise. The holder either has to store the undesirable object or organize its disposal. Costs of collection, transport, storage and final disposal of wastes, as well as of the respective infrastructure and its maintenance, either rest with the producer of waste, are formally borne by the municipalities and the state or – especially in the case of dumping – are otherwise passed on to the public at large or specific population segments in the form of negative externalities. Wastes have not only important economic implications but also various impacts on public health and the environment.

a) Social and Environmental Impacts

In the absence of appropriate collection and waste management services provided by or on behalf of municipalities, the informal sector often plays an important role in the collection of wastes, recycling and resource recovery. Dump sites in cities can be home to thousands of waste pickers who survive on the recovery of discarded materials.[193] The scavengers, as the waste pickers are called, are heavily exposed to the risks associated with dumping sites, as they live under unhygienic conditions in a dangerous environment, while they often lack the minimum protective equipment.[194]

Waste disposal in *open dumps* or poorly operated landfills is generally associated with different forms of health and environmental risks, including the

190 ibid 14.

191 'Waste Atlas – Interactive Map with Visualized Waste Management Data' (n 182).

192 See, in general, Singh and others (n 151).

193 Thaddeus Chidi Nzeadibe and Ignatius Ani Madu, 'Open Dump' in Carl Zimring and William Rathje, *Encyclopedia of Consumption and Waste: The Social Science of Garbage* (SAGE Publications, Inc 2012) 632.

194 Scheinberg, Wilson and Rodic (n 152) 16.

risk of direct physical harm by accidents, explosions and fires, as well as biological contamination of wastes with subsequent transmission of bacteriological pathogens through direct contact or food and water contamination. Dumps can be breeding grounds for disease-carrying rodents or insects. Chemical contamination of soil, food or water also counts among the risks and may have negative impacts on reproductive activities, notably stillbirth, low birth weights or specific birth defects.[195] Rainwater absorbs soluble and suspended contaminants while it percolates the waste layers. Eventually, the contaminated water will leak out from the site and enter surface watercourses or groundwater aquifers, while polluting drink water supplies. Contaminants are ingested by fish and other animals, and bioaccumulate throughout the food chain.[196] Health risks are moreover associated with the inhalation of noxious vapours that are emitted when dumped wastes decompose, or from toxic fumes that are caused by fires in the dump sites. Municipal wastes in open dump sites are often mixed with hazardous wastes, such as contaminated medical equipment, pesticides and other toxic chemical substances, batteries, mercury-containing wastes or explosives. Finally, open dumps often exacerbate the incidence of urban flooding and encourage poor sanitation habits.[197] In cities and municipalities that rely on open dumping, it is mostly poor segments of the urban population that live close to dumping sites and are directly exposed to these risks and to contaminants in air, water and soil in particular. In these population segments, diarrhoea is twice as high and acute respiratory infections six times higher as in other segments benefitting from better waste management services.[198] Children are especially vulnerable to the risks associated with wastes.[199] Also, solid waste workers and informal waste pickers, who are frequently exposed to the dangers of waste, have higher risks of infections and parasites, diarrhoea and pulmonary problems, especially in developing countries.[200]

Open – or uncontrolled – *burning* of plastics and other types of wastes is strictly prohibited in many countries, but is common in regions with poor

195 Philip Rushbrook, *Solid Waste Landfills in Middle- and Lower-Income Countries: A Technical Guide to Planning, Design, and Operation* (The World Bank 1999) 12. See also Hoornweg and Bhada-Tata (n 152) 6 and 26.

196 Rushbrook (n 195) 16.

197 Nzeadibe and Madu (n 193) 632. For a list of impacts of open dumping sites on human health and the environment, see also International Solid Waste Association ISWA, 'Closing of Open Dumps: Key Issue Paper' (2007) 2–4.

198 Hoornweg and Bhada-Tata (n 152) 26.

199 Scheinberg, Wilson and Rodic (n 152) 15.

200 ibid.

waste management services. It can produce large amounts of smoke, particulates and noxious odours. Persistent organic pollutants such as dioxins can be generated as by-products of incomplete incineration processes, especially when PVC or other chlorinated compounds are involved. Air pollution from open burning of wastes may cause severe health problems.[201]

Environmental impacts of *landfills* comprise 'emissions of hazardous substances to soil and groundwater, emissions of methane into the atmosphere, dust, noise, explosion risks and deterioration of land'.[202] Landfills and dumps are an important contributor to global methane generation and account for up to 20 per cent of anthropogenic methane production.[203] According to the Intergovernmental Panel on Climate Change (IPCC), methane is a greenhouse gas with a global warming potential 34 times stronger than that of carbon dioxide if compared over a 100-year period.[204] Since only a fraction of landfill facilities capture methane (and the ones that do, on average, recover only small percentages of total methane emissions), wastes in landfills significantly add to global warming.[205] Biodegradable fractions of plastic wastes contribute to this effect.[206] On the other hand, non-biodegradable plastics, which account for about 25 per cent of all solid wastes in landfills, are responsible for a decrease in landfill capacities, while they increase the risk of accidental fires with highly polluting emissions.[207] Groundwater pollution by dump or landfill leachate also remains a widespread problem, even though it is technically

---

201 CIEL, 'Plastic & Health' (n 10) 43, with reference; International Solid Waste Association ISWA (n 197) 3; Abhijit Roy, 'Open Burning' in Carl Zimring and William Rathje, *Encyclopedia of Consumption and Waste: The Social Science of Garbage* (SAGE Publications, Inc 2012) 629–30.

202 European Commission, Proposal for a Council Directive on the Landfill of Waste 1997 [COM (97) 105 final [1997] OJ C156/10], as cited in Williams (n 149) 174.

203 Michiel RJ Doorn, Morton A Barlaz and Susan A Thorneloe, *Estimate of Global Methane Emissions from Landfills and Open Dumps* (US Environmental Protection Agency EPA 1995) 1.

204 IPCC, 'Climate Change 2013: The Physical Science Basis. Contribution of Working Group I to the Fifth Assessment Report of the Intergovernmental Panel on Climate Change' (Cambridge University Press 2013) 714. Greenhouse gases are gases which, when in the atmosphere, allow transmission of short-wave radiation from the sun, but withhold long-wave radiation reflected from the Earth's surface, which causes global warming: Williams (n 149) 174 and 215. The global warming potential is the ratio of change in global mean surface temperature at a chosen point in time from the substance of interest relative to that from CO_2: see IPCC 663.

205 International Solid Waste Association ISWA (n 197) 3.

206 Gómez and Michel (n 116) 2589.

207 Aguado and Serrano (n 187) 15.

feasible to collect the leachate, as is done in modern landfills.[208] However, low- and middle-income countries often lack the necessary means for these technologies. Even in high-income countries, many landfills have been installed before high standards of groundwater protection were introduced. The remediation of old landfill sites is, therefore, an important task of waste management authorities.[209] Because of leaking additives, plastics can be an important contributor to leachate toxicity.[210]

Solid waste disposal also plays an important role in terms of landuse: Wastes take up more and more land, especially within and close to cities. The availability of disposal sites within the collection areas becomes limited, and siting is often opposed by local residents.[211] In small concentrations, wastes spoil landscapes and decrease their recreation value. In large concentrations, they pollute and severely deteriorate the land. The impact of plastic wastes in this regard is considerable. Because of their low density, plastics take more space when dumped and cause a greater visual impact on disposal than many other materials.[212] In urban regions, poor segments of the population are often closer and more exposed to waste disposal sites. The placing of dumps or landfills therefore poses concerns of environmental justice.[213]

Incineration of wastes causes carbon dioxide and, thus, contributes to global warming. The burning of certain types of wastes, including PVC, also produces persistent organic pollutants,[214] which are either released to the atmosphere or, when captured through efficient gas clean-up systems, contained in the solid residues and have to be landfilled. Air pollution and ash disposal are, thus, further challenges associated with waste incineration.[215] Incinerators also require high investment and may be, for different reasons, an unsuitable disposal option for a specific municipality. If designed as waste-to-energy facilities, however, incinerators allow heat or energy recovery and electricity generation.[216] In their solid form, plastic and other wastes may also serve as

208 See Idris, Inanc and Hassan (n 168) 105.

209 Heike Weber, 'Landfills, Modern' in Carl Zimring and William Rathje, *Encyclopedia of Consumption and Waste: The Social Science of Garbage* (SAGE Publications, Inc 2012) 473.

210 Aguado and Serrano (n 187) 15.

211 Hoornweg and Bhada-Tata (n 152) 4; Idris, Inanc and Hassan (n 168) 104.

212 Aguado and Serrano (n 187) 15.

213 Weber (n 209) 471.

214 Shah and others (n 102) 248.

215 Hoornweg and Bhada-Tata (n 152) 4. For detailed information about quantities and impacts of different incineration emissions, see Williams (n 149) 263–304.

216 Gupta and Lilley (n 186) 630.

refuse-derived fuel in industrial processes. With this, fossil-fuel-derived energy can be partially substituted and reduced.

Negative effects of improperly managed *composting* facilities include potential pollution and health risks because of leachate and aerosols, odours, fires, dust and vermin.[217] Gaseous emissions from composting often are malodorous and might be toxic. Bioaerosols can contain microbial organisms such as bacteria or fungi, the spores of which can lead to allergic responses.[218] As a substitute for other disposal methods, however, composting of wastes can have a net positive environmental impact. Globally, about 46 per cent of municipal solid waste, especially food and garden wastes, is considered putrescible. Along with paper, card and certain types of (natural fibre) textiles, about three-quarters of global waste is potentially biodegradable. Separate collection of some fractions of this waste with subsequent composting removes large parts of biodegradable waste from the waste stream. Composting processes as a substitute for landfilling may reduce greenhouse gas emissions, ecotoxicity potential and eutrophication. The use of compost as a substitute for synthetic fertilizers entails additional positive effects, including with regard to water and electricity consumption.[219]

b) Economic Implications

From an economic point of view, wastes bear extremely high costs for individuals, private companies and municipalities. The collection and disposal of wastes often represents the largest budget item of cities and municipalities.[220] Wastes, however, also bear secondary, less visible economic costs, including in the form of land degradation, lower agricultural yields or a decline in tourism. Waste-related clean-up costs and costs for soil and groundwater remediation can be important as well. Waste may also raise costs in health care and social protection. Furthermore, wastes impose opportunity costs in terms of land use and the allocation of financial resources. Finally, waste generation implies temporary or final loss of material or energy resources. The loss is temporary if efforts are made for resource and energy recovery, which again impose costs.

---

217 MPM Taha and others, 'Bioaerosol Releases from Compost Facilities: Evaluating Passive and Active Source Terms at a Green Waste Facility for Improved Risk Assessments' (2006) 40 Atmospheric Environment 1159, 1159.

218 See, in general, Peter Sykes, Ken Jones and JohnD Wildsmith, 'Managing the Potential Public Health Risks from Bioaerosol Liberation at Commercial Composting Sites in the UK: An Analysis of the Evidence Base' (2007) 52 Resources, Conservation and Recycling 410; Taha and others (n 217).

219 Greene (n 114) 133, including references.

220 Hoornweg and Bhada-Tata (n 152) 1; Kaza and others (n 167) 102.

If recovery is possible, wastes provide an important potential source of valuable resources and energy. Waste management, including the recovery of resources, is an important economic sector. Also, the contribution of the informal waste sector to local economies often is substantial. Not only in low- and middle-income countries may the informal waste sector, including both individuals and micro-enterprises, compete with municipal collection and disposal systems.[221] In China, about 20 per cent of discards are recovered for recycling, mostly by informal waste pickers.[222] China also used to be the main importer of post-consumer waste plastics. In 2017, an estimated US$4.3 billion worth of plastic waste and scrap was exported worldwide, most of it by developed countries (71 per cent). The majority of importing countries are developing countries (75 per cent). China alone imported 64 per cent of plastic waste in 2017. China, however, banned the import of non-industrial plastic waste in 2018.[223] China's action triggered other countries in the East Asian and Pacific region to impose import restrictions on plastic wastes, including Indonesia, Malaysia, the Republic of Korea, Thailand, Viet Nam, and Taiwan Province of China. In 2019, global trade in plastic waste was 46 per cent lower than before the introduction of these import restrictions.[224]

C *Life-cycle Analysis and Impact Assessments*

Informed decisions play a decisive role in sustainable development. Without knowing the impacts of different options for action, diverse interests cannot be weighed against each other and balanced with the necessary diligence and care. It is not only the state, as the central regulatory authority and important procurer, but also private manufacturers and consumers that are important

---

221 See, in general, Kaveri Gill, *Of Poverty and Plastic: Scavenging and Scrap Trading Entrepreneurs in India's Urban Informal Economy* (Paperback edn, Oxford University Press 2012). See also Scheinberg, Wilson and Rodic (n 152) 1–2; Hoornweg and Bhada-Tata (n 152) 15.

222 Hoornweg and Bhada-Tata (n 152) 28; Roland Linzner and Stefan Salhofer, 'Municipal Solid Waste Recycling and the Significance of Informal Sector in Urban China' (2014) 32 Waste Management & Research 896, 905.

223 See WTO Notification G/TBT/N/CHN/1211 of 18 July 2017; WTO Notification G/TBT/N/CHN/1228 of 15 November 2017. See also Amy L Brooks, Shunli Wang and Jenna R Jambeck, 'The Chinese Import Ban and Its Impact on Global Plastic Waste Trade' (2018) 4 Science Advances eaat0131.

224 WTO Committee on Trade and Environment, 'Communication on Trade in Plastics, Sustainability and Development by the United Nations Conference on Trade and Development (UNCTAD)' (2020) JOB/TE/63 5–6.

decision makers. They form our production and consumption patterns by their daily decisions, including with regard to material and product choices.

Environmental performance of plastic materials is currently gaining weight as a factor in the decision process, especially because of an increasing demand for environmentally sound materials.[225] However, environmental and health impacts are often not easily measurable, quantifiable or foreseeable. Life-cycle assessments (LCA) are a tool to evaluate potential impacts of different product alternatives, materials or disposal methods and compare them with one another. Given the many relevant factors and uncertainties in the life cycle of a product, LCAs are highly complex, while their quality depends on the availability of extensive sets of useful data. They potentially measure the impacts of a product throughout its life cycle (from 'cradle to grave'), 'starting from the extraction of raw materials from the earth and ending at the waste products being returned to the earth'.[226] LCAs are commonly used in green or sustainable chemistry and engineering, a discipline tailored to advance sustainable development.[227] They can play an important role in public and private environmental management, for instance in green procurement.[228] Eco-labels and eco-design are also increasingly based on LCAs. LCA is only one out of several environmental management techniques and can be used along with other, complementary assessment tools.[229]

Although the approach was first used to assess life cycle-costs of investment goods, in particular in public procurement (e.g. weapon systems), the scope of

225 Other relevant factors for material selection include feedstock and processing costs, processability, service performance of the material with regard to the object's final purpose, market conditions, legal requirements, available technologies and consumer preferences.

226 Yates and Barlow (n 50) 55. See also Domininghaus (n 30) 2.

227 Shawn Hunter, Richard Helling and Dawn Shiang, 'Integration of LCA and Life-Cycle Thinking within the Themes of Sustainable Chemistry & Engineering' in Mary Ann Curran (ed), *Life Cycle Assessment Handbook: A Guide for Environmentally Sustainable Products* (John Wiley & Sons 2012) 369–73.

228 See Jeroen B Guinée and others, *Handbook on Life Cycle Assessment: Operational Guide to the ISO Standards*, vol 7 (Jeroen B Guinée ed, Kluwer Academic Publishers 2004) 6; ISO 14040:2006 (n 150).

229 While product footprints usually are subject to bottom-up LCA, environmentally extended input–output analysis (EEIOA) is used to assess footprints at global or national level: see Julien Boucher and others, *Review of Plastic Footprint Methodologies: Laying the Foundation for the Development of a Standardised Plastic Footprint Measurement Tool* (IUCN 2019) 7. Further tools or techniques include, for instance, risk assessment, environmental performance evaluation, environmental auditing and environmental impact assessment. See Guinée and others (n 228) 9; Mary Ann Curran, 'Life Cycle Assessment: A Review of the Methodology and Its Application to Sustainability' (2013) 2 Current Opinion in Chemical Engineering 273, 275–76.

LCA traditionally focuses on environmental issues.[230] The ISO played a key role in the standardization of environmental LCA (i). In more recent years, however, the assessment technique has been more and more applied in a broader context, and may include impacts beyond the environment. UN Environment increasingly promotes LCA as a tool to better achieve sustainable development objectives and includes social and socio-economic impacts in what is called life-cycle sustainability assessment (LCSA) (ii). With regard to plastics, impact assessments generally serve to compare environmental footprints of different types of materials or different disposal options (iii).

i The ISO Standard Series on LCA

Building on the work of other international bodies, ISO elaborated a series of standards to harmonize the application and interpretation of LCA. The standard series increases comparability of different LCA studies. In its main standard ISO 14040:2006 (first published in 1997), the ISO defines LCA as 'compilation and evaluation of the inputs, outputs and potential environmental impacts of a product system throughout its life cycle'.[231] A product system in the sense of the ISO standard is the total system of unit processes involved in the life cycle of a product.[232] Input refers to the 'product, material or energy flow that enters a unit process', including 'raw materials, intermediate products and co-products'.[233] Energy and water consumption are covered by the standard. Land use is not directly referred to in the ISO standard but is broadly accepted as an impact category.[234] Output, on the other hand, refers to the 'product, material or energy flow that leaves a unit process', including 'raw materials, intermediate products, co-products and releases'.[235] Output as analysed in LCAs generally includes waste generation and the emission of (hazardous) substances as caused by the extraction (or production) of input resources or by the production, transportation, use or disposal of the product.

The set of data on input and output of a product system is recorded in what is called a life-cycle inventory. Impact assessment methodologies help to

---

230 Gjalt Huppes and Mary Ann Curran, 'Environmental Life Cycle Assessment: Background and Perspective' in Mary Ann Curran (ed), *Life Cycle Assessment Handbook: A Guide for Environmentally Sustainable Products* (John Wiley & Sons 2012) 1–4.

231 ISO 14040:2006 (n 150). See also Guinée and others (n 228) 5.

232 Guinée and others (n 228) 5.

233 ISO 14040:2006 (n 150).

234 See, for instance, Thomas Koellner and Roland Scholz, 'Assessment of Land Use Impacts on the Natural Environment. Part 1: An Analytical Framework for Pure Land Occupation and Land Use Change' (2007) 12 The International Journal of Life Cycle Assessment 16, 16.

235 ISO 14040:2006 (n 150).

translate this data into environmental impacts, for instance on human health, ecosystem quality or resource availability.[236] LCAs are, thus, mostly quantitative in nature. Where quantitative data is missing, qualitative aspects are taken into account.[237] Once the impacts have been evaluated and quantified, different impact categories can be defined and compared, in order to identify unintended environmental trade-offs between such impact categories. Moreover, the environmental burden of different product alternatives can be directly compared.[238]

ii The Life Cycle Initiative

Even though the concept of LCA was designed for assessing environmental impacts, the discussion on how to deal with social and socio-economic impacts within the LCA framework is almost as old as the concept itself.[239] In 2002, the Life Cycle Initiative was launched, a public–private, multi-stakeholder partnership which is hosted by UN Environment. The initiative is a response to the call for a life-cycle economy that was formulated by states around the world in the Malmö Ministerial Declaration in 2000.[240] It moreover contributes to the 10-Year Framework of Programmes to promote sustainable consumption and production patterns,[241] as requested at the World Summit on Sustainable Development in Johannesburg in 2002 and adopted at the UN Conference on Sustainable Development in Rio de Janeiro, Brazil, in 2012. With the initiative, UN Environment promotes life-cycle thinking, a concept to take into account environmental, social and economic impacts of a product over its entire life cycle in decision-making processes, as well as in the development of policies and products. The goals of life-cycle thinking

236 See Yates and Barlow (n 50) 55.

237 Guinée and others (n 228) 6. The availability of reliable data is one of the biggest challenges related to LCAs. Databases in increasingly standardized formats are being developed in different countries. See ibid 8.

238 Michaelangelo D Tabone and others, 'Sustainability Metrics: Life Cycle Assessment and Green Design in Polymers' (2010) 44 Environmental Science & Technology 8264, 8264.

239 See James Fava and others (eds), *Conceptual Framework for Life-Cycle Impact Assessment* (SETAC 1993); as cited in Evan Stuart Andrews and others, *Guidelines for Social Life Cycle Assessment of Products: Social and Socio-Economic LCA Guidelines Complementing Environmental LCA and Life Cycle Costing, Contributing to the Full Assessment of Goods and Services within the Context of Sustainable Development* (Catherine Benoît and Bernard Mazijn eds, UNEP 2009) 17.

240 Global Ministerial Environment Forum, 'Malmö Ministerial Declaration' (Sixth Special Session of the UNEP Governing Council 2000) UNEP/GC/DEC/SS.VI/1.

241 UN Conference on Sustainable Development, 'A 10-Year Framework of Programmes on Sustainable Consumption and Production Patterns' (2012) A/CONF.216/5.

are to reduce a product's resource use and emissions to the environment and to improve its socio-economic performance throughout its life cycle. Within the concept of life cycle thinking, LCA serves as a tool to find the potentials to reach these goals in each life-cycle stage, including production, packaging, distribution, use, maintenance, and eventually recycling, reuse, recovery or final disposal.

Under the auspices of the Life Cycle Initiative, LCA methodologies as described in the ISO standard are applied to aspects other than environmental ones. In 2009, UN Environment published guidelines for social LCA of products that show how 'production and consumption impacts on the workers, the local communities, the consumers, the society and all value chain actors' can be included in the assessment.[242]

Similar assessment methodologies have also been applied to evaluate the overall costs of a product. Life-cycle costing takes into account all costs related to the production, use (or maintenance) and disposal of a product. In fact, the purchase price often reflects only a small part of the costs that are caused by a product throughout its life cycle.[243] Costs that are not reflected in the product price and have to be borne by others are referred to as (negative) externalities. In life-cycle costing, these kinds of costs are anticipatorily included in the assessment if it can be assumed that they are to be internalized (due to new regulations) in the near future.[244]

When combining the traditional model of (environmental) LCA with social LCA and life-cycle costing, life-cycle thinking can be applied to the three pillars of sustainability (environmental, social and economic).[245] Under the umbrella of the Life Cycle Initiative, this kind of holistic perspective is promoted as overarching LCSA. LCSA 'offers a way of incorporating sustainability in decision-making processes' and fosters the development of sustainable policies and products.[246]

---

242 Andrews and others (n 239) 5.

243 ibid 35.

244 See David Hunkeler and others (eds), *Environmental Life Cycle Costing* (SETAC; CRC Press 2008) 173. Life-cycle costing was developed by the US military in the 1960s and is broadly used in different industry sectors, especially for investment goods: see Andrews and others (n 239) 35; Huppes and Curran (n 230) 1.

245 On the concept of sustainable development in international law, see Section 2.1.A.ii.2 below.

246 Andreas Ciroth and others, *Towards a Life Cycle Sustainablity Assessment: Making Informed Choices on Products* (Sonia Valdivia and others eds, UNEP/SETAC Life Cycle Initiative 2011) 1.

iii LCAs and Plastics

A number of studies have used LCAs to examine and compare the environmental performance of different types of plastics and other materials, in order to provide guidance towards a more sustainable use, design and disposal of products. The majority of the studies compare conventional with biodegradable (bio-based) plastics, which have been synthesized in the quest for more sustainable materials. Some studies compare the environmental performance of plastics when used in specific applications to the environmental performance of other materials such as glass or paper. A small number of studies focus on recycling or compare different end-of-life options. Even when existing LCAs consider waste management scenarios, they usually ignore environmental leakage of packaging. LCA can be used not only to quantify product footprints, but also to evaluate the plastic footprint of individuals, companies, sectors or countries.[247]

The studies usually include different impact categories, particularly fossil resource depletion, carbon footprint and global warming potential. Further impact categories include smog creation, eutrophication, acidification, and human and ecosystem toxicity.[248] The results of the assessments, and their comparability, heavily depend on the chosen system boundaries (cradle to granule, cradle to gate, cradle to grave or cradle to cradle), the materials (PLA, starch-based polymers etc.) and kind of objects (packaging, disposable or durable objects) that are assessed, the impact categories that are observed, variable geographical or other conditions and basic assumptions made for the assessment, including with regard to allocation methods, the use fertilizers in (bio-based) feedstock production, the use of (non-) renewable energy in the whole production process and disposal options in cradle-to-grave analyses.[249] Owing to these variables, results diverge from one study to another, while overall comparability is limited and may require normalization of the results and sensitivity or scenario analysis. The studies, however, provide an overview of the environmental and human health impacts of plastics within the system boundaries of the studies and show what trade-offs there can be between plastics and other materials, between biodegradable, bio-based and conventional polymer production or between different disposal options.[250]

247 Boucher and others (n 229) 7.

248 Hottle, Bilec and Landis (n 49) 1901–02; Tabone and others (n 238) 8266; Yates and Barlow (n 50) 55.

249 Yates and Barlow (n 50) 62.

250 See Hottle, Bilec and Landis (n 49) 1901.

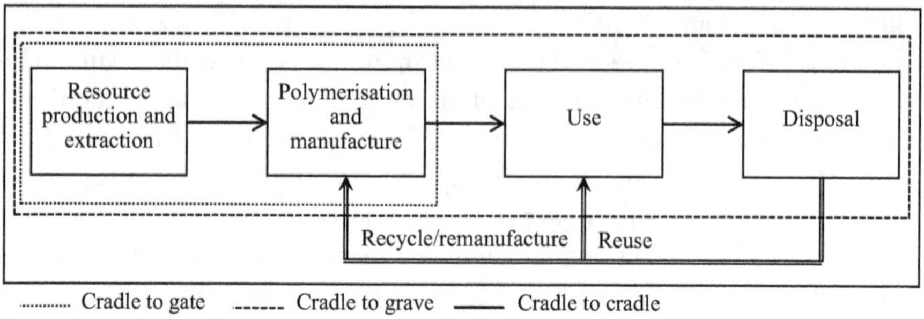

FIGURE 9 System boundaries of life-cycle assessments
ADAPTED FROM TROY A HOTTLE, MELISSA M BILEC AND AMY E LANDIS, 'SUSTAINABILITY ASSESSMENTS OF BIO-BASED POLYMERS' (2013) 98 POLYMER DEGRADATION AND STABILITY 1898 DOI:10.1016/J.POLYMDEGRADSTAB.2013.06.016, P. 1900. © 2013 WITH PERMISSION FROM ELSEVIER.

With regard to the system boundaries, many studies are confined to cradle-to-granule or cradle-to-gate analyses, excluding the use and end-of-life phases of the products (see Figure 9). Even cradle-to-grave studies sometimes omit the use or transportation phases.[251] Including the end-of-life phase in the assessment provides more comprehensive results, but also introduces greater amounts of uncertainty and variability, as there is, for instance, little life-cycle data available on the specific impacts of different disposal options.[252]

Throughout their life cycle, the different types of plastics have different impacts on human health and the environment:

– Fossil feedstock of *petrochemical, non-biodegradable polymers* can be calculated in energy rather than a material input by multiplying the amount consumed by its heat of combustion.[253] To calculate total fossil fuel depletion of the product from cradle to gate, the energy necessary for processing the feedstock has to be added, as well as the energy for transportation. Cradle-to-grave analyses have to be based on assumptions on disposal methods. When the products are landfilled, the carbon in the plastic is not likely to contribute to global warming, since it is locked in the landfills for an indefinite period of time. In this scenario, the discarded products take a relatively large amount of space for the same period of time. When the products are incinerated, their carbon content, which before has been fixed within the fossil resource for several millennia, is set free and emitted to

251 Yates and Barlow (n 50) 55.
252 Hottle, Bilec and Landis (n 49) 1898.
253 Yates and Barlow (n 50) 55.

the atmosphere.[254] When incinerated in waste-to-energy facilities, energy recoveries can be deducted from the total amount of used energy and fossil fuel depletion if they are used to substitute for fossil-based energy sources.[255] Recycled plastics may have a smaller effect on global warming if less energy is used to recycle them than is needed for the production of virgin materials.[256]

- *Bio-based polymers* which are derived from agricultural products require prior cultivation of the crop that provides the feedstock. LCAs on respective polymers thus include the fuel required for farming activities, as well as for the manufacture and transport of fertilizers, herbicides and pesticides. They might also include other impact categories such as land use, water consumption or soil depletion.[257] Since their feedstock contains atmospheric CO_2, bio-based plastics that are landfilled at the end of their service life potentially reduce greenhouse gases in the atmosphere by sequestering carbon.[258] This effect is, however, extenuated by the carbon released to the environment due to the production and use of these plastics, as well as through the collection, transport and processing of the garbage. Also, in some environmental impact categories, such as eutrophication, ozone depletion and non-carcinogenic human health, bio-based polymers might have higher impacts when compared to petroleum-based plastics.[259]
- *Biodegradable polymers* can be incorporated into organic recycling schemes based on anaerobic digestion or composting. As a consequence, less waste has to be sent for incineration or landfill, which reduces the impacts that are associated with these disposal methods.[260] In composting processes, the carbon content of the materials is converted into CO_2 rather than methane, as would be the case in landfilling.[261] Composting and anaerobic digestion

254 A kilogram of plastic produces an average of 2.8 kg of carbon dioxide: Hottle, Bilec and Landis (n 49) 1899.

255 Tarja Häkkinen and Sirje Vares, 'Environmental Impacts of Disposable Cups with Special Focus on the Effect of Material Choices and End of Life' (2010) 18 Journal of Cleaner Production 1458, 1462.

256 Gómez and Michel (n 116) 2584.

257 Yates and Barlow (n 50) 55. A complete replacement of polyolefins by bio-based plastics in packaging could cause serious competition between polymer feedstock and food production: see Gerald Scott, 'Science and Standards' in Emo Chiellini and Roberto Solaro (eds), *Biodegradable Polymers and Plastics* (Springer Science & Business Media 2003) 5.

258 Gómez and Michel (n 116) 2584.

259 See Hottle, Bilec and Landis (n 49) 1901.

260 Gómez and Michel (n 116) 2590.

261 ibid 2584.

can, however, also have negative impacts on the environment.[262] Also, the actual disposal route of plastic products is mostly uncertain. Even if a product is compostable in industrial facilities, relevant infrastructure in a specific region is not necessarily sufficiently developed. Biodegradable plastics therefore often follow the main waste stream and predominant disposal methods. Landfilling of biodegradable plastics can negatively influence their environmental profile if they have the potential for methane emissions.[263] Owing to a lack of data on the extent of biodegradation of different biopolymers in the different environments, on the main disposal routes of biopolymers and on the impacts of these disposal methods, 'the environmental impacts associated with the creation, use, and disposal of [biodegradable] polymers remains unclear'.[264]

– *Biodegradable plastics made from petrochemical feedstocks* probably have the greatest potential to contribute to greenhouse gas emissions.[265] When they degrade, they release fossil carbon dioxide to the atmosphere. If they biodegrade in a landfill, they might generate methane. Also, the environmental performance of *hybrid plastics* that are made from both bio-based and petrochemical feedstocks is relatively poor from a greenhouse gas emissions perspective. These materials usually are neither recyclable nor truly biodegradable.[266]

Figure 10 shows cradle-to-gate impact assessment results in ten different impact categories for a number of petrochemical and bio-based polymers, as well as a hybrid material. Results from the respective study show a disparity between bio-based and petroleum-based polymers: although bio-based polymers rank highly in terms of green design,[267] they exhibit relatively large

262 Yates and Barlow (n 50) 62.

263 Hottle, Bilec and Landis (n 49) 1905.

264 ibid 1905. See also Yates and Barlow (n 50) 62.

265 Gómez and Michel (n 116) 2584.

266 ibid.

267 The assessment on green design was based on the Twelve Principles of Green Chemistry as developed by Paul Anastas and John Warner (Prevention; Atom Economy; Less Hazardous Chemical Syntheses; Designing Safer Chemicals; Safer Solvents and Auxiliaries; Design for Energy Efficiency; Use of Renewable Feedstocks; Reduce Derivatives; Catalysis; Design for Degradation; Real-time analysis for Pollution Prevention; Inherently Safer Chemistry for Accident Prevention) and the Twelve Principles of Green Engineering as developed by Paul Anastas and Julie Zimmerman (Inherent Rather Than Circumstantial; Prevention Instead of Treatment; Design for Separation; Maximize Efficiency; Output-Pulled Versus Input-Pushed; Conserve Complexity; Durability Rather Than Immortality; Meet Need, Minimize Excess; Minimize Material Diversity; Integrate Material and Energy Flows;

environmental impacts from production and, therefore, rank in the middle in LCA rankings. Polyolefins perform well in cradle-to-gate LCA analyses, whereas complex polymers (PET, PVC, and polycarbonate (PC)) place at the bottom of both LCA and green design ranking.[268]

Most of the studies that have been reviewed for this chapter conclude that bio-based and/or biodegradable polymers that are currently available on the market are not necessarily more environmentally friendly than the petrochemical polymers.[269] However, it is repeatedly emphasized that the environmental profile of this relatively young class of polymers is supposed to rapidly improve in the future.

LCAs have also been used to assess the environmental performance and impact of recycled plastics. As the raw material extracting and manufacturing processes have the biggest share of the carbon footprint of a plastic product, recycling can considerably reduce the carbon footprint. The best results can be achieved if the proportion of recycled raw material is maximized and processing optimized.[270] On the other hand, recycling often implies higher water usage due to the large amounts of water used in the washing process of recycled plastics.[271] In spite of this, recycling offers substantial environmental advantages for petroleum-based plastics when compared to other disposal options, also due to a reduction of feedstock requirements and energy input.[272]

The recycling of biodegradable polymers is more complex. Traditional recycling facilities might not be properly equipped for dealing with these materials and cannot prevent them from fouling other recycling streams. Although it is technically feasible to mechanically recycle some biodegradable polymers, it

Design for Commercial "Afterlife"; Renewable Rather Than Depleting): Tabone and others (n 238) 8265. See also Paul T Anastas and JC Warner, *Green Chemistry: Theory and Practice* (Oxford University Press 1998); Paul T Anastas and Julie B Zimmerman, 'Design through the 12 Principles of Green Engineering' (2003) 37 Environmental Science & Technology 94A.

268 Tabone and others (n 238) 8264.

269 See, for instance, Yates and Barlow (n 50) 65.

270 Aaron Dormer and others, 'Carbon Footprint Analysis in Plastics Manufacturing' (2013) 51 Journal of Cleaner Production 133, 133. Up to 90 per cent of the energy used in the production of plastics from virgin materials can be saved if plastics are recycled instead. One tonne of recycled plastic saves 5,774 kWh of energy, 16.3 barrels of oil and 22 cubic metres of landfill. See BIR, 'BIR – Bureau of International Recycling: Plastics' <https://archive.bir.org/industry/plastics/> accessed 19 February 2022.

271 Greene (n 114) 120.

272 Hottle, Bilec and Landis (n 49) 1905.

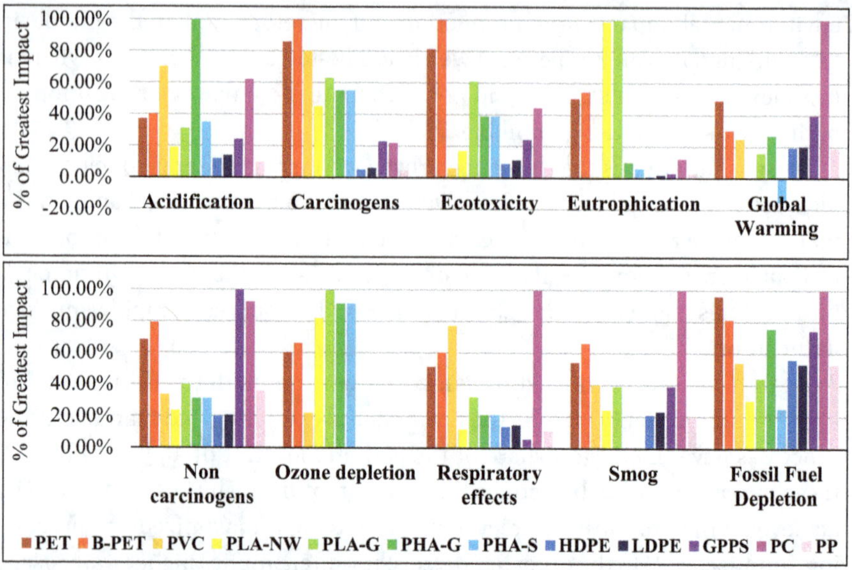

FIGURE 10 Cradle-to-gate LCA results for petroleum-based, bio-based and mixed polymers
The figure shows crade-to-gate impact assessment results for seven polymers that are generated from fossil-fuel feedstocks (PET; PVC; HDPE; LDPE; PS; PC; PP), two bio-based polymers, each in two different varieties (polylactic acid made via a general process (PLA-G) and a process reported by Nature-Works LLC (PLA-NW); polyhydroxyalkanoate derived from corn grain (PHA-G) and from corn stover (PHA-S)), as well as one hybrid bio/petroleum polymer (biopolyethylene terephthalate (B-PET)). Cradle-to-gate assessments only include impacts resulting from the production stage, but not from use or disposal. Ten different impact categories have been assessed.
REPRINTED WITH PERMISSION FROM MICHAELANGELO D TABONE AND OTHERS, 'SUSTAINABILITY METRICS: LIFE CYCLE ASSESSMENT AND GREEN DESIGN IN POLYMERS' (2010) 44 ENVIRONMENTAL SCIENCE & TECHNOLOGY 8264, 8266. © 2010 AMERICAN CHEMICAL SOCIETY.

currently is not economically attractive owing to the lack of continuous and reliable supply of corresponding waste materials.[273]

LCAs can also be useful to compare the environmental performance of plastics and of other materials in specific applications. The results of such studies are ambiguous and strongly depend on the system boundaries of the studies and the chosen parameters.[274] Plastic leakage to the environment and related

273 JH Song and others, 'Biodegradable and Compostable Alternatives to Conventional Plastics' (2009) 364 Philosophical Transactions of the Royal Society B: Biological Sciences 2127, 2130.

274 Disposable PET cups were, for instance, reported to have greater use of resources and release of harmful emissions than PE- or PLA-coated carton-based cups: Häkkinen

impacts are often not included among the parameters examined.[275] There are also information gaps relating to long-term impacts on ecosystems and health by microplastics. Furthermore, a LCA-based report by UN Environment has clearly shown that the design and type of use of a product may have a greater influence on its environmental impact than the material itself. Reusable products usually have lower environmental impacts than single-use products. Replacing one disposable product (e.g. made of plastic) with another disposable product made of a different material (e.g. paper, biodegradable plastic) is only likely to transfer the burdens and create other problems. UN Environment therefore encourages states to replace single-use plastic products with reusable products as part of a circular economy approach.[276]

While they allow us to compare potential impacts of different materials or products, LCAs circumvent the question whether a specific product is needed at all. However, the key to effective marine plastic pollution mitigation strategies may not only include careful, sustainable product design and recycling management, but also moderate, needs-based, environmentally sound consumer behaviour.

2 Plastic Pollution in the Seas

All through the history of human civilization, waste has been dumped in and close to the oceans or in rivers, lakes and other waterways. As long as populations were small and refuses mostly biodegradable, there was only little evidence of resulting human impacts on marine environments.[277] Even today,

---

and Vares (n 255) 1461. By contrast, plastic baby food pots were found to impose a slightly smaller burden to the environment than glass jars in three European countries: Sebastien Humbert and others, 'Life Cycle Assessment of Two Baby Food Packaging Alternatives: Glass Jars vs. Plastic Pots' (2009) 14 The International Journal of Life Cycle Assessment 95. In an assessment of different sorts of shopping bags in China, Hong Kong and India, bags made from non-woven fabrics, especially PP, showed the least global warming potential, followed by woven cotton bags. When compared to these two groups, both plastic and paper bags were found to have high global warming potential, especially because reuse rates are considerably lower for plastic and paper bags than for non-woven and woven bags: Subramanian Senthilkannan Muthu and others, 'Carbon Footprint of Shopping (Grocery) Bags in China, Hong Kong and India' (2011) 45 Atmospheric Environment 469, 472.

275 A report published by IUCN found that there is still no robust impact assessment method in place to allow full alignment of plastic leakage approaches with the LCA framework: Boucher and others (n 229) 35.

276 UNEP, *Addressing Single-Use Plastic Products Pollution Using a Life Cycle Approach* (n 159).

277 Gregory and Andrady (n 133) 379.

there is a widespread belief that the ocean is resilient to human influences, no matter 'how much we take out of – or put into – it'.[278] Yet, with the industrial age, the tide has turned. Related phenomena such as rapid population growth, global warming and the widespread use and disposal of bio-stable materials that find their way into the oceans have brought about some fundamental changes. Our impact on the oceans has been detrimental in the last century and probably is, at least to some extent, irreversible.[279] Human activities on land and the seas put increasing stresses and strains on the oceans and marine biodiversity to the extent that the capacity of the marine environment to regenerate may have passed its limit.[280] Ocean pollution through marine littering, and plastics in particular, is only one out of a wide range of factors that drastically disturb the natural balance of the ocean.[281] However, the issue presents us with enormous challenges, and is likely to do even more so in the future, as the full scale of the problem is still unknown.[282]

Marine pollution is generally defined as the 'direct or indirect introduction by humans of substances or energy into the marine environment (including estuaries), resulting in harm to living resources, hazards to human health, hindrances to marine activities including fishing, impairment of the quality of sea water and reduction of amenities'.[283] *Marine litter*, as one form of marine pollution, can be defined as 'any persistent, manufactured or processed solid

278 Earle (n 14) 17–18.

279 A study on anthropogenic impact on different marine ecosystems concluded in 2008 that 'no area is unaffected by human influence and that a large fraction (41 per cent) is strongly affected by multiple drivers': Benjamin S Halpern and others, 'A Global Map of Human Impact on Marine Ecosystems' (2008) 319 Science 948, 948.

280 See United Nations, 'UNCLOS at 30' (United Nations 2012) 6 <http://www.un.org/depts/los/convention_agreements/pamphlet_unclos_at_30.pdf> accessed 19 February 2022; Tullio Treves, 'Principles and Objectives of the Legal Regime Governing Areas Beyond National Jurisdiction' in AG Oude Elferink and EJ Molenaar (eds), *The International Legal Regime of Areas beyond National Jurisdiction: Current and Future Developments* (Koninklijke Brill NV 2010) 22.

281 Other factors include overfishing, the widespread use of destructive fishing techniques and the destruction of habitats, the continuous loss of biological diversity, ocean acidification due to global warming, eutrophication and noise pollution, as well as pollution due to the release of oil and other persistent pollutants into the sea or nuclear testing.

282 See Gregory and Andrady (n 133) 380.

283 United Nations, 'Glossary of Environment Statistics' (United Nations 1997) Series F, No. 67 (UN Doc. ST/ESA/STAT/SER.F/67) 47; GESAMP, 'The State of the Marine Environment' (UNEP 1990) Reports and Studies No 39, preliminary notes. cf United Nations Convention on the Law of the Sea (UNCLOS) (opened for signature on 10 December 1982, entered into force on 16 November 1994) 1833 UNTS 397, 21 ILM 1261 (1982) art 1(4).

material discarded, disposed of or abandoned in the marine and coastal environment'.[284] It consists of:

> items that have been made or used by people and deliberately discarded into the sea or rivers or on beaches; brought indirectly to the sea with rivers, sewage, storm water or winds; accidentally lost, including material lost at sea in bad weather (fishing gear, cargo); or deliberately left by people on beaches and shores.[285]

Such items not only include plastic products or fragments but also glass, metals, natural fibres, paper and wood. Plastics, however, represent the biggest proportion of marine debris, and entail a number of particular challenges, especially their 'nearly indestructible morphology' and toxic substances they accumulate and/or release.[286] Although plastics constitute only about 12 per cent of global municipal wastes, they comprise 60–80 per cent of wastes that are accumulated in marine environments, including beaches and coastal waters, ocean water columns and the seabed.[287] *Marine plastic pollution* thus primarily involves the accumulation of plastic debris of all sizes in marine environments. The presence of widespread plastic debris – or litter – and microplastics in the sea poses a severe problem with a wide range of significant implications for the marine environment and its inhabitants, but also for human activities and health.

While representing one of the youngest generations of anthropogenic litter, which originated in the mid-twentieth century only, plastics are now ubiquitous in the marine environment.[288] Although the problem of marine plastic

284 UNEP, *Marine Litter: A Global Challenge* (UNEP 2009) 13. See also Gregory and Andrady (n 133) 379.

285 UNEP, *Marine Litter* (n 284) 13.

286 Hammer, Kraak and Parsons (n 102) 2.

287 See David KA Barnes, 'Remote Islands Reveal Rapid Rise of Southern Hemisphere Sea Debris' (2005) 5 Scientific World Journal 915, 918; Barnes and others (n 133) 1987; José GB Derraik, 'The Pollution of the Marine Environment by Plastic Debris: A Review' (2002) 44 Marine Pollution Bulletin 842, 843; Gregory and Andrady (n 133) 380; MR Gregory and PG Ryan, 'Pelagic Plastics and Other Seaborne Persistent Synthetic Debris: A Review of Southern Hemisphere Perspectives' in James M Coe and Donald B Rogers (eds), *Marine Debris: Sources, Impacts and Solutions* (Springer New York 1997) 63; Carey Morishige and others, 'Factors Affecting Marine Debris Deposition at French Frigate Shoals, Northwestern Hawaiian Islands Marine National Monument, 1990–2006' (2007) 54 Marine Pollution Bulletin 1162, 1167; Slat and others (n 103) 38.

288 First indications of plastic debris accumulation in the marine environment were provided in the 1960s, when plastic fragments and pellets were discovered in the guts of

pollution is commonly recognized, continuously rising production levels of plastics and quantities of existing marine plastic litter, as well as the current inexistence of valuable clean-up technologies make it seem inevitable that the abundance of plastic fragments will continue to increase in the years and decades to come. Owing to the low degradability of plastics, marine plastic debris is likely to persist for many centuries – even if input were stopped immediately.[289]

The current chapter will briefly summarize some findings on abundance and distribution of marine plastic litter (A), its composition (B), main sources (C) and impacts (D).

A *Abundance and Spatial Distribution*

About 10 per cent of all plastic wastes end up in the sea.[290] Estimates reach from a daily input of around 27,000 tonnes and an annual input of 10 million tonnes to an annual input of 12.7 million tonnes of plastics to the ocean.[291] Plastics make up 60–80 per cent of marine debris. They occur nearly everywhere in the world's oceans, including polar regions, remote islands and the

---

dead sea birds: see Karl W Kenyon and Eugene Kridler, 'Laysan Albatrosses Swallow Indigestible Matter' (1969) 86 Auk 339, 340–41; Barnes and others (n 133) 1988 and 1993. First direct records of plastic fragments in open seawater and other marine environments date from the 1970s: see JB Buchanan, 'Pollution by Synthetic Fibres' (1971) 2 Marine Pollution Bulletin 23; Edward J Carpenter and others, 'Polystyrene Spherules in Coastal Waters' (1972) 178 Science 749; EJ Carpenter and KL Smith, 'Plastics on the Sargasso Sea Surface' (1972) 175 Science 1240; JB Colton, BR Burns and FD Knapp, 'Plastic Particles in Surface Waters of the Northwestern Atlantic' (1974) 185 Science 491; H Hays and G Cormons, 'Plastic Particles Found in Tern Pellets, on Coastal Beaches and at Factory Sites' (1974) 5 Marine Pollution Bulletin 44; S Kartar, F Abou-Seedou and M Sainsbury, 'Polystyrene Spherules in the Severn Estuary – A Progress Report' (1976) 7 Marine Pollution Bulletin 52; S Kartar, RA Milne and M Sainsbury, 'Polystyrene Waste in the Severn Estuary' (1973) 4 Marine Pollution Bulletin 144; AW Morris and EI Hamilton, 'Polystyrene Spherules in the Bristol Channel' (1974) 5 Marine Pollution Bulletin 26. In the subsequent decades, there was a substantial increase in anthropogenic debris in the seas: see Barnes (n 287); Barnes and others (n 133) 1988; Derraik (n 287); Trevor R Dixon and TJ Dixon, 'Marine Litter Surveillance' (1981) 12 Marine Pollution Bulletin 289.

289 Barnes and others (n 133) 1985; UNEP, *Marine Litter: An Analytical Overview* (UNEP 2005) 1.

290 Richard C Thompson, 'Plastic Debris in the Marine Environment: Consequences and Solutions' in Jochen C Krause, Henning von Nordheim and Stefan Bräger (eds), *Marine Nature Conservation in Europe 2006: Proceedings of the Symposium held in Stralsund, Germany, 8th–12th May 2006* (German Federal Agency for Nature Conservation 2007) 108.

291 See Boucher and others (n 229) 3; Jenna R Jambeck and others, 'Plastic Waste Inputs from Land into the Ocean' (2015) 347 Science 768, 768.

deep seabed.[292] Geographical distribution and accumulation of the debris are not homogenous but strongly depend on ocean currents, winds, seasons and geomorphology, but also the proximity of urban settlements, shore use and other factors, including mass, buoyancy and persistence of the material.[293] Since plastic materials are persistent and about 49–60 per cent of them are positively buoyant, many plastic objects travel long distances on ocean currents, including to remote places.[294] Unless they are washed ashore and not retaken by the sea, and assumed that they are not consumed by animals or otherwise removed from the ocean, most objects will eventually become waterlogged or fouled by biota growing on their surface, which makes them heavy and causes them to sink.[295] Marine litter is constantly exposed to external stresses that cause the items to fragment into ever-smaller pieces, including microplastics and possibly nano-sized particles. Particles of all sizes can be found in surface water, shallow waters, beaches and deep-sea sediments.[296]

i Floating Plastic Debris

In 2014, it was estimated that there were more than 5.25 trillion pelagic plastic particles floating in the oceans, with a total weight of about 268,940 tonnes.[297]

---

292 Gregory and Andrady (n 133) 384; Hammer, Kraak and Parsons (n 102) 13; UNEP, *Marine Litter: An Analytical Overview* (n 289) ii; UNEP, *UNEP Year Book 2014: Emerging Issues in Our Global Environment* (UNEP 2014) 49.

293 See Barnes and others (n 133) 1989 and 1995; CJ Moore and others, 'A Comparison of Plastic and Plankton in the North Pacific Central Gyre' (2001) 42 Marine Pollution Bulletin 1297, 1299; Kershaw and others (n 96) 22.

294 Hammer, Kraak and Parsons (n 102) 5; L Lebreton and others, 'Evidence That the Great Pacific Garbage Patch Is Rapidly Accumulating Plastic' (2018) 8 Scientific Reports 12 <http://www.nature.com/articles/s41598-018-22939-w> accessed 19 February 2022.

295 Barnes and others (n 133) 1988; Hammer, Kraak and Parsons (n 102) 13. Plastic fragments may also sink if their density changes due to the leaching of additives: Francois Galgani, Georg Hanke and Thomas Maes, 'Global Distribution, Composition and Abundance of Marine Litter' in Melanie Bergmann, Lars Gutow and Michael Klages (eds), *Marine Anthropogenic Litter* (Springer 2015) 36.

296 Richard C Thompson, 'Microplastics in the Marine Environment: Sources, Consequences and Solutions' in Melanie Bergmann, Lars Gutow and Michael Klages (eds), *Marine Anthropogenic Litter* (Springer 2015) 192. From all plastic debris at the sea, it is estimated that about 15 per cent is floating on the surface, 15 per cent is washed ashore and 70 per cent eventually sinks to the sea bottom: see Hammer, Kraak and Parsons (n 102) 13; UNEP, *Marine Litter – Trash That Kills* (2001) 4.

297 Marcus Eriksen and others, 'Plastic Pollution in the World's Oceans: More than 5 Trillion Plastic Pieces Weighing over 250,000 Tons Afloat at Sea' (2014) 9 PLoS ONE e111913, 7. cf Andrés Cózar and others, 'Plastic Debris in the Open Ocean' (2014) 111 Proceedings of the National Academy of Sciences 10239.

A 2018 study predicted about 1.8 trillion pieces of floating plastic debris, corresponding to at least 79,000 tonnes, inside an area of 1.6 million km^2. The results of the study suggest that abundance of pelagic plastics have previously been underestimated and misinterpreted.[298] Past and current input rates of plastics from land- and sea-based sources indicate concentration levels that exceed observed quantities by two orders of magnitude. There seem to be mechanisms either removing most of the plastic mass from the ocean surface or fragmenting them into smaller pieces that are not covered by the sampling methods. The fate of 99 per cent of marine plastic wastes thus remains unknown – a sobering number reflecting fundamental knowledge gaps with regard to the fate of microplastics in the ocean.[299]

The spatial distribution of floating plastic debris is governed by ocean currents. Ocean surface currents can be studied on the basis of data on traceable flotsam.[300] The data on the release and recovery of the flotsam was used to develop and refine computer-based ocean current models, which predicted a number of debris accumulation zones, one of which is situated in the high-pressure zone between Hawaii and the US west coast. With the discovery of high amounts of plastic debris in this very zone by research vessels in the 1980s and late 1990s, first records of large plastic accumulation in a subtropical gyre have been established.[301] In subsequent years, many sampling studies followed. They provided further evidence of the phenomenon, which is also taking place in other areas.[302]

---

298 Lebreton and others (n 294).

299 See Eriksen and others (n 297) 10; Lebreton and others (n 294) 12; AE Schwarz and others, 'Sources, Transport, and Accumulation of Different Types of Plastic Litter in Aquatic Environments: A Review Study' (2019) 143 Marine Pollution Bulletin 92; Erik van Sebille and others, 'A Global Inventory of Small Floating Plastic Debris' (2015) 10 Environmental Research Letters 124006; Alexandra ter Halle and others, 'Understanding the Fragmentation Pattern of Marine Plastic Debris' (2016) 50 Environmental Science & Technology 5668.

300 In the past, oceanographers repeatedly tracked flotsam, including some of the spilled cargo from thousands of containers that annually fall overboard, to better understand global patterns of oceanic currents: see Curtis C Ebbesmeyer and Ingraham W James, 'Shoe Spill in the North Pacific' (1992) 73 Eos, Transactions American Geophysical Union 361; 'Pacific Toy Spill Fuels Ocean Current Pathways Research' (1994) 75 Eos, Transactions American Geophysical Union 425.

301 See Robert H Day and David G Shaw, 'Patterns in the Abundance of Pelagic Plastic and Tar in the North Pacific Ocean, 1976–1985' (1987) 18 Marine Pollution Bulletin 311; Moore and others (n 293). See also Moore and Phillips (n 3) 53.

302 See, for instance, Kara Lavender Law and others, 'Plastic Accumulation in the North Atlantic Subtropical Gyre' (2010) 329 Science 1185; CJ Moore, GL Lattin and AF Zellers, 'Density of Plastic Particles Found in Zooplankton Trawls from Coastal Waters of

Pathways of floating debris have also been studied by the use of data from satellite-tracked drifting surface buoys (drifters) as used, for instance, by the US National Oceanic and Atmospheric Administration's (NOAA) Global Ocean Drifter Program.[303] Drifter data is used in global ocean circulation models that simulate input, transport and accumulation of floating debris in the ocean over a specific period of time. The models predict that ocean currents transporting debris tend to accumulate them in five different subtropical convergence zones or gyres in the North and South Atlantic Ocean, the North and South Pacific and the Indian Ocean, respectively (see Figure 11).[304] Distribution patterns as revealed by sampling studies largely agreed with those predicted by the ocean surface circulation models.[305]

Gyres are spiralling ocean surface currents driven by the global wind system (see Figure 12). The currents tend to force the debris towards a central area, where debris concentration is elevated. A plastic particle or item which is released into the ocean is hence likely to be gathered with other plastic objects towards the centre of the convergence zones, after travelling for several years around the gyres.[306]

The high incidence of plastic debris in the accumulation zones has been receiving increasing media attention during the last couple of years. The zones have commonly been called 'plastic garbage patches', 'plastic soup', 'trash vortexes' or 'plastic islands', although all of these terms are quite misleading. Most floating plastic items in the accumulation zones are small fragments that are barely visible. The zones are, therefore, not distinguishable on satellite images but have to be explored by sampling.

California to the North Pacific Central Gyre', *The Plastic Debris Rivers to Sea Conference, Redondo Beach, california, USA* (2005); Peter G Ryan, 'Litter Survey Detects the South Atlantic "Garbage Patch"' (2014) 79 Marine Pollution Bulletin 220; Rei Yamashita and Atsushi Tanimura, 'Floating Plastic in the Kuroshio Current Area, Western North Pacific Ocean' (2007) 54 Marine Pollution Bulletin 485.

303 Law and others (n 302) 1186. For more information on the Global Ocean Drifter Program, see NOAA Physical Oceanography Division, 'Project Report 2017' (NOAA 2018) 9 <http://www.aoml.noaa.gov/phod/docs/PhOD_programs.pdf> accessed 19 February 2022.

304 See LCM Lebreton, SD Greer and JC Borrero, 'Numerical Modelling of Floating Debris in the World's Oceans' (2012) 64 Marine Pollution Bulletin 653; Nikolai Maximenko, Jan Hafner and Peter Niiler, 'Pathways of Marine Debris Derived from Trajectories of Lagrangian Drifters' (2012) 65 Marine Pollution Bulletin 51. See also Kershaw and others (n 96) 22 and 24; IPRC (International Pacific Research Center), 'Tracking Ocean Debris' (2008) 8 IPRC Cimate 14, 16; UNEP, *UNEP Year Book 2014: Emerging Issues in Our Global Environment* (n 292) 49.

305 See, for instance, Cózar and others (n 297) 10240.

306 Slat and others (n 103) 39.

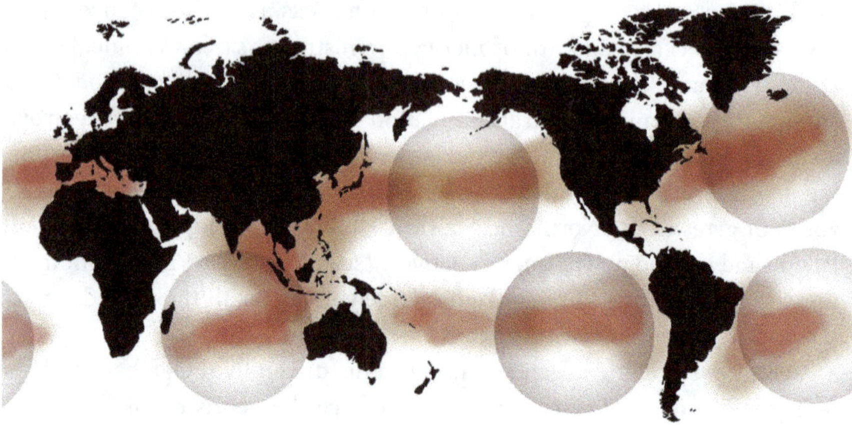

FIGURE 11 Accumulation zones of floating debris
JUDITH SCHÄLI, 'MARINE PLASTIC POLLUTION AS A COMMON CONCERN OF HUMANKIND' IN THOMAS COTTIER AND ZAKER AHMAD (EDS), THE PROSPECTS OF COMMON CONCERN OF HUMANKIND IN INTERNATIONAL LAW (CAMBRIDGE UNIVERSITY PRESS 2021) 161. REPRODUCED WITH PERMISSION OF CAMBRIDGE UNIVERSITY PRESS THROUGH PLSCLEAR.

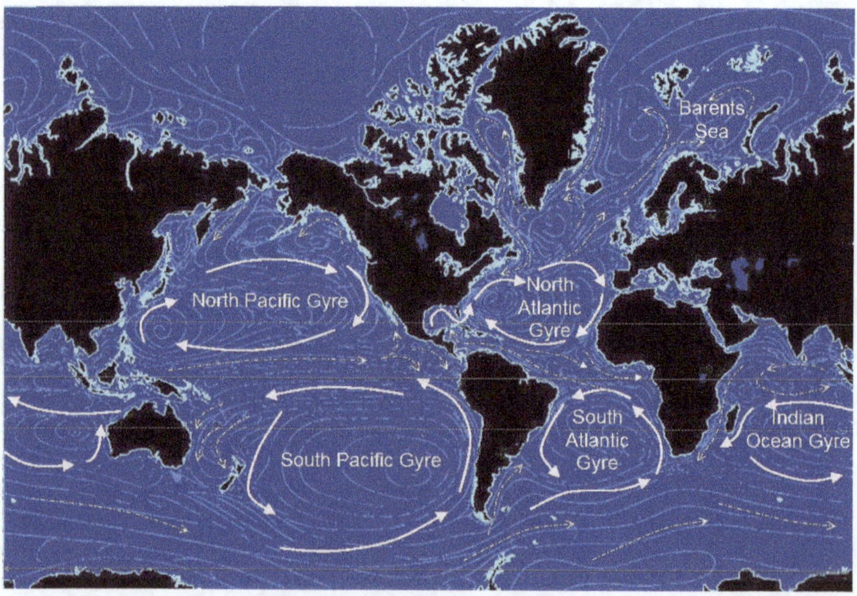

FIGURE 12 Ocean currents forming the five subtropical gyres
AUTHOR

Marine biodiversity greatly varies from one gyre to another. The *North Atlantic gyre* holds the Sargasso Sea, a region of about four million square kilometres situated in the middle of the gyre. The Sargasso Sea is a hotspot for marine wildlife, as it contains a wide range of habitats and provides a resting, feeding and breeding area for many species.[307] By contrast, the *South Pacific gyre* has been described as a desert zone, as its sediments belong to the least inhabited zones ever explored for evidence of life.[308]

Plastic accumulation in the *North Pacific gyre* is densest in two peak areas. The western peak is situated south-west of Japan; the eastern peak is located in the high-pressure zone between Hawaii and the United States. Exact venue and size of the accumulation zones are difficult to determine, as they constantly vary. Sampling studies and circulation models suggest that the eastern accumulation zone in the North Pacific Ocean is the biggest and densest 'patch'. Its surface area is about 1.6 million km^2.[309]

Several sampling studies have been undertaken in different regions and time frames.[310] Sampling studies use different methods to estimate the abundance of floating plastic debris. The quantity of larger items can be extrapolated from visual observations and counting, while the abundance of smaller items is generally estimated by means of samples collected with net trawls. Two of the studies are global in scope.[311]

---

307 D d'A Laffoley and others, 'The Protection and Management of the Sargasso Sea: The Golden Floating Rainforest of the Atlantic Ocean: Summary Science and Supporting Evidence Case' (Sargasso Sea Alliance 2011) 9.

308 University of Rhode Island, 'Subseafloor Sediment In South Pacific Gyre One Of Least Inhabited Places On Earth' (*ScienceDaily*, 1 July 2009) <http://www.sciencedaily.com/releases/2009/06/090622171408.htm> accessed 19 February 2022.

309 See Lebreton and others (n 294).

310 See, for example Barnes and others (n 133); Cózar and others (n 297); Eriksen and others (n 297); 'Plastic Pollution in the South Pacific Subtropical Gyre' (2013) 68 Marine Pollution Bulletin 71; Galgani, Hanke and Maes (n 295); Hammer, Kraak and Parsons (n 102); Kara Lavender Law and others, 'Distribution of Surface Plastic Debris in the Eastern Pacific Ocean from an 11-Year Data Set' (2014) 48 Environmental Science & Technology 4732; Lebreton and others (n 294); Moore and others (n 293); Moore and others (n 302); Peter G Ryan, 'The Characteristics and Distribution of Plastic Particles at the Sea-Surface off the Southwestern Cape Province, South Africa' (1988) 25 Marine Environmental Research 249; 'A Simple Technique for Counting Marine Debris at Sea Reveals Steep Litter Gradients between the Straits of Malacca and the Bay of Bengal' (2013) 69 Marine Pollution Bulletin 128; 'Litter Survey Detects the South Atlantic "Garbage Patch"' (n 302); Yamashita and Tanimura (n 302). For a detailed overview of sampling studies on the abundance and distribution of marine (plastic) debris, see Slat and others (n 103) 42–47.

311 Cózar and others (n 297); Eriksen and others (n 297).

There are only a few datasets spanning more than a decade. Yet, studies overall suggest that there was a dramatic increase in marine plastic debris of more than 20 millimetres until the 1990s. Since then, quantities of pelagic plastic debris of measurable sizes seem to have stabilized in the Northern Hemisphere.[312] It remains unclear whether this is due to sedimentation, shore deposition, ingestion by marine organisms or fragmentation to smaller debris sizes that were not retained by the sampling nets.[313] Data moreover suggest that accumulation rates in the Southern Hemisphere are slightly lower than in the Northern Hemisphere, but still increasing significantly (see Table 3).[314] A study from 2012 modelling the pathways of surface marine debris for a period of more than 1,000 years suggests that, over the centuries, exchanges between the ocean basins play an important role in the spreading of marine debris, and stabilization takes several centuries.[315]

Plastic debris does not only occur within the five gyres but is ubiquitous and can be found across all the oceans from Arctic to Antarctic regions. High occurrence has been observed in enclosed and semi-enclosed seas, including the Mediterranean Sea,[316] the North Sea,[317] the Barents Sea[318] and northern South China Sea.[319] Estimations of global total weight of floating plastic debris lie at 233,400 tonnes for larger plastic items and 35,540 tonnes for microplastics.[320]

---

312 Barnes and others (n 133) 1995. cf ibid 1988.

313 Law and others (n 302) 1187.

314 Barnes and others (n 133) 1995. The fact that plastic abundance in the Southern Hemisphere is almost as high as in the Northern Hemisphere seems surprising, given that inputs are substantially higher in the Northern Hemisphere. Whether the balanced distribution between the Northern and the Southern Hemisphere is due to cross-equatorial movements of the particles or to unknown sources in the Southern Hemisphere is yet unclear: see Eriksen and others (n 297) 10.

315 Erik van Sebille, Matthew H England and Gary Froyland, 'Origin, Dynamics and Evolution of Ocean Garbage Patches from Observed Surface Drifters' (2012) 7 Environmental Research Letters 044040.

316 See Eriksen and others (n 297) 8; Olivia Gerigny and others, 'Déchets en mer et sur le fond', *Plan d'action pour le milieu marin: Sous-région marine Méditerranée Occidentale: Évaluation initiale des eaux marines* <http://www.dirm.mediterranee.developpement-durable.gouv.fr/IMG/pdf/Evaluation_initiale_des_eaux_marines_web.pdf> accessed 19 February 2022.

317 See Martin Thiel and others, 'Spatio-Temporal Distribution of Floating Objects in the German Bight (North Sea)' (2011) 65 Journal of Sea Research 368.

318 See Andrés Cózar and others, 'The Arctic Ocean as a Dead End for Floating Plastics in the North Atlantic Branch of the Thermohaline Circulation' (2017) 3 Science Advances e1600582.

319 See Peng Zhou and others, 'The Abundance, Composition and Sources of Marine Debris in Coastal Seawaters or Beaches around the Northern South China Sea (China)' (2011) 62 Marine Pollution Bulletin 1998.

320 According to Eriksen and others, differences in numbers when compared to the results of the circumnavigation from 2010/11 are due to the fact that Cózar and others focused on microplastics only: Eriksen and others (n 297) 10.

TABLE 3 Estimates of total abundance and mass of floating plastic debris in different oceanic regions

	Abundance (pieces)	Mass (t)
North Pacific Ocean	1,990,000,000,000	96,400
North Atlantic Ocean	930,000,000,000	56,470
South Pacific Ocean	491,000,000,000	21,020
South Atlantic Ocean	297,000,000,000	12,780
Indian Ocean	1,300,000,000,000	59,130
Mediterranean Sea	247,000,000,000	23,150
Total	**5,255,000,000,000**	**268,940**

DATA SOURCE: MARCUS ERIKSEN AND OTHERS, 'PLASTIC POLLUTION IN THE WORLD'S OCEANS: MORE THAN 5 TRILLION PLASTIC PIECES WEIGHING OVER 250,000 TONS AFLOAT AT SEA' (2014) 9 PLOS ONE E111913, 8.

Overall, litter is more abundant close to cities and tourist beaches, which are important sources of discarded bottles, shopping bags and cigarette filters, napkins and other consumer goods.[321] Yet, since plastic litter travels long distances more easily than other debris, the share of plastics from total debris increases as the distance from the debris source increases.[322] Also, average density increases towards the centres of the accumulation zones, as predicted by the simulation models. In general, ocean margins are areas of plastic migration, while subtropical gyres are areas of accumulation.[323] In the centre of the gyres, pieces tend to be smaller, older and more weathered.[324]

ii Plastic Debris in Beaches

It is estimated that about as much plastic particles that are afloat in the oceans are washed ashore.[325] Plastic debris is, hence, commonly found in beaches and beach sediments all around the world. The abundance of beached plastic litter has been studied in different regions, including in the North Atlantic,[326]

321 Kershaw and others (n 96) 21.

322 Hammer, Kraak and Parsons (n 102) 13.

323 Eriksen and others (n 297) 7.

324 See, for instance, Galgani, Hanke and Maes (n 295) 39.

325 See, for instance, Hammer, Kraak and Parsons (n 102) 13, estimating that while most fragments evenually sink towards the ocean floor, half of the remaining plastic debris is washed ashore.

326 E.g. Michiel Claessens and others, 'Occurrence and Distribution of Microplastics in Marine Sediments along the Belgian Coast' (2011) 62 Marine Pollution Bulletin 2199; AM

the North Pacific[327] and the Southern Hemisphere, especially the beaches and shores of New Zealand.[328] Observed numbers greatly vary, depending on the survey technique, accounted fragment sizes and location.[329] High densities can be found close to sources, after flooding events or container spills.[330]

Cundell, 'Plastic Materials Accumulating in Narragansett Bay' (1973) 4 Marine Pollution Bulletin 187; Trevor R Dixon and A Joy Cooke, 'Discarded Containers on a Kent Beach' (1977) 8 Marine Pollution Bulletin 105; Murray R Gregory, 'Virgin Plastic Granules on Some Beaches of Eastern Canada and Bermuda' (1983) 10 Marine Environmental Research 73; G Scott, 'Plastics Packaging and Coastal Pollution' (1972) 3 International Journal of Environmental Studies 35.

327 E.g. Gregory, 'Virgin Plastic Granules on Some Beaches of Eastern Canada and Bermuda' (n 326); Theodore R Merrell, 'Accumulation of Plastic Litter on Beaches of Amchitka Island, Alaska' (1980) 3 Marine Environmental Research 171; C Rosevelt and others, 'Marine Debris in Central California: Quantifying Type and Abundance of Beach Litter in Monterey Bay, CA' (2013) 71 Marine Pollution Bulletin 299.

328 E.g. Murray R Gregory, 'Plastic Pellets on New Zealand Beaches' (1977) 8 Marine Pollution Bulletin 82; 'Accumulation and Distribution of Virgin Plastic Granules on New Zealand Beaches' (1978) 12 New Zealand Journal of Marine and Freshwater Research 399; 'Plastics and Other Seaborne Litter on the Shores of New Zealand's Sub-Antarctic Island' (1987) 7 New Zealand Antarctic Record 32.

329 In 2009, about 2,000 items of anthropogenic debris were estimated to strand on North Atlantic Ocean shores per linear kilometre per year, and about 500 items on South Atlantic Ocean shores. More than half of the debris is plastic: Barnes and others (n 133) 1988. See also DKA Barnes and P Milner, 'Drifting Plastic and Its Consequences for Sessile Organism Dispersal in the Atlantic Ocean' (2005) 146 Marine Biology 815.

330 There are reports of more than 100,000 items, especially plastic pellets, per square metre of beach sediment near Auckland, New Zealand: Gregory, 'Accumulation and Distribution of Virgin Plastic Granules on New Zealand Beaches' (n 328) 400; RC Thompson and others, 'Plastics, the Environment and Human Health: Current Consensus and Future Trends' (2009) 364 Philosophical Transactions of the Royal Society B: Biological Sciences 2153, 2154. In Bootless Bay, Papua New Guinea, debris densities of up to 78.3 items per square metre were reported, almost 90 per cent of which was plastic: Stephen DA Smith, 'Marine Debris: A Proximate Threat to Marine Sustainability in Bootless Bay, Papua New Guinea' (2012) 64 Marine Pollution Bulletin 1880, 1880. After a typhoon in 2009, 3,227 items were found in a random 100 metres × 5 metres beach transect in the south-west of Taiwan; 78.3 per cent of the items were plastic: Ta-Kang Liu, Meng-Wei Wang and Ping Chen, 'Influence of Waste Management Policy on the Characteristics of Beach Litter in Kaohsiung, Taiwan' (2013) 72 Marine Pollution Bulletin 99, 101. After a flooding event in the Turkish Western Black Sea also in 2009, beach litter densities of up to 5,058 pieces per square metre were reported, with over 90 per cent plastics: Eda N Topçu and others, 'Origin and Abundance of Marine Litter along Sandy Beaches of the Turkish Western Black Sea Coast' (2013) 85 Marine Environmental Research 21, 24. Densities of anthropogenic marine debris found in Chilean beaches and shores ranged from ten to over 250 pieces per kilometre. About 86 per cent of the debris was plastic: M Thiel and others, 'Anthropogenic Marine Debris in the Coastal Environment: A Multi-Year Comparison between Coastal Waters and Local Shores' (2013) 71 Marine Pollution Bulletin 307, 310.

Some of the highest densities of debris was reported from Henderson Island, a remote, uninhabited island in the South Pacific. Although the island is far away from any kind of input sources, an estimated 37.7 million debris items weighing a total of 17.6 tons were present on Henderson in 2017, with up to 26.8 new items per metre accumulating daily.[331] Coast sediment-surface counts do not take into account buried litter and, hence, underestimate abundance.[332]

The main sources of beach litter are land-based, originating from both adjacent and distant countries.[333] Accumulation is greater near densely populated areas and on beaches that are frequently visited.[334] Other factors that influence the accumulation of debris in coastal areas include the shape of the beach and geographical location.[335] Relatively high densities of plastic debris, but also high variability, can be found in enclosed or semi-enclosed seas, as well as in open-ocean coastlines such as Hawaii. Changes in oceanic circulation driven by weather phenomena such as El Niño events increase interannual variability.[336]

As is the case for floating plastic debris, cleaning of beached plastic debris is extremely difficult, especially with regard to small size fragments and buried pieces. While beach clean-up days are organized around the world, success is limited, as more debris is washed ashore on a daily basis.

iii Plastic Debris on the Seabed

A possible explanation for the missing fraction of plastic debris in open-ocean surveys lies in the particles' tendency to travel towards the ground. Approximately 70 per cent of all floating plastic fragments are believed to eventually sink to the seabed.[337] A reason for their sinking is the weight of fouling by bacteria, algae, barnacles, shellfish and other organisms. Fouling may increase the density of plastic objects, causing them to sink, with particles being redistributed throughout the whole water column. When ingested, microplastic particles might also sink with the bodies of dead fish or with faecal pellets.[338]

---

331 Jennifer L Lavers and Alexander L Bond, 'Exceptional and Rapid Accumulation of Anthropogenic Debris on One of the World's Most Remote and Pristine Islands' (2017) 114 Proceedings of the National Academy of Sciences 6052.

332 Galgani, Hanke and Maes (n 295) 33.

333 See, for instance, Topçu and others (n 330) 25.

334 Hammer, Kraak and Parsons (n 102) 15.

335 Galgani, Hanke and Maes (n 295) 33.

336 See Barnes and others (n 133) 1988, including references.

337 Hammer, Kraak and Parsons (n 102) 17.

338 Cózar and others (n 297) 10242; Eriksen and others (n 297) 11.

The deep-sea sediments have shown to be a major sink for plastics, including microplastics.[339] Settling of plastic litter on the deep-sea bed seems to be permanent in most cases.[340] If, however, the biological surface layer is removed by grazing organisms or reduced due to adverse conditions for the fouling organisms in the depths, the objects may float upwards again.[341] Investigation of the presence and abundance of plastic particles in the deep sea, as well as of their aging, is hampered by sampling difficulties and high costs. Large-scale studies on seabed debris are, hence, scarce.[342] It is widely assumed that plastic objects or fragments degrade at much lower rates at the seafloor, where they are shielded from UV radiation. However, some plastics may be susceptible to bacterial decay at sea.[343]

It is assumed that bottom debris, including from land-based sources, tends to become trapped in areas of low circulation, especially bays and semi-enclosed seas.[344] Studies suggest that in the North Sea, a total of 600,000 m^3 of marine debris is present on the seabed.[345] High densities of marine debris, particularly plastic, have also been found on the Mediterranean seabed.[346]

339 Lucy C Woodall and others, 'The Deep Sea Is a Major Sink for Microplastic Debris' (2014) 1 Royal Society Open Science 140317, 1. See also Lisbeth Van Cauwenberghe and others, 'Microplastic Pollution in Deep-Sea Sediments' (2013) 182 Environmental Pollution 495.

340 See Gregory and Andrady (n 133) 384–85, with references.

341 Cózar and others (n 297) 10241; Kershaw and others (n 96) 26.

342 See, however, F Galgani and others, 'Litter on the Sea Floor Along European Coasts' (2000) 40 Marine Pollution Bulletin 516; C Ioakeimidis and others, 'A Comparative Study of Marine Litter on the Seafloor of Coastal Areas in the Eastern Mediterranean and Black Seas' (2014) 89 Marine Pollution Bulletin 296; Andreas Koutsodendris and others, 'Benthic Marine Litter in Four Gulfs in Greece, Eastern Mediterranean; Abundance, Composition and Source Identification' (2008) 77 Estuarine, Coastal and Shelf Science 501; DI Lee, HS Cho and SB Jeong, 'Distribution Characteristics of Marine Litter on the Sea Bed of the East China Sea and the South Sea of Korea' (2006) 70 Estuarine, Coastal and Shelf Science 187; Juying Wang and others, 'Chapter 25: Marine Debris', *First World Ocean Assessment* (United Nations 2016) 397–98.

343 See Peter G Ryan, 'A Brief History of Marine Litter Research' in Melanie Bergmann, Lars Gutow and Michael Klages (eds), *Marine Anthropogenic Litter* (Springer 2015) 16, with references.

344 See Barnes and others (n 133) 1991. cf Hammer, Kraak and Parsons (n 102) 17.

345 Hammer, Kraak and Parsons (n 102) 17.

346 See Murray R Gregory, 'Environmental Implications of Plastic Debris in Marine Settings – Entanglement, Ingestion, Smothering, Hangers-on, Hitch-Hiking and Alien Invasions' (2009) 364 Philosophical Transactions of the Royal Society B: Biological Sciences 2013, 2017.

B *Composition of Marine Plastic Debris*

While plastics constitute only about 12 per cent of global municipal solid waste mass, they constitute about 60–80 per cent of total marine debris.[347] Plastic debris is often categorized into different size classes, including nano-, micro-, meso-, macro- and megadebris.[348] Microplastic fragments of sizes up to 4.75 mm are predominant in terms of numbers, with trillions of them floating in surface waters. In terms of mass, however, they only represent about 13 per cent of the total available buoyant material.[349] The average size of plastic particles in the marine environment seems to be decreasing, while the abundance and global distribution of microplastics have increased over the last few decades.[350] Microplastics comprise primary microplastics (such as microbeads[351] from cosmetic products, abrasives or pellets) and secondary microplastics, consisting of fragments, fibres or powders breaking from bigger objects. Abrasion of tyres is considered the largest source of microplastics, followed by city dust, abrasion of road markings and releases due to the laundry of synthetic textiles.[352] Owing to their high numbers and small size, microplastics are almost impossible to be removed from the environment.[353]

---

347 Barnes and others (n 133) 1987; Slat and others (n 103) 38.

348 Size classification varies among different studies. Nanoplastics, which represent the least known group of marine litter, are plastic particles that are less than 0.0001 mm in at least one of their dimensions. Microplastics usually comprise plastic fragments of sizes up to 0.2 or 0.5 cm, mesoplastics are up to 2 or 5 cm. The term macroplastics usually refers to items bigger than 2 or 5 cm. Large plastic objects of more than 50 cm are sometimes referred to as megaplastics: see Hammer, Kraak and Parsons (n 102) 5; Lebreton and others (n 294) 5.

349 Lebreton and others (n 294) 2; Eriksen and others (n 297) 9.

350 Barnes and others (n 133) 1985.

351 Microbeads are found in a wide range of personal care products such as toothpaste, shower gels and facial cleansers, but also in air-blast or sandblast cleaning media, sometimes replacing natural ingredients. In the absence of effective wastewater treatment, the microplastics are released directly to the ocean or other water bodies such as lakes and rivers: see UNEP, *UNEP Year Book 2014: Emerging Issues in Our Global Environment* (n 292) 50. cf WHO (n 69).

352 Julien Boucher and Damien Friot, 'Primary Microplastics in the Oceans: A Global Evaluation of Sources' (IUCN 2017) 21; UNEP, 'Mapping of Global Plastics Value Chain' (n 90) 52. See also Edgar Hernandez, Bernd Nowack and Denise M Mitrano, 'Polyester Textiles as a Source of Microplastics from Households: A Mechanistic Study to Understand Microfiber Release During Washing' (2017) 51 Environmental Science & Technology 7036.

353 Conventional and advanced treatment in wastewater and drinking water systems can effectively remove microplastic particles. However, approximately 67 per cent of the

The vast majority of floating objects are made of PE and PP rigid plastics and bundled fishing nets and ropes. Foamed PS items also belong to the most commonly occurring marine macroplastics. Derelict fishing buoys are important contributors in terms of weight.[354] By contrast, denser types of plastic, such as PET, tend to sink more readily.[355] Studies moreover suggest that the objects' volume-to-surface ratios play a significant role for their movement patterns and fate. Objects such as films, which have small volume-to-surface ratios, seem to be more susceptible to biofouling and therefore to sink more rapidly or fragmentize into microscopic pieces that are removed from surface layers.[356]

The most commonly found plastic litter items in the marine environment, especially beaches, include cigarette butts, plastic beverage bottles and bottle caps, food wrappers, plastic grocery bags and other bags, plastic lids, straws and stirrers, foam takeaway containers, and plastic cups and plates.[357] Plastic pellets or nurdles are also commonly found on beaches and water surfaces all over the world.[358] User plastics are predominant near densely populated areas. Abandoned, discarded or lost fishing gear is prevalent in offshore places.[359] In particular, abandoned fishing nets and ropes are common in many places.

C *Main Pollution Sources*

From a regulatory point of view, a distinction is often drawn between ocean- or sea-based pollution sources on the one hand and land-based sources on the other hand. Ocean-based sources of marine pollution include deliberate dumping of wastes at sea (that is, from vessels, aircraft or offshore installations) and disposal or accidental loss of wastes, cargo and gear by commercial and recreational shipping, fishing and military fleets. In particular, derelict fishing nets and ropes, as well as container spills are important sources of marine plastics.

---

population in low- and middle-income countries lack access to sewage connections and about 20 per cent of household wastewater collected in sewers does not undergo at least secondary treatment: WHO (n 69) xi, with references.

354 Patrick ten Brink and others, 'Plastics Marine Litter and the Circular Economy: A Briefing by IEEP for the MAVA Foundation' (IEEP 2016) 4.

355 Kershaw and others (n 96) 22.

356 Lebreton and others (n 294) 12.

357 See Ocean Conservancy, 'International Coastal Cleanup 2017 Report' (2017) 13 <https://oceanconservancy.org/wp-content/uploads/2017/04/2017-Ocean-Conservancy-ICC-Report.pdf> accessed 19 February 2022. The 2016 International Coastal Cleanup involved 504,583 volunteers in 112 countries around the world, who removed 8,346 tonnes of debris (13,840,398 items) from 24,136 km of beaches and inland waterways.

358 Hammer, Kraak and Parsons (n 102) 6, with references.

359 See ibid 18; Galgani, Hanke and Maes (n 295) 39.

Sea-based sources also include wastes resulting from other sea-based activities (including from the aquaculture industry, offshore platforms and other installations at sea).[360]

Land-based pollution sources, on the other hand, consist of municipal, industrial or agricultural wastes or discharges, as well as dumped wastes or otherwise irregular waste streams that reach the marine environment from land through different pathways, including rivers, severe weather events such as floods, and wind.[361] Marine debris from land-based sources typically includes beach and urban litter, wastes from unprotected landfills that are located near the coast, sewage outflows and storm water drainage outlets.[362] Pollution through the atmosphere that results from land-based activities is usually also counted as land-based pollution (e.g. atmospheric deposition of microplastics from tyre wear and from wear and tear of plastic products during normal use).[363]

Land-based sources account for about 80 per cent of marine pollution, with sewage being the largest source of contamination.[364] Similarly, it is widely cited that about 80 per cent of marine plastic debris stems from land-based sources.[365] The portion of plastics from land-based sources tends to be lower

---

360 See Galgani, Hanke and Maes (n 295) 31; Yoshifumi Tanaka, *The International Law of the Sea* (2nd edn, Cambridge University Press 2015) 271–72.

361 See, for instance, 'Montreal Guidelines for the Protection of the Marine Environment Against Pollution from Land-Based Sources' (Decision 13/18/II of the Governing Council of UNEP, of 24 May 1985) para 1(b); Gregory and Andrady (n 133) 382; Tanaka, *International Law of the Sea* (n 360) 270.

362 See Galgani, Hanke and Maes (n 295) 31.

363 Peter Sundt, Per-Erik Schulze and Frode Syversen, 'Sources of Microplastics-Pollution to the Marine Environment' (Norwegian Environment Agency 2015) M-321|2015 33–42; Yoshifumi Tanaka, 'Regulation of Land-Based Marine Pollution in International Law: A Comparative Analysis between Global and Regional Legal Frameworks' (2006) 66 Zeitschrift fuer Ausländisches Öffentliches Recht und Völkerrecht [Heidelberg Journal of International Law] 535, 553.

364 UNGA, 'Report of the Secretary-General: Oceans and the Law of the Sea' (2004) UN Doc A/59/62/Add.1 29 para 97; GESAMP, 'The State of the Marine Environment' (n 283) 104 para 431; Daud Hassan, *Protecting the Marine Environment from Land-Based Sources of Pollution: Towards Effective International Cooperation* (Ashgate 2006) 15–16; Donald R Rothwell and Tim Stephens, *The International Law of the Sea* (2nd edn, Hart Publishing 2016) 366; Tanaka, 'Regulation of Land-Based Marine Pollution' (n 363) 535. According to the 1990 GESAMP Report, 44 per cent of marine pollution can be attributed to land-based discharge, 33 per cent to atmospheric input from land, 12 per cent to maritime transport, 10 per cent to dumping and 1 per cent to oil exploration and production: GESAMP, 'The State of the Marine Environment' (n 283) 88. Sea-based pollution sources together account for less than 20 per cent of marine pollution.

365 See Anthony L Andrady, 'Microplastics in the Marine Environment' (2011) 62 Marine Pollution Bulletin 1596, 1597; Galgani, Hanke and Maes (n 295) 31; Gregory and Andrady

in offshore places, where marine-sourced plastics are often predominant. This might be due either to the latter's purposely engineered durability in the marine environment or the fact that plastics entering the ocean from land-based sources often accumulate in coastal environments, including through beaching.[366]

A distinction can also be made between *point sources of pollution*, referring to sources with a single, geographically identifiable entry point into the environment, and *non-point sources*, which are much more diffuse. Main point sources of anthropogenic pollutants include industrial plants, sewage discharges and storm water runoff, as well as offshore platforms. The more problematic (mainly) non-point sources include agriculture, forestry and development activities, maritime transportation and dumping.

Plastic input into the sea from land is mainly caused by improper material, product and waste management, improper human behaviour, including littering, unsustainable production and consumption patterns, involving the wide use of single-use plastic goods, and unintentional losses during use, especially due to the abrasion of products.[367] Plastic debris from land-based sources includes plastics from all life-cycle stages, including pre-production resins or nurdles, user goods and plastic wastes. A high number of activities contribute to marine plastic pollution from land-based sources, including industrial activities, sewage, urban development and tourism. Key sources of primary microplastics in the marine environment are plastic pellets, synthetic textiles, tyres, road markings, city dust and personal care products. Most of these sources generate unintentional losses through abrasion, weathering or unintentional spills during production, transport, use or disposal. Only losses from personal care products, such as toothpastes or shampoos, can be considered intentional losses.[368] Households activities generate about 77 per cent of

---

(n 133) 382; Lebreton, Greer and Borrero (n 304) 654; Michael Liffmann and Laura Boogaerts, 'Linkages Between Land-Based Sources of Pollution and Marine Debris' in James M Coe and Donald B Rogers (eds), *Marine Debris: Sources, Impacts and Solutions* (Springer New York 1997) 359. cf Jambeck and others (n 291) 768. The predominance of marine plastics from land-based sources is questioned by a 2019 study suggesting major debris inputs from ships, especially by dumped PET bottles from Chinese vessels: see Peter G Ryan and others, 'Rapid Increase in Asian Bottles in the South Atlantic Ocean Indicates Major Debris Inputs from Ships' [2019] Proceedings of the National Academy of Sciences 201909816.

366 Data from coastal clean-ups may therefore lead to overestimations of the portion of plastics from land-based sources: see Lebreton and others (n 294) 12.

367 See Boucher and Friot (n 352) 21; Barnes and others (n 133) 1986–87; Hammer, Kraak and Parsons (n 102) 6.

368 Boucher and Friot (n 352) 14.

microplastics releases, especially through passenger transport in private cars, laundry of synthetic textiles and the use of personal care products.[369]

It has been estimated that, in 2010, 275 million tonnes of plastic waste were generated in 192 coastal countries, with 4.8 to 12.7 million tonnes entering the ocean.[370] Main contributors in terms of land-based sources of marine plastic debris are countries with large coastal populations, widespread use of plastic goods and packaging, and high rates of mismanaged wastes. Mismanaged waste includes disposal in dumps or open, uncontrolled landfills. Such waste potentially enters the ocean via inland waterways, wastewater outflows, and transport by wind or tides.[371] If the share of mismanaged wastes cannot be diminished, plastic input to the oceans is expected to rise significantly, since coastal population is increasing.[372]

Sixteen of the top 20 polluters are middle-income countries with fast economic growth but lacking essential waste management infrastructure. Several East and South East Asian countries rank among the top ten polluters.[373] Studies suggest that effective input reduction would require substantial infrastructure investment primarily in low- and middle-income countries, as well as a reduction in waste generation in higher-income countries.[374]

D *Impacts of Marine Plastic Pollution*

i Impact on the Marine Environment and Marine Biodiversity

Marine plastic litter is known to cause physical hazard to marine wildlife. An estimated 817 marine species are directly affected through ingestion of plastics and microplastic particles, entanglement in marine debris, ghost fishing by derelict fishing nets or ropes, dispersal by rafting on marine debris, especially plastics, and provision of new habitats due to marine littering.[375] Marine

369 ibid 24. See also Hernandez, Nowack and Mitrano (n 352); Sundt, Schulze and Syversen (n 363).

370 Jambeck and others (n 291) 768. cf UNEP, 'Mapping of Global Plastics Value Chain' (n 90) 53.

371 Jambeck and others (n 291) 768.

372 See Melanie Bergmann, Lars Gutow and Michael Klages, 'Preface' in Melanie Bergmann, Lars Gutow and Michael Klages (eds), *Marine Anthropogenic Litter* (Springer 2015) ix.

373 Including China, Indonesia, Philippines, Vietnam, Thailand, and Malaysia. Sri Lanka, Egypt, Nigeria, Bangladesh, South Africa and India are also considered major contributors. The United States rank twentieth: see Jambeck and others (n 291) 769. See also Cózar and others (n 297) 10240.

374 See Jambeck and others (n 291) 770.

375 CBD Secretariat, 'Marine Debris: Understanding, Preventing and Mitigating the Significant Adverse Impacts on Marine and Coastal Biodiversity' (McGraw-Hill Education, 2016) CBD Technical Series No 83 16.

plastics affect marine organisms at every trophic level, from small filter-feeding organisms at the bottom of the food chain to marine mammals such as whales.[376] Effects can be observed in all different kinds of marine habitats, including coastal habitats, the seabed and open waters.[377] They can also be observed in remote locations with negligible local sources of plastics. Most of observed and reported impacts occur at suborganismal levels (e.g. molecular, cellular, tissue). However, lethal effects on individual organisms have also been widely observed.[378] Impacts on populations, assemblages and species are more difficult to quantify but cannot be excluded.[379]

Wildlife entanglement is one of the most visible effects of marine debris (see Figure 13). Entangled animals are hindered in their ability to move, feed and breathe. They may not be able to avoid predators or may die from exhaustion. Wounds from entanglement can inflame and thus bring some additional risk. One hundred per cent of marine turtle species, 67 per cent of seal species, 31 per cent of whales and 25 per cent of seabird species have been recorded as entangled. Of a particular concern in this respect are derelict fishing gear, especially nets that continue to trap and kill organisms (ghost fishing) and damage benthic habitats, but also ropes, balloons, plastic bags, sheets and six-pack drink holders.[380]

---

376 Matthew Cole and others, 'Microplastics as Contaminants in the Marine Environment: A Review' (2011) 62 Marine Pollution Bulletin 2588, 2593; David W Laist, 'Impacts of Marine Debris: Entanglement of Marine Life in Marine Debris Including a Comprehensive List of Species with Entanglement and Ingestion Records' in James M Coe and Donald B Rogers (eds), *Marine Debris* (Springer New York 1997). See also Susanne Kühn, Elisa L Bravo Rebolledo and Jan A van Franeker, 'Deleterious Effects of Litter on Marine Life' in Melanie Bergmann, Lars Gutow and Michael Klages (eds), *Marine Anthropogenic Litter* (Springer 2015) 75–105, with references; UNEP and GRID-Arendal, *Marine Litter: Vital Graphics* (2016) 15, with references.

377 The presence of ingested microplastics has been detected in amphipod populations in the Mariana Trench and other deep ocean trenches: see AJ Jamieson and others, 'Microplastics and Synthetic Particles Ingested by Deep-Sea Amphipods in Six of the Deepest Marine Ecosystems on Earth' (2019) 6 Royal Society Open Science 180667. Particularly high concentrations of microplastic particles have been found in arctic sea ice: see Ilka Peeken and others, 'Arctic Sea Ice Is an Important Temporal Sink and Means of Transport for Microplastic' (2018) 9 Nature Communications 1505.

378 See Chelsea M Rochman and others, 'The Ecological Impacts of Marine Debris: Unraveling the Demonstrated Evidence from What Is Perceived' (2016) 97 Ecology 302.

379 See Kershaw and others (n 96) 25.

380 See Kühn, Bravo Rebolledo and van Franeker (n 376) 76–83, with references. See also Geremy Cliff and others, 'Large Sharks and Plastic Debris in KwaZulu-Natal, South Africa' (2002) 53 Marine and Freshwater Research 575; Amanda Johnson and others, 'Fishing Gear Involved in Entanglements of Right and Humpback Whales' (2006) 21 Marine Mammal Science 635; Laist (n 376); J Orós and others, 'Diseases and Causes of Mortality

FIGURE 13 Turtle entangled in marine debris
NOAA MARINE DEBRIS PROGRAM, 'ENTANGLED GREEN SEA TURTLE' (2012) <HTTPS://WWW.FLICKR.COM/PHOTOS/NOAAMARINEDEBRIS/7656597150/> ACCESSED 19 FEBRUARY 2022, LICENSED UNDER CC BY 2.0, <HTTPS://CREATIVECOMMONS.ORG/LICENSES/BY/2.0> ACCESSED 19 FEBRUARY 2022.

Ingestion of marine debris is a less visible but widely reported phenomenon (see Figure 14).[381] A broad range of marine species ingest marine plastic debris intentionally – because they mistake the particles for food – or unintentionally, by filter feeding or via their prey (secondary ingestion).[382] Offshore-feeding birds such as fulmars and albatrosses have been found to contain plastic objects in their guts and pass them on to chicks.[383] When accumulating in the stomach,

among Sea Turtles Stranded in the Canary Islands, Spain (1998–2001)' (2005) 63 Diseases of Aquatic Organisms 13.

381 See, for instance, Derraik (n 287) 844–46; Cecilia Eriksson and Harry Burton, 'Origins and Biological Accumulation of Small Plastic Particles in Fur Seals from Macquarie Island' (2003) 32 Ambio 380; Ryan, 'A Brief History of Marine Litter Research' (n 343) 3–12.

382 Filter-feeding organisms, including different species of plankton, crustaceans, shellfish, fish and whales, obtain their nutrition by filtering large volumes of water, and thus are widely exposed to pelagic plastics. Microplastics have been identified as a threat to endangered surface-feeding baleen whales: see UNEP, *UNEP Year Book 2014: Emerging Issues in Our Global Environment* (n 292) 50.

383 Kershaw and others (n 96) 24; Peter G Ryan and others, 'Monitoring the Abundance of Plastic Debris in the Marine Environment' (2009) 364 Philosophical Transactions of the

FIGURE 14 Ingestion of marine plastic debris. The unaltered stomach contents of a dead albatross chick photographed on Midway Atoll in the Pacific in 2009 include plastic marine debris.

© 2009 CHRIS JORDAN. REPRINTED WITH PERMISSION BY CHRIS JORDAN.

plastics affect the organism's fitness and may have consequences for reproduction and survival. Ingestion of plastics has been documented for 100 per cent of marine turtle, 59 per cent of whale, 36 per cent of seal and 40 per cent of seabird species.[384] In some species, ingestion is reported in over 80 per cent of a population sampled.[385] Plastics in the digestive tract often contribute to malnutrition and dehydration. They may block the gastrointestinal tract or severely damage it, with possible lethal effects.[386] Implications of marine plastic litter for invertebrates and other species with low public focus on are less well studied.[387]

Royal Society of London B: Biological Sciences 1999; Lindsay C Young and others, 'Bringing Home the Trash: Do Colony-Based Differences in Foraging Distribution Lead to Increased Plastic Ingestion in Laysan Albatrosses?' (2009) 4 PLOS ONE e7623.

384 See Kühn, Bravo Rebolledo and van Franeker (n 376) 85.

385 Rochman and others, 'The Ecological Impacts of Marine Debris' (n 378) 303.

386 Kühn, Bravo Rebolledo and van Franeker (n 376) 85–95, with references.

387 Bergmann, Gutow and Klages (n 372) x.

Marine plastic debris not only poses physical hazards through entanglement or ingestion but also chemical hazards with potential toxicological impacts on marine ecosystems and biodiversity. Plastics can leach chemicals that have been added during production or are by-products of the production process. Some of these leaching chemicals have potential negative health effects.[388] In addition, plastic debris tend to accumulate chemicals, including persistent, bioaccumulative and toxic substances,[389] from the surrounding seawater. Persistent organic pollutants can become several orders of magnitude more concentrated on the surface of plastic debris than in the surrounding seawater.[390] As a result, marine plastics may transfer a complex mixture of potentially hazardous chemicals to the tissues of organisms upon direct ingestion or via the food web.[391] The chemicals can penetrate cells and harm ecophysiological functions performed by organisms, for instance by increasing liver toxicity or disrupting the endocrine system.[392] It has been shown

388 Released substances include phthalates, brominated flame retardants, bisphenol A, formaldehyde, acetaldehyde, 4-nonylphenol and possibly polyfluoronated compounds, triclosan, phthalate plasticizers and lead heat stabilizers: see Kennedy Bucci and others, 'Impacts to Larval Fathead Minnows Vary between Preconsumer and Environmental Microplastics' [2021] Environmental Toxicology and Chemistry <https://onlinelibrary.wiley.com/doi/abs/10.1002/etc.5036> accessed 19 February 2022; Frederic Gallo and others, 'Marine Litter Plastics and Microplastics and Their Toxic Chemicals Components: The Need for Urgent Preventive Measures' (2018) 30 Environmental Sciences Europe <https://www.ncbi.nlm.nih.gov/pmc/articles/PMC5918521> accessed 19 February 2022; Chelsea M Rochman, 'The Complex Mixture, Fate and Toxicity of Chemicals Associated with Plastic Debris in the Marine Environment' in Melanie Bergmann, Lars Gutow and Michael Klages (eds), *Marine Anthropogenic Litter* (Springer 2015) 131, with references. See also Section 1.1.A.ii above.

389 Such as polychlorinated biphenyls (PCBs), polyaromatic hydrocarbons (PAHs), hexachlorocyclohexane (HCH), dichlorodiphenyldichloroethylene (DDE), nonylphenol and phenanthrene. Because of their persistent, bioaccumulative and toxic characteristics, the European Union lists several of these chemicals as priority substances: European Parliament and Council Directive 2008/105/EC of 16 December 2008 on environmental quality standards in the field of water policy [2008] OJ L348/84, Annex II.

390 The sorptive capacity of a plastic particle and the rate at which chemicals are absorbed depend on the surface-to-volume ratio of the particle. In general, the effect is greater the smaller a fragment is. At the same time, smaller fragments enter the food chain more easily, thereby potentially transferring the chemicals to marine organisms: see Barnes and others (n 133) 1995.

391 Rochman and others, 'The Ecological Impacts of Marine Debris' (n 378) 303. See also Andrady (n 365) 1601–02; Emma L Teuten and others, 'Transport and Release of Chemicals from Plastics to the Environment and to Wildlife' (2009) 364 Philosophical Transactions of the Royal Society B: Biological Sciences 2027.

392 See Mark Anthony Browne and others, 'Microplastic Moves Pollutants and Additives to Worms, Reducing Functions Linked to Health and Biodiversity' (2013) 23 Current Biology

that these contaminants are bioavailable to a wide range of marine species, including whales, sharks, seabirds, fish and other organisms upon ingestion.[393] Plastics cause and enhance bioaccumulation of such chemicals in animal tissues, including in a range of commercially important fish and shellfish.[394] Toxicant concentrations potentially increase through transfer within the food web (biomagnification). Studies of seafood, sea salt and other products intended for human consumption suggest that humans are also affected.[395] More research is needed on potential effects on humans and other non-marine mammals.[396]

Plastics may also serve as a vector for chemicals by absorbing chemicals in contaminated areas and leaching them in more pristine regions, with unknown effects on local ecosystems in these areas.[397] Floating plastic debris also facilitates transport of microorganisms, pathogens and other plant and animal species. It may thereby contribute to increased invasion of ecosystems by alien species. The dispersal of organisms related to floating plastic debris takes place horizontally, from one region to another, and vertically, through the water column to the seafloor. Biological invasions by non-indigenous species are considered a major threat to coastal ecosystems. While so-called 'hitch-hiking' also occurs on natural floating debris, marine plastic litter substantially enhanced rafting opportunities for marine organisms. It is widely assumed that change in the temporal and spatial availability of rafts dramatically affects the dynamics of rafting transport and colonization by associated organisms.[398]

2388, 2388; Chelsea M Rochman and others, 'Ingested Plastic Transfers Hazardous Chemicals to Fish and Induces Hepatic Stress' (2013) 3 Scientific Reports 3263, 3–4; Chelsea M Rochman and others, 'Early Warning Signs of Endocrine Disruption in Adult Fish from the Ingestion of Polyethylene with and without Sorbed Chemical Pollutants from the Marine Environment' (2014) 493 The Science of the Total Environment 656.

393 Barnes and others (n 133); Rochman (n 388) 119, with references.

394 See Mark A Browne and others, 'Ingested Microscopic Plastic Translocates to the Circulatory System of the Mussel, Mytilus Edulis (L)' (2008) 42 Environmental Science & Technology 5026.

395 See CIEL, 'Plastic & Health' (n 10) 52–55, with references; WWF, *No Plastic in Nature: Assessing Plastic Ingestion from Nature to People* (2019) 7–8.

396 Rochman (n 388) 130. cf WHO (n 69) 31–34.

397 See Rochman (n 388) 128, with references.

398 T Kiessling, L Gutow and M Thiel, 'Biodiversity: Invasions by Marine Life on Plastic Debris' in Melanie Bergmann, Lars Gutow and Michael Klages (eds), *Marine Anthropogenic Litter* (Springer 2015) 157. See also Stefano Aliani and Anne Molcard, 'Hitch-Hiking on Floating Marine Debris: Macrobenthic Species in the Western Mediterranean Sea' (2003) 503 Hydrobiologia 59; David KA Barnes, 'Biodiversity: Invasions by Marine Life on Plastic Debris' (2002) 416 Nature 808.

Plastic debris may also cause habitat alterations. When accumulating on the seafloor, it reduces the available oxygen content of the water, with detrimental effects for aerobic benthic organisms – a phenomenon that is often referred to as *smothering*.[399] When accumulating on beaches, it potentially alters graininess, density and permeability of the sediment. Microplastic contents in sediments also reduce heat transfer, causing the sediments to warm more slowly or reach lower maximum temperatures. It has been assumed that these changes can have a serious effect on beach organisms, including those that have temperature-dependent sex-determination, such as sea turtle eggs.[400]

ii Economic and Social Impacts

Marine plastic pollution entails considerable costs that are related to the clean-up of litter, to the reparation and replacement of damaged ship components and gear, to health impacts (including costs of emergency rescue services due to physical or navigational hazards of plastic debris and hospitalization costs), and to the reduction of ecosystem services (including food provision) and other economic benefits derived from the marine environment. Marine litter-related costs include costs related to additional expenditure and costs related to losses of output and revenue, as well as social or welfare costs, which are generally associated with broader health impacts and the reduction of aesthetic, recreational, cultural or other intangible values of marine environments.[401] Not all of these costs are easily quantifiable in financial or economic terms. Quantifications thus usually do not reflect full costs. The total natural capital cost of plastic used in the consumer goods industry is estimated to be more than US$75 billion per year.[402] Global costs related to marine litter have been estimated at US$13 billion per year.[403] These costs are partly borne by a broad range of industry sectors – including the shipping and fishing industries,

399 See Kühn, Bravo Rebolledo and van Franeker (n 376) 83–85, with references.

400 Henry S Carson and others, 'Small Plastic Debris Changes Water Movement and Heat Transfer through Beach Sediments' (2011) 62 Marine Pollution Bulletin 1708; Hammer, Kraak and Parsons (n 102) 16.

401 See Stephanie Newman and others, 'The Economics of Marine Litter' in Melanie Bergmann, Lars Gutow and Michael Klages (eds), *Marine Anthropogenic Litter* (Springer 2015) 368.

402 The natural capital cost of plastic includes costs related to a range of environmental impacts, including those on oceans and impacts related to greenhouse gas emissions released from producing plastic feedstock or the loss of resources when plastic waste is not recycled: see UNEP, 'Valuing Plastic: The Business Case for Measuring, Managing and Disclosing Plastic Use in the Consumer Goods Industry' (UNEP 2014) 7.

403 See ibid.

tourism, aquaculture and agriculture – and partly by municipalities and the public at large.

Clean-up costs include costs for the collection, transportation and disposal of litter and the construction and maintenance of waste management infrastructure, as well as related administrative costs. They are mostly borne by coastal municipalities, tourism companies or privately organized voluntary groups. In 2010, coastal municipalities in the UK spent about €18–19 million in total for cleaning up beaches from marine litter. Yearly costs seem to be increasing considerably.[404] In Belgium and the Netherlands, municipalities incur beach clean-up costs of about €10.4 million per year.[405] Local communities relying on coastal tourism often have to bear additional costs in the form of loss of revenue or income when marine litter affects people's perceptions of the quality of the marine environment and causes numbers of visitors to decline. The economic impact of a single marine litter event in South Korea in 2011 was estimated to be between €23 and €29 million as a result of over 500,000 fewer visitors when compared to 2010.[406] The loss can affect national economies and level of employment when dependent on coastal tourism and associated economic activities.[407] Coastal municipalities, governments and local communities also often spend money for awareness-raising activities and education in order to address littering and other behavioural sources of marine plastics.

Much like coastal tourism, fisheries and, to a lesser extent, the aquaculture industry are extremely vulnerable to the hazards posed by marine litter. In the Asia-Pacific region, marine litter costs more than US$1 billion per year to marine industries, equivalent to 0.3 per cent of the gross domestic product for the marine sector of the region.[408] Economic impacts are related to reparation

---

404 John Mouat, Rebeca Lopez Lozano and Hannah Bateson, 'Economic Impacts of Marine Litter' (KIMO International 2010) 37–40.

405 ibid 43. It was estimated that removing litter from South Africa's waste water streams would cost about US$279 million per year: see ten Brink and others (n 354) 22, including reference.

406 Yong Chang Jang and others, 'Estimation of Lost Tourism Revenue in Geoje Island from the 2011 Marine Debris Pollution Event in South Korea' (2014) 81 Marine Pollution Bulletin 49.

407 See P ten Brink and others, *Guidelines on the Use of Market-Based Instruments to Address the Problem of Marine Litter* (UNEP 2009) 22; Kershaw and others (n 96) 28.

408 Estimated damage cost across the 21 APEC-Countries is US$364 million for the fishing industry, US$279 million for the shipping industry and US$622 million for the marine tourism industry: see Alistair McIlgorm, Harry F Campbell and Michael J Rule, 'The Economic Cost and Control of Marine Debris Damage in the Asia-Pacific Region' (2011) 54 Ocean & Coastal Management 643.

and replacement costs of vessels and gear damaged due to encounters with marine litter, as well as lost fishing opportunities due to time spent cleaning litter from nets, propellers and blocked water intakes.[409] Marine litter costs the Scottish fishing industry the equivalent of 5 per cent of the total revenue of affected fisheries.[410] In addition, fisheries suffer from a loss of revenues due to reduced or contaminated catches. Ghost nets especially can contribute to a decline in fish stocks. The introduction of alien invasive species or pathogens with plastic flotsam can result in serious economic losses, too.[411] Economic impacts that are related to a loss of fish or shellfish quality due to plastic ingestion and contamination have not yet been properly assessed.

As a significant navigational hazard for vessels, marine litter also considerably affects the shipping and yachting industries. In order to keep their facilities safe and attractive, harbours have to constantly remove marine litter. Vessel incidents related to the obstruction of motors due to plastics or interferences with propellers, anchors, rudders or blocked intake pipes and valves are more and more common.[412] Collisions with marine litter also poses a threat to mariners.

When ocean debris is blown to or washed upon coastal farmland, it may also affect agriculture. It may cause damage to property and equipment or present a risk to livestock.[413]

The costs related to marine plastic pollution are considered avoidable losses to the economy to the extent that prevention of marine plastic litter can reduce such costs.[414] It is assumed that costs of inaction are often higher than costs of action.[415] Action against marine litter can be taken throughout the life

409 Newman and others (n 401) 372.

410 See Kershaw and others (n 96) 28. See also Mouat, Lopez Lozano and Bateson (n 404) 56–58.

411 It was estimated that the introduction of the carpet sea squirt (*Didemnum vexillum*) in Holyhead Harbour (Wales, UK) would have cost the local mussel fisheries up to €8.6 million in the next ten years if no mitigation measures were taken: Rohan Holt, 'The Carpet Sea Squirt Didemnum Vexillum: Eradication from Holyhead Marina – Progress to October 2009' (Presentation to the Scottish Natural Heritage Conference 'Marine Non-native Species: Responding to the threat', Battleby, UK, 27 October 2009). See also Newman and others (n 401) 369.

412 See Kershaw and others (n 96) 28; Newman and others (n 401) 371.

413 Newman and others (n 401) 375.

414 UNEP, 'Combating Marine Plastic Litter and Microplastics: An Assessment of the Effectiveness of Relevant International, Regional and Subregional Governance Strategies and Approaches' (2017) (UNEA-3 Legal Report) UNEP/EA.3/INF/5 99.

415 See Emma Watkins and others, 'Marine Litter: Socio-Economic Study – Scoping Report' (IEEP 2015), summary.

cycle of plastics in the form of either preventive or remedial measures. The two types of measures are complementary. However, prevention in the form of systemic upstream approaches have been identified as more efficient and effective when compared to mere remedial actions such as litter removal. They are also more cost-effective in the long run.[416]

The question of who has to bear the costs related to marine plastic pollution raises a number of equity concerns, both with regard to intra- and intergenerational equity (referring to equity within a generation and between generations, respectively).[417] The *intragenerational* aspect is related to the fact that costs associated with marine plastic debris are not necessarily borne by those who cause the problem in the first place.[418] On the one hand, producers and users of plastic goods do usually not have to fully bear the costs related to these products and the damage they cause when released into the environment. Costs in the form of negative externalities of such products are borne by others, including the different actors as discussed in the prior paragraphs. On the other hand, the level at which countries are affected by the issue is highly uneven. It depends on a country's geographic location, national economy and level of income. Developing countries, and especially small island developing countries, are generally most affected, even though their contribution to the problem may be negligible. From an *intergenerational* perspective, it is important to note that the full dimension of the consequences, including economic, of marine plastic litter may only be revealed in the future. It is conceivable that costs related to currently existing levels of plastic pollution will increase over time and be borne by future instead of current generations.

In order to respond to such equity concerns, a number of measures seems necessary. From an international law perspective, an appropriate response involves the whole international community. Cooperation among the countries, including all the polluters and both countries with weak waste management infrastructures and technologically advanced countries, seems inevitable in order to find common responses. Technological and financial support of countries in need seems a necessary feature for such a response. From an industry perspective, costs would have to be internalized and thus be fully borne by the polluters. Possible approaches and instruments allowing for cost internalization are discussed in Part 1.[419]

---

416 UNEP, 'UNEA-3 Legal Report' (n 414) 98.

417 For more information on the concepts of intra- and intergenerational equity, see Section 2.1.A.ii.1) below.

418 See ten Brink and others (n 407) 22.

419 See Section 2.1.A.ii.2) in particular.

3 Summary and Interim Conclusions

Plastics, as we know them today, are a relatively young material. During their rather short history, a great number of scientists, entrepreneurs, inventors, discoveries, events and coincidences, as well as a considerable amount of both endeavour and serendipity contributed to their development. The history of plastics was shaped by the pursuit of power in imperialistic times and during wars, by economic drivers and profit-related motives, but also by an inexhaustible desire for knowledge and discovery, the joy of experimenting and the wish for well-performing, easily processible materials that are not only affordable but allow new designs and applications which were not imaginable before. Plastics reflect the inventiveness of their developers in their extreme versatility. In some regards, they outstripped natural materials in their performance, and played a decisive role in the development of modern communication, transportation and space technologies, as well as in housing, sanitation and alimentation.

Along with rising income levels and new economic models, plastics also considerably influenced our production and consumption patterns and have become an integral feature of the consumer society – a society which is increasingly reflecting on the consequences of waste proliferation, both within society and beyond. Public awareness of the risks and costs of wastes, and plastic wastes in particular, is rising. The accumulation of plastics in remote areas, including the high seas and the deep seabed, triggers feelings of indignation and concern. In these places, and out of human surveillance and control, the downside of many of the outperforming characteristics of plastics is revealed: their high degree of biological inertness, the toxic or ecotoxic effects of some of their components or additives and, above all, their sheer abundance.

As shown in Part 1, pollution in the form of marine plastic debris and microplastics brings about a particular set of challenges and hazards that are unknown to other forms of marine pollution. Plastic debris barely degrades and is difficult to clean up with current technologies. With continuous input from land and, in a more limited way, from sea-based sources, plastic litter is rapidly accumulating in the oceans. Projected scenarios with regard to quantities and impacts are alarming.[420] When compared with other forms of marine pollution, marine plastic debris spreads more easily and more widely.

420 According to a study presented at the World Economic Forum 2016, oceans are expected to contain more plastics than fish (by weight) by 2050 in a business-as-usual scenario: World Economic Forum (n 13) 7.

Plastic fragments from nano to macro sizes can be found across the oceans and occur in all compartments of the sea, including surface waters, pelagic waters, beaches and the seabed. Notably, open-ocean accumulation zones are often situated in areas beyond national jurisdiction. Plastic fragments serve as a vector for contaminants and pathogenic microorganisms, facilitate the dispersal of invasive species, and affect a wide range of marine species and ecosystems. Moreover, marine plastic pollution affects national economies, poses a threat to human health, and impedes legitimate uses of the sea, including marine transportation, fishing and recreation. Coastal zones, many of which may be considered biodiversity hotspots, are probably the most vulnerable to the negative impacts of plastic debris. Yet, plastics are ubiquitous in the ocean. While marine plastic pollution certainly poses a problem to local families and communities, its scope is far wider than that. It is, indeed, a global problem, calling for responses at various levels of governance, from local to global.

Part 1 has also shown that the bulk of marine plastic pollution stems from land-based sources. It mainly includes mismanaged wastes, including from urban centres and dumping sites situated close to the coast or from tourist beaches. Single-use plastic items, such as bags, cups, bottles, films and cutlery, represent a large proportion of the wastes encountered in marine environments, especially coasts. Plastic pollution from land-based sources also includes primary and secondary microplastic particles from tyre wear, city dust, cosmetics, plastic production, laundering and other sources and activities. The particles and fragments, both micro and macro, enter the marine environment from the land through rivers, tides, floods, winds, sewage outflows or the atmosphere.

Costs related to marine plastic pollution are not necessarily borne by the ones who cause them. There are many complicating factors in the establishment of a causal link between the production, use or disposal of plastic products and any consequential loss or damage that may occur in the marine environment. Comparable to the emission of greenhouse gases and the related impact of global warming, the release of plastic particles into the environment (and the marine environment in particular) from land is continuous, dispersed and diffuse in character. The complex life cycle of plastic products suggests that the many actors involved in it share a potential responsibility. Due to the wide dispersal, complicated distribution patterns and continuous fragmentation processes of marine plastic debris, it is usually difficult to trace it back to its exact source when harm occurs. However, a collective responsibility is incontrovertible, while the degree to which a specific country or private actor contributes to the problem is highly variable and difficult to measure.

Marine plastic pollution entails high environmental, social and economic costs that are potentially irreversible and (at least partially) avoidable. With the exception of incinerated plastics, almost every piece of plastic ever made and released into the environment still remains there in the form of whole items or as fragments – and poses a potential risk to the marine environment.[421] Plastic production is gradually rising, while the average service life of plastic products has continually decreased in the last years. As a consequence, plastic waste generation rates continue to grow. Plastic accumulation in the seas will not stop or slow down until there is a change not only in perception but in action by all the actors involved: governments, producers, consumers and waste management operators.

A change in action may require, or be facilitated by, a change in policies and law. While the legal aspects and possibilities will be examined in the next part, the insights as provided by Part 1 give some guidance with regard to the direction in which such a change may go in order to contribute to a solution. It can be expressed in targets at which potential legal adjustments should aim:

- *consumer responsibility*: a change in consumption habits, including through more reasonable, needs-based consumption; gradual substitution of durable products for disposable ones; lower packaging consumption; thorough waste separation at disposal; extended user responsibility;
- *producer responsibility*: green design, including product design for a longer service life and recyclability; life-cycle-based approaches in material selection; no obsolescence; declaration of materials and additives; use of safe chemicals only; reduced packaging where possible; cost internalization; extended producer responsibility;
- *sustainable resource management*: considering new economic models, approaching a circular economy; revalorization of resources and their reintroduction into the production and consumption cycles through reuse, recycling and composting; integrative waste management, including waste prevention, waste reduction, effective waste collection systems with cost recovery and safe waste disposal with energy recovery, if possible. In particular, the improvement of waste management infrastructure in developing countries seems of paramount importance but will require substantial resources and time.[422]

The cumulative and indirect nature of the risk associated with the production, use and disposal of plastics, the diffuseness of this form of pollution and

421 Barnes and others (n 133) 1993.

422 See Jambeck and others (n 291) 770. See also UNEP, 'Mapping of Global Plastics Value Chain' (n 90) 17–18.

its global scale are important characteristics. They need to be given particular attention in the analysis of the legal and policy framework that applies to the problem. Part 2 will give an overview of this very framework and the relevant rules at global and regional levels, as well as their implementation at the national level. Insights from Part 1 suggest that with respect to marine plastic pollution from land-based sources, such implementing measures need to address waste and resource management in the first place, as well as unsustainable production and consumption patterns. The wide and improvident use of disposable or non-recoverable items plays an important role in this regard and calls for particular attention.

PART 2

The Protection of the Marine Environment from Land-based Sources of Plastic Pollution in International Law

Marine plastic debris is a form of marine pollution that has been receiving increasing attention from international institutions in recent years.[423] So far, no global instrument is specifically tailored to the issue at stake. At an international level, marine plastic pollution is regulated in a more general way, along with other forms of marine pollution. The very core of the relevant legal framework consists of a set of general obligations related to the protection and preservation of the marine environment and a number of state duties regarding pollution prevention and control. These obligations are partly derived from general international law and reflected in UNCLOS Part XII,[424] as well as in several regional legal instruments. They apply to all sources of marine pollution.

More concrete rules and standards much depend on the specific sources of pollution: sea-based sources of marine pollution are regulated by a number of global legal instruments.[425] UNCLOS incorporates the rules and standards contained therein by reference. It plays an important role in their widespread application, even beyond the membership of corresponding treaties. Regional schemes, on the other hand, play a secondary role. This contrasts with the regime applying to land-based pollution sources, in which global standards are mainly set within a non-legal policy framework. As these standards are not legally binding and their adherence not compulsory, regional rules play a much more important role in this field. Reference to corresponding rules and standards in UNCLOS is much weaker, and so is the role UNCLOS plays in their

---

423 See Section 2.1.A.i.5) below.

424 1982 UNCLOS.

425 With regard to plastics, two of them are of particular importance: The Convention on the Prevention of Marine Pollution by Dumping of Wastes and Other Matter (1972 London Dumping Convention) (adopted on 13 November 1972, entered into force on 40 August 1975) strictly prohibits dumping of wastes at sea from vessels, aircraft or offshore-installations. Disposal of plastics from vessels is also prohibited by Annex V of the International Convention for the Prevention of Pollution from Ships (signed on 2 November 1973) 1340 UNTS 184, 12 ILM 1319 (1973) and Protocol Relating to the International Convention for the Prevention of Pollution from Ships (adopted on 17 February 1978) 1340 UNTS 61, 17 ILM 546 (1978), both entered into force on 2 October 1983 (1973/78 MARPOL).

© JUDITH SCHÄLI, 2022 | DOI:10.1163/9789004508613_004
This is an open access chapter distributed under the terms of the CC BY-NC 4.0 license.

application. Both regimes – on land- and sea-based sources – have their deficiencies and *lacunae*, for instance with respect to compliance, enforcement and liability issues.[426] Challenges with regard to the regulation of land-based pollution sources are, however, more far-reaching, and more fundamental. Pertinent regulation – on the prevention and control of marine pollution from land-based sources – will be the focus of this part.

As has been shown in Part 1, distinguishing features of marine plastic pollution include its global and cumulative character and the fact that its sources are continuous, dispersed and diffuse. These features are of a peculiar interest in the analysis of the relevant legal framework and need to be taken into account. Finally, the framework will be tested against these special features in order to see whether it does or does not provide a sufficient and adequate response to them.

The analysis in Part 2 starts with the global regime (Chapter 1). It examines its major traits and their practical impacts on the challenge of massive accumulation of plastics and microplastics in marine environments. In a second step, Part 2 deals with the regional schemes and their major strengths and deficiencies with regard to the issue at stake (Chapter 2). It then turns to national implementation measures and provides a general overview of some of the relevant approaches, policies and tools that have been explored at the national and supranational levels so far (Chapter 3). Part 2 concludes that, while providing a relatively strong general framework on the protection of the marine environment and the regulation of marine pollution, the current regime does not give a sufficient response to the specific problem of marine plastic pollution from land-based sources. It is precisely the above-mentioned characteristics – the dispersed nature of the problem, as well as its diffuse sources and cumulative effects – that reveal the most evident limits of the framework.

1 The Global Framework

The view that marine resources are inexhaustible and the ocean's assimilative capacities infinite has been widely accepted for a long period of human history. Until the middle of the twentieth century, oceans were largely treated as a mere transportation route, continuous source of food and convenient dumping site. A number of alarming signs, such as mercury pollution in Japanese Minamata Bay and the discovery of the related Minamata disease in the 1950s,

---

426 See, for instance, Derraik (n 287) 848.

as well as increasing scientific evidence that the ocean's capacity to assimilate human discharges and wastes is both limited and quantifiable induced an irrevocable change of mind. A better understanding of the functions performed by the oceans and their importance to human survival laid the basis for the now prevailing understanding that oceans need to be managed in a much more holistic way. Environmental considerations form an indispensable part of such management. Also, increasing knowledge and awareness with regard to the sensitivity of marine ecosystems and the threats posed on them by human activities contributed to a profound adaptation of global policies and rules in the past 50 years. Today, the protection and preservation of the marine environment is one of the core objectives of the international law of the sea, with environmental concerns figuring prominently and with increasing emphasis in today's global political agenda related to ocean governance. Regulations regarding pollution control and – more recently and more importantly – pollution prevention are at the very heart of the regime on the protection of the marine environment.

The control of vessel-based pollution, especially by oil, was the first concern to be addressed in this regard. In the course of the twentieth century, a treaty regime was developed on sea-based sources of marine pollution. The regulation of land-based sources took longer and has been much more controversial. The push towards a global solution by some actors repeatedly clashed with the reluctance of most countries towards a global convention on land-based sources. The development of non-binding instruments and the promotion of regional programmes are two aspects of a strategy to fill the regulatory void and hence avoid a deadlock in the development of a regime on land-based pollution sources. In view of changing perceptions that come along with today's environmental challenges, including the ones posed by marine plastic pollution, this strategy is increasingly challenged.

Section A of the current chapter outlines the global policy framework relevant to the problem of marine plastic pollution, which is rooted in the global conferences of 1972 and 1992 and has become increasingly specific in recent years. Section B gives a detailed account of the relevant provisions of UNCLOS and its Part XII in particular. Section C addresses matters of coherency between UNCLOS and international trade regulation and gives an introduction into the relevant provisions of the law of the World Trade Organization (WTO). The protection of the marine environment from land-based sources of plastic pollution is, of course, very closely related to other regulatory fields, including the regulation of hazardous chemicals, the protection of biodiversity, and waste management. Possible implications from these other fields are discussed in Section D.

A *Global Policy, Principles and Concepts*

i The Global Policy Framework

While evidence of the detrimental effects of marine plastic pollution has been known since the early 1970s, it was much more recently that the real scale of the problem has been recognized and that action has been taken. The UN Environment Programme (UNEP), today often referred to as UN Environment, played an important role in global policy formulation with respect to marine pollution from land-based sources and plastics. Major events in the development of a policy framework on land-based pollution sources include the 1972 Stockholm Conference and the subsequent establishment of UN Environment, the adoption of Agenda 21 at the 1992 Rio Conference, and the adoption of the Global Programme of Action for the Protection of the Marine Environment from Land-Based Activities (GPA) in 1995. About a decade later, the UN set marine debris and plastics on its permanent agenda and initiated a belated debate. In parallel, the issue was taken up and addressed by other fora, including in a multi-stakeholder dialogue.

1) *UN Environment's Role in Policy Formulation and Regulation with Regard to Land-based Sources of Marine Pollution*

Although still with less emphasis than was put on it at later occasions, the problem of land-based pollution sources was seized on at the 1972 Stockholm Conference on the Human Environment. The event marked the start of a new era of global environmental policy formulation. The Stockholm Declaration[427] was one of its main outcomes. Its Principle 7 requests states to 'take all possible steps to prevent pollution of the seas by substances that are liable to create hazards to human health, to harm living resources and marine life, to damage amenities or to interfere with other legitimate uses of the sea'. The attached action plan recommends that national controls over land-based sources of marine pollution be strengthened. In the following year, the UN General Assembly established UN Environment. The Environment Programme was given a leading role in the implementation of the action plan.[428] Prevention and control of marine pollution was considered to play a key role in this regard. Most notably, UN Environment recognized the control

427 Declaration of the United Nations Conference on the Human Environment (1972 Stockholm Declaration) in Report of the Stockholm Conference, UN Doc. A/CONF.48/14/Rev. 1 (1972) 3, reprinted in 11 ILM 1416 (1972).

428 UNGA Res 2994 (XXVII) (1972), 'United Nations Conference on the Human Environment' para 2.

of land-based sources of pollution as a major aspect in the protection of the human environment.[429]

Yet, the set-up of a global instrument on land-based pollution sources proved much more difficult than the adoption of instruments dealing with other pollution sources, despite the fact that land-based pollution sources are more important in terms of pollution quantity. They are, however, also more diffuse and variable than sea-based sources. Monitoring, control and mitigation are, therefore, more complicated with regard to land-based sources. Also, land-based pollution is often caused by activities that are closely linked to economic, industrial and social development of the respective countries. Their international regulation involves areas that are often considered to fall under the national sovereignty of states and is, therefore, particularly challenging.[430] That is why a global legal agreement on land-based pollution sources was, at the time, not considered feasible.[431]

UN Environment thus adopted a different approach and focused on the development of regional frameworks. The idea behind this approach was to concentrate global regulatory efforts on the development of internationally acceptable guidelines and general principles, while setting region-specific strategies and standards in corresponding programmes.[432] For the time being, the formulation of general principles was left to the Third United Nations Conference on the Law of the Sea, which started negotiations in 1973. In 1974, UN Environment launched the Regional Seas Programme.[433] In the early 1980s,

429 See Thomas A Mensah, 'The International Legal Regime for the Protection and Preservation of the Marine Environment from Land-Based Sources of Pollution' in Alan E Boyle and David Freestone (eds), *International Law and Sustainable Development: Past Achievements and Future Challenges* (Oxford University Press 1999) 299.

430 See Robin Rolf Churchill and Alan Vaughan Lowe, *The Law of the Sea* (3rd edn, Manchester University Press 1999) 379; Mensah (n 429) 312; Edward L Miles, 'The Approaches of UNCLOS and Agenda 21 – A Synthesis' in Mochtar Kusuma-Atmadja, Thomas A Mensah and Bernard H Oxman (eds), *Sustainable Development and Preservation of the Oceans: The Challenges of UNCLOS and Agenda 21 – Proceedings the Law of the Sea Institute Twenty-Ninth Annual Conference (Despansar, Bali, Indonesia, 1995)* (Law of the Sea Institute 1997) 37.

431 UNEP, 'Review of Development Activities Since 1985 – Note by the Secretariat' UNEP/MG/IG/1/2 of 29 April 1994 515; Miles (n 430) 37.

432 Mensah (n 429) 300.

433 The Programme will be discussed more in detail in the second chapter of this part. In a nutshell, it comprises 14 regional programmes and four partner programmes, each of which addresses a region's particular environmental challenges in an action plan. The regional programmes involve different legal settings: some of them have adopted a regional convention and a number of specific protocols in the subsequent years, while others do still not have any legal foundations. No conventions have yet been developed

it also explored the possibilities for the adoption of an international agreement on land-based sources of marine pollution.[434] The attempt faced strong resistance, however, and so the efforts remained unsuccessful.

In 1987, the World Commission on Environment and Development (WCED) released its report *Our Common Future* (the Brundtland Report), which is known for its contribution to the promotion of the concept of sustainable development.[435] In its report, the commission acknowledged that 'the living resources of the sea are under threat from overexploitation, pollution, and land-based development' and that '[t]he major land-based threats to the oceans require effective national actions based on international cooperation'.[436] The commission recognized UN Environment's role as a key agent in the preparation of global guidelines and principles on marine pollution from land-based sources. It invited UN Environment to extend its Regional Seas Programme and to develop a similar programme for international river basins.[437]

---

for the East Asian Seas, South Asian Seas, North-East Pacific or North-West Pacific regions. Also, there is no relevant legal agreement for the Arctic region.

434 In 1980, UN Environment convened a Working Group for this purpose, which led to the adoption by the UN Environment Governing Council, in 1985, of the Montreal Guidelines for the Protection of the Marine Environment against Pollution from Land-based Sources: UNEP, '1985 Montreal Guidelines' (n 361). Though not legally binding in character, the Montreal Guidelines are one of the first global instruments on the subject. They address issues that are not regulated in UNCLOS, such as the development of control strategies, the periodic adoption of implementation reports and the setup of institutional arrangements at the appropriate regional or global level. Three Annexes provide additional guidance for implementation. In addition, UN Environment established the Montevideo Programme for the Development and Periodic Review of Environmental Law (Montevideo Programme) in 1981. Marine pollution from land-based sources was one of three major subject areas of the programme. The involved experts generally approved UN Environment's regional approach and referred to the work of the Third United Nations Conference on the Law of the Sea, the conclusion of which was now imminent. They expected the adoption of a global convention (UNCLOS) that was to include guidelines and principles and address land-based sources of marine pollution: UNEP, 'Montevideo Programme for the Development and Periodic Review of Environmental Law (1981)' (UNEP Governing Council Decision 10/21 of 31 May 1982) 4. Calls for a specific convention on land-based sources have also been formulated and discussed by other bodies, but without any concrete results: see, for instance, IMO, 'Report of the 13th Consultative Meeting of the Contracting Parties to the 1972 London Dumping Convention' (1990) UN Doc IMO/LDC.13/15 Annex 4 para 2.

435 WCED, *Our Common Future* (*Brundtland Report*) (Oxford University Press 1987). The UN General Assembly transmitted the report to all governments and UN bodies and invited them to take account of the report in determining their policies and programmes: UNGA Res 42/187 (1987), 'Report of the World Commission on Environment and Development' para 6.

436 WCED (n 435) ch 10.I.

437 ibid ch 12.II.2.2.1.

In 1990, the Joint Group of Experts on the Scientific Aspects of Marine Environmental Protection (GESAMP) – a body that was established in 1969 in order to provide scientific advice to the UN system with respect to the protection of the marine environment – published a report on the state of the marine environment. In the report, GESAMP identified land-based sources as the main contributors to marine pollution and recognized a need for strengthening their regulation at all levels.[438] At the same time, GESAMP acknowledged that 'the establishment of a globally applicable and all-embracing convention on the protection of the marine environment from land-based sources of pollution seems unlikely, taking into account the many different stages of development in the various regions of the world'.[439] The 1990 report is one of the first of its kind to explicitly refer to the problem of 'plastic and other litter' and to call for awareness-raising measures and a more rigorous enforcement of corresponding rules.[440]

2) *The 1992 Rio Conference*

The regime on land-based sources of marine pollution was also a subject of discussion during the preparation of the 1992 UN Conference on Environment and Development (1992 Rio Conference, UNCED). The aim of UNCED was the elaboration of 'strategies and measures to halt and reverse the effects of environmental degradation in the context of increased national and international efforts to promote sustainable and environmentally sound development in all countries'.[441]

In the run-up to the 1992 Conference, UN Environment participated in the organization of the Intergovernmental Meeting on Land-Based Sources of Marine Pollution, which was held in May 1991 in Halifax, Canada.[442] Participants of the Halifax Meeting concluded that, in order to effectively

438 GESAMP, 'The State of the Marine Environment' (n 283) para 431. According to the report, 'major changes in long-established agricultural and industrial practices' may be required, as well as 'the development or expansion of waste treatment facilities both along the coast and far inland, sometimes well beyond the boundaries of the coastal states concerned': ibid.

439 GESAMP, 'The State of the Marine Environment' (n 283) para 376.

440 ibid 403–04.

441 UNGA Res 44/228 (1989), 'United Nations Conference on Environment and Development' ch I para 3.

442 John Karau, 'The Control of Land-Based Sources of Marine Pollution' (1992) 25 Marine Pollution Bulletin 80, 80; Mensah (n 429) 303; Netherlands Institute for the Law of the Sea, *International Organizations and the Law of the Sea: Documentary Yearbook*, vol 8 (1992) xxv. The main findings of the Halifax Meeting are summarized in UNEP, 'Review of Development Activities Since 1985' (n 431) 517 para 26–27.

address land-based sources of marine pollution, a coherent strategy was necessary at all levels of governance. They recommended that states should adopt such a strategy 'based on a commonly accepted set of principles, and containing a set of goals to be achieved'.[443] The outcome of the Halifax Meeting was fed into the preparatory process of UNCED. Countries preferred, however, national and regional solutions and were not willing to commit for a global convention on the issue.[444]

UNCED was the first 'Earth Summit' at which nations where represented by their heads of state or government. Main outcomes of the conference included, among other things, a Declaration of Principles (later known as the Rio Declaration)[445] and *Agenda 21*, a comprehensive plan of action covering the period beyond 1992 and into the twenty-first century.[446] As they are universally endorsed and reflect a global consensus, the Rio Principles play an important role in the interpretation and application of existing rules of environmental law, as well as in the formation of new rules in this field. They are valuable environmental management tools, representing prevalent approaches to existing environmental challenges.[447]

443 Karau (n 442) 80.

444 As discussed at the UNCED Preparatory Committee's third meeting in August 1991: see ibid 81.

445 Rio Declaration on Environment and Development (1992 Rio Declaration) in Report of the United Nations Conference on Environment and Development (1992), UN Doc A/CONF.151/26 (Vol. I).

446 Important outcomes of the conference further include the UN climate and biodiversity conventions and the Forest Principles: United Nations Framework Convention on Climate Change (UNFCCC) (opened for signature on 9 May 1992, entered into force on 21 March 1994) 1771 UNTS 107; United Nations Convention on Biological Diversity (CBD) (opened for signature on 5 June 1992, entered into force on 29 December 1993) 1760 UNTS 79; Non-Legally Binding Authoritative Statement of Principles for a Global Consensus on the Management, Conservation and Sustainable Development of All Types of Forests (Forest Principles) (adopted on 14 June 1992) UN Doc A/CONF.151/26 (Vol. III). UNCED also paved the way for the adoption of a convention on sustainable land use: United Nations Convention to Combat Desertification in Countries Experiencing Serious Drought and/or Desertification, Particularly in Africa (UNCCD) (opened for signature on 17 June 1994, entered into force on 26 December 1996) 1954 UNTS 3, 33 ILM 1328 (1994).

447 For more information, see Alan Boyle and David Freestone, 'Introduction' in Alan Boyle and David Freestone (eds), *International Law and Sustainable Development: Past Achievements and Future Challenges* (Oxford University Press 1999); Philippe Sands and Jacqueline Peel, *Principles of International Environmental Law* (3rd edn, Cambridge University Press 2012) in particular ch 6; Jorge E Viñuales (ed), *The Rio Declaration on Environment and Development: A Commentary* (Oxford University Press 2015). See also Nicolas de Sadeleer, *Environmental Principles: From Political Slogans to Legal Rules* (Oxford University Press 2002).

Agenda 21 established a work programme for the international community in respect to all areas of human impacts on the environment.[448] Chapter 17 of Agenda 21 is fully dedicated to the protection of the oceans and its resources.[449] In the chapter, the importance of land-based pollution sources, including, for instance, with regard to litter and plastics, is acknowledged. It is further held that 'there is currently no global scheme to address marine pollution from land-based sources'.[450] Agenda 21 calls on states to 'commit themselves, in accordance with their policies, priorities and resources, to prevent, reduce and control degradation of the marine environment so as to maintain and improve its life-support and productive capacities'. To this end, states should apply preventive, precautionary and anticipatory approaches; ensure prior assessment of activities that may have significant adverse impacts upon the marine environment; integrate protection of the marine environment into relevant general environmental, social and economic development policies; develop economic incentives consistent with the internalization of environmental costs and the polluter pays principle; and take into account equity concerns.[451] Finally, states are invited to consider 'updating, strengthening and extending' relevant instruments and to assess the effectiveness of existing frameworks.[452]

Follow-up of UNCED and the implementation of Agenda 21 were originally monitored by the Commission on Sustainable Development (CSD), a body established by the UN General Assembly in December 1992. The CSD reported to the UN through the Economic and Social Council (ECOSOC). At its seventh session, the commission recommended that priority be given to the 'prevention of pollution and degradation of the marine environment from landbased and other activities' and emphasized the need for cooperation at all levels and capacity-building to this purpose.[453] In 2012, the CSD was replaced by a high-level political forum. Implementation of Agenda 21 involves all levels of governance and different actors, including UN bodies and state governments.

448 See Alicia Barcena, 'An Overview of the Oceans in Agenda 21 of the 1992 United Nations Conference on Environment and Development' (1992) 25 Marine Pollution Bulletin 107, 107.

449 The chapter is entitled 'Protection of The Oceans, All Kinds of Seas, Including Enclosed and Semi-Enclosed Seas, and Coastal Areas and the Protection, Rational Use and Development of their Living Resources'.

450 Agenda 21, *Report of the United Nations Conference on Environment and Development, Rio de Janeiro, 3–14 June 1992, Vol I, Resolutions Adopted by the Conference* (United Nations publication, Sales No E93I8 and corrigendum) para 17.18.

451 ibid para 17.22.

452 ibid para 17.25.

453 CSD Decision 7/1, 'Ocean and Sea' (1999) E/1999/25 para 3(b).

UNCLOS provides the legal framework for the programme of action as contained in Chapter 17, and implementation has to be consistent with the provisions of UNCLOS.[454]

3) *The 1995 Washington Conference and the GPA*

In Agenda 21, UN Environment was invited to convene an intergovernmental meeting on the protection of the marine environment from land-based activities.[455] UN Environment followed the invitation and organized a conference that took place from 23 October to 3 November 1995 in Washington.[456] At the conference, two documents were successfully adopted by 108 countries and the European Union: the Washington Declaration[457] and the *Global Programme of Action for the Protection of the Marine Environment from Land-Based Activities* (GPA).[458]

The Washington Declaration is a political statement of participating countries confirming their commitment to protect and preserve the marine environment from the impacts of land-based activities, including litter. It is moreover a declaration of intention with respect to the implementation of the GPA, especially with regard to: the development of national action programmes and their implementation; capacity-building and the mobilization of resources; immediate preventive and remedial action; access to cleaner technologies; public–private partnerships; better wastewater management and treatment; the development of a legally binding instrument on persistent organic pollutants; the establishment of a clearing-house mechanism; and institutional follow-up.

Perhaps more impressively, the second instrument that was adopted at the Washington Conference, the GPA, is probably the most comprehensive international initiative addressing land-based activities. The GPA 'aims at preventing

454 See Alexander Yankov, 'The Law of the Sea Convention and Agenda 21: Marine Environmental Implications' in Alan Boyle and David Freestone (eds), *International Law and Sustainable Development: Past Achievements and Future Challenges* (Oxford University Press 1999) 273. On Chapter 17 of Agenda 21, see also Hassan (n 364) 93–95.

455 Agenda 21 (n 450) para 17.26.

456 Three preparatory expert meetings were held prior to the Washington Conference. At the final preparatory meeting, which was held in Reykjavik, Iceland, in March 1995, participants agreed on the objective to produce an effective programme of action instead of a legally binding instrument. They agreed that action should be taken at the global, regional and national levels: see Miles (n 430) 38.

457 'Washington Declaration on Protection of the Marine Environment from Land-Based Activities' (UNEP 1995).

458 UNEP, 'Global Programme of Action for the Protection of the Marine Environment from Land-Based Activities' (1995) UN Doc UNEP(OCA)/LBA/IG.2/7.

the degradation of the marine environment from land-based activities by facilitating the realization of the duty of States to preserve and protect the marine environment' – a duty that is stipulated in UNCLOS.[459] In addition to the prevention, reduction and control of marine pollution, the GPA refers to pollution elimination and measures that lead to the recovery of the marine environment from the impacts of pollution.[460] In this respect, the GPA goes beyond the scope of corresponding provisions in UNCLOS. The Programme of Action 'is designed to be a source of conceptual and practical guidance' for implementing existing obligations and commitments, including under UNCLOS and Agenda 21, as well as for devising further action. Guidance for action at the national, regional and global level is provided in three chapters of the GPA.[461]

At the *national* level, the GPA urges states to develop national programmes of action (NPAS) within the framework of integrated coastal area management. The NPAS should include provisions for: identifying and assessing problems; establishing priorities; setting management objectives for priority problems; selecting management strategies and measures; defining criteria for evaluating the effectiveness of strategies and programmes; and ensuring programme support elements (such as financing, human resources and legal and enforcement mechanisms).[462] The GPA calls on states to apply a number of principles and approaches, including integrated coastal area management; watershed management; poverty alleviation; environmental impact assessment; the protection of critical habitats and endangered species; vertical policy integration; cooperation; precaution and intergenerational equity.[463] For their strategies and measures, states are invited to use best available techniques (BATS) and best environmental practices (BEPS); clean production practices; environmentally sound and efficient technologies; and product substitution. Possible measures include market-based instruments, with due regard for the polluter pays principle and cost internalization; regulatory measures; technical assistance and cooperation; education; and awareness-raising activities. Particular reference is made to waste recovery, recycling and waste treatment, as well as to the importance of institutional arrangements, monitoring and reporting,

---

459 ibid para 3; 1982 UNCLOS art 192.

460 UNEP, 'GPA' (n 458) para 3.

461 ibid paras 14–15.

462 ibid para 18. See David VanderZwaag and Ann Powers, 'The Protection of the Marine Environment from Land-Based Pollution and Activities: Gauging the Tides of Global and Regional Governance' (2008) 23 The International Journal of Marine and Coastal Law 423, 427–28.

463 UNEP, 'GPA' (n 458) para 23.

and resource mobilization.[464] Environmental effectiveness, cost-effectiveness, equity and flexibility are some of the suggested criteria for evaluating the NPAs.[465]

At the *regional* level, the GPA calls for enhanced cooperation in protecting the marine environment from land-based activities. It encourages states to strengthen existing regional conventions and programmes and to negotiate new ones, if appropriate.[466] The GPA provides guidance for the adoption of regional action programmes following the methodology as specified with regard to NPAs.[467] It points out a list of issues to be considered in this regard, including policy harmonization and capacity-building schemes. The involvement of landlocked states in regional schemes is strongly encouraged in the GPA.[468] With respect to the institutional aspects of regional and subregional arrangements, states are recommended to invite multilateral financing agencies and other institutions to cooperate in programming and implementing regional agreements in the developing-country regions.[469]

The importance of effective *international* cooperation for the successful implementation of the GPA is also stressed, especially with regard to capacity-building, technology transfer and financial support.[470] The development of a clearing-house mechanism is suggested as a means of mobilizing experience and expertise.[471] Regular review of the implementation of the GPA, but also of the state of the marine environment is encouraged.[472] Resource mobilization and effective institutional arrangements are considered key objectives of international cooperation under the GPA. With reference made to the commitments contained in Chapters 33 (financial resources and mechanisms) and 34 (transfer of environmentally sound technology, cooperation and capacity-building)

464 ibid para 26.
465 ibid para 27.
466 ibid para 31.
467 ibid paras 32–33.
468 ibid para 34. Reference to land-locked states is in line with Article 23 of the United Nations Convention on the Law of the Non-navigational Uses of International Watercourses (1997 Watercourse Convention) (adopted on 21 May 1997, entered into force on 17 August 2014) 36 ILM 700 (1997), UN Doc A/RES/51/229 (1997). According to the Article,

> Watercourse States shall, individually and, where appropriate, in cooperation with other States, take all measures with respect to an international watercourse that are necessary to protect and preserve the marine environment, including estuaries, taking into account generally accepted international rules and standards.

469 UNEP, 'GPA' (n 458) para 32(a).
470 ibid para 36.
471 ibid para 42.
472 ibid paras 36–37.

of Agenda 21, the GPA calls for support to countries in need of assistance for the implementation of the programme.[473]

A special role is assigned to the Global Environmental Facility (GEF) in this regard. The GEF is invited to support GPA implementation under its focal areas, especially international waters and biodiversity protection.[474] The GEF's Operational Strategy, which was adopted in 1995, defines the control of land-based pollution sources as a priority area for action in its focal area on international waters.[475] Marine plastic pollution has been an issue under GEF-6 and GEF-7 replenishment and in several publications supported by the GEF.[476]

Also, the GPA dedicated a section to the treatment of wastewater and sewage, and urged countries to develop an international legally binding instrument on the application of the prior informed consent (PIC) procedure for certain hazardous chemicals in international trade and one on persistent organic pollutants (POPs).[477] Such instruments have been adopted in 1998 and 2001, respectively.[478] Their specific implications for plastic production, use and disposal will be discussed in the Section D.

Besides the chapters guiding action at the national, regional and international levels, a full chapter of the GPA is devoted to source categories.[479] One

473 ibid para 38.
474 ibid paras 69–70.
475 GEF, 'Operational Strategy' (1995) GEF/C.6/3 ch 4 para 4.10.
476 See, for instance, UNDP and GEF, 'Plastics and Circular Economy Community Solutions' (2019). The GEF also assists 'Addressing Marine Plastics: A Systemic Approach', a project by UN Environment in collaboration with the New Plastics Economy, Ocean Conservancy, and GRID-Arendal. The aim of the project is the developent of a strategic roadmap to help guide the transition to circular plastic economies at local, national and global scales, and stem the flow of plastic waste to the ocean.
477 UNEP, 'GPA' (n 458) paras 90 and 88, respectively. The request is consistent with two related decisions of the UNEP General Council: UNEP, 'Development of an International Legally Binding Instrument for the Application of the Prior Informed Consent Procedure for Certain Hazardous Chemicals in International Trade, and Consideration of Further Measures to Reduce the Risks from Hazardous Chemicals' (1995) UNEP/GC.18/12; UNEP, 'Persistent Organic Pollutants' (1995) UNEP/GC.18/32.
478 Rotterdam Convention on the Prior Informed Consent Procedure for Certain Hazardous Chemicals and Pesticides in International Trade (Rotterdam PIC Convention) (adopted on 10 September 1998, entered into force on 24 February 2004, last revised on 10 May 2013) 2244 UNTS 393, 38 ILM 1 (1999); Stockholm Convention on Persistent Organic Pollutants (Stockholm POPs Convention) (adopted on 22 May 2001, entered into force on 17 May 2004, last amended in 2015) 2256 UNTS 119, 40 ILM 532 (2001).
479 The nine main source categories identified are sewage, POPs, radioactive substances, heavy metals, oils, nutrients, sediment mobilization, litter plastics, and physical alterations and degradation of habitats. See Biliana Cicin-Sain, 'Earth Summit Implementation: Progress since Rio' (1996) 20 Marine Policy 123, 131.

of the examined source categories is litter.[480] The chapter acknowledges the negative impacts associated with plastic litter in particular, sets objectives for improvement and proposes a set of actions. With reference made to paragraph 21.39 of Agenda 21, a defined objective is the significant reduction of the amount of litter reaching the marine and coastal environment 'by the prevention or reduction of the generation of solid waste and improvements in its management, including collection and recycling of litter'.[481] Proposed objectives include the introduction of appropriate measures (regulatory measures and/or economic instruments) to encourage reduction in the generation of solid wastes, as well as '[c]ooperation with countries in need of assistance, through financial, scientific and technological support, in developing and establishing environmentally sound waste-disposal methods and alternatives to disposal'.[482]

In 1997, the UN General Assembly adopted a resolution on institutional arrangements of the GPA and designated UN Environment as the lead agency in the implementation of the GPA.[483] In the same year, a UN Environment coordinating office was established in The Hague, the Netherlands. Acting in its role as secretariat of the GPA,[484] UN Environment developed a clearing-house mechanism in cooperation with a number of UN agencies involved in the implementation of the GPA. It has promoted cooperation between relevant actors and mainstreaming of issues related to the implementation of the programme into different fora.[485] While, in general, the GPA has been well received, implementation is slow and insufficient.[486] Key challenges with

480 UNEP, 'GPA' (n 458) paras 140–48.

481 ibid para 144.

482 ibid paras 146 and 148.

483 UNGA Res 51/189 (1996), 'Institutional Arrangements for the Implementation of the Global Programme of Action for the Protection of the Marine Environment from Land-Based Activities'. UN Environment made the implementation of the GPA a top priority: see UNEP, 'Implementation of the Global Programme of Action for the Protection of the Marine Environment from Land-Based Activities' (1997) UNEP/GC.19/14A. See also Mensah (n 429) 309.

484 See UNEP, 'GPA' (n 458) paras 74–75.

485 Mainstreaming work was successful in that different bodies (such as the CSD and the UN General Assembly) referred to the GPA and addressed a number of issues relevant to their fields of work.

486 Effectiveness of the GPA is discussed in Hassan (n 364) 98–100; Bettina Meier-Wehren, 'The Global Programme of Action for the Protection of the Marine Environment from Land-Based Activities' (2013) 17 NZJ Envtl. L. 1, 36–40; VanderZwaag and Powers (n 462) 429–42. See also implementation reports by UN Environment: UNEP, 'Report of the First Intergovernmental Review Meeting on the Implementation of the Global Programme of Action for the Protection of the Marine Environment from Land-Based Activities' (2001)

regard to implementation of the GPA include: limited national participation and implementation; limited national reporting; limited coverage of pollutant source categories; limited financing; the non-legally binding character of the GPA; and deficiencies in international environmental governance.[487]

At an international level, states committed themselves to advance implementation of the GPA at the World Summit on Sustainable Development (WSSD) held in Johannesburg, South Africa, in 2002.[488] In the Johannesburg Plan of Implementation, one of the main outcomes of the WSSD, states are also called on to 'strengthen the capacity of developing countries [...] to mainstream the objectives of the Global Programme of Action and to manage the risks and impacts of ocean pollution'.[489] Since 2001, the UN General Assembly has referred to the GPA, with increasing emphasis, in its annual resolutions on oceans and the law of the sea.[490]

Every five to six years, there is an intergovernmental review meeting on the implementation of the GPA.[491] In preparation for the second meeting in 2006, a report was issued assessing the state of the marine environment.[492]

UNEP/GPA/IGR.1/9; 'Report of the Second Session of the Intergovernmental Review Meeting on the Implementation of the Global Programme of Action for the Protection of the Marine Environment from Land-Based Activities' (2006) UNEP/GPA/IGR.2/7.

487 These key challenges are discussed in VanderZwaag and Powers (n 462) 438–42.

488 Johannesburg Plan of Implementation in Report of the World Summit on Sustainable Development (2002), UN Doc A/CONF.199/20 para 33. After the conferences in Stockholm in 1972 and in Rio in 1992, the WSSD was the third UN Conference on environment and development. The conference mainly served for reaffirming and refining existing principles and policies, including Agenda 21: see Patricia Birnie, Alan Boyle and Catherine Redgwell, *International Law and the Environment* (3rd edn, OUP Oxford 2009) 53.

489 Johannesburg Plan of Implementation para 33(b). At the WSSD, the establishment of a regular process under the UN for global reporting and assessment of the state of the marine environment was recommended: see UNGA Res 57/141 (2002), 'Oceans and the Law of the Sea' Preamble. The Regular Process for Global Reporting and Assessment of the State of the Marine Environment Including Socioeconomic Aspect was subsequently established through a number of resolutions. Its first cycle ran from 2010 to 2014, the second cycle from 2015 to 2020. The two World Ocean Assessment reports are available online: 'Regular Process' <https://www.un.org/regularprocess/> accessed 19 February 2022. Chapters 25 and 12 deal with marine debris: see Wang and others (n 342); Francois Galgani and others, 'Chapter 12: Changes in Inputs and Distribution of Solid Waste, Other Than Dredged Material, in the Marine Environment', *Second World Ocean Assessment* (United Nations 2021).

490 See UNGA Res 55/7 (2001) para 27; Res 75/239 (2021) paras 217 and 244–46.

491 Meetings were held in Montreal, Canada (2001), in Beijing, China (2006), in Manila, the Philippines (2012), and in Bali, Indonesia (2018).

492 UNEP and GPA, *The State of the Marine Environment: Trends and Processes* (UNEP/GPA Coordination Office 2006).

While progress was noted with regard to some source categories of marine pollution, including POPs, the report showed that the problem of marine litter had worsened, despite control measures.[493] Marine plastic litter has, therefore, been identified as a priority for action.[494] At the third review meeting on the implementation of the GPA in Manila in 2012, a declaration on furthering the implementation of the GPA was adopted. In the declaration, generally referred to as the Manila Declaration, 64 governments and the European Commission recognized that:

> marine litter is a problem that is global in scale and underestimated in impact; that it directly threatens coastal and marine habitats and species, economic growth, human health and safety, and social values; that a significant portion of marine litter originates from land-based activities; and that movement of litter and debris, exacerbated by storm events, has significant impacts on the marine environment.[495]

They therefore decided that the GPA coordination office focus its work on marine litter as one out of three priority source categories.[496] The governments moreover called for the establishment of a global partnership on marine litter. The Manila Declaration provided UN Environment with a strong mandate to continue its work on marine litter.

4) *The 2011 Honolulu Strategy: Plastics Coming into Focus*

In March 2011, almost a year before the Manila review meeting, the NOAA and UN Environment co-organized the Fifth International Marine Debris Conference (5IMDC) which was held in Honolulu, Hawai'i, US. About 450 people from 38 countries and with different institutional backgrounds participated in the conference. The theme of the conference was *Waves of Change:*

---

493 ibid 28.

494 ibid 34.

495 'Manila Declaration on Furthering the Implementation of the Global Programme of Action for the Protection of the Marine Environment from Land-Based Activities' (2012) UNEP/GCSS.XII/INF/10, Annex Preamble.

496 ibid para 5. To this purpose, they defined strategic directions, including:

> Working with all stakeholders concerned to find innovative solutions and initiatives to the problem of marine litter, including by sharing best practices, technical information about capacity-building and legal, policy, community-based, economic and market-based means of preventing, reducing and managing marine litter, and working to establish a global partnership on marine litter.

Global Lessons to Inspire Local Action.[497] The 5IMDC was an awareness-raising event that kicked off and promoted a cross-sectoral and multi-stakeholder dialogue by gathering representatives from governments, industry, academia and civil society,[498] who all committed to 'reduce waste in order to halt and reverse the occurrence of marine debris' and to 'advocate mechanisms that emphasise the prevention or minimisation of waste'.[499] The conference had much broader outreach than its four precedents. At its 66th session, the UN General Assembly took note of the conference and encouraged states 'to further develop partnerships with industry and civil society to raise awareness of the extent of the impact of marine debris on the health and productivity of the marine environment and consequent economic loss'.[500]

The event contributed significantly to the development of the *Honolulu Strategy: A Global Framework for Prevention and Management of Marine Debris*.[501] As a framework for a comprehensive and global effort to reduce the global impacts of marine debris, the Honolulu Strategy 'provides a focal point for improved collaboration and coordination among the multitude of stakeholders across the globe concerned with marine debris'. It is designed as a planning and monitoring tool for programmes and projects dealing with the prevention and reduction of marine debris.[502] Three goals and 19 strategies are the core of the Honolulu Strategy (see Table 4). *Goal A* consists of a 'reduced amount and impact of land-based sources of marine debris introduced into the sea'. The seven strategies that come within the ambit of Goal A much focus on waste minimization, improved waste and wastewater management, and improved regulatory frameworks and compliance in this regard. The annex to the document contains a list of possible action for each of the proposed strategies. While the scope of the Honolulu Strategy includes all sorts of (anthropogenic) marine debris, the document much focuses on plastic debris in its

497 See UNEP and NOAA, 'Summary Proceedings of the 5th International Marine Debris Conference, Held on 20–25 March 2011 in Honolulu, HI, USA' (2011) 4.

498 Stakeholder engagement rapidly increased in the last couple of years. Several national agencies, private companies and business associations have organized international conferences on the topic of marine debris and marine plastic pollution.

499 These are two out of 12 commitments: see 'Honolulu Commitment' (2011) <https://5imdc.files.wordpress.com/2011/03/honolulucommitment.pdf> accessed 19 February 2022.

500 UNGA Res 66/231 (2011), 'Oceans and the Law of the Sea' para 141.

501 UNEP and NOAA, 'The Honolulu Strategy: A Global Framework for Prevention and Management of Marine Debris' (2011).

502 ibid Executive Summary.

TABLE 4 Honolulu strategy: goals and strategies

Goal A:	**Reduced amount and impact of land-based sources of marine debris introduced into the sea**
Strategy A1.	Conduct education and outreach on marine debris impacts and the need for improved solid waste management
Strategy A2.	Employ market-based instruments to support solid waste management, in particular waste minimization
Strategy A3.	Employ infrastructure and implement best practices for improving stormwater management and reducing discharge of solid waste into waterways
Strategy A4.	Develop, strengthen, and enact legislation and policies to support solid waste minimization and management
Strategy A5.	Improve the regulatory framework regarding stormwater, sewage systems, and debris in tributary waterways
Strategy A6.	Build capacity to monitor and enforce compliance with regulations and permit conditions regarding litter, dumping, solid waste management, stormwater, and surface runoff
Strategy A7.	Conduct regular cleanup efforts on coastal lands, in watersheds, and in waterways – especially at hot spots of marine debris accumulation
Goal B:	**Reduced amount and impact of sea-based sources of marine debris, including solid waste; lost cargo; abandoned, lost, or otherwise discarded fishing gear (ALDFG); and abandoned vessels, introduced into the sea**
Strategy B1.	Conduct ocean-user education and outreach on marine debris impacts, prevention, and management
Strategy B2.	Develop and strengthen implementation of waste minimization and proper waste storage at sea, and of disposal at port reception facilities, in order to minimize incidents of ocean dumping
Strategy B3.	Develop and strengthen implementation of industry best management practices (BMP) designed to minimize abandonment of vessels and accidental loss of cargo, solid waste, and gear at sea

TABLE 4 Honolulu strategy: goals and strategies (*cont.*)

Strategy B4.	Develop and promote use of fishing gear modifications or alternative technologies to reduce the loss of fishing gear and/or its impacts as ALDFG
Strategy B5.	Develop and strengthen implementation of legislation and policies to prevent and manage marine debris from at-sea sources, and implement requirements of MARPOL Annex V and other relevant international instruments and agreements
Strategy B6.	Build capacity to monitor and enforce (1) national and local legislation, and (2) compliance with requirements of MARPOL Annex V and other relevant international instruments and agreements
Goal C:	**Reduced amount and impact of accumulated marine debris on shorelines, in benthic habitats, and in pelagic waters**
Strategy C1.	Conduct education and outreach on marine debris impacts and removal
Strategy C2.	Develop and promote use of technologies and methods to effectively locate and remove marine debris accumulations
Strategy C3.	Build capacity to co-manage marine debris removal response
Strategy C4.	Develop or strengthen implementation of incentives for removal of ALDFG and other large accumulations of marine debris encountered at sea
Strategy C5.	Establish appropriate regional, national, and local mechanisms to facilitate removal of marine debris
Strategy C6.	Remove marine debris from shorelines, benthic habitats, and pelagic water

analysis of the problem. Also, proposals for action as contained in the annex are well designed for plastics.

5) *Plastic Marine Debris as a Raising Concern in Formal UN Processes*

Although the 1990 GESAMP report on the state of the marine environment, Agenda 21 and the GPA all referred to the challenges related to plastic litter and marine debris, it took another decade for the topic to be set on the permanent agenda of the UN. The Open-Ended Informal Consultative Process on Oceans and the Law of the Sea (ICP) played an important role in this regard.[503] Following a recommendation of the UN General Assembly,[504] it discussed the issue of marine debris at its sixth meeting in 2005[505] and again at its seventeenth meeting, which was convened in June 2016 in New York, USA. The topic suits well, as the ICP serves as a forum to 'foster productive exchange of information and ideas on complex ocean issues that do not yet have a single institutional "home"'.[506] During the discussions in 2016, it was highlighted that the size of the problem had increased exponentially since the topic of marine debris was addressed at the sixth meeting in 2005. There was wide agreement that 'marine debris in general, and plastics in particular, were some of the greatest environmental concerns of our time, along with climate change, ocean acidification and loss of biodiversity'.[507] Several delegates emphasized the need to address the issue, 'both downstream, through improved mechanisms for waste management, disposal and recycling, and upstream, by addressing consumption and production patterns, including through awareness-raising campaigns'.[508]

Since ICP-6 in 2005, marine debris has featured in the General Assembly's annual resolution on oceans and the law of the sea. Plastic debris, specifically, has come into focus more recently, especially after UN Environment had issued a series of information documents and guidelines on marine (plastic) litter.[509] Since about the year 2010, other international bodies started to pick up the topic, including, for instance, the UN Convention on Biological Diversity

503 The ICP was established by UNGA Res 54/33 (1999) para 2, in consistency with the legal framework provided by UNCLOS and the goals of chapter 17 of Agenda 21. The primary task of the ICP is to facilitate the annual review by the General Assembly of developments in ocean affairs 'by suggesting particular issues to be considered by it, with an emphasis on identifying areas where coordination and cooperation at the intergovernmental and inter-agency levels should be enhanced'.

504 UNGA Res 59/24 (2004), 'Oceans and the Law of the Sea' para 92.

505 See UNGA, 'Report on the Work of the United Nations Open-Ended Informal Consultative Process on Oceans and the Law of the Sea at Its Sixth Meeting' (2005) UN Doc A/60/99.

506 IISD, 'Summary of the Seventeenth Meeting of the United Nations Open-Ended Informal Consultative Process on Oceans and the Law of the Sea: 13–17 June 2016' (2016) 25 Earth Negotiations Bulletin: ICP-17 Final 12 <https://enb.iisd.org/events/icp-17/summary-report-13-17-june-2016> accessed 19 February 2022.

507 UNGA, 'Report of ICP-17 (2017)' (n 11) para 12; UNGA Res 72/73 (2017) (n 11) para 188.

508 UNGA, 'Report of ICP-17 (2017)' (n 11) para 23.

509 While UN Environment had published on the subject before, a first series of information documents was issued in 2009: see UNEP, *Marine Litter – Trash That Kills* (n 296); *Marine Litter: An Analytical Overview* (n 289); *Marine Litter* (n 284); G Macfadyen, Tim Huntington and Rod Cappell, *Abandoned, Lost or Otherwise Discarded Fishing Gear* (UNEP/FAO 2009);

(CBD).[510] Only since 2012, the General Assembly's law of the sea resolutions have referred to plastics as a source of concern for the marine environment.[511]

2012 was also the year of the UN Conference on Sustainable Development (UNCSD, also known as Rio+20) held 20 years after the 1992 Rio Conference. Like its predecessor, the UNCSD was hosted by Brazil and took place in the city of Rio de Janeiro. The conference was attended by representatives from 191 states, including 79 heads of state or government. They adopted an extensive political document suggesting practical measures for implementing sustainable

---

Anthony Cheshire and others, *UNEP/IOC Guidelines on Survey and Monitoring of Marine Litter* (UNEP/IOC 2009); ten Brink and others (n 407). Since 2015, UN Environment supported a broad range of publications focusing on marine plastic pollution or related subjects: see UNEP, *Plastic in Cosmetics: Are We Polluting the Environment through Our Personal Care?* (2015); *Biodegradable Plastics & Marine Litter: Misconceptions, Concerns and Impacts on Marine Environments* (n 51); UNEP and GRID-Arendal (n 376); UNEP, 'Marine Litter Legislation: A Toolkit for Policymakers' (UNEP 2016); 'Marine Plastic Debris and Microplastics: Global Lessons and Research to Inspire Action and Guide Policy Change' (2016) (UNEA-2 Technical Report on Marine Plastic Debris); 'Combating Marine Plastic Litter and Microplastics: An Assessment of the Effectiveness of Relevant International, Regional and Subregional Governance Strategies and Approaches – Summary for Policy Makers' (2018) UNEP/AHEG/2018/1/INF/3; 'Addressing Marine Plastics: A Systemic Approach – Stocktaking Report' (2018); 'Mapping of Global Plastics Value Chain' (n 90); *Single-Use Plastics: A Roadmap for Sustainability* (n 94); 'Legal Limits on Single-Use Plastics and Microplastics: A Global Review of National Laws and Regulations' (2018); 'Plastics and Shallow Water Coral Reefs: Synthesis of the Science for Policy-Makers' (2019); GESAMP, 'Guidelines for the Monitoring and Assessment of Plastic Litter in the Ocean' (2019) 99 Reports and Studies; GA Circular, 'The Role of Gender in Waste Management: Gender Perspectives on Waste in India, Indonesia, the Philippines and Vietnam' (Report commissioned by Ocean Conservancy 2019); UNEP, *Addressing Single-Use Plastic Products Pollution Using a Life Cycle Approach* (n 159). In 2015, UN Environment also launched a massive open online course on marine litter with more than 6,500 participants. The course has been relaunched every two years.

510 The issue has been addressed by the CBD in reports, special workshops and in COP decisions: see STAP, 'Marine Debris as a Global Environmental Problem: Introducing a Solutions Based Framework on Plastic' (GEF 2011); CBD Secretariat and STAP, 'Impacts of Marine Debris on Biodiversity: Current Status and Potential Solutions' (2012) CBD Technical Series 67; CBD COP Decision XI/18 (2012), 'Marine and Coastal Biodiversity: Sustainable Fisheries and Addressing Adverse Impacts of Human Activities, Voluntary Guidelines for Environmental Assessment, and Marine Spatial Planning' UNEP/CBD/COP/DEC/XI/18 paras 25–27; CBD, 'Report of the Expert Workshop to Prepare Practical Guidance on Preventing and Mitigating the Significant Adverse Impacts of Marine Debris on Marine and Coastal Biodiversity and Habitats' (2014) UNEP/CBD/MCB/EM/2014/3/2. See also Section 2.1.D.i.1) below.

511 UNGA Res 67/78 (2012) para 142; Res 68/70 (2013) paras 152 and 164; Res 69/245 (2014) paras 163, 181 and 298; Res 70/235 (2015) paras 170, 188–90 and 192; Res 71/257 (2016) paras 182–84 and 204–10; Res 72/73 (2017) paras 186–88 and 208–14; Res 73/124 (2018) paras 207–14 and 221; Res 74/19 (2019) paras 217 ff; Res 75/239 (2021) paras 217 ff.

development. The document is known under its title *The Future We Want*. A full section is devoted to oceans and seas. In this section, states committed to:

> protect, and restore, the health, productivity and resilience of oceans and marine ecosystems, and to maintain their biodiversity, enabling their conservation and sustainable use for present and future generations, and to effectively apply an ecosystem approach and the precautionary approach in the management, in accordance with international law, of activities impacting on the marine environment.[512]

Also, as the participating states noted with concern that 'the health of oceans and marine biodiversity are negatively affected by marine pollution, including marine debris, especially plastic', they committed 'to take action to, by 2025, [...] achieve significant reductions in marine debris to prevent harm to the coastal and marine environment'.[513] In line with these commitments and in response to a respective call in the Manila Declaration, the Global Partnership on Marine Litter (GPML) was launched at the UNCSD. The GPML is a voluntary multi-stakeholder coordination mechanism focusing on the prevention, reduction and better management of marine litter. The mechanism operates under the auspices of the GPA and is open to governments, NGOs, academia, the private sector, civil society and individuals.[514]

Moreover, states launched a process at the UNCSD to develop a set of Sustainable Development Goals (SDGs). In 2015, the UN General Assembly adopted the 2030 Agenda on Sustainable Development and, with it, 17 SDGs and 169 targets to be achieved by 2030.[515] The SDGs are not legally binding. Their implementation is, however, monitored and reviewed at the global level by the use of a set of global indicators. Many of the goals and targets relate to marine litter in a direct or indirect way. Most importantly, *Goal 14* is to conserve and sustainably use the oceans, seas and marine resources. Target 14.1 is to prevent and significantly reduce marine pollution of all kinds by 2025, in particular pollution from land-based activities, including marine debris and nutrient pollution. Table 5 shows a number of targets that are relevant for the prevention and control of marine plastic litter.

---

512 UNGA Res. 66/288 (2012), annex, 'The Future We Want' para 158.

513 ibid para 163.

514 For more information, see GPML Secretariat, 'GPML Framework Document' (October 2018) <https://marinelitternetwork.engr.uga.edu/wp-content/uploads/2018/03/gpml_framework_document.pdf> accessed 19 February 2022.

515 UNGA Res 70/1 (2015), 'Transforming Our World: The 2030 Agenda for Sustainable Development'.

TABLE 5 SDG targets related to marine litter[a]

6.3	**by 2030 the proportion of untreated wastewater should be halved**
11.6	By 2030, reduce the adverse per capita environmental impact of cities, including by paying special attention to air quality and municipal and other waste management
12.1	Implement the **10-year framework of programmes on sustainable consumption and production**, all countries taking action, with developed countries taking the lead, taking into account the development and capabilities of developing countries
12.2	By 2030, achieve the sustainable management and efficient use of natural resources
12.4	By 2020, achieve the **environmentally sound management of chemicals and all wastes throughout their life cycle**, in accordance with agreed international frameworks, and significantly reduce their release to air, water and soil in order to minimize their adverse impacts on human health and the environment
12.5	**By 2030, substantially reduce waste generation through prevention, reduction, recycling and reuse**
12.b	Develop and implement tools to monitor sustainable development impacts for **sustainable tourism** that creates jobs and promotes local culture and products
14.1	**By 2025, prevent and significantly reduce marine pollution of all kinds, in particular from land-based activities, including marine debris and nutrient pollution**
14.2	By 2020, sustainably manage and **protect marine and coastal ecosystems** to avoid significant adverse impacts, including by strengthening their resilience, and take action for their **restoration** in order to achieve healthy and productive oceans
14.7	By 2030, increase the economic benefits to Small Island developing States and least developed countries from the sustainable use of marine resources, including through sustainable management of fisheries, aquaculture and tourism
14.a	Increase scientific knowledge, develop research capacity and transfer marine technology, taking into account the Intergovernmental Oceanographic Commission Criteria and Guidelines on the Transfer of Marine Technology, in order to **improve ocean health** and to enhance the contribution of marine biodiversity to the development of developing countries, in particular small island developing States and least developed countries

TABLE 5 SDG targets related to marine litter (*cont.*)

14.c	**Enhance the conservation and sustainable use of oceans and their resources by implementing international law as reflected in UNCLOS**, which provides the legal framework for the conservation and sustainable use of oceans and their resources, as recalled in paragraph 158 of The Future We Want
15.5	**Take urgent and significant action to reduce the degradation of natural habitats, halt the loss of biodiversity and, by 2020, protect and prevent the extinction of threatened species**

a See UNEP, 'UNEA-2 Technical Report on Marine Plastic Debris' (n 514) 6–7.

In June 2017, a high-level UN conference to support the implementation of SDG 14 was held at the UN Headquarters in New York.[516] The conference aimed to identify ways and means to support the implementation of SDG 14, enhance stakeholder involvement and provide input to the High-Level Political Forum on Sustainable Development (HLPF), a body established to boost efforts to achieve the SDGs.[517] The conference produced three outcomes: an intergovernmentally agreed Call for Action; a registry of voluntary commitments (with 1328 initial registrations and more than 150 commitments submitted to reduce plastic waste); and key messages from the partnership dialogues. Plastics and microplastics were widely discussed at the conference. In the Call for Action, states called on all stakeholders to:

- accelerate actions to prevent and significantly reduce marine pollution of all kinds, particularly from land-based activities, including marine debris, plastics and microplastics;
- promote waste prevention and minimization;
- develop sustainable consumption and production patterns;
- implement long-term and robust strategies to reduce the use of plastics and microplastics, in particular plastic bags and single-use plastics.[518]

516 See IISD, 'Summary of the Ocean Conference: 5–9 June 2017' (2017) 32 Earth Negotiations Bulletin: Ocean Conference Final.

517 The HLPF meets annually. HLPF 5 (July 2017) addressed the implementation of five SDGs, including SDG 14. Plastic discharge into the oceans was also discussed at the first HLPF meeting that took place under the auspices of the General Assembly at the level of Heads of State and Government in September 2019: UNGA Res 74/4 (2019), 'Political Declaration of the High-Level Political Forum on Sustainable Development Convened under the Auspices of the General Assembly' para 20.

518 UNGA, 'Our Ocean, Our Future: Call for Action' (A/CONF230/11, Annex 2017) para 13(g–i).

At the UNCSD in 2012, states decided to strengthen UN Environment and establish universal membership to its Governing Council.[519] This decision laid the foundations for the first UN Environment Assembly (UNEA), which was convened in June 2014 in Nairobi, Kenya. In its Resolution 1/6, UNEA recognized 'that plastics, including microplastics, in the marine environment are a rapidly increasing problem due to their large and still increasing use combined with the inadequate management and disposal of plastic waste'.[520] For this reason, the UN Environment Executive Director was requested to undertake a study on marine plastic debris and marine microplastics and to present it at the second UNEA in May 2016. Based on this report[521] and a set of policy recommendations by the executive director, UNEA-2 adopted a second resolution on marine plastic litter and microplastics and requested that the executive director assess the effectiveness of international, regional and subregional governance strategies and corresponding regulatory frameworks relevant to marine plastic litter and microplastics, and to identify possible gaps and options for addressing them.[522] In his report, the executive director judged the existing framework to be insufficient. He recommended the establishment of a global umbrella mechanism specific to marine plastic litter and microplastics and proposed the establishment of a new international legally binding architecture as one out of several measures to effectively tackle the problem in a multilayered governance approach.[523] The report was presented at UNEA-3 in December 2017. UNEA hence established an Ad Hoc Open-Ended Expert Group on Marine Litter and Microplastics (AHEG) to make recommendations to strengthen international governance structures for combating marine plastic litter and microplastics.[524] The mandate of the ad hoc expert group was extended at UNEA-4 in March 2019 and the group was mandated to analyse potential response options related to marine plastic litter and microplastics.[525]

---

519 UNGA Res. 66/288 (2012), annex (n 512) para 88.

520 UNEA Resolution 1/6 (2014), 'Marine Plastic Debris and Microplastics' UNEP/EA.1/Res.6 para 4.

521 UNEP, 'UNEA-2 Technical Report on Marine Plastic Debris' (n 509).

522 UNEA Resolution 2/11 (2016), 'Marine Plastic Litter and Microplastics' UNEP/EA.2/Res.11 para 21.

523 UNEP, 'UNEA-3 Legal Report' (n 414). See also UNEP, 'UNEA-3 Legal Report – Summary for Policy Makers' (n 509).

524 UNEA Resolution 3/7 (2017), 'Marine Litter and Microplastics' UNEP/EA.3/Res.7. See also UNEP, 'Report of the First Meeting of the Ad Hoc Open-Ended Expert Group on Marine Litter and Microplastics' (2018) UNEP/AHEG/2018/1/6.

525 UNEA Resolution 4/6 (2019) (n 11); IISD, 'Summary of the Fourth Session of the United Nations Environment Assembly: 11–15 March 2019' (2019) 16 Earth Negotiations Bulletin: UNEA-4 FINAL 6–7 <http://enb.iisd.org/download/pdf/enb16153e.pdf>

After four meetings between 2018 and 2020,[526] the AHEG forwarded a Chair's Summary to UNEA-5.1, held virtually in February 2021. In the summary, the AHEG identified a range of national, regional and international response options. It suggested considering the establishment of an Intergovernmental Negotiation Committee (INC), aimed to frame and coordinate a new global instrument on marine plastics and microplastics.[527] The AHEG proposal reflects a widespread call for collective action at the global level and was promply taken up by the governments of Ecuador, Germany, Ghana, and Viet Nam. In order to make concrete suggestions at the resumed fifth session of UNEA in February 2022, they co-convened a Ministerial Conference under the auspices of UN Environment in September 2021. At the conference, states called on UNEA to establish an INC towards a new global agreement.[528] Suggested elements of such an agreement include:

- global and national reduction targets;
- design standards;
- phasing out avoidable plastic products;
- facilitation of national and regional action plans;
- sharing of scientific knowledge through a scientific panel and utilizing globally harmonized monitoring methodology;
- international coordination of financial and technical resources.

---

accessed 19 February 2022. See also UNEP, 'Draft Report of the Third Meeting of the Ad Hoc Open-Ended Expert Group on Marine Litter and Microplastics' (2019) UNEP/AHEG/2019/3/L.1. Also at UNEA-4, a multi-stakeholder platform was established within UN Environment to take immediate action towards the long-term elimination of discharges of litter and microplastics into the oceans. Finally, a resolution was adopted proposing various measures to combat single-use plastic products pollution: UNEA Resolution 4/9 (2019), 'Addressing Single-Use Plastic Products Pollution' UNEP/EA.4/Res.9. See also UNEP, 'Analysis of Voluntary Commitments Targeting Marine Litter and Microplastics Pursuant to Resolution 3/7 – Report of the Executive Director' (2018) UNEP/EA.4/11; 'Progress in the Work of the Ad Hoc Open-Ended Expert Group on Marine Litter and Microplastics Established by Resolution 3/7 – Report of the Executive Director' (2018) UNEP/EA.4/12.

526 In Nairobi, Kenya, in May 2018; in Geneva, Switzerland, in December 2018; again in Nairobi in March 2019; in Bangkok, Thailand, in December 2019; and virtually in November 2020.

527 AHEG, 'Chair's Summary of the Work of the Ad Hoc Open-Ended Expert Group on Marine Litter and Microplastics for Consideration by the United Nations Environment Assembly at Its Fifth Session' (November 2020) <https://wedocs.unep.org/bitstream/handle/20.500.11822/34635/K2100061.pdf?sequence=11&isAllowed=y> accessed 19 February 2022.

528 See IISD, 'Ministerial Conference on Marine Litter and Plastic Pollution: 1–2 September 2021' [2021] Marine Litter & Plastic Pollution Bulletin <https://enb.iisd.org/sites/default/files/2021-09/ministerial_conference_on_marine_litter_and_plastic_pollution_summary.pdf> accessed 19 February 2022.

Marine plastic pollution has also been addressed in regional political and economic fora. In June 2015, the Group of Seven (G7)[529] adopted an Action Plan to Combat Marine Litter and committed to support: development and implementation of national or regional action plans; existing platforms and tools for cooperation such as the GPA, the GPML and the Regional Seas Conventions and Action Plans; other countries, especially developing countries, in their efforts to deal with the problem; and the use of a broad range of policy toolkits and available instruments, including economic incentives, market-based instruments, and public–private partnerships to combat marine litter. They also committed to prioritize sound waste management, including with regard to waste minimization, reuse and recycling; prevention of microplastics entering the marine environment; reduction of disposable single-use items; and promotion of best practices along the whole plastics manufacturing and value chain from production to transport.[530] In June 2018, the G7 further strengthened its commitment by launching the Ocean Plastics Charter. Since its launch, an increasing number of governments and business organizations adopted the charter, pledgeding, among other tings, to significantly reduce the unnecessary use of single-use plastics.[531]

In November 2017, the Association of Southeast Asian Nations (ASEAN) held a Conference on Reducing Marine Debris in the ASEAN Region in cooperation with Thailand and the International Union for Conservation of Nature and Natural Resources (IUCN). Fifteen member economies of the Asia-Pacific Economic Cooperation (APEC) met in June 2018 in Busan, Korea, and proposed wide-ranging measures to prevent and manage the problem of marine debris. Similarly, the Group of 20 (G20) adopted the G20 Action Plan on Marine Litter at its summit in Germany in 2017.[532] Building on the framework, the G20 Ministerial Meeting on Energy Transitions and Global Environment for Sustainable Growth adopted an implementation framework for action on marine plastic litter in June 2019.[533]

529 The G7 is a group of the seven major advanced economies: Canada, France, Germany, Italy, Japan, the United Kingdom and the United States, with a representative of the European Union.

530 G7, 'G-7 Action Plan to Combat Marine Litter' (White House Press Release 2015) Annex to the G-7 Leaders' Declaration <https://www.whitehouse.gov/the-press-office/2015/06/08/annex-g-7-leaders-declaration> accessed 19 February 2022.

531 G7, 'Ocean Plastics Charter' (2018) <https://www.consilium.europa.eu/media/40516/charlevoix_oceans_plastic_charter_en.pdf> accessed 19 February 2022.

532 G20, 'Annex to G20 Leaders Declaration: G20 Action Plan on Marine Litter' (2017) <https://www.g20germany.de/Content/DE/_Anlagen/G7_G20/2017-g20-marine-litter-en__blob=publicationFile&v=4.pdf> accessed 19 February 2022.

533 G20, 'G20 Implementation Framework for Actions on Marine Plastic Litter' (2019) <https://www.mofa.go.jp/policy/economy/g20_summit/osaka19/pdf/documents/en/annex_14.pdf > accessed 19 February 2022.

Marine pollution, including plastic, is also on the permanent agenda of the annual Our Oceans Conference. The fifth Our Ocean Conference was held from 29 to 30 October 2018 in Bali, Indonesia. Several countries committed to take measures to reduce marine plastic pollution in the oceans. The EU and Norway committed to assist developing countries, especially Asian countries, to combat marine litter and microplastics. The World Bank committed US$250 million to address marine litter and pollution. In addition, a number of multinational companies, such as Nestlé, Coca-Cola and Unilever, committed to increase the proportion of recycled plastic in products and packaging.[534] The sixth Our Oceans Conference was held in October 2019 in Olso, Norway, and generated 370 pledges for a clean and healthy ocean, 76 of which relate directly to marine debris.[535] The seventh Our Ocean Conference is scheduled for April 2022.

ii Relevant Principles and Concepts

Two legal principles or concepts that are highly relevant to marine plastic pollution mitigation are introduced in this subsection. Further environmental principles, such as the precautionary approach, are addressed in the subsequent section, where relevant.

1) *Sustainable Development*

The concept of sustainable development was brought up in answer to a number of fundamental challenges that have confronted the international community for the better part of a century. Against the backdrop of decolonization, widespread poverty and inequalities, and raising environmental concerns, the international community struggled with the reconciliation of differing interests and policy concerns. Regulatory and policy approaches were fragmentary and incoherent, and debates hampered by a North–South divide.[536] With the rise of the concept of sustainable development, emphasis is increasingly put

534 For more information on pledges, see 'Fifth Our Ocean Conference 2018' <https://ourocean2018.org/?l=our-ocean-commitments> accessed 19 February 2022.

535 IISD's SDG Knowledge Hub, 'Our Ocean Conference Participants Pledge USD 64 Billion to Protect Oceans' (29 October 2019) <http://sdg.iisd.org/news/our-ocean-conference-participants-pledge-usd-64-billion-to-protect-oceans/> accessed 19 February 2022.

536 For more information on corresponding debates, see Elisabeth Bürgi Bonanomi, *Sustainable Development in International Law Making and Trade: International Food Governance and Trade in Agriculture* (Edward Elgar Publishing 2015) 9–21; Nico Schrijver, *The Evolution of Sustainable Development in International Law: Inception, Meaning and Status* (Martinus Nijhoff Publishers 2008) ch 2.

on the integration and reconciliation of different needs and interests, and policy coherence.

In 1983, the UN General Assembly commissioned a report on 'long-term environmental strategies for achieving sustainable development to the year 2000 and beyond'.[537] The respective report was prepared by the WCED and issued in 1987. In the report, commonly known as the Brundtland Report,[538] sustainable development was defined as 'development that meets the needs of the present without compromising the ability of future generations to meet their own needs'.[539] According to the report, the principle 'contains within it two key concepts:

- the concept of 'needs', in particular the essential needs of the world's poor, to which overriding priority should be given; and
- the idea of limitations imposed by the state of technology and social organization on the environment's ability to meet present and future needs.[540]

The concept of sustainable development, as defined in the Brundtland Report, was endorsed at the 1992 Rio Conference and introduced into the outcome documents, including the Rio Declaration, Agenda 21, the UN Framework Convention on Climate Change (UNFCCC), the CBD, and the Forest Principles.[541] Most notably, the concept informed a number of Rio Principles.[542] With the Rio endorsement, the concept gained rapidly traction in public international law and greatly influenced its further development. By now, the concept has been firmly established as an international legal concept. It forms an integral part of a great number of international instruments and is recognized in all regions of the world.[543] Yet, while there is wide agreement on the existence and significance of the concept *per se*, there is still a certain vagueness in the concept's concrete contours.[544]

---

537 UNGA Res 38/161 (1983), 'Process of Preparation of the Environmental Perspective to the Year 2000 and Beyond' para 8(a).

538 WCED (n 435).

539 ibid ch 2.

540 ibid.

541 See 1992 UNFCCC art 3; 1992 CBD arts 8 and 10; Non-Legally Binding Authoritative Statement of Principles for a Global Consensus on the Management, Conservation and Sustainable Development of All Types of Forests (Forest Principles) (adopted on 14 June 1992) UN Doc A/CONF.151/26 (Vol. III) Preamble and art 2(a). See also 1994 UNCCD arts 2,4 and 5.

542 Rio Principles 3–8, 10 and 17.

543 Sands and Peel (n 447) 206–07, including references; *Gabčíkovo-Nagymaros Project (Hungary v Slovakia), Judgment* [1997] ICJ Rep 1997 7 78, para 140.

544 See Birnie, Boyle and Redgwell (n 488) 125–27; Bürgi Bonanomi (n 536) 189–93; Günther Handl, 'Environmental Security and Global Change: The Challenge to International Law'

The most essential elements inherent to the concept are reflected in the Rio Declaration and its Principles 3–8 in particular, as well as in the New Delhi Declaration of Principles of International Law Relating to Sustainable Development as adopted by the International Law Association (ILA) at its 70th Conference in 2002.[545] From a substantive point of view, these elements include the conservation and sustainable use of natural resources;[546] integration of environmental protection and economic development;[547] the right to development;[548] and the concepts of intra- and intergenerational equity.[549] *Intra*generational equity implies that in its use of natural resources and in the context of other activities, a state must take account of the needs of other states (especially developing and least developed states). The concept also refers to a fair distribution of resources and justice within a single state. The principle of *inter*generational equity implies that there is a need to preserve natural resources for the benefit of future generations.[550] Intergenerational

(1990) 1 Yearbook of International Environmental Law 3, 24–28; Vaughan Lowe, 'Sustainable Development and Unsustainable Arguments' in Alan Boyle and David Freestone (eds), *International Law and Sustainable Development: Past Achievements and Future Challenges* (Oxford University Press 1999) 31–37; Schrijver, *Evolution of Sustainable Development* (n 536) 219–27; Marie-Claire Cordonier Segger and Ashfaq Khalfan, *Sustainable Development Law: Principles, Practices and Prospects* (Oxford University Press 2004), forword by Judge Christopher G. Weeramantry; Christina Voigt, *Sustainable Development as a Principle of International Law: Resolving Conflicts between Climate Measures and WTO Law* (Martinus Nijhoff Publishers 2009) 160–77. cf *Gabčíkovo-Nagymaros Project (Hungary v Slovakia), Separate Opinion of Vice-President Weeramantry* [1997] ICJ Rep 1997 88; *Pulp Mills on the River Uruguay (Argentina v Uruguay), Judgment* [2010] ICJ Rep 2010 14 48 and 74–75 paras 75–76 and 177, respectively.

545 'ILA New Delhi Declaration of Principles of International Law Relating to Sustainable Development' 2 International Environmental Agreements 209 (ILA Principles on Sustainable Development). See also CSD, 'Report of the Expert Group Meeting on Identification of Principles of International Law for Sustainable Development' (1996) Prepared by the Division for Sustainable Development for the CSD 4th session; Sumudu A Atapattu, *Emerging Principles of International Environmental Law* (Transnational Publishers 2006) 93–126; Birnie, Boyle and Redgwell (n 488) 116; Cordonier Segger and Khalfan (n 544) ch 2; Schrijver, *Evolution of Sustainable Development* (n 536) ch 5.

546 Rio Principles 7 and 8; ILA Principles 1, 3 and 4.

547 Rio Principle 4; ILA Principle 7. See *Gabčíkovo-Nagymaros* (n 543) 78 para 140; *The Iron Rhine Arbitration (Belgium v the Netherlands)* [2005] 27 UN Rep Int'l Arb Awards 35 66 para 59; *Pulp Mills on the River Uruguay (Argentina v Uruguay), Provisional Measures, Order of 13 July 2006* [2006] ICJ Rep 2006 113 133 para 80; *Pulp Mills Judgment* (n 544) 48 para 76.

548 Rio Principle 3; ILA Principle 2.

549 Stockholm Principle 1; Rio Principles 3, 5 and 6; ILA Principles 1, 2, 3 and 7.

550 On intergenerational equity, see, in general, Edith Brown Weiss, *In Fairness to Future Generations: International Law, Common Patrimony, and Intergenerational Equity*

equity stands for the temporal dimension of sustainable development. While there is a broad discussion with regard to the exact nature and content of our obligations towards future generations, or the rights future generations hold, it goes from the Brundtland definition that current generations are requested (at least on moral grounds) to make sure not to compromise the ability of future generations to satisfy their needs and solve their problems. Sustainable development is, hence, not a preservationist approach in a strict sense. With reference taken to the needs of future generations, the concept is based on a utilitarian approach in promotion of development 'of a special qualitative nature'.[551]

Public participation in decision-making and environmental impact assessment have been referred to as the main procedural elements of sustainable development.[552] Also, it has been argued that sustainable development can serve as a concept of legal methodology framing the discretionary space of decision makers in legislative and judiciary processes. As such, it requires the involvement of stakeholders; the integration and reconciliation of social, economic, environmental and future-related aspects 'in such a way that they mutually reinforce each other or avoid the impacts of trade-offs'; and compliance with basic substantial and procedural principles with respect to coherence, proportionality, efficiency, transparency, equity and public participation.[553] The procedural dimension of the concept is considered highly relevant. It requires 'development decisions to be the outcome of a process which promotes sustainable development'.[554]

In this sense, the principle of sustainable development provides guidance for decision makers on how to deal with conflicting interests or norms and sets the leading goals – and compulsory objectives – 'in shaping and applying the law, both domestically and internationally'.[555] This is particularly important with regard to plastic pollution mitigation, which involves extremely diverse

(Transnational Pub/United Nations University 1989). See also *Nuclear Tests case (New Zealand v France) Dissenting opinion of Judge Weeramantry* ICJ Rep 1995 317 341.

551 Handl, 'Environmental Security' (n 544) 24–25.

552 Rio Principles 10 and 17; ILA Principles 5 and 6. See Birnie, Boyle and Redgwell (n 488) 116; Boyle and Freestone (n 447) 15–16.

553 Katja Gehne, *Nachhaltige Entwicklung als Rechtsprinzip: normativer Aussagegehalt, rechtstheoretische Einordnung, Funktionen im Recht* (Mohr Siebeck 2011) 349–50. See also Atapattu (n 545) 93. cf ILA Principles 5 and 6.

554 Birnie, Boyle and Redgwell (n 488) 126.

555 Bürgi Bonanomi (n 536), Forword by Thomas Cottier. See also Birnie, Boyle and Redgwell (n 488) 127; Handl, 'Environmental Security' (n 544) 27; Lowe (n 544) 31–37; Reinhard Stockmann, 'Understanding Sustainability Evaluation and Its Contributions to Policy-Making' in Anneke von Raggamby and Frieder Rubik (eds), *Sustainable development, evaluation and policy making: theory, practise and quality assurance* (Edward Elgar 2012) 3–20.

interests of an ecological, economic and social nature. The principle requires states to take into account environmental, economic and social impacts of plastic pollution, and to assess and weigh up costs of action and inaction, including for poor country regions and future generations. Assessment results are to be communicated and fed in decision-making procedures. Sustainable development thus demands a coherent, transparent and equitable formulation of policy and law.

2) *The Polluter Pays Principle*

The polluter pays principle is an economic principle guiding the allocation of costs for environmental damage or pollution in such a way that, as a general rule, the polluter is charged with the costs of pollution prevention and control measures. As will be explained below, the principle is closely related to the notion of cost internalization, the question of permissible state subsidies and the rules governing liability for environmental damage.[556]

The polluter pays principle is well established in OECD and EU countries where it has been influencing environmental regulation for more than 40 years.[557] Beyond this geographic scope, the implications of the principle are less clear. The principle was endorsed at the Rio Conference in 1992 and is expressed in Rio Principle 16. The vague formulation in Rio Principle 16 gives rise to the supposition that it is the result of a delicate compromise:

> National authorities should endeavour to promote the internalization of environmental costs and the use of economic instruments, taking into account the approach that the polluter should, in principle, bear the cost of pollution, with due regard to the public interest and without distorting international trade and investment.

The normative character of Rio Principle 16 is questionable, not only because of the soft law nature of the Rio Declaration but also because of the weak

---

556 From a global perspective, the principle raises the question of whether and to what extent developed countries bear a responsibility towards developing countries 'in the international pursuit of sustainable development in view of the pressures their societies place on the global environment': Rio Principle 7. Many states, however, do not consider the principle to be applicable to inter-state relations and the responsibilities of states towards each other, even if they support the principle's applicability at a national level: see Sands and Peel (n 447) 229.

557 OECD, *Extended Producer Responsibility: A Guidance Manual for Governments* (OECD Publishing 2001) 21; *The Polluter Pays Principle: Definition, Analysis, Implementation* (OECD Publishing 2008) 5.

wording of Principle 16 and incoherent state practice.[558] If any obligations can be drawn from the polluter pays principle in a general way, then they are coupled with a high degree of flexibility in national implementation. There are, however, a number of multilateral and regional treaties that refer to the principle in their preambles[559] or include it in the operative part.[560]

The OECD was the first international body to expressly refer to the polluter pays principle in an instrument and to promote its use. According to an OECD Council Recommendation of 1972, the principle means that:

> the polluter should bear the expenses of carrying out [pollution prevention, reduction and control] measures decided by public authorities to ensure that the environment is in an acceptable state. In other words, the cost of these measures should be reflected in the cost of goods and services which cause pollution in production and/or consumption. Such measures should not be accompanied by subsidies that would create significant distortions in international trade and investment.[561]

---

558 According to Birnie et al., 'Principle 16 simply lacks the normative character of a rule of law': Birnie, Boyle and Redgwell (n 488) 322. cf *The Rhine Chlorides Arbitration Concerning the Auditing of Accounts* (*Netherlands–France*) *Award* PCA 2004 para 103.

559 Eg Protocol for the Protection of the Mediterranean Sea against Pollution from Land-Based Sources and Activities (1996 Syracuse Protocol) (originally adopted in 1980 in Athens, amended on 7 March 1996, entered into force on 11 May 2008); International Convention on Oil Pollution Preparedness, Response and Co-operation (1990 OPRC) (adopted on 30 November 1990, entered into force on 13 May 1995) 1891 UNTS 51, 30 ILM 735 (1990); Protocol on Preparedness, Response and Co-operation to Pollution Incidents by Hazardous and Noxious Substances (2000 OPRC-HNS Protocol) (adopted on 15 March 2000, entered into force on 14 June 2007). In some treaties, the polluter pays principle is referred to as a 'general principle of international environmental law'.

560 Convention for the Protection of the Marine Environment of the North-East Atlantic (1992 OSPAR Convention) (adopted on 22 September 1992, entered into force on 25 March 1998, text last updated on 18 May 2006) 32 2354 UNTS 67, ILM 1069 (1993) art 2.2(b); Convention on the Protection and Use of Transboundary Watercourses and International Lakes (1992 UNECE Water Convention) (adopted on 17 March 1992, entered into force on 6 October 1996) 1936 UNTS 269, 31 ILM 1312 (1992) art 2.5(b); Convention on the Protection of the Marine Environment of the Baltic Sea Area (1992 Helsinki Convention) (adopted in 1992, entered into force on 17 January 2000) art 2(5); Convention for the Protection of the Mediterranean Sea against Pollution (1995 Barcelona Convention) (opened for signature on 16 February 1976, entered into force on 12 February 1978, amended on 10 June 1995, amended version entered into force on 9 July 2004) 1102 UNTS 44, 15 ILM 290 (1976) art 4(3)(a); Protocol to the 1972 London Convention on the Prevention of Marine Pollution by Dumping of Wastes and Other Matter (1996 London Protocol) (adopted on 7 November 1996, entered into force on 24 March 2006) 36 ILM 1 (1997) art 3(2).

561 OECD, 'Recommendation of the Council on Guiding Principles Concerning International Economic Aspects of Environmental Policies' (1972) C(72)128. See also OECD,

The polluter pays principle implies the notion of cost internalization, according to which negative external effects of production and consumption (generally referred to as negative externalities) are to be charged to producers or consumers by means of economic and other instruments.[562] Producers may pass on, fully or in part, their environmental costs into prices. In this way, product and service prices more properly reflect real costs, including the ones otherwise borne by public authorities or the victims of pollution. If such costs are hidden, 'markets will react to distorted price signals and make inefficient economic choices'.[563] However, the polluter pays principle, as commonly understood and defined in the OECD Council Recommendation, does not require full internalization of environmental costs but serves as an efficiency principle providing guidance for cost allocation.[564] The main instruments for public authorities to implement the polluter pays principle, especially with regard to its function of cost internalization, consist of market-based instruments, including taxation and charges, as well as regulatory measures and standards.[565]

The principle is closely related to the notion of *extended producer responsibility*, an important instrument for the promotion of recyclable materials and green design. Extended producer responsibility shifts the responsibility for waste management from the state to the private industry. It is based on the assumption that producers have the greatest control over product design and thus over the product's recyclability or toxicity. In order to incentivize sustainable product design, producers are obliged to organize for and pay the costs related to the disposal of their products. This may be done in the form of a reuse, take-back or recycling programme. In this way, producers and retailers have to internalize waste management costs in their product prices.[566]

'Recommendation of the Council on the Implementation of the Polluter-Pays Principle' (1974) C(74)223; OECD, 'Recommendation of the Council Concerning the Application of the Polluter-Pays Principle to Accidental Pollution' (1989) C(89)88.

562 Accordingly, environmental costs that are caused by the operation of a facility are to be charged on the operator to the extent that the operator is considered 'the polluter'.

563 Sadeleer (n 447) 21.

564 The principle refers to an 'acceptable state' of the environment. What is acceptable corresponds to a collective choice and decisions by public authorities. Zero pollution and, accordingly, full cost internalization, is not necessarily envisaged. Costs have to be internalized to the level at which the advantage of a further reduction in pollution is perceived as smaller than the social costs related to additional pollution regulation and control. Internalization beyond this level is optional and does not fall under the polluter pays principle within the OECD meaning: see OECD, *The Polluter Pays Principle* (n 557) 6 and 15.

565 Examples of such measures are discussed in the third chapter of this part (2.3).

566 OECD, *Extended Producer Responsibility* (n 557) 9.

The polluter pays principle as applied within the OECD serves as an objective to member countries rather than a strict rule, and allows for exceptions. This being the case, the OECD aims at policy harmonization among countries and at promoting a level playing field. In order to avoid distortions in international trade and investment, especially through the subsidization of polluting activities by states, the OECD examined the question of allowable exceptions to the principle.[567]

As it guides cost allocation in the case of pollution and environmental damage, the principle is related to the rules dealing with liability and compensation for environmental damage.[568] It can influence the choice of the legislator between strict liability for environmental damages and a fault-based regime. As a tendency, it would do so in favour of the former to the detriment of the latter, that is, pushing towards a duty by polluters to compensate harmful consequences of their activities irrespective of their own fault.[569] Non-compensation for environmental damage (for instance because fault cannot be proved in a fault-based liability system) is not compatible with the polluter pays principle, as it transfers the costs of pollution to the victims or the public at large.[570]

The concept of civil liability is of little use if victims are confronted with pollution from a diffuse nature. This includes cases in which damage is caused collectively or by the accumulation of many small acts of pollution, each of which is lawful.[571] In such contexts, it is often impossible to identify individual polluters. Even if they can be identified, their contribution to the damage is negligible and does not justify compensation for damage. Marine plastic pollution from land-based sources is a suitable example in this regard. Usually, such pollution is caused by the combined acts of a high number of small actors rather than by the activity of a single large operator. If, as is assumed, large operators are involved, for instance the operator of a badly maintained landfill located

567 OECD, *The Polluter Pays Principle* (n 557) 6–7.

568 In the commentaries to its 2006 Draft Principles on the Allocation of Loss, the International Law Commission (ILC) held that the polluter pays principle forms an essential component 'in underpinning the present draft principles to ensure that victims that suffer harm as a result of an incident involving a hazardous activity are able to obtain prompt and adequate compensation': ILC, 'Draft Principles on the Allocation of Loss in the Case of Transboundary Harm Arising Out of Hazardous Activities', *Report of the ILC 60th session* (UN doc A/61/10 ch VE1 2006) Commentary to the Preamble at 115 para 2.

569 See Sadeleer (n 447) 51.

570 See ibid 56. The same is true if liability is based on negligence: if negligence cannot be proved, or if the environmental damage caused was 'neither reasonably foreseeable nor avoidable', there will be no compensation by the polluter. As a result, the costs will be borne by the victims or the taxpayer: see Birnie, Boyle and Redgwell (n 488) 324.

571 See Sadeleer (n 447) 53.

close to the coast and leaking into the ocean, it is difficult to attribute plastic debris to this specific operator once it has entered the marine environment. If damage is attributable to an operator, compensation will still not be guaranteed, as it depends on the operator's solvency. Also, civil compensation is not a useful concept for avoiding harm to the environment that does not have any prompt and direct consequences for humans. The entanglement of protected or otherwise unexploited marine species in plastic debris, for instance, may not entail a quantifiable loss for any individual person or social group. If so, a legal interest in compensation for damage is questionable.

In the case of plastics, the polluter pays principle's inherent request for cost internalization seems particularly interesting. Respective measures, whether economic or regulatory in character, have a great potential to influence the behaviour of all actors involved in the life cycle of plastic products. Applied within a coherent policy framework, the polluter pays principle provides a useful approach to pollution prevention and may play an important role in the shift towards more sustainable production and consumption patterns.[572] Rather than obliging states to take specific measures, the principle thus serves as a guiding tool for the adoption and implementation of an effective and coherent policy framework that provides an enabling environment for sustainable development.

Conclusion of Section A

This section provided an overview on the development of global policies related to plastics and the mitigation of marine pollution from land-based sources. It showed that since the 1990 GESAMP report on the state of the marine environment, marine pollution from land-based sources has increasingly been accepted as a major concern by relevant bodies and the international community. With the firm mission to effectively tackle the problem, UN Environment established the Regional Seas Programme[573] and adopted the GPA in 1995. The GPA provides for valuable guidance for action at different levels of governance and remains one of the most important fora in this respect.

It took more than another decade for plastics to get wider attention by the international community. Thenceforth, awareness grew rapidly. In the last few

572 In a coherent policy framework aiming at more sustainable production and consumption patterns, the polluter pays principle may well be complemented by a user pays principle – a notion that has emerged more recently and has been referred to in a number of OECD decisions: see ibid 42.

573 The programme will be discussed in the second chapter of Part 2 (2.2).

years, the international community has been stressing the problem of marine plastic pollution, particularly from land-based sources, in many occasions, including at UNCSD in 2012, UNEA, the UN General Assembly and the Ocean Conferences. States recognized the urgency of action, set goals and targets to guide that action and launched a process under UNEA to investigate possible solutions. Today, many countries and other actors call for an international agreement as a form of collective response to an issue of global concern.

Intergovernmental action is complemented by broader stakeholder involvement, such as in the Honolulu Strategy, under the aegis of the GPML or in form of the partnership dialogue of the Ocean Conference. Policy formulation is moreover guided by a number of concepts and principles, including sustainable development and the polluter pays principle.

B *The UN Convention on the Law of the Sea*

This section will examine the relevant provisions of UNCLOS, which is the most central global legal instrument with regard to the protection of the marine environment from land-based sources of plastic pollution. UNCLOS 'provides the legal framework for the conservation and the sustainable use of the oceans and their resources',[574] sets out a set of principles on the protection and conservation of the marine environment and works as an umbrella instrument in this regard. The treaty was adopted at the Third United Nations Conference on the Law of the Sea (1973–1982) on 10 December 1982 and entered into force on 16 November 1994. Today, it has 168 parties, including the European Union.[575] While the convention 'sets out the legal framework within which all activities in the oceans and seas must be carried out',[576] its material scope goes beyond such activities and includes land-based activities with potential effects on the

574 UNGA Res. 66/288 (2012), annex (n 512) para 158; UNGA Res 69/245 (2014), 'Oceans and the Law of the Sea' 2. See also Agenda 21 (n 450) resolution 1, annex II, para 17.1. According to Agenda 21, UNCLOS 'provides the international basis upon which to pursue the protection and sustainable development of the marine and coastal environment and its resources'.

575 As of February 2022, UNCLOS has been ratified by the EU and 167 countries, excluding Cambodia; Colombia; El Salvador; Eritrea; Iran; Israel; Libya; North Korea; Peru; Syria; Turkey; United Arab Emirates; United States and Venezuela: see United Nations, 'United Nations Convention on the Law of the Sea' (*UN Treaty Collection*, 2021) <https://treaties.un.org/Pages/ViewDetailsIII.aspx?src=TREATY&mtdsg_no=XXI-6&chapter=21&Temp=mtdsg3&clang=_en#1> accessed 19 February 2022.

576 See Preamble to the annual UNGA Resolution on oceans and the law of the sea: UNGA Res 63/111 (2008); Res 64/71 (2009); Res 65/37 (2010); Res 66/231 (2011); Res 67/78 (2012); Res 68/70 (2013); Res 69/245 (2014); Res 70/235 (2015); Res 71/257 (2016); Res 72/73 (2017).

marine environment. Because of its supposed comprehensiveness and wide participation, UNCLOS is often seen as a 'constitution for the ocean'.[577]

The adoption of UNCLOS has been pivotal to the codification and evolution of the law of the sea: many of the convention's substantive provisions are widely recognized to reflect customary international law – either because they are a codification of pre-existing customary rules or because they have acquired such status in the course of the negotiations or after adoption.[578] In its different parts, the convention seeks to coordinate and reconcile the interests of individual states in what is called the zonal management approach. At the same time, it provides a framework for international cooperation in marine affairs in order to protect the common interests of the international community as a whole (integrated management approach). This double approach is another particularity of UNCLOS.[579]

With regard to common interests, UNCLOS has significantly contributed to, and reflects, an expansion of the thematic scope of the law of the sea to issues such as pollution prevention and the protection of the marine environment.[580] Under the pre-UNCLOS regime, only a few internationally agreed

577 See remarks by Tommy TB Koh, President of the Third United Nations Conference on the Law of the Sea, at its final session in Montenegro Bay, Jamaica, 11 December 1982, reprinted in *The Law of the Sea: Official Text of the United Nations Convention on the Law of the Sea* (United Nations 1983) xxxiii; Shirley V Scott, 'The LOS Convention as a Constitutional Regime for the Oceans' in Alex G Oude Elferink (ed), *Stability And Change in the Law of the Sea: The Role of the LOS Convention* (Martinus Nijhoff Publishers 2005) 12.

578 Respective rules are, thus, also binding on non-member states. On the customary nature of rules related to the protection of the marine environment, see Birnie, Boyle and Redgwell (n 488) 387; Alan E Boyle, 'Land-Based Sources of Marine Pollution: Current Legal Regime' (1992) 16 Marine Policy 20, 25; Sands and Peel (n 447) 350. For a list of UNCLOS provisions that have been recognized to reflect customary law, see, in general, J Ashley Roach, 'Today's Customary International Law of the Sea' (2014) 45 Ocean Development & International Law 239.

579 See Tanaka, *International Law of the Sea* (n 360) 4 and 37.

580 Growing demand for maritime resources, both living and non-living, gradually expanded the scope of the law of the sea to questions related to resource allocation and control. In the context of major geopolitical rearrangements that came along with the decolonialization process, the struggle among countries for newly accessible resources, including energy resources and manganese nodules from the seafloor, had significant impacts on the development of the law of the sea. On the one hand, it favoured the enclosure of the seas. The enclosure movement is also known as the territorialisation of the seas and basically refers to the extension of the territorial sea of coastal states to 12 nautical miles, as well as to the development of the regimes of the continental shelf and the Exclusive Economic Zone, and their consolidation in UNCLOS: see Thomas Cottier, *Equitable Principles of Maritime Boundary Delimitation: The Quest for Distributive Justice in International Law* (Cambridge University Press 2015) 46–47. As a result of the enclosure movement, there has been a substantial reduction in the area of the high seas, as the admissible limits

regulations imposed any kind of limits to the freedom of states to pollute the marine environment, and none of these applied to land-based pollution sources or airborne pollution.[581] A number of maritime disasters, such as the sinking of a Liberian oil tanker (*Torrey Canyon*) off the coast of England in 1967, played a crucial role for the subsequent regulatory efforts towards a more stringent regime. The regulation of marine conservation and the protection of the marine environment, including from land-based pollution sources, gained impetus on the international agenda in the early 1970s, shortly before UNCLOS was negotiated. The text of UNCLOS has been greatly influenced by the development of international environmental law during that time. This

---

of coastal state jurisdiction have been 'gradually extended away from the coast': David Anderson, 'Freedoms of the High Seas in the Modern Law of the Sea' in David Freestone, Richard Barnes and David Ong (eds), *The Law of the Sea: Progress and Prospects* (Oxford University Press 2006) 328. cf Bernard H Oxman, 'The Territorial Temptation: A Siren Song at Sea' (2006) 100 The American Journal of International Law 830. The enclosure movement therefore represents a shift of balance between two of the main governing principles in the law of the sea – the principles of the freedom of the high seas and of sovereignty – for the benefit of the latter. On the other hand, the struggle for resources strongly influenced the development of an unprecedented regime for the deep seabed, which is governed by the principle of the common heritage of mankind. For more information on the evolution of the law of the sea, its governing principles and codification efforts, see Churchill and Lowe (n 430) 71–79 and 204–22; Cottier, *Equitable Principles of Maritime Boundary Delimitation* 45–66; Rothwell and Stephens (n 364) 2–4; Nico Schrijver, *Sovereignty over Natural Resources: Balancing Rights and Duties* (Cambridge University Press 1997) 203–4 and 215–29; Tanaka, *International Law of the Sea* (n 360) 17–21; Davor Vidas, 'Responsibility for the Seas' in Davor Vidas (ed), *Law, Technology and Science for Oceans in Globalisation: IUU Fishing, Oil Pollution, Bioprospecting, Outer Continental Shelf* (Brill 2010) 17–24.

581 Under the Convention on the High Seas (entered into force on 30 September 1962) 450 UNTS 11 arts 24 and 25, states were required to regulate oil pollution from ships, pipelines and seabed operations and to take measures in order to prevent nuclear pollution. From the late 1960s, a number of conventions were concluded to regulate further issues, including pollution from vessels, dumping at sea, maritime casualties and civil liability for pollution from vessels: International Convention for the Prevention of Pollution of the Sea by Oil (1954 OILPOL) (opened for signature on 12 May 1954, entered into force on 26 July 1958) 327 UNTS 3; 1973/78 MARPOL; 1972 London Dumping Convention; International Convention Relating to Intervention on the High Seas in Cases of Oil Pollution Casualties (1969 INTERVENTION) (adopted on 29 November 1969, entered into force on 6 May 1975) and Protocol Relating to Intervention on the High Seas in Cases of Pollution by Substances other than Oil (adopted on 2 November 1973); International Convention on Civil Liability for Oil Pollution Damage (1969/92 CLC) (adopted on 29 November 1969, entered into force on 19 June 1975), as replaced by 1992 Protocol (adopted on 27 November 1992, entered into force on 30 May 1996). See Alan E Boyle, 'Marine Pollution under the Law of the Sea Convention' (1985) 79 The American Journal of International Law 347, 347–48.

being said, the problem of plastic accumulation in the oceans was not widely recognized yet as a matter of major concern at the time when the convention was adopted.

In view of the increasing degradation of marine ecosystems, the establishment of an agreed and more comprehensive framework was one of the major objectives – and achievements – of the Third United Nations Conference on the Law of the Sea.[582] The aim to establish

> a legal order for the seas and oceans which will facilitate international communication, and will promote the peaceful uses of the seas and oceans, the equitable and efficient utilization of their resources, the *conservation of their living resources*, and the *study, protection and preservation of the marine environment*[583]

is prominently laid down in the preamble of the treaty. The protection and preservation of the marine environment specifically refers to the prevention, reduction and control of pollution from all sources, but also includes the conservation of living resources and ecosystems.[584]

---

582 See Boyle, 'Marine Pollution under the Law of the Sea Convention' (n 581) 347; Birnie, Boyle and Redgwell (n 488) 387; Center for Oceans Law and Policy, University of Virginia, 'PART XII – Protection and Preservation of the Marine Environment (IV)', *United Nations Convention on the Law of the Sea* (Brill Online 2016) 3 <http://referenceworks.brillonline.com/entries/united-nations-convention-on-the-law-of-the-sea/part-xii-LAOS_Part12> accessed 19 February 2022; Jonathan I Charney, 'The Marine Environment and the 1982 United Nations Conventions on the Law of the Sea' (1994) 28 International Lawyer 879, 882; Pierre-Marie Dupuy and Jorge E Viñuales, *International Environmental Law* (Cambridge University Press 2015) 97–98; Catherine Redgwell, 'From Permission to Prohibition: The 1982 Convention on the Law of the Sea and Protection of the Marine Environment' in David Freestone, Richard Barnes and David Ong (eds), *The Law of the Sea: Progress and Prospects* (Oxford University Press 2006) 180–81; Rothwell and Stephens (n 364) 365; Sands and Peel (n 447) 349–50. See also UNGA Res 2750 C (XXV) (1970) para 2.

583 Emphasis added.

584 In an order concerning the *Southern Bluefin Tuna Cases*, the International Tribunal for the Law of the Sea (ITLOS) held that 'the conservation of the living resources of the sea is an element in the protection and preservation of the marine environment': *Southern Bluefin Tuna Cases (New Zealand v Japan; Australia v Japan), Provisional Measures* [1999] ITLOS cases Nos. 3 and 4 para 70; *Request for an Advisory Opinion Submitted by the Sub-regional Fisheries Commission, Advisory Opinion* [2015] ITLOS case No. 21 34 para 120; *Chagos Marine Protected Area Arbitration (Mauritius v United Kingdom)* [2015] PCA (Arbitral Tribunal 2015) 211 para 538; *South China Sea Arbitration (the Philippines v China)* [2016] Arbitral Tribunal 2016 Case No 2013-19, PCA 380–84 paras 956–66. For more information on the regime on the conservation of marine living resources and

Rules that touch upon environmental protection can be found throughout the convention. Most fundamentally, UNCLOS Part XII is fully devoted to the issue and provides a unifying framework on marine environmental protection. UNCLOS is the first global instrument to articulate a general obligation of states to protect and preserve the marine environment[585] and to address all sources of pollution, including, in particular, pollution from land-based sources, seabed activities within or beyond national jurisdiction, and vessels, by dumping and from or through the atmosphere.[586] With the introduction of these general obligations[587] UNCLOS brought about a major shift in marine environmental protection from a substantial freedom to pollute the oceans towards a global regime of diligent pollution control. Under UNCLOS, a sound marine environment is considered a matter of common concern beyond the interests of individual states.[588]

The structure of the treaty reflects its wide thematic scope: in addition to its spatial regulations dividing the ocean into a number of jurisdictional zones (UNLCOS Parts I–XI) and its provisions on the protection and preservation of the marine environment (Part XII), the convention addresses further issues, such as marine scientific research (Part XIII) and development and transfer of marine technology (Part XIV). It moreover lays down a comprehensive dispute settlement system (Part XV) and established the International Tribunal for the Law of the Sea (ITLOS) as an independent judicial body with the power to adjudicate disputes with respect to the interpretation and application of the convention (UNCLOS Annex VI).

This chapter starts with an introduction into the convention's jurisdictional provisions in order to provide an overview of the different maritime zones (i).

---

marine biodiversity, including under UNCLOS, see Birnie, Boyle and Redgwell (n 488) ch 13; Dupuy and Viñuales (n 582) 162–67; Rothwell and Stephens (n 364) 315–45; Sands and Peel (n 447) 396–448; Tanaka, *International Law of the Sea* (n 360) 334–58. See also related contributions in David Freestone, Richard Barnes and David Ong (eds), *The Law of the Sea: Progress and Prospects* (Oxford University Press 2006) 210–307; Davor Vidas (ed), *Law, Technology and Science for Oceans in Globalisation: IUU Fishing, Oil Pollution, Bioprospecting, Outer Continental Shelf* (Brill 2010) 77–210; Davor Vidas and Peter Johan Schei (eds), *The World Ocean in Globalisation: Climate Change, Sustainable Fisheries, Biodiversity, Shipping, Regional Issues* (Brill 2011) Part III.

585 UNCLOS art 192. See Myron H Nordquist, Shabtai Rosenne and Alexander Yankov (eds), *United Nations Convention on the Law of the Sea 1982: A Commentary, Vol IV: Articles 192 to 278* (Center for Oceans Law and Policy and Kluwer Law International 2002) 36.

586 UNCLOS arts 194 and 207–12.

587 The obligations will be discussed in more detail in subsection ii below.

588 See Birnie, Boyle and Redgwell (n 488) 383; Boyle, 'Marine Pollution under the Law of the Sea Convention' (n 581) 347–51; Tanaka, *International Law of the Sea* (n 360) 268.

A basic understanding of the jurisdictional set-up under UNCLOS is important to better understand the convention's regime on the protection of the marine environment from different sources of pollution, respective obligations of states arising from the convention, and the possibilities for future action in addressing the problem of marine plastic pollution. Subsection ii starts with the treaty's definition of marine pollution, before it turns to the general provisions of Part XII, which are deliberately drafted in an open-textured way. It shows how these provisions can be and must be interpreted and applied in the light of contemporary international environmental law. It also shows how respective obligations evolved in scope and must be applied in coherence with other instruments, including, for instance, the UN Convention on Biological Diversity.[589] Finally, Subsection ii addresses the more specific obligations under Part XII: it discusses the relevance of global standards and non-binding instruments that have been adopted with regard to marine plastic pollution from land-based sources, issues related to due diligence and the differentiation in the standard of care, the role of risk evaluation and precaution, environmental impact assessment, and cooperation. Subsection iii analyses the main challenges related to the enforcement of UNCLOS Part XII. In its concluding remarks, the section recaps the main gaps and challenges of the UNCLOS regime when applying it to the issue of marine plastic pollution. The subsequent sections C and D will discuss other relevant instruments and treaty regimes.

i Maritime Zones

Marine spaces include the seabed and its subsoil, the superjacent water column and the airspace above the sea. In Parts I–XI, UNCLOS divides these spaces into a number of jurisdictional zones, each of which entails different rights and duties pertaining to either individual states or the international community. Most fundamentally, the ocean spaces are divided into zones under national jurisdiction over which coastal states exercise full territorial sovereignty or (limited) sovereign rights, and areas beyond national jurisdiction, which are governed by the concept of the freedom of the high seas, unless otherwise provided.[590]

589 1992 CBD.

590 A major exception to the principle of freedom of the high seas refers to the deep seabed (Area) and its mineral resources in particular, which are governed by the principle of the common heritage of mankind: see Section i.2) below. For more information on the different maritime zones, see Churchill and Lowe (n 430) ch 2–12; Cottier, *Equitable Principles of Maritime Boundary Delimitation* (n 580) Part I; AG Oude Elferink and EJ Molenaar (eds), *The International Legal Regime of Areas beyond National Jurisdiction: Current and*

Plastic debris and microplastics that enter the marine environment from land-based sources may travel through or end up in all the different areas of the sea, including domestic coasts, areas under foreign jurisdiction and common spaces. They often accumulate on shores, but also in waters of the global vortexes situated in the high seas, and on the deep seabed. UNCLOS sets the jurisdictional framework that applies to these different areas and defines the very basic rights and responsibilities that states hold in each of them, including with respect to marine plastic pollution. Pursuant to the relevant provisions under UNCLOS Part XII and related rules, preventive obligations with regard to land-based sources of plastic pollution are incumbent on the state in the territory of which the pollution source is located. In the case of sea-based pollution, they are incumbent on the flag state. States have an obligation to reduce and control pollution that occurs under their jurisdiction or control, and to prevent its spreading to other jurisdictions or areas.[591]

Acts or omissions contrary to UNCLOS Part XII may result in damage purely within the jurisdiction of the respective state, transboundary damage and/or damage to areas beyond national jurisdiction. These three constellations have different implications with regard to the enforceability of UNCLOS provisions: if pollution affects a neighbouring or other state, this state may react in one way or another, including through legal means. By contrast, cases of pollution in domestic areas or areas beyond national jurisdiction are very unlikely to entail any legal consequences at all. At least in the past, there has been a high reluctance of states to resort to the traditional means of enforcement in such cases. Yet, a few recent counterexamples possibly reflect a change in the interpretation and application of respective duties and may indicate the emergence of a different trend.[592]

Future Developments (Martinus Nijhoff Publishers 2010); Myron H Nordquist, Satya N Nandan and Shabtai Rosenne, *United Nations Convention on the Law of the Sea 1982: A Commentary, Vol II: Articles 1 to 85* (Center for Oceans Law and Policy and Kluwer Law International 2002); *United Nations Convention on the Law of the Sea 1982: A Commentary, Vol III: Articles 86 to 132* (Center for Oceans Law and Policy and Kluwer Law International 2002); *United Nations Convention on the Law of the Sea 1982: A Commentary, Vol VI: Articles 133 to 191* (Center for Oceans Law and Policy and Kluwer Law International 1985); Daniel P O'Connell, *The International Law of the Sea*, vol 1 (Ivan Anthony Shearer ed, Clarendon Press 1983); Daniel P O'Connell, *The International Law of the Sea*, vol 2 (Ivan Anthony Shearer ed, Clarendon Press 1984); Rothwell and Stephens (n 364) ch 2–9; Tanaka (n 360) Part I.

591 See Section 2.1.B.ii below.

592 Two recent examples of cases in which states brought claims against other states for acts that resulted in negative effects in common spaces or domestic areas of the polluting state include the *Whaling* case and the *South China Sea* case: *Whaling in the Antarctic*

1) *Areas under National Jurisdiction*

UNCLOS defines a so-called baseline to delimit the internal waters of a coastal state. Internal waters include inland waters such as rivers, but also harbours, estuaries and bays.[593] The first zone as defined by UNCLOS beyond internal waters is the territorial sea of coastal states (UNCLOS Part II). The territorial sea is a belt of sea (including seabed, its subsoil, the water column and airspace) adjacent to the coast upon which the coastal state basically exercises full sovereignty.[594] Full sovereignty implies 'legislative and enforcement jurisdiction over all matters and all people in an exclusive manner unless international law provides otherwise'.[595] Unlike in internal waters, ships of all states enjoy the right of innocent passage through the territorial sea.[596] The zone may not exceed 12 nautical miles from the baseline.[597] This first zone is bordered by a contiguous zone, which may not extend beyond 24 nautical miles from the baseline and allows the coastal state to exercise the control necessary to prevent and punish infringement of its laws and regulations within its territory or territorial sea.[598]

Beyond and adjacent to the territorial sea (thus including the contiguous zone), coastal states may claim their Exclusive Economic Zone (EEZ).[599] The EEZ is regulated by UNCLOS Part V and covers an area that extends up to 200 nautical miles from the baselines.[600] In the EEZ, coastal states exercise sovereign rights 'for the purpose of exploring and exploiting, conserving and managing the natural resources […] and with regard to other activities for the economic exploitation and exploration of the zone'.[601] Similarly, coastal states have jurisdiction over the EEZ with regard to further issues, including marine scientific research and the protection and preservation of the marine environment.[602] In particular, they have legislative and enforcement powers with

---

(Australia v Japan: New Zealand intervening), Judgment [2014] ICJ Rep 2014 226; *South China Sea Arbitration* (n 584). See discussion in subsection 2.1.B.iii below.

593 1982 UNCLOS arts 8–11. The baseline usually is the low-water line along the coast (normal baseline): ibid art 5. Alternative methods for baseline determination may be applied under special geographical conditions, including for straights, bays and archipelagic states.

594 1982 UNCLOS art 2(1).

595 Tanaka, *International Law of the Sea* (n 360) 6.

596 1982 UNCLOS art 17. Innocent passage excludes, for instance, military, fishing or research activities: ibid art 19(2).

597 1982 UNCLOS art 3.

598 ibid art 23.

599 ibid art 55.

600 ibid art 57.

601 ibid art 56(1)(a).

602 ibid art 56(1)(b).

regard to the conservation and use of living resources.[603] Sovereign rights in the EEZ are exclusive; other nations need the express consent of the coastal state for engaging in any of these activities.[604] In the EEZ, foreign states enjoy the freedoms of the high seas to the extent that these freedoms are not restricted by the coastal state's sovereign rights under Part V of the convention.[605] The EEZ comprises the water column, the seabed and its subsoil, as well as the airspace above the sea. With regard to the seabed, the provisions governing the continental shelf have to be taken into account.

The continental shelf is regulated in UNCLOS Part VI.[606] It is defined as 'the seabed and subsoil of the submarine areas that extend beyond [the coastal state's] territorial sea throughout the natural prolongation of its land territory to the outer edge of the continental margin'.[607] Where the outer edge of the continental margin does not extend up to 200 nautical miles from the baseline, the continental shelf of a coastal state is expanded to 200 nautical miles through a legal fiction, even if geological conditions are different. If, on the other hand, the natural prolongation of the land territory exceeds 200 nautical miles, the continental shelf may also go beyond this limit.[608] UNCLOS Part VI attributes sovereign rights to coastal states over the continental shelf 'for the purpose of exploring it and exploiting its natural resources'.[609] Exploration or

603 ibid arts 61–68 and 73. See *Fisheries Advisory Opinion* (n 584).

604 Tanaka, *International Law of the Sea* (n 360) 130–31.

605 1982 UNCLOS art 58(1). Freedoms applying to the EEZ include the freedoms of navigation, overflight and the lying of submarine cables and pipelines.

606 The continental-shelf doctrine harks back to 'the long range world-wide need for new sources of petroleum and other minerals' and the corresponding proclamation of United States President Harry S. Truman of 28 September 1945, in which he declared the outer continental shelf to be under US jurisdiction and control: Harry S Truman, 'Presidential Proclamation No. 2667 – Policy of the United States With Respect to the Natural Resources of the Subsoil and Sea Bed of the Continental Shelf' (1945) 10 Fed. Reg. 12,303. Many countries followed the example of the United States and claimed exclusive economic jurisdiction over the natural resources of the continental shelf or, in the absence of a continental shelf, of the seabed up to 200 nautical miles from the coast. UNCLOS Part VI reflects this doctrine.

607 1982 UNCLOS art 76(1).

608 The seaward limits of the continental shelves exceeding 200 nautical miles are currently being set by the coastal states according to specifically defined criteria: ibid art 76(4–7). The process is accompanied and monitored by the Commission on the Limits of the Continental Shelf, a body set up under Annex II of the convention on the basis of equitable geographical representation (see art 2(1) of UNCLOS Annex II).

609 ibid art 77(1). Specific activities falling under exclusive jurisdiction of the coastal state include drilling operations for all purposes and the construction, operation and use of artificial islands, installations and structures on the continental shelf: ibid arts 80–81. Natural resources of the continental shelf include mineral and other non-living resources

exploitation of the continental shelf and its natural resources by third states is subject to the express consent of the coastal state.[610] In the exercise of its rights over the continental shelf, however, the coastal state must not unduly affect the rights and freedoms of other states.[611]

Maritime zones under national jurisdiction are thus either characterized by territorial sovereignty of the coastal state, which implies comprehensive jurisdiction *ratione materiae* and *ratione personae*, or by sovereign rights of the coastal state, comprising exclusive rights limited to the material scope as defined by law. Specifically, coastal states exercise territorial sovereignty over their internal waters and territorial sea and sovereign rights over their EEZ and continental shelf.[612] In all these areas, coastal states do not only have jurisdiction with regard to the protection and preservation of the marine environment,[613] but have a duty to adopt measures to this aim, including by adopting and enforcing corresponding legislation.[614] This duty flows from Part XII and is a corollary of the sovereign rights they enjoy.

---

of the seabed and its subsoil. They also include sedentary species that, 'at the harvestable stage, either are immobile on or under the seabed or are unable to move except in constant physical contact with the seabed': ibid art 77(4). Such species include oysters, clams and abalone, and, arguably, also crabs and lobsters: see Churchill and Lowe (n 430) 151–52. Non-natural resources, such as wrecks, are, though, not covered. When exploiting non-living resources of the outer continental shelf (beyond 200 nautical miles from the baseline), coastal states have to make payments or contributions in kind to the International Seabed Authority (ISA). Payments are made according to a specific formula and equitably distributed among the parties, taking into account the interests and needs of developing and disadvantaged states: 1982 UNCLOS art 82.

610 1982 UNCLOS art 77(2) and, with regard to marine scientific research, art 246(2).

611 ibid art 78(2). In particular, other states are entitled to lay submarine cables and pipelines on the continental shelf. The delineation of the course for the laying of such pipelines is subject to the consent of the coastal state. Also, the coastal state may establish conditions for cables or pipelines entering its territory or territorial sea: ibid art 79(1–4).

612 See Tanaka, *International Law of the Sea* (n 360) 6–7.

613 Part VI of the convention, which sets out the regime on the continental shelf, is silent about the matter of environmental protection. Within the EEZ, the coastal states' jurisdiction in this respect comprises the seafloor and its subsoil. In the outer continental shelf, coastal states have jurisdiction with regard to the protection of the marine environment to the extent that it forms part of their exploration and exploitation of the natural resources and does not unduly restrict the freedoms of other states.

614 In an advisory opinion that ITLOS adopted at the request of the Sub-Regional Fisheries Commission, the tribunal held that 'laws and regulations adopted by the coastal State in conformity with the provisions of the Convention for the purpose of conserving the living resources and protecting and preserving the marine environment within its exclusive economic zone, constitute part of the legal order for the seas and oceans established by the Convention'. It also held that in the EEZ, the primary responsibility for taking such

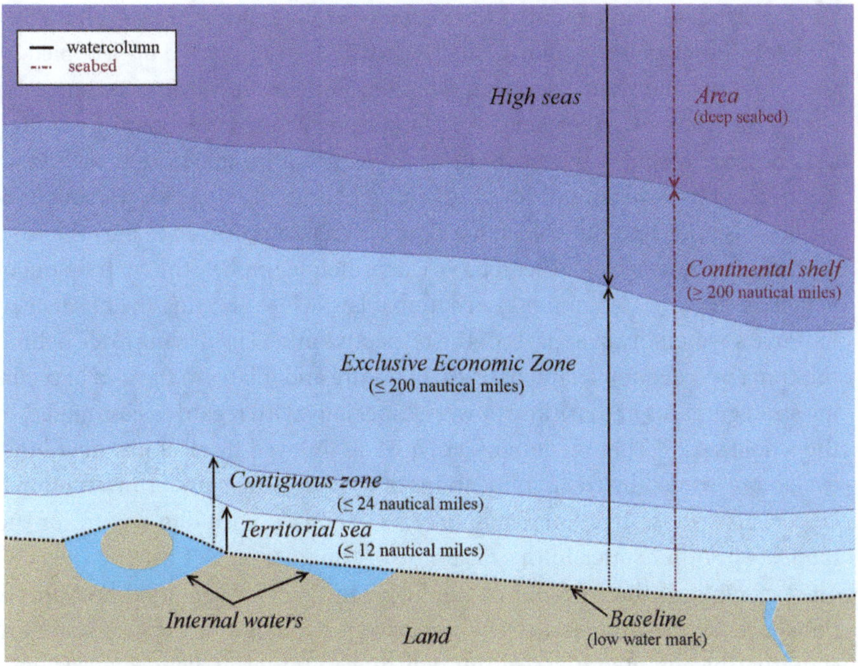

FIGURE 15 Maritime zones according to UNCLOS
ADAPTED FROM A PICTURE BY HISTORICAIR, <HTTPS://DE.WIKIPEDIA.ORG/WIKI/DATEI:ZONMAR-EN.SVG>, ACCESSED 19 FEBRUARY 2022, LICENSED UNDER CC BY-SA 3.0, <HTTPS://CREATIVECOMMONS.ORG/LICENSES/BY-SA/3.0/DEED.EN> ACCESSED 6 DECEMBER 2021.

2) *Areas beyond National Jurisdiction*

Areas beyond national jurisdiction comprise the high seas and the deep seabed, the latter of which is known as the *Area*. The two zones are governed by two fairly different principles: the high seas, consisting of the water columns and airspace beyond the EEZ (or, in the event that a coastal state did not claim an EEZ, beyond its territorial sea), are governed by the principle of the freedom of the high seas.[615] The Area (that is, the seabed beyond the continental shelves), on the other hand, is governed by the principle of the common heritage of mankind.[616] The two principles represent different regulatory approaches with regard to the management of common spaces and common resources.

---

measures rests with the coastal state: *Fisheries Advisory Opinion* (n 584) 30–31 paras 102 and 106. See also ibid 34–35 para 120.

615 1982 UNCLOS arts 86 and 87.

616 ibid art 136.

The high seas are regulated in UNCLOS Part VII. While they are reserved for peaceful purposes[617] and, as such, cannot be appropriated or occupied,[618] the high seas and their resources, whether living or non-living, are open for use by all states, whether coastal or landlocked.[619] The freedom of the high seas notably includes the freedom of navigation, the freedom of overflight, the freedom to lay submarine cables and pipelines, the freedom to construct artificial islands and other installations, the freedom of fishing and the freedom of marine scientific research.[620] The principle implies, thus, a freedom of activities as permitted under international law, while granting the absence of national sovereignty over parts of the respective area. The driving force behind the concept is economic and political in nature and relates to the aim of securing strategic gains of maritime powers, especially with regard to commerce, in the whole sea.[621] The freedom of activities as enjoyed by all states may, however, be restricted by treaty obligations and other duties under international law.[622] Also, these freedoms may only be exercised with due regard for the interests of other states in their exercise of the freedoms of the high seas.[623] The principle of the freedom of the high seas is complemented and operationalized by the principle of the exclusive jurisdiction of the flag state: the state that has granted a vessel the right to sail under its flag exercises both exclusive legislative and enforcement jurisdiction over it (and the people on board) while the ship sails on the high seas.[624] The principle implies that it is the responsibility of the flag state to ensure that ships flying its flag comply with international law when engaging in activities in the high seas.[625] This is

617 ibid art 88.

618 ibid art 89.

619 ibid art 87(1).

620 ibid art 87(1)(a–f).

621 Churchill and Lowe (n 430) 78; Oxman (n 580) 837; Vidas, 'Responsibility for the Seas' (n 580) 27.

622 Such obligations may be included in UNCLOS itself or other treaties such as the UN Fish Stock Agreement, which, for instance, restricts the freedom to fish for the states parties to it: United Nations Agreement for the Implementation of the Provisions of the United Nations Convention on the Law of the Sea of 10 December 1982 Relating to the Conservation and Management of Straddling Fish Stocks and Highly Migratory Fish Stocks (adopted on 4 August 1995, entered into force on 11 December 2001) 2167 UNTS 88, 34 ILM 1542 (1995).

623 1982 UNCLOS art 87(2).

624 ibid art 92(1); *The M/V 'Saiga' Case* (*Saint Vincent and the Grenadines v Guinea*) [1999] ITLOS case No. 2 para 106.

625 For more information on the principle of the exclusive jurisdiction of the flag state, see Tanaka, *International Law of the Sea* (n 360) 157–77.

also true with regard to rules related to plastic pollution from ships and dumping at sea.[626]

The regime of the high seas contrasts with the regime applying to the Area, which is regulated in UNLCOS Part XI: the deep seabed and its resources are defined as the common heritage of mankind,[627] whereas the term *resources* refers to mineral resources only.[628] Similar to the high seas, the Area is reserved for peaceful purposes[629] and cannot be appropriated or occupied.[630] In contrast to the regime of the high seas, however, the freedom of activities does not apply to the Area and its resources. The convention explicitly provides that activities in the Area shall be carried out for the benefit of mankind as a whole, while taking into particular consideration the interests and needs of developing states.[631] Thus, while the resources of the high seas are freely exploitable (as long as in accordance with respective obligations under international law), states are *not* free to exploit the resources of the Area. Instead, resource exploitation in the Area is administered by the International Seabed Authority (ISA) "International Seabed Authority (ISA)", which acts on behalf of mankind as a whole.[632] The tasks of ISA include providing for 'the equitable sharing of financial and other economic benefits derived from activities in the Area through any appropriate mechanism, on a non-discriminatory basis'.[633] The Authority

626 See 1982 UNCLOS arts 211(2) and 217(1). See also 1973/78 MARPOL.

627 1982 UNCLOS art 136.

628 ibid art 133.

629 ibid art 141. See also art 138.

630 Hence, the Area cannot be considered a *res nullius* over which states can claim ownership. Claims of sovereignty or sovereign rights over parts of the Area are explicitly excluded: ibid art 137(1).

631 ibid art 140(1).

632 ibid arts 137(2) and 153(1). ISA (referred to in the treaty as 'the Authority') was established by the adoption of UNCLOS art 156(1) and has its seat in Jamaica (art 156(4)). All parties to UNCLOS are member to ISA (art 156(2)) and its supreme organ, the Assembly [regulated by arts 159–60 and Annex Section 3 of the Agreement Relating to the Implementation of Part XI of the United Nations Convention on the Law of the Sea of 10 December 1982 (Implementing Agreement) (adopted on 28 July 1994, entered into force on 28 July 1996) 33 ILM 1309 (1994)]. Further organs include the Council (UNCLOS arts 161–65; Implementing Agreement Annex Section 3) serving as the executive organ of ISA; the Secretariat (arts 166–69); and the Enterprise, the operative arm of the organization (art 170; Implementing Agreement Annex Section 2). ISA has legislative and enforcement jurisdiction with respect to the exploration and exploitation of mineral resources ('activities') in the Area (art 17(1) of UNCLOS Annex III and UNCLOS art 153(5)).

633 1982 UNCLOS art 140(2). In the context of increasing self-determination of the global south, equity concerns and a call for distributive justice have, in fact, been a driving factor in the development of the regime. In the run up to the negotiations of UNCLOS,

can also adopt rules, regulations and procedures for 'the prevention, reduction and control of pollution and other hazards to the marine environment' and 'the prevention of damage to the flora and fauna of the marine environment'.[634]

The core elements of the principle of the common heritage of mankind include the principle of non-appropriation, the reservation for peaceful purposes and the principle of use for the benefit of mankind as a whole.[635] Features

---

developing countries feared to lose out against technologically advanced states in the accession and exploitation of deep-seabed resources: see Churchill and Lowe (n 430) 223–26; Tullio Scovazzi, 'The Seabed beyond the Limits of National Jurisdiction: General and Institutional Aspects' in AG Oude Elferink and EJ Molenaar (eds), *The International Legal Regime of Areas beyond National Jurisdiction: Current and Future Developments* (Koninklijke Brill NV 2010) 44; Tanaka, *International Law of the Sea* (n 360) 179–80. In a speech before the UN General Assembly in 1967, the Maltese Ambassador Arvid Pardo thus suggested the deep seabed to be defined as the common heritage of mankind that 'should be used and exploited for peaceful purposes and for the exclusive benefit of mankind as a whole': Speech by Arvid Pardo at the UN General Assembly, of 1st November 1967, as contained in UNGA, 'Twenty-Second Session Official Records: First Committee, 1515th Meeting' (1967) UN Doc A/C.1/PV.1515; and UNGA, 'Twenty-Second Session Official Records: First Committee, 1516th Meeting' (1967) UN Doc A/C.1/PV.1516 (1967). Quotation at ibid para 13. See also Cottier, *Equitable Principles of Maritime Boundary Delimitation* (n 580) 45–66; Schrijver, *Sovereignty over Natural Resources* (n 580) 215–29; Scovazzi, 'The Seabed beyond the Limits of National Jurisdiction: General and Institutional Aspects' 44. Pardo's speech led to a moratorium of resource exploitation in the deep seabed in 1969 and to the adoption of a 'Declaration of Principles' by the General Assembly in 1970, which consolidated Pardo's claim: UNGA Res 2574 (XXIV) (1969), 'Question of the Reservation Exclusively for Peaceful Purposes of the Sea-Bed and the Ocean Floor, and the Subsoil Thereof, Underlying the High Seas beyond the Limits of Present National Jurisdiction, and the Use of Their Resources in the Interests of Mankind'; UNGA Res 2749 (XXV) (1970), 'Declaration of Principles Governing the Sea-Bed and the Ocean Floor, and the Subsoil Thereof, beyond the Limits of National Jurisdiction' para 1. In spite of continuing disagreement, especially between the Group of 77 (G77) and developed states, over the exact nature and design of the regime, it was embedded in UNCLOS Part XI: Churchill and Lowe (n 430) 228–29. On the role of the G77 during UNCLOS negotiations, see Rothwell and Stephens (n 364) 12–14.

634 UNCLOS art 145. In this competence, the ISA adopted regulations on prospecting and exploration for polymetallic nodules and sulphides in the Area. The UN General Assembly repeatedly emphasized the importance of the ISA's on-going work in this field.

635 See Tanaka, *International Law of the Sea* (n 360) 191. The original text provided for a rather interventionist regime with elements of supranational control and administration, and differential treatment for developing countries. Yet, even before the convention entered into force in 1994, the application of the concept of common heritage of mankind was restricted. Several aspects, mainly opposed by industrialized countries, were amended or eliminated by an implementing agreement adopted by the General Assembly on 28 July 1994: 1994 Agreement on the Implementation of UNCLOS Part XI. Eliminated elements particularly include obligatory technology transfer, financial obligations of states and miners, as well as production limitation from seabed resources that

such as (limited) international management, access and benefit sharing and the principle of sustainable development, which, arguably, are inherent to the concept, are among the particularities of the regime.[636] Yet, the scope of the concept is geographically limited and becomes even more so with the ongoing extension of the continental shelves beyond the limit of 200 nautical miles – a process which continually reduces the area of the deep seabed. Also, the thematic scope of the concept, which is confined to mineral resources, further curtails the practical relevance of the concept.

While Parts VII and XI say little about the protection of the marine environment (beyond resource management) in these areas,[637] the obligations of states arising from Part XII generally also apply to the high seas and the deep seabed.[638] States do, for instance, have to take the necessary measures to ensure that pollution occurring in areas under their jurisdiction does not spread to the high seas or the deep seabed.[639] States also have to enforce the

---

ought to benefit developing country economies dependant on the export of land-mined minerals. Amended elements notably include decision-making procedures of the ISA Council and Assembly with a shift towards a consensus requirement; budgetary issues, and rules regarding compensation and economic assistance of developing countries. Only with the corresponding adjustments – in particular towards a more market-based approach – UNLCOS became universally acceptable. For more information, see Churchill and Lowe (n 430) 229–53; Cottier, *Equitable Principles of Maritime Boundary Delimitation* (n 580) 54; Scovazzi, 'The Seabed beyond the Limits of National Jurisdiction: General and Institutional Aspects' (n 633) 45–48; Tanaka, 'Regulation of Land-Based Marine Pollution' (n 363) 186–92. As one of the major opponents of UNCLOS Part XI in its original form, the United States actively participated in the negotiations which led to the adoption of the 1994 Implementing Agreement. Yet, it has ratified neither the convention nor the implementing agreement, although it recognizes UNCLOS (in most of its parts) as a codification of customary international law. For a historical summary of the United States' main concerns with regard to the regulation of the deep seabed and its role in the set-up of the 1994 Implementing Agreement, see Charney, 'The Marine Environment and UNCLOS' (n 582) 880, in particular fn 3.

636 Schrijver, *Sovereignty over Natural Resources* (n 580) 218–20.

637 In the high seas, conservation of living resources is to be achieved by international cooperation: 1982 UNCLOS art 118. This is also true for the determination of the allowable catch of living resources in the high seas (art 119). For the currently 90 parties of the Fish Stocks Agreement of 4 August 1995, the respective provisions in UNCLOS are to be read in conjunction with those of the agreement. In order to provide effective mechanisms for compliance and enforcement on the high seas and to ensure coherence in the management of straddling or highly migratory fish stocks, the Fish Stocks Agreement establishes detailed minimum international standards for the conservation and management of these species. With the exception of arts 5–7, the agreement applies exclusively to areas beyond national jurisdiction.

638 See *Fisheries Advisory Opinion* (n 584) 34–35 para 120.

639 See 1982 UNCLOS art 194(2).

laws and regulations they adopt in the discharge of their obligations under Part XII, including with respect to ships flying their flag on the high seas. With regard to activities in the Area, ISA "International Seabed Authority (ISA)" is the competent authority for the adoption of rules and regulations with regard to pollution prevention and environmental protection.

While the freedom of the high seas does not include a freedom to pollute (which would be against Part XII and related rules), it certainly includes the freedom to clean up plastic pollution, as long as this measure does not unduly restrict the freedoms of other states. Clean-up activities may form an important element of the range of measures that a state can take in order to fulfil its obligations under UNCLOS Part XII, especially because pollution reduction is explicitly required. Yet, technology for the clean-up of marine debris at sea is still in its infant stage. This might be one out of several reasons why no argument for a duty of states to clean up plastic debris in the high seas (not to mention the deep seabed) has ever been made. Another such reason is certainly the lack of jurisdiction, which, arguably, is the corollary of environmental responsibilities. This further adds to the importance of prevention and the secondary role of pollution reduction in this field, especially in areas beyond national jurisdiction.

ii UNCLOS Part XII: The Protection and Preservation of the Marine Environment

UNCLOS Part XII comprises 46 articles and is structured into 11 sections. The first section contains a number of legal principles governing the Part XII regime. The principles were drafted in line with the language and spirit of Principle 7 of the 1972 Stockholm Declaration[640] and other coeval documents.[641] At the very outset of Part XII, it expresses in Article 192 a general duty of states to protect and preserve the marine environment. This duty is both the core and foundation of the global legal regime on marine plastic pollution mitigation. The current subsection sheds light on its normative content (2) and discusses the more specific obligations as contained in UNCLOS Part XII (3). Before that,

640 Stockholm Principle 7 calls on states to 'take all possible steps to prevent pollution of the seas by substances that are liable to create hazards to human health, to harm living resources and marine life, to damage amenities or to interfere with other legitimate uses of the sea': 1972 Stockholm Declaration.

641 E.g. United Nations, 'Report of the Intergovernmental Working Group on Marine Pollution on Its Second Session' (1971) UN doc A/CONF.48/IWGMP.II/5 3 Principle 1: 'Every state has a duty to protect and preserve the marine environment and, in particular, to prevent pollution that may affect areas where an internationally shared resource is located'. See also Nordquist, Rosenne and Yankov (n 585) para 192.3.

it takes a look at the convention's definition of marine pollution and examines whether and to what extent marine plastic debris is covered by the term (1).

1) *Definition of Marine Pollution*

For the purposes of the convention, *pollution of the marine environment* is defined as

> the introduction by man, directly or indirectly, of substances or energy into the marine environment, including estuaries, which results or is likely to result in such deleterious effects as harm to living resources and marine life, hazards to human health, hindrance to marine activities, including fishing and other legitimate uses of the sea, impairment of quality for use of sea water and reduction of amenities.[642]

This definition widely corresponds to the common understanding of the term.[643] It contains three main elements that seem of particular relevance. It so goes from the definition that marine pollution usually involves elevated concentrations of substances in water, soil, organisms or other media within the marine environment. Such elevated concentration levels are generally referred to as *contamination*, respective substances as *contaminants*. The definition also points to the anthropogenic origin of pollution: the alteration in concentration levels has, hence, to be caused by human activities ('introduction by man'). Finally, the definition shows that pollution involves any kind of negative or deleterious effects, for instance in the form of impaired use. High concentrations of substances in seawater do, thus, not necessarily mean that the water is polluted, even if the contamination was caused by humans. The water is, however, polluted if there are negative effects that can be associated with the contamination.

---

642 1982 UNCLOS art 1(1)(4).

643 See GESAMP, 'Report of the First Session' (1969) UN Doc GESAMP I/11 5; United Nations, 'Report of the United Nations Conference on the Human Environment' (1972) UN Doc A/CONF.48/14/Rev. 1 (1972) Annex III, 73; Hassan (n 364) 12–15; E Pontavice, 'Pollution' in Leo J Bouchez and L Kaijen (eds), *The Future of the Law of the Sea: Proceedings of the Symposium on the Future of the Sea organized at Den Helder by the Royal Netherlands Naval College and the International Law Institute of Utrecht State University 26 and 27 June 1972* (Martinus Nijhoff 1973) 104; Meng Qing-Nan, *Land Based Marine Pollution: International Law Development* (Graham & Trotman/Martinus Nijhoff 1987) 3–5. For a critical review of the evolution of the definition and its inclusion and adoption in UNCLOS, see, in general, M Tomczak, 'Defining Marine Pollution: A Comparison of Definitions Used by International Conventions' (1984) 8 Marine Policy 311.

Common contaminants or potential pollutants include:

- biological substances (such as pathogenic microorganisms or invasive species);
- chemical substances (including petroleum hydrocarbons; persistent organic pollutants such as chlorinated hydrocarbons; inorganic pollutants, including heavy metals; endocrine disruptors; nutrients, especially nitrogen and phosphorus; sediment mobilization; and marine debris, including plastic litter);
- radionuclides from a variety of activities; and
- substances altering the physic-chemical properties of the sea water (due to a different pH, salinity or oxygen demand).[644]

The UNCLOS definition also covers the introduction of energy (for instance in the form of heat from power plants) into the marine environment with potentially harmful effects, and possibly also noise.[645]

Importantly, the definition does not exclusively refer to negative effects on *human* activities and interests but refers in this respect to marine life in general.[646] Also, it includes not only acts that actually result in negative effects to the marine environment but also acts that are 'likely to result' in such effects. The definition is thus not confined to an established cause–effect relationship but includes in its scope the introduction into the marine environment of substances or energy with potentially harmful effects.[647] Implicitly, this definition refers to, and goes in line with, broader concepts such as risk evaluation, precaution and due diligence, which will be discussed later in this section.[648]

---

644 See, for instance, GESAMP, 'Protecting the Oceans from Land-Based Activities: Land-Based Sources and Activities Affecting the Quality and Uses of the Marine, Coastal and Associated Freshwater Environment' (UNEP 2001) Reports and Studies No 71 at 9, 16 and 20; Michael Hardy, 'International Control of Marine Pollution' (1971) 11 Nat. Resources J. 296, 303–05; UNEP and GPA (n 492). See also Churchill and Lowe (n 430) 331; Hassan (n 364) 23–34.

645 See IMO, 'Guidelines for the Reduction of Underwater Noise from Commercial Shipping to Address Adverse Impacts on Marine Life' (2014) MEPC.1/Circ.833; UNGA Res 71/257 (2016), 'Oceans and the Law of the Sea' para 266. On the impacts of anthropogenic noise on whales and other cetaceans see LS Weilgart, 'The Impacts of Anthropogenic Ocean Noise on Cetaceans and Implications for Management' (2007) 85 Canadian Journal of Zoology 1091.

646 See *South China Sea Arbitration* (n 584) 382 para 960.

647 cf *Southern Bluefin Tuna Cases* (n 584) paras 77–79; *Responsibilities and Obligations of States Sponsoring Persons and Entities with Respect to Activities in the Area (Advisory Opinion)* [2011] ITLOS (Seabed Disputes Chamber) case No. 17 40 paras 131–32. See also Qing-Nan (n 643) 5; Tanaka, *International Law of the Sea* (n 360) 269.

648 See 2.1.B.ii.3)b) and c) below.

Marine plastic debris refers to objects or substances that are produced, used and disposed of by humans and find their way into the marine environment from different sources and through different pathways. They are directly or indirectly introduced by man into the marine environment.[649] The debris has actual or potential harmful effects on all the categories as mentioned in the UNCLOS definition of marine pollution: it damages marine wildlife and entire ecosystems, poses a risk to human health and safety, hampers maritime transport and other marine activities, adversely affects economic activities such as tourism and fisheries and reduces the cultural, aesthetic and amenity values of the marine environment to human society.[650] Plastic debris thus clearly falls under the definition of marine pollution and into the scope of UNCLOS Part XII.

2) *General Obligations under UNCLOS Part XII*

The starting point and basis of UNCLOS Part XII is the obligation of states to protect and preserve the marine environment (Article 192). Its normative content is informed by the subsequent articles of Chapter 1, but also by the more specific provisions contained in the other sections of Part XII. Deliberately worded in a broad and open way, UNCLOS Article 192 clearly needs to be interpreted and applied in light of contemporary international environmental law.[651] Recent case law and an advisory opinion issued by the ITLOS Seabed Disputes Chamber in 2011[652] give particular attention to three elements in this respect: due diligence, environmental impact assessment, and precaution. Moreover, as the subject of marine environmental protection is also addressed by or closely related to the subject area of a number of other international legal instruments, the broader legal environment has to be taken into account, including with regard to related multilateral environmental agreements.[653]

---

649 Indirect introduction into the marine environment includes any loss of control of plastic wastes allowing them to enter the environment and to eventually end up in the sea. *Introduction into the marine environment* may therefore refer to the use of microbeads in showers in case sewage treatment plants cannot filter them out, or to the dumping of plastics on land or at sea, unsustainable landfill sites or the introduction of plastics into rivers of upstream states.

650 See UNEP and GPA (n 492) 26.

651 See *South China Sea Arbitration* (n 584) 373 para 941.

652 *Responsibilities of States in the Area* (n 647).

653 cf art 31(3)(c) of the Vienna Convention on the Law of Treaties (1969 VCLT) (adopted on 23 May 1969, entered into force on 27 January 1980) 1155 UNTS 331, 8 ILM 679 (1969). See also the comments by the ILC in 'Fragmentation of International Law: Difficulties Arising From the Diversification and Expansion of International Law (Fragmentation Report)' (Study Group of the International Law Commission 2006) A/CN.4/L.682 212 para 423.

Recent judgments show how the development of new instruments has influenced the evolution of the scope of UNCLOS Article 192 and related provisions. Landmark rulings in this respect include, in particular, two arbitral decisions: the first involves a dispute between Mauritius and the United Kingdom regarding the establishment by the latter of a marine protected area around the Chagos Archipelago;[654] the second is a case brought by the Philippines against the People's Republic of China dealing with, among other things, environmental concerns in the South China Sea.[655] Especially in the second case, the arbitral tribunal referred to a number of multilateral agreements in the interpretation of UNCLOS provisions. Considering concerns of legal coherence and the principle of systemic integration, the current and subsequent subsections discuss the linkages between UNCLOS environmental provisions and a number of related instruments.

a) The Text of the Convention

In presumably simple terms, Article 192 of the convention provides that 'States have the obligation to protect and preserve the marine environment'. While the term *marine environment* is not explicitly defined in the convention, it clearly comprises all parts of the sea and the living and non-living resources contained therein, and cannot be confined to, for instance, parts under national jurisdiction or control.[656] Remarkably, the provision is addressed to *states* rather than *states parties* to the convention, so that its scope of application seems to go beyond the treaty's membership and include all the states. There are several possible interpretations to this choice of terminology, including that the duty to protect and preserve the marine environment reflects a customary rule or a general principle of international law.[657]

According to UNCLOS Article 193, the duty to protect and preserve the marine environment as contained in Article 192 explicitly qualifies the sovereign

---

654 *Chagos Marine Protected Area Arbitration* (n 584).

655 *South China Sea Arbitration* (n 584).

656 In the *South China Sea Arbitration,* the tribunal noted that 'the environmental obligations in Part XII apply to States irrespective of where the alleged harmful activities took place': ibid 370 para 927. The tribunal also held that 'the obligations in Part XII apply to all States with respect to the marine environment in all maritime areas, both inside the national jurisdiction of States and beyond it' and that 'questions of sovereignty are irrelevant to the application of Part XII of the Convention': ibid 373 para 940. See also *Fisheries Advisory Opinion* (n 584) 35 para 120.

657 Nordquist, Rosenne and Yankov (n 585) para 192.8 and 194.10(c). See also Birnie, Boyle and Redgwell (n 488) 387; Dupuy and Viñuales (n 582) 99.

right of states to exploit their natural resources.[658] While the right of states to exploit their resources is confirmed in UNCLOS, states, in the exercise of their right, need to weigh up purely economic interests against environmental concerns. Environmental considerations thus form a compulsory part of marine resource management by states. In this sense, UNCLOS Article 193 implicitly refers to a balancing of interests as suggested by the concept of sustainable development.[659] Article 193 is reminiscent of Stockholm Principle 21 and Rio Principle 2, both of which link the right of states to exploit their own resources to their 'responsibility to ensure that activities within their jurisdiction or control do not cause damage to the environment of other states or of areas beyond the limits of national jurisdiction'. The UNCLOS provision, however, shifts the emphasis from a negative obligation not to cause harm to a positive duty to protect and preserve the environment.[660]

---

658 UNCLOS art 193 reads as follows: 'States have the sovereign right to exploit their natural resources pursuant to their environmental policies and in accordance with their duty to protect and preserve the marine environment'.

659 With respect to the overarching goal of sustainable development, Rio Principle 4 explicitly expresses a state duty to reconcile economic development with environmental protection: 'In order to achieve sustainable development, environmental protection shall constitute an integral part of the development process and cannot be considered in isolation from it'. The International Court of Justice (ICJ) confirmed the principle: *Gabčíkovo-Nagymaros* (n 543) 78 para 140; *Iron Rhine Arbitration* (n 547) 66–67 para 59; *Pulp Mills, Provisional Measures* (n 547) 133 para 80. In return, interests related to environmental protection cannot generally invalidate the right to economic development. On sustainable development, see Section 2.1.A.ii.1) above.

660 The interlinkage of rights coupled to territorial sovereignty and the sovereignty over natural resources on the one hand and of corresponding responsibilities on the other hand has long been established in international law. In a territorial dispute between the Netherlands and the United States in 1928, the arbitral tribunal held that sovereignty implies as a corollary duty 'the obligation to protect within the territory the rights of other States': *Island of Palmas case (Netherlands v USA)* [1928] 2 UN Rep Int'l Arb Awards 829 839. The reasoning is, in fact, inherent to the principle of sovereignty itself and the principle of sovereign equality of states which was later expressed in art 2.1 of the UN Charter. The ICJ came to a similar conclusion in its *Barcelona Traction* case. In the judgment, known for its reference to *erga omnes* obligations of states (that is, obligations of a state towards the international community), the court held that '[r]esponsibility is the necessary corollary of a right': *Barcelona Traction, Light and Power Company, Limited (Belgium v Spain) Judgment* [1970] ICJ Rep 1970 3 33 para 36. The same must be true with respect to sovereignty over natural resources: it entails both rights and duties, which form the legal room to manoeuvre with respect to a state's resource management. This applies even more so to shared resources. In fact, with respect to marine living resources, it is usually difficult to determine into which jurisdiction they fall. See Franz Xaver Perrez, *Cooperative Sovereignty: From Independence to Interdependence in the Structure of*

UNCLOS Article 194 reflects one of the core components of the duty to protect and preserve the marine environment. In its paragraph 1, it requires states (and not merely states parties) to

> take [...] all measures [...] necessary to prevent, reduce and control pollution of the marine environment from any source, using for this purpose the best practicable means at their disposal and in accordance with their capabilities [and to] endeavour to harmonize their policies in this connection.

It follows from the text that the adoption of three types of measures – namely to prevent pollution, reduce pollution and control pollution – constitutes a crucial element in the protection and preservation of the marine environment. Four issues as expressed in paragraph 1 are particularly striking in this regard: first, the provision does not prohibit pollution *per se* but, instead, requires states to take preventive and reactive measures. It does, therefore, not require a specific result, such as a pollution-free environment, but obliges states to take action, or adopt conduct, that leads towards a desired result. Second, reference in paragraph 1 to terms such as 'best practicable means', 'at their disposal' and 'in accordance with their capabilities' seem to qualify the request for states to take 'all measures necessary' to prevent, reduce and control pollution. Capability will thus be an essential issue in the determination of the exact nature and content of the duty to take measures to prevent, reduce and control pollution or to ensure not to cause harm to the environment beyond the areas under their jurisdiction. Third, the provision refers to *any source* of pollution. The inclusion of all pollution sources, including land-based and atmospheric sources, was a novelty at the time of adoption of the convention. Even today, UNCLOS is still an exception among global environmental treaties in this regard. Finally, paragraph 1 indicates that harmonization of national policies plays a key role in global pollution prevention, reduction and control.

Paragraph 2 requires states to:

> take all measures necessary to ensure that activities under their jurisdiction or control are so conducted as not to cause damage by pollution to other States and their environment, and that pollution arising from

International Environmental Law (Kluwer Law International 2000) ch 6; Sands and Peel (n 447) 193. cf Schrijver, *Sovereignty over Natural Resources* (n 580) 391–92.

incidents or activities under their jurisdiction or control does not spread beyond the areas where they exercise sovereign rights.

In the context of Article 194(2), the term *activities* mainly refers to the introduction of potentially harmful substances or energy into the marine environment, as expressed in the UNCLOS definition of marine pollution.[661] The provision does not necessarily include an absolute prohibition to introduce such substances into the marine environment. Rather, it obliges states to do their best efforts to ensure no such activities cause *significant* transboundary pollution.[662] Among its procedural aspects, the rule involves an obligation of states to provide necessary information in order to assess the magnitude of transboundary harm and the causal link between a state's activities and the harm.[663]

Article 194 paragraphs 1 and 2 slightly differ in focus and scope: paragraph 1 primarily aims at protecting the marine environment as such, independently from its social or economic value or any human uses. The provision therefore includes in its scope purely domestic pollution, as well as pollution caused to the global commons.[664] By contrast, paragraph 2 arguably protects the interests of states in the first place. It specifically applies to transboundary contexts, in which activities in one state bear the risk of causing damage in another state or in an area beyond national jurisdiction. With regard to damages caused to other states, it might be argued that the norm is mainly bilateral in scope. Yet, in cases of damage caused to the environment of the high seas or the deep seabed, remedy must be open to third states. In this specific regard, the provision is *erga omnes* in character.[665]

661 See 1982 UNCLOS art 1(4). See also Section 2.1.B.ii.1) above.

662 Whether or not transboundary pollution is significant depends on the specific circumstances of a case. According to the ILC, significant harm leads to 'a real detrimental effect' that 'must be susceptible of being measured by factual and objective standards': ILC, 'Draft Articles on Prevention of Transboundary Harm from Hazardous Activities', *Report of the International Law Commission 53th session* (UN Doc A/56/10 ch VE1 2001) article 2 and commentary para 4 at 388. Criteria for determining the threshold of significant harm include the likelihood and severity of harmful effects. Transboundary effects involving serious irreversible impacts on the environment or on human health 'are likely to be *a priori* deemed significantly harmful': Günther Handl, 'Transboundary Impacts' in Daniel Bodansky, Jutta Brunnée and Ellen Hey (eds), *The Oxford Handbook of International Environmental Law* (Oxford University Press 2007) 536.

663 Handl, 'Transboundary Impacts' (n 662) 535–36.

664 See Birnie, Boyle and Redgwell (n 488) 129; Sadeleer (n 447) 64; Sands and Peel (n 447) 201.

665 See Jonathan I Charney, 'Third State Remedies for Environmental Damage to the World's Common Spaces' in Fancesco Francioni and Tullio Scovazzi (eds), *International*

The prescribed measures have to deal with all sources of pollution of the marine environment and to be designed to minimize to the fullest possible extent the release of toxic or harmful substances from land-based sources, from and through the atmosphere or by dumping, as well as pollution from vessels, mining installations or other installations at sea (paragraph 3). The measures taken in accordance with Article 194 must not unjustifiably interfere with other lawful activities in the marine environment (paragraph 4). The protection and preservation of 'rare or fragile ecosystems as well as the habitat of depleted, threatened or endangered species and other forms of marine life' is given special attention (paragraph 5).

Article 195 provides that in taking measures to prevent, reduce and control pollution of the marine environment, states have to make sure 'not to transfer [...] damage or hazards from one area to another or transform one type of pollution into another'. Also, states have to prevent, reduce and control pollution resulting from the use of technology or the introduction of new or alien species into parts of the marine environment (Article 196).

Sections 2–11 of UNCLOS Part XII contain more specific obligations that form part of the duty to protect and preserve the marine environment. Part XII Sections 5 and 6 specify the obligation of states to take and enforce measures (especially laws and regulations) to prevent, reduce and control pollution of the marine environment from all different sources, including land-based. The two sections also address policy harmonization, as well as the establishment and implementation of global and regional rules and standards. Similarly important are the duties of states to cooperate as expressed in Part XII Section 2, as well as the duties related to technical assistance (Section 3), monitoring and assessment (Section 4), liability (Section 9) and compliance with other rules of international law (Section 11). These specific obligations are discussed in Subsection 3) below.

b) Systemic Integration and the Interpretation of Part XII: a Case Law Study

In the *South China Sea* Arbitration, the arbitral tribunal examined China's compliance with its general duties under Part XII of the convention. It found that China breached its obligations under Article 192 and other provisions because of harmful fishing practices, harvesting of endangered species and the destruction of coral reefs through unsustainable artificial island building.[666] In

---

Responsibility for Environmental Harm (Graham & Trotman/Martinus Nijhoff 1991) 165–66. See also Section 2.1.B.iii below.

666 *South China Sea Arbitration* (n 584) 384 paras 964 and 966, as well as 394 para 983.

its analysis, the tribunal observed that the proper content of the obligation to protect and preserve the marine environment is 'informed by the other provisions of Part XII and *other applicable rules of international law*'.[667]

The tribunal's reference to other rules of international law in the interpretation and application of Article 192 conforms to a perceptible preference in international litigation of what has been called an integrated conception of international law over a fragmented one.[668] It also conforms to the principle of systemic integration.[669] According to the principle of systemic integration, international law obligations, whether treaty-based or other, form part of 'some coherent and meaningful whole', which is why they must be 'applied and interpreted against the background of the general principles of international law'.[670] The same principle suggests that 'customary law, general principles of law and general treaty provisions form the interpretative background for specific treaty provisions' and must be taken into account as such.[671] Practical examples in which courts and tribunals refer to general norms of contemporary international law in the interpretation of specific treaty provisions, and environmental obligations in particular, are manifold.[672]

---

667 ibid 373 para 941 (emphasis added).

668 Alan E Boyle, 'Relationship between International Environmental Law and Other Branches of International Law' in Daniel Bodansky, Jutta Brunnée and Ellen Hey (eds), *The Oxford Handbook of International Environmental Law* (Oxford University Press 2007) 128. On fragmentation and coherence in international law, see ILC, 'Fragmentation Report' (n 653); Joost Pauwelyn, *Conflict of Norms in Public International Law: How WTO Law Relates to Other Rules of International Law* (Cambridge University Press 2003); Philippe Sands, 'Sustainable Development: Treaty, Custom, and the Cross-Fertilization of International Law' in Alan Boyle and David Freestone (eds), *International Law and Sustainable Development: Past Achievements and Future Challenges* (Oxford University Press 1999); Bruno Simma, 'Universality of International Law from the Perspective of a Practitioner' (2009) 20 European Journal of International Law 265.

669 See, in general, ILC, 'Fragmentation Report' (n 653) ch F; Campbell McLachlan, 'The Principle of Systemic Integration and Article 31(3)(c) of the Vienna Convention' (2005) 54 International and Comparative Law Quarterly 279.

670 Arnold Duncan McNair, *The Law of Treaties* (2nd edn, Clarendon Press 1961) 466, as cited in ILC, 'Fragmentation Report' (n 653) 208 para 414. In an award of 1928, the arbitral tribunal nicely held that: 'Every international convention must be deemed tacitly to refer to general principles of international law for all questions which it does not itself resolve in express terms and in a different way': *Georges Pinson Case* (*France v United Mexican States*) [1928] Arbitral Award 5 RIAA 327 422. See also Alan Boyle and Christine Chinkin, *The Making of International Law* (OUP Oxford 2007) 244–46; McLachlan (n 669) 280.

671 ILC, 'Fragmentation Report' (n 653) 211 para 421.

672 See, for instance, *United States – Standards for Reformulated and Conventional Gasoline* (*US Gasoline*) [1996] Appellate Body Report WT/DS2/AB/R 17; *European Communities – Measures Concerning Meat and Meat Products* (*Hormones*) (*EC Hormones*) [1998] Appellate

Courts and tribunals do, however, not only refer to general international law when interpreting specific rules and norms: in order to avoid potential conflicts of norms and ensure coherence between different legal obligations, they also often take account of other treaties and instruments applicable to the parties.[673] The practice of placing a treaty into its legal environment accords with the principle of systemic integration and its specific reflection in Article 31(3)(c) of the Vienna Convention on the Law of Treaties (VCLT). The article depicts a general rule of interpretation and provides that in the interpretation of a treaty instrument, 'any relevant rules of international law applicable in the relations between the parties' shall be taken into account. While the exact substantive and temporal scope of the rule is unclear and disputed, it clearly implies that courts and tribunals must interpret and apply a treaty in its relationship to its normative environment, even with regard to instruments over which they may not have jurisdiction in the respective case.[674] In other words, systemic integration forms a mandatory part of the interpretation process related to norms and rules of international law.

The link to external sources, both general and specific, may be particularly useful for clarifying the ordinary meaning of terms used in a treaty and determining their object and purpose. It may provide evidence of what might be a common understanding by the parties. Instruments may be relevant in this regard even when they were adopted after the treaty the provisions of which are to be interpreted.[675] This is especially true with respect to terms that are *evolutionary* in nature (that is, terms which the parties to the treaty did not intend 'to have a fixed content regardless of the subsequent evolution of international law').[676] In such cases, the legal environment to be considered is the one that exists at the time of application, not at the time of adoption of the treaty. In this way, progressive developments can be taken into account. Evolutionary terms are common in provisions related to the protection of the

---

Body Report WT/DS26/AB/R 47–8 paras 123–25; *Case Concerning Oil Platforms (Islamic republic of Iran v United States of America), Judgment* [2003] ICJ Rep 2003 161 182 para 41. Some examples of environmental cases will be discussed below.

673 In an 1971 case, the ICJ held that treaties are to be 'interpreted and applied within the framework of the entire legal system prevailing at the time of the interpretation': *Legal Consequences for States of the Continued Presence of South Africa in Namibia (South West Africa) Notwithstanding Security Council Resolution 276 (1970), Advirory Opinion* [1971] ICJ Rep 1971 16 31 para 53.

674 See ILC, 'Fragmentation Report' (n 653) 212–13 para 423.

675 For more information about the issue of inter-temporality, see ILC, 'Fragmentation Report' (n 653) 240–43 paras 475–78.

676 *Aegean Sea Continental Shelf, Judgment* [1978] ICJ Rep 1978 3 32 para 77.

environment. This is a dynamic field of regulation, as environmental concerns have been increasing and new scientific insights are provided at a fast pace.[677] The regulatory density in this field has been increasing accordingly. Newer and more specific instruments may thus offer valuable clues to a meaningful and coherent interpretation of a term – one that reflects contemporary common values and the latest stage of scientific knowledge.[678]

Reference to General Norms of International Environmental Law in Legal Practice

Without mentioning the principle of systemic integration in explicit terms, the International Court of Justice (ICJ) repeatedly referred to general norms of contemporary international law in its interpretation even of old treaties. Two of the Court's decisions are particularly interesting in this respect:

The *Pulp Mills Case* was decided in 2010 and deals with an environmental dispute between Argentina and Uruguay. In the case, Argentina claimed that the authorization and construction of two pulp mills by Uruguay on the banks of a shared watercourse were in violation of a statute that was adopted by the two countries in 1975. In its interpretation of the relevant provisions of the 1975 statute, especially the ones related to the prevention of transboundary pollution, the ICJ widely referred to contemporary rules of international environmental law. It held that the 'obligation to adopt regulatory or administrative measures either individually or jointly and to enforce them is an obligation of conduct',[679] which is generally referred to as an obligation of *due diligence*. The Court made similar observations with regard to the specific obligation under the 1975 statute to prevent pollution and preserve the aquatic environment by prescribing appropriate rules and measures:

677 In a 1997 ruling, the ICJ recalled the dynamic character of the science and law related to the protection of the environment: 'Owing to new scientific insights and to a growing awareness of the risks for mankind [...] new norms and standards have been developed [...]. Such new norms have to be taken into consideration, and such new standards given proper weight, not only when States contemplate new activities but also when continuing with activities begun in the past': *Gabčíkovo-Nagymaros* (n 543) 77–78 para 140. See also the WTO Appellate Body's reference to a number of environmental treaties in its interpretation of the term 'exhaustible natural resources': *United States – Import Prohibition of Certain Shrimp and Shrimp Products* (*US Shrimp*) [1998] Appellate Body Report WT/DS58/AB/R paras 130–31.

678 See ILC, 'Fragmentation Report' (n 653) 211 para 419.

679 *Pulp Mills Judgment* (n 544) 77 para 187 and 79 para 197.

> [It] is an obligation to act with due diligence in respect of all activities which take place under the jurisdiction and control of each party. It is an obligation which entails not only the adoption of appropriate rules and measures, but also a certain level of vigilance in their enforcement and the exercise of administrative control applicable to public and private operators.[680]

The Court recalled that it had recognized the principle of prevention (which it identified as an obligation of due diligence) as a customary rule in an advisory opinion issued in 1996.[681] It further held that the obligation to protect and preserve, as addressed in the statute,

> has to be interpreted in accordance with a practice, which in recent years has gained so much acceptance among States that it may now be considered a requirement under general international law to undertake an *environmental impact assessment* where there is a risk that the proposed industrial activity may have a significant adverse impact in a transboundary context, in particular, on a shared resource.[682]

The Court explained that

> due diligence, and the duty of vigilance and prevention which it implies, would not be considered to have been exercised, if a party [...] did not

680 ibid 79 para 197. See also *Fisheries Advisory Opinion* (n 584) 38 para 131; *South China Sea Arbitration* (n 584) 375–76 para 944.

681 *Pulp Mills Judgment* (n 544) 55–56 para 101 and 78 para 193. See *Legality of the Threat or Use of Nuclear Weapons in Armed Conflict, Advisory Opinion* [1996] ICJ Rep 1996 226 242 para 29. See also *Iron Rhine Arbitration* (n 547) 66–67 para 59. The principle of prevention, which is also reflected in UNCLOS art 194(2), is expressed in Stockholm Principle 21 and Rio Principle 2, and has been repeatedly stressed by the General Assembly: e.g. UNGA Res 2995 (XXVII) (1972), 'Co-Operation between States in the Field of the Environment' para 1; UNGA Res 3281 (XXIX) (1974), 'Charter of Economic Rights and Duties of States' art 30. The rule has also been embedded in a number of international environmental treaties, such as in 1992 CBD art 3.

682 *Pulp Mills Judgment* (n 544) 83 para 204 (emphasis added). See also Argumentation by New Zealand in *Request for an Examination of the Situation in Accordance with Paragraph 63 of the Court's Judgment of 20 December 1974 in the Nuclear Tests (New Zealand v France) Case* [1995] ICJ Rep 1995 288; *Request for an Examination of the Situation, Dissenting Opinion of Judge Weeramantry* [1995] ICJ Rep 1995 312 344–45; *Gabčíkovo-Nagymaros* (n 543) 77–78 paras 139–41; *Gabčíkovo-Nagymaros Project (Hungary v. Slovakia), Separate Opinion of Vice-President Weeramantry* (n 544) 111–13. See also Handl, 'Transboundary Impacts' (n 662) 541.

> undertake an environmental impact assessment on the potential effects of such works.[683]

Finally, the ICJ acknowledged that the *precautionary approach* might be relevant in the interpretation and application of the provisions of the statute, even though this would not necessarily imply a reversal of the burden of proof.[684] While in the judgment, the ICJ does not discuss it further, reference to the precautionary principle or approach is common in international and regional environmental treaties and other instruments. The most prominent reference may be found in the 1992 Rio Declaration on Environment and Development: Rio Principle 15 provides that in the event of threats of serious or irreversible damage, 'lack of full scientific certainty shall not be used as a reason for postponing cost-effective measures to prevent environmental degradation'. Rio Principle 15 also requires states to apply the precautionary approach widely according to their capabilities.

The *Pulp Mills* ruling suggests that today, *due diligence* with regard to the prevention of transboundary harm, the undertaking of *environmental impact assessment* and *precaution* form important elements of duties related to the protection of the environment and the sustainable management of shared resources. The Court's findings in the case are highly relevant for the interpretation of UNCLOS Part XII, as the obligation to protect and preserve the marine environment is inextricably linked with the principle of prevention. It notably includes the obligation to adopt 'regulatory or administrative measures', which the Court identified as an obligation of due diligence that implies, as the case may be, an obligation to undertake environmental impact assessment and to adopt precautionary measures.

The ICJ confirmed the conclusions reached in its *Pulp Mills* judgment in two cases between Nicaragua and Costa Rica that were jointly decided in 2015. In the *Nicaragua/Costa Rica* Cases, both applicants claimed that their respective neighbour state had violated international environmental law (Nicaragua by dredging of the San Juan River, Costa Rica by carrying out major route construction works along the same river). The parties accused each other of a breach of procedural and substantive obligations related to the prevention of significant transboundary environmental harm. The Court observed in this respect that

683 *Pulp Mills Judgment* (n 544) 83 para 204.

684 ibid 71 para 164.

> the fact that the 1858 Treaty may contain limited obligations concerning notification or consultation in specific situations does not exclude any other procedural obligations with regard to transboundary harm which may exist in treaty or customary international law.

In this vein, the Court addressed the procedural obligations to carry out an environmental impact assessment and to notify and consult, all of which were identified as customary rules. It also addressed the substantial obligation not to cause significant transboundary harm. Paraphrasing the *Pulp Mills* judgment, the ICJ described the latter as an obligation not of result but of due diligence, namely the obligation of a state 'to use all the means at its disposal in order to avoid activities which take place in its territory, or in any area under its jurisdiction, causing significant damage to the environment of another State'.[685] The Court also explained that the obligation to undertake environmental impact assessments is not confined in its scope to industrial activities (as the wording in *Pulp Mills* might suggest) but 'applies generally to proposed activities which may have a significant adverse impact in a transboundary context'. It concluded in this respect that

> to fulfil its obligation to exercise due diligence in preventing significant transboundary environmental harm, a State must, before embarking on an activity having the potential adversely to affect the environment of another State, ascertain if there is a risk of significant transboundary harm, which would trigger the requirement to carry out an environmental impact assessment.[686]

The findings by the ICJ have been supported and confirmed by other tribunals, including in maritime contexts: in an advisory opinion issued in 2011, the ITLOS Seabed Disputes Chamber identified due diligence, environmental impact assessment and precaution as important elements for the discharge of UNCLOS Part XI obligations. The advisory opinion was rendered at the request of the Council of the International Seabed Authority in response to three questions related to the legal responsibilities and obligations of states under UNCLOS and its implementing agreement with respect to the sponsorship

685 *Certain Activities Carried Out by Nicaragua in the Border Area* (*Costa Rica v Nicaragua*) *and Construction of a Road in Costa Rica Along the San Juan River* (*Nicaragua v Costa Rica*) [2015] ICJ General List Nos 150 and 152 45 para 104.

686 ibid 45 para 104.

of activities in the Area. In this context, the Chamber found that the obligation 'to ensure' – to which it also referred as an obligation 'of conduct' and of 'due diligence' – is an obligation 'to deploy adequate means, to exercise best possible efforts, to do the utmost, to obtain this result'.[687] As an example of such an obligation of due diligence, the tribunal explicitly referred to UNCLOS Article 194(2).[688] It moreover noted that 'the obligation to conduct an environmental impact assessment is a direct obligation under the [Law of the Sea] Convention and a general obligation under customary international law'.[689]

In its general observations on due diligence and environmental impact assessment, the Seabed Disputes Chamber closely followed the ICJ's main argument in *Pulp Mills* and the comments by the International Law Commission (ILC) in its 2001 Draft Articles on Prevention of Transboundary Harm from Hazardous Activities.[690] With regard to the content of due diligence, the Chamber went an important step further by asserting that the *precautionary approach* formed an integral part of due diligence obligations. It explained that the due diligence obligation to prevent damage also applied 'in situations where scientific evidence concerning the scope and potential negative impact of the activity in question is insufficient but where there are plausible indications of potential risks'.[691] It specifically pointed out that a disregard of these risks would amount to a failure to comply with the precautionary approach and the obligation of due diligence. In the view of the Chamber, Rio Principle 15 and reference to it

687 *Responsibilities of States in the Area* (n 647) 34 para 110.

688 ibid 35 para 13.

689 ibid 44 para 145. See also *The MOX Plant Case (Ireland v United Kingdom), Provisional Measures* [2001] ITLOS case No. 10 para 84; *Case Concerning Land Reclamation by Singapore in and Around the Straits of Johor (Malaysia v, Singapore), Provisional Measures* [2003] ITLOS case No. 12 para 99; *South China Sea Arbitration* (n 584) 377 para 948.

690 In its comments, the ILC held that:

> The obligation of the State of origin to take preventive or minimization measures is one of due diligence. It is the conduct of the State of origin that will determine whether the State has complied with its obligation under the present articles. [...] the State of origin is required [...] to exert its best possible efforts to minimize the risk. In this sense it does not guarantee that the harm would not occur:

ILC, '2001 ILC Draft Articles on Prevention of Transboundary Harm' (n 662) 391–92 para 7. See also Alan E Boyle, 'Codification of International Environmental Law and the International Law Commission: Injurious Consequences Revisited' in Alan Boyle and David Freestone (eds), *International Law and Sustainable Development: Past Achievements and Future Challenges* (Oxford University Press 1999) 76; Sadeleer (n 447) 63.

691 *Responsibilities of States in the Area* (n 647) 40 para 131. See also *Southern Bluefin Tuna Cases* (n 584) paras 77–80.

in a growing number of international treaties reflect 'a trend towards making this approach part of customary international law'.[692]

Valuable clues about the interpretation of UNCLOS Part XII are offered by the *South China Sea Arbitration*, a case decided by an arbitral tribunal in 2016. The case is outstanding as it contains a rather detailed analysis of the obligation to protect and preserve the marine environment under UNCLOS. In the case, the Philippines alleged that China violated its obligation to protect and preserve the marine environment by conducting harmful fishing practices and harmful construction activities. In its legal analysis, the tribunal directly drew on the observations by the ICJ in *Pulp Mills* and the Seabed Disputes Chamber in its 2011 advisory opinion.[693] It fully applied the respective conclusions with regard to prevention, due diligence and environmental impact assessment to the obligations under UNCLOS Part XII. By contrast, the tribunal did not have to address questions related to the precautionary approach, considering the amount of scientific evidence that had been provided to it with regard to the devastating and long-lasting effects of the activities by China or under China's control.

---

692 *Responsibilities of States in the Area* (n 647) 41 para 135. In spite of the high number of references to the precautionary principle or approach in international and regional law, its status and meaning are not undisputed. On the one hand, interpretations vary with regard to the exact meaning of the principle or approach: it is, for instance, controversial whether it requires activities and substances susceptible to cause harm to be regulated and possibly prohibited, even where full scientific evidence cannot be provided, or whether preventive actions are merely allowed, but not necessarily requested, in such case. On the other hand, there is some disagreement with regard to its legal nature: the terms of Rio Principle 15 suggest that it is of obligatory character – a view that is particularly supported by the European Union (which argues that the principle forms part of customary law) but denied by the United States. See *EC Hormones* (n 672) 46ff paras 120–25. Moreover, terminology with regard to the precautionary approach – or principle – is not uniform. Global agreements usually refer to the precautionary approach or, alternatively, precautionary measures: see, for instance, Vienna Convention for the Protection of the Ozone Layer (1985 Vienna Convention) (adopted on 22 March 1985, entered into force on 22 September 1988) 1513 UNTS 323, 26 ILM 1529 (1987) Preamble; Montreal Protocol on Substances that Deplete the Ozone Layer (1987 Montreal Protocol) (adopted on 16 September 1987, entered into force on 1 January 1989, last amended in 1999) 1522 UNTS 3, 26 ILM 1550 (1987) Preamble; 1992 OSPAR Convention art 2(2)(a); 1992 UNFCCC art 3(3); 1996 London Protocol art 3(1); Cartagena Protocol on Biosafety to the Convention on Biological Diversity (Cartagena Protocol) (adopted on 29 January 2000, entered into force on 11 September 2003) 2226 UNTS 208, 39 ILM 1027 (2000) Preamble; 2001 Stockholm POPs Convention art 1. Meanwhile, EU law and European treaties generally refer to the precautionary principle: see, in particular, Consolidated Version of the Treaty on the Functioning of the European Union (TFEU) [2016] OJ C202/1 art 191(2).

693 See *South China Sea Arbitration* (n 584) 375 para 944.

The tribunal observed that the obligation under Article 192 extended 'both to "protection" of the marine environment from future damage and "preservation" in the sense of maintaining or improving its present condition'.[694] It further noted that the provision entailed 'the positive obligation to take active measures to protect and preserve the marine environment, and [...] the negative obligation not to degrade the marine environment'.[695] It recalled in this regard that 'Articles 192 and 194 set forth obligations not only in relation to activities directly taken by States and their organs, but also in relation to ensuring activities within their jurisdiction and control do not harm the marine environment'.[696] Finally, the tribunal confirmed the importance of cooperation and environmental impact assessment in the context of UNCLOS Article 192 and related obligations. It identified the failure by China to cooperate and to undertake an environmental impact assessment (or to deliver assessment results) with regard to activities that bore an obvious risk of causing significant and harmful effects to the marine environment as a breach of respective obligations.[697]

The Role of Related Treaties on Environmental Protection

In the *Chagos* case, which was decided in 2015, Mauritius challenged the establishment by the United Kingdom of a marine protected area (MPA) around the Chagos Archipelago, sovereignty over which is claimed by both states.[698] The arbitral tribunal analysed the compatibility of the MPA and its establishment with relevant obligations under UNCLOS. The case involved, among other things, a clash of environmental considerations on the one side with social or economic considerations on the other side. Specifically, Mauritius

694 ibid 373 para 941.

695 ibid 373 para 941. The Philippines' allegations with regard to the harmful fishing techniques by vessels flying under Chinese flag fall into the first category: China had a positive obligation to take active measures to protect and preserve the marine environment. In line with the cases discussed above, the tribunal held that beyond the adoption of appropriate rules and measures to prohibit a harmful practice, enforcement of such rules was an indispensable part of the due diligence obligation of states. As China 'must have known of, and deliberately tolerated, and protected the harmful acts', the tribunal found that China breached its obligations under Article 192 of the convention: ibid 383 para 964. China's construction activities on seven reefs, on the other hand, contrasted with China's negative obligation not to degrade the marine environment, as the activities were part of 'an official Chinese policy and program implemented by organs of the Chinese State': ibid 388 para 976.

696 *South China Sea Arbitration* (n 584) 375 para 944.

697 ibid 394–97 paras 984–91.

698 *Chagos Marine Protected Area Arbitration* (n 584).

claimed that the declaration of the MPA infringed on Mauritian fishing rights in the territorial sea. In this respect, the case touched on questions related to the conservation and sustainable use of living resources. The tribunal notably observed that the obligation of the United Kingdom to protect and preserve the marine environment extended to measures focused primarily on conservation and the preservation of ecosystems. As a consequence, the establishment of the MPA could potentially be justified even if Mauritian fishing rights were infringed. The tribunal's assertions illustrate the importance it accords to ecosystem protection and conservational issues. Given the specific situation of the Chagos Archipelago, however, the adoption of a measure such as the declaration of an MPA would have required meaningful consultation and cooperation with Mauritius – a requirement that the United Kingdom failed to fulfil.[699]

The *South China Sea Arbitration* deals with strongly related issues. It is a showcase for systemic integration through a living interpretation and application of UNCLOS Part XII. Although the tribunal did not explicitly refer to Article 31(3)(c) of the Vienna Convention, its interpretation of UNCLOS Articles 192 and 194 was guided and informed by principles and standards as they are defined in other conventions. The tribunal recalled that, in the light of UNCLOS Article 237, the obligation to protect and preserve the marine environment must be interpreted by reference to the subsequent provisions of Part XII and '*to specific obligations set out in other international agreements*'.[700] In line with this observation, the tribunal made full use of such references in its interpretation of the general obligations under Part XII.

The tribunal's examination is remarkable in that it clearly depicts the importance of ecosystem protection, conservation of endangered species and sustainable use of living resources of the sea in the protection and preservation of the marine environment. The tribunal recalled the finding by ITLOS that '[t]he conservation of the living resources of the sea is an element in the protection and preservation of the marine environment'.[701] It gave particular attention to Article 194(5) in this respect. The provision sets out an obligation to take the measures necessary 'to protect and preserve rare or fragile ecosystems as well as the habitat of depleted, threatened or endangered species and other forms of marine life'. According to the tribunal, the wording of this provision confirms that in order to fulfil the obligation to protect and preserve

699 ibid 210–12 paras 537–41.

700 *South China Sea Arbitration* (n 584) 374 para 942 (emphasis added).

701 ibid 380 para 956, citing *Southern Bluefin Tuna Cases* (n 584) 295 para 70.

the marine environment, measures may be required that go beyond simple pollution control.[702]

In order to determine the full scope of Article 194(5) and the terms used therein, the tribunal particularly referred to the Convention on International Trade in Endangered Species of Wild Fauna and Flora (CITES)[703] and the CBD. Specifically, it referred to CBD Article 2 in the determination of what consists a (rare and fragile) ecosystem, and to the CITES annexes with regard to the question whether a targeted species is generally qualified as threatened or endangered.[704] Given the fact that the two instruments are nearly universally ratified (including by China and the Philippines), the tribunal did not find it necessary to analyse whether there is precise congruence between the membership of UNCLOS and these treaties. Instead, it pointed out that CITES and the CBD contain 'internationally accepted definitions' of relevant terms, as well as standards forming 'part of the general corpus of international law that informs the content of Article 192 and 194(5)'.[705]

With due regard to recent developments in international law related to the conservation and sustainable use of living resources, as reflected in the CBD and other instruments, the tribunal gave new emphasis to conservation issues in the interpretation of Article 192. Taking account of the scientific evidence before it, it acknowledged that the duty to protect and preserve the marine environment nowadays necessarily includes the due diligence obligation to prevent the harvesting of species that are 'recognised internationally as being at risk of extinction and requiring international protection', especially in the context of fragile ecosystems. It moreover follows from the tribunal's considerations that harm to the marine environment 'as such' may be sufficient for

702 *South China Sea Arbitration* (n 584) 376 para 945; *Chagos Marine Protected Area Arbitration* (n 584) 211 para 538.

703 Convention on International Trade in Endangered Species of Wild Fauna and Flora (CITES) (adopted on 3 March 1973, entered into force on 1 July 1975, as amended in 1979 and 1983) 993 UNTS 243.

704 The tribunal moreover took notice of references made in the scientific reports before it to the FAO 'Code of Conduct for Responsible Fisheries' (1995). The code supported the reports' findings that the fishing methods applied by Chinese fishing vessels were to be qualified as irresponsible and unsustainable: see *South China Sea Arbitration* (n 584) 386 para 970.

705 *South China Sea Arbitration* (n 584) 376 para 945, and 380 para 956. Informed by these definitions and standards, the tribunal concluded that it had 'no doubt from the scientific evidence before it that the marine environments where the allegedly harmful activities took place [...] constitute "rare or fragile ecosystems"' and that '[t]hey are also the habitats of "depleted, threatened or endangered species"'.

constituting a breach of the obligations under Part XII, regardless of whether any country suffered a measurable loss.[706]

Interim Conclusions

A contemplation of the above-discussed cases provides important guidance on how to interpret and apply UNCLOS Part XII obligations. It also points out the key elements of the obligation to protect and preserve the marine environment. Interpretation of Article 192 and related provisions in the light of contemporary international environmental law strongly suggests that:

- the obligation to protect and preserve the marine environment, as provided by Article 192, is an obligation of *due diligence*, the content of which is informed by the other provisions of Part XII and other applicable rules of international law;
- to fulfil its obligation to exercise due diligence in protecting and preserving the marine environment, a state must ascertain if there is a risk of significant environmental harm related to its planned activities, which would trigger the requirement to carry out an *environmental impact assessment*;
- in cases of scientific uncertainty with regard to the potential negative impact of such activities, *precaution* is an increasingly relevant factor in the determination whether preventive obligations have been duly fulfilled.

The relevant provisions moreover suggest that the obligation to protect and preserve the marine environment is an obligation of conduct, which notably includes:

- the *obligation to take regulatory and other measures* necessary to prevent, reduce and control pollution of the marine environment, as provided by Article 194, with due regard for the *conservation and the preservation of ecosystems* (national implementation);
- the *obligation to cooperate* at different levels of governance and to provide assistance (global and regional cooperation); and
- the *obligation to comply with other conventions* and take the legal environment into account (coherence).

3) *Specific Obligations and Their Relevance to Plastics*

The general duty of states to protect and preserve the marine environment is specified in Part XII Sections 2–11. Elements include the adoption and enforcement of laws and regulations; differential treatment; precaution; monitoring

706 ibid 380–82 paras 956–60.

and environmental impact assessment; global and regional cooperation and technical assistance; and compliance with other conventions.

a) The Adoption and Enforcement of Laws and Regulations

According to Article 194(1), national implementation of the obligation to protect and preserve the marine environment requires the adoption of national measures – legislative, administrative and other – to prevent, reduce and control pollution of the marine environment from any source, including land-based. Rather than specifying the content of the measures to be taken or the precise level of protection to be achieved, UNCLOS uses a mechanism of reference to international standards established in other fora. The rules of reference can be seen as a major strength of the regime. They allow for the incorporation of standards, where they exist, that regulate various aspects of marine pollution, including, for instance, those related to the regulation of hazardous substances, waste disposal or the management of international watercourses.

Prevention, Reduction and Control

Among the threesome of pollution *prevention*, *reduction* and *control*, prevention seems of paramount importance. It can be seen as a primary duty under UNCLOS Part XII.[707] While there evidently is a partial overlap in meaning with respect to the three terms, pollution *prevention* clearly refers to source reduction and thus tackles marine pollution at its roots. With regard to plastics, prevention especially encompasses measures related to:

- the sound management of resources and wastes, including waste-reduction measures, improved collection, increasing recycling quantity and quality, safer disposal (no unprotected dumping sites along the coasts etc.);
- sustainable production and consumption, including with regard to consumption rates, especially of single-use plastics and other disposables,

707 In its *Gabčíkovo-Nagymaros Judgment*, the ICJ held that 'in the field of environmental protection, vigilance and prevention are required on account of the often irreversible character of damage to the environment and of the limitations inherent in the very mechanism of reparation of this type of damage': *Gabčíkovo-Nagymaros* (n 543) 78 para 140. See also Ulrich Beyerlin, 'New Developments in the Protection of the Marine Environment: Potential Effects of the Rio Process' (1995) 55 Zeitschrift für ausländisches öffentliches Recht und Völkerrecht 544, 553; Alexandre Kiss and Dinah Shelton, *International Environmental Law* (2nd edn, Transnational Publishers 2000) 263; Sadeleer (n 447) 61–90; Sands and Peel (n 447) 200–03; Edith Brown Weiss and others, *International Environmental Law and Policy* (2nd edn, Aspen Publishers 2007) 257–383.

non-recoverable plastics such as plastic microbeads, non-recyclable compounds, and materials leaking persistent organic pollutants into the soil, water, human body or other environments;
- the safe regulation of chemicals, including persistent organic pollutants and endocrine disruptors in plastics; and
- the regulation of packaging quantity and materials or product designs.

In the event that preventive measures are, for any reason, not reasonable, effective or sufficient, measures must also be taken for pollution reduction and control.[708] Pollution *control* most usually refers to so-called 'end-of-pipe solutions' serving to isolate contaminants from the environment.[709] Control measures are necessary to deal with potentially harmful substances the discharge or release of which can hardly be avoided and that are likely to enter the marine environment in hazardous quantities if not properly controlled. According measures include, for instance, the prescription of filter systems for the removal of plastic particles and, if possible, plastic microfibres, from waste water and sewage.

Pollution *reduction* mainly refers to the reduction of anthropogenic contaminants in the environment through clean-up activities. Reduction measures are necessary with regard to substances that have been introduced into the marine environment in the past and, if not removed, are likely to persist there for an indefinite period of time and cause damage to humans or the environment. The collection of floating or beached plastics would fall under this term.

Some guidance with regard to the measures that states shall take can be found in Part XII Section 5 (international rules and national legislation)[710] and Section 6 (enforcement).[711] In these sections, UNCLOS explicitly distinguishes between five sources of marine pollution: (1) land-based sources; (2) seabed activities;[712] (3) dumping; (4) vessels; and (5) the atmosphere. Part XII

---

708 cf ILC, '2001 ILC Draft Articles on Prevention of Transboundary Harm' (n 662) 390–91 para 3.

709 The concept of pollution control assumes that environmental damage can be avoided by 'controlling the manner, time and rate at which pollutants enter the environment': ILO, 'Chapter 55 – Environmental Pollution Control', *Encyclopaedia of Occupational Health and Safety* (4th edn, ILO 2016) Part VII <https://www.iloencyclopaedia.org/part-vii-86401/environmental-pollution-control> accessed 19 February 2022. See also Vinish Kathuria, 'Pollution: Prevention vs Control: Is EOP Treatment the Solution?' (2001) 36 Economic and Political Weekly 2745, 2747.

710 1982 UNCLOS arts 207–12.

711 ibid arts 213–22.

712 UNCLOS distinguishes between seabed activities subject to national jurisdiction and activities in the Area.

Sections 5 and 6 contain specific provisions for each of these types of sources and thus add more detail to the general provision of Article 194. The provisions reflect Rio Principle 11, expressing the duty of states to enact effective environmental legislation.[713]

General Mechanism of Reference

The convention does not specify the content of the laws and regulations to be adopted by states, or define any minimum level of protection that states should apply. In particular, it does not include a list of prohibited substances.[714] Instead, the convention refers to relevant 'internationally agreed rules, standards and recommended practices and procedures' that may contain more specific requirements with regard to the content of the measures to be taken and the level of protection to be applied. In this respect, the provisions, especially of Section 5, are unconventional in that they define the relations between national laws and regulations on the one hand and international 'rules, standards and recommended practices and procedures' on the other hand. Specifically, the provisions lay down the degree of conformity with the international rules and standards required on the national level.[715]

Specifications with regard to the national measures and their relation to international rules and standards vary according to the type of pollution sources. The differences are especially due to non-uniform language with regard to the reference to international standards: for most sources, including seabed activities, dumping and vessel-based pollution, clear preference is given to internationally agreed rules and standards.[716] The preference is reflected in three aspects:

1. States have to *establish* global and regional rules and standards to prevent, reduce and control pollution of the marine environment from seabed activities or vessels.[717]

---

713 1982 UNCLOS arts 207(1–2); 208(1–2); 209(2); 210(1–2); 211(2) and (4); 212(1–2).

714 UNCLOS has been criticized for its failure to set concrete standards and because it does not contain any concrete provisions with regard to the actual reduction in pollution levels: see Boyle, 'Marine Pollution under the Law of the Sea Convention' (n 581) 353–55; Hassan (n 364) 5 and 82–83; Qing-Nan (n 643) 103–05; Diana L Torrens, 'Protection of the Marine Environment in International Law: Toward an Effective Regime of the Law of the Sea' (1994) 19 Queens Law Journal 613, 625; VanderZwaag and Powers (n 462) 425; Yankov (n 454) 281.

715 Nordquist, Rosenne and Yankov (n 585) 65.

716 See Boyle, 'Marine Pollution under the Law of the Sea Convention' (n 581) 352.

717 1982 UNCLOS arts 208(5) and 211(1).

2. States have to *adhere to the international rules and standards* in the adoption of national legislation and other measures.[718]
3. States have to adopt laws and regulations and take other measures necessary to *implement* and *enforce* applicable international rules and standards established through competent international organizations or diplomatic conference to prevent, reduce and control pollution of the marine environment from these sources.[719]

With this mechanism, UNCLOS incorporates international standards that were agreed under the auspices of competent organizations, for instance the International Maritime Organization (IMO),[720] or within other fora. These standards serve as minimum standards, while allowing states to choose a higher level of protection, with stricter standards.[721] One of the strengths of the use of reference standards is that the regime can evolve more easily, as

---

718 With regard to seabed activities, such laws, regulations and measures 'shall be no less effective than international rules, standards and recommended practices and procedures': UNCLOS arts 208(3) (pollution from seabed activities subject to national jurisdiction) and 209(2) (pollution from seabed activities in the Area). With regard to dumping, they 'shall be no less effective in preventing, reducing and controlling such pollution than the global rules and standards': UNCLOS art 210(6). Regulation of pollution from vessels by the flag state 'shall at least have the same effect as that of generally accepted international rules and standards established through the competent international organization or general diplomatic conference': UNCLOS art 211(2).

719 1982 UNCLOS arts 214, 216(1) and 217(1).

720 The IMO (originally called the Inter-Governmental Maritime Consultative Organization) was created in 1948 by the UN Maritime Conference in Geneva. IMO is a specialized agency of the UN responsible for global standard-setting in the field of maritime safety and security, and of environmental performance of international shipping. In 1975, the IMO Marine Environment Protection Committee (MEPC) was formed. Conventions concluded under the auspices of or administered by IMO include: 1969/92 CLC; 1969 INTERVENTION; International Convention on the Establishment of an International Fund for Compensation for Oil Pollution Damage (adopted on 18 December 1971, entered into force on 16 October 1978, ceased to be in force from 24 May 2002), superseded by its 1992 Protocol (1992 FUND) (adopted on 27 November 1992, entered into force on 30 May 1996); 1972 London Dumping Convention; 1996 London Protocol; 1973/78 MARPOL; 1990 OPRC; Protocol on Preparedness, Response and Co-operation to Pollution Incidents by Hazardous and Noxious Substances (2000 OPRC-HNS Protocol) (adopted on 15 March 2000, entered into force on 14 June 2007); International Convention on the Control of Harmful Anti-fouling Systems on Ships (2001 AFS) (adopted on 5 October 2001, entered into force on 17 September 2008); International Convention on Liability and Compensation for Damage in Connection with the Carriage of Hazardous and Noxious Substances by Sea (HNS) (adopted on 3 May 1996, not in force) superseded by its 2010 Protocol (adopted on 30 April 2010, not yet in force).

721 Coastal states are generally bound to international standards and may only be allowed to adopt stricter standards under restrictive conditions: 1982 UNCLOS art 211(5) and (6).

standards can be re-examined and regularly adjusted to changing conditions, including knowledge increase or technological developments. The mechanism of incorporation by reference thus allows for a more dynamic evolution of the regime. It is also crucial for the convention's role as a global framework on marine environmental protection. At the same time, the UNCLOS system promotes a minimum harmonization of rules with regard to these pollution sources at the international level: through their incorporation by UNCLOS, standards such as contained in the annexes to MARPOL[722] or the London

722 MARPOL is one of the key conventions for the protection of the marine environment from sea-based sources of marine plastic debris. The instrument covers pollution arising from the normal operation of ships and, to a more limited extent, from accidental loss. It was adopted in 1973 and was substantially amended by its 1978 protocol before entering into force. MARPOL currently includes six annexes providing for technical regulations on the prevention of pollution by oil, noxious liquid substances in bulk, harmful substances in packaged form, sewage from ships, garbage from ships, and air pollution, respectively. Annex V, which came into force on 31 December 1988 and was substantially revised in 2013, regulates the prevention of pollution by garbage from ships. It prohibits discharge of all garbage into the sea, except as provided otherwise in the Annex. The disposal of plastics at sea – irrespective of the type of plastic and the region of the sea – is strictly prohibited by Annex V (reg 3(2)). The disposal is exceptionally permitted if it is deemed 'necessary for the purpose of securing the safety of a ship and those on board or saving life at sea' or in the event of damage to a ship (reg 7(1.1–1.2)). Accidental loss of synthetic fishing nets is not covered if 'all reasonable precautions have been taken to prevent such loss' (reg 7(1.3)). Parties to Annex V must provide garbage receptacles at their ports in order for ships to dispose of their garbage in a sound manner when entering a port (reg 8). It is mainly incumbent on the state a ship is registered with (flag state) to ensure the ship's compliance with MARPOL standards. For this purpose, it has to enact domestic laws and implementing regulations and to set in place a certification and control system. As of September 2021, MARPOL Annex V has been ratified by 155 countries the combined merchant fleets of which constitute approximately 98.5 per cent of the gross tonnage of the world's merchant fleet. For further information on MARPOL 73/78 and its Annex V in particular, including discussions on successes and challenges in enforcement, see, in general, Rebecca Becker, 'MARPOL 73/78: An Overview in International Environmental Enforcement' (1998) 10 Georgetown International Environmental Law Review 625; Jeff B Curtis, 'Vessel-Source Oil Pollution and MARPOL 73/78: An International Success Story' (1984) 15 Envtl. L. 679; Andrew Griffin, 'MARPOL 73/78 and Vessel Pollution: A Glass Half Full or Half Empty?' (1994) 1 Indiana Journal of Global Legal Studies 489; Paul E Hagen, 'International Community Confronts Plastics Polluting from Ships: MARPOL Annex V and the Problem That Won't Go Away' (1990) 5 Am. UJ Int'l L. & Pol'y 425; John R Henderson, 'A Pre- and Post-MARPOL Annex V Summary of Hawaiian Monk Seal Entanglements and Marine Debris Accumulation in the Northwestern Hawaiian Islands, 1982–1998' (2001) 42 Marine Pollution Bulletin 584; Bruce S Maheim Jr, 'Annex V of the MARPOL Convention: Will It Stop Marine Plastic Pollution?' (1988) 1 Georgetown International Environmental Law Review 71; Gerard Peet, 'The MARPOL Convention: Implementation and Effectiveness' (1992) 7 Int'l J. Estuarine

Dumping Convention[723] can possibly become binding on states that have never ratified these conventions. System wide and consistent application within the UNCLOS regime may provide a basis for their customary status.[724]

The Particular Case of Land-based Pollution Sources

With respect to land-based pollution sources, the wording is weaker. Article 207(1) provides that

> States shall adopt laws and regulations to prevent, reduce and control pollution of the marine environment from land-based sources, including rivers, estuaries, pipelines and outfall structures, *taking into account*

& Coastal L. 277; Andrew Rakestraw, 'Open Oceans and Marine Debris: Solutions for the Ineffective Enforcement of MARPOL Annex V' (2012) 35 Hastings Int'l & Comp. L. Rev. 383.

723 The London Dumping Convention and its 1996 Protocol address the prevention of marine pollution by dumping at sea. For the purposes of the convention, dumping is defined as 'any deliberate disposal at sea of wastes or other matter from vessels, aircraft, platforms or other man-made structures at sea', as well as 'any deliberate disposal at sea of vessels, aircraft, platforms or other man-made structures at sea' (art 3(1)(a) of the Convention). Parties to the convention and the protocol are obliged to prohibit dumping into the sea of any wastes or other matter (except for a limited number of clearly defined substances, the dumping of which requires a permit) and the incineration at sea of waste or other matter (London Protocol art 4–5 and Annex 1). Dumping and incineration of plastic wastes is prohibited; respective permits are not envisaged. The objective of the protocol not only includes pollution prevention, but also the elimination of pollution caused by dumping or incineration at sea to the maximum practicable extent (London Protocol art 2). The protocol obliges states to apply a precautionary approach and the polluter-pays principle (London Protocol art 3(1–2)). It moreover urges parties to control dumping of wastes and other matter from vessels and aircraft in internal waters at their 'discretion' (London Protocol art 7(2)). While both the convention and the protocol call for parties to protect and preserve the marine environment from all sources of pollution, they do not contain any specific obligations with regard to land-based pollution sources. Rather, internal waters and watersheds are excluded explicitly from the definition of 'sea' for the purposes of the convention and the protocol. Major land-based pollution sources such as industrial discharges into rivers do, thus, not fall into the scope of the London dumping regime. As of September 2021, 87 countries had ratified the London Convention and 53 countries had ratified its protocol.

724 See IMO, 'Implications of the United Nations Convention on the Law of the Sea for the International Maritime Organization' (2014) LEG/MISC/8 10–12. See also Birnie, Boyle and Redgwell (n 488) 150 and 404; Boyle, 'Marine Pollution under the Law of the Sea Convention' (n 581) 356; Rothwell and Stephens (n 364) 372; Tanaka, *International Law of the Sea* (n 360) 277.

internationally agreed rules, standards and recommended practices and procedures'.[725]

States shall moreover take 'other measures as may be necessary to prevent, reduce and control such pollution'[726] and 'endeavour to harmonize their policies in this connection at the appropriate regional level'.[727] States do not have a strict obligation to establish global rules, standards and recommended practices but shall *endeavour* to establish them, 'taking into account characteristic regional features, the economic capacity of developing States and their need for economic development'. Such rules, standards and recommended practices and procedures shall be re-examined from time to time as necessary.[728] Similar wording was used with regard to pollution from atmospheric sources, though without reference to different capacities and re-examination of standards.[729]

Article 213 finally provides that states shall enforce their laws and regulations adopted in accordance with Article 207 and shall adopt laws and regulations and take other measures necessary for the implementation of relevant international rules and standards.[730] Article 213, like any other provision under Section 6, is subject to the safeguards provisions in Section 7.[731]

The weaker formulation in Article 207 ('taking into account') leaves states wider discretion in national implementation than they have with regard to other sources of pollution, except for atmospheric pollution.[732] It is important to note, however, that the freedom of states in choosing their level of protection is not absolute: the wording of Article 207(1) and related provisions does

725 Emphasis added. An almost identical wording is used in art 23 of the 1997 Watercourses Convention.

726 1982 UNCLOS art 207(2).

727 ibid art 207(3).

728 ibid art 207(4).

729 ibid arts 212 and 222. For more information on the regulation of atmospheric sources under UNCLOS, see James Harrison, 'Pollution of the Marine Envrionment from or Through the Atmosphere' in David Joseph Attard and others (eds), *The IMLI Manual on International Maritime Law Volume III: Marine Environmental Law and International Maritime Security Law* (Oxford University Press 2016).

730 It is not perfectly clear from the text of the provision whether the word *necessary* refers to 'other measures' only or also to 'laws and regulations'. In any case, it plays a double-edged role in this context. It can be interpreted as an (abstract) minimum standard or as a qualifying factor. As an indefinite legal term, it will probably add to the discretionary space of states in the implementation of the provision.

731 Safeguards include, for instance, the principle of non-discrimination (UNCLOS Article 227) and the observance of recognized rights of the accused (UNCLOS art 230).

732 See Nordquist, Rosenne and Yankov (n 585) 132.

not allow states to take no action but obliges them to take preventive and other measures in good faith. Article 207(5) moreover provides that laws and regulations 'shall include those designed to minimize, to the fullest extent possible, the release of toxic, harmful or noxious substances, especially those which are persistent, into the marine environment'. The provision indicates that persistency is an important factor in the classification of substances, and in the determination of toxic, harmful or noxious substances in particular. Plastics are clearly covered by the provision, given their harmful effect on marine life and ecosystems, their tendency to contain or accumulate pollutants and their high degree of bioinertness and persistence.

The difference in reference and the greater leeway given to states with respect to land-based sources might be due to the fact that at the time when UNCLOS was negotiated and adopted, no agreement had been reached yet on how to best address land-based sources of marine pollution. The reasons are manyfold:

- *Low awareness:* The first global scientific assessment on the effects of specific substances on the marine environment was published in 1982.[733] The significance of land-based pollution was only recognized in the 1990 report.[734] Awareness of the scale of negative impacts of marine plastic debris and their relation to land-based activities is much more recent. The global character of marine plastic pollution had not yet been recognized when UNCLOS was adopted.
- *Complexity:* Land-based pollution involves a high number of substances, actors and activities, which implies complex policy choices. This is true for plastics, too: the materials are used in nearly all industry sectors and for a broad range of social activities. Actors involved in the life cycle of plastics range from the petrochemical industry to machine manufacturers, recyclers and waste management companies.
- *Regional differences:* Policy preferences highly depend on the geographic, ecological and economic situation of a state. A low level of development and high poverty are restraining factors in the adoption and implementation of effective environmental regulation. If not strongly incentivized, concerned countries might not readily engage in the development of high international standards.[735]

733 GESAMP, 'The Review of the Health of the Oceans' (UNESCO 1982) Reports and Studies No 15.

734 GESAMP, 'The State of the Marine Environment' (n 283) para 16. See also Yankov (n 454) 281.

735 See Tanaka, *International Law of the Sea* (n 360) 280–81.

- *Economic concerns and national sovereignty:* Finally, international regulation of land-based pollution sources, and the development of a respective legal framework, has long been hampered by fears of interference in domestic affairs and of inhibiting effects on industrial development. The regulation of relevant sectors, including industry, agriculture, forestry and household, is a most sensitive issue, which is often put under the protective shell of national sovereignty.[736] Under UNCLOS, land-based pollution sources and pathways, 'including rivers, estuaries, pipelines and outfall structures'[737] fall within the exclusive jurisdiction of the coastal state.[738]

States remained reluctant to regulate land-based sources even after the adoption of UNCLOS. No such reluctance existed with regard to dumping at sea or vessel-based pollution: regulation in this aera developed at a much faster pace, especially under the auspices of IMO.[739] Unlike for other pollution sources, UNCLOS does not impose a hard obligation on states to adopt such standards for land-based sources. To date, therefore, there are largely only non-binding instruments at the global level that deal with prevention and mitigation of land-based sources of pollution – and plastics in particular. Nevertheless, relevant environmental agreements are increasingly including provisions that relate to plastic pollution mitigation, especially in the chemicals and waste sector.[740] Furthermore, in certain marine regions, regional agreements have been adopted that are, in principle, able to specify and supplement the provisions in UNCLOS.

The Role of Regional Rules and Non-binding Instruments

The regime under UNCLOS on land-based sources of pollution thus has two special features: First, with few exceptions, there is a lack of global, legally binding plastics-specific rules and standards. Existing instruments are mostly non-binding or regional in character. In this context, the question arises whether

736 See, for instance, Hassan (n 364) 40. For relevant discussions in the negotiation history of UNCLOS see Boyle, 'Marine Pollution under the Law of the Sea Convention' (n 581) 354.

737 1982 UNCLOS art 207(1).

738 See Yankov (n 454) 280.

739 Arguably, a need for cooperation is more obvious in these fields, because pollution by dumping and accidental or operational discharge from vessels often involves legislative or enforcement jurisdiction of two or more states, namely the state a vessel is registered with (flag state) and the states that exercise territorial jurisdiction over areas (coastal state) and ports (port state) entered by the vessel: see 1982 UNCLOS arts 210(5); 211(2–6); 216(1); 217; 220.

740 See Section 2.1.D.ii below.

such instruments are covered by Articles 207 and 213 at all. Secondly, the reference to these instruments is weaker, at least in Article 207. This raises the question of whether there is a difference in impact when compared to other pollution sources.

Article 207 seems to take account of a broad range of instruments by referring to 'internationally agreed rules, standards and recommended practices and procedures'. The list clearly covers regional conventions on the protection and preservation of the marine environment and their protocols on land-based sources. Article 207(4) particularly refers to the establishment of regional rules and standards and allows states to take into account characteristic regional features. Regional rules and standards are thus meant to be taken into account by the states concerned.[741] If such rules provide suitable solutions for other regions, too, respective countries may well take them into consideration. The more regions share a specific approach to land-based sources and enshrined it in a convention or protocol, the more the respective rules must be considered to be internationally agreed in the sense of UNCLOS Article 207(1).[742]

The list of instruments in Article 207 potentially also covers non-binding instruments, including Chapter 17 of Agenda 21, the GPA, the Honolulu Strategy and SDG 14.[743] In Article 213, on the other hand, a more restrictive formulation

741 In view of the references made in UNCLOS to regional cooperation, regional agreements may be seen as instruments covered by VCLT Article 31(2)(b) and are thus relevant to the interpretation of UNCLOS Part XII. Article 31(2)(b) 1969 VCLT reads as follows: 'The context for the purpose of the interpretation of a treaty shall comprise, in addition to the text, including its preamble and annexes: [...] Any instrument which was made by one or more parties in connexion with the conclusion of the treaty and accepted by the other parties as an instrument related to the treaty'.

742 Widespread ratification or acceptance might be a relevant criterion for a rule or standard to be considered internationally agreed: see discussion in Boyle, 'Marine Pollution under the Law of the Sea Convention' (n 581) 355–56.

743 Agenda 21 and the SDGs are outcomes of global summits and thus clearly fulfil the criteria of 'internationally agreed'. The same is true for the GPA, which was adopted by 108 countries and has been broadly supported and repeatedly highlighted by General Assembly resolutions and other documents, including the 'Montreal Declaration on the Protection of the Marine Environment from Land-Based Activities' (2001); 'Beijing Declaration on Furthering the Implementation of the Global Programme of Action for the Protection of the Marine Environment from Land-Based Activities' (2006); 'Manila Declaration on Furthering the Implementation of the Global Programme of Action for the Protection of the Marine Environment from Land-Based Activities' (n 495). The qualification of the Honolulu Strategy is less certain, especially in view of the fact that it was never formally agreed on by states but was drafted as a guiding tool for both public and private actors and then launched at a multi-stakeholder event. However, by suggesting a global framework for the prevention and management of marine debris, the Honolulu Strategy is the most concise instrument in response to a problem the severity, scale and acuteness of which

is used. The provision provides that, in order to prevent, reduce and control pollution of the marine environment from land-based sources, states:

> shall adopt laws and regulations and take other measures necessary to implement *applicable* international rules and standards *established through competent international organizations or diplomatic conference*.[744]

The scope of Article 213 is confined to rules and standards and does not, in contrast to Article 207, refer to recommended practices and procedures. This supports a more restrictive interpretation, assuming that instruments that were not intended to be binding on states and have never been formally ratified would fall, if at all, into the category of recommended practices and procedures. Neither Article 213 nor any of the provisions under Section 6 covers this category of instruments. This interpretation finds further support in the fact that Section 6 consistently refers to *applicable* international rules and standards, which seems to confine the scope of the provisions to rules and standards the state concerned is clearly bound to.[745] Reference to *international* rules and standards implies that corresponding rules form part of treaties that have been subject to widespread ratification or are widely accepted as customary rules.[746] Such rules have to be established through either competent international organizations or a diplomatic conference. The term *diplomatic conference* most usually refers to plenipotentiary conferences involving state representatives, which includes UNEA.[747]

The role of standard-setting institutions, especially the IMO (former IMCO), was widely discussed during UNCLOS negotiations.[748] Yet, the *travaux preparatoires* do not provide final clarification with regard to the meaning that was

---

has been increasingly emphasized by the UN General Assembly and other international fora. While it might not formally be covered by Article 207, it is surely relevant in this context and may provide suitable guidance to states in the implementation of their duties.

744 Emphasis added.

745 The UNCLOS *travaux preparatoires* are silent about the exact meaning of the term *applicable* in this context but seem to suggest a restrictive interpretation of the term: see Nordquist, Rosenne and Yankov (n 585) 216 and 220.

746 See discussion in Boyle, 'Marine Pollution under the Law of the Sea Convention' (n 581) 356.

747 See Nordquist, Rosenne and Yankov (n 585) 133.

748 See UN Doc A/CONF.62/C.3/SR.19, '19th Meeting of the Third Committee' in United Nations (ed), *Official Records of the Third United Nations Conference on the Law of the Sea*, vol IV (2009); UN Doc A/CONF.62/C.3/SR.33, '33rd Meeting of the Third Committee' in United Nations (ed), *Official Records of the Third United Nations Conference on the Law of the Sea*, vol VI (2009).

attached to the term 'applicable international rules and standards' by the drafters of the convention. In a case decided in 2014, the ICJ acknowledged that resolutions by the International Whaling Commission (IWC), even though non-binding in nature, may be relevant for the interpretation of the International Convention for the Regulation of Whaling (ICRW)[749] when they were adopted by consensus or by a unanimous vote.[750] The Court also referred to guidelines issued by the commission as a supplementary means of interpretation in order to confirm the meaning it gave to a specific treaty provision.[751] However, the Court rejected Australia's assertion that IWC resolutions lacking the support of some IWC members, especially the defendant party, are to be seen as a subsequent agreement between the parties to the interpretation of the relevant provision, or a subsequent practice establishing such an agreement, within the meaning of VCLT Article 31(3)(a) and (b), respectively.[752] When reversing the Court's argument, VCLT Article 31(3)(a) suggests that non-binding instruments may be relevant for the interpretation of a provision as a 'subsequent agreement between the parties regarding the interpretation of the treaty or the application of its provisions' if it has been supported by all the parties.

In light of these arguments, it can be concluded that:

1. With few exceptions, there is a lack of global binding instruments on land-based pollution sources, and plastic pollution in particular;
2. most of the non-binding instruments are covered by the formulation in Article 207: states are thus obliged to take them into account in the adoption of national measures;
3. non-binding instruments do not generally meet the higher threshold of Article 213: states do therefore not have a strict obligation to adopt the measures necessary to implement them;
4. if, however, the instruments have been endorsed by all the parties, a case can be made for their applicability within the context of VCLT Article 31(3)(a).
5. Regional conventions are covered by both provisions, at least with regard to their parties.

The question of how the weaker wording in Article 207 affects its regulatory content is difficult to assess. Arguably, the combination of the absence of sufficient global rules and standards on land-based sources of marine pollution and

749 International Convention for the Regulation of Whaling (1946 ICRW) (adopted on 2 December 1946, entered into force on 10 November 1948) 161 UNTS 72.

750 *Whaling in the Antarctic* (n 592) 248 para 46.

751 ibid 252 para 58.

752 ibid 257 para 83.

the priority UNCLOS Part XII gives to national regulation in this field results in a regime in which there is little international control with regard to the most problematic type of pollution sources.[753] Only by the incorporation of plastic-specific instruments, whether directly or by reference, the convention can give sufficient guidance on the content of the measures to be taken or the level of protection to be applied. Only plastic-specific instruments can give effective content to the general provisions under Section 1 of Part XII.[754] Without the effective incorporation of such instruments, the regulatory framework with respect to land-based sources is largely confined to customary obligations to which UNCLOS does not add much of substance. At best, UNCLOS promotes the implementation of relevant instruments by its call on states to take them into account in the adoption of national measures. It possibly also promotes harmonization of national rules and policies, even if the convention's actual impact in this regard is difficult to evaluate. Only if the incorporation of specific standards on land-based sources of pollution can be significantly strengthened, either through better implementation or through the further adoption of binding rules, UNCLOS may provide a sufficient framework for the protection of the marine environment from land-based pollution sources or for achieving a sustainable ocean management and the 2030 Agenda for Sustainable Development.

b) Due Diligence and the Differentiation of the Standard of Care

In order to fulfil its obligations under Part XII, a state is obliged to act with due diligence and care. It is required to use 'all the means at its disposal'[755] and 'to exert its best possible efforts to minimize the risk'[756] by applying the degree of care that can be expected of a 'good government'.[757] The concept of due diligence results in a rather wide policy space for states in the choice of their implementing measures.

Variation in the Standard of Care as a Form of Differential Treatment

As due diligence obligations do not require a specific result in the first place but efforts to be taken towards such a result, the concept of due diligence allows for graduation in the scope of effective commitments – or in the standard of

753 See Boyle, 'Marine Pollution under the Law of the Sea Convention' (n 581) 354.

754 See Birnie, Boyle and Redgwell (n 488) 389 and 454; Boyle, 'Marine Pollution under the Law of the Sea Convention' (n 581) 356–57.

755 *Pulp Mills Judgment* (n 544) 45–46 para 101.

756 ILC, '2001 ILC Draft Articles on Prevention of Transboundary Harm' (n 662) 392 para 7.

757 ibid 395 para 17.

care. Graduation in this context means that the degree of expected care, or of what is considered 'reasonably appropriate',[758] depends on the capabilities of the state in question. UNCLOS Article 194(1) directly refers to this characteristic element of due diligence by stipulating that for the purpose of the provision, states should use 'best practicable means at their disposal and *in accordance with their capabilities*'.[759] A state's capabilities with regard to the respective obligation depend on available financial means, technologies and knowhow, but also governance structures and other factors, including policy constraints.[760] Most evidently, states with a well-developed economy, abundant financial and other resources and sound governance structures are expected a higher standard of care than countries under less favourable conditions.[761]

Graduation in the standard of care is a typical feature of due diligence obligations and can be seen as a form of (implicit) differential treatment.[762] Yet, in the context of UNCLOS Article 194, this does not imply that basic implementation is conditional on a certain level of economic development. While the economic level of a state is one of the factors to be taken into account in determining whether the state has complied with its obligation, it cannot be used as an argument to fully exempt a state from the corresponding obligation.[763] Regardless of its level of development, a state is obliged to use available means and infrastructure ('at their disposal') in good faith to control and

758 cf art 4(4) of UNCLOS Annex III.

759 Emphasis added.

760 Policy decisions regarding the allocation of scarce resources in developing countries can entail high opportunity costs with regard to either developmental projects or environmental protection.

761 See ILC, '2001 ILC Draft Articles on Prevention of Transboundary Harm' (n 662) 395 para 17.

762 Differential treatment is a mutually accepted exception to reciprocity in international law with the aim to bring about substantive equality among states instead of formal equality. Differential treatment in the event of unequal factual conditions can foster cooperation and effective action at the international level, as well as facilitate implementation of international law, including multinational environmental agreements. It may consist in positive discrimination (e.g. lower commitments) of disadvantaged states, a redistribution of resources towards such countries or flexibility measures such as different timescales (e.g. longer phase-out periods) for developing states. For more information on differential treatment in international law, see, in general, Philippe Cullet, 'Differential Treatment in International Law: Towards a New Paradigm of Inter-State Relations' (1999) 10 European Journal of International Law 549; Duncan French, 'Developing States and International Environmental Law: The Importance of Differentiated Responsibilities' (2000) 49 International and Comparative Law Quarterly 35.

763 See ILC, '2001 ILC Draft Articles on Prevention of Transboundary Harm' (n 662) 394 para 13.

monitor activities, especially hazardous activities, within its territory or under its control.[764] In doing so, states should use 'the best practicable means', and thus have to take into account scientific and technological advances and keep up with these developments to the best of their ability.[765]

With regard to plastics, the greatest challenge for many countries remains waste collection. If to be provided or supervised by the state, effective waste collection requires a solid infrastructure (including streets, trucks, bins etc.), minimal governance structures and a lot of money. Especially in rural or sparsely populated areas, or in conflict zones, these conditions are hardly met. In some countries, more than half of the wastes therefore remain uncollected.[766] Sorting for recycling and safe disposal are further challenges. The construction and maintenance of both sanitary landfills and incineration plants are costly, which is why most of the wastes are dumped or stored in poorly managed landfills. From there, they easily enter the waterways and marine environments. Poor waste management often comes along with widespread poverty, poor infrastructure, poor sanitation, low education and a wide range of related hurdles that tend to mutually aggravate each other as part of a vicious circle. Given these circumstances, positive change is extremely difficult to achieve. In the context of due diligence, states concerned are not expected to apply the same measures and solutions as high-income countries. However, they have to investigate other solutions more suitable to their case. Such solutions may include the integration of the informal waste picking and recycling sector into the formal economy. It may also include a stricter regulation of plastic materials or specific products at a different stage of their lifecycle, for instance at the stage of production or import, retail or use.

The Role of International Standards

International standards play a crucial role in the determination of the standard of care with respect to a state's duty to take all necessary measures to prevent, control and reduce pollution of the marine environment. According to the ILC, such standards 'constitute a necessary reference point to determine whether measures adopted are suitable'.[767] In the context of graduation and differential treatment, reference standards have to be agreed internationally and cannot solely reflect standards as applied by, for instance, high-income countries. It is acknowledged in Rio Principle 11 that environmental standards, as applied

764 See ibid 395 para 17.

765 See ibid 394 para 11.

766 See Section 1.1.B.ii.1)b) above.

767 ILC, '2001 ILC Draft Articles on Prevention of Transboundary Harm' (n 662) 391 para 4.

by some countries, may be 'inappropriate and of unwarranted economic and social cost' in others.[768] In view of the principle of non-discrimination, countries that choose a high domestic standard are, however, expected to apply it also to their activities abroad or activities with extraterritorial effects.[769]

The development of international standards, and their implementation, forms an integral part of the duty of prevention. It may also be seen as a prerequisite for policy harmonization in this regard, which is requested by UNCLOS Article 194(1). The development of such standards requires mutual support, and support of low-income countries by higher-income countries in particular.[770] Countries will only agree on specific standards if they have, or if they are granted, the means to implement them. Capacity-building schemes and the transfer of technology and financial resources therefore play an important role in the development of uniform standards.

Even if standards are not duly adjusted, changing conditions may influence the degree of expected care. According to the ITLOS, due diligence is 'a variable concept', one which may 'change over time as measures considered sufficiently diligent at a certain moment may become not diligent enough in light, for instance, of new scientific or technological knowledge'.[771] While its responsiveness to changing conditions may be considered an advantage, the concept of due diligence does not provide further guidance with regard to the expected level of protection and the content of the measures to be taken by states.[772] The concept of due diligence cannot, therefore, compensate for the regulatory deficiencies with regard to land-based pollution sources.

The Role of Assistance and the (Non-)Applicability of CBDR

In UNCLOS Part XII, reference to capabilities and according flexibility in the standard of care comes along with the obligation of (developed) states to provide scientific, educational, technical and other assistance to developing states[773] and the explicit intention for developing countries to be granted preference by international organizations in the allocation of funds.[774] Of course, the provision of assistance by developed countries ideally entails an increase

768 cf Sockholm Principle 23.

769 See Birnie, Boyle and Redgwell (n 488) 152.

770 ILC, '2001 ILC Draft Articles on Prevention of Transboundary Harm' (n 662) 395 para 16; Sadeleer (n 447) 64.

771 *Responsibilities of States in the Area* (n 647) 36 para 117; *Fisheries Advisory Opinion* (n 584) 38 para 132.

772 See Birnie, Boyle and Redgwell (n 488) 149.

773 1982 UNCLOS art 202.

774 ibid art 203.

of the means at the disposal of those countries benefitting from the support. Similarly, technology and knowhow transfer may open up new opportunities for pollution prevention and control. Hence, the provision of assistance to countries in need of support may influence the standard of expected care. This does not, however, imply that developing countries only have to implement the provision if such assistance is provided. In this sense, the principle of common but differentiated responsibilities (CBDR)[775] does not apply to UNCLOS Part XII obligations if CBDR means that implementation is conditional on the provision of financial assistance and transfer of technology by developed states.[776]

While affirming a common responsibility of all states for the protection of the environment, the concept of CBDR explicitly recognizes different contributions of developed and developing countries to global environmental degradation and acknowledges their different capacities for adaptation and mitigation measures. In view of these differences with regard to responsibilities and capacities, CBDR allows for different standards for developed and developing states. Also, developed countries have to provide assistance to developing countries if they wish the latter to implement the standards.[777] With regard

775 CBDR is reflected in Rio Principles 6, 7, 11 and 15. For more information on CBDR in international law, see Philippe Cullet, 'Common but Differentiated Responsibilities' in Malgosia Fitzmaurice, David M Ong and Panos Merkouris (eds), *Research Handbook on International Environmental Law* (Edward Elgar Publishing 2010); French (n 762); Tuula Honkonen, *The Common but Differentiated Responsibility Principle in Multilateral Environmental Agreements: Regulatory and Policy Aspects* (Kluwer Law International 2009); 'The Principle of Common but Differentiated Responsibility in Post-2012 Climate Negotiations' (2009) 18 Review of European Community & International Environmental Law 257; Fabio Morosini, 'Trade and Climate Change: Unveiling the Principle of Common but Differentiated Responsibilities from the WTO Agreements' (2010) 42 George Washington International Law Review 713; Lavanya Rajamani, 'The Principle of Common but Differentiated Responsibility and the Balance of Commitments under the Climate Regime' (2000) 9 Review of European Community & International Environmental Law 120; Christopher D Stone, 'Common but Differentiated Responsibilities in International Law' (2004) 98 The American Journal of International Law 276; Michael Weisslitz, 'Rethinking the Equitable Principle of Common but Differentiated Responsibility: Differential versus Absolute Norms of Compliance and Contribution in the Global Climate Change Context' (2002) 13 Colorado Journal of International Environmental Law and Policy 473.

776 CBDR is reflected in this sense in 1987 Montreal Protocol art 5(5); 1992 CBD art 20(4); 1992 UNFCCC art 3.

777 See Agenda 21 (n 450) ch 17.2. Differential treatment and CBDR in particular is a nearly universally accepted principle. It played a crucial role in the design of different environmental regimes, especially the ones dealing with global or common concerns that are not equally attributable to all the states but affect the international community as a whole. These include the ozone, climate, desertification, biodiversity and forests regimes: see

to the applicability of the principle of CBDR to the obligations under UNCLOS Article 194, several issues have to be taken into account.

First, marine pollution, and marine plastic pollution from land-based sources in particular, is a global problem to which, arguably, some countries have contributed much more than others. Hence, it seems reasonable to argue that the main contributors should bear the main responsibility for it and support affected countries accordingly when they are suffering from beached debris, especially if we assume that the debris was generated elsewhere. However, studies show that main contributors are not necessarily developed countries in the traditional sense but include China, Indonesia, the Philippines, Vietnam, Sri Lanka and other middle- and low-income countries.[778] As explained above, marine pollution from land-based sources is often linked to inadequate waste management, which, in turn, is usually due to limited capacities of municipalities and local governments. The principle of CBDR can thus hardly be applied in its strict sense, since contribution and capability – as the two elements at the basis of differentiation in responsibility – do not match.

Second, core obligations of Article 194(1–2) are pollution prevention and the prevention of transboundary harm. The provision clearly focuses on each country's own responsibilities. In contrast to global environmental degradation that, in the past, has been mainly caused by developed countries, domestic pollution and transboundary harm are attributable to the state that caused the pollution or harm by its activities and failed to prevent it.[779] CBDR does therefore not apply, at least with respect to the aspect of conditionality.[780]

1985 Vienna Convention for the Protection of the Ozone Layer arts 2(2) and 4(2); 1987 Montreal Protocol arts 5(1) and 10A; 1992 UNFCCC arts 3 and 4; Kyoto Protocol to the United Nations Framework Convention on Climate Change (Kyoto Protocol) (adopted on 11 December 1997, entered into force on 16 February 2005) UN Doc FCCC/CP/1997/7/Add.1, 2303 UNTS 148, 37 ILM 22 (1998) art 10; 1994 UNCCD arts 3(d) and 6; 1992 CBD arts 16 and 20 in particular; Non-Legally Binding Authoritative Statement of Principles for a Global Consensus on the Management, Conservation and Sustainable Development of All Types of Forests (Forest Principles) (adopted on 14 June 1992) UN Doc A/CONF.151/26 (Vol. III) para 9(a). The classical and rigid distinction between developing and developed states (or typically of Annex I and non-Annex I countries in the UNFCCC context) has been challenged under the 2015 Paris Agreement, in which all countries are required to contribute to reducing greenhouse-gas emissions, while recognizing that emission peaking will take longer for developing countries: Paris Agreement (adopted by UNFCCC COP decision on 12 December 2015, entered into force on 4 November 2016) in Report of the COP 21, FCCC/CP/2015/10/Add.1, Annex art 4(1–4).

778 See Jambeck and others (n 291) 769.

779 See *South China Sea Arbitration* (n 584) 373–75 paras 941 and 944.

780 See *Responsibilities of States in the Area* (n 647) 48–49 paras 158–62. The concept does also not apply to treaties regulating ultrahazardous activities or pollution from ships (1973/78

c) Risk Evaluation and Precaution

The standard of care to be applied in the context of UNCLOS Part XII does not only depend on a country's capabilities but also on the severity of the risk and of hazard involved. The ITLOS held in this respect that '[t]he standard of due diligence has to be more severe for the riskier activities'.[781] Risk assessment therefore plays an important role in the discharge of the obligations under Part XII, especially with regard to pollution prevention and ecosystem protection. For the purpose of the convention, *pollution* is defined as the 'introduction [...] of substances [...] into the marine environment, [...] which results or *is likely to result* in such deleterious effects as harm to living resources and marine life, hazards to human health [etc.]'.[782] In order to fulfil its obligations as contained in Article 194, a state must thus assess whether and to what degree a substance is, in whatever form, susceptible of being introduced into or otherwise ending up in the marine environment, and whether or not its introduction into the marine environment is likely to result in deleterious effects. This goes beyond measuring real and actual effects and includes an anticipatory element, namely the assessment or evaluation of potential impacts that are *likely to* occur. In the event that risk of significant harm is to be expected ('likely to result in such deleterious effects'), states have a duty to take all measures necessary to prevent, reduce and control the introduction of the corresponding substances into the marine environment.

When a risk assessment is carried out and a certain degree of risk is asserted, a state has to decide on how to deal with that risk.[783] This decision depends on the chosen level of protection of a state and the standards it adopts, as well as on other factors such as available means, policy priorities and cost-efficiency of possible measures. According to Article 194, a state is not free in choosing its level of protection but has to strive for the highest level possible within the limits of its capabilities and take all measures necessary to prevent marine pollution. For this purpose, it has to 'take into account'[784] internationally

MARPOL); dumping at sea (1972 London Dumping Convention); or the conduct of activities on the deep seabed (UNCLOS Part XI): Birnie, Boyle and Redgwell (n 488) 136.

781 *Responsibilities of States in the Area* (n 647) 37 para 117; *Fisheries Advisory Opinion* (n 584) 38 para 132.

782 1982 UNCLOS art 1(4) (emphasis added).

783 See *EC Hormones* (n 672) 179–86. Risk assessment is therefore not to be confused with risk management, where States have to decide how to deal with a given risk: see Thomas Cottier, 'Technology and the Law of International Trade Regulation' in Roger Brownsword, Eloise Scotford and Karen Yeung (eds), *The Oxford Handbook of Law, Regulation and Technology* (Oxford University Press 2017) 1039–40.

784 1982 UNCLOS art 207(1).

agreed minimal standards and use the best practicable means at its disposal. Best available technology and best environmental practices as defined in different fora can be used as a reference to determine whether a state exercises due diligence and care with regard to the prevention and mitigation of marine pollution.

According to the ILC, the *risk* of causing significant transboundary harm refers to the combined effect of the probability of occurrence of harmful effects and their magnitude. It includes 'risks taking the form of a high probability of causing significant transboundary harm and a low probability of causing disastrous transboundary harm'.[785] Objective determination of such a risk is based on scientific criteria. Where there is scientific proof of a risk of significant environmental damage by pollution, measures need to be taken. However, both the probability of certain effects to occur and the magnitude of potential hazard involved are parameters that are not necessarily easy to assess or to prove. They depend on a multitude of factors, not all of which can clearly be determined.[786] Sometimes, risk assessment results are ambiguous and experts do not agree about the degree of risk a certain activity involves. In such cases, it might not be possible to provide full scientific proof before harm occurs. Situations of scientific uncertainty (in which there are reasonable grounds to assume a threat of harm but the risk cannot be fully scientifically proved in a timely manner) have been receiving increasing attention in contemporary international environmental law, and are usually linked with precaution.[787]

785 ILC, '2001 ILC Draft Articles on Prevention of Transboundary Harm' (n 662) 386–90 Article 2 with commentaries. Activities generally considered ultra-hazardous require a high standard of care. An ultra-hazardous activity has been defined as 'an activity with a danger that is rarely expected to materialize but might assume, on that rare occasion grave (more than significant, serious or substantial) proportions': ibid 381 para 2. See comments by Handl, 'Transboundary Impacts' (n 662) 539–40.

786 In the case of marine pollution, such factors may include weather conditions, geographical location, ocean currents, the occurrence and behaviour of affected marine species, as well as the occurrence and abundance of other toxic substances and their combined effect on human health and the environment.

787 See *EC Hormones* (n 672) 46–48 paras 120–25; *Southern Bluefin Tuna Cases* (n 584) paras 77–80; *European Communities – Measures Affecting Asbestos and Asbestos-Containing Products* (*EC Asbestos*) [2001] Appellate Body Report WT/DS135/AB/R 60–63 paras 164–75; *Responsibilities of States in the Area* (n 647) 40–41 paras 131–35. Particularly with regard to land-based pollution sources, the Preparatory Committee of the UN Conference on Environment and Development stressed the importance of precautionary measures in its report to the Secretary General:

> Given the present uncertainty of the impact of many anthropogenic substances in the marine environment and the risks they may present to important resources,

In general, the duty of diligent control and regulation arises if significant harm is foreseeable and the risk of causing such harm can be objectively determined. In this respect, the precautionary approach implies that states are entitled, if not obliged, to take preventive measures even if a risk of significant[788] harm cannot be fully proved by scientific means. Applying a precautionary approach does not rule out scientific criteria from policymaking or rule-making processes. Scientific evidence is still the basis of risk evaluation. However, a precautionary approach lowers the standard of proof of risk (or, as the case may be, reverses the burden of proof): even if full scientific certainty cannot be provided, or if there are divergent views in this regard, preventive measures may be justified. In other words: the lack of full scientific certainty with regard to the severity of a risk may not justify inaction if, based on scientific evidence, a threat of significant harm can be assumed.[789] With regard to UNCLOS Article 194, this means that the conduct of a state may be considered in breach of the state's obligation of due diligence if the state did not properly evaluate a risk according to its capacities or decided not to take measures to encounter a risk of serious pollution on the sole ground that this risk was not fully scientifically proved. Precaution thus suggests that the failure to adopt

> precautionary approaches are clearly needed in determining the amounts of many substances that should be allowed to enter the oceans and the priorities for the implementation of control measures:

United Nations, 'Report of the Secretary-General of the Conference on the Protection of the Oceans, All Kinds of Seas Including Enclosed and Semi-Enclosed Seas, Coastal Areas and the Protection Rational Use and Development of Their Living Resources' (1991) UN Doc A/CONF.151/PC/30 and Corr. 1 para 54, reprinted in Netherlands Institute for the Law of the Sea, *International Organizations and the Law of the Sea: Documentary Yearbook*, vol 7 (1991) 302. In recent UNGA resolutions, the precautionary approach is increasingly stressed with regard to activities having an impact on the marine environment. For more information on precaution in international environmental law, see David Freestone, 'The Road from Rio: International Environmental Law After the Earth Summit' (1994) 6 Journal of Environmental Law 193, 211; Jacqueline Peel, *Science and Risk Regulation in International Law* (Cambridge University Press 2010) 111–70; Sadeleer (n 447) 91–223; Sands and Peel (n 447) 217–28; Jonathan B Wiener, 'Precaution' in Daniel Bodansky, Jutta Brunnée and Ellen Hey (eds), *The Oxford Handbook of International Environmental Law* (Oxford University Press 2007) 558–610.

788 In international law, there are various differing thresholds of potential harm for precautionary measures to be taken: Rio Principle 15 refers to 'threats of serious or irreversible damage' and sets a relatively high threshold. In contrast, 1992 OSPAR Convention Article 2(a) holds that 'preventive measures are to be taken when there are reasonable grounds for concern that substances [...] may bring about hazards [...]'.

789 See Birnie, Boyle and Redgwell (n 488) 153 and 163. On the relation between precautionary measures and the allocation of the burden of proof, see ibid 158.

sufficient preventive measures may not be justified by the lack of full scientific evidence and may be considered a breach of the due diligence obligation if a risk of significant damage could be presumed.[790]

There is no lack of scientific evidence with regard to a wide range of harmful effects caused by marine plastic debris. The focus of the states' risk assessments must therefore lie on the probability of plastics to enter the marine environment. If there is high probability of plastics entering the marine environment, measures need to be taken to lower or eliminate that risk. Such measures can include moving landfills away from the coast, requiring beach resorts to collect waste, or disincentivising the use of single-use plastic and non-recyclable plastics.[791] Precaution may be relevant for issues related to nanoplastics, the exact impact of which is still disputed, or the use of certain additives, including substances with potentially endocrine-disrupting properties.

d) Monitoring and Environmental Impact Assessment

A further component of the general duties to protect and preserve the marine environment and to prevent pollution, including from land-based sources, consists of the undertaking of prior environmental impact assessments and environmental monitoring. Environmental impact assessment has been defined as an 'examination, analysis and assessment of planned activities with a view to ensuring environmentally sound and sustainable development'[792] or as 'a national procedure for evaluating the likely impact of a proposed activity on the environment'.[793] The aim of such an assessment is not only to anticipate possible impacts on the environment but also to propose ways to prevent or minimize them.[794] Ideally, assessment results provide the necessary information for states to properly evaluate the risks involved in a specific activity. Based on the assessment results, states are in a better position to decide whether and

790 *Responsibilities of States in the Area* (n 647) 40 para 131.

791 See Chapter 2.3 below.

792 UNEP, 'Goals and Principles of Environmental Impact Assessment (UNEP 1987 EIA Principles)' (1987) Governing Council Res 14/25 (1987), endorsed by UN General Assembly Res 42/184 (1987) Preamble. On environmental impact assessments, see Atapattu (n 545) 273–77 and 289–378; Birnie, Boyle and Redgwell (n 488) 164–75; Neil Craik, *The International Law of Environmental Impact Assessment: Process, Substance and Integration* (Cambridge University Press 2008); 'Principle 17: Environmental Impact Assessment' in Jorge E Viñuales (ed), *The Rio Declaration on Environment and Development: A Commentary* (Oxford University Press 2015).

793 Convention on Environmental Impact Assessment in a Transboundary Context (1991 Espoo Convention) (adopted on 25 February 1991, entered into force on 10 September 1997) 1989 UNTS 309, 30 ILM 802 (1991) art 1(vi).

794 Atapattu (n 545) 277.

to what degree precaution is indicated. Environmental impact assessments allow for proper integration of environmental concerns into decision-making processes and therefore facilitate law and policy formulation in the context of sustainable development.[795] Best available options can in this way be identified among different alternatives.

From a substantive point of view, environmental impact assessments are an important instrument for the prevention of damage by pollution and, thus, for states to fulfil respective duties. From a procedural point of view, they provide a suitable (and usually necessary) basis for a meaningful notification and consultation process with states that are potentially affected by envisaged industrial and other activities. In this vein, the assessments play an important role with respect to a state's duty to cooperate.[796] Yet, the relevance of environmental impact assessments is not confined to interstate relations. In domestic contexts, they may be indispensable for compliance with human rights law, especially with regard to the rights of access to environmental information, public participation in environmental decision-making and access to justice in environmental matters. Environmental impact assessment studies provide for the necessary transparency in this regard.[797] The nature of the duty to undertake environmental impact assessment may vary according to the context. Its customary nature is most evident for transboundary contexts and contended with regard to impacts to the global commons and purely domestic effects.[798]

Environmental impact assessments are usually carried out *ex ante*, that is, at the planning stage of a project or proposed activity or in the drafting phase of new regulations, plans or policies. However, due diligence of states does not

795 On sustainable development, see Section 2.1.A.ii.1) above.

796 See *South China Sea Arbitration* (n 584) 395–97 paras 987–91; ILC, '2001 ILC Draft Articles on Prevention of Transboundary Harm' (n 662) arts 4–9, especially art 7.

797 See Convention on Access to Information, Public Participation in Decision-Making and Access to Justice in Environmental Matters (1998 Aarhus Convention) (adopted on 25 June 1998, entered into force on 30 October 2001) 2162 UNTS 447, 38 ILM 517 (1999). On the relevance of environmental impact assessment in relation to the Aarhus Convention, see Atapattu (n 545) 356–77. See also Birnie, Boyle and Redgwell (n 488) 164–75; Handl, 'Transboundary Impacts' (n 662) 543. cf ILC, '2001 ILC Draft Articles on Prevention of Transboundary Harm' (n 662) 422 art 13 with commentary.

798 See Craik, 'Principle 17: Environmental Impact Assessment' (n 792) 458. Birnie and others conclude that 'at present general international law neither requires states to assess possible global effects nor effects wholly within their own borders': Birnie, Boyle and Redgwell (n 488) 167. cf Alex G Oude Elferink, 'Environmental Impact Assessment in Areas beyond National Jurisdiction' (2012) 27 The International Journal of Marine and Coastal Law 449, arguing that the duty to undertake environmental impact assessments also applies to impacts that are caused or arise in areas beyond national jurisdiction.

end with the start of a project or activity. Rather, states have to thoroughly measure and evaluate the effects on the environment during the whole term of an activity, and possibly beyond it. The process of measuring environmental impacts after the start of an activity is generally referred to as monitoring.[799]

UNCLOS Part XII Section 4 contains three articles that deal with monitoring, assessment and reporting. Article 206 provides that:

> When States have reasonable grounds for believing that planned activities under their jurisdiction or control may cause substantial pollution of or significant and harmful changes to the marine environment, they shall, as far as practicable, assess the potential effects of such activities on the marine environment and shall communicate reports of the results of such assessments in the manner provided in article 205.[800]

Article 205 provides that

> States shall publish reports of the results obtained [...] or provide such reports at appropriate intervals to the competent international organizations, which should make them available to all States.

The obligation to undertake an environmental impact assessment, as expressed in Article 206, is not an absolute one but contains several elements of discretion on the part of the state concerned. First, the term 'reasonable grounds' implies that for the duty to be triggered, there has to be an element of foreseeability with regard to the pollution that might be caused by the activity.[801] Second, only *substantial* pollution or *significant* changes to the marine

799 In the *Gabčíkovo-Nagymaros Judgment*, the ICJ held that not only with regard to new activities but also when continuing with activities begun in the past, states 'should look afresh at the effects on the environment of [their] operation' and take into account new norms and standards that have been developed: *Gabčíkovo-Nagymaros* (n 543) 77–78 para 140.

800 A request for states to undertake environmental impact assessment for 'proposed activities that are likely to have a significant adverse impact on the environment' is also expressed in Rio Principle 17. Much like UNCLOS art 206, Rio Principle 17 does not refer to the risk of *transboundary* harm in particular. Instead, it is formulated in more general terms and includes in its scope all activities that are 'subject to a decision of a competent national authority', including state-driven activities and activities or projects that are subject to licensing or approval by the state.

801 On the threshold of foreseeability with regard to environmental impact assessments, see Birnie, Boyle and Redgwell (n 488) 171.

environment fall under the scope of the provision.[802] Third, even when states have reasonable grounds for believing that there is a risk of substantial pollution or significant changes to the marine environment, they only have to assess potential effects 'as far as practicable'. The decision on whether an assessment is practicable is largely left to the state's own discretion and principally depends on its capabilities.

The scope of the provision is moreover confined to *activities*. While the term is not clearly defined, it typically refers to the construction and operation of factories, plants, streets, dams and other facilities potentially involving significant impacts on (shared) resources. Large irrigation or deforestation projects are also covered. The term equally refers to the issuance of corresponding construction permits and operating approvals to private actors. Domestic environmental impact assessment requirements may go further than that and also apply to, for instance, public procurement, free trade agreements or investment treaties. The 1991 Espoo Convention and, more importantly, its 2003 Protocol on Strategic Environmental Assessment (SEA)[803] break with the traditional approach that limits the scope of environmental impact assessments to activities or projects. In contrast to UNCLOS Article 206, the SEA Protocol applies to plans and programmes and, in a more limited way, to policies and legislation.[804]

Finally, Article 206 does not specify the required content or documentation of impact assessments.[805] The duty to communicate assessment reports, however, is an absolute obligation.[806] Again, the Espoo Convention goes further in this regard: its Appendix II describes the minimum information that should be contained in the environmental impact assessment documentation.

---

802 See n 662.

803 Protocol on Strategic Environmental Assessment to the 1991 Espoo Convention (SEA) (adopted on 21 May 2003, entered into force 11 July 2010) Doc. ECE/MP.EIA/2003/2. All 45 countries that are currently parties to the Espoo Convention and the 33 parties to the SEA Protocol (status of September 2021) are members of the UN Economic Commission for Europe (UNECE). In 2014, the convention was opened to accession by non-UNECE countries. The Espoo Convention and its protocol do not reflect customary rules. The ICJ thus denied their applicability to non-parties: *Pulp Mills Judgment* (n 544) 83 para 205.

804 SEA Protocol arts 1(a–b), 4 and 13.

805 Birnie and others note in this regard that in contrast to Articles 207–11, no reference is made to internationally agreed rules and standards: Birnie, Boyle and Redgwell (n 488) 173–74.

806 See Nordquist, Rosenne and Yankov (n 585) 124 para 206.6(b); *South China Sea Arbitration* (n 584) 378 para 948. Because China failed to communicate any assessment results, the tribunal found that China did not fulfil its obligations under UNCLOS art 206: *South China Sea Arbitration* (n 584) 396–97 para 991.

Such information includes, among other things, a description of the proposed activity and its purpose; a description of reasonable alternatives (including no action); a description of the potential environmental impacts of the project and alternatives; possible mitigation measures; knowledge gaps and uncertainties; and an outline for monitoring and management programmes.[807]

In addition to assessing impacts of planned activities, states have to monitor the effects of ongoing activities. For some activities, such as landfilling, monitoring may be required even a long time after the activity has been terminated. Article 204(1) provides in this respect that states shall 'endeavour, as far as practicable, [...] to observe, measure, evaluate and analyse, by recognized scientific methods, the risks or effects of pollution of the marine environment'. Article 204(2) specifies that states shall, in particular, 'keep under surveillance the effects of any activities which they permit or in which they engage in order to determine whether these activities are likely to pollute the marine environment'. Again, the language of the article leaves considerable discretion to the state concerned. It is, for instance, not perfectly clear what kind of specific measures the term *surveillance* refers to.[808] In any case, the place in which the activities are carried out and the nationality of the individual or entity undertaking the activity are not relevant for the purpose of Article 204 if the state is engaged in or has permitted the activity.[809]

Proper environmental impact assessment, monitoring and reporting are important factors in determining whether a state has fulfilled its obligation to protect and preserve the marine environment with due diligence. It will be difficult for a state to prove compliance with its general duties under UNCLOS Part XII if it failed to undertake impact assessment and to correctly monitor its activities.[810]

With respect to marine plastic pollution, the provisions of UNCLOS Part XII Section 4 are particularly relevant with regard to state-controlled activities relating to the extraction and production of raw materials for plastics, pellet production and transport, converting, recycling and the disposal of plastic wastes. Especially with regard to disposal activities and waste management,

807 For more information on the Espoo convention, see, for instance, Atapattu (n 545) 309–18. On the content of environmental impact assessments, see Craik, 'Principle 17: Environmental Impact Assessment' (n 792) 459–60.

808 See Nordquist, Rosenne and Yankov (n 585) 115 para 204.8(d).

809 See ibid.

810 See *Responsibilities of States in the Area* (n 647) 72 and 43–46 paras 141–50; *South China Sea Arbitration* (n 584) 395–97 paras 987–91. See also Handl, 'Transboundary Impacts' (n 662) 543; Tanaka, *International Law of the Sea* (n 360) 286.

municipalities often play an important role. Environmental impact assessments may form part of the regular building application process, spatial planning and other administrative procedures. By contrast, activities that are not directly controlled by the state (and do not require its explicit permission) do not fall under the scope of Section 4. This includes the bulk of activities related to the use and disposal of plastics. Moreover, while point sources of plastic pollution, such as landfills and production facilities, can be relatively easily assessed in terms of environmental impacts, the same is not true for non-point sources. In fact, the concept of environmental impact assessment is difficult to apply to widespread plastic consumption and disposal practices, at least in a direct sense. It can, however, be applied to laws and regulations that regulate consumption and disposal behaviours. Life-cycle assessments of plastic products and packaging are a valuable tool in this regard: by evaluating environmental impacts of plastics in specific applications accross their entire life cycle, they provide key information for sustainable policy choices and decision-making in government procurement and legislative processes.[811]

In this vein, the scope of the UNCLOS provisions is unsatisfactory, as it does not include laws, regulations, policies and programmes. The provisions do not directly require states to assess their regulatory framework and strategies and, thus, to continually optimize their effect on activities of privately owned companies and individuals. However, since much of marine plastic pollution is due to behavioural failures, regulatory measures and market-based instruments are important to provide incentives and disincentives in order to bring about desired behavioural change.[812] A requirement for states to assess the impacts of respective policies, laws and other measures and to regularly report the results could be a useful component of an effective regime for the prevention of marine plastic pollution.

e) Cooperation and Assistance

Global and Regional Cooperation

UNCLOS Section 2 on global and regional cooperation may be seen as an expression of the underlying understanding that the protection and preservation of the marine environment cannot be achieved by individual states alone, but has to be based on common efforts, while taking into account different views, values and conditions. The *South China Sea* case perfectly shows the extent of damage that can be caused to the marine environment when a

811 On Life-Cycle Assessment of plastic products, see Section 1.1.C above.

812 See Section 1.2.C above on the main sources of marine plastic pollution and Chapter 2.3 below on national measures.

state refuses to effectively cooperate in the protection and preservation of the marine environment and fails to fulfil respective obligations under Part XII of the convention.[813] The significance of effective cooperation in the protection of the environment has been repeatedly stressed by international courts and tribunals. Most prominently, ITLOS held that 'the duty to cooperate is a fundamental principle in the prevention of pollution of the marine environment under Part XII of the [Law of the Sea] Convention and general international law'.[814]

The convention's Section 2 and related provisions are one of the novelties of UNCLOS: not only did UNCLOS introduce a general duty for states to protect and preserve the marine environment; it was also the first global instrument to stipulate a firm duty to cooperate in this regard and to define relevant aspects of this duty. In spite of the use of some qualifying terms, the provisions are formulated as strict obligations and to be implemented in good faith.[815]

According to UNCLOS Article 197, states have a duty to cooperate on a global basis and, as appropriate, on a regional basis in developing international rules, standards and recommended practices and procedures for the protection and preservation of the marine environment. They may do so directly or through competent international organizations. Particularly relevant in this regard are the IMO and the Food and Agriculture Organization of the UN (FAO). Both organizations have been serving as important fora for cooperation and the definition of international standards in treaties and soft law. With respect to plastics and marine debris, UNEA (through UN Environment) would seem a suitable forum for international legal standards to be set. Regional cooperation, on the other hand, is mainly realized in the context of UN Environment's Regional Seas Programme and related programmes.[816] UNCLOS Article 197 explicitly provides that states have to take into account characteristic regional features in the formulation and elaboration of common rules.[817]

---

813 *South China Sea Arbitration* (n 584) 394–95 paras 984–86. The arbitral tribunal held that China failed to cooperate with other states with regard to its land reclamation and construction of artificial islands, which caused 'severe, irreparable harm to the coral reef ecosystem'. The tribunal concluded that China had breached its obligations under UNCLOS art 197 and other provisions: ibid 475–76.

814 *MOX Plant* (n 689) para 82. See also *Case Concerning Land Reclamation* (n 689) para 92; *Lac Lanoux Arbitration (Spain v France)* (1957) 7 UN Rep Int'l Arb Awards 281 para 22; *North Sea Continental Shelf, Judgment* [1969] ICJ Rep 1969 3 47 para 85; *Gabčíkovo-Nagymaros* (n 543) 78 para 141; *Southern Bluefin Tuna Cases* (n 584) para 78.

815 See Nordquist, Rosenne and Yankov (n 585) 78.

816 See Chapter 2.2 below.

817 1982 UNCLOS art 197. cf Rio Principles 7 and 27.

UNCLOS further provides that, in the event of imminent or actual damage to the marine environment, states have an obligation to immediately notify the states 'likely to be affected by such damage, as well as the competent international organizations'.[818] The obligation to notify is considered a rule of customary law.[819] States in areas affected by imminent or actual damage and the competent international organizations have to cooperate 'in eliminating the effects of pollution and preventing or minimizing the damage'. To this purpose, states 'shall jointly develop and promote contingency plans for responding to pollution incidents in the marine environment'.[820] The duty to cooperate in the event of imminent or actual damage is qualified by the reference in Article 199 to the respective capabilities of states concerned.

A duty to cooperate is also expressed with regard to studies, research programmes and exchange of information and data acquired about pollution of the marine environment.[821] Finally, cooperation is required for the establishment of 'appropriate scientific criteria for the formulation and elaboration of rules, standards and recommended practices and procedures for the prevention, reduction and control of pollution of the marine environment'.[822] These obligations are highly relevant to marine plastic debris and microplastics: a lack of detailed knowledge and data has been repeatedly identified with regard to quantities, exact sources and pathways of micro- and macroplastics, as well as with respect to their degradation, distribution and impacts, including on human health. In its Resolution 2/11 on Marine Plastic Litter and Microplastics, UNEA therefore encouraged 'the establishment of a harmonized international size definition and terminology and compatible standards and methods for the monitoring and assessment of marine plastic debris and microplastics'.[823] The use of common scientific criteria is, in fact, a prerequisite for a common understanding of the problem and of possible solutions. The same is true with regard to criteria measuring the performance and effectiveness of governance structures and specific practices.[824]

818 ibid art 198. See also Rio Principles 18 and 19.

819 See Nordquist, Rosenne and Yankov (n 585) 83.

820 1982 UNCLOS art 199.

821 ibid art 200.

822 ibid art 201.

823 UNEA Resolution 2/11 (2016) (n 521) para 17. For a summary of key research needs, see UNEP, 'UNEA-2 Technical Report on Marine Plastic Debris' (n 509) 175–79.

824 In the report of the Executive Director on Resolution 1/6, joint development of key performance indicators is recommended to monitor plastic litter and assess related measures and strategies: UNEP, 'Resolution 1/6: Marine Plastic Debris and Microplastics – Report of the Executive Director' (2016) UNEP/EA.2/5 6 para 8(h)(vi).

With regard to enclosed or semi-enclosed seas, UNCLOS Part XII Section 2 is supplemented by Article 123. The provision requires states bordering an enclosed or semi-enclosed sea to *endeavour* to coordinate management, conservation efforts and research. Other obligations that are not directly covered by Section 2 but closely linked to it include, for instance, the duty to undertake environmental impact assessments as provided by Article 206.

Technical Assistance

Mismanaged wastes are one of the most important sources of marine plastic debris from land. According to a study published in 2015, the mass of mismanaged plastic wastes would decrease by 41 per cent within ten years, if the 20 most polluting countries (that is, the biggest contributors to marine plastic pollution from land-based sources) doubled their rates of adequate waste disposal.[825] Twelve of these countries are low- or lower-middle-income countries. Seven of the 20 top-ranking countries are upper-middle-income economies. The United States is the only high-income country to be on the list, ranking twentieth.[826]

A significant reduction of mismanaged wastes, especially in low- and middle-income countries, is of paramount importance for achieving a reduction in global plastic input into the marine environment. In order to tackle the problem, improvement of waste collection systems and infrastructure in these countries is therefore essential. Yet, the respective countries face a wide range of challenges, including a lack of financial resources, technologies and knowhow. At the same time, they are extremely vulnerable to the negative impacts of marine plastic pollution, especially if their coastal populations are not sufficiently protected against negative health impacts or if their economies rely on fishing and tourism. Rapid improvement of waste management infrastructure is inconceivable without the support of high-income countries.

Much like in other fields of environmental protection, effective participation of developing countries in global efforts to protect and preserve the marine environment depends on support provided by developed countries. Without such support, developing countries often lack the necessary means

825 Jambeck and others (n 291) 770.

826 For 2021, low-income economies are defined as those with a gross national income (GNI) per capita of US$1,045 or less in 2020; lower middle-income economies are those with a GNI per capita between US$1,046 and US$4,095; upper middle-income economies are those with a GNI per capita between US$4,096 and US$12,695; high-income economies are those with a GNI per capita of US$12,696 or more. World Bank, 'World Bank Country and Lending Groups – Data' (2021) <https://datahelpdesk.worldbank.org/knowledgebase/articles/906519-world-bank-country-and-lending-groups> accessed 10 October 2021.

for effectively engaging in common programmes and activities and implementing jointly agreed standards. It is an essential component of the principle of cooperation in a (global) partnership as referred to in Rio Principles 7 and 27.[827] Hence, UNCLOS Section 3 on technical assistance complements the previous section on global and regional cooperation.

The section is to be read in conjunction with the general obligations as contained in the first section of Part XII. In fact, the duty to protect and preserve the marine environment does not exclusively refer to domestic activities, including with transboundary effects, but includes extraterritorial components. The duty to provide technical assistance is one of these components. It is closely related not only to the notion of intragenerational equity, but also to the notion that the state of the marine environment is a matter of common concern of humankind. In this sense, the duty to protect and preserve the marine environment is incumbent upon the international community as a whole. The duty of a state to protect the marine environment therefore includes a duty to support less-developed countries in the fulfilment of their obligation.

Specifically, Article 202 deals with the provision of scientific and technical assistance to developing states for the protection and preservation of the marine environment and the prevention, reduction and control of marine pollution. While the obligation to provide such assistance is formulated as a strict one, states are only obliged to '*promote* programmes of scientific, educational, technical and other assistance to developing States'.[828] Article 202(a) provides a list of specific forms of assistance that shall be promoted. Appropriate assistance shall also be provided for the minimization of damage to the marine environment caused by 'major incidents'[829] and for the preparation of environmental assessments.[830] The term *appropriate* gives states a considerable discretionary space in their decision on the type and degree of assistance they intent to provide.

Article 203 deals with preferential treatment for developing states. It stipulates that developing states shall be provided preference by international organizations with regard to the allocation of marine pollution funds and technical assistance and with regard to the utilization of the specialized agencies of respective organizations. Indirectly, the provision is addressed to the

827 See CSD, 'Report of the Expert Group Meeting on Identification of Principles of International Law for Sustainable Development, Background Paper (CSD Report on Principles for Sustainable Development)' (1995) para 81; Atapattu (n 545) 119.

828 1982 UNCLOS art 202(a) (emphasis added).

829 ibid art 202(b).

830 ibid art 202(c).

member states of these organizations: they are called on to distribute available funds according to the needs of states, with the developing states having priority. The term developing countries is not defined in UNCLOS, but seems to be used according to the criteria established by the UN.[831] None of the provisions of Section 3 affects the general responsibility of the developing states for applying the substantive rules of Part XII.[832]

Overall, the obligations under Part XII Section 3 are deliberately open worded. The section gives states considerable discretionary space in their decision on the form and degree of assistance they intent to provide. It does not prescribe financial support or refer to any financial mechanism such as the GEF. Also, it does not provide the institutional basis for concerted action in this regard. This is despite the fact that the need for technology transfer, capacity building and financial support for developing countries in relation to plastic pollution mitigation is widely undisputed.[833]

f) Compliance with Other Conventions

UNCLOS Article 237 governs the relationship between Part XII and other conventions and agreements. It is considered a *lex specialis* with regard to Article 311 on the general relation between UNCLOS and other treaties.[834] By virtue of Article 237, special conventions and agreements have priority over the more general provisions of UNCLOS Part XII as long as they are compatible with its general principles.[835]

Article 237 is consistent with the rules of treaty interpretation in general international law, including VCLT Article 31(3)(c) and the principle of systemic integration.[836] It can be seen as a corollary to the mechanism of reference

---

831 See Nordquist, Rosenne and Yankov (n 585) 104.

832 See ibid 107–8.

833 As confirmed at the Ministerial Conference on Marine Litter in September 2021: see IISD, 'Ministerial Conference on Marine Litter and Plastic Pollution: 1–2 September 2021' (n 528).

834 Dupuy and Viñuales (n 582) 100; Nordquist, Rosenne and Yankov (n 585) 425.

835 According to Article 237(1), the provisions of Part XII are 'without prejudice to the specific obligations assumed by States [or international organizations parties to the convention in accordance with Article 305(1)(f)] under special conventions and agreements' relating to the protection and preservation of the marine environment, regardless of whether these conventions and agreements were concluded prior to or after the adoption of UNCLOS, provided that they have been concluded 'in furtherance of the general principles set forth in [UNCLOS]'. Article 237(2) provides that special obligations as referred to in the first paragraph 'should be carried out in a manner consistent with the general principles and objectives' of UNCLOS.

836 See Section 2.1.B.ii.2)b) above.

by which UNCLOS incorporates internationally agreed rules and standards dealing with the prevention and control of marine pollution from different sources.[837] In this sense, the obligation to protect and preserve the marine environment includes an obligation to take other relevant instruments into account and implement corresponding duties to the extent that they are applicable and compatible with UNCLOS Part XII.

As a rule of conflict, Article 237 plays an important role with regard to the continuous evolution of the UNCLOS framework and its relation to other treaties and bodies of law. A revision of UNCLOS provisions is nearly inconceivable and would, if envisaged, probably take several years or decades of negotiations. Against this backdrop, the further development of related international rules and standards by the competent authorities, and their incorporation by UNCLOS, allows the convention to adjust to new conditions and developments more easily.[838]

The relevance of a number of international agreements, and their relation to Part XII, will be discussed in Sections C and D below. Besides these agreements, regional conventions for the protection and preservation of the marine environment seem particularly important for the purposes of UNCLOS Article 237. Especially in view of the protracted regulatory standstill with

837 The duty of states to comply with international rules and standards in the adoption of laws and regulations to prevent, reduce and control marine pollution (or, in the case of land-based pollution sources and pollution from and through the atmosphere, to *take into account* such rules and standards) presupposes the applicability of corresponding instruments and their compatibility with the UNLCOS Part XII regime.

838 Another way of changing and expanding the framework is by means of implementing agreements: see Birnie, Boyle and Redgwell (n 488) 382. So far, two such agreements have been adopted: the 1994 Agreement on the Implementation of UNCLOS Part XI was adopted shortly before UNCLOS entered into force in 1994 in order to restrict the application of the concept of common heritage of mankind as defined in Part XI of the convention. The 1995 Fish Stock Agreement sets out principles for the conservation and management of straddling fish stocks and of highly migratory fish stocks. In addition, in June 2015, the UN General Assembly decided to develop an international legally binding instrument, possibly under UNCLOS, on the conservation and sustainable use of marine biological diversity of areas beyond national jurisdiction (BBNJ): see UNGA Res 69/292 (2015), 'Development of an International Legally Binding Instrument under the United Nations Convention on the Law of the Sea on the Conservation and Sustainable Use of Marine Biological Diversity of Areas beyond National Jurisdiction'. At its 72nd session, it decided to convene an intergovernmental conference to this purpose: see UNGA Res 72/249 (2017), 'International Legally Binding Instrument under the United Nations Convention on the Law of the Sea on the Conservation and Sustainable Use of Marine Biological Diversity of Areas beyond National Jurisdiction'. Three sessions of the conference were held in September 2018, March–April 2019 and August 2019, respectively.

regard to land-based pollution sources at the global level, regional conventions may have the potential to fill the gap. Whether and to what extent they do so will be discussed in Chapter 2.2 below.

Interim Conclusions

Along with its general provisions on the protection and preservation of the marine environment, UNCLOS provides for a comprehensive framework setting out valuable principles for action to be taken at the national, regional and international levels. Specifically, it requires states to adopt laws and regulations and take other measures at the national level, to assess environmental impacts and monitor activities, to effectively cooperate at the regional level, to provide assistance to developing countries, and to establish global rules and standards to prevent marine pollution and harmonize policies in this regard. UNCLOS moreover offers a set of useful features, including its mechanism of reference allowing for the incorporation of international standards and, as discussed below, its dispute settlement system.

With regard to land-based sources of marine pollution, UNCLOS does not give clear priority to international standards over national regulations. In addition, states have been very reluctant to adopt binding regulations on land-based sources in the past. Although states also have to take non-binding instruments into account when adopting national mitigation measures, the exact content of the obligations under UNCLOS remains blurred and the level of protection to be achieved is not defined. This is a difficult hurdle to overcome, including for the enforcement of UNCLOS Part XII obligations in a plastics-related context. Against the background of the continuing and rapid increase of plastics in the marine environment, clearer goals and requirements are needed to abate them effectively and in a timely manner. The status and impact of such requirements can be strengthened through the reference mechanism in UNLCOS.

iii Compliance and Enforcement: The Challenges of Plastics

Before addressing a number of challenges related to plastic pollution and the enforcement of UNCLOS Part XII, the present subsection provides a brief overview of the legal setting regarding the international responsibility of states and liability for damage. In a third part, it explains the UNCLOS dispute settlement system and its relevance to plastics.

1) *The Legal Framework*

UNCLOS Part XII Section 9 refers to the rules related to the responsibility and liability for damage caused to the marine environment. In a nutshell, Article 235 confirms the applicability of the international law on state responsibility and liability and, at the same time, serves as a safeguard provision to accommodate later developments in this field.[839] It also requires states to ensure that recourse is available for prompt and adequate compensation 'in respect of damage caused by pollution of the marine environment by natural or juridical persons under their jurisdiction'.[840] It does not, however, give any clarification with regard to a number of unresolved issues and challenges inherent to the current international law of responsibility and liability.[841] With regard to plastic pollution, such challenges relate, in particular, to the diffuse, dispersed and accumulative nature of the problem.

If damage is caused by the breach of an international obligation, liability becomes an essential feature of the obligations that arise from the wrongful act (or omission) under the law of state responsibility. However, damages may occur even if there is no act or omission contrary to international law. Such

---

839 The article reads as follows:

1. States are responsible for the fulfilment of their international obligations concerning the protection and preservation of the marine environment. They shall be liable in accordance with international law.
2. States shall ensure that recourse is available in accordance with their legal systems for prompt and adequate compensation or other relief in respect of damage caused by pollution of the marine environment by natural or juridical persons under their jurisdiction.
3. With the objective of assuring prompt and adequate compensation in respect of all damage caused by pollution of the marine environment, States shall cooperate in the implementation of existing international law and the further development of international law relating to responsibility and liability for the assessment of and compensation for damage and the settlement of related disputes, as well as, where appropriate, development of criteria and procedures for payment of adequate compensation, such as compulsory insurance or compensation funds.

Article 235(3) has to be read together with Article 304, which specifically refers to 'existing rules and the development of further rules regarding responsibility and liability under international law'. The two provisions reflect the general uncertainty prevailing in this field of law. cf Stockholm Principle 22 and Rio Principle 13.

840 1982 UNCLOS art 235(2). See *Responsibilities of States in the Area* (n 647) 43 paras 139–40.

841 These challenges relate to the discharge of due diligence obligations such as the duty of prevention; the threshold level environmental damage must have to be actionable; the burden of proof, especially in situations in which a party resorts to the precautionary approach; the question of liability without fault and other potential implications of the polluter-pays principle; and the right of states to bring a claim in the event of a breach of *erga omnes* obligations: see, for instance, Robert V Percival, 'International Responsibility and Liability for Environmental Harm' in Shawkat Alam and others (eds), *Routledge Handbook of International Environmental Law* (Routledge 2015) 683; Nordquist, Rosenne and Yankov (n 585) 412 para 235.10(b–c).

damages include, for instance, the ones associated with hazardous but lawful activities, including the operation of power plants, the shipping of oil or the transport of other hazardous substances. Liability is, therefore, not a concept that is confined to states. Under the realm of civil liability, other actors, including private operators, can be held liable for the damages they cause.

There are different sets of rules that are relevant in this regard:

- The first set of rules concerns the responsibility and liability of a state (or, alternatively, of an international organization) in breach of an international obligation. Besides customary rules, the ILC Draft Articles on Responsibility of States for Internationally Wrongful Acts as adopted in 2001 play an important role in this regard.[842] In 2011, they were complemented by the ILC Draft Articles on the Responsibility of International Organizations.[843]
- The second set of rules, or principles, deals with liability for damage arising from acts *not prohibited* by international law. The ILC has been active in this field, too. Its Draft Articles on Prevention of Transboundary Harm[844] define a certain minimum standard of due diligence for states in the management of activities posing a risk of significant transboundary harm. When transboundary harm occurs even though states comply with the required degree of due diligence, the question of compensation for damage falls outside the scope of state responsibility. Regulation in this field was widely unclear until recently. Only in 2006 did the ILC adopt a set of draft principles applying to

842 ILC, 'Draft Articles on Responsibility of States for Internationally Wrongful Acts', *Report of the International Law Commission 53th session* (UN Doc A/56/10 ch IVE1 2001). Every breach of an obligation by (and attributable to) a state constitutes an internationally wrongful act and entails the international responsibility of that state (Draft Articles 1–2). State responsibility includes an obligation of the state to cease the wrongful act and, if circumstances so require, assure or guarantee non-repetition (Draft Article 30). It moreover includes an obligation to make full reparation for the injury caused by the wrongful act (Draft Article 31). Full reparation may consist in restitution, compensation or satisfaction, in this order of preference (Draft Articles 34–37). If the responsible state does not comply with the obligations arising from its responsibility and fails to cease the wrongful act or fully repair the damage, injured states are entitled to take peaceful countermeasures (Draft Articles 49–54). They may do so only after they have requested reparation, duly notified the responsible state on planned countermeasures and offered to negotiate with that state (Draft Article 52). The Draft Articles widely reflect customary rules but include a number of provisions that rather reflect progressive development of the law of state responsibility.

843 ILC, 'Draft Articles on the Responsibility of International Organizations', *Report of the ILC 63th session* (UN doc A/66/10 ch VE1 2011).

844 ILC, '2001 ILC Draft Articles on Prevention of Transboundary Harm' (n 662).

such cases.[845] They establish a regime of liability for transboundary damage and specify the duties of states in this regard. It is important to note in this respect that state practice does not, in general, suggest that states are liable in the absence of fault.[846]
- In addition to the ILC Draft Principles, there are a number of special, treaty-based schemes, including sectoral, on state and civil liability in international law dealing with the compensation for damage arising from specific activities that are generally considered as hazardous or ultra-hazardous. All these rules of international law are, of course, supplemented by national and regional liability systems.[847] In the absence of contrary rules in international or regional treaties, national liability regimes are often the only ones to potentially cover cases of purely domestic damage.

Whether and to what degree liability regimes apply to a case depends on their design: in regimes based on strict liability, the occurrence of damage associated with a specific activity may be enough to trigger liability of some of the actors involved. By contrast, this would not be the case in a fault-based regime. In such a regime, a state or private operator is only liable for wrongful acts or omissions. Subjective elements (such as intention or recklessness) may be required in addition to the objective elements of a wrongful act.

In the context of environmental disputes in international law, the term *fault* usually refers to the failure of a state to act with due diligence (or to duly discharge procedural obligations, including to cooperate), which, in principle, is enough to trigger the state's responsibility.[848] While, thus, depending on the applicable rules, subjective elements of a fault may be required (or not!) for a state or private actor to be held *liable*, they play a minor role with respect to the international responsibility of a state. Most environmental treaty regimes, including UNCLOS Part XII, do not provide for strict liability: if a state acts with the required degree of diligence, it cannot be held liable for damage under the convention.[849]

845 ILC, '2006 Draft Principles on the Allocation of Loss' (n 568).

846 See R Lefeber, *Transboundary Environmental Interference and the Origin of State Liability* (Martinus Nijhoff Publishers 1996) 187. See also Alexandre Kiss and Dinah Shelton, 'Strict Liability in International Environmental Law' in Tafsir Malick Ndiaye and Rüdiger Wolfrum (eds), *Law of the Sea, Environmental Law and Settlement of Disputes* (Martinus Nijhoff Publishers 2007) 1139.

847 See Percival (n 841) 681.

848 See *Responsibilities of States in the Area* (n 647).

849 See Birnie, Boyle and Redgwell (n 488) 215–16; Antonio Cassese, *International Law* (OUP Oxford 2005) 250–51.

2) *The Challenge of Plastics*

Plastic pollution of the oceans poses a number of particular challenges with regard to the enforcement of UNLCOS Part XII provisions. These challenges become apparent when we imagine the case of large-scale plastic accumulation in the coastal waters and beaches of a specific country, causing a broad range of negative externalities. Not only do local communities have to bear the clean-up costs; it might well be also the case that many families and local businesses suffer a considerable loss of income or profit, respectively, because fishing has become more difficult and tourists do no longer come to that beach. In addition, a wide range of marine species, including endangered species, are severely affected through entanglement, ingestion and habitat pollution. Finally, local communities feel that there is a considerable health risk from the plastics due to the contamination of fish and physical injury. Because of these adverse effects, the people concerned wonder:

a. whether the plastic pollution in their region can be associated with a breach of UNCLOS Part XII by their own country or any other country;
b. whether the countries in breach of their obligation can be held responsible for it; and
c. whether compensation is available to people living close to that beach and being affected by the pollution.

a) Whether There is a Breach of the Duty to Protect and Preserve the Marine Environment

The first challenge relates to the question of which state the pollution is attributable to. Marine debris mostly consists of fragmented pieces, many of which will have lost their original properties, including colour, shape or possible inscriptions. Proofing their origin is a difficult task. Plastic pollution from land-based sources, such as inadequate waste management, typically accumulates in domestic areas in the first place, including river deltas and domestic shores. This is especially true for urban or tourist areas close to the coasts. However, pollution may also originate in upstream, possibly landlocked, states, and be transported by rivers to the shores of downstream states. Besides, marine plastic debris is easily transported to other shores, even of remote countries, or to the global gyres, which mostly form part of the high seas. The geographic location of some countries, including (but not only) some island countries, is such that ocean currents continuously wash ashore high amounts of plastic fragments from remote places. Marine plastic pollution from land-based sources is therefore generally not attributable to the actions or inactions of any single state or operator.

This difficulty is aggravated by the fact that sources of marine plastic pollution on land are widely continuous and dispersed, such as laundry and tyre wear. Marine plastic pollution is a problem to which nearly all the countries are contributing in a continuous way, although to different degrees. Hence, it can be argued that there is a shared responsibility by the international community. At best, contributions can be estimated to the extent that relevant data is available. In this respect, marine plastic pollution is comparable to the issue of climate change, the loss of biodiversity and similar concerns in that it is connected to a collective action problem.

Even if the pollution could be traced back to a single state, it would not be clear whether it constituted a violation of obligations under international law. Most usually, the actual polluters are private actors involved in the production, transport, use and disposal of plastic products, or products containing microplastics. As described in the previous subsection, there is a breach of the duty to protect and preserve the marine environment in the sense of UNCLOS Article 192 when a state does not make use of its regulatory competence to prevent, reduce and control marine pollution with the diligence due, or when it fails to duly discharge its procedural obligations, inclusidng its obligation to cooperate. Although UNCLOS refers to international rules and standards to better identify necessary regulatory and other measures to prevent plastic input into the ocean, the exact content of the duty under Articles 192 and 194 remains vague.[850] The question of compliance with a due diligence obligation largely depends on the standard of care and thus on the capacities of a specific state. A second challenge is hence related to the variable nature of due diligence obligations, in particular with regard to the standard of care.

The obligation to prevent transboundary environmental harm traditionally relates to hazardous activities.[851] Transboundary movement of lower-quality, mixed and contaminated plastics is considered a hazardous activity subject to international regulation.[852] The duty to protect and preserve the marine environment, however, goes beyond the prevention of transboundary harm and potentially includes an obligation to address a broad range of activities that

850 Measures may, for instance, consist of prohibitions and sanctions of littering and dumping, careful regulation of landfills, especially if they are located close to watersheds or the sea, the set in place of an effective and sound waste management system, and the control of point sources of plastic pollution. They may also consist of research programms on input reduction related to sources of plastic pollution that are more difficult to address with current technologies, such as, for instance, the millions of tonnes of micro- (or nano-) plastic particles from tyre wear or microfibres in wastewater. Implementation measures will be discussed in more detail in Chapter 2.3 below.

851 See ILC, '2001 ILC Draft Articles on Prevention of Transboundary Harm' (n 662).

852 See Section 2.1.D.ii.1) below.

are not traditionally considered hazardous, but relate to normal production, use and disposal of plastics and plastic goods.[853] The risk associated with the production, use and disposal of plastics is a cumulative one. Corresponding damage is caused by an extremely large number of activities and actors, the contribution by each of which is little and uncertain.[854] The ILC acknowledges that claims are not commonplace in the event that harm occurs because of gradually accumulated adverse effects over a period of time. They are not commonplace because it is difficult in these cases to establish a causal link between the (hazardous) activity and the damage incurred.[855] This significantly adds to the unsettled character of the case.

Lastly, there is the question of threshold environmental damage must take in order for the responsibility of a state to be triggered. Under general international environmental law, the scope of application of the duty to prevent transboundary environmental damage is generally confined to activities involving a risk of causing *significant* transboundary harm.[856] UNCLOS Articles 192 and 194 do not, however, refer to any sort of qualifying factor with regard to the threshold of environmental damage. The wording of the provision suggests that the threshold question is less relevant in the context of due diligence, as respective obligations are obligations of conduct, and not of result.

Both risk and damage related to marine plastic pollution are difficult to quantify. While the effects of entanglement and ingestion are widely known and recognized, the exact impacts of micro- and nanoplastics perhaps seem less evident, and further research is required. Further research is also required

853 For instance, a case can be made in favour of a phase-out of non-recoverable plastic materials that potentially accumulate in marine environments (e.g. microplastics in personal care products). Such a phase out has been recommended by UN Environment Executive Director: UNEP, 'Resolution 1/6: Marine Plastic Debris and Microplastics – Report of the Executive Director' (n 824) 6.

854 The degree to which states would have to (or do have to) intervene in production and consumption patterns, in both important national industries and daily individual behaviour, is the main reason for the reluctance of states to tackle the problem of marine plastic pollution, whether through more effective substantial provisions, binding standards or better enforcement.

855 ILC, '2006 Draft Principles on the Allocation of Loss' (n 568) 119 commentary to Draft Principle 1, para 7.

856 According to the ILC, significant harm leads to 'a real detrimental effect' that 'must be susceptible of being measured by factual and objective standards': ILC, '2001 ILC Draft Articles on Prevention of Transboundary Harm' (n 662) art 2 and commentary para 4 at 388. Criteria for determining the threshold of significant harm include the likelihood and severity of harmful effects.

with regard to chemical contamination, bioaccumulation and -magnification, and impacts on human health, but also with regard to the spread of invasive species facilitated through plastic debris, and related threats to marine ecosystems. The precautionary principle is, thus, highly relevant in this context. Moreover, plastic pollution may be one out of several causes for a gradual decrease in fish stocks, along with overfishing, climate change and other causes, the cumulative effect of which is difficult to foresee. Traditional enforcement mechanisms, as available under UNCLOS, typically struggle to deal with cases in which damage is not quantifiable or financially assessable.[857]

Overall, the question whether wide accumulation of plastics in the marine environment is related to a breach of UNCLOS Part XII obligations cannot be answered in a general way and depends on the specific case. The main challenges in this regard are related to:

- the identification of a single state to which the pollution is attributable;
- the establishment of a causal link between causes and effects, especially with regard to diffuse sources and cumulative effects;
- the determination of the standard of care with respect to marine plastic pollution mitigation in the absence of binding international standards; and
- the quantification of environmental, social and economic damage related to marine plastic pollution.

b) Whether the Countries in Breach of Their Obligation Can Be Held Responsible for It

The principle of state responsibility is tailored to interstate constellations in which the acts or omissions of one state cause injury to another state or a group of states.[858] In the case of coastal plastic pollution, such a transboundary

---

857 See ILC, '2001 ILC Draft Articles on State Responsibility' (n 842) art 36 para 2. However, the UN Security Council held Iraq liable for any direct damage, 'including environmental damage and the depletion of natural resources', as caused by Iraq's unlawful invasion and occupation of Kuwait: UNSC (1991) S/RES/687 7 para 16. Compensation was provided for a wide range of environmental damages: UNCC, 'Report and Recommendations Made by the Panel of Commissioners Concerning the Fifth Instalment of "F4" Claims' (2005) S/AC.26/2005/10. See Philippe Gautier, 'Environmental Damage and the United Nations Claims Commission: New Directions for Future International Environmental Cases?' in Tafsir Malick Ndiaye and Rüdiger Wolfrum (eds), *Law of the Sea, Environmental Law and Settlement of Disputes* (Martinus Nijhoff Publishers 2007) 177–214; Mojtaba Kazazi, 'The UNCC Follow-up Programme for Environmental Awards' in Tafsir Malick Ndiaye and Rüdiger Wolfrum (eds), *Law of the Sea, Environmental Law and Settlement of Disputes* (Martinus Nijhoff Publishers 2007) 1109–29.

858 Such as in *The Trail Smelter Arbitration (United States v Canada)* [1941] 3 UN Rep Int'l Arb Awards 1905; *Lac Lanoux Arbitration* (n 814); *Gabčíkovo-Nagymaros* (n 543); *MOX Plant* (n

constellation is conceivable. In the commentary to its Draft Articles on State Responsibility, the ILC specifically refers to the case of pollution of the high seas in breach of UNCLOS Article 194. It holds that such pollution 'may particularly impact on one or several States whose beaches may be polluted by toxic residues or whose coastal fisheries may be closed', in which case the respective states can be considered injured by the breach.[859] The affected state would have to proof that the plastics were introduced into the marine environment by activities under the jurisdiction or control of the allegedly responsible state. It would moreover have to establish a causal link to significant damage.[860] So far, no state has brought a claim against another state for transboundary plastic pollution in marine environments.

Acts or omissions contrary to UNCLOS Part XII may not only result in transboundary damage, but could result also in damage purely within the borders of the respective state or damage to areas beyond national jurisdiction, including the high seas and the deep seabed. Both domestic areas and areas beyond national jurisdiction are covered by UNCLOS Part XII, especially its Article 194.[861]

According to the ILC Draft Articles on State Responsibility, states are entitled to act in the collective public interest in protection of fundamental values shared by a group of states to which they are party, or, as the case may be, of values deemed of universal significance.[862] In the case of a multilateral treaty regime established in protection of a collective interest, each party to that treaty has the right to enforce the obligations arising from the treaty *vis-à-vis*

---

689); *Pulp Mills Judgment* (n 544); *South China Sea Arbitration* (n 584). In the law of state responsibility, a distinction is generally made between *injured states* and third states. Accordingly, it is distinguished between cases in which only the former are entitled to invoke the responsibility of a state and cases of 'aggravated' responsibility that may also be invoked by the latter if certain conditions are fulfilled: see Cassese (n 849) 244.

859 ILC, '2001 ILC Draft Articles on State Responsibility' (n 842) 299–300 Commentary to art 42(12).

860 See ibid art 42. cf 1969 VCLT art 60.

861 On the suggestion that a coastal state is obliged towards the world at large to prevent pollution of its territorial sea, see Louis Cavaré, 'Les problèmes juridiques posés par la pollution des eaux maritimes au point de vue interne et international' [1964] Revue Generale de Droit International Public 617, 631; O'Connell, *The International Law of the Sea* (n 590) 987–88.

862 ILC, '2001 ILC Draft Articles on State Responsibility' (n 842) art 48(1). The article provides that *any state other than an injured state* is entitled to invoke the responsibility of another state if: (a) 'The obligation breached is owed to a group of States including that State, and is established for the protection of a collective interest of the group; or (b) The obligation breached is owed to the international community as a whole'.

other parties, even if it has not suffered any direct form of damage. Similarly, remedy is also open to states in the event that the obligation breached is owed to the 'international community as a whole'. Respective obligations include *erga omnes* customary obligations such as the duty to protect and preserve the marine environment.[863]

It is to be noted that the relevant ILC Draft Article depicts a progressive development of the law of state responsibility that, though widely accepted in literature,[864] is not so much reflected in state practice yet. The ICJ acknowledged the existence of obligations of a state towards the international community as a whole in its *Barcelona Traction* judgment of 1970. According to the Court, such obligations are, by 'their very nature [...] the concern of all states'. Also, the Court held that '[i]n view of the importance of the rights involved, all States can be held to have a legal interest in their protection; they are obligations *erga omnes*'.[865] Since then, the concept has gained importance in human rights law and humanitarian law.[866] In at least two cases decided by arbitral

863 See *Responsibilities of States in the Area* (n 647) 54 para 180. On public interest standing, see Charney, 'Third State Remedies for Environmental Damage to the World's Common Spaces' (n 665) 165–66.

864 See, for instance, Birnie, Boyle and Redgwell (n 488) 233–34; James Crawford, 'Overview of Part Three of the Articles on State Responsibility' in James Crawford, Alain Pellet and Simon Olleson (eds), *The Law of International Responsibility* (Oxford University Press 2010) 934; Bruno Simma, 'Doctrinal Expressions of Community Interest in International Law', *Collected Courses of the Hague Academy of International Law*, vol 250 (The Hague Academy of International Law/Brill Online 1994) 293–301; Christian J Tams, 'Individual States as Guardians of Community Interests' in Ulrich Fastenrath and others (eds), *From Bilateralism to Community Interest: Essays in Honour of Judge Bruno Simma* (Oxford University Press 2011); Anne-Laure Vaurs-Chaumette, 'The International Community as a Whole' in James Crawford, Alain Pellet and Simon Olleson (eds), *The Law of International Responsibility* (Oxford University Press 2010) 1024.

865 *Barcelona Traction* (n 660) 32 para 33. See also *East Timor (Portugal v Australia)* [1995] ICJ Rep 1995 90 102 para 29; *Application of the Convention on the Prevention and Punishment of the Crime of Genocide, Preliminary Objections, Judgment* [1996] ICJ Rep 1996 595 616 para 31. Four years after *Barcelona Traction*, some of the ICJ judges explicitly rejected the notion of an *actio popularis*, that is, the right of a state to bring a claim on behalf of the international community as a whole, in the *1974 Nuclear Tests Cases*: see, in particular, *Nuclear Tests (Australia v France), Dissenting opinion of Judge de Castro* ICJ Rep 1974 372 390. cf *Nuclear Tests (Australia v France), Joint dissenting opinion of Judges Onyeama, Dillard, Jiménez de Aréchaga and Sir Humphrey Waldock* ICJ Rep 1974 312 369–70. Following a unilateral decision by France that it would cease to carry out atmospheric nuclear tests, the ICJ did not address the merits of the case.

866 Human rights law is particularly well developed with respect to collective or institutional responses to violations. Several human rights treaties set up mechanisms through which individual states or treaty bodies can invoke the responsibility of a non-compliant state and, for instance, demand cessation of a violation of treaty provisions. Some of these

tribunals, public interest standing has been granted in contexts related to the protection of the marine environment to enforce rules applicable to all the parties to an agreement.[867] The *South China Sea* case is the first example of a public interest claim referring to UNCLOS Part XII.

The general reluctance of the states to take action against other states is probably greatest when the damage mainly affects areas under the territorial sovereignty of the non-compliant state. In spite of the international obligation at stake, such situations are often treated as an internal affair of the polluting state. International responses to 'domestic' actions with no extraterritorial effects are confined to a number of gross infringements of values that are 'deemed of universal significance and not derogable by States'.[868] They can be found in cases related to human rights law, humanitarian law and international criminal law.

International practice suggests that states, when acting in a public interest and on behalf of the community, tend to do so through institutional bodies, such as UN bodies, other international organizations, treaty bodies or human rights bodies. Especially within the context of multilateral treaty systems, responses to a violation of treaty obligations are most usually decided by the Meeting of the Parties or other treaty bodies with supervisory powers. Individual responses rarely go beyond diplomatic protests.[869] If, however, they involve measures with potential impact on international trade, such measures have to be consistent with respective rules as adopted under the auspices of the WTO.[870]

Overall, there are numerous hurdles associated with state responsibility claims, whether in terms of the burden of proof or political reciprocity in interstate relations. In the law regulating specific aspects of marine pollution, states thus often fall back on special liability regimes. These usually focus on

---

treaties set up judicial or quasi-judicial bodies with the competence to consider individual complaints relating to the compliance by the respective states with the treaty provisions. Similar developments can be observed in international humanitarian law and international criminal law: see Cassese (n 849) 265–67.

867 *Whaling in the Antarctic* (n 592); *South China Sea Arbitration* (n 584).

868 Cassese (n 849) 263.

869 The ILC Draft Articles do not specify whether any state other than an injured state is entitled to take countermeasures. In the drafting of the ILC Articles, no agreement could be reached on the matter. A saving clause was introduced in Article 54, leaving the issue to be resolved by later developments in international law. Crawford (n 864) 936–39. However, in the case of a serious breach by a state of an obligation arising under a peremptory norm of general international law, see ILC, '2001 ILC Draft Articles on State Responsibility' (n 842) arts 40–41.

870 See Section 2.1.C below.

the polluter, including private operators, and hence provide a valuable alternative to state responsibility claims.[871]

c) Whether Compensation Is Available

A certain risk of causing damage is inherent to many ordinary, though potentially harmful activities, whether industrial, commercial or other. Liability addresses the question of compensation, including for damage caused by lawful activities.[872] Such activities are often not attributable to the state, and states are usually unwilling to be held liable for damage caused by these activities.[873] On the one hand, state compensation for losses caused by hazardous activities would imply that the risks associated with hazardous activities and their financial consequences could be transferred to the state. This could be seen as a dubious subsidization of hazardous activities and an incentive for operators to accept higher risks, taking advantage of possible grey areas of

871 See Birnie, Boyle and Redgwell (n 488) 431.

872 On liability in international law, see Michael Bowman and Alan E Boyle (eds), *Environmental Damage in International and Comparative Law: Problems of Definition and Valuation* (Oxford University Press 2002); Alan E Boyle, 'Globalising Environmental Liability: The Interplay of National and International Law' (2005) 17 Journal of Environmental Law 3; 'Liability for Injurious Consequences of Acts Not Prohibited by International Law' in James Crawford, Alain Pellet and Simon Olleson (eds), *The Law of International Responsibility* (Oxford University Press 2010); Edward Brans, *Liability for Damage to Public Natural Resources: Standing, Damage and Damage Assessment* (Kluwer Law International 2001); Jutta Brunnée, 'Of Sense and Sensibility: Reflections on International Liability Regimes as Tools for Environmental Protection' (2004) 53 The International and Comparative Law Quarterly 351; Gautier (n 857); Philippe Guttinger, 'Allocation of Responsibility for Harmful Consequences of Acts Not Prohibited by International Law' in James Crawford, Alain Pellet and Simon Olleson (eds), *The Law of International Responsibility* (Oxford University Press 2010); Kazazi (n 857); Lefeber, *Origin of State Liability* (n 846); Ruth Mackenzie and Ruth Khalastchi, 'Liability and Compensation for Environmental Damage in the Context of the Work of the United Nations Compensation Commission' (1996) 5 Review of European Community & International Environmental Law 281; Michel Montjoie, 'The Concept of Liability in the Absence of an Internationally Wrongful Act' in James Crawford, Alain Pellet and Simon Olleson (eds), *The Law of International Responsibility* (Oxford University Press 2010); Percival (n 841); Hanqin Xue, *Transboundary Damage in International Law* (Cambridge University Press 2003).

873 In general, state practice does not suggest strict liability of states in cases of transboundary damage. At the most, strict liability for *ultrahazardous* activities might be considered a general principle of law: see Boyle, 'Liability for Injurious Consequences of Acts Not Prohibited by International Law' (n 872) 98; Kiss and Shelton, 'Strict Liability in International Environmental Law' (n 846); Lefeber, *Origin of State Liability* (n 846) 187; Sands and Peel (n 447) 712–13. See also discussion in Birnie, Boyle and Redgwell (n 488) 221–23.

national regulations – a result that is inconsistent with the polluter pays principle and hardly compatible with the aim and purpose of environmental legislation. On the other hand, there is also no good reason why the loss should be borne by the victims of the damage, or by the state where the victims live. None of these possibilities would, in any way, be consistent with the polluter pays principle.[874]

For these reasons, the ILC came up with a different approach to liability for transboundary damage. In 2006, it adopted its Draft Principles on the Allocation of Loss.[875] According to the principles, 'each State should take all necessary measures to ensure that prompt and adequate compensation is available for victims of transboundary damage caused by hazardous activities located within its territory or otherwise under its jurisdiction or control'.[876] Notably, such measures should include 'the imposition of liability on the operator or, where appropriate, other person or entity'. The ILC's approach is, hence, not based on the liability of states in the absence of fault but on the duty of states to ensure that the ones who cause the damage also provide reparation and compensation. The liability regime as reflected in and provided by the ILC Draft Principles and specific conventions is complementary to the regime of state responsibility, and also to national civil or criminal law regimes or criminal prosecution under MARPOL and other conventions.[877]

The ILC Draft Principles require states to prescribe a regime based on strict liability, in which there is no need to prove fault.[878] Also, states should require the operator (or other person or entity) to provide financial security to cover claims of compensation, and they should ensure the establishment of industry-wide funds and provide additional funds if necessary.[879] In the event of an incident involving a hazardous activity, states are required to ensure that appropriate response measures are taken and to cooperate with affected states

874 On the polluter pays principle, see Section 2.1.A.ii.2) above. See also Mensah (n 429) 314–15.

875 ILC, '2006 Draft Principles on the Allocation of Loss' (n 568). At the regional level, the Council of Europe adopted a Convention on liability in 1993, but it has not yet entered into force: Convention on Civil Liability for Damage Resulting from Activities Dangerous to the Environment (1993 Lugano Convention) (adopted by the Council of Europe on 21 June 1993, not yet in force) 32 ILM 1228, CETS 150.

876 ILC, '2006 Draft Principles on the Allocation of Loss' (n 568) Principle 4(1).

877 See ILC, '2006 Draft Principles on the Allocation of Loss' (n 568) 111 general commentary para 6. Some cases of transboundary damage are preferably addressed via national courts and claims relying on civil liability. The *Sandoz* chemical spill of 1986, which polluted the Rhine river, is an example of such a case: see Birnie, Boyle and Redgwell (n 488) 219.

878 ILC, '2006 Draft Principles on the Allocation of Loss' (n 568) Principle 4(2).

879 ibid Principle 4(3–5).

in mitigating and eliminating the effects of transboundary damage.[880] The ILC Draft Principles define the term *damage* in a manner to include damage to the environment *per se* (in form of a 'loss or damage by impairment of the environment'), as well as 'the costs of reasonable measures of reinstatement of the [...] environment, including natural resources'.[881] In the commentary to the draft principle, the ILC notes that this definition reflects a recent and emerging notion of damage, and that some questions related to this notion are, at the current state of affairs, left to be answered by national law (including the questions of who may take redress in the event of damage to the environment and how such damage is best to be assessed).

The ILC principles further provide that states have to ensure non-discriminatory access for victims of transboundary damage to national remedies.[882] Such remedies have to be prompt, adequate and effective. The wording of the ILC draft principle strongly reminds of UNCLOS Article 235(2), requiring states to 'ensure that recourse is available in accordance with their legal systems for prompt and adequate compensation or other relief'.[883]

Finally, the ILC Draft Principles encourage states to conclude specific global, regional or bilateral agreements regulating compensation for damage and related issues, as well as providing for supplementary funding for compensation, with regard to particular categories of hazardous activities.[884] Such specific agreements are especially desirable for ultra-hazardous activities and other activities for which, for any reason, the general regime seems unsuitable or insufficient.[885] Specific treaty regimes can be tailored to particular activities. While, for instance, strict state liability might make sense for damage associated with activities in outer space, it will probably not be the right approach to deal with oil spill damage, in which case the shipowner or, possibly, the

880 ibid Principle 5.

881 ibid Principle 2(a)(iii–iv). See also ILC, '2006 Draft Principles on the Allocation of Loss' (n 568) commentary to Principle 2, paras 11–18.

882 ILC, '2006 Draft Principles on the Allocation of Loss' (n 568) Principle 6(1–2).

883 See also 1998 Aarhus Convention art 9 para 4 and Rio Principle 10. Both the ILC Draft Principles and UNCLOS art 235(2) require the *state of origin* (under the jurisdiction or control of which the hazardous activity is carried out) to ensure access to national remedies. In fact, there are a number of arguments in favour of access for the victims to local remedies in their own state where transboundary damage occurred: see Boyle, 'Marine Pollution under the Law of the Sea Convention' (n 581) 368.

884 ILC, '2006 Draft Principles on the Allocation of Loss' (n 568) Principle 7.

885 Specific agreements have been concluded in a number of fields, including with regard to nuclear damage, damage caused by space objects, oil pollution damage, damage in connection with the carriage of hazardous and noxious substances by sea, and damage resulting from transboundary movements of hazardous wastes and their disposal.

receivers of the cargo, are the main source of redress. The different treaty-based liability regimes also have different approaches with regard to their geographic scope of applicability, compensation limits, compulsory insurances or possible defences.

With regard to marine plastic pollution from land-based sources, no specific treaty-based liability regime has been adopted. UNCLOS only provides in this respect that states 'shall be liable in accordance with international law'.[886] Also, neither state practice nor any international treaty provides, in a general way, for strict state liability for damage caused by the introduction of plastics into the sea. Rather, UNCLOS Article 235 indicates that states are only liable for their failure to comply with their obligations under the convention (they are 'responsible for the fulfilment' of respective obligations), but not without fault.[887] The case of marine plastic pollution thus falls under the general regime as reflected and developed by the ILC Draft Principles on the Allocation of Loss.

The absence of a clearly identifiable polluter might be one of the reasons why no compensation schemes have been adopted at the international level for marine plastic pollution from land-based sources. Admittedly, the exact design of such a regime is, perhaps, less obvious than with regard to oil pollution or nuclear plants. In the case of plastic pollution, obligatory insurances or direct resort to operators only makes sense for a limited number of the actors involved, for instance for plastic producers or converters in the case of pellet loss, for the operators of landfills, or for the pellet transport industry.[888] In practice, such insurances will only take effect in formalized and well-organized systems. It is difficult to imagine how such a system could address the informal waste sector, including illegal dumpsites and related marine debris. Otherwise, alternative sources for compensation funds have to be developed in line with

---

886 1982 UNCLOS art 235(1).

887 The same model is reflected in UNCLOS Article 139 with regard to the responsibility of states for deep seabed operations. States are only liable for their own failure, but not for damage caused by national operators: see *Responsibilities of States in the Area* (n 647) 52–53 paras 176–77 and 56 para 189; Birnie, Boyle and Redgwell (n 488) 430. In addition, UNCLOS Article 232 provides that states are liable for damage arising from the measures taken by the states for enforcing their laws and regulations 'when such measures are unlawful or exceed those reasonably required in the light of available information'.

888 While the ILC liability scheme focuses on the liability of operators, it also allows for alternatives: see Boyle, 'Liability for Injurious Consequences of Acts Not Prohibited by International Law' (n 872) 102. Civil liability schemes for marine plastic pollution could be adopted at the regional level, if this is more appropriate or practical: see Mensah (n 429) 322.

the polluter pays principle. This would best be done by the internalization of these costs and extended producer responsibility.

3) *UNCLOS Dispute Settlement*

a) The Mechanisms

UNCLOS Part XV sets out a comprehensive dispute settlement system. In principle, it is a two-tier system involving, as a first tier, voluntary procedures, including conciliation. Where no settlement can be reached by recourse to such voluntary procedures, compulsory procedures apply, all of which entail binding decisions. UNCLOS is, hence, one out of very few treaties to provide compulsory jurisdiction on environmental disputes, while giving the parties a relatively large freedom of choice with regard to the procedures.[889] Notwithstanding any scepticism towards the effectiveness of traditional means of enforcement in international environmental law, UNCLOS dispute settlement is one of the particularities of the regime and well deserves a mention. ITLOS, a special tribunal established under the convention, and a number of ad hoc arbitration tribunals have adjudicated a growing number of

889 For further information, see AO Adede, *The System for Settlement of Disputes Under the United Nations Convention on the Law of the Sea: A Drafting History and a Commentary* (BRILL 1987); Alan E Boyle, 'Dispute Settlement and the Law of the Sea Convention: Problems of Fragmentation and Jurisdiction' (1997) 46 International and Comparative Law Quarterly 37; 'The Environmental Jurisprudence of the International Tribunal for the Law of the Sea' (2007) 22 The international journal of marine and coastal law 369; Jonathan I Charney, 'The Implications of Expanding International Dispute Settlement Systems: The 1982 Convention on the Law of the Sea' (1996) 90 The American Journal of International Law 69; John G Collier and Alan Vaughan Lowe, 'Dispute Settlement in the Law of the Sea' in John G Collier and Alan Vaughan Lowe (eds), *The Settlement of Disputes in International Law: Institutions and Procedures* (Oxford University Press 1999); Natalie Klein, *Dispute Settlement in the UN Convention on the Law of the Sea* (Cambridge University Press 2005); Thomas A Mensah, 'The Dispute Settlement Regime of the 1982 United Nations Convention on the Law of the Sea' (1998) 2 Max Planck Yearbook of United Nations Law 307; Myron H Nordquist, Shabtai Rosenne and Louis B Sohn (eds), *United Nations Convention on the Law of the Sea 1982: A Commentary, Vol V: Articles 279 to 320* (Center for Oceans Law and Policy and Kluwer Law International 1989); Rosemary Rayfuse, 'Future of Compulsory Dispute Settlement under the Law of the Sea Convention' (2005) 36 Victoria University of Wellington Law Review 683; Tullio Treves, 'A System for the Law of the Sea Dispute Settlement' in David Freestone, Richard Barnes and David Ong (eds), *The Law of the Sea: Progress and Prospects* (Oxford University Press 2006); Helmut Tuerk, 'The Work of the International Tribunal for the Law of the Sea' (2012) 26 Ocean Yearbook Online 181; Rüdiger Wolfrum, 'The Settlement of Disputes Before the International Tribunal for the Law of the Sea – A Progressive Development of International Law or Relying on Traditional Mechanisms?' (2008) 51 Japanese Yearbook of International Law.

environmental cases. They have addressed substantial issues, including with regard to the interpretation and application of UNCLOS Part XII and pollution prevention,[890] due diligence,[891] cooperation,[892] and environmental impact assessment.[893] They have also dealt with the question of provisional measures for the protection and preservation of the marine environment.[894] In addressing these issues, the tribunals have substantively contributed to the consistent application of the law and its continued evolution.[895] The present subsection will shortly explain the mechanisms.

The dispute settlement procedures as set out in Part XV constitute an integral part of the convention. Part XV is divided into three sections: Section 1 contains a number of general provisions, including with regard to voluntary procedures; Section 2 addresses compulsory procedures entailing binding decisions; and Section 3 deals with the limitations and exceptions to these procedures.

In Section 1, parties are required 'to settle any dispute between them concerning the interpretation or application of the Convention by peaceful means' as indicated in Article 33 of the UN Charter.[896] Such means include 'negotiation, enquiry, mediation, conciliation, arbitration, judicial settlement, resort to regional agencies or arrangements, or other peaceful means of their own choice'.[897] Some of these means are diplomatic in nature and do not produce legally binding decisions (e.g. mediation or conciliation). In contrast, arbitration and judicial settlement are the classical means for parties to obtain binding decisions. UNCLOS does not, in principle, prefer one of these means

890 *Chagos Marine Protected Area Arbitration* (n 584); *Fisheries Advisory Opinion* (n 584); *South China Sea Arbitration* (n 584).

891 *Responsibilities of States in the Area* (n 647); *Fisheries Advisory Opinion* (n 584); *South China Sea Arbitration* (n 584).

892 *Southern Bluefin Tuna Cases* (n 584); *MOX Plant* (n 689); *Case Concerning Land Reclamation* (n 689); *Chagos Marine Protected Area Arbitration* (n 584); *Fisheries Advisory Opinion* (n 584); *South China Sea Arbitration* (n 584).

893 *MOX Plant* (n 689); *Case Concerning Land Reclamation* (n 689); *Responsibilities of States in the Area* (n 647); *South China Sea Arbitration* (n 584).

894 *Southern Bluefin Tuna Cases* (n 584); *MOX Plant* (n 689); *Case Concerning Land Reclamation* (n 689).

895 See, in particular, Boyle, 'The Environmental Jurisprudence of the International Tribunal for the Law of the Sea' (n 889) 380–81.

896 1982 UNCLOS art 279.

897 On the different means of dispute settlement, see Cassese (n 849) 278–95; Collier and Lowe (n 889); JG Merrills, *International Dispute Settlement* (Cambridge University Press 2011); Sands and Peel (n 447) 159–83; Tim Stephens, 'The Settlement of Disputes in International Environmental Law' in Shawkat Alam and others (eds), *Routledge Handbook of International Environmental Law* (Routledge 2015) 180–83.

over another. Rather, parties are free to choose any peaceful means to settle a dispute at any time.[898]

When a dispute arises, the parties have an obligation to 'proceed expeditiously to an exchange of views' regarding the choice of dispute settlement procedure.[899] Article 284 provides for the possibility of conciliation. If parties agree to submit a dispute to voluntary conciliation, they may do so in accordance with the procedure under UNCLOS Annex V or any other conciliation procedure. If the parties are not able to settle the dispute by use of the means of their own choice, or if an agreed time-limit expires, the procedures provided for in Part XV Section 2 apply.[900] Parties may also agree to settle a dispute between them by the means provided for in Section 2 without prior resort to voluntary means under Section 1.

Section 2 addresses compulsory dispute settlement. By accepting the terms of the convention at the time of ratification or accession, parties also accept the compulsory dispute settlement procedures laid down in Part XV Section 2 and related provisions.[901] They apply whenever the following three conditions are met cumulatively:

1) A dispute arises between parties concerning the interpretation or application of the convention;
2) the requirements of Section 1 are satisfied, unless otherwise agreed by the parties; and
3) none of the exceptions under Section 3 applies.[902]

Parties are free to choose one or more of the suggested procedures. There are four options: the ITLOS; the ICJ; an arbitral tribunal constituted in accordance with Annex VII; or a special arbitral tribunal constituted in accordance with Annex VIII. The last option is reserved to disputes relating to: fisheries; the protection and preservation of the marine environment; marine scientific

898 1982 UNCLOS art 280. If the parties have agreed, through a general, regional or bilateral agreement or otherwise, that a dispute concerning the interpretation or application of the convention shall be submitted to a specific procedure that entails a binding decision, that procedure applies, unless the parties to the dispute agree otherwise: ibid art 282.

899 1982 UNCLOS art 283(1). The choice is, of course, limited to peaceful means. Recourse to non-peaceful means for the settlement of disputes under the convention is not permitted: see Patibandla Chandrasekhara Rao, 'Law of the Sea, Settlement of Disputes', *Max Planck Encyclopedia of Public International Law* (2011) para 7.

900 1982 UNCLOS art 281. For disputes related to seabed activities (submitted pursuant to Part XI of the convention), Section 1 also applies if entities other than states are involved in a dispute: see ibid art 285.

901 See Chandrasekhara Rao (n 899) para 16.

902 1982 UNCLOS art 286.

research; or navigation, including pollution from vessels and by dumping. Parties may give effect to their choice of procedure by means of a written declaration when signing, ratifying or acceding the convention or at any time thereafter.[903] If a party has not submitted a written declaration before a dispute arises, it is deemed to have accepted arbitration in accordance with Annex VII.[904] Arbitration in accordance with Annex VII also applies to disputes between parties that have not accepted the same procedure, unless they agree otherwise.[905] The choice by the parties does not affect the jurisdiction of the ITLOS Seabed Disputes Chamber in cases related to activities in the Area.[906]

The court or tribunal adjudicating on a case in accordance with Part XV has jurisdiction over any dispute concerning the interpretation or application of the convention or any other international agreement related to its purposes.[907] Applicable law includes UNCLOS and other rules of international law that are compatible with the convention.[908] At the request of a party or *proprio motu*, the court or tribunal may select scientific or technical experts without a right to vote.[909] If the parties so agree, it may decide a case *ex aequo et bono*.[910] Decisions taken by the court or tribunal are final and binding on the parties to the dispute for the particular dispute at stake.[911] Even in the event that a party refuses to participate in proceedings and does not appear in hearings, it remains bound by the decision taken by the tribunal or court.[912]

Under certain conditions, the court or tribunal may prescribe provisional measures, including for the prevention of serious harm to the marine environment or for the protection of marine resources.[913] ITLOS has granted provisional measures when a party was able to establish a serious risk, even if full scientific proof could not be provided.[914] It ordered parties to consult and negotiate, exchange information, and assess and monitor environmental risks. It does not, however, order cessation of a potentially harmful activity by means

903 ibid art 287(1).
904 ibid art 287(3).
905 ibid art 287(5).
906 ibid art 287(2).
907 ibid art 288.
908 ibid art 293(1).
909 ibid art 289.
910 ibid art 293(2).
911 ibid art 296.
912 Art 9 of UNCLOS Annex VII. See *South China Sea Arbitration* (n 584) 45 paras 117–18.
913 1982 UNCLOS art 290(1).
914 See *Southern Bluefin Tuna Cases* (n 584); *MOX Plant* (n 689); *Case Concerning Land Reclamation* (n 689).

of an interim order.[915] Parties to the dispute have to comply promptly with provisional measures that have been prescribed in this way.[916]

UNCLOS Part XV, Section 3 provides for a number of limitations on the applicability of Section 2 and optional exceptions to it. Specifically, the tribunal or court may only exercise limited jurisdiction over disputes concerning the exercise by a coastal state of its sovereign rights or jurisdiction provided for in UNCLOS. However, Section 2 applies to cases in which it is alleged that a coastal state 'has acted in contravention of specified international rules and standards for the protection and preservation of the marine environment'.[917] Under Section 3, parties have also the possibility to activate exceptions from compulsory settlement. A state may declare that it does not accept such procedures with regard to disputes concerning sea boundary delimitations; historic bays and titles; military activities and law enforcement activities.[918]

The ITLOS Statute is contained in UNCLOS Annex VI. The tribunal has 21 members with 'recognized competence in the field of the law of the sea'.[919] It has a Special Chamber for Marine Environment Disputes consisting of nine members. The expertise of the judges may be counted among the benefits of the regime. In other respects, opinions on the UNCLOS dispute settlement system vary. While its substantial contribution to environmental jurisprudence is widely acknowledged, a certain risk is associated by some with what has been referred to as the proliferation of international courts and tribunals.[920] Whether under UNCLOS dispute settlement or any comparable regime, the most conspicuous feature about the judgments dealing with environmental matters is, perhaps, that they most commonly require parties to cooperate better and negotiate further.[921] They may provide that an environmental

---

915 See Birnie, Boyle and Redgwell (n 488) 226–27.

916 1982 UNCLOS art 290(6).

917 ibid art 297(1)(c).

918 ibid art 298(1). In the *South China Sea Arbitration*, the tribunal concluded that certain claims brought by the Philippines concerning the exceptions activated by China 'were not exclusively preliminary and would be deferred for further consideration in conjunction with the merits': *South China Sea Arbitration* (n 584) 62–63 paras 161–63.

919 1982 UNCLOS Annex VI art 2(1).

920 Simma, 'Universality of International Law from the Perspective of a Practitioner' (n 668) 278. Simma notably argues that there is more convergence than divergence in international jurisprudence and that, 'if various international courts do disagree on a point of law, the ensuing judicial dialogue may possibly further progressive development of the law'.

921 See, for instance, *Southern Bluefin Tuna Cases* (n 584); *MOX Plant* (n 689); *Case Concerning Land Reclamation* (n 689). See also *Lac Lanoux Arbitration* (n 814); *Gabčíkovo-Nagymaros* (n 543); *Pulp Mills Judgment* (n 544). See also Birnie, Boyle and Redgwell (n 488) 213 and 226; Sands and Peel (n 447) 160–61.

obligation has been breached[922] or require parties to cease activities or take further measures.[923] By contrast, they are usually silent about matters related to liability and compensation for environmental damage.[924] In any case, the jurisprudence of international courts and tribunals plays an important role for the (evolving) interpretation of treaty provisions and general law. Beyond that, their implications are mainly political in nature. As has been said: 'Community pressure remains in practice the only real sanction for enforcing compliance with arbitral awards, or with judgments of the ICJ or other international tribunals, and it is only in that very limited sense that we can talk about courts "enforcing" international law at all'.[925]

b) Lack of Compliance Facilitation

With the treaty's reliance on state responsibility and dispute settlement, UNCLOS enforcement is mainly based on traditional means of international enforcement. Especially in international environmental law, a number of disadvantages are associated with these traditional means of enforcement, including their bilateral and confrontational character, the *ex post* approach that is inherent to them (while damage to the environment is often irreversible), the inappropriate response they provide with respect to a wide range of environmental problems or common concerns, and a perceptible reluctance of states to resort to them.[926] Owing to these weaknesses, the last few decades have seen the rise of alternative regimes, which generally facilitate dispute

922 See *Chagos Marine Protected Area Arbitration* (n 584); *South China Sea Arbitration* (n 584).

923 In *Case Concerning Land Reclamation* (n 689) ITLOS ordered Singapore not to conduct its land reclamation in ways that might cause serious harm to the marine environment. In the *Kishenganga Arbitration*, the court decided that India shall release a minimum flow of water to a river below a dam: *Indus Waters Kishenganga Arbitration (Pakistan v India), Final Award* [2013] PCA (Arbitral Tribunal 2015). See also *Award between the United States and the United Kingdom relating to the rights of jurisdiction of United States in the Bering's sea and the preservation of fur seals* (1893) XXVIII Rep Int Arbitr Awards 263; *Trail Smelter Arbitration* (n 858).

924 A well-known exception in this respect is the *Trail Smelter Arbitration* (n 858). Also, the UN Security Council held Iraq liable for any direct damage, 'including environmental damage and the depletion of natural resources', caused by Iraq's unlawful invasion and occupation of Kuwait: UNSC (n 857) 7 para 16. Compensation was provided for a wide range of environmental damages: see UNCC (n 857). See also Gautier (n 857); Kazazi (n 857).

925 Birnie, Boyle and Redgwell (n 488) 213.

926 See ibid 211–12; Jan Klabbers, 'Compliance Procedures' in Daniel Bodansky, Jutta Brunnée and Ellen Hey (eds), *The Oxford Handbook of International Environmental Law* (Oxford University Press 2007) 1001.

avoidance and are based on new approaches to deal with cases of alleged non-compliance.

Traditional enforcement mechanisms provide states with a means to respond to an infringement of their rights, for instance by taking countermeasures or retaliatory action until the wrongful act is ceased and damage compensated, or by suspending or terminating a treaty.[927] Environmental regimes, however, often address global concerns rather than (or on top of) the interests of individual states. With regard to the general aim of such a regime – including the protection of the environment and the prevention of damage – retaliation or the suspension or termination of a treaty are, arguably, counterproductive responses to a failure by a particular state to comply with its environmental obligations.

This becomes even more evident when taking into account the fact that non-compliance – especially with environmental obligations – is not necessarily due to bad faith or intentions but may have many reasons, including limited capacities and a lack of necessary financial, institutional and other resources.[928] It may be due to policy constraints, for instance when environmental degradation is accepted for the sake of developmental projects pushed for by domestic stakeholders and foreign investors.[929] Also, since norms and standards of environmental protection are not always very well defined and without ambiguity, there might be competing interpretations of the law, which complicates enforcement. With regard to UNCLOS Part XII, such uncertainties are, for instance, related to the standard of care in due diligence obligations, the threshold of acceptable environmental harm and precaution.[930]

New approaches to non-compliance, such as reflected in a number of regional seas instruments, try to better accommodate some of the particularities associated with compliance with environmental obligations.[931] Instead of *ex post* responses to infringements, they allow for active compliance management.

927 In accordance with art 60 of the 1969 VCLT.

928 This is why, *prima facie*, non-compliance with multilateral environmental treaties seems to be a 'poor nation's problem' in the first place: Klabbers (n 926) 996–98.

929 Non-compliance may, in this sense, also be due to discrepancies in priority setting among countries. As Sands appositely observed in this respect: 'The limitations inherent in international arrangements for ensuring compliance with international environmental obligations are well apparent, and developments in international law alone will not be sufficient to overcome the political, economic and social reasons lying behind non-compliance': Sands and Peel (n 447) 182.

930 See Klabbers (n 926) 1001–02.

931 Whether and to what extent these approaches achieve in doing so is disputed: see ibid 1003–05.

Most importantly, such compliance mechanisms facilitate the identification of non-intentional causes of non-compliance, including the lack of capacities or resources. Additionally, they allow the addressing of such causes in a more anticipatory manner, ideally before serious or irreversible damage occurs. In doing so, they transpose the principle of preventive action into the procedural and institutional setting. Recourse to state responsibility and formal dispute settlement procedures may be avoided by the use of non-adversarial procedures. Non-compliance procedures do not, however, preclude the use of traditional enforcement mechanisms but offer an additional way of addressing compliance.[932]

Given the difficulties in the enforcement of the duty to protect and preserve the marine environment with regard to marine plastic pollution mitigation, a compliance facilitation procedure would seem necessary and useful. It would have to be tailored to the problem related to plastics and be linked to compliance review mechanisms. Compliance and implementation review usually comprises reporting obligations and may also have financial implications. In the case of plastic pollution, reporting obligations require harmonised monitoring methods. Whether UNCLOS would be the most suitable institutional home for such a mechanism is questionable. In view of the ongoing discussions under the auspices of UN Environment, the adoption of a new instrument specifically dealing with marine plastic pollution mitigation seems conceivable. The adoption of such an instrument would be a perfect opportunity to complement well-defined substantive requirements, such as the phase-out of certain products or national reduction targets, with an effective compliance facilitation mechanism and capacity-building scheme.

Conclusion of Section B

The adoption of UNCLOS was an important step forward in the development of a global regime on the protection and preservation of the marine environment. Its comprehensiveness, the package-deal approach, the fact that it represents a nearly global consensus and the customary status of most of its norms are some of the evident particularities of the convention. Also, UNCLOS set up a dispute settlement mechanism that is unique among environmental treaties and contributed considerably to the jurisprudence in this field of law. Part XII of the convention is innovative in that it introduced a general obligation to protect and preserve the marine environment and to prevent, reduce and

932 On the relation between non-compliance procedures and traditional enforcement mechanisms, see ibid 1005–07.

control marine pollution from all sources by the adoption, implementation and enforcement of appropriate measures, including regulatory. The UNCLOS regime is based on diligent control and regulation, and thus set an end to the former freedom of states to pollute the marine environment.

The obligation to protect and preserve the marine environment constitutes the core and foundation of the regime applying to marine plastic pollution mitigation from land-based sources. As an obligation of due diligence, it has to be interpreted in the light of contemporary international environmental law. Its content is informed by UNCLOS Part XII and other applicable rules of international law. The obligation not only consists of a negative duty not to cause significant damage to the marine environment but also comprises a positive obligation to proactively take measures to prevent, reduce and control pollution of the marine environment, including through the adoption of national measures, international cooperation, standard-setting activities, technical assistance, environmental impact assessment and monitoring of potentially harmful activities. Risk evaluation, precaution and cooperation play an important role in the fulfilment of respective obligations. Recent case law moreover suggests that states, in their obligation to adopt regulatory and other measures, have to give sufficient attention to the conservation and preservation of ecosystems.

Instead of defining a certain level of protection and regulating specific activities or substances within the convention or annexes, UNCLOS incorporates standards as adopted by the relevant international organizations. With this mechanism, it allows for a continuous development and evolution of the regime.

In view of the above, UNCLOS provides a relatively strong general framework on the protection of the marine environment and the regulation of marine pollution. The merits of the regime must, however, be put into perspective when it comes to the specific problem of marine plastic pollution from land-based sources. On closer inspection, several diluting factors attenuate the advantages of the convention and lead to the conclusion that it does not give a sufficient response by itself to this particular problem. Evidence of continuously increasing amounts of plastics in the oceans supports this conclusion.

There are many reasons why the regime does not take the desired effect. UNCLOS is not tailored to the issue of marine plastic pollution and does not provide for specific solutions, neither at a substantive level nor at the level of enforcement. For the purpose of plastic pollution mitigation, UNCLOS Part XII provisions are too general in nature. In the absence of a more specific instrument that fills the gaps and gives more specific content to them, many of these provisions are either inappropriate or insufficient – or simply not enforceable.

From a substantive point of view, the following factors deserve particular attention in this respect:

- *Due diligence in the absence of relevant legally binding international standards:* While the concept of due diligence is a valuable one to reflect different realities and take into account geographic, economic and other factors, it is accompanied by a range of legal uncertainties. Overall, there is little guidance in the convention on how exactly to interpret the obligation to prevent pollution with respect to plastics, and how to define the standard of care. In order to give effective content to the general obligations, UNCLOS depends highly on the existence of international standards. Reference to such standards is weaker with regard to land-based sources than with regard to other pollution sources. Also, existing international standards that are specifically relevant to plastics from land-based sources are mostly non-binding in nature. While states are generally obliged to take them into account in the adoption of national measures, there is no strict obligation to implement them. As a consequence, reference to international standards does not sufficiently clarify the uncertainties related to the general obligations with regard to plastics. The case would arguably be different if there was a legally binding international instrument providing for sufficiently clear standards on marine plastic pollution mitigation.
- *Lack of reference to relevant environmental management principles:* UNCLOS does not directly refer to sustainable development (including policy integration and the accommodation of the needs of future generations), the precautionary approach, the polluter pays principle (including cost internalization), clean production or integrated coastal zone management. These and other principles are, however, fundamental in the combat of marine plastic pollution.
- *Lack of reference to plastic-specific tools providing for additional guidance:* Also, UNCLOS does not define control measures for point and non-point pollution sources, or provide a list of substance categories and activities to be covered by preventive measures. Neither does it refer to the waste management hierarchy (or related reduce–reuse–recycle paradigms), best available techniques or best environmental practices, or any similar tool that would provide for additional guidance. There is no direct requirement in UNCLOS to include business and civil society. Similarly, public–private partnerships and environmental education are not addressed. The experience gained in regional frameworks and at the national level, however, shows that these can be important aspects in plastic pollution mitigation. While the regional instruments do not have global reach, they may serve as example models for

a more effective international regime. Also, they provide some important building blocks for such a regime.[933]

- *Environmental impact assessment and monitoring:* UNCLOS requires that environmental impact assessment and environmental monitoring be undertaken with regard to activities, but does not define the minimum content of the reports. It is not evident how the obligation to undertake environmental impact assessment can best be applied to plastics, and to non-point sources of plastic pollution in particular. Again, it is the continuous, diffuse and accumulative nature of plastic pollution that poses the main challenge here. Reference to life-cycle assessment would perhaps be more suitable in this respect. Moreover, UNCLOS does not require states to assess environmental policies and legislation. Yet, impact assessment of policies seems essential, including when it comes to changing production and consumption patterns and other behavioural issues.
- *Capacity-building:* UNCLOS allows for graduation, taking account of the fact that a low level of development and widespread poverty are restraining factors in the adoption and implementation of effective environmental regulation. Yet, while UNCLOS takes into account different levels of capacity and provides for the necessary flexibility in the standard of care, it does not counterbalance this flexibility with a sufficiently strong capacity-building scheme. In view of the problematic waste management conditions prevailing in many countries worldwide and the high costs related to their improvement, the provision of targeted and coordinated support, including financial, is absolutely necessary.[934] The convention does not provide the legal and institutional basis for concerted action in this regard.

While states have substantive obligations under UNLCOS to adopt a conduct towards the prevention and mitigation of marine plastic pollution, enforcement of such obligations is an extremely challenging task. Challenges include the difficulties associated with the identification of the polluter in a specific case and the provision of the necessary evidence in this regard; the determination of the standard of care with respect to marine plastic pollution mitigation in the absence of binding international standards; the lack of capacities in a context of due diligence obligations; the reluctance of states to bring cases solely related to areas beyond national jurisdiction or domestic pollution; the fact that all states contribute to the problem (collective action problem); the

933 Regional conventions will be discussed in the following Chapter (2.2).

934 See Cottier, 'Technology and the Law of International Trade Regulation' (n 783) 1041–42.

definition of hazardous activities and the question to what extent plastic production, use and disposal fall under this term; the gradual accumulation of negative effects and the quantification of environmental damage in this context. The absence or weak effect of principles and obligations specifically tailored to the problem at stake and the lack of guidance for implementation at the substantive level add to the problem. These challenges constitute a relatively high hurdle for a case to be brought even in interstate constellations.

With its reference to the law of state responsibility and liability on the one hand and its solid dispute settlement mechanism on the other hand, UNCLOS widely relies on traditional means of enforcement. These traditional, interstate enforcement mechanisms have not, so far, provided a means to appropriately address the 'incremental and gradual harmful effects of normal activities'.[935] They presuppose that the wrongdoer, if there is one, can clearly be identified. Yet, marine plastic pollution, as massive and problematic as it may be, does not result from a single act or omission that can easily be associated with a particular polluter. Rather, damage is insidious, cumulative and dispersed. This continuous, dispersed and diffuse character of plastic pollution is the main hurdle to UNCLOS enforcement. It is related to – or, indeed, at the root of – many of the above identified challenges. In this specific plastic-related context, traditional dispute settlement seems more of a theoretical option than of a way to give the provisions real effect. Also, the general reluctance of states to resort to public interest standing means that, in practice, large parts of marine plastic pollution are not *effectively* covered by the convention's enforcement mechanism. These parts include large accumulation zones in the high seas and the deep seabed, as well as domestic pollution on tourist beaches or from landfills, plastic factories and population centres situated close to the coast when evidence of transboundary damage cannot be provided.

In order to enhance compliance and increase practical enforceability of the duty to protect the marine environment from plastic pollution, some basic features, which respond to the identified challenges, seem necessary. One of these features is the improvement of the substantive rules by defining clear and legally binding standards, taking into account relevant environmental principles and management tools. Another such feature is the creation of a compliance facilitation procedure complementing and supplementing the UNCLOS dispute settlement regime. Effective compliance facilitation usually comes along with reporting obligations by states on national implementation, as well as global implementation review and a strong capacity-building

935 Xue (n 872) 195.

scheme. International coordination of financial and technical resources seems necessary in this context.

These elements could be covered by a special instrument directly addressing marine plastic pollution, especially from land-based sources. Working towards such an instrument goes in line with the obligations under UNCLOS to cooperate at the appropriate level, including international, to harmonize policies and to adopt and enforce international standards.[936] By virtue of Article 237, a special instrument on marine plastic pollution in furtherance of the principles as set forth in UNCLOS would have priority over the more general provisions of UNCLOS Part XII. At the same time, the adoption of such an instrument would give much greater effect to the general provisions under UNCLOS, as these provisions would be informed by the adopted standards on plastic pollution mitigation. On the other hand, UNCLOS would strengthen the effect of international standards on marine plastic pollution mitigation adopted by a competent international organization or a diplomatic conference. According to UNCLOS Article 213, states would have to adopt laws and regulations and take other measures necessary to implement them. Thanks to the incorporated reference to such standards, UNCLOS would thus not need to be amended to include plastic-specific obligations, but could effectively fulfil its role as a framework convention. Within this framework and appropriate regional cooperation, countries have a policy space with regard to national implementation. The model corresponds to the doctrine of multilayered governance, or the *Five Storey House*, which allows assigning regulations to appropriate levels of governance, from local to global.[937]

In order to better apprehend the need of such an instrument, Sections C and D discuss the relevance of other global instruments to marine plastic pollution mitigation and their relationship to UNCLOS. Most of the instruments that are relevant to plastics are mutually supportive with respect to the objectives and

936 Indeed, the emphasis UNCLOS puts on global and regional cooperation and an equitable balance of interests ideally lowers the need for recourse to dispute settlement mechanisms.

937 Allocations essentially depend upon the public good to be produced: see Cottier, 'Technology and the Law of International Trade Regulation' (n 783) 1038–39. On multilayered governance and the theory of the five storey house, see Thomas Cottier, 'Multilayered Governance, Pluralism, and Moral Conflict' (2009) 16 Indiana Journal of Global Legal Studies 647; 'Towards a Five Storey House' in Christian Joerges and Ernst-Ulrich Petersmann (eds), *Constitutionalism, Multilevel Trade Governance and International Economic Law* (Hart 2011); Thomas Cottier and Maya Hertig, 'The Prospects of 21st Century Constitutionalism' (2003) 7 Max Planck Yearbook of United Nations Law 261, ch IV.

obligations under Part XII. Even if there are competing objectives, conform interpretation is usually possible and corresponds to the practice of international courts and tribunals.[938] In fact, a real conflict of norms is rare in this context.[939] External norms that are relevant to the protection and preservation of the marine environment, be it in a direct or indirect way, inform the content and interpretation of the duties of states under UNCLOS Part XII, and vice versa. This is also true if, as the case may be, there are slight differences in the membership of the respective treaties.[940]

The most delicate relationship with regard to regulatory coherence may be the one between UNCLOS Part XII and international trade regulation. Trade law is relevant in that it defines and limits the leeway of states in taking implementing measures with potentially trade-distorting effects. A smooth interplay between environmental obligations and trade law is possible and corresponds to the normal case. However, environmental measures with extraterritorial effects have repeatedly been challenged before the WTO dispute settlement bodies and have usually been won by the complaining party (that is the foreign state affected by the measure). The same constellation is conceivable with regard to national measures taken in the prevention and combat of marine plastic pollution. Section C gives a brief overview on the law of the WTO and discusses its relation to UNLCOS Part XII.[941] The specific role of WTO law with regard to national implementation measures in marine plastic litter mitigation will be discussed in Section 2.3.B.

C *The Law of the World Trade Organization*

In contrast to the environmental agreements that will be discussed in Section D, trade law, and the related fields of investment law and intellectual property rights law, have primarily an economic and developmental rationale.

938 See, for instance, reference to the CBD and other multilateral environmental agreements in *South China Sea Arbitration* (n 584) 376–84 paras 945–64; *US Shrimp* (n 677) paras 130–4 and 168.

939 On conflicts and coherence in international environmental law, see: Boyle, 'Relationship between International Environmental Law and Other Branches of International Law' (n 668); ILC, 'Fragmentation Report' (n 653); Pauwelyn, *Conflict of Norms* (n 668); Simma, 'Universality of International Law from the Perspective of a Practitioner' (n 668); Rüdiger Wolfrum and Nele Matz, *Conflicts in International Environmental Law* (Springer 2003).

940 In *US Shrimp*, the WTO Appellate Body relied on a number of environmental agreements to which the US (as defending party to the dispute) is not a party: *US Shrimp* (n 677).

941 The analysis in this book focuses on the WTO regime and does not take special account of other trade-related instruments or look into related fields, such as investment protection. However, many of the findings may be valid for these instruments as well.

According to the preamble of the Agreement Establishing the World Trade Organization (Marrakesh Agreement), the general objective of WTO-covered agreements is to raise standards of living, ensure full employment and economic growth, and expand the production of and trade in goods and services. To this purpose, the agreements aim at substantially reducing tariffs and other barriers to trade and eliminating discriminatory treatment in international trade relations.[942] These policy objectives may well compete with the desire to protect and preserve the environment, which has been a main driver in the adoption of UNCLOS Part XII.

The fact that WTO-covered agreements and UNCLOS are based on different, potentially competing policy objectives does not, however, mean that the respective provisions are *per se* incompatible. In fact, conflicts or inconsistencies between the two regimes are the exception and not the rule. There is little case law related to interferences between UNCLOS and WTO commitments, and none of the cases focused on Part XII obligations.[943] Adjudicating bodies and the legal doctrine suggest that these commitments can be reconciled, since both sets of treaties focus on international cooperation as

942 Agreement Establishing the World Trade Organization (Marrakesh Agreement) (adopted on 15 April 1994, entered into force on 1 January 1995) 1867 UNTS 154, 33 ILM 1144 (1994), Preamble.

943 In *US Shrimp*, the WTO Appellate Body considered a US measure in protection of migratory sea turtles as unjustifiable because of the failure by the United States to engage in meaningful negotiations with a number of shrimp-exporting countries, while it conducted such negotiations with other countries. In the judgment, much emphasis was put on the need for prior negotiation and international cooperation in furtherance of the principles set forth in UNCLOS Articles 64, 65 and 118: *US Shrimp* (n 677) 65–72 para 166–76. The *Swordfish Stocks Case* involved a unilateral ban by Chile on the importation and transit of swordfish catches and their processing in Chilean ports when these catches did not conform to Chilean conservation rules. Chile had adopted conservation rules in accordance with the Framework Agreement for the Conservation of the Living Marine Resources of the High Seas of the South Pacific (Galapagos Agreement) (adopted on 14 August 2000), which was being negotiated and to which Chile is a signatory. In response to the ban, the European Union initiated a WTO dispute settlement proceeding against Chile in April 2000. While the case was pending before the WTO, Chile started proceedings against the European Union under UNCLOS by instituting an arbitral tribunal. In the case, which was later dealt with by a special chamber instituted by the ITLOS, Chile argued that the European Union had violated UNCLOS provisions by bringing the case before a WTO panel: *Conservation and Sustainable Exploitation of Swordfish Stocks in the South-Eastern Pacific Ocean* (*Chile v European Union*) [2000] ITLOS case No. 7 para 3 lit d. Eventually, both the WTO and ITLOS cases were withdrawn and the dispute was solved by a series of negotiations between Chile and the European Union. For more information on the case, see Peter-Tobias Stoll and Silja Vöneky, 'The Swordfish Case: Law of the Sea v. Trade' (2002) 62 ZAÖRV 21.

a preferred approach when compared to unilateral action by individual states.[944]

Discussion on the interrelation between UNCLOS and WTO-covered agreements forms part of the broader debate on the nexus between environment and trade in international law. It is not merely theoretical but is practically relevant at different levels (comparable to the ones identified under the concept of common concern[945]):

- First, it is relevant at the level of the states' *domestic obligations*. While UNCLOS Part XII and WTO-covered agreements are not *per se* incompatible, tensions may arise at the level of implementation. Measures taken in the fulfilment of environmental obligations may be *a priori* inconsistent with rules of WTO law and related agreements. Such inconsistencies may especially arise when implementing measures, possibly taken on a unilateral basis, have negative effects on other states, either by limiting their market access or because the measures discriminate in their effect against foreign products when compared to like domestic products. In general, WTO rules play a potentially inhibiting role with regard to trade measures that aim at influencing the behaviour of actors abroad and enforce self-set standards in other countries, including in protection of the global commons. In fact, policy measures with trade effects are sometimes a preferred method for states to address environmental problems caused outside their own jurisdiction. Discussions on the interface of environmental and trade law often focus on this particular aspect and are thus closely related to the issue of extraterritorial jurisdiction and unilateralism.[946] Trade restrictions of goods based on

944 See, for instance, Brian K Myers, 'Trade Measures and the Environment: Can the WTO and UNCLOS Be Reconciled?' (2005) 23 UCLA J. Envtl. L. & Pol'y 37, 70–71. See also Franz Xaver Perrez, 'The Mutual Supportiveness of Trade and Environment' (2006) 100 ASIL Proceedings 26.

945 See Schäli (n 20).

946 On extraterritorial jurisdiction and unilateralism in a trade-environment context, see Erich Vranes, *Trade and the Environment: Fundamental Issues in International Law, WTO Law, and Legal Theory* (Oxford University Press 2009) Part II. In general, it is assumed that the jurisdiction of a state is strongly linked with – and in principle confined to – its territory. Extraterritorial jurisdiction is the exception and requires justification by the state resorting to such measures. The exact definition of extraterritorial jurisdiction is not evident but involves more than mere extraterritorial effects of a specific measure. It arguably consists of a direct interference with a foreign state's competence to determine its domestic affairs. The question of whether and under what circumstances trade measures are to be classified as extraterritorial and thus require justification under general international law is particularly difficult: on the one hand they are applied within a state or at its border and do not regulate the behaviour of actors outside the state's jurisdiction in a coercive

(non-product-related) processes and production methods (so-called PPMs) are of a particular concern in this regard and highly controversial in the context of WTO law.[947]

- Second, the WTO potentially fosters *international cooperation* in the development and implementation of environmental law: the efforts taken under the aegis of the WTO to collaborate with the secretariats of multilateral environmental agreements, and the approach taken by the WTO dispute settlement bodies in respect of such agreements, strongly encourage states to adopt common solutions to environmental problems and to cooperate at the global and appropriate regional levels.[948]
- Third, international trade regulation plays a restraining role with regard to the adoption of *unilateral measures* in terms of trade sanctions towards a non-complying state that, as a free rider, possibly benefits from specific efforts of other states but does not fulfil its own duties in this respect. The effectiveness of such sanctions is disputed with regard to environmental duties, especially if non-compliance is mainly due to low capacities.

---

way. On the other hand, they can strongly influence such behaviour. Some measures have therefore been classified as extraterritorial in a number of panel and Appellate Body reports: ibid 157–68. The *US Tuna* panel reports of 1991 and 1994, both unadopted, suggest the disputed US measure, consisting in a non-product-related PPM, to be extraterritorial in character: *United States – Restrictions on Imports of Tuna* (*US Tuna I*) [1991] GATT Panel Report (unadopted) DS21/R, BISD 39S/55; *United States – Restrictions on Imports of Tuna* (*US Tuna II* (*EEC*)) [1994] GATT Panel Report (unadopted) DS29/R. The position on this issue by the Appellate Body in *US Shrimp* is less clear. In its report, the Appellate Body refers to a 'sufficient nexus' between the sea turtle species protected by the measure and the US: *US Shrimp* (n 677) para 133. Unilateral trade measures can be defined as 'regulations that serve to protect the environment, but incur trade impacts and are adopted by one or more states without the consent of the affected state': Vranes 174.

947 On PPMs see, for instance, Christiane R Conrad, *Processes and Production Methods (PPMs) in WTO Law: Interfacing Trade and Social Goals* (Cambridge University Press 2011); Kateryna Holzer, *Carbon-Related Border Adjustment and WTO Law* (Edward Elgar Publishing 2014) ch 5; OECD, 'Processes and Production Methods (PPMs): Conceptual Framework and Considerations on Use of PPM-Based Trade Measures' (OECD 1997) OCDE/GD(97)137; Robert Read, 'Process and Production Methods and the Regulation of International Trade' in Nicolas Perdikis and Robert Read (eds), *The WTO and the Regulation of International Trade: Recent Trade Disputes Between the European Union and the United States* (Edward Elgar 2005); Vranes (n 946) Part III ch 3; Jochem Wiers, 'WTO Rules and Environmental Production and Processing Methods (PPMs)' (2001) 2 ERA-Forum 101. See also Section 2.1.C.ii.1).b) below.

948 See, in particular, *US Shrimp* (n 677) 65–70 paras 166–172. See also Alan E Boyle, 'Further Development of the 1982 Convention on the Law of the Sea: Mechanisms for Change' in David Freestone, Richard Barnes and David Ong (eds), *The Law of the Sea: Progress and Prospects* (Oxford University Press 2006) 59.

- Finally, the relationship between UNCLOS and WTO law is relevant with regard to *dispute settlement*: WTO dispute settlement may offer countries affected by a measure a possibility to challenge the measure in question. Competing dispute resolution between UNCLOS and WTO dispute settlement bodies is therefore conceivable and has been an issue in at least one case.[949] A further issue that may arise in this regard is the question of whether and to what extent dispute settlement bodies of one regime may, or have to, take into account agreements associated with the other regime in the interpretation of their own treaties.

The current subsection starts with a brief introduction into the institutional set-up of the WTO (i) and the core principles and obligations under WTO law (ii). It then examines the interrelation between the WTO and UNCLOS Part XII (iii) and generally addresses some issues of coherence, including with regard to national implementation, the role of international cooperation and a potential international agreement on plastics, and unilateral measures (iv).

i The WTO in a Nutshell

The WTO system has its roots in the post-Second World War spirit that coined major trade liberalization efforts in the promotion of global economic growth. Along with the International Monetary Fund and the International Bank for Reconstruction and Development (today's World Bank), the 1947 General Agreement on Tariffs and Trade (GATT 1947)[950] formed one of the three pillars of the Bretton Woods system. The GATT induced substantial tariff reductions in global trade in goods and also tackled non-tariff barriers to trade, trade in services and trade-related aspects of intellectual property rights. Commitments were defined in eight multilateral trade negotiation rounds, the last of which was held in Uruguay in 1994. At the so-called Uruguay Round, the WTO was established through the Marrakesh Agreement. The WTO administers a revised version of the GATT as well as a number of other agreements, all of which are annexed to the Marrakesh Agreement. Its organizational structure includes the Committee on Trade and Environment (CTE), which addresses various aspects of the relationship between international trade and the protection of the environment.

In 2001, the Doha programme of work was launched, which is sometimes referred to as a ninth negotiation round or the 'Doha Round'. In the Doha Round, the CTE was charged with focusing on the relationship between WTO rules

949 *Swordfish Stocks Case* (n 943).

950 General Agreement on Tariffs and Trade (GATT 1947) (entered into force on 1 January 1948) 55 UNTS 194 1947.

and multilateral environmental agreements, collaboration between the WTO and secretariats of environmental agreements, and the reduction of barriers to trade in environmental goods and services. More generally, Doha negotiations focused on a number of highly contentious subjects, including agriculture trade. They have been hampered by strong tensions between developing and developed countries, and have not yielded the results that were hoped for. The round was concluded in 2015 without major achievements. Arguably, it marks a crisis in multilateral trade negotiations, which led to the negotiation of a number of 'mega-regional' trade agreements seemingly competing with the multilateral trading system, until negotiations came to an abrupt halt with the election of President Trump in the United States in 2016.[951]

Current discussions within the WTO are still marked by the ongoing crisis, but also the management of global challenges related to the environment and the corona pandemic in 2019. The role of the WTO and global trade in relation to plastic pollution is also increasingly an issue in this context.[952] In November 2020, a group of WTO members launched an Informal Dialogue on Plastics Pollution and Environmentally Sustainable Plastics Trade. The purpose of the Informal Dialogue is to identify key opportunities for enhanced trade cooperation to support domestic, regional, and global efforts against plastic pollution.[953]

---

951 These agreements notably include the Trans-Pacific Partnership (TPP) Agreement among Australia, Canada, Japan, Mexico, the United States, and seven more countries (the US withdrew from negotiations on 23 January 2017) and the Transatlantic Trade and Investment Partnership (TTIP) between the United States and the European Union (EU). For an outline and assessment of recent structural changes in world trade law, see Thomas Cottier, 'International Economic Law in Transition from Trade Liberalization to Trade Regulation' (2014) 17 Journal of International Economic Law 671; 'The Common Law of International Trade and the Future of the World Trade Organization' (2015) 18 Journal of International Economic Law 3; 'The Changing Structure of International Trade Law' (2018) 21 Zeitschrift für europarechtliche Studien 421.

952 See Barrowclough, Deere Birkbeck and Christen (n 91); Carolyn Deere Birkbeck, 'Strengthening International Cooperation to Tackle Plastic Pollution: Options for the WTO' (2020) Global Governance Brief 1; Deere Birkbeck and others (n 134); UNCTAD, 'Material Substitutes to Address Marine Plastic Pollution and Support a Circular Economy: Issues and Options for Trade Policymakers' (2021) UNCTAD/DITC/TED/INF/2021/5; WTO Committee on Trade and Environment (n 224).

953 Identified key elements include: improving transparency; monitoring trade trends; promoting best practices; strengthening policy coherence; identifying the scope for collective approaches; assessing capacity and technical assistance needs; and cooperating with other international processes and efforts: see WTO, 'Plastics Pollution Dialogue Advances Discussions, Eyeing MC12 Outcome' (*Informal Dialogue on Plastics Pollution and Environmentally Sustainable Plastics Trade*, 21 June 2021) <https://www.wto.org/english/news_e/news21_e/ega_21jun21_e.htm> accessed 19 February 2022.

Dispute settlement is one of the core functions of the WTO. The Dispute Settlement Understanding (DSU)[954] is one of the instruments annexed to the Marrakesh Agreement. It fundamentally reformed dispute settlement as practised under the 1947 GATT and established a solid, unparalleled trade dispute settlement system which is at the heart of international trade regulation.[955] The system involves several steps: in the event of a dispute being raised, parties first have to consult and strive for a mutually acceptable solution. Only if consultations fail may the complaining party request the establishment of an ad hoc panel.[956] In the event of such a request, a panel is established by the Dispute Settlement Body (DSB), a body consisting of representatives from all member governments.[957] The panel will examine the case referred to it and report its findings to the DSB. If the panel's report is appealed by either of the parties, the case is heard by the Appellate Body, a standing body with its seat in Geneva, Switzerland. The Appellate Body usually consists of seven persons.[958] Normally, it can uphold, modify or reverse the legal findings and conclusions of the panel.[959] Parties have to accept Appellate Body reports unconditionally.[960] The report (not appealed or as revised by the Appellate Body) is adopted by the DSB, unless the DSB decides by consensus not to adopt it.[961] Based on the report, the DSB can request a party to bring a measure that is found inconsistent with a covered agreement into conformity with the party's obligations under that agreement. The party has to report on implementation of the report in a reasonable period of time.[962] If it fails to implement it, the parties may agree on compensation measures or the DSB may authorize the winning party to retaliate by suspending concessions owed to the non-implementing party.[963]

---

954 Understanding on Rules and Procedures Governing the Settlement of Disputes (DSU) Marrakesh Agreement Establishing the World Trade Organization, Annex 2, 1869 UNTS 401, 33 ILM 1226 (1994).

955 Cottier, 'The Common Law of International Trade and the Future of the World Trade Organization' (n 951) 12.

956 DSU art 4(7).

957 The same representatives meet as General Council, which is the WTO's highest-level decision-making body.

958 The US has been blocking new appointments in the past few years, so that with the expiring of terms Appellate Body membership was reduced to below the minimum of three members needed to consider appealed panel reports. As of 11 December 2019, it is no longer able to hear new appeals, which leaves the future of the WTO dispute settlement system uncertain.

959 DSU art 18(13).

960 ibid art 18(14).

961 ibid arts 16.4 and 17.14.

962 ibid arts 19 and 21.

963 ibid art 22.

ii Core Principles and Agreements

Core objectives of the WTO regime include fair competition and the improvement of market access through the lowering of tariff and non-tariff barriers to trade, non-discrimination and transparency. These disciplines form an integral part of the covered agreements, each of which addresses a particular aspect related to international trade. For the purposes of this book, three instruments are of particular relevance: the GATT, as revised in 1994, provides for the general rules on trade in goods, including, of course, plastic products.[964] The Agreement on Technical Barriers to Trade (TBT) is relevant for measures involving technical regulations and standards, including labelling and product or packaging regulations that relate to the life cycle of plastics or refer to their properties, basic ingredients, degradability, or related processes and production methods.[965] Finally, the Agreement on the Application of Sanitary and Phytosanitary Measures (SPS) may be of some relevance in the food packaging and beverage sectors.[966] Further covered agreements, such as the Agreement on Trade-Related Aspects of Intellectual Property Rights (TRIPS),[967] the Agreement on Subsidies and Countervailing Measures (SCM)[968]

---

964 General Agreement on Tariffs and Trade (GATT 1994) Marrakesh Agreement Establishing the World Trade Organization, Annex 1A, 1867 UNTS 190, 33 ILM 1153 (1994).

965 Agreement on Technical Barriers to Trade (TBT) Marrakesh Agreement Establishing the World Trade Organization, Annex 1A, 1868 UNTS 120. See *United States – Measures Concerning the Importation, Marketing and Sale of Tuna and Tuna Products* (*Tuna II (Mexico)*) [2012] Appellate Body Report WT/DS381/AB/R 72–80 paras 178–99.

966 Agreement on the Application of Sanitary and Phytosanitary Measures (SPS) Marrakesh Agreement Establishing the World Trade Organization, Annex 1A, 1867 UNTS 493.

967 Agreement on Trade-Related Aspects of Intellectual Property Rights (TRIPS) Marrakesh Agreement Establishing the World Trade Organization, Annex 1C, as amended on 23 January 2017, 1869 UNTS 299, 33 ILM 1197 (1994). The law on the protection of intellectual property rights seems particularly relevant to questions related to technology transfer. While from an environmental point of view, there is an interest in the rapid dissemination of sustainable packaging designs and waste management technologies, the developer of such designs and technologies has an economic interest in controlling the use of his or her innovation in order to recoup the investment undertaken in research and development. The TRIPS Agreement sets minimum standards on the laws used by states to protect intellectual property rights. It allows member states to exclude certain inventions from patentability, especially when the *ordre public* or morality is at stake, or to protect human, animal or plant life or health, as well as to avoid serious prejudice to the environment (see art 27(2)). On the TRIPS Agreement and technology regulation, see Cottier, 'Technology and the Law of International Trade Regulation' (n 783).

968 Agreement on Subsidies and Countervailing Measures (SCM) Marrakesh Agreement Establishing the World Trade Organization, Annex 1A, 1869 UNTS 14. WTO rules on export subsidies could come into play if, for instance, mandatory take-back schemes of plastic packaging lead to an oversupply of recyclable plastics and are, as a consequence, dumped

or the Agreement on Government Procurement (GPA), as well as international treaties on investment protection, might also be relevant with regard to measures on plastics and marine litter prevention but will not be further discussed here.

1) *The General Agreement on Tariffs and Trade*

a) Basic Disciplines under GATT

In order to improve general conditions of market access, WTO law defines and limits permitted measures by members for regulating trade. Under GATT, the only admitted trade barriers are import or export taxes (often referred to as tariffs[969]) and other charges of an equivalent effect, as well as import licences.[970] In the Uruguay multilateral negotiation round, countries agreed to further cut tariff rates and 'bind' them to a certain level. Bound tariff rates may not be raised without compensating affected parties. For the sake of transparency and predictability, countries' commitments in this regard are defined in their schedules of concession.[971]

WTO obligations are fundamentally based on the principle of non-discrimination, which has been referred to as the 'critical discipline' of WTO law.[972] The principle is reflected in the most favoured nation and national treatment principles. The *most favoured nation* principle (MFN), which is prominently reflected in GATT Article I, requires that if special treatment is given to the goods and services of one country, the same treatment (or treatment no less favourable) be accorded to like goods and services of all WTO member states.[973]

---

on international markets at low or negative prices in order to dispose of stock piles: see OECD, *Extended Producer Responsibility* (n 557) 70–71.

969 A tariff is defined as ‚a pecuniary tax on a product levied upon importation or exportation, i.e. upon its crossing the border into, or from, another country or jurisdiction': Thomas Cottier and Matthias Oesch, *International Trade Regulation: Law and Policy in the WTO, the European Union and Switzerland: Cases, Materials and Comments* (Staempfli Publishers 2005) 577–78. GATT Article II:2(a) explicitly excludes from the notion of tariffs charges levied on imported products equivalent to an internal tax imposed on domestic goods (so-called border tax adjustment measures): ibid 580–81. See also Peter van den Bossche and Werner Zdouc, *The Law and Policy of the World Trade Organization: Text, Cases, and Materials* (3rd edn, Cambridge University Press 2013) ch 6.

970 See Marion Panizzon, Luca Arnold and Thomas Cottier, 'Handel und Umwelt in der WTO: Entwicklungen und Perspektiven' [2010] Umweltrecht in der Praxis 206.

971 See GATT 1994 art II.

972 IISD and UNEP, *Environment and Trade: A Handbook* (IISD 2005) 31.

973 GATT 1994 art I; TBT art 2.1. cf General Agreement on Trade in Services (GATS) Marrakesh Agreement Establishing the World Trade Organization, Annex 1B, 1869 UNTS 183, 33 ILM 1167 (1994) art II; TRIPS art 4.

Through the MFN, tariff and other trade concessions by a state towards another state apply between that state and all other WTO members.[974]

Perhaps more crucial with regard to the subject at hand, the *national treatment* principle, as enshrined in GATT Article III, requires that imported goods from other countries be treated no less favourably than like domestic goods.[975] The provision requires equality of competitive conditions and aims at protecting expectations of equal competitive relationships.[976] According to its paragraph 1,

> contracting parties recognize that internal taxes and other internal charges, and laws, regulations and requirements affecting the internal sale, offering for sale, purchase, transportation, distribution or use of products [...] should not be applied to imported or domestic products *so as to afford protection to domestic production.*[977]

Paragraphs 2 and 4 define national treatment obligations with respect to internal taxation and internal regulations, respectively. An internal tax or other internal charge applied to imported products is inconsistent with GATT Article III:2, first sentence, when it exceeds taxes or charges applied to *like* domestic products.[978] According to GATT Article III:2, second sentence, internal taxes or other internal charges are not to be applied to imported or domestic products so as to afford protection to domestic production. The Note Ad Article III provides in this respect that a tax 'would be considered to be inconsistent with the provisions of the second sentence [...] where competition was involved between, on the one hand, the taxed product and, on the other hand, a *directly competitive or substitutable product* which was *not similarly taxed*'.[979]

974 Under the GATT regime, there are two exceptions to the MFN rule: first, states party to regional trade agreements are allowed to apply preferential tariff rates among each other: see GATT 1994 art XXIV. Second, GATT allows its members to apply preferential tariff rates to developing countries, and least developed countries in particular.

975 The principle of National Treatment is also reflected in other covered agreements: see TBT art 2.1; GATS art XVII; TRIPS art 3.

976 *Korea – Taxes on Alcoholic Beverages* (*Korea Alcoholic Beverages*) [1999] Appellate Body Report WT/DS75/AB/R, WT/DS84/AB/R para 120.

977 Emphasis added.

978 The consistency test for GATT art III:2, first sentence, is, thus, three-tired and examines whether the measure at issue is an internal tax or other internal charge on products; whether the imported and domestic products are like products; and whether the imported products are taxed in excess of the domestic products: see Bossche and Zdouc (n 969) 356.

979 Emphasis added. This results in a four-tired test of consistency, examining whether the measure at issue is an internal tax or other internal charge on products; whether the

GATT Article III:2 thus provides for a stricter requirement with regard to the taxation of like products than with regard to the taxation of the broader category of directly competitive or substitutable products: while no tax differential whatsoever is allowed between imported and like domestic products to the detriment of the imported product (first sentence), an internal tax imposed on imported products may slightly exceed taxes on directly competitive or substitutable domestic products (second sentence).[980] Inconsistency with GATT Article III:2, second sentence moreover presupposes an element of protectionism, namely that the tax measure in question be 'applied to imported or domestic products so as to afford protection to domestic production'.[981] According to the Appellate Body, the protective application of a measure can most often be discerned from its design, its architecture, and its revealing structure.[982]

Internal taxes or other internal charges in the sense of GATT Article III:2 are distinct from border measures in that they 'accrue due to an internal event, such as the distribution, sale, use or transportation of the imported product'.[983] The characterization of a measure in a state's domestic law is not decisive in itself for the measure's qualification as an internal measure under WTO law, nor is the intent of the legislators.[984] GATT Article III:2 also covers indirect taxation, such as taxes imposed on raw materials used in the products,[985] or border tax adjustment measures.[986]

imported and domestic products are directly competitive or substitutable; whether the imported and domestic products are dissimilarly taxed; and whether the dissimilar taxation is applied so as to afford protection to domestic production: see ibid 371. See also *Japan – Taxes on Alcoholic Beverages* (*Japan Alcoholic Beverages II*) [1996] Appellate Body Report WT/DS8/AB/R, WT/DS10/AB/R, WT/DS11/AB/R 24.

980 See *Japan Alcoholic Beverages II* (n 979) 26–27.

981 GATT 1994 art III:1.

982 *Japan Alcoholic Beverages II* (n 979) 29.

983 *China – Measures Affecting Imports of Automobile Parts* (*China Auto Parts*) [2009] Appellate Body Report WT/DS339/AB/R, WT/DS340/AB/R, WT/DS342/AB/R para 162.

984 See ibid para 178.

985 See *Japan – Customs Duties, Taxes and Labelling Practices on Imported Wines and Alcoholic Beverages* (*Japan Alcoholic Beverages I*) [1987] GATT Panel Report L/6216, BISD 34S/83 para 5.8.

986 Border tax adjustments are 'any fiscal measures which put into effect, in whole or in part, the destination principle (i.e. which enable exported products to be relieved of some or all of the tax charged in the exporting country in respect of similar domestic products sold to consumers on the home market and which enable imported products sold to consumers to be charged with some or all of the tax charged in the importing country in respect of similar domestic products)': GATT, 'Report of the Working Party on Border Tax Adjustments (Adopted on 2 December 1970)' (1972) BISD 18th Supp. 97 para 4.

The principle of national treatment also applies to internal regulation. According to GATT Article III:4, imported products 'shall be accorded treatment no less favourable than that accorded to like products of national origin in respect of all laws, regulations and requirements affecting their internal sale, offering for sale, purchase, transportation, distribution or use'.[987] The provision covers any laws or regulations which might adversely modify the conditions of competition between the domestic and imported products on the internal market, for instance by imposing additional administrative burdens on imported products.[988] Voluntary private action may fall under the term *requirement* if the government can be hold responsible for the private action due to a close link to a government action.[989]

While the use of tariffs is, under certain constraints, accepted under GATT, its Article XI prohibits *quantitative restrictions*, including import and export bans, quotas or measures with similar trade-distorting effects. The prohibition is based on the rationale that volume-based measures are assumed to have a more trade-distorting effect than price-based measures. To the extent that quantitative restrictions are justified or exceptionally allowed, they must be applied in a non-discriminatory way.[990] WTO members are required to notify the secretariat of any quantitative restrictions which they maintain, as well as of any changes in these restrictions.[991] The secretariat maintains a public database on quantitative restrictions.

---

987 According to the Appellate Body, three elements must be satisfied for a violation of Article III:4 to be established: that the imported and domestic products at issue are 'like products'; that the measure at issue is a 'law, regulation, or requirement affecting their internal sale, offering for sale, purchase, transportation, distribution, or use'; and that the imported products are accorded 'less favourable' treatment than that accorded to like domestic products: *Korea – Measures Affecting Imports of Fresh, Chilled and Frozen Beef* (*Korea Beef*) [2000] Appellate Body Report WT/DS161/AB/R, WT/DS169/AB/R para 133.

988 The Appellate Body however held that 'the existence of a detrimental effect on a given imported product resulting from a measure does not necessarily imply that this measure accords less favourable treatment to imports if the detrimental effect is explained by factors or circumstances unrelated to the foreign origin of the product, such as the market share of the importer': *Dominican Republic – Measures Affecting the Importation and Internal Sale of Cigarettes* (*Dominican Republic Cigarettes*) [2005] Appellate Body Report WT/DS302/AB/R para 96.

989 See *Canada – Certain Measures Affecting the Automotive Industry* (*Canada Autos*) [2000] WTO Panel Report WT/DS139/R, WT/DS142/R para 10.107.

990 GATT 1994 Article XIII.

991 Such notifications must contain a general description of the restriction, its administration and the product concerned, and indicate the type of restriction, the relevant tariff line code, the national legal basis for the restriction and the WTO justification for the measure concerned: Bossche and Zdouc (n 969) 482.

In order to determine whether a specific measure falls under GATT Article III or GATT Article XI, or both, it is important to take into account the different aims of the two provisions (i.e. equal conditions for competition in internal markets versus market access) and to differentiate between internal measures on the one hand and border measures on the other hand. The differentiation is not always obvious, especially if the measure is applied to imported products at the time or point of importation. The Note Ad Article III holds in this respect:

> Any internal tax or other internal charge, or any law, regulation or requirement of the kind referred to in paragraph 1 which applies to an imported product and to the like domestic product and is collected or enforced in the case of the imported product at the time or point of importation, is nevertheless to be regarded as an internal tax or other internal charge, or a law, regulation or requirement of the kind referred to in paragraph 1, and is accordingly subject to the provisions of Article III.

It follows that, when the importation of a product is denied on the reason that the product does not conform to domestic environmental legislation (applying also to domestic products), the consistency of the measure with the GATT is to be examined under its Article III rather than Article XI.[992] The cumulative applicability of GATT Articles III and XI is exceptional but not excluded.[993]

In the past, states have sometimes resorted to import bans in order to halt the import of goods they considered particularly environmentally destructive. Moreover, some multilateral environmental agreements require import and export bans of specific product categories, such as endangered species or hazardous wastes.[994] The WTO dispute settlement bodies basically respect environmental obligations of parties that arise from such agreements. Seemingly, trade measures that are based on multilateral environmental obligations have never been challenged under WTO law. The case is a different one with regard to unilateral trade measures that do not find a direct basis in an international treaty: although the GATT provides for environmental exceptions, none of the members that resorted to such measures has been able to actually justify them on environmental grounds in a WTO case.[995]

---

992 See ibid 354.

993 See *India – Measures Affecting the Automotive Sector* (*India Autos*) [2002] WTO Panel Report WT/DS146/R, WT/DS175/R and Corrigendum para 7.224.

994 See 1973 CITES; 1989 Basel Convention. See also 1987 Montreal Protocol.

995 Examples include *US Tuna I* (n 946); *US Shrimp* (n 677). Also in *US Gasoline* (n 672) the US measure, which was found in violation of GATT Article III, did not meet the requirements

b) The Likeness of Products and PPM-based Measures

With regard to trade in goods, non-discrimination principles are based on the idea of 'like products', a concept that must be taken into account whenever discriminatory treatment is at stake. In a case of alleged discriminatory treatment between two products, the likeness of these products – or, in the case of GATT Article III:2, second sentence, their direct competitiveness or substitutability – has to be established on a preliminary basis. The exact meaning of the concept varies from one provision to another and has to be determined on a case-by-case basis. The Appellate Body held in this respect that 'the determination of "likeness" under Article III:2, first sentence, of the GATT 1994 is, fundamentally, a determination about the nature and extent of a competitive relationship between and among imported and domestic products'.[996] In this context, the concept of 'like products' is narrow. General criteria that have been used by panels and the Appellate Body to determine the likeness of products include:

- the product's properties, nature and quality;
- the product's end uses in a given market;
- consumers' tastes and habits; and
- international tariff classification.[997]

These criteria, which are often referred to as the *border tax criteria*, serve as tools for assessing the evidence relating to the competitive relationship between and among the products.[998] They are not necessarily exclusive. Also,

---

for an environmental exception. However, the Appellate Body accepted a French measure prohibiting the manufacture, processing, sale and import of asbestos and asbestos-containing products to be 'necessary to protect human life or health' and thus to be justifiable as an exception under GATT.

996 *Philippines – Taxes on Distilled Spirits* (*Philippines Distilled Spirits*) [2011] Appellate Body Report WT/DS396/AB/R, cWT/DS403/AB/R para 170.

997 The first three criteria were defined in GATT (n 986) 102 para 18. Uniform and sufficiently detailed classification in tariff nomenclatures based on the Harmonized System (a universal classification tool administered by the World Customs Organization) was also recognized as providing a useful basis for confirming 'likeness' in products: see *EEC – Measures on Animal Feed Proteins* (*EEC Animal Feed*) [1978] GATT Panel Report BISD 25S/49 para 4.2; *Japan Alcoholic Beverages II* (n 979) 20–22; *Canada – Certain Measures Concerning Periodicals* (*Canada Periodicals*) [1997] Appellate Body Report WT/DS31/AB/R 20–21; *Philippines Distilled Spirits* (n 996) paras 112–83. See also Won-Mog Choi, *'Like Products' in International Trade Law: Towards a Consistent GATT/WTO Jurisprudence* (Oxford University Press 2003); Robert E Hudec, '"Like Product": The Differences in Meaning in GATT Articles I and III' in Thomas Cottier and Petros Mavroidis (eds), *Regulatory Barriers and the Principle of Non-Discrimination in World Trade Law* (University of Michigan Press 2000).

998 *Philippines Distilled Spirits* (n 996) para 131.

evidence under one of the criteria is not sufficient in itself to establish the likeness of two products. The Appellate Body explained in this respect that

> products that have very similar physical characteristics may not be 'like', within the meaning of Article III:2, if their competitiveness or substitutability is low, while products that present certain physical differences may still be considered 'like' if such physical differences have a limited impact on the competitive relationship between and among the products.[999]

The category of directly competitive or substitutable products, as referred to in GATT Article III:2, second sentence, is construed less narrowly and refers to products that are interchangeable or offer 'alternative ways of satisfying a particular need or taste'.[1000] The potential substitutability of products has been recognized as sufficient for the conditions of the provision to be met.[1001]

Much like in the case of Article III:2, first sentence, the determination of likeness under Article III:4 is, fundamentally, a determination about the nature and extent of a competitive relationship between and among products.[1002] However, the Appellate Body found that the meaning of 'likeness' under Articles III:2, first sentence, and III:4 is not exactly congruent, as the product scope of Article III:4 and that of Article III:2, first *and* second sentence, cannot be significantly different. The term is, therefore, accorded a broader meaning under Article III:4.[1003]

The border tax criteria invariably focus on the products themselves, and not on the way in which they have been produced. However, it is questionable whether products should be considered to be like products if environmental impacts associated with their production process greatly vary. In fact, there has been a long-lasting debate on whether and to what extent products may be treated differently because of the way in which they have been produced even if the production method does not influence the physical properties of the end product (non-product-related PPMs).[1004] The wish of some states

999 ibid para 120.

1000 *Korea Alcoholic Beverages* (n 976) para 115. See also *Philippines Distilled Spirits* (n 996) para 205.

1001 See *Korea Alcoholic Beverages* (n 976) para 114.

1002 EC *Asbestos* (n 787) para 99.

1003 See ibid paras 96–99.

1004 PPM s have been defined in different ways. For instance, the OECD defined them as 'the way in which products are manufactured or processed and natural resources are extracted or harvested': OECD, 'PPMs' (n 947) 7. In literature, they have also been defined as the 'sum of all activities necessary to place the product on the market': Sebastian Puth, *WTO und Umwelt: Die Produkt-Prozess-Doktrin* (Duncker & Humblot 2003) 44. See also

to discriminate between products based on environmental considerations clashes with the fear by other, mostly developing, countries of environmental protectionism and a loss of market access.[1005]

With regard to fish and other natural resources, PPM-based measures may for instance refer to harvesting methods. With regard to the life cycle of plastics, diverging environmental footprints (that is, environmental product performance) may be due to a range of product-related or non-product-related PPMs. Some examples are given in Table 6.

The likeness test as traditionally applied by WTO dispute settlement bodies only takes environmental and health concerns into account to the extent that they are directly reflected in the product itself.[1006] For instance, the Appellate

---

Conrad (n 947) 25–31. Product-related PPMs alter the physical characteristic of the end-product. In contrast, non-product-related PPMs do not leave any detectable physical traces on the product. Measures based on product-related PPMs usually aim at internalizing externalities that are linked to consumption or disposal, while measures based on non-product-related PPMs are often concerned with production externalities. The former category typically falls into the scope of the TBT and SPS agreements (see Sections 2) and 3) below). With regard to the latter category, the regulatory situation is less obvious. See, however, *Tuna II (Mexico)* (n 965).

1005 See Shahrukh Rafi Khan, 'Trade Liberalization and the Environment: Northern and Southern Perspectives' in Shahrukh Rafi Khan (ed), *Trade and Environment: Difficult Policy Choices at the Interface* (Zed Books 2002).

1006 Two panels have used a different test based on the regulatory motivation of the measure: see *United States – Measures Affecting Alcoholic and Malt Beverages* [1992] GATT Panel Report DS23/R, BISD 39S/206 76–77 paras 5.74–77; *United States – Taxes on Automobiles* [1994] GATT Panel Report DS44/R, BISD 41S/131 101–2 paras 5.29–30. The so-called *aims-and-effect* test was rejected by the Appellate Body in later decisions: see *Japan Alcoholic Beverages II* (n 979) 27; *European Communities – Regime for the Importation, Sale and Distribution of Bananas* (*EC Bananas III*) [1997] Appellate Body Report WT/DS27/AB/R 92 para 216. However, the Appellate Body also held that in order to determine whether a measure affords protection to domestic production (as prohibited by GATT Article III(1)), the design, architecture and structure of the measure need to be thoroughly examined: *Japan Alcoholic Beverages II* (n 979) 29; *Korea Alcoholic Beverages* (n 976) 42–45 paras 146–54. Moreover, in *EC Asbestos*, the Appellate Body attributed some importance to the effect of a measure, albeit under its analysis of whether there was less favourable treatment rather than as part of the likeness test: *EC Asbestos* (n 787) 38 para 100. cf *European Communities – Measures Affecting the Approval and Marketing of Biotech Products* (*EC Biotech*) [2006] WTO Panel Report WT/DS291/R, WT/DS292/R, WT/DS293/R 865 para 7.2514. Interestingly, the motivation or objective of a measure was also considered a relevant factor for the *chapeau* test (see Subsection c) below) in *Brazil – Measures Affecting Imports of Retreaded Tyres* (*Brazil Retreaded Tyres*) [2007] Appellate Body Report WT/DS332/AB/R 90 para 227. In the inconsistent jurisprudence of GATT and WTO dispute settlement bodies, the aim and effect of a measure has therefore been taken into account at different stages of the analysis and with different emphasis. See Conrad (n 947) 206–22; Arwel Davies, 'Interpreting the Chapeau of GATT Article XX in Light of

TABLE 6 Examples of PPMs with regard to plastic products

Product-related PPMs:	Non-product-related PPMs:
– the use of different plastic materials or composites in a product (e.g. polystyrene cups vs polypropylene cups) – the use of different additives in a plastic material (recipes are, however, often not disclosed) – quantitative and qualitative differences in packaging at different stages of the production chain – different product designs, reflected in their reusability, recyclability, biodegradability, leakage of additives etc.	– the use of different raw materials (renewable or non-renewable) for the production of the same plastic material – the use of different energy sources (renewable or non-renewable) for the production of the same plastic material – the use of different technologies (such as filters) and chemicals in the production process – pellet leakages and dissimilar management of production wastes – different transportation modes

Body refused to introduce a separate criterion to examine health risks associated with a specific product in the *EC Asbestos* case.[1007] It instead used the traditional criteria to deal with health concerns. It emphasized that the health risks associated with the products were reflected in their physical properties and influenced their end use, consumer behaviour with respect to the products and the competitive relationship between the products.[1008] The Appellate Body concluded that the evidence brought by the complaining party was 'far from sufficient' to satisfy its burden of proving the likeness of the products.[1009]

While in *EC Asbestos* the criterion of consumers' tastes and habits gained in importance, panels and the Appellate Body have not (yet) accepted non-product-related PPMs to form part of the likeness test in GATT and WTO case law, in spite of their potential to influence consumer behaviour. Perhaps more fundamentally, PPM-based measures have often been dealt with under the

the "New" Approach in Brazil – Tyres' (2009) 43 Journal of World Trade Law 507, 534–38; Panizzon, Arnold and Cottier (n 970) 226–31.

1007 *EC Asbestos* (n 787) 43 para 113.

1008 ibid 42–46 paras 111–26.

1009 ibid 53 para 141.

prohibition of quantitative restrictions rather than the national treatment obligation, even when the challenged measure regulated not only import but also the use of domestic products.[1010] Both the prohibition of quantitative restrictions and the principle of national treatment have significant practical implications as they limit the regulatory autonomy of states with regard to environmental concerns.[1011] However, an argument can be made under Article III that two products are not like products if one has been produced in a more sustainable way when compared to the other, and that they thus are not in a direct competitive relationship (an argument not accepted by WTO dispute settlement bodies so far). Under GATT Article XI, even less policy space is accorded to member states for environmental considerations, as the prohibition of quantitative restrictions is not based on the competitive relationship and likeness of products. In this case, countries have to resort to the GATT exception clauses in order to possibly justify their measure.

c) Environmental and Health Exceptions

The general exceptions under GATT Article XX allow states to adopt measures in pursuance of legitimate policy objectives even if these measures are inconsistent with any provision of the GATT. Thus, regardless of whether a measure is considered inconsistent with GATT Article III or XI, the exception clauses allow states to justify their measure if certain – fairly restrictive – conditions are fulfilled. In the analysis of Article XX, a two-tier test is applied: for a measure to be justified as a general exception, it must:

1. fall under one of the particular exceptions enumerated in paragraphs a–j (provisional justification); and
2. satisfy the requirements imposed by the opening clauses of the provision, generally referred to as the *chapeau*.[1012]

Legitimate policy objectives include, among other things, the protection of human, animal or plant life or health (paragraph b)[1013] and the conservation of

1010 Since the Note Ad Article III refers to products only, and not to PPMs, the *US Tuna I* and *US Tuna II* (*EEC*) panels concluded that the US measures fell under GATT Article XI rather than Article III. The approach has been criticized in literature: see Panizzon, Arnold and Cottier (n 970) 220–21. See also Holzer (n 947) 194.

1011 Thomas Cottier, Elisabeth Tuerk and Marion Panizzon, 'Handel und Umwelt im Recht der WTO: Auf dem Wege zur praktischen Konkordanz' [2003] Zeitschrift für Umweltrecht 155, 157.

1012 See *US Gasoline* (n 672) 22; *US Shrimp* (n 677) 44 paras 119–20; *Brazil Retreaded Tyres* (n 1006) 55 para 139.

1013 Measures taken in protection against asbestos, nicotine, genetically modified organisms, hormone-treated beef, frozen fish, or pandemic risk have been treated under

exhaustible natural resources (paragraph g). Legal measures that are relevant to the protection of animal welfare and the biodiversity have also been provisionally justified under the public morals exception (paragraph a).[1014] The approaches under these paragraphs are similar, although requirements with regard to the link between the measure and the policy objective are stricter under paragraphs a and b than under paragraph g: in order to be provisionally justified under the former two, measures need to be *necessary* to protect public morals or human, animal or plant life or health, respectively;[1015] under paragraph g, it is sufficient if the measures are *relating to* the conservation of exhaustible natural resources.[1016] However, in order for an environmental measure to be provisionally justified under paragraph g, it has to be 'made effective in conjunction with restrictions on domestic production or consumption'.

With regard to the exception clauses, the Appellate Body held that 'a balance must be struck between the *right* of a Member to invoke an exception under Article XX and the *duty* of that same Member to respect the treaty rights of the other Members'.[1017] To this purpose, the specific exception clauses

---

paragraph b: see EC *Asbestos* (n 787); *Thailand – Restrictions on Importation of and Internal Taxes on Cigarettes* (*Thailand Cigarettes*) [1990] GATT Panel Report DS10/R, BISD 37S/200; *Dominican Republic Cigarettes* (n 988); EC *Biotech* (n 1006); EC *Hormones* (n 672); *Australia – Measures Affecting Importation of Salmon* (*Australia Salmon*) [1998] Appellate Body Report WT/DS18/AB/R; *Brazil Retreaded Tyres* (n 1006).

1014 *European Communities – Measures Prohibiting the Importation and Marketing of Seal Products* (EC *Seals Products*) [2014] Appellate Body Report WT/DS400/AB/R, WT/DS401/AB/R 174 para 5.289. The implications of the decision by the Appellate Body in the case are discussed in Thomas Cottier, 'The Implications of EC – Seal Products for the Protection of Core Labour Standards in WTO Law' in Henner Gött (ed), *Labour Standards in International Economic Law* (Springer International Publishing 2018); Robert Howse, Joanna Langille and Katie Sykes, 'Pluralism in Practice: Moral Legislation and the Law of the WTO after Seal Products' (2015) 48 Geo. Wash. Int'l L. Rev. 81; Pelin Serpin, 'The Public Morals Exception after the WTO Seal Products Dispute: Has the Exception Swallowed the Rules' [2016] Colum. Bus. L. Rev. 217.

1015 In *Thailand Cigarettes*, the panel held that a measure imposed by a country 'could be considered to be "necessary" in terms of Article XX(b) only if there were no alternative measure consistent with the General Agreement, or less inconsistent with it, which [that country] could reasonably be expected to employ to achieve its health policy objectives': *Thailand Cigarettes* (n 1013) 21 para 75. Later reports are less restrictive in this respect. Under the WTO regime, the Appellate Body notably based its analysis with respect to the necessity of a measure on a weighing of interests: see *Korea Beef* (n 987) 49 para 162; EC *Seals Products* (n 1014) 140 para 5.169. cf *Brazil Retreaded Tyres* (n 1006) 56 para 143. In EC *Seals Products*, the Appellate Body notes that scientific risk assessment methods are not a suitable tool with regard to the protection of public morals, while they play an important role in protecting animal or plant life or health: EC *Seals Products* (n 1014) para 5.198.

1016 See *US Taxes on Automobiles* (n 1006) 111 para 5.63; *US Gasoline* (n 672) 14–19.

1017 *US Shrimp* (n 677) 60 para 156.

are complemented by the *chapeau*. As an introductory clause, the chapeau addresses the manner in which a measure is applied and sets out a number of negative conditions in this regard. A measure that is provisionally justified under one of the exception clauses must hence not be 'applied in a manner which would constitute a means of arbitrary or unjustifiable discrimination between countries where the same conditions prevail, or a disguised restriction on international trade'.[1018] The requirements of the chapeau are a major stumbling block for unilateral measures with coercive, extraterritorial effects when these measures are not based on prior consultation and cooperative efforts.[1019] The burden of proving that a measure which is provisionally justified does not, in its application, constitute a means of arbitrary or unjustifiable discrimination or a disguised restriction on international trade, rests on the party invoking the exception.[1020]

US Shrimp is considered a landmark decision with regard to the justification of a PPM-based measure. The case deals with the justification of a measure discriminating between shrimp products based on the way the shrimp was harvested. It marks a milestone in that the Appellate Body considered the measure, which aimed at protecting marine turtles, to be provisionally justified under GATT in spite of its extraterritorial effects.[1021] It notably held that 'there is a sufficient nexus between the migratory and endangered marine populations involved and the United States for purposes of Article XX(g)'.[1022] PPM-based measures are, thus, not automatically considered inconsistent with WTO law.[1023] In the end, however, the measure was found to constitute an unjustifiable discrimination because of the way it was applied. Aggravating factors included the measure's 'intended and actual coercive effect on other governments' to 'adopt essentially the same policy' as the United States, the failure by the US to have 'prior consistent recourse to diplomacy', the lack of flexibility of the measure with regard to the different conditions prevailing in the exporting countries, and its lack of transparency and predictability.[1024]

1018 On the interpretation of the chapeau, see, in particular, *US Gasoline* (n 672) 23; *US Shrimp* (n 677) 56–57 para 150; *Brazil Retreaded Tyres* (n 1006) 95–99 paras 240–52.

1019 See, for instance, *US Shrimp* (n 677) 63–72 paras 161–76.

1020 *US Gasoline* (n 672) 22–23.

1021 *US Shrimp* (n 677) 53–54 paras 141–42.

1022 ibid 51 para 133.

1023 The *EC Seals Products* Appellate Body report indicates in this regard that partial bans of products cannot operate without PPM-based measures: see Cottier, 'The Implications of EC – Seal Products' (n 1014) 85.

1024 *US Shrimp* (n 677) 63–76 paras 161–86. cf *Tuna II* (*Mexico*) (n 965) 324–31 paras 124–28.

2) *The Agreement on Technical Barriers to Trade*

The TBT covers measures related to technical regulations and standards. The agreement defines technical regulations as any document 'which lays down product characteristics or their related processes and production methods [...] with which compliance is mandatory'.[1025] It further provides that such a regulation 'may also include or deal exclusively with terminology, symbols, packaging, marking or labelling requirements'. As the Appellate Body explained,

> the 'characteristics' of a product include [...] any objectively definable 'features', 'qualities', 'attributes', or other 'distinguishing mark' of a product. Such 'characteristics' might relate, inter alia, to a product's composition, size, shape, colour, texture, hardness, tensile strength, flammability, conductivity, density, or viscosity.[1026]

The Appellate Body further noted that product characteristics may be prescribed or imposed in either a positive form (i.e. that products must possess certain characteristics) or a negative form (i.e. that products must not possess certain characteristics).

Standards, on the other hand, are defined as any document 'approved by a recognized body, that provides [...] rules, guidelines or characteristics for products or related processes and production methods, with which compliance is *not* mandatory'.[1027] Standards are regulated less strictly in the TBT.

Regulations or standards, which may refer to any life-cycle stage of a product, are potential non-tariff barriers to trade. The TBT defines the circumstances under which such measures are allowed and the conditions that must be met in their adoption and application. The agreement sets out a national treatment and MFN requirement.[1028] It moreover requires that technical regulations be not 'more trade-restrictive than necessary to fulfil a legitimate objective'.[1029]

1025 TBT Annex 1.1. The test for determining whether a measure is a 'technical regulation' under the TBT is three-tiered: the measure must apply to an identifiable product or group of products; the measure must lay down product characteristics; and compliance with the product characteristics laid down in the measure must be mandatory: see Bossche and Zdouc (n 969) 857.

1026 *EC Asbestos* (n 787) para 67.

1027 TBT Annex 1.2 (emphasis added).

1028 ibid art 2.1. While the TBT Agreement does not contain a general exceptions clause similar to GATT Article XX, the Appellate Body acknowledged that member states also have a right to regulate under the TBT, and that Article 2.1 'does not operate to prohibit *a priori* any restriction on international trade': see *EC Seals Products* (n 1014) 128 para 5.124.

1029 TBT art 2.2. In *US Tuna II (Mexico)*, the Appellate Body found that the US did not justify its measure as non-discriminatory because it did not demonstrate that the detrimental

In this regard, the TBT introduces disciplines that go beyond the GATT non-discrimination approach.[1030] The TBT also provides that states shall base their technical regulations on relevant international standards to the extent that such standards exist and may effectively contribute to the legitimate objective pursued.[1031] It obliges member states to take all reasonable measures to ensure that local government and non-governmental bodies comply with their obligations under the agreement.[1032]

Whether a specific measure, or a norm that forms part of it, falls under the GATT or the TBT depends on its structure and content: a ban of specific products, such as polystyrene cups, would fall under GATT, as it constitutes an *unconditional prohibition* on market access for this particular product. By contrast, a measure prohibiting single-use cups from containing polystyrene would instead be considered a technical regulation and thus fall under the TBT, as it constitutes a *conditional* regulation of market access for a group of products (cups). The market access for this group of products is then dependent on specific product characteristics, namely whether they contain polystyrene.[1033] Accordingly, a ban of certain additives in plastics would be assessed as a technical regulation of plastics under the TBT, as would be mandatory product specifications (allowable thickness etc.) of single-use plastic carrier bags in shops. A document that lays down products specifications is regarded as a standard under the TBT agreement if compliance is voluntary. Examples include labels related to the biodegradability of plastic products, provided that they are voluntary and that non-compliance does not preclude market access. Packaging regulations typically fall under the TBT, too. PPM-based measures usually also constitute technical regulations or standards and thus fall under the TBT.[1034]

---

impact of the measure stemmed 'exclusively from a legitimate regulatory distinction': *Tuna II (Mexico)* (n 965) 115 para 298. See also Vranes (n 946) 303–05.

1030 Vranes (n 946) 286.

1031 For more information, see Panagiotis Delimatsis, '"Relevant International Standards" and "Recognised Standardisation Bodies" Under the TBT Agreement' in Panagiotis Delimatsis (ed), *The Law, Economics and Politics of International Standardisation* (Cambridge University Press 2015).

1032 TBT arts 3, 4, 7 and 8.

1033 See Vranes (n 946) 290–91. See also *EC Asbestos* (n 787) 27–28 paras 71–72; *European Communities – Trade Description of Sardines* (*EC Sardines*) [2002] Appellate Body Report WT/DS231/AB/R 49–50 para 190; *EC Seals Products* (n 1014) 106–14 paras 5.26–5.60.

1034 In *US Tuna II (Mexico)*, the Appellate Body characterized a US non-product-related PPM-based measure as a 'technical regulation' within the meaning of Annex 1.1 to the TBT Agreement. The measure was found to establish the conditions for the use of a 'dolphin-safe' label on tuna products and to set out 'a single and legally mandated definition of a

The applicability of the TBT does not, however, suspend the applicability of the GATT, unless there is a conflict of norms *stricto sensu*.[1035]

3) *The Agreement on the Application of Sanitary and Phytosanitary Measures*

The SPS applies to all sanitary and phytosanitary measures which may affect international trade. Sanitary and phytosanitary measures are for instance taken to minimize risks from pests and diseases, the spread of which is facilitated by the international movement of plants, animals or foodstuffs. More relevant to plastics, the SPS also covers measures regulating additives and contaminants in food and beverages.[1036] The agreement allows member states to adopt such measures on a national treatment and MFN basis to the extent that they are *necessary* for the protection of human, animal or plant life or health and based on scientific principles.[1037] The SPS prescribes the use of international standards but allows members to adopt stricter standards resulting in a higher level of protection if there is scientific justification.[1038] It also requires that covered measures be based on a risk assessment.[1039] Precautionary measures are allowed on a provisional basis, but must be reviewed within a reasonable period of time.[1040] The interpretation of the precautionary approach under

"dolphin-safe" tuna product' while disallowing the use of other labels on tuna products that did not satisfy this definition: *Tuna II (Mexico)* (n 965) 80 para 199.

1035 Vranes (n 946) 298–302.

1036 IISD and UNEP (n 972) 39.

1037 SPS art 2 para 2–3.

1038 ibid art 3.

1039 ibid art 5 para 1.

1040 ibid art 5 para 7. The application of the precautionary approach under the SPS Agreement was addressed in *EC Hormones* (n 672) 46–48 paras 120–25; *EC Biotech* (n 1006) 1019–20 paras 7.3260–61; *Canada – Continued Suspension of Obligations in the EC – Hormones Dispute* (*Canada Continued Suspension*) [2008] Appellate Body Report WT/DS321/AB/R 282–306 paras 674–736. In *Canada Continued Suspension*, the Appellate Body pleaded for a broad policy space of member states as to risk factors and scientific evidence and took into account non-scientific policy considerations, such as the acceptable level of protection. See discussion in Alessandra Arcuri, 'Food Safety at the WTO After "Continued Suspension": A Paradigm Shift?' in Antonis Antoniadis, Robert Schütze and Eleanor Spaventa (eds), *The European Union and Global Emergencies: A Law and Policy Analysis* (Hart Publishing 2010); Sungjoon Cho, 'United States-Continued Suspension of Obligations in the EC-Hormones Dispute' (2009) 103 Am. J. Int'l L. 299; Caroline E Foster, 'Precaution, Scientific Development and Scientific Uncertainty under the WTO Agreement on Sanitary and Phytosanitary Measures' (2009) 18 Review of European Community & International Environmental Law 50; Markus W Gehring and Marie-Claire Cordonier Segger, *Precaution in World Trade Law: The Precautionary Principle and Its Implications for the World Trade Organization* (CISDL 2002).

the SPS Agreement is far more restrictive than under other treaties, such as the CBD Cartagena Protocol on Biosafety.[1041]

iii General Remarks Regarding the Relationship between UNCLOS Part XII and WTO Law

When contemplating the relationship between UNCLOS Part XII and WTO law, several points have to be taken into account:

- *Relation of WTO law to general international law:* While WTO law has been referred to as a 'self-contained regime',[1042] there is wide agreement that WTO law is not a closed system but has to be read in the context of general international law.[1043] The Appellate Body held in this respect that WTO agreements should not be read 'in clinical isolation from public international law'.[1044] International law applies to WTO law to the extent that the covered agreements do not 'contract out' from it.[1045] WTO dispute settlement bodies have hence frequently sought 'additional interpretative guidance' from the general principles of international law.[1046]

1041 The protocol provides that lack of scientific certainty 'shall not prevent [the party] from taking a decision […] with regard to the import of the living modified organism in question […] in order to avoid or minimize such potential adverse effects': 2000 Cartagena Protocol art 10 para 6.

1042 See PJ Kuyper, 'The Law of GATT as a Special Field of International Law: Ignorance, Further Refinement or Self-Contained System of International Law?' (1994) 25 Netherlands Yearbook of International Law 227, 252.

1043 According to the ILC, '[t]here is no doubt that the *WTO dispute settlement system is a self-contained regime* in the sense that article 23 of the Dispute Settlement Understanding (DSU) excludes unilateral determinations of breach or countermeasures outside the "specific subsystem" of the WTO-regime' (emphasis added). At the same time, the ILC held that no regime is self-contained in the sense that it is to be regarded as isolated from general international law. General international law always provides the normative background and a fall back regime: ILC, 'Fragmentation Report' (n 653) 100 paras 192–93. See also Marina Foltea, *International Organizations in WTO Dispute Settlement: How Much Institutional Sensitivity?* (Cambridge University Press 2012) ch 3; Anja Lindroos and Michael Mehling, 'Dispelling the Chimera of "Self-Contained Regimes" International Law and the WTO' (2005) 16 European Journal of International Law 857; Bruno Simma, 'Of Planets and the Universe: Self-Contained Regimes in International Law' (2006) 17 European Journal of International Law 483, 519–23; JHH Weiler, 'The Rule of Lawyers and the Ethos of Diplomats Reflections on the Internal and External Legitimacy of WTO Dispute Settlement' (2001) 35 Journal of World Trade 191.

1044 *US Gasoline* (n 672) 17.

1045 *Korea – Measures Affecting Government Procurement* (*Korea Procurement*) [2000] WTO Panel Report WT/DS163/R 181 para 7.96.

1046 *US Shrimp* (n 677) 62 para 158; ILC, 'Fragmentation Report' (n 653) 71 para 134.

– *WTO law and the protection of the environment:* The international community repeatedly emphasized the importance of coordinating policies on trade and the environment.[1047] It was also acknowledged under the aegis of the WTO, including in case law.[1048] Different perhaps from early rulings under the GATT, the WTO Appellate Body more seriously accepted the need to find a balance between safeguarding market access and protecting the environment. It underscored the autonomy of member states 'to determine their own policies on the environment (including its relationship with trade), their environmental objectives and the environmental legislation they enact and implement'.[1049] The acceptance of environmental considerations as legitimate policy objectives particularly finds expression in the exceptions clause of the GATT[1050] and its counterparts in other agreements.
– *Relation of WTO law to multilateral environmental agreements:*[1051]

Rule of conflict: WTO-covered agreements do not address the issue of potential conflict of norms with other treaties. The relationship between multilateral environmental agreements and WTO-covered agreements is thus governed by principles of general international law, including as reflected in VCLT Articles 30 and 41, as well as by possible rules of conflict forming part of multilateral environmental agreements relevant to the case. In view of these rules, multilateral environmental obligations tend to prevail over trade obligations to the extent that they are of an integral character (as opposed to the mostly reciprocal obligations under trade law). Integral obligations are not merely reciprocal or bilateral in scope but are due to all the parties of the respective agreement (*erga omnes partes*) or, if general in nature, to the international community as a whole (*erga omnes*). A violation of such a rule does hence infringe on the rights of all the other states parties to the agreement or all states, respectively. As Pauwelyn expounds:

1047 See Agenda 21 (n 450) para 17.118; Johannesburg Plan of Implementation para 154; UNGA Res. 66/288 (2012), annex (n 511) paras 26, 58(h) and 78. More generally, the integration of economic and environmental aspects is demanded under the concept of sustainable development such as reflected in Rio Principle 4. The principle reads as follows: 'In order to achieve sustainable development, environmental protection shall constitute an integral part of the development process and cannot be considered in isolation from it'. See also Edith Brown Weiss, 'Environment and Trade as Partners in Sustainable Development: A Commentary' [1992] American Journal of International Law 728.

1048 See Marrakesh Agreement Preamble; WTO, 'Ministerial Decision on Trade and Environment' (1994); *US Gasoline* (n 672) 30.

1049 *US Gasoline* (n 672) 30.

1050 GATT 1994 art XX.

1051 For an overview, see ILC, 'Fragmentation Report' (n 653) 138–43 paras 272–82.

> In summary, when integral obligations are involved, conflicting WTO rules must normally give way [...] irrespective of whether the multilateral environmental rule comes earlier or later in time. If it comes later in time, it prevails as the *lex posterior* under [VCLT] Article 30(4)(a). If it is the earlier in time, it cannot, as an integral obligation, be validly deviated from *inter se* by the later WTO rule pursuant to [VCLT Articles 41 and 58].[1052]

This means, as a consequence, that integral obligations under UNCLOS Part XII, although adopted prior to the establishment of the WTO, prevail over trade obligations of a reciprocal nature to the extent that there is a true conflict between the norms. This conclusion is in line with UNCLOS Article 311, which focuses on the mutual supportiveness between the convention and other agreements[1053] and according to which UNCLOS prevails over later *inter se* agreements to the extent that they are incompatible with the effective execution of the object and purpose of UNCLOS or its basic principles.[1054]

Mutual supportiveness and treaty interpretation: There is no true conflict of norms as long as the norms can be interpreted in a compatible way, allowing them both to apply in a mutually supportive way. Treaty interpretation is, therefore, a valuable means for avoiding such conflicts.[1055] In the interpretation of WTO-covered agreements, reference to multilateral environmental agreements may be necessary in order to appropriately capture an internationally agreed meaning of environment-related terms.[1056] WTO dispute settlement bodies draw their competence to consult such agreements from Article 3(2) DSU in conjunction with Article 31(3) VCLT. Pursuant to Article 3(2) DSU, WTO panels and the Appellate Body are required to rely on the general rules of interpretation of public international law, including VCLT Article 31(3)(c) and the principle of systemic integration. Wherever relevant and applicable, UNCLOS Part XII and other environmental agreements thus form part of the interpretative background of legal provisions

1052 Pauwelyn, *Conflict of Norms* (n 668) 323. See also Boyle, 'Relationship between International Environmental Law and Other Branches of International Law' (n 668) 136–38; ILC, 'Fragmentation Report' (n 653) 83 para 154. cf Perrez, 'The Mutual Supportiveness of Trade and Environment' (n 944) 27.

1053 1982 UNCLOS art 311(2).

1054 ibid art 311(3). See Boyle, 'Further Development of the 1982 Convention on the Law of the Sea: Mechanisms for Change' (n 948) 60; ILC, 'Fragmentation Report' (n 653) 141–42 paras 278–80.

1055 See Wolfrum and Matz (n 939) 6.

1056 See *US Shrimp* (n 677) 48–51 paras 130–34.

under WTO law.[1057] The competence of WTO dispute settlement bodies to examine non-WTO rules (and their obligation to do so) is also reflected in Article 11 of the DSU and allows for more coherence between the different fields of law.[1058] It is further strengthened by a reference to sustainable development in the preamble to the Marrakesh Agreement. There is, however, certain inconsistency in WTO case law with regard to the question of whether there is a need for congruent membership for non-WTO agreements to be taken into account.[1059] The increasingly integrative approach especially by the Appellate Body towards multilateral environmental agreements arguably reflects increasing environmental concerns and the growing importance of the concept of global commons in international law.[1060]

Impact on policy space: Multilateral environmental treaties have a potential to strengthen the member states' authority to enact environmental legislation under the WTO regime. International environmental obligations, such as defined in UNCLOS Part XII or other multilateral environmental agreements, play an important role in the definition of the scope of the member states' regulatory autonomy under WTO law. There is a general presumption of mutual supportiveness between such instruments and WTO-covered agreements.[1061] That is to say, whenever a state is required to adopt a measure by an international treaty, this measure is presumed to be consistent with WTO obligations. However, in the case of UNCLOS Part XII, the situation is slightly more complex: UNCLOS does not directly require trade measures to be taken but sets out principles and objectives instead, and leaves to its parties a wide room to manoeuvre in the implementation of their obligations. While trade-related measures may be an efficient and effective means to achieve the objectives of the treaty, the need to take such measures is not spelled out. Yet, trade measures, including, for instance,

1057 See ILC, 'Fragmentation Report' (n 653) 88–89 para 167. For more information on potential conflicts between WTO law and other rules of international law see Vranes (n 946) 68–92.

1058 According to DSU Article 11, 'a panel should [...] make such other findings as will assist the DSB in making the recommendations or in giving the rulings provided for in the covered agreements'. The rule has been referred to as an 'implied powers' clause that 'should be interpreted broadly so that the panels and Appellate Body can decide all aspects of a dispute': Thomas J Schoenbaum, 'WTO Dispute Settlement: Praise and Suggestions for Reform' (1998) 47 The International and Comparative Law Quarterly 647, 653. See also Myers (n 944) 72; Joost Pauwelyn, 'The Role of Public International Law in the WTO: How Far Can We Go?' (2001) 95 American Journal of International Law 535, 557.

1059 cf *US Tuna II* (*EEC*) (n 946) 19 para 3.38 and 50–51 paras 5.18–5.20; *US Shrimp* (n 677) for instance 48 para 130; *EC Biotech* (n 1006) 334 para 7.70.

1060 Panizzon, Arnold and Cottier (n 970) 210–12. See also, in general, Foltea (n 1043).

1061 See, for instance, IISD and UNEP (n 972) 65.

bans of microbeads in products and of other non-recoverable plastics destined to end up in waterways, may prove necessary in order to effectively protect the marine environment from microplastics, taking into account the specific level of protection pursued by that state. Consistency of such measures with WTO law strongly depends on their exact design and has to be examined on a case-by-case basis.[1062]

iv The Role of WTO Law with Regard to Domestic Implementation, Cooperation and Unilateral Enforcement

As we have seen in the previous section, the implementation of UNCLOS Part XII requires both international and regional cooperation through harmonized policies, the definition of common standards and support for developing countries, as well as measures at the national and, where appropriate, local levels to ensure the implementation and enforcement of the internationally agreed standards. The legal concept of common concern of humankind as developed by Cottier and others[1063] addresses these levels of action in relation to global problems and goes further into the question of how the creation of global public goods can be strengthened by a state or group of states in the interest of the international community when confronted to institutional deficiencies, the refusal of other states to cooperate due to the pursuit of purely national interests, and free riding. The concept 'seeks to structure the interactive process of producing public goods by defining duties to negotiate and cooperate, the obligations to do homework, and the scope of second best unilateral action of States or of the EU furthering solutions to the problem identified'.[1064]

The concept of common concern is based on the assumption that 'collective action problems occurring in the process of globalisation are mainly caused by the lack of appropriate and effective global institutions that ensure the sustainable production of global public goods'.[1065] It further assumes that issues of common conern are those that 'inevitably transcend the boundaries of a single state and require collective action in response'.[1066] When collective

1062 Implementing measures and their consistency with WTO law will be discussed in Chapter 2.3 below.

1063 Thomas Cottier and Zaker Ahmad (eds), *The Prospects of Common Concern of Humankind in International Law* (Cambridge University Press 2021).

1064 Thomas Cottier, 'The Principle of Common Concern of Humankind' in Thomas Cottier and Zaker Ahmad (eds), *The Prospects of Common Concern of Humankind in International Law* (Cambridge University Press 2021) 25–26.

1065 ibid 3.

1066 Dinah Shelton, 'Common Concern of Humanity' (2009) 5 Iustum Aequum Salutare 33, 34. Common concerns of humankind potentially affect all of humanity and the international

action problems threaten the international system as a whole, there is a need to 'secure that all countries alike are engaged in making contributions and commitments to their mutual support, commensurate with their levels of social and economic development and powers they may exert'.[1067] According to the concept, recognition by the international community of a grave and shared problem as a common concern of humankind triggers an enhanced duty to negotiate and cooperate in the first place, but also a firm obligation for each state to address the problem domestically, including, as the case may be, by regulatory means (obligation to to homework).[1068] Under specific circumstances, the concept also supports the use of unilateral trade measures against free riding. International trade regulation, and WTO law in particular, has implications at all these levels of action: international cooperation, domestic implementation and unilateral enforcement measures.

With regard to marine plastic pollution,[1069] states can choose between a broad range of domestic measures in fulfilment of their obligations, including: product bans; packaging regulations (both with regard to packaging quantity and quality); market-based instruments such as taxes and levies; technical minimum standards, for instance with regard to the recyclability, biodegradability or durability of products; labels; legal requirements related to extended producer responsibility; etc. Such measures will primarily target domestic behaviour. However, domestic measures, including, for instance, sales regulations of plastic bags, often include provisions that regulate trade specifically or have impacts on trade.

When taxes, bans, mandatory standards and other measures have obstructive effects on international trade in the goods subject to respective regulations (or like products), they are challengeable under WTO law. If affected countries decide to bring a case before a WTO panel, the measure will be tested for its consistency with WTO-covered agreements. In order to justify a measure that, for its trade-restrictive effect, is incompatible with any provision under the GATT, a state must prove that the measure is adopted in pursuance of a legitimate policy objective and fulfils the restrictive conditions as set out in

---

system as a whole in terms of stability and viability, thus bearing the risk to threaten international stability, peace and welfare: see Cottier, 'The Principle of Common Concern' (n 1064) 39. It was also suggested that 'issues of common concern are linked to the recognition of *erga omnes* obligations and the formation of collective compliance institutions': Shelton 34.

1067 Cottier, 'The Principle of Common Concern' (n 1064) 9.

1068 The concept implies a 'shift of classical international law from coexistence to cooperation, and ultimately perhaps even to integration and legal harmonisation in specific regulatory areas': see ibid 24.

1069 See Schäli (n 20).

the agreement.[1070] WTO jurisprudence suggests that this proof is difficult to establish.

A state can more easily justify a measure if it manages to prove that the measure is necessary for the implementation of an international standard, private or as defined in a multilateral environmental agreement. In the absence of common standards, serious efforts to cooperate with potentially affected countries are usually required.[1071] Cooperation, collective action and conformity with international standards generally make a strong case in favour of the measures taken. Besides that, the wording and design of the measure play a fundamental role. An arbitrarily discriminatory design of the measure, disguised protectionism, 'unnecessary' unilateralism and unreasonable interferences in the domestic affairs of other states are hardly justifiable under WTO law.

In this sense, international trade regulation may be seen as a constraining factor in the free implementation of environmental obligations, and of UNCLOS Part XII and related obligations in particular. Generally speaking, trade law disciplines states in the adoption of measures, particularly with regard to arbitrariness and discriminatory treatment. It does particularly curtail the states' freedom to take unilateral actions and gives preference to concerted action instead. The same preference can be derived from Article 1 of the UN Charter and is reflected in Rio Principle 12[1072] and Agenda 21.[1073] States have thus an

1070 Specifically the *chapeau* of GATT 1994 Article XX. For more information, see Section 2.3.B below.

1071 In the *US – Tuna I* case the measure adopted by the US did not pass the necessity test under GATT Article XX because the US was not able to demonstrate that 'it had exhausted all options reasonably available to it to pursue its [...] objectives through measures consistent with the General Agreement, in particular through the negotiation of international cooperative arrangements': *US Tuna I* (n 946) 36 para 5.28.

1072 According to Rio Principle 12,

> [t]rade policy measures for environmental purposes should not constitute a means of arbitrary or unjustifiable discrimination or a disguised restriction on international trade. Unilateral actions to deal with environmental challenges outside the jurisdiction of the importing country should be avoided. Environmental measures addressing transboundary or global environmental problems should, as far as possible, be based on an international consensus.

1073 In the Ocean Chapter of Agenda 21, states recognized that:

> environmental policies should deal with the root causes of environmental degradation, thus preventing environmental measures from resulting in unnecessary restrictions to trade. Trade policy measures for environmental purposes should not constitute a means of arbitrary or unjustifiable discrimination or a disguised restriction on international trade. Unilateral actions to deal with environmental challenges outside the jurisdiction of the importing country should be avoided. Environmental measures addressing international environmental problems should, as far as possible, be based on an international consensus. Domestic

obligation to seek compatible solutions through cooperation, which is an obligation of conduct.[1074]

However, sometimes cooperation does not give a sufficient answer to collective action problems and the problem of free riders benefitting from the efforts taken by others. Free riding potentially impairs the positive effects of international cooperation in a specific field and frustrates legitimate expectations. If, by way of assumption, a number of states commonly agree to apply strict standards in the production and transport of plastics and plastic products in order to avoid pellet loss, another state not joining the cooperative effort will possibly benefit from the situation and expand its market share due to lower production costs. Business companies may outsource production to such countries where they benefit from lower environmental standards.

Unilateral trade restrictions may provide an effective means to address environmental concerns and the problem of free riders.[1075] WTO law provides for justifiable exceptions, but, in the absence of international treaties and common action, it usually requires a full use of diplomatic means prior to the adoption of the measure, including serious international negotiations with potentially affected states.[1076] Only if affected states refuse to negotiate in good faith may unilateral trade measures be a legitimate option.[1077] Exhaustion of diplomatic means can be time-consuming, while trade measures allow for a relatively fast reaction. The concept of common concern therefore suggests a revision of the doctrine of extraterritorial effects of domestic law and the of law of sanctions and countermeasures in support of addressing collective action problems in the pursuit of creating global public goods. Specifically, it suggests that the introduction of differential tariffs and additional tariff lines for sustainable modes of production of a specific good may be justified under GATT Article XX and related provisions when in support of a solution to a

---

> measures targeted to achieve certain environmental objectives may need trade measures to render them effective. Should trade policy measures be found necessary for the enforcement of environmental policies, certain principles and rules should apply:

Agenda 21 (n 450) para 17.118.

1074 See Vranes (n 946) 176–77. On the justification of unilateral actions in general international law, see ibid 176–83.

1075 See Myers (n 944) 68–69.

1076 See *United States – Import Prohibition of Certain Shrimp and Shrimp Products, Recourse to Article 21.5 of the DSU by Malaysia* [2001] Appellate Body Report WT/DS58/AB/RW 42–43 para 134.

1077 See Boyle, 'Further Development of the 1982 Convention on the Law of the Sea: Mechanisms for Change' (n 948) 59.

problem that was identified by the international community as an issue of common concern.

Like in the case of marine plastic pollution, '[h]arm to a matter of common concern is often widespread and diffuse in origin, making it difficult if not impossible to rely on traditional bilateral notions of state responsibility to enforce international norms'.[1078] With regard to compliance and enforcement of the obligations to cooperate and do homework, Cottier and others note that 'problems of vetoing decisions in the Security Council and frequent reliance upon consensus diplomacy in international organizations require implementation to be backed up by individual states'. They call on large markets to use their leverage and bargaining power and to take action against states that do not comply. Economic and trade sanctions should serve as a means of exerting pressure in this context. However, WTO law allows such measures only to a very limited extent.[1079] Countermeasures in terms of withdrawal of concession can only be taken with regard to products that are directly related to the alleged violation. The concept therefore argues in favour of future acceptance within WTO law of measures taken in response to a common concern of humankind, whether or not they are directly linked to the targeted product. More generally, it argues in favour of a public interest standing and the possibility of taking lawful countermeasures[1080] on behalf of the international community in the sense of ILC Draft Articles 48 and 54, respectively, on state responsibility.[1081]

Conclusion of Section C

A closer examination of the relationship between UNCLOS Part XII and WTO law underscores the importance of clear internationally agreed environmental standards. With regard to plastics, such standards would potentially clarify the content of state obligations under UNCLOS Part XII and provide valuable guidance on the kind of implementing measures that are justifiable under WTO

1078 Shelton (n 1066) 34.

1079 Trade 'sanctions' bear the risk of a *tit-for-tat* scenario in which targeted nations respond with economic countermeasures and potentially prejudice the cooperative spirit among nations (such as in the 2018 trade war between the US and China): see Myers (n 944) 70. On the limitations imposed to the concept of common concern by the disciplines of WTO law, see Thomas Cottier and Sofya Matteotti-Berkutova, 'International Environmental Law and the Evolving Concept of "Common Concern of Mankind"' in Thomas Cottier, Olga Nartova and Sadeq Z Bigdeli (eds), *International Trade Regulation and the Mitigation of Climate Change* (Cambridge University Press 2009) 44–46.

1080 Such measures are subject to the principle of proportionality and must not exceed of what is required to achieve compensation for damage and losses incurred.

1081 ILC, '2001 ILC Draft Articles on State Responsibility' (n 842) art 48(1).

law. This being the case, an international agreement that defines such standards would promote coherence between the two regimes and their mutual supportiveness. A firm duty to closely cooperate in the fight against marine plastic pollution and define common and effective standards does not only emerge from UNCLOS itself, but, according to a modern conception of international law, is further strengthened by the fact that the international community has repeatedly acknowledged and underlined the gravity and global scope of the problem.

Regardless of its restrictive effects, trade law does not in any way exempt states from their environmental obligations. All to the contrary: as discussed above, in the event of a true conflict of norms, integral environmental obligations usually prevail over trade obligations that are reciprocal or bilateral in scope. In view of the supposed mutual supportiveness of the two regimes (and in avoidance of a conflict of norms), WTO rules do not in principle prevent states from taking measures to address environmental concerns or enforce environmental policies. If such measures are based on or backed by multilateral efforts, which are reflected in multilateral environmental agreements and other instruments, they are more easily justified even if there are extraterritorial effects. Reference to such (external) instruments by WTO dispute settlement bodies is increasingly common, both in their legal assessment of a specific measure and the interpretation of covered agreements more generally.[1082] Assuming that the concept of common concern as described by Cottier and others gains a foothold in international law, extraterritorial effects of domestic measures can also be justified if they serve to solve an issue of common concern. The same applies to trade measures directed against free riders in matters of common concern.

D *Multilateral Environmental Agreements Relevant to Marine Plastic Pollution Mitigation*

Other fields that are relevant to the mitigation of plastic pollution from land-based sources include the protection and preservation of marine and coastal biodiversity (i), the law related to the management of hazardous chemicals

1082 The Appellate Body report in the *US – Shrimp* case serves as a prime example in this regard: in order to determine the meaning of the term 'natural resources' within the context of GATT Article XX – a meaning that it held was 'by definition evolutionary' – the Appellate Body referred to the 1992 Rio Declaration, the CBD, UNCLOS and a number of other instruments. Based on this reference, it concluded that the term included both living and non-living resources: *US Shrimp* (n 677) 48–50 paras 130–31.

and wastes (ii), the management of watercourses (iii), the prevention of sea-based marine pollution (iv) and climate change mitigation (v).

i The Protection and Preservation of Marine Species and Ecosystems

Marine plastic debris and microplastics pose a severe threat to marine species and ecosystems. In 2016, 817 marine species were identified to be affected by marine debris, especially plastics.[1083] Effects include ingestion, entanglement, the effects of microplastics and persistent, bioaccumulative and toxic substances, habitat alterations, dispersal via rafting and the transport of invasive alien species, as well as ecosystem-level effects. Microplastics are present in all marine habitats and readily available to every level of the food web. They provide a new habitat in the oceans for microbial communities and can be absorbed by the tissue of marine organisms or transmit hazardous chemicals to it. Plastics and their regulation are therefore relevant to multilateral environmental agreements and other instruments dealing with the protection of biological diversity and marine living resources. Respective institutions have been addressing the issue with increasing emphasis. These particularly include different treaty bodies of the CBD and the Convention on the Conservation of Migratory Species of Wild Animals (CMS).[1084]

1) *The Convention on Biological Diversity*

The CBD was adopted at UNCED in 1992 and entered into force in 1993. It is hosted by UN Environment and nearly universally ratified.[1085] The convention's objectives include the conservation of biological diversity, the sustainable use of its components and the fair and equitable sharing of the benefits arising out of the utilization of genetic resources.[1086] For the purpose of the convention, the term *biodiversity* includes diversity within species, between species and of ecosystems.[1087] The convention is based on the ecosystem approach.[1088] It further stresses the importance of scientific assessment, technology transfer and stakeholder involvement. The CBD has a protocol on

1083 CBD Secretariat (n 375) 16.

1084 Convention on the Conservation of Migratory Species of Wild Animals (CMS) (adopted on 23 June 1979, entered into force on 1 November 1983) 1651 UNTS 333, 19 ILM 15 (1980).

1085 As of September 2021, the CBD has 196 parties, excluding the United States.

1086 1992 CBD art 1.

1087 ibid art 2.

1088 For a description of the ecosystem approach and a number of guiding principles related to it, see CBD COP Decision V/6 (2000), 'Ecosystem Approach' UNEP/CBD/COP/5/23, 103.

living modified organisms[1089] and one on access to genetic resources and the sharing of benefits.[1090] Its institutional set-up includes, along with the conference of the parties and the secretariat, the Subsidiary Body on Scientific, Technical and Technological Advice (SBSTTA) and the Subsidiary Body on Implementation (SIB). The GEF operates as the financial mechanism of the agreement. The convention requires countries to prepare a national biodiversity strategy or action plan. These strategies and action plans are the principal instruments for implementing the convention at the national level. A clearing-house mechanism has been established under the convention in order to facilitate implementation, including in view of the Strategic Plan for Biodiversity 2011–2020.[1091] The mechanism provides effective information services in order to promote and facilitate scientific and technical cooperation, knowledge sharing and information exchange.

The CBD COP identified seven thematic programmes of work, one of which is marine and coastal biodiversity. Increasing attention is given to the impacts of marine debris on marine and coastal biodiversity. In its work, the CBD closely collaborates with the GEF Scientific and Technical Advisory Panel (GEF-STAP).[1092] Shortly after the 5th International Marine Debris Conference in Honolulu and the adoption of the Honolulu Commitment in 2011,[1093] the GEF-STAP circulated a report on marine debris in which it stressed the global dimension of the problem.[1094] A year later, the CBD Secretariat and the

1089 2000 Cartagena Protocol.

1090 Nagoya Protocol on Access to Genetic Resources and the Fair and Equitable Sharing of Benefits Arising from their Utilization to the Convention on Biological Diversity (2010 Nagoya Protocol) (adopted on 29 October 2010, entered into force on 12 October 1914).

1091 The Strategic Plan for Biodiversity 2011–2020 was adopted in 2010 and includes a number of strategic goals, as well as the Aichi Biodiversity Targets. See CBD COP Decision X/2 (2010), 'The Strategic Plan for Biodiversity 2011–2020 and the Aichi Biodiversity Targets' UNEP/CBD/COP/DEC/X/2.

1092 In COP decision X/29, parties noted an urgent need to further assess and monitor the impacts and risks of human activities on marine and coastal biodiversity and requested the executive secretary to mainstream biodiversity concerns into assessment work undertaken by other competent organizations, including the UN Regular Process for the Global Reporting and Assessment of the State of the Marine Environment, Including Socioeconomic Aspects ('Regular Process' <https://www.un.org/regularprocess/> accessed 19 February 2022), FAO, UNEP, the UNESCO-IOC, IMO and ISA. Pursuant to this request, the Executive Secretary collaborated with the GEF-STAP on the impacts of marine debris on marine and coastal biodiversity: CBD, 'Synthesis Document on the Impacts of Marine Debris on Marine and Coastal Biodiversity: Note by the Executive Secretary' (2012) UNEP/CBD/SBSTTA/16/INF/15.

1093 See Section 2.1.A.i.4) above.

1094 STAP (n 510).

GEF-STAP co-published an extensive study on the impacts of marine debris on biodiversity.[1095] The CBD also convened an expert workshop on marine debris in Baltimore, United States, in December 2014.[1096] In 2016, it published a second study on prevention and mitigation of marine debris.[1097] The study includes a list of examples of management tools and measures with a focus on plastics. In the same year, parties to the CBD adopted the 'voluntary practical guidance on preventing and mitigating the impacts of marine debris on marine and coastal biodiversity and habitats'.[1098] The document suggests a detailed list of approaches and priority actions, including the promotion of 'structural economic changes that would reduce the production and consumption of plastics, increase production of environmentally friendlier materials, and support the development of alternative materials'. Further priority actions include increasing recycling and reuse and supporting 'an enabling environment for these changes through capacity-building, regulations and standards and cooperation among industry, governments and consumers'.[1099] Proposed actions are closely related to the measures as suggested by UN Environment in its marine litter legislation toolkit published a few months earlier.[1100] With regard to plastics, they play a fundamental role in the national implementation of UNCLOS Part XII obligations, even though they are not legally binding.[1101]

In 2018, the CBD COP urged its parties to increase their efforts with regard to avoiding, minimizing and mitigating the impacts of plastic pollution on marine and coastal biodiversity and habitats.[1102] The COP CBD is currently in the process of including a target for the elimination of plastic waste discharge in the Post-2020 Global Biodiversity Framework.[1103]

1095 CBD Secretariat and STAP (n 510).

1096 See CBD, 'Expert Workshop Report 2014' (n 510).

1097 CBD Secretariat (n 375).

1098 CBD COP Decision XIII/10 (2016), 'Addressing Impacts of Marine Debris and Anthropogenic Underwater Noise on Marine and Coastal Biodiversity' CBD/COP/DEC/XIII/10 Annex.

1099 ibid Annex para 8(b).

1100 UNEP, 'Marine Litter Legislation: A Toolkit for Policymakers' (n 509).

1101 See Chapter 2.3 below. Overlaps in the scope, objective and purpose between the CBD and UNCLOS go well beyond concerns related to plastic pollution. Potential areas of conflict particularly include questions related to the conservation and sustainable use of marine living resources, the scope of the ecosystem approach, the establishment of marine protected areas and access and benefit-sharing with regard to marine genetic resources. For more information, see Wolfrum and Matz (n 939) 15–31.

1102 CBD COP Decision 14/10 (2018), 'Other Matters Related to Marine and Coastal Biodiversity' CBD/COP/DEC/14/10.

1103 See CBD, 'Report of the Open-Ended Working Group on the Post-2020 Global Biodiversity Framework on Its Third Meeting (Part I)' (2021) CBD/W2020/3/4.

2) *Convention on the Conservation of Migratory Species of Wild Animals*

Another convention that is administered by UN Environment and concerned with the impacts of plastics on marine biodiversity is the CMS. The CMS is dedicated to the conservation of migratory species, their habitats and migration routes on a global scale. It promotes concerted action among the countries concerned with the migration of certain species. Appendix I contains a list of migratory species that are threatened with extinction. The parties are obliged to make every effort to protect these animals and their habitats and mitigate obstacles to their migration. Appendix II lists migratory species that need or would significantly benefit from international cooperation. The convention encourages the conclusion of agreements to their conservation and management, and acts as a framework convention for seven species-oriented agreements and several memoranda of understanding that have been concluded under its auspices. Species covered by such agreements include, among other species, turtles, sharks, marine mammals and migratory birds with marine migration routes. Each of the agreements concluded in this context can be tailored to the specific needs of a certain range of migratory species, which is an important strength of the CMS family.

In 2011, the CMS COP acknowledged the negative impacts of marine debris on substantial numbers of migratory marine wildlife that are threatened with extinction.[1104] It required the secretariat to provide available information on the impact of marine debris on listed migratory species to the Scientific Council, a subsidiary body of the convention providing scientific advice for the identification of research and conservation priorities. The COP further required the parties to adopt national action plans addressing the negative impacts of marine debris, and to properly cover the topic in their national reports. CMS commissioned three reports on the management of marine debris, vessel best practice, and public awareness and education, respectively.[1105] Based on these reports, the COP invited its members in 2014 to implement cost-effective measures for the prevention of debris and encouraged them to establish public awareness campaigns.[1106] Following up on the UNEA resolutions on marine litter and

1104 CMS COP Resolution 10.4 (2011), 'Marine Debris' UNEP/CMS/Resolution 10.4.

1105 CMS, 'Report I: Migratory Species, Marine Debris and Its Management' (2014) UNEP/CMS/COP11/Inf.27; 'Report II: Marine Debris and Commercial Marine Vessel Best Practice' (2014) UNEP/CMS/COP11/Inf.28; 'Report III: Marine Debris Public Awareness and Education Campaigns' (2014) UNEP/CMS/COP11/Inf.29.

1106 CMS COP Resolution 11.30 (2014), 'Management of Marine Debris' UNEP/CMS/Resolution 11.30.

microplastics, the CMS COP called on its members at its 2017 and 2020 meetings to collect and exchange information on the impact of plastic pollution on migratory species, especially Annex I and II species, and take appropriate measures to protect them.[1107] In 2021, the CMS Secretariat published a report supporting evidence that migratory species are likely to be among the most vulnerable to plastic pollution. The study focused on the impacts of plastic pollution on animals that live on land and in freshwater environments in the Asia-Pacific region. Particular attention was given to the Ganges and Mekong river basins, which together contribute an estimated 200,000 tonnes of plastic pollution to the Indian Ocean and the Pacific Ocean each year.[1108]

3) *Other Biodiversity-related Conventions*

The UN Fish Stock Agreement, which has been concluded under the auspices of UNCLOS, sets out principles for the conservation and management of straddling and highly migratory fish stocks. The agreement facilitates the implementation of UNCLOS and advances and expands the convention's rules and principles in this regard.[1109] It prescribes the application of the precautionary approach in this respect, as well as the use of best available scientific information.[1110] It also requires its parties to minimize pollution and wastes and protect biodiversity in the marine environment. With respect to plastics, parties are particularly concerned with the issue of abandoned, lost or otherwise discarded fishing gear (ALDFG). The so-called ghost nets – nets that were lost or discarded in the ocean and continue to catch target and non-target species over an indefinite period of time – cause substantial ecological and socio-economic problems. In spite of growing awareness in this respect, their number is rapidly increasing, and so are their impacts. ALDFG is therefore addressed by a number of institutions dealing with marine living resources and sea-based pollution sources in the first place, including the FAO.[1111]

1107 See CMS COP Resolution 12.20 (2017), 'Management of Marine Debris' UNEP/CMS/Resolution 12.20; CMS COP Decisions 13.122 to 13.125 (2020), 'Impacts of Plastic Pollution on Aquatic, Terrestrial and Avian Species'.

1108 See CMS and UNEP, *Impacts of Plastic Pollution on Freshwater Aquatic, Terrestrial and Avian Migratory Species in the Asia and Pacific Region* (2021).

1109 See Moritaka Hayashi, 'The 1995 UN Fish Stocks Agreement and the Law of the Sea' in Davor Vidas and Willy Østreng (eds), *Order for the Oceans at the Turn of the Century* (Kluwer Law International 1999) 38.

1110 1995 Fish Stock Agreement arts 5–6.

1111 The FAO plays an important role in the development of fisheries law. On ALDFG, see FAO and UNEP, 'Abandoned, Lost or Otherwise Discarded Fishing Gear' (2009) FAO Fisheries and Aquaculture Technical Paper 523 UNEP Regional Seas Reports and Studies 185; FAO, *International Guidelines on Bycatch Management and Reduction of Discards*

Other biodiversity-related conventions may also be relevant with respect to the protection and preservation of the marine environment in general and plastic pollution mitigation from land-based sources in particular. In the *South China Sea* case, the tribunal referred to the appendices of CITES to point out the fact that the species at stake were generally considered to be threatened with extinction.[1112] The Ramsar Convention on Wetlands,[1113] on the other hand, is relevant to plastic pollution in the context of site management. The convention provides a framework for national action and international cooperation for the conservation and wise use of wetlands and their resources. For this purpose, each state party has to designate suitable wetlands for the List of Wetlands of International Importance (Ramsar List).[1114] Litter is a common problem in many areas covered by the list, and a number of large clean-up events have been organized.[1115]

Marine plastic debris is also a concern under the International Convention for the Regulation of Whaling.[1116] The IWC held three workshops on entanglement of large whales in 2010, 2011 and 2015, respectively,[1117] as well as

(2011); 'Abandoned, Lost or Otherwise Discarded Gillnets and Trammel Nets: Methods to Estimate Ghost Fishing Mortality, and the Status of Regional Monitoring and Management' (2016) FAO Fisheries and Aquaculture Technical Paper 600; 'Report of the Expert Consultation on the Marking of Fishing Gear, Rome, Italy, 4–7 April 2016' (2016) FAO Fisheries and Aquaculture Report R1157. See also IWC Res 2018-3, 'Resolution on Ghost Gear Entanglement Among Cetaceans'.

1112 *South China Sea Arbitration* (n 584) 380–84 paras 956–64.

1113 Convention on Wetlands of International Importance especially as Waterfowl Habitat (1971 Ramsar Convention) (adopted on 2 February 1971, entered into force on 21 December 1975, as last amended on 28 May 1987) 996 UNTS 245, 11 ILM 963 (1972).

1114 More than 2,400 sites are included in the list, covering a surface area of more than 2.5 million km^2. The aim of the Ramsar List is mainly the recording of relevant data, as well as the exchange of information among the parties or between the parties and the secretariat. Where a site runs the risk of undergoing a change in its ecological character brought about by human action, technical assistance is provided.

1115 The same is true for sites protected under the Convention Concerning the Protection of the World Cultural and Natural Heritage (World Heritage Convention) (adopted on 23 November 19, entered into force on 15 December 1975) 1037 UNTS 151, 11 ILM 1358 (1972).

1116 International Convention for the Regulation of Whaling (1946 ICRW) (adopted on 2 December 1946, entered into force on 10 November 1948) 161 UNTS 72.

1117 IWC, 'Report of the Workshop on Welfare Issues Associated with the Entanglement of Large Whales' (2010) IWC/62/15; 'Report of Second IWC Workshop on Welfare Issues Associated with the Entanglement of Large Whales With a Focus on Entanglement Response' (2011) IWC/64/WKM&AWI REP1; 'Report of the Third Workshop on Large Whale Entanglement Issues, Provincetown, MA, USA, 21–23 April 2015' (2015) IWC/66/WK-I-Rep01. IWC also manages an entanglement response capacity building programme and coordinates an Expert Advisory Panel on Entanglement Response.

three workshops on marine debris in 2013, 2014 and 2019. The 2013 workshop focused on threats, knowledge gaps and further research requirements.[1118] The follow-up workshop focused on the mitigation and management of threats to cetaceans from marine debris. The workshop report includes a number of recommendations with regard to further work on marine plastic debris.[1119] The third workshop reviewed the latest evidence of ingestion, entanglement, microdebris and toxicology.[1120] The IWC assesses the impacts of microplastics on cetaceans in its Pollution 2020 project.[1121]

With regard to their work on plastic pollution, the CBD, CMS and IWC emphasized the importance of cooperation among them and with further institutions, including IMO, FAO, ISO and the regional conventions.

ii Waste Management and the Regulation of Wastes and Hazardous Chemicals

Inadequate disposal behaviours and insufficient or unsound waste management are major sources of plastic pollution. Also, plastics contain chemicals that are inclined to migrate and leak into the environment. At the same time, they absorb toxic chemicals from ambient seawater. When ingested, they transfer the chemicals to marine organisms. These toxic substances are susceptible to bioaccumulate throughout the food chain. Both waste management law and the regulation and control of hazardous chemicals are thus of fundamental importance for the mitigation of marine plastic pollution from land-based sources. From an international law perspective, the two issues are dealt with in a single cluster of multilateral environmental agreements, generally referred to as the chemicals and wastes cluster. The cluster includes the Basel Convention on the Control of Transboundary Movements of Hazardous Wastes and Their Disposal,[1122] the Rotterdam Convention on the Prior Informed Consent Procedure for Certain Hazardous Chemicals and Pesticides in International Trade[1123] and the Stockholm Convention on Persistent Organic Pollutants.[1124]

1118 IWC, 'Report of the 2013 IWC Scientific Committee Workshop on Marine Debris' (2013) SC/65a/Rep06.

1119 IWC, 'Report of the IWC Workshop on Mitigation and Management of the Threats Posed by Marine Debris to Cetaceans' (2014) IWC/65/CCRep04.

1120 IWC, 'Report of IWC Workshop on Marine Debris: The Way Forward' (2019) SC/68B/REP/03.

1121 IWC, 'Understanding the Threat to Cetaceans from Microplastics and PAHs – Pollution 2020' <https://iwc.int/understanding-the-threat-to-cetaceans-from-micropl> accessed 19 February 2022.

1122 1989 Basel Convention.

1123 1998 Rotterdam PIC Convention.

1124 2001 Stockholm POPs Convention.

It is also closely related to the Minamata Convention on Mercury.[1125] The four conventions share a life-cycle approach to chemicals and waste management. Their common objective is to protect human health and the environment from hazardous chemicals and wastes and to assist parties to manage these at different stages of their life cycle. Because of the thematic and organizational proximity, the conferences of parties to the Basel, Rotterdam and Stockholm Conventions decided to enhance cooperation and coordination among them and launched a synergies process in 2008.[1126] Among the foursome of the chemicals and wastes agreements, the Basel and Stockholm Conventions are especially relevant to the regulation of plastic pollution from land-based sources.

1) *The Basel Convention on the Control of Transboundary Movements of Hazardous Wastes and Their Disposal*

The Basel Convention aims at protecting the environment and human health from negative impacts of hazardous wastes and other wastes throughout their lifecycle. It requires its parties to reduce the generation of hazardous and other wastes to a minimum and dispose of them domestically where possible and in an environmentally sound manner.[1127] The convention thus aims to reduce the generation and international movement of hazardous wastes and promotes environmentally sound waste management. It applies the concept of waste management hierarchy in this regard, a concept that gives priority to the least environmentally harmful management or disposal option (see Figure 16).[1128]

From a substantive point of view, the Basel Convention restricts the transboundary movement of hazardous and other wastes. Export of covered wastes requires prior informed consent by the states of import and transit.[1129] Exports to Antarctica, to non-parties or to parties having banned the import

1125 Minamata Convention on Mercury (adopted on 10 October 2013, entered into force on 16 August 2017).

1126 In February 2010, simultaneous Extraordinary Meetings of the Conferences of the Parties (ExCOPs) to the three conventions were held in Bali, Indonesia, at the margins of the special session of the UNEP Governing Council. The COPs of the three conventions took identical decisions on cooperation and coordination regarding joint activities, joint managerial functions, joint services, synchronization of budget cycles, joint audits, and review arrangements: Omnibus decisions BC.Ex-1/1, RC.Ex-1/1 and SC.Ex-1/1. The synergies process was further strengthened by biennial COP decisions in 2011, 2013, 2015, 2017 and 2019.

1127 1989 Basel Convention art 4(2).

1128 See Basel Convention COP decision BC 10/2 (2011), 'Strategic Framework for the Implementation of the Basel Convention for 2012–2021' Annex para 3(a).

1129 1989 Basel Convention arts 6 and 7.

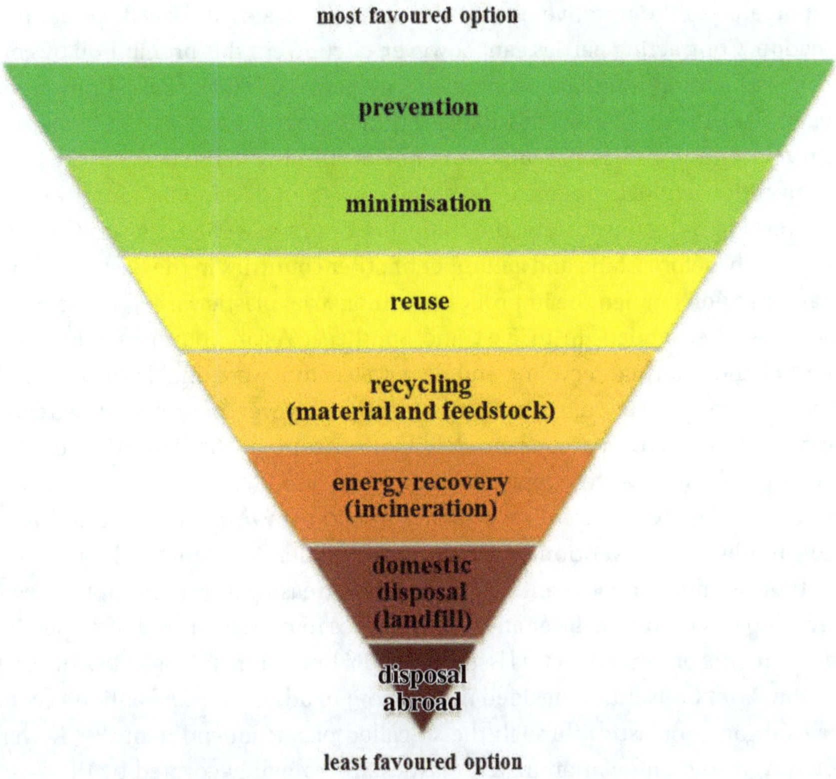

FIGURE 16 Waste management hierarchy
AUTHOR

of hazardous wastes are prohibited.[1130] Since December 2019, when the so-called Ban Amendment entered into force, exports from OECD countries to non-OECD countries have also been prohibited.[1131] The amendment reflects wide agreement among parties that developing countries are particularly

1130 ibid art 4(1) and (5–6).

1131 The ban was originally agreed on in COP Decision II/12 in 1994. At its third meeting (1995), the COP decided to amend the convention accordingly, by introducing a new preambular paragraph '[r]ecognizing that transboundary movements of hazardous wastes, especially to developing countries, have a high risk of not constituting an environmentally sound management of hazardous wastes': BC-III/1. The Ban Amendment also includes Article 4A, which obliges OECD parties, parties to the European Union and Lichtenstein to prohibit all transboundary movements to all other parties to the convention of hazardous wastes that are intended for final disposal, and to phase out transboundary movements to these countries of hazardous wastes that are exported for other purposes, including reuse, recycling or recovery operations.

vulnerable to the negative effects of hazardous wastes and need special protection. Contracting parties can, however, circumvent this prohibition by concluding bilateral, multilateral or regional agreements.[1132] The Basel Convention explicitly provides for this possibility if these agreements meet the standard of the convention and do not run counter to its purpose. In this context, the Basel Convention explicitly refers to the specific needs of developing countries.

Developing countries are the main importers of various types of waste. Especially before China and a number of other countries in the East Asian and Pacific region banned the import of non-industrial plastic waste, plastic waste streams often ended up in East and Southeast Asian countries, where the formal and informal recycling and disposal sectors were unable to cope with the imported waste volumes. Until recently, however, plastic waste streams have not been covered appropriately by the scope of the Basel Convention. Solid plastic wastes were typically considered non-hazardous under the convention.[1133] Only plastics disposed of in *household wastes* and collected were covered by the convention as 'other wastes' under Article 1(2) when subject to transboundary movement.[1134] In view of increasing awareness of the negative impacts of marine litter and microplastics in particular, and of respective assessments presented on this issue at the UN Environment Assembly, the COP to the Basel Convention decided in May 2019 to adjust the convention's scope with regard to plastics through the so-called plastic amendments.[1135] Lower-quality, mixed and contaminated plastics are now fully covered by the Basel

1132 1989 Basel Convention art 11(1).

1133 Basel Convention Annex IX item B3010 before amendment by COP19.

1134 For the purposes of the Basel Convention, hazardous wastes are wastes that belong to specific categories (as defined in Annex I of the convention), possessing certain characteristics (as defined in Annex III), such as toxicity or ecotoxicity. Plastics containing specific flame retardants, such as polybrominated biphenyls, would fall into this category. Substances or wastes are considered *toxic* if their inhalation or ingestion may involve delayed or chronic effects, including carcinogenicity. They are considered *ecotoxic* if their release 'may present immediate or delayed adverse impacts to the environment by means of bioaccumulation and/or toxic effects upon biotic systems': see codes H11 and H12, respectively, according to Annex III to the 1989 Basel Convention. See also Basel Convention, 'Approach to Basel Convention Hazard Characteristic H11: Characterization of Chronic or Delayed Toxicity' (2004) UNEP/CHW. 7/11/Add.2/Rev. 1; 'Interim Guidelines on the Hazardous Characteristics H12-Ecotoxic' (2003). Categories of 'other wastes' are listed in Annex II, such as wastes collected from households.

1135 Basel Convention COP decision BC 14/12 (2019), 'Amendments to Annexes II, VIII and IX to the Basel Convention' UNEP/CHW.14/12; IISD, 'Summary of the Meetings of the Conferences of the Parties to the Basel, Rotterdam and Stockholm Conventions: 29 April – 10 May 2019' (2019) 15 Earth Negotiations Bulletin: COPS FINAL 18 <http://enb.iisd.org/download/pdf/enb15269e.pdf> accessed 19 February 2022.

Convention. These plastics are difficult to recycle and therefore usually end up in landfills. They also make up the majority of the plastic scrap exported to low or lower-middle-income countries.[1136] General obligations with regard to waste minimization, sound waste management and the regulation of transboundary movement therefore apply to these plastics now.[1137] As a consequence, contracting parties are, for example, not allowed to import mixed plastic wastes from non-parties (such as the US) any more, as long as there are no bilateral or regional agreements between these states within the meaning of Article 11 of the Basel Convention.

The COP to the Basel Convention adopted a series of non-binding technical guidelines that assist parties in ensuring the environmentally sound management of hazardous and other wastes. Some of them are relevant to plastics, including, for instance, the ones dealing with household wastes, waste incineration, engineered landfills, the sound management of waste tyres, and the sound management of wastes containing persistent organic pollutants.[1138] In 2002, the COP also adopted technical guidelines for the identification and environmentally sound management of plastic wastes and for their disposal.[1139] The original version of the document focuses on technical aspects of the management of plastic wastes, and of plastic recycling in particular. As it does not address the problem of marine plastic debris and microplastics, or health and environmental impacts of plastics in general, the COP decided at

---

1136 See Dominique Mosbergen, 'How America Is Sabotaging The Global War On Plastic Waste' (*HuffPost*, 54:41 400AD) <https://www.huffpost.com/entry/plastic-regulation-us-obstruction-basel-convention_n_5cde76f0e4b00e035b8da236> accessed 19 February 2022.

1137 See Basel Convention Secretariat, 'Report on Possible Options Available under the Basel Convention to Further Address Marine Plastic Litter and Microplastics' (2018) UNEP/CHW/OEWG.11/INF/22 para 28. For a critical view on the suitability of the Basel Convention to more properly regulate plastics and plastic pollution from land-based sources, see Nils Simon and Maro Luisa Schulte, 'Stopping Global Plastic Pollution: The Case for an International Convention' (Heinrich Böll Stiftung 2017) Ecology Publication Series 43 26–29. See also European Commission, 'Green Paper on a European Strategy on Plastic Waste in the Environment' (2013) COM(2013) 123 final 19.

1138 Basel Convention, 'Basel Convention Technical Guidelines on Wastes Collected from Households (Y46)' (1994); 'Basel Convention Technical Guidelines on Incineration on Land (D10)' (1995); 'Basel Convention Technical Guidelines on Specially Engineered Landfill (D5)' (1995); 'Revised Technical Guidelines for the Environmentally Sound Management of Used and Waste Pneumatic Tyres' (2011) UNEP/CHW.10/6/Add.1/Rev.1; 'General Technical Guidelines on the Environmentally Sound Management of Wastes of Wastes Consisting of, Containing or Contaminated with Persistent Organic Pollutants' (2015) UNEP/CHW.12/5/Add.2/Rev.1.

1139 Basel Convention, 'Technical Guidelines for the Identification and Environmentally Sound Management of Plastic Wastes and for Their Disposal' (2002) UNEP/CHW.6/21.

its fourteenth meeting in May 2019 to update the guidelines accordingly.[1140] The COP also followed a suggestion by the Open-Ended Working Group (OEWG),[1141] an advisory body under the Basel Convention, to establish a new Partnership on Plastic Waste[1142] in addition to the Partnership on Household Waste that was established at BC COP 13 in 2017 for further exploring the environmentally sound management of household wastes.[1143] The Plastic Waste Partnership comprises more than a hundred actors from governments, private sector and civil society organisations. Under its auspices, numerous pitot projects have been launched to promote the implementation of the 2019 plastic waste amendments. Finally, the COP decided to take advantage of the convention's potentials with regard to public awareness, data collection and information exchange[1144] and took note of the capacity-building work by the convention's regional and coordinating centres, which had been encouraged at BC COP 13 to work on the impact of plastic waste, marine plastic litter and microplastics.[1145]

The Basel Convention is administered by UN Environment and currently has 188 parties.[1146] In 1999, the Basel Protocol on Liability and Compensation

1140 IISD, 'Summary of COP BC/RC/SC 2019' (n 1135) 18.

1141 At the BC COP 13, which took place from 24 April to 5 May 2017, new areas of work were added to the work programme of the OEWG. The new areas of work notably include waste containing nanomaterials, as well as marine plastic litter and microplastics. In view of the assessment work under the auspices of UN Environment in this field and any relevant decision by the UNEA at its third meeting, the OEWG was tasked to '[c]onsider relevant options available under the Convention to further address marine plastic litter and microplastics [...] and develop a proposal for possible further actions': Basel Convention COP decision BC 13/17 (2017), 'Work Programme and Operations of the Open-Ended Working Group for the Biennium 2018–2019' UNEP/CHW.13/17 Annex; Basel Convention, 'Report of COP to the Basel Convention on the Work of Its 13th Meeting' (2017) UNEP/CHW.13/28 81.

1142 Basel Convention Secretariat, 'Marine Plastic Litter and Microplastics' (2019) UNEP/CHW.14/11 paras 25–30.

1143 See Basel Convention COP decision BC 13/14 (2017), 'Partnership on Household Waste' UNEP/CHW.13/14.

1144 See Basel Convention Secretariat, 'Marine Plastic Litter and Microplastics' (n 1142) paras 31–33. See also Basel Convention OEWG decision 11/8, 'Draft Elements as a Basis for a Decision on Marine Plastic Litter' Annex; Basel Convention Secretariat, 'Report on Possible Options Available under the Basel Convention to Further Address Marine Plastic Litter and Microplastics' (n 1137).

1145 See Basel Convention COP decision BC 13/11 (2017), 'Technical Assistance' UNEP/CHW.13/11 para 14; Basel Convention Secretariat, 'Basel Convention Regional and Coordinating Centres' (2019) UNEP/CHW.14/17 para 23(2).

1146 Status of ratification in September 2021.

was adopted.[1147] Once it enters into force, it will apply to damage 'due to an incident occurring during a transboundary movement of hazardous wastes and other wastes and their disposal, including illegal traffic'.[1148] The protocol will provide for strict civil liability and, as the case may be, fault-based liability.[1149] Three years after the adoption of the protocol, the legal and institutional framework of the Basel Convention has been further complemented by the establishment of a compliance committee. The committee assists parties in complying with their obligations under the convention and facilitates, monitors and reports on implementation.[1150]

2) *The Stockholm Convention on Persistent Organic Pollutants*

The Stockholm Convention on Persistent Organic Pollutants is another important agreement associated with the chemicals and wastes cluster. It was adopted in 2001 and entered into force in 2004. It currently has 184 parties.[1151] 'Mindful of the precautionary approach', the convention aims at protecting human health and the environment from the exposure to POPs.[1152] POPs are organic chemical substances that, when released into the environment, remain intact for exceptionally long periods of time (as they resist degradation), become widely distributed throughout the environment, accumulate in the fatty tissue of living organisms, are susceptible to bioaccumulation and are toxic to both humans and wildlife. The Stockholm Convention requires its parties to take measures to eliminate or reduce the release of POPs into the environment. Specifically, parties shall prohibit the production and use of the chemicals listed in Annex A and ban their import and export (unless

1147 Protocol on Liability and Compensation for Damage Resulting from Transboundary Movements of Hazardous Wastes and Their Disposal (1999 Basel Protocol) (adopted on 10 December 1999, not yet in force) UN Doc. UNEP/CHW.1/WG/1/9/2. The protocol will enter into force after the ratification by twenty states. Twelve instruments of ratification have been deposited so far (as of September 2021).

1148 ibid art 3(1).

1149 ibid arts 4 and 5.

1150 See Alessandro Fodella, 'Mechanism for Promoting Implementation and Compliance with the 1989 Basel Convention on the Transboundary Movements of Hazardous Wastes and Their Disposal' in Tullio Treves and others (eds), *Non-Compliance Procedures and Mechanisms and the Effectiveness of International Environmental Agreements* (TMC Asser Press 2009) 33. See also Basel Convention, 'The Basel Convention Mechanism for Promoting Implementation and Compliance' (2006); 'The Basel Convention Mechanism for Promoting Implementation and Compliance: Celebrating a Decade of Assistance to Parties' (2011).

1151 As of September 2021.

1152 2001 Stockholm POPs Convention art 1.

the party has a specific exemption that applies to the case). They moreover shall restrict the production and use of the chemicals listed in Annex B.[1153] Furthermore, parties have to take measures to reduce or eliminate releases from unintentional production for chemicals listed in Annex C and to reduce or eliminate releases from stockpiles and wastes.[1154] Initially, 12 chemicals were listed under the three annexes, including a range of pesticides, industrial chemicals and by-products. Since then, several new POPs have been added to the list.

The Stockholm Convention covers a range of substances that have been widely used in the production of plastics. Such substances include, as one example out of many, polybrominated diphenyl ethers (PBDEs), which have been used since the 1970s as additive flame retardants in a wide range of consumer products such as car interiors or upholstery (made from polyurethane foam) and housings or casings of electronic or electrical equipment (made from ABS or other polymers).[1155] While the production of listed chemicals has declined since they are subject to international regulation, many products that contain such substances are still in use or in their disposal stage.[1156] Both end-of-life vehicles and electronic wastes are still traded to or dumped in developing countries, where sound disposal of these goods is difficult.

Annex C to the Stockholm Convention covers POPs that may be released from uncontrolled plastic waste combustion, including dump fires and other open burning practices. In particular, incineration of PVC plastics may generate a range of irritant, corrosive and toxic substances such as polychlorinated dibenzodioxins (PCDDs) and polychlorinated dibenzofurans (PCDFs), which

1153 ibid art 3(1). Annex B allows for the registration of acceptable purposes or specific exemptions for the production and use of the listed POPs. The import and export of chemicals listed in Annex A or B can take place under specific restrictive conditions, as set out in Article 3(2).

1154 ibid arts 5–6. Further obligations under the convention relate to the development of implementation plans (art 7), information exchange (art 9), public information, awareness and education (art 10), research, development and monitoring (art 11), technical assistance (art 12), financial resources and mechanisms (art 13), and reporting (art 15).

1155 Stockholm Convention, 'Guidance on Best Available Techniques and Best Environmental Practices for the Recycling and Disposal of Articles Containing Polybrominated Diphenyl Ethers (PBDEs) Listed under the Stockholm Convention on Persistent Organic Pollutants' 17–19.

1156 Decabromodiphenyl ether and short-chain chlorinated paraffins (which are widely used in plastics as additive flame retardant or fillers) as well as perfluorooctanoic acid (as used in non-stick cookware and other applications) are chemicals that were recently added to Stockholm Convention Annex A.

are listed in Stockholm Convention Annex C.[1157] In the absence of the necessary infrastructure for a sound management of wastes and affordable, accessible and safe disposal facilities, open burning often seems the cheapest and easiest means of volume reduction and disposal of plastics. Article 5 of the Stockholm Convention requires states to take measures to reduce and possibly eliminate releases of the chemicals listed in Annex C. To this purpose, parties are strongly recommended to undertake measures against open and other uncontrolled burning of wastes, including the burning of landfill sites.[1158]

The annexes to the Stockholm Convention moreover cover a broad range of chemicals that originate from anthropogenic sources and are widely present in aquatic environments. Plastic fragments, and microplastics in particular, tend to accumulate such substances from the ambient seawater at their surface. When ingested, they serve as a vector for the contaminants to animal tissues and the food chain.

The listing of additives in plastics with acknowledged endocrine-disrupting properties is currently being discussed.[1159] Such additives, which include phthalates, are widely used in plastics.

The Stockholm Convention is complemented by soft law instruments such as the Strategic Approach to International Chemicals Management (SAICM), a policy framework to promote chemical safety around the world. It was adopted by the First International Conference on Chemicals Management (ICCM) in 2006. The framework's objective is 'the achievement of the sound management of chemicals throughout their life cycle so that by the year 2020,

1157 WV Titow, *PVC Technology* (4th edn, Elsevier Applied Science Publishers 1984) 10; Ren-De Sun and others, 'Suppressing Effect of CaCO3 on the Dioxins Emission from Poly(Vinyl Chloride) (PVC) Incineration' (2003) 79 Polymer Degradation and Stability 253, 253.

1158 2001 Stockholm POPs Convention Annex C Part V para A(f). See also Stockholm Convention, 'Guidelines on Best Available Techniques and Provisional Guidance on Best Environmental Practices Relevant to Article 5 and Annex C of the Stockholm Convention on Persistent Organic Pollutants: Open Burning of Waste, Including Burning of Landfill Sites' (2008) 9–14.

1159 See, for instance, Food Packaging Forum, 'UV-328 Qualifies for Screening as POP' (22 January 2021) <https://www.foodpackagingforum.org/news/uv-328-qualifies-for-screening-as-pop> accessed 19 February 2022; COP to the Basel and Stockhom conventions, 'Report on the Activities of the Basel and Stockholm Conventions Regional Centres (Joint Document)' (2017) UNEP/CHW.13/INF/29/Rev.1 and UNEP/POPS/COP8/INF26/Rev.1 Annex VI. The process for listing of new POPs in Annexes A, B or C is set out in Article 8 of the convention. Any party may submit a proposal to the secretariat for listing a chemical to the annexes. The proposal will be examined by the Persistent Organic Pollutants Review Committee and must fulfil the requirements in Annexes D, E and F of the convention.

chemicals are produced and used in ways that minimize significant adverse impacts on the environment and human health'.[1160] The ICCM has adopted eight resolutions on *emerging policy issues* and called for cooperative action in their regard. Two of these resolutions address manufactured nanomaterials and endocrine-disrupting chemicals as used in plastics, respectively.

iii International Watercourses

Rivers and streams are an important pathway allowing plastics to travel from inland places to the shore. A study found that of the total 100,887 river and stream outlets included in the model, about 32,000 locations discharge macroplastic waste into the ocean, resulting in 0.8 to 2.7 million tonnes entering the marine environment in 2015. About 1,600 rivers account for 80 per cent of global riverine plastic emissions to the ocean. Urban rivers, including small rivers, in Southeast Asia and West Africa have been identified as the main hotspots for plastic emissions.[1161] The regulation of watercourses and their management is, therefore, crucial for the prevention of marine plastic debris from land-based sources. Yet, while environmental concerns have been relevant in the development of this body of law, its regulatory impacts on plastic pollution prevention remains limited. Existing instruments do not add much to the global and regional frameworks addressing land-based sources of marine pollution. Also, plastics seem not to figure on the agenda of the relevant bodies in this field. In many regions, assessments of plastic pollution in rivers and its impacts on these environments are, therefore, still at the beginning.

The core principles of international watercourse law include the principle of equitable and reasonable utilization, the obligation not to cause significant damage, the obligation to cooperate and the obligation of prior notification.[1162]

1160 UNEP, 'SAICM: Overview' (*International Chemicals Management*) <http://www.saicm.org/About/SAICMOverview/tabid/5522/language/en-US/Default.aspx> accessed 19 February 2022.

1161 Lourens JJ Meijer and others, 'More Than 1000 Rivers Account for 80% of Global Riverine Plastic Emissions into the Ocean' (2021) 7 Science Advances eaaz5803.

1162 Historically, shared water resources have played a significant role in the development of these principles and of general international environmental law: see *Lac Lanoux Arbitration* (n 814); *Pulp Mills Judgment* (n 544). See also Laurence Boisson de Chazournes and Mara Tignino, 'Introduction' in Laurence Boisson de Chazournes and Mara Tignino (eds), *International Water Law* (Edward Elgar 2015); Laurence Boisson de Chazournes, *Fresh Water in International Law* (Oxford University Press 2013) ch 1; Owen McIntyre, *Environmental Protection of International Watercourses Under International Law* (Routledge 2016) ch 3–4; Salman MA Salman, 'The Helsinki Rules, the UN Watercourses

These principles are enshrined in the UN Watercourses Convention[1163] and the UNECE Water Convention,[1164] as well as in a number of bilateral and regional treaties. Part IV of the UN Watercourses Convention deals with the protection and preservation of ecosystems and the prevention, reduction and control of pollution. Parties to the convention have to protect the water quality and to cooperate to this aim. At the request of a party, riparian states have to consult on measures such as the establishment of 'lists of substances the introduction of which into the waters of an international watercourse is to be prohibited, limited, investigated or monitored'.[1165] Such lists of substances have been established under a number of agreements.[1166] The UNECE Water Convention, on the other hand, obliges its parties to apply the precautionary principle and the polluter pays principle in this regard.

The two conventions also recognize the important link between freshwater and marine pollution: in its Article 23, the UN Watercourses Convention provides that watercourse states 'shall [...] take all measures with respect to an international watercourse that are necessary to protect and preserve the marine environment, including estuaries, taking into account generally accepted international rules and standards'. The provision essentially reflects the object and purpose of UNCLOS Part XII but does not add substance to it. Much like UNCLOS Article 207, it obliges states to ensure that the measures they are planning or implementing on an international watercourse 'be at least

---

Convention and the Berlin Rules: Perspectives on International Water Law' (2007) 23 International Journal of Water Resources Development 625.

1163 1997 Watercourses Convention. While the convention applies only to international watercourses, the concept of a watercourse is a broad one. It refers to 'a system of surface waters and groundwaters constituting by virtue of their physical relationship a unitary whole and normally flowing into a common terminus': ibid art 2(a).

1164 Convention on the Protection and Use of Transboundary Watercourses and International Lakes (UNECE Water Convention) (adopted on 17 March 1992, entered into force on 6 October 1996, as amended in 1999 by the Protocol on Water and Health) 1936 UNTS 269, 31 ILM 1312 (1992). In 2003, the convention's Articles 25 and 26 were amended so as to enable states outside the UNECE region to accede to it. The amendment entered into force in 2015. Hence, the convention has universal scope. For more information, see UNECE Watercourse Convention, 'Guide to Implementing The Water Convention' (United Nations 2013) ECE/MP.WAT/39; 'The Global Opening of the 1992 Water Convention' (United Nations 2016) ECE/MP.WAT/43/Rev.1.

1165 1997 Watercourses Convention art 21(3)(c).

1166 e.g. Convention for the Protection of the Rhine Against Chemical Pollution (adopted on 3 December 1976, entered into force on 1 February 1979) 1124 UNTS 375; Agreement Between Canada and the United States of America on Great Lakes Water Quality (adopted and entered into force on 22 November 1978) 1153 UNTS 187.

consistent with the pertinent rules and standards governing the protection and preservation of the marine environment'.[1167]

The UNECE Water Convention obliges riparian parties to cooperate and harmonize their policies 'aimed at the protection of the environment of transboundary waters or the environment influenced by such waters, including the marine environment'.[1168] Moreover, parties are required to establish joint bodies on transboundary water resources and to cooperate through them with such bodies established by coastal states for the protection of the marine environment.[1169]

iv Prevention and Mitigation of Plastic Pollution from Sea-based Sources

The IMO serves as the principal forum for the further development of rules and regulations with respect to pollution from ships.[1170] The organization administers a large number of treaties on marine pollution prevention from vessels and dumping at sea, and on civil liability. As discussed above, the London Dumping Convention, its 1996 Protocol and MARPOL are of particular relevance to plastic pollution mitigation. The IMO Secretariat repeatedly examined the implications of UNCLOS for IMO and the instruments concluded under its auspices. In an assessment of 1987, the secretariat held that UNCLOS does not preclude the existence of special rules or their future adoption by IMO but presupposes their existence and 'depends on them for the effective implementation of its general principles'.[1171] In support of SDG 14, the IMO Marine Environment Protection Committee adopted an action plan in 2018 to reduce and prevent marine plastic litter from ship-based sources.[1172]

1167 Attila Tanzi and Maurizio Arcari, *The United Nations Convention on the Law of International Watercourses: A Framework for Sharing* (Kluwer Law International 2001) 278. See also Aldo Chircop, 'Marine Pollution from Land-Based Activities: Legal Regimes and Management Frameworks' in Davor Vidas and Willy Østreng (eds), *Order for the Oceans at the Turn of the Century* (Kluwer Law International 1999) 181.

1168 UNECE Water Convention art 2(6).

1169 ibid art 9(2)(4).

1170 See Section 2.1.B.ii.3)a) above.

1171 See IMO, 'Implications of the United Nations Convention on the Law of the Sea for the International Maritime Organization' (1987) LEG/MISC/1, as cited in Nordquist, Rosenne and Yankov (n 585) 426. See also IMO, LEG/MISC/3/Rev.1 (2003); LEG/MISC/8 (2014).

1172 IMO Marine Environment Protection Committee Resolution MEPC.310(73), 'Action Plan to Address Marine Plastic Litter from Ships' (2018) MEPC 73/19/Add.1 Annex 10.

v Climate Change Mitigation

The vast majority of plastics are made from petrochemical products derived from fossil fuels such as petroleum and natural gas. Nearly all intermediates for plastics can be produced more cheaply from petroleum than from other sources.[1173] The share of petroleum used in plastics amounts to about 5 per cent of global petroleum consumption. If trends in oil consumption and plastic production continue as expected, this share will increase to 20 per cent by 2050.[1174] Petroleum fractions are either used as feedstock in the chemical plants or as energy source in the production process. The plastics industry is therefore geographically, economically and commercially linked to the fossil fuel industry and the chemical industry.

Currently, major investments are being made in plastics infrastructure in the United States, the Middle East, China and Europe. This massive capacity expansion will affect plastics production for decades and could underpin mitigation efforts.[1175] The future of the petroleum industry, on which these investments are based, is in turn shaped by the climate policy objectives and commitments of the international community, such as formulated under the Paris Agreement.[1176] As even small changes in the price of oil or gas can have significant consequences for the plastics industry, a shift in fossil fuel markets will fundamentally affect the long-term economic prospects of the plastics industry. A phase-out of fossil fuels 'will force plastic producers to bear more of their upstream costs, dramatically altering the investment risk facing their production facilities'.[1177]

Plastic production is itself an energy-intensive and carbon-emitting process and is likely to be impacted by regulation that applies a cost to carbon. According to estimates, combined emissions from plastics production and embedded carbon could be as much as 287 billion tonnes by 2100. Net CO_2 emissions from plastics in the European Union could grow by as much as 76 per cent by 2050.[1178] As part of its climate strategy, France therefore enacted a regulation on petroleum-based disposable plastic products in 2016. The measure forms part of France's Energy Transition for Green Growth Act. It stipulates

1173 Brydson (n 38) 10.
1174 CIEL, 'Feedstocks' (n 83) 2; CIEL, 'Driving the Plastics Boom' (n 83).
1175 See CIEL, 'Driving the Plastics Boom' (n 83); CIEL, 'Untested Assumptions in the Plastics Boom' (n 129).
1176 2015 Paris Agreement.
1177 CIEL, 'Untested Assumptions in the Plastics Boom' (n 129).
1178 Deere Birkbeck (n 952) 7.

that, by the year 2025, at least 60 per cent of the material used to produce targeted items will have to be produced from renewable sources.[1179]

Climate change mitigation commitments can have an effect not only on plastic production and trade policy choices with respect to plastic goods, but possibly also on the choice between different disposal options, as these have different effects on the carbon footprint.

Conclusion of Section D

Marine plastic pollution is increasingly addressed under the aegis of the biodiversity conventions and, within their scope of application, the chemicals and waste conventions. Convention bodies and parties have acknowledged the particular threats associated with marine plastic debris and have been approaching them from their specific perspective. CBD and CMS have adopted recommendations for action or developed guidelines on mitigation. The Basel Convention has adapted its scope of application and now fully covers lower-quality, mixed and contaminated plastics, which make up the majority of the plastic scrap exported to low or lower-middle-income countries. Under its auspices, the Partnership on Household Wastes and the Partnership on Plastic Waste have been established to promote action and encourage stakeholder dialogue towards the ultimate goal of eliminating the discharge of plastic waste and microplastics into the environment, in particular the marine environment. The Stockholm Convention may increase the range of hazardous substances that are regulated or banned, including with regard to substances that are used in plastics. It could therefore contribute to a more sustainable design of plastic materials and goods. The watercourse conventions, on the other hand, have not yet explored their potential role with regard to marine plastic pollution mitigation from land-based sources.

Overall, the regulatory framework related to marine plastic pollution mitigation from land-based sources remains fragmented and elusive. Owing to their particular and constrictive scope of application, none of the instruments can provide a holistic approach to plastic pollution mitigation from land-based sources in a sufficiently effective way. While increasing reception of the topic in the various relevant fora and growing institutional cooperation have a positive impact on coherence, it does not suffice to provide the necessary guidance on how to best implement UNCLOS Part XII with regard to plastics, or facilitate compliance or enforcement.

1179 France, 'Décret N° 2016-1170 Du 30 Août 2016 Relatif Aux Modalités de Mise En Œuvre de La Limitation Des Gobelets, Verres et Assiettes Jetables En Matière Plastique'.

Marine plastic pollution has been identified as a cross-cutting concern that involves different fields of law and a number of international bodies and instruments. While the subject cannot currently be assigned to a single institutional home (at least with regard to land-based sources), UN Environment seems the most central actor among international institutions in this regard. It administers not only a number of global environmental treaties that are relevant for marine plastic pollution mitigation (such as the CBD, the Basel Convention and the Stockholm Convention) but also the Regional Seas Programme, several regional seas conventions, the GPA and the GPML. UN Environment moreover has launched several studies on the matter and has gained a lot of expertise.[1180] While it provides for the operational structure, UN Environment's mandate is defined at UNEA, which is the political forum for action to be taken.

2 Regional Schemes

The global regime is complemented and supplemented by regional schemes, the development of which is required, 'as appropriate', in UNCLOS Article 197. In the establishment of regional rules and standards, characteristic regional features, the economic capacity of developing states and their need for economic development are to be taken into account.[1181] The relation between regional conventions and UNCLOS is governed by UNCLOS Article 237, which refers to 'special conventions and agreements' dealing with the protection and conservation of the marine environment. Along with specific multilateral treaties as concluded under the auspices of IMO and other organizations, regional conventions are an important example in this regard. Article 237 holds that the provisions of Part XII are 'without prejudice' to the obligations assumed by states under such instruments, regardless of whether they were adopted before or after UNCLOS.[1182] By virtue of Article 237, priority is given to the more stringent rules, as long as they are consistent with the general principles and objectives of UNCLOS.[1183]

1180 In the legal assessment for UNEA-3, UN Environment has been identified as a strong candidate for the institutional home of a new global architecture on marine plastic litter and microplastics: UNEP, 'UNEA-3 Legal Report – Summary for Policy Makers' (n 509) 11.

1181 1982 UNCLOS art 207(4). The article also provides that such rules and standards shall be re-examined from time to time.

1182 cf conditions as set out in 1982 UNCLOS art 311.

1183 See Section 2.1.B.ii.3)f) above.

A need for regional cooperation in marine pollution mitigation is particularly evident with regard to enclosed and semi-enclosed seas. States bordering enclosed or semi-enclosed seas are, therefore, called on to cooperate with each other and, among other things, to coordinate the implementation of their rights and duties with respect to the protection and preservation of the marine environment.[1184] Enclosed or semi-enclosed seas represent geographical entities that are widely independent from the wider ocean. They often embrace highly sensitive ecosystems with relatively high numbers of potentially endemic species. As major oceanic currents play no or only a minor role in these areas, pollution does often not as easily dissipate as in other places. The usually slow renewal of such water bodies implicates that, even in the event of reversible damage, it may take very long periods of time for corresponding ecosystems to recover from pollution incidents.

Not surprisingly, some of the oldest, most comprehensive and progressive regional cooperation regimes focus on enclosed or semi-enclosed seas. This is especially true for regions mainly consisting of industrialized countries, such as the Baltic Sea region.[1185] Regional cooperation has, however, also been sought by states sharing a common coastline or being part of the same archipelago. UN Environment has been the central driving force in this regard: under the auspices of its Regional Seas Programme, it established regional cooperation programmes in 14 regions, mainly comprising developing countries. Most of these programmes, as will be discussed below, are based on legal agreements.[1186]

Cooperation mechanisms for the protection and preservation of the marine environment or ocean governance are not confined to the UN Environment Regional Seas Programme or comparable regimes. Rather, a wide range of bodies or programmes may be active in the same geographic area. The geographic scope of these programmes or of related projects may not be congruent. While the regions covered by the Regional Seas Programme are largely defined on the basis of political considerations, GEF-sponsored projects are usually based on the concept of large marine ecosystems (LMEs). LMEs are

1184 1982 UNCLOS art 123.

1185 Other examples for regional cooperation around enclosed or semi-enclosed seas include the Black Sea, Caspian Sea, and Mediterranean schemes, as well as the Red Sea and Gulf of Aden and ROPME Sea (Persian/Arabian Gulf and Gulf of Oman) regimes.

1186 Examples of coastline-state cooperation schemes under UN Environment include the North-East and South-East Pacific, West and Central Africa, and Western Indian Ocean regimes. The Pacific region and Wider Caribbean region are examples for regional cooperation mainly between island states.

areas defined by purely ecological criteria for the purpose of ecosystem-based ocean management.[1187]

The present chapter starts with an overview on the regional schemes (A). It briefly outlines the Regional Seas Family, including with regard to the typical contents of the regional conventions and protocols on land-based sources. Two example regions are discussed in more detail. The chapter will then shed light on some particularities of these regimes, especially with regard to their specific strengths, potentials and deficiencies (B). The chapter focuses on the question of whether and to what extent regional schemes can compensate for the deficits of the global regime. Table 7 and Figure 17 give an overview of existing programmes and instruments.

A *Overview on the Regional Schemes*

i The Regional Seas Family

Regional schemes currently cover 18 regions. Fourteen of these regions are covered by programmes established under the auspices of UN Environment. Four more regions are covered by independent programmes that UN Environment considers as partner programmes. Together, they form the so-called Regional Seas Family. About 146 countries participate in one or more regional seas or partner programmes. Global meetings of the Regional Seas Programme are held on an almost yearly basis.

The Regional Seas Programme was initiated in 1974 and is headquartered in Nairobi. It aims to promote the sustainable management and use of marine environments, including coastal areas, foster regional cooperation for their protection and contribute to the implementation of Agenda 2030, SDG 14 and similar instruments. Seven of these programmes are directly administered by UN Environment. They cover the East Asian Seas, Mediterranean, North-West Pacific, West and Central Africa, Western Indian Ocean and Wider Caribbean regions, as well as, on an interim basis, the Caspian Sea.[1188] In UN Environment-administered regions, UN Environment mainly operates through regional

1187 For more information on the interplay between the UN Environment Regional Seas Programme, LMEs and other governing bodies, see Julien Rochette and others, 'Regional Oceans Governance Mechanisms: A Review' (2015) 60 Marine Policy 9; UNEP, 'Regional Oceans Governance: Making Regional Seas Programmes, Regional Fishery Bodies and Large Marine Ecosystem Mechanisms Work Better Together' (UNEP 2016) UNEP Regional Seas Reports and Studies No 197.

1188 The Caspian regional programme is the youngest under UNEP administration. Parties to the Teheran Convention decided to entrust UN Environment with the task at their fifth meeting in 2014. The Teheran Convention covers four protocols, including one on land-based sources and one dealing with environmental impact assessment.

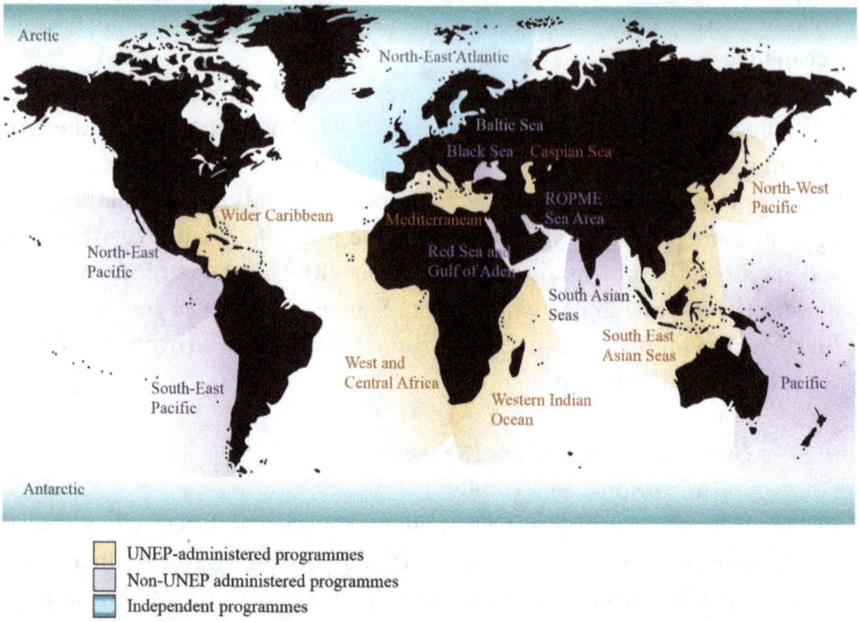

FIGURE 17 The Regional Seas Family
SOURCE: ADAPTED FROM UNEP, MARINE LITTER: A GLOBAL CHALLENGE (UNEP 2009) 16.

cooperating units (RCUs). The Black Sea, North-East Pacific, Pacific, Red Sea and Gulf of Aden, ROPME Sea (Persian/Arabian Gulf, Gulf of Oman and parts of the Arabian Sea), South Asian Seas and South-East Pacific regions are also covered by the Regional Seas Programme but are administered by special commissions, secretariats or other bodies.[1189] Independent programmes have been concluded in the North-East Atlantic and Baltic Sea regions. UN Environment also considers the Antarctic and Arctic regions to be partner programmes (see Figure 17). While the independent programmes are not formally part of the Regional Seas Programme, they support it and participate in corresponding activities, meetings and policy discussions.[1190]

1189 These include the Black Sea Commission BSC (Black Sea Region); the Secretariat of the Pacific Regional Environment Programme SPREP (Pacific Region); the Regional Organization for the Conservation of the Environment of the Red Sea and Gulf of Aden PERSGA (Red Sea and Gulf of Aden); the Kuwait Regional Organization for the Protection of the Marine Environment ROPME (ROPME Sea Area); the South Asia Co-operative Environment Programme SACEP (South-Asian Seas); and the Permanent Commission for the South Pacific CPPS (South-East Pacific Region).

1190 See VanderZwaag and Powers (n 462) 443.

The UN Environment regional seas programmes are based on (non-legally binding) action plans related to the environmental conservation and management of the regional seas while engaging states sharing a common body of water in policy coordination and cooperative efforts. The action plans are a relatively flexible tool and allow focusing on the particular environmental concerns, challenges and conditions of the respective regions. They facilitate concerted action in this regard. Most of the action plans or strategies are implemented by regional legal conventions.[1191] UN Environment regional conventions on the protection of the marine environment are designed as framework conventions that envisage the adoption of more specific protocols. Protocols on land-based pollution sources have been adopted in nine regions.[1192] To date, five of them have entered

---

1191 1995 Barcelona Convention; Convention for Co-operation in the Protection and Development of the Marine and Coastal Environment of the West and Central African Region (1981 Abidjan Convention) (adopted in March 1981, entered into force on 5 August 1984); Convention for the Protection, Management and Development of the Marine and Coastal Environment of the Eastern African Region (1985 Nairobi Convention) (adopted on 21 June 1985, entered into force on 30 May 1996, to be replaced by the 2010 Nairobi Convention); Amended Nairobi Convention for the Protection, Management and Development of the Marine and Coastal Environment of the Western Indian Ocean (2010 Nairobi Convention) (adopted on 31 March 2010, not yet in force); Convention for the Protection and Development of the Marine Environment of the Wider Caribbean Region (1983 Cartagena Convention) (adopted on 24 March 1983, entered into force on 11 October 1986) 1506 UNTS 157, TIAS 11085; Convention on the Protection of the Black Sea Against Pollution (1992 Bucharest Convention) (adopted on 21 April 1992, entered into force on 15 January 1994); Convention for Cooperation in the Protection and Sustainable Development of the Marine and Coastal Environment of The Northeast Pacific (2002 Antigua Convention) (adopted on 18 February 2002, not yet in force); Convention for the Protection of the Natural Resources and Environment of the South Pacific Region (1986 Noumea Convention) (adopted on 24 November 1986, entered into force on 22 August 1990); Regional Convention for the Conservation of the Red Sea and Gulf of Aden Environment (1982 Jeddah Convention) (adopted in February 1982, entered into force on 20 August 1985); Kuwait Regional Convention for Cooperation on the Protection of the Marine Environment from Pollution (1978 Kuwait Convention) (adopted on 24 April 1978, entered into force on 1 July 1979); Convention for the Protection of the Marine Environment and Coastal Area of the South-East Pacific (1981 Lima Convention) (adopted on 12 November 1981, entered into force on 19 May 1986).

1192 Caspian Sea Region: Protocol for the Protection of the Caspian Sea Against Pollution from Land-Based Sources and Activities to the 2003 Tehran Convention (2012 Moscow Protocol) (adopted on 12 December 2012, not yet in force). Mediterranean Region: Protocol for the Protection of the Mediterranean Sea against Pollution from Land-Based Sources (1980 Athens Protocol) (signed on 17 May 1980, entered into force on 17 June 1983) 19 ILM 869 (1980); 1996 Syracuse Protocol. West and Central Africa Region: Additional Protocol to the Abidjan Convention Concerning Cooperation in the Protection and Development of Marine and Coastal Environment from Land-Based Sources and Activities in the Western, Central and Southern African Region (2012 Abidjan Protocol) (adopted on 22 June 2012,

into force (see Table 7). Three regional seas programmes, including in the North-West Pacific, East Asian Seas and South Asian Seas regions, are not based on any legally binding instrument. The South-West Atlantic region is one of the last regions not to be covered by any (even non-legally binding) instrument.

The regimes of the North-East Atlantic region and the Baltic Sea predate the UN Environment regimes: the Oslo and Paris Conventions were adopted in 1972 and 1974, respectively, and the Helsinki Convention in 1974.[1193] Like some of the instruments adopted under the auspices of the UN Environment Regional Seas Programme, the originally three independent conventions have been fundamentally revised in the aftermath of 1992 UNCED to now include some of the concepts and principles endorsed at the Rio Conference. The Paris and Oslo Conventions were merged and replaced by the OSPAR Convention.[1194] The structure and approaches of both the OSPAR and Helsinki Conventions are different from the UN Environment model. They do not work as framework conventions but address specific issues, including land-based sources, within the convention itself in a more substantial way. The use of annexes and

---

not yet in force). Western Indian Ocean Region: Protocol for the Protection of the Marine and Coastal Environment of the Western Indian Ocean from Land-Based Sources and Activities (2010 Nairobi Protocol) (adopted on 31 March 2010; not yet in force). Wider Caribbean Region: Protocol Concerning Pollution from Land-Based Sources and Activities to the Convention for the Protection and Development of the Marine Environment of the Wider Caribbean Region (1999 Aruba Protocol) (adopted on 6 October 1999, entered into force on 13 August 2010). Black Sea Region: Protocol on Protection of the Black Sea Marine Environment Against Pollution from Land Based Sources (1992 Bucharest Protocol) (adopted on 21 April 1992, entered into force on 15 January 1994) 32 ILM 1122 (1993); Protocol on the Protection of the Marine Environment of the Black Sea from Land-Based Sources and Activities (2009 Sofia Protocol) (originally adopted in Bucharest in 1992, fully revised in 2009, revised version not yet in force). Red Sea and Gulf of Aden: Protocol concerning the Protection of the Marine Environment from Land-Based Activities in the Red Sea and Gulf of Aden (2005 Jeddah Protocol) (adopted on 25 September 2005, not yet in force). ROPME Sea Area (Kuwait): Protocol for the Protection of the Marine Environment against Pollution from Land-Based Sources (1990 Kuwait Protocol) (adopted in 1990, entered into force on 2 January 1993). South East Pacific Region: Protocol for the Protection of the South-East Pacific against Pollution from Land-based Sources (1983 Quito Protocol) (signed on 22 July 1983, entered into force in 1986).

1193 Convention for the Prevention of Marine Pollution by Dumping from Ships and Aircraft (1972 Oslo Convention) (adopted on 15 February 1972, entered into force on 7 April 1974, later replaced by the 1992 OSPAR Convention) 932 UNTS 3, 11 ILM 262 (1972); Convention for the Prevention of Marine Pollution from Land-Based Sources (1974 Paris Convention) (adopted on 4 June 1974, entered into force on 6 May 1978, later replaced by the 1992 OSPAR Convention); Convention on the Protection of the Marine Environment of the Baltic Sea Area (1974 Helsinki Convention) (adopted on 24 March 1974, entered into force on 3 May 1980, later replaced by the 1992 Helsinki Convention).

1194 1992 OSPAR Convention.

appendices, as well as the power of the OSPAR and Helsinki Commissions to adopt recommendations and, as in the case of the OSPAR Convention, binding decisions, allow for a relatively flexible regulation of scientific issues and a quite dynamic evolution of the regime.[1195] The strong institutional setting, high commitments by the contracting parties and a solid funding base are some of the particularities of these two regimes.[1196]

The Arctic and Antarctic regimes are considered partner programmes, too. The Antarctic is governed by the Antarctic Treaty[1197] and related instruments,

---

1195 The OSPAR Commission and its predecessors have adopted a substantive number of recommendations, decisions and other documents providing for additional guidance on the implementation of the convention. These include, for instance: the OSPAR Recommendation 2016/01 on the reduction of marine litter through the implementation of fishing for litter initiatives; the 2014 Regional Action Plan for Prevention and Management of Marine Litter in the North-East Atlantic and the 2015 Guidelines for Monitoring and Assessment of plastic particles in stomachs of Fulmars in the North Sea area.

1196 For more information on the OSPAR regime, see Louise Angélique de La Fayette, 'The OSPAR Convention Comes into Force: Continuity and Progress' (1999) 14 The International Journal of Marine and Coastal Law 247; Peter Heslenfeld and E Lisette Enserink, 'OSPAR Ecological Quality Objectives: The Utility of Health Indicators for the North Sea' (2008) 65 ICES Journal of Marine Science: Journal du Conseil 1392; David Johnson, 'Environmental Indicators: Their Utility in Meeting the OSPAR Convention's Regulatory Needs' (2008) 65 ICES Journal of Marine Science: Journal du Conseil 1387; 'Can Competent Authorities Cooperate for the Common Good: Towards a Collective Arrangement in the North-East Atlantic' in Paul Arthur Berkman and Alexander N Vylegzhanin (eds), *Environmental Security in the Arctic Ocean* (Springer Netherlands 2013); Erik J Molenaar and Alex G Oude Elferink, 'Marine Protected Areas in Areas beyond National Jurisdiction: The Pioneering Efforts under the OSPAR Convention' (2009) 5 Utrecht Law Review; Alan Simcock, 'OSPAR Convention on the Protection of the Marine Environment of the North-East Atlantic' in Ulrich Beyerlin, Peter-Tobias Stoll and Rüdiger Wolfrum (eds), *Ensuring Compliance with Multilateral Environmental Agreements: A Dialogue between Practitioners and Academics* (Martinus Nijhoff Publishers 2006). For more information about the HELCOM regime, see Hermanni Backer and others, 'HELCOM Baltic Sea Action Plan – A Regional Programme of Measures for the Marine Environment Based on the Ecosystem Approach' (2010) 60 Marine Pollution Bulletin 642; Peter Ehlers, 'The Baltic Sea Area: Convention on the Protection of the Marine Environment of the Baltic Sea Area (Helsinki Convention) of 1974 and the Revised Convention of 1992' (1994) 29 Marine Pollution Bulletin 617; Kristine Kern, 'Governance For Sustainable Development in the Baltic Sea Region' (2011) 42 Journal of Baltic Studies 21. See also Michael Gilek and Kristine Kern (eds), *Governing Europe's Marine Environment: Europeanization of Regional Seas Or Regionalization of EU Policies?* (Ashgate 2015); Jesper Raakjaer and others, 'Ecosystem-Based Marine Management in European Regional Seas Calls for Nested Governance Structures and Coordination – a Policy Brief' (2014) 50, Part B Marine Policy 373; Judith van Leeuwen, Luc van Hoof and Jan van Tatenhove, 'Institutional Ambiguity in Implementing the European Union Marine Strategy Framework Directive' (2012) 36 Marine Policy 636.

1197 Antarctic Treaty (adopted on 1 December 1959, entered into force on 23 June 1961) 402 UNTS 71, 19 ILM 860 (1980).

including the 1980 CAMLR Convention.[1198] The scope of the latter is particular in that it does not focus on pollution mitigation in the first place but on the conservation of living resources in the covered area. The Commission for the Conservation of Antarctic Marine Living Resources (CCAMLR) and its Scientific Committee, however, address the monitoring of marine debris and its impact on the marine environment and marine species on a regular basis. By contrast, no convention has been adopted with regard to the protection of the marine environment in the Arctic region. Marine pollution in the Arctic is addressed by the Arctic Council's Working Group on the Protection of the Arctic Marine Environment (PAME). The Arctic region is, thus, the only independent regime that is not treaty-based.

Altogether, there are 14 regional conventions (one of which is not in force yet) dealing with the protection and preservation of the marine environment. Two of these conventions directly address the problem of land-based sources of marine pollution. In nine more regions, protocols on land-based sources have been adopted. Five of them have entered into force. There are at least five regions which are not covered by a convention.[1199] Seven of the regional programmes do not specifically address land-based sources of marine pollution in detail and in a legally binding way. Land-based sources of marine pollution are, however, recognized as a major concern in almost all the regional programmes.[1200] Also, the potentially important role the regional programmes may play in the protection of the marine environment from land-based sources is widely acknowledged.[1201]

Within the framework of the Regional Seas Programme, UN Environment strongly promotes action on marine litter and encourages the establishment of partnerships in this regard, including between regional seas conventions

1198 Convention for the Conservation of Antarctic Marine Living Resources (1980 CAMLR Convention) (adopted on 20 May 1980, entered into force on 7 April 1982) 1329 UNTS 48, 19 ILM 841 (1980).

1199 North-West Pacific Region; East Asian Seas; South Asian Seas; Arctic Region; South-West Atlantic Region.

1200 Other shared priorities include ship-generated marine pollution; destruction of ecosystems and habitats due to coastal development and urbanization; conservation and management of marine and coastal ecosystems; Integrated Coastal Zone Management and Integrated Coastal Area and River Basin Management; over-exploitation and depletion of living marine resources; and monitoring, reporting and assessment of the marine environment. See UNEP, *Marine Litter* (n 284) 16.

1201 See, for instance, VanderZwaag and Powers (n 462) 443; Leila Mead, 'The "Crown Jewels" of Environmental Diplomacy: Assessing the UNEP Regional Seas Programme' (IISD Earth Negotiation Bulletin 2021) Still only one Earth: Lessons from 50 years of UN sustainable development policy Brief#17.

and action plans, UN bodies, funding institutions and the private sector. It promoted review and assessment activities, the adoption of regional action plans and strategies on marine litter and the participation in regional clean-up days.[1202] Based on a number of regional assessment reports, UN Environment identified a knowledge gap, in combination with the lack of specific legislation, adequate law enforcement and funding, as the primary reasons for the continuing aggravation of the problem of marine litter.[1203]

A number of regions have adopted specific regional action plans on the sustainable management of marine litter.[1204] In their action plans, participating regions all emphasized the important role of integrated waste management efforts, education and outreach, behavioural changes, implementation of economic instruments and concerted clean-up actions. They also agreed that existing legislation needed to be adapted and better enforced. The need for a harmonized marine litter monitoring strategy was also stressed in the action plans, as well as the need for national funding programmes and international support. Marine litter and microplastics are hence regularly discussed at the annual global meeting of the Regional Seas Programme.

1202 Regional assessment reports address institutional arrangements, capacities and funding resources and identify gaps and needs: see UNEP-MAP, *Marine Litter Assessment in the Mediterranean* (2015); UNEP-NOWPAP, *Marine Litter in the Northwest Pacific Region* (2008); UNEP-COBSEA, *Marine Litter in the East Asian Seas Region* (2008); UNEP and WIOMSA, *Marine Litter in the Eastern Africa Region: An Overview Assessment* (2008); UNEP-CEP, *Marine Litter in the Wider Caribbean: A Regional Overview and Action Plan* (2008); BSC, *Marine Litter in the Black Sea Region: A Review of the Problem* (2007); PERSGA, *Marine Litter in the PERSGA Region* (2008); SACEP, *Marine Litter in the South Asian Seas Region* (2007); CPPS, *Marine Litter in the Southeast Pacific Region: A Review of the Problem* (2007); HELCOM-MARLIN, 'Final Report of Baltic Marine Litter Project Marlin: Litter Monitoring and Raising Awareness 2011–2013' (2014); CEP, *Marine Litter in the Caspian Region: Review and Framework Strategy* (2009); OSPAR Commission, *Marine Litter in the North-East Atlantic Region: Assessment and Priorities for Response* (2009).

1203 UNEP, *Marine Litter* (n 284) 11. See also UNGA Res 60/30 (2005), 'Oceans and the Law of the Sea' para 65.

1204 HELCOM, 'Regional Action Plan for Marine Litter in the Baltic Sea' (2015); OSPAR Commission, 'Regional Action Plan for Prevention and Management of Marine Litter in the North-East Atlantic' (2014); SACEP, 'Towards Litter Free Indian Ocean: Summary of the Regional Marine Litter Action Plan for South Asian Seas Region' (2018); SPREP, 'Cleaner Pacific 2025: Pacific Regional Waste and Pollution Management Strategy 2016–2025' (2016); UNEP-CAR/RCU, 'Regional Action Plan on Marine Litter Management (RAPMali) for the Wider Caribbean Region 2014' (2014); UNEP-COBSEA, 'Regional Action Plan on Marine Litter' (2019); UNEP-MAP, 'Regional Plan for the Marine Litter Management in the Mediterranean' (2013) UNEP (DEPI)/MED WG.379/5; UNEP-NOWPAP, 'NOWPAP Regional Action Plan on Marine Litter' (2008).

TABLE 7 Regional programmes and instruments

	Region	RAP ma Li	Coordinating body	Convention	Protocol on land-based sources
UNEP administered programmes	Caspian Sea	2009*	UNEP	2003 Tehran Convention (EIF 2006)	2012 Moscow Protocol, not yet in force
	East Asian Seas (EAS)	2019	UNEP/COBSEA	–	–
	Mediterranean Region	2013	UNEP/MEDU	1976 Barcelona Convention (EIF 1978), rev. in 1995 (EIF 2004)	1980 Athens Protocol (EIF 1983), rev. in 1996 in Syracuse (EIF 2008)
	North-West Pacific Region (NOWPAP)	2008	UNEP	–	–
	West and Central Africa Region (WACAF)	–	UNEP	1981 Abidjan Convention (EIF 1984)	2012 Abidjan Protocol, not yet in force
	Western Indian Ocean Region (WIO)	–	UNEP	1985 Nairobi Convention (EIF 1996, rev. in 2010, rev. version not yet in force)	2010 Nairobi Protocol, not yet in force
	Wider Caribbean Region (WCR)	2014	UNEP-CAR/RCU	1983 Cartagena Convention (EIF 1986)	1999 Aruba Protocol (EIF 2010)

TABLE 7 Regional programmes and instruments (*cont.*)

	Region	RAP ma Li	Coordinating body	Convention	Protocol on land-based sources
Non-UNEP administered programmes	Black Sea Region	MoU on ML 2015	BSC	1992 Bucharest Convention (EIF 1994)	1992 Bucharest Protocol (EIF 1994) rev. in 2009 in Sofia, rev. version not yet in force
	North-East Pacific Region	–	–	2002 Antigua Convention (not yet in force)	–
	Pacific Region	2016**	SPREP	1986 Noumea Convention (EIF 1990)	–
	Red Sea and Gulf of Aden	2008*	PERSGA	1982 Jeddah Convention (EIF 1985)	2005 Jeddah Protocol, not yet in force
	ROPME Sea Area	–	ROPME	1978 Kuwait Convention (EIF 1979)	1990 Kuwait Protocol (EIF 1993)
	South Asian Seas (SAS)	2018	SACEP	–	–
	South-East Pacific Region	2007*	CPPS	1981 Lima Convention (EIF 1986)	1983 Quito Protocol (EIF 1986)

TABLE 7 Regional programmes and instruments (*cont.*)

	Region	RAP ma Li	Coordinating body	Convention	Protocol on land-based sources
Independent programmes	Antarctic Region	–	CCAMLR	1959 Antarctic Treaty (EIF 1961); 1980 CAMLR Convention (EIF 1982)	–
	Arctic Region	–	Artic Council; PAME	–	–
	Baltic Sea	2015	HELCOM	1972 Helsinki Convention (EIF 1974), rev. in 1992 (EIF 2000)	LBS are addressed in the convention
	North-East Atlantic Region	2014	OSPAR Commission	1992 OSPAR Convention (EIF 1998), combining former Oslo and Paris Conventions)	LBS are addressed in the convention

RAP Ma Li = Regional action plan on marine litter
EIF = Entry into force
LBS = Land-based sources of marine pollution
MoU = Memorandum of understanding

* Strategic objectives in review document; no specific action plan on marine litter
** Regional Waste and Pollution Management Strategy; marine litter is not the main focus

TABLE 8 Membership of regional conventions and protocols on land-based sources

	Region	Convention/LBS protocol	Parties
UNEP administered programmes	Caspian Sea	2003 Tehran Convention	Azerbaijan, Iran, Kazakhstan, Russian Federation, Turkmenistan
		2012 Moscow Protocol	
	East Asian Seas		
	Mediterranean Region	1976/95 Barcelona Convention	Albania, Algeria, Bosnia and Herzegovina, Croatia, Cyprus, Egypt, European Union, France, Greece, Israel, Italy, Lebanon, Libya, Malta, Monaco, Montenegro, Morocco, Slovenia, Spain, Syria, Tunisia, Turkey
		1980 Athens Protocol	Albania, Algeria, Bosnia and Herzegovina, Croatia, Cyprus, Egypt, European Union, France, Greece, Israel, Italy, Lebanon, Libya, Malta, Monaco, Montenegro, Morocco, Slovenia, Spain, Syria, Tunisia, Turkey
		1996 Syracuse Protocol	Albania, Croatia, Cyprus, European Union, France, Greece, Israel, Italy, Malta, Monaco, Montenegro, Morocco, Slovenia, Spain, Syria, Tunisia, Turkey
	North-West Pacific		
	West and Central Africa Region	1981 Abidjan Convention	Angola, Benin, Cameroon, Congo, Côte d'Ivoire, Democratic Republic of Congo, Gabon, Gambia, Ghana, Guinea, Guinea-Bissau, Liberia, Mauritania, Namibia, Nigeria, Senegal, Sierra Leone, South Africa and Togo
		2012 Abidjan Protocol	

TABLE 8 Membership of regional conventions and protocols on land-based sources (*cont.*)

	Region	Convention/LBS protocol	Parties
	Western Indian Ocean Region	1985 Nairobi Convention 2010 Nairobi Convention 2010 Nairobi Protocol	Comoros, France, Kenya, Madagascar, Mauritius, Mozambique, Seychelles, Somalia, Tanzania, South Africa
	Wider Caribbean Region	1983 Cartagena Convention	Antigua and Barbuda, Bahamas, Barbados, Belize, Colombia, Costa Rica, Cuba, Dominica, Dominican Republic, France, Grenada, Guatemala, Guyana, Jamaica, Mexico, Netherlands Antilles, Nicaragua, Panama, St Kitts and Nevis, Saint Lucia, St. Vincent and the Grenadines, Trinidad and Tobago, UK, USA, Venezuela
		1999 Aruba Protocol	Antigua and Barbuda, Bahamas, Belize, Costa Rica, Dominican Republic, France, Grenada, Guyana, Jamaica, Panama, Saint Lucia, Trinidad and Tobago, USA
Non-UNEP administered programmes	Black Sea Region	1992 Bucharest Convention	Bulgaria, Georgia, Romania, Russian Federation, Turkey and Ukraine

TABLE 8 Membership of regional conventions and protocols on land-based sources (*cont.*)

Region	Convention/LBS protocol	Parties
	1992 Bucharest Protocol	Bulgaria, Georgia, Romania, Russian Federation, Turkey and Ukraine
	2009 Sofia Protocol	
North-East Pacific Region	2002 Antigua Convention	
Pacific Region	1986 Noumea Convention	Australia, Cook Islands, Federated States of Micronesia, Fiji, France, Marshall Islands, Nauru, New Zealand, Papua New Guinea, Western Samoa, Solomon Islands, USA
Red Sea and Gulf of Aden	1982 Jeddah Convention	Djibouti, Egypt, Jordan, Saudi Arabia, Somalia, Sudan, Yemen
	2005 Jeddah Protocol	
ROPME Sea Area	1978 Kuwait Convention	Bahrain, Iran, Iraq, Kuwait, Oman, Qatar, Saudi Arabia, United Arab Emirates
	1990 Kuwait Protocol	Bahrain, Iran, Kuwait, Oman, Qatar, Saudi Arabia
South Asian Seas		
South-East Pacific Region	1981 Lima Convention	Chile, Colombia, Ecuador, Panama, Peru
	1983 Quito Protocol	Chile, Colombia, Ecuador, Panama, Peru

TABLE 8 Membership of regional conventions and protocols on land-based sources (*cont.*)

	Region	Convention/LBS protocol	Parties
Independent programmes	Antarctic Region	1980 CAMLR Convention	Australia, Argentina, Belgium, Brazil, Bulgaria, Canada, Chile, People's Republic of China, Cook Islands, European Union, Finland, France, Germany, Greece, India, Italy, Japan, Republic of Korea, Mauritius, Namibia, Netherlands, Nez Zealand, Norway, Pakistan, Panama, Peru, Poland, Russia, South Africa, Spain, Sweden, Ukraine, UK, USA, Uruguay, Vanuatu
	Baltic Sea	1992 Helsinki Convention	Denmark, Estonia, European Union, Finland, Germany, Latvia, Lithuania, Poland, Russian Federation and Sweden
	North-East Atlantic	1992 OSPAR Convention	Belgium, Denmark, European Union, Finland, France, Germany, Iceland, Ireland, Luxembourg, Netherlands, Norway, Portugal, Spain, Sweden, Switzerland, UK

ii The Legal and Non-legal Frameworks

1) *The Regional Conventions*

a) Structure and General Contents

The 14 regional seas conventions that have been adopted since the mid-1970s are consistent with and widely reflect UNCLOS Part XII, while some conventions – especially the Helsinki and OSPAR conventions as well as some instruments of the so-called second generation – present a stronger and clearer wording or more stringent obligations (both with regard to substantive and procedural provisions) and address some additional issues.

In the preambles of the regional conventions, reference is often made to 'the special hydrographical and ecological characteristics of the region and its vulnerability to pollution'. In some regions, the contracting parties note that global agreements 'do not cover all aspects of environmental deterioration and do not entirely meet the special requirements' of their region.[1205] The aim to enhance cooperation on a regional basis is, therefore, stressed in the conventions, and parties are encouraged to enter into bilateral and multilateral agreements.

Except for the CAMLR Convention, all the regional conventions oblige their parties to take preventive and responsive measures against pollution. They define the different pollution sources and oblige their parties to address land-based sources. They moreover require parties to cooperate in cases of pollution emergencies, call for scientific and technical cooperation, including with regard to pollution monitoring, and oblige parties to undertake environmental impact assessment with regard to planned activities. The conventions also generally contain the relevant definitions, address dispute settlement and provide for institutional arrangements. Finally, most conventions require their parties to designate a focal point or competent national authority and provide the other parties with respective information.

The common denominator of the regional conventions thus largely corresponds to the obligations as contained in UNCLOS Part XII. However, exact formulations and the corresponding level of commitment greatly vary from one region to another. For instance, while the Lima Convention only requires its parties to *endeavour* to adopt appropriate measures,[1206] others explicitly

1205 cf 1992 OSPAR Convention, in which the contracting parties recognize that 'it may be desirable to adopt, on the regional level, more stringent measures [...] than are provided for in international conventions or agreements with a global scope'.

1206 See 1981 Lima Convention, particularly Article 3(1) and (3), as well as Article 4. Unlike most of the other conventions, the Lima Convention refers to existing international standards.

oblige their parties to adopt plans, programmes and environmental legislation for implementing the conventions and their protocols, to set time limits for the full implementation of adopted measures and to apply a range of environmental management principles such as the precautionary principle, the polluter pays principle, integrated coastal area (and river basin) management, and sustainable development.[1207] Remarkably, the OSPAR and Helsinki conventions apply a rather rigorous interpretation of some of these principles, especially the precautionary principle.[1208] There are also differences in wording with regard to obligations related to scientific and technical cooperation, assistance, monitoring and environmental impact assessment. A number of conventions address the issue of particularly sensible areas or endangered species and require parties to establish protected areas. Very few conventions refer to the use of best available techniques and best environmental practices, clean production and the role of the private sector. Some conventions address further issues which are of particular concern in their region.[1209]

In contrast to UNCLOS Part XII, the regional conventions oblige their parties to regularly report on implementation to the governing body or some other institution. Such reports at least include a description of the measures taken for the implementation of the convention. Some instruments also require an evaluation of the effectiveness of these measures and, as the case may be, a report on problems encountered in the implementation of the convention. Most conventions provide for a dispute settlement procedure, either in a single provision or in a separate annex. By contrast, compliance procedures are not commonly envisaged in the conventions. The most remarkable exception in this regard is, perhaps, the OSPAR Commission's supervisory and control power, which is widely unique in the field of environmental protection from land-based pollution sources. The commission assesses compliance by parties with the convention and recommendations or decisions taken thereunder. It bases its assessment on the country reports and may decide upon necessary steps 'to bring about full compliance'.[1210] Most conventions do also not contain

1207 See, for instance, 1995 Barcelona Convention.

1208 According to the definition as used in the 1992 OSPAR Convention, the precautionary principle means that 'preventive measures are to be taken when there are reasonable grounds for concern [...] even when there is no conclusive evidence of a causal relationship between the inputs and the effects': art 2(2)(a). See also 1992 Helsinki Convention art 3(2).

1209 Such region-specific concerns include, for instance, the transboundary movement of hazardous wastes and their disposal, coastal erosion, coastal dredging or the storage of radioactive wastes.

1210 1992 OSPAR Convention art 23. The commission's supervisory power is somewhat curtailed by the possibility for parties to opt out from a decision, in which case a decision is not binding on these parties: see ibid art 13(2). See also Simcock (n 1196).

any specific requirements with regard to liability and compensation.[1211] An exception in this regard is the 1992 Bucharest Convention, which obliges its parties to adopt rules and regulations on the liability for damage caused by natural or juridical persons to the marine environment of the Black Sea, and to ensure that recourse is available.[1212]

The conventions set up the necessary institutional arrangements, generally including a governing body, in which all the parties are represented, and a secretariat. The governing bodies of UN Environment-administered conventions are referred to as meeting of the parties, while UN Environment is responsible for carrying out secretariat functions. With regard to the conventions concluded under the auspices of non-UN Environment-administered or independent programmes, the institutional set-up is more diverse. Their governing bodies either consist of a conference or meetings of the parties, commissions or the governing council of a specific organization established for the protection and conservation of the regional marine environment. The core functions of the governing bodies include: the supervision of the implementation of the convention, the state of the marine environment and the effectiveness of the measures taken; the review of the content of the convention and related instruments; the adoption, review and amendment of protocols and annexes; the adoption of procedural and financial rules; and the determination of the budget and financial participation of the parties. Under some conventions, they can also adopt recommendations or decisions, set up subsidiary bodies or review compliance by contracting parties. Governing bodies usually meet on a yearly or biennial basis and take unanimous decisions with regard to substantive matters. Besides the governing body and a secretariat, two conventions include a judicial commission or committee for the settlement of disputes. Very few conventions have technical and scientific bodies.

UN Environment granted its regional seas programmes substantial financial support during their initial phase. The programmes were supposed to take on full financial responsibility after a certain period of time. To this purpose, most

1211 Most regional conventions contain a *pactum de contrahendo* provision, envisaging the future adoption of a liability regime by the contracting parties. Implementation of these provisions is slow or inexistent, which is why they have been referred to as 'dead letters in the sea': see R Lefeber, 'The Liability Provisions of Regional Sea Conventions: Dead Letters in the Sea?' in Davor Vidas and Willy Østreng (eds), *Order for the Oceans at the Turn of the Century* (Kluwer Law International 1999); Tullio Scovazzi, 'The Mediterranean Guidelines for the Determination of Environmental Liability and Compensation: The Negotiations for the Instrument and the Question of Damage That Can Be Compensated' (2009) 13 Max Planck Yearbook of United Nations Law 183, 185.

1212 1992 Bucharest Convention art XVI.

conventions request their governing bodies to adopt financial rules and determine the annual contributions by the parties. Such contributions are usually paid to a regional trust fund that is administered by the respective secretariat. However, transition to financial autonomy was – and still is – a major challenge in developing-country regions.

An overview on the general contents of the regional conventions is provided by Table 9.

b) Covered Area

The geographical scope of the regional conventions greatly varies. Conventions applying to enclosed or semi-enclosed seas, including the Mediterranean Sea, Black Sea, Baltic Sea and Caspian Sea, usually apply to the entire maritime area of the respective enclosed or semi-enclosed sea. Two of these conventions allow or require the inclusion of internal waters as defined by each party.[1213] By contrast, the Bucharest and Tehran Conventions do not refer to coastal areas or internal waters with regard to their geographical scope. The Kuwait and Jeddah Conventions, which also apply to a strictly defined geographical sea area, explicitly exclude the application of the conventions to internal waters, unless otherwise provided.

The landward and seaward limits of the areas covered by conventions applying to open coastlines also vary: four of these conventions explicitly include internal waters or the coastal environment in their scope of application. The amended Nairobi Convention even includes the watershed of the contracting parties as specified in each protocol. The outer limit of the covered area at least includes the 200-nautical mile zone falling under the jurisdiction of the contracting states. The Cartagena, Noumea, Lima and OSPAR Conventions also include parts of the high seas as defined in the respective conventions. Least concise is, perhaps, the formulation used in the Antigua Convention, which defines its scope of application as 'the maritime areas of the Northeast Pacific, defined in conformity with the United Nations Convention on the Law of the Sea'.[1214]

Remarkably, there are no regional legal instruments on the protection of the marine environment applying to the South Asian Seas, the South-East Asian Seas, the North-West Pacific and the South-West Atlantic regions. In some of these regions, land-based pollution, and marine plastic pollution in particular, are a major concern, as 14 of the 20 most polluting countries and the most

1213 1995 Barcelona Convention art 1(2); 1992 Helsinki Convention art 1.
1214 2002 Antigua Convention art 2 para 1.

polluting rivers are located in these areas.[1215] For an overview on the area covered by the different regional conventions, see Figure 18.

2) *Legal Instruments on Land-based Sources of Pollution*

a) Structure and General Contents

The thematic scope of the instruments on land-based sources mostly includes discharges originating from land-based point and diffuse sources and activities that may affect the marine environment of the regional sea, as well as input of polluting substances from land-based sources that are transported through the atmosphere.

The protocols usually aim explicitly at eliminating pollution from land-based sources and phasing out the inputs of polluting substances. To this end, they establish a national system of discharge limitations and control, which is based on environmental assessment and monitoring[1216] and strongly builds on the use of best available technologies and best environmental practices. The protocols usually distinguish between point and diffuse sources of pollution and other harmful activities. Point sources, such as factory outlets, are to be strictly regulated by the competent national authorities. Most of the protocols and the OSPAR and Helsinki Conventions require such regulation to prescribe a system of prior authorization, monitoring, inspection and, possibly, sanctions.[1217] Some instruments provide further guidance on how to address specific sources of land-based pollution, including diffuse sources such as agriculture and forestry.[1218]

1215 See Jambeck and others (n 291) 769; Meijer and others (n 1161) 2.

1216 A relatively strong wording on environmental impact assessment can be found in the 2010 Nairobi Protocol. According to its Article 4(2)(c), states parties have to ensure:

> that new or existing activities, developments, programmes, plans, policies and processes that are likely to cause significant adverse impacts to the marine and/or coastal environment are subjected to environmental impact assessment, environmental audit or strategic environmental assessment, as appropriate, and prior authorization by a competent national authority or authorities as a matter of law.

See also 2010 Nairobi Protocol Article 13 on environmental impact assessment and audit.

1217 While the requirement of prior authorisation with regard to pollution discharges is common to the instruments on land-based sources, there are differences with regard to the quantities that require an authorisation. Under the Helsinki Convention, for instance, a permit is required when discharges are more than negligible: 1992 Helsinki Convention art 6 para 3. In contrast, the OSPAR Convention and the Syracuse Protocol require a permit for point source discharges that affect the marine environment: 1992 OSPAR Convention Annex I art 2 para 1; 1996 Syracuse Protocol art 6 para 1.

1218 See, for instance, 2009 Sofia Protocol Annex II; 1992 Helsinki Convention Annex III; 2012 Moscow Protocol Annex II.

TABLE 9 Content of regional conventions

Region	Instrument	EIF	Parties	Applies to internal waters	General aim to enhance cooperation	General obligation to take preventive and responsive measures against pollution	Explicit duty to adopt environmental legislation	Addresses LBS in a general way	Provides for specific measures on LBS	Refers to transboundary movements of hazardous wastes and their disposal	Requires parties to cooperate in cases of pollution emergencies	Calls for scientific and technical cooperation, including with regard to monitoring
Caspian Sea	2003 Tehran C.	2006	5		X	X		X	X		X	X
East Asian Seas	–											
Mediterranean	1995 Barcelona C.	2004	22*		X	X	X	X		X	X	X
North-West Pacific	–											
West & Central Africa	1981 Abidjan C.	1984	17	X	X	X	X	X			X	X
Western Indian Ocean	1985 Nairobi C.	1996	10	(X)	X	X		X			X	X
	2010 Nairobi C.	(n.i.f.)		X	X	X		X		X	X	X
Wider Caribbean	1983 Cartagena C.	1986	25		X	X		X			X	X
Black Sea	1992 Bucharest C.	1994	6		X	X		X	(X)	X	X	X
North-East Pacific	2002 Antigua C.	(n.i.f.)			X	X	X	X			X	X
Pacific	1986 Noumea C.	1990	12		X	X	(X)	X		(X)	X	X
Red Sea & Gulf of Aden	1982 Jeddah C.	1985	7		X	X	X	X			X	X
ROPME Sea	1978 Kuwait C.	1979	8		X	X	X	X			X	X
South Asian Seas	–											
South-East Pacific	1981 Lima C.	1986	5	(X)	X	(X)	(X)	X			X	X
Antarctic	1980 CAMLR C.	1982	36*		X							
Arctic	–											
Baltic Sea	1992 Helsinki C.	2000	10*	X	X	X	X	X	X		X	X
North-East Atlantic	1992 OSPAR C.	1998	16*	X	X	X		X	X		(X)	X
Global	**1982 UNCLOS**	**1994**	168		X	X	X	X			X	X

EIF = entry into force
n.i.f. = not in force

* including European Union

X = criterion is fulfilled; direct reference
(X) = criterion is fulfilled to some extent or implicitly; indirect reference

Specific provisions on liability and compensation	EIA with regard to planned activities	Marine protected areas; hotspots; sensitive areas; endangered species	Public access to information	Public participation	Education and awareness	Duty to report on implementation	National focal points	Compliance procedure	Dispute settlement procedure	Budget; funding; financial mechanisms	Institutional arrangements (Secretariat/CoP, MoP, Council or Commission)	Advisory committee; technical body	Envisages the adoption of protocols	Reference to:	- precautionary principle or approach	- polluter pays principle	- Sustainable development; integration	- ICZM	- clean production	- BAT/BEP	- EQS/EQO
	X		X			X	X		(X)	(X)	X		X		X	X		(X)	X	X	
	X		X	X		X	(X)	X	X	(X)	X		X		X	X	X	X	X	X	
	X	X				X	X		X	(X)	X		X				X				
	X	X				X	(X)		X	(X)	X		X								
	X	X				X		(X)	X	(X)	X		X		X	X		X			
	X	X				X	X		X	(X)	X		X								
X						X	X		(X)	(X)	X		X						X		
	X	X	X	X	X	X	(X)		(X)	(X)	X		X		X	X	X	X	(X)	(X)	
	X	X				X	X		X	(X)	X		X								
	X					X	X	(X)	X	X	X	(X)	X								
	X					X	X		X	(X)	X	(X)	X								
(X)	X					X	X			(X)	X		X								
	X	X				X		(X)	X	X	X	X									
	X	X	X			X			X	X	X				X	X				X	
	(X)	X	X		(X)	X		X	X	(X)	X	X			X	X			X	X	(X)
(X)	X	(X)							X												

BS = Land-based sources of marine pollution
IA = Environmental impact assessment
CZM = Integrated coastal zone (and river basin) management
AT = Best available technique
EP = Best environmental practice
QS = Environmental quality standard
QO = Environmental quality objective

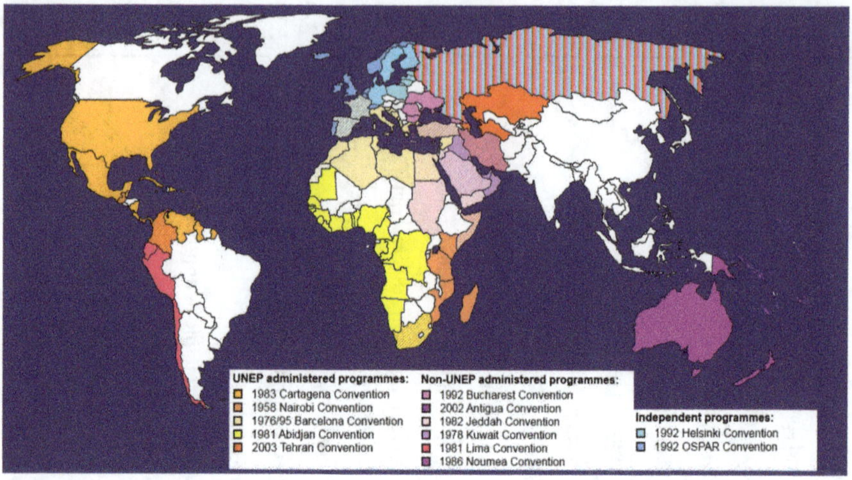

FIGURE 18 Parties to regional conventions
AUTHOR

A list of substances and activities that need particular consideration is contained in the annexes to the protocols or OPSAR and Helsinki conventions.[1219] Sectors of priority activities include, for instance, the textile, recycling, beverages, rubber and plastic industries, as well as tourism, agriculture, aquaculture and waste water and solid waste management. Categories of priority substances notably include litter. They also often include endocrine-disrupting

1219 Most of the older instruments on land-based sources of pollution used to follow the so-called black and grey lists approach. Much like in (older) instruments regulating dumping at sea, prohibited substances were listed in black lists, while grey lists contained substances that were to be strictly limited. With the adoption of the 1996 London Dumping Protocol, the black and grey list approach of the London Dumping Convention was replaced by the revised-list approach, according to which dumping is prohibited except for the listed substances: see Redgwell (n 582) 188. A revised-list approach is also applied under the OSPAR regime on dumping (in contrast to the black and grey lists as used under its predecessor, the 1974 Paris Convention). For land-based sources of pollution, however, the 'prohibited unless permitted' approach does not apply in this strict sense. Instead, in most of the instruments that have been revised since the 1990s, a list of priority substances and activities was substituted for the black and grey lists. The new approach, generally referred to as uniform approach, takes account of the fundamental goal of preventing *all* marine pollution, including pollution by traditionally grey list substances. Today, the 1983 Quito and the 1992 Bucharest Protocols are the only protocols on land-based sources to use black and grey lists. For more information, see David Joseph Attard and others (eds), *The IMLI Manual on International Maritime Law Volume III: Marine Environmental Law and International Maritime Security Law* (Oxford University Press 2016) ch 5.3.2; Tanaka, 'Regulation of Land-Based Marine Pollution' (n 363) 553–58; Tanaka, *International Law of the Sea* (n 360) 282–84.

substances and non-toxic substances that may interfere with any legitimate use of the sea. Plastics are, therefore, covered in various ways. Persistency, toxicity and bioaccumulation are among the characteristics of targeted substances that need to be taken into account in the implementation of the protocols and agreements.[1220]

A majority of the protocols use the concepts of best available techniques (or technology) and best environmental practices. Best available techniques are usually defined as 'the latest stage of development (state of the art) of processes, of facilities or of methods of operation which indicate the practical suitability of a particular measure for limiting discharges, emissions and waste'.[1221] The use of such techniques or technologies shall emphasize the use of non-waste technology. Best environmental practices, on the other hand, refer to the application of the most appropriate combination of measures. Such measures may include:

- the provision of information and education to the public and to users about the environmental consequences of choice of particular activities and choice of products, their use and ultimate disposal;
- the development and application of codes of good environmental practice which cover all aspects of the activity in the product's life;
- the mandatory application of labels informing users of environmental risks related to a product, its use and ultimate disposal;
- saving of resources, including energy;
- making collection and disposal systems available to the public;
- avoiding the use of hazardous substances or products and the generation of hazardous waste;
- recycling, recovery and reuse;
- the application of economic instruments to activities, products or groups of products; and
- the establishment of a system of licensing, involving a range of restrictions or a ban.[1222]

1220 See, for instance, 1996 Syracuse Protocol Annex I; 2012 Abidjan Protocol Annex I; 2010 Nairobi Protocol Annex II; 2009 Sofia Protocol Annex I; 1992 Helsinki Convention Annex I; 2012 Moscow Protocol Annex I. The Jeddah Protocol does not contain a list but directly refers to the GPA and the substances and properties as listed therein: 2005 Jeddah Protocol Annex I.

1221 1996 Syracuse Protocol Annex IV; 2012 Abidjan Protocol Annex I; 2012 Moscow Protocol Annex V.

1222 See 1996 Syracuse Protocol Annex IV; 2012 Abidjan Protocol Annex II; 2010 Nairobi Protocol Annex I; 2009 Sofia Protocol Annex V; 2012 Moscow Protocol Annex V; 1992 OSPAR Convention Appendix 1.

Reference to environmental management principles such as the precautionary principle, the polluter pays principle or clean(-er) production are more common than in the parent conventions. Also, when compared to the regional conventions, more land-based sources protocols oblige their parties to provide public access to environmental information, to involve the public in the formulation and adoption of measures and in impact assessment procedures, and to take measures related to education and awareness with respect to the problem of marine pollution.

With regard to regional cooperation, many of the protocols require their parties to adopt common guidelines, standards or criteria dealing with some technical aspects, limitation values of discharges and emissions, seawater quality, the progressive replacement of products causing significant pollution of the marine environment, etc. Some protocols use the concepts of *environmental quality objectives*[1223] and *environmental quality standards*[1224] for this purpose. The required level of detail with regard to cooperation and policy harmonization is, therefore, much higher when compared to corresponding requirements under UNCLOS or the regional conventions. Duties related to technical assistance tend to be more specific than in the parent conventions, too.

Most of the protocols require the parties to assess the effectiveness of regulatory and other measures they have taken for implementation of the protocols and to report on results and possible difficulties. Some instruments establish or envisage the establishment of compliance procedures, providing the governing body with the necessary competences to review compliance and decide upon steps to bring about full compliance with the provisions of the respective instrument.[1225]

In the parent conventions, notification and, possibly, consultation with affected parties is often required in cases of pollution emergency and (imminent) transboundary damage. Reference to prior notification, exchange of information and consultation among parties is also common with regard

1223 Environmental quality objectives are defined as clearly identified objectives or goals 'for purposes of environmental quality whether in specific or general application to relevant environmental resources, activities or programmes': see 2010 Nairobi Protocol art 1(viii). In 2008, the OSPAR Commission adopted an Ecological Quality Objective on the number of plsstic particles in seabird stomachs: OSPAR Commission, *Background Document for the EcoQO on Plastic Particles in Stomachs of Seabirds* (2008). See also Heslenfeld and Enserink (n 1196) 1394; Johnson, 'Environmental Indicators' (n 1196) 1390.

1224 Environmental quality standards refer to 'the concentration of a particular substance or group of substances in water, sediment or biota that should not be exceeded to protect human health or the environment': see 1985 Nairobi Convention art 1(ix).

1225 See, for instance, 2009 Sofia Protocol art 17.

to projects and, as the case may be, programmes subject to environmental impact assessment. There is, however, usually no strict obligation for prior consultation. Rather, most conventions either allow their parties to invite other parties to consult with them,[1226] or require their parties to develop procedures for the dissemination of information and, if necessary, for consultations among the parties concerned.[1227] Also, none of the instruments provides that parties have to consult with their neighbours or the supervisory treaty bodies with regard to the emission authorizations and licences they issue in accordance with the conventions or protocols and their annexes. This means that other parties and the supervisory bodies have only limited means to influence respective decision-making in a state party. Especially in cases of domestic (non-transboundary) damage, they can at best intervene *ex post*, that is, after damage has occurred – if the treaties allow for it. This potential *lacuna* is slightly attenuated by some other duties of the states, including the general duty to cooperate among each other in the implementation of the convention and the protocols, the duty to adopt and implement regional guidelines and standards, the duty to report on measures and their effectives, and the duty to settle disputes peacefully.

It follows from the above that implementation of the regional instruments on land-based sources is multilayered: from a regulatory point of view, it includes the adoption of common standards and practices at a regional level and policy harmonization. It also includes the adoption and enforcement of national implementation measures and the adherence to the regional standards by the parties. Enforcement of regional standards, including with respect to the issuance of permits, monitoring activities and inspection, is down to the parties; the power of supervisory bodies is very limited in this regard. The realization of mitigation and conservation projects within or across countries also contributes to the implementation of the agreements. Such projects are usually funded by multiple actors, including external actors such as the GEF.

Finally, most protocols address budgetary and financial issues, as fundraising remains one of the most fundamental challenges with regard to the implementation of the regimes. In addition to the financial mechanisms as provided for in the conventions, some protocols invite contracting parties to provide

1226 See, for instance, 1983 Cartagena Convention art 12 para 3. The Noumea and Helsinki Conventions provide for stricter duties in this regard: 1986 Noumea Convention art 16 para 3(b); 1992 Helsinki Convention art 7.

1227 See, for instance: 2002 Antigua Convention art 5 para 6(c); 1995 Barcelona Convention art 4 para 3(d); 1985 Nairobi Convention art 13 para 3; 2010 Nairobi Convention art 14 para 3. See also 1990 Kuwait Protocol art VIII para 4.

additional funding in form of voluntary contributions. They require states to ensure that adequate financial resources are available for implementation, as well as for the operation of the secretariats and other bodies. Moreover, they oblige their parties to 'explore innovative methods and incentives for mobilizing and channelling resources, including those of foundations, non-governmental organizations and other private sector entities'.[1228] The private sector and public–private partnerships are identified as an important potential source of funding.

An overview on the general contents of the protocols and conventions on land-based sources is provided in Table 10.

b) Covered Area

The geographical scope of most of the protocols on land-based sources of pollution is broader than that of their parent convention, as they mostly apply to (parts of the) internal waters (usually up to the freshwater limit or to a limit designated by the contracting parties). The 1996 Syracuse, 2012 Abidjan and 2010 Nairobi Protocols apply to the entire watershed situated within the territory of one of the contracting parties.

So far, regional legal instruments on land-based sources of marine pollution have only been in force in Northern Europe and the Mediterranean region, as well as the Black Sea, ROPME Sea, Caribbean and South-East Pacific regions. With regard to the instruments currently in force, the ones applying to the European and Mediterranean room tend to be both more stringent and more comprehensive than others. However, regional differences in the level of obligations as reflected in the legal instruments will be reduced considerably once the newer protocols enter into force. More or less recently adopted protocols are being ratified in the African regions, as well as in the Black Sea, Caspian Sea and Red Sea and Gulf of Aden regions.

For an overview of the area covered by the protocols, see Figure 19.

3) *Specific Examples*

The present subsection presents examples of both a legal and a non-legal regional scheme. The example regions involve different continents and legal cultures and illustrate opposing approaches to pollution-related problems. They moreover reflect different levels of capacity and funding. Both programmes are administered by UN Environment.

1228 See, for instance, 2010 Nairobi Protocol art 20 para 3(c).

Special attention is given to the Mediterranean regime. The Mediterranean regime exhibits several characteristics that make it particularly suitable as a testing field for a potential global instrument on plastic pollution. First, when compared to the OSPAR and Helsinki or the African regimes, the Mediterranean region involves a more representative mix of countries, including both developed and developing, with different legal traditions and economic and cultural backgrounds. Second, the regime has experienced both progressive forces and restraints in its development, much as may be expected in a global regime. Thanks to an acceptable level of available resources and the driving influence by the European Union, performance of the regime ranks in the (upper) mid-range, in spite of the absence of country leadership. Third, the Barcelona system represents a widely applied model based on a framework convention, issue-specific protocols, a decentralized structure and UN Environment administration. The East Asian Seas programme serves as the second example. The region is confronted with major problems and challenges related to marine plastic pollution. At the same time, the affected states have, so far, decided against a strong regional scheme.

a) Mediterranean Region

The Mediterranean Sea is a semi-enclosed sea of high strategic and ecological importance. It takes about a hundred years for its waters to be fully renewed. Bordering states include both industrialized and developing countries. In spite of the differences in their needs, legal systems or levels of economic development and wealth, they share a long tradition of cooperation for the protection of the Mediterranean environment.[1229]

Governing Instruments

The Mediterranean Action Plan (MAP) was adopted by 16 countries in 1975. Under the umbrella of UN Environment, it was the first of its kind. The MAP focused on pollution assessment and control, policy formulation, sustainable coastal development and sustainable resource management. The plan called for the adoption of a framework convention and specific protocols for the protection of the Mediterranean environment. Only a year after the adoption of

1229 See Tullio Scovazzi, 'The Governance of the Mediterranean Sea' in Joseph F DiMento and Alexis Jaclyn Hickman (eds), *Environmental Governance of the Great Seas: Law and Effect* (Edward Elgar Publishing 2012) 89–96. On the negotiation history of the Barcelona system see, in particular, Arsen Pavasovic, 'The Mediterranean Action Plan Phase II and the Revised Barcelona Convention: New Prospective for Integrated Coastal Management in the Mediterranean Region' (1996) 31 Ocean & Coastal Management 133.

TABLE 10 Content of LBS protocols and the OSPAR and Helsinki conventions

Region	Instrument	EIF	Parties	Applies to internal waters	Applies to the entire watershed	Includes inputs through the atmosphere	Objective to eliminate pollution; phase out	Asks for timetables for implementation	Common guidelines and standards	Refers to the progressive replacement of products & processes	National system of authorization, monitoring, inspection, possibly sanctions	Emission control; discharge limitations	List of substance categories and activities to
Caspian Sea	2012 Moscow P.	(n.i.f.)		X		X	X	X	X	X	X	X	X
Mediterranean	1996 Syracuse P.	2008	17*	X	X	X	X	X	X	X	X	X	X
West & Central Africa	2012 Abidjan P.	(n.i.f.)		X	X	X	(X)		X	X	X	X	X
Western Indian Ocean	2010 Nairobi P.	(n.i.f.)		X	(X)	X	(X)	X	X	X	X	X	X
Wider Caribbean	1999 Aruba P.	2010	13			X		X				X	X
Black Sea	1992 Bucharest P.	1994	6	X		X			X			(X)	X
	2009 Sofia P.	(n.i.f.)		X		X	X	X	X	X	X	X	X
Red Sea & Gulf of Aden	2005 Jeddah P.	(n.i.f.)		X		X	X	X	X	(X)	X	X	X
ROPME Sea	1990 Kuwait P.	1993	6	X		X		X	X	X	(X)	X	(X)
South-East Pacific	1983 Quito P.	1986	5	X		X	(X)		X		(X)	X	X
Baltic Sea	1992 Helsinki C.	2000	10*	X	(X)	X	X		X		X	X	X
North-East Atlantic	1992 OSPAR C.	1998	16*	X		X		X	X	(X)	X	X	X
Global	**1982 UNCLOS**	**1994**	168			(X)							

EIF = entry into force
n.i.f. = not in force

* including European Union

X = criterion is fulfilled; direct reference
(X) = criterion is fulfilled to some extent or implicitly; indirect reference

Contains guidance on how to address point and diffuse sources (and other activities)	Monitoring; EIA; assessment of measures	Marine protected areas; hotspots, sensitive areas: endangered species	Public access to information	Public participation	Education and awareness	Scientific and technical cooperation; assistance	Duty to report on implementation	National focal points	Compliance procedure	Addresses additional funding sources	Advisory committee; technical body	Reference to:	- precautionary principle	- polluter pays principle	- Sustainable development; integration	- ICZM	- clean production	- BAT/BEP	- EQS/EQO	- GPA
X	X	X	X	X	(X)	X	X	X	X	X			X	X	X	X	X	X	X	X
X	X					X	X		X				X	X			X	X		X
X	X	X	X	X	X	X	X	X		X			X	X	(X)	X	X	X	X	X
X	X	X	X	X	X	X	X	X	(X)	X			X	X	(X)			X	X	
X	X		X	X	X	X	X	X		X	X				X	X				X
	(X)						X													
X	X	X	X	X		X	X	X	X	X			X	X	X	X		X	X	X
(X)	X	X	(X)		(X)	X	X	X	(X)	X				X	(X)	X	X	X		X
(X)	X					X	X	(X)												
	(X)					X	X	X												
X	(X)	(X)	X			X	X			X			X	X				X	(X)	
(X)	X	X	X		(X)	X	X		X		X		X	X			X	X	(X)	
	(X)					X														

BS = Land-based sources of marine pollution
IA = Environmental impact assessment
CZM = Integrated coastal zone (and river basin) management
AT = Best available technique
EP = Best environmental practice
QS = Environmental quality standard
QO = Environmental quality objective
PA = 1995 UNEP Global Programme of Action

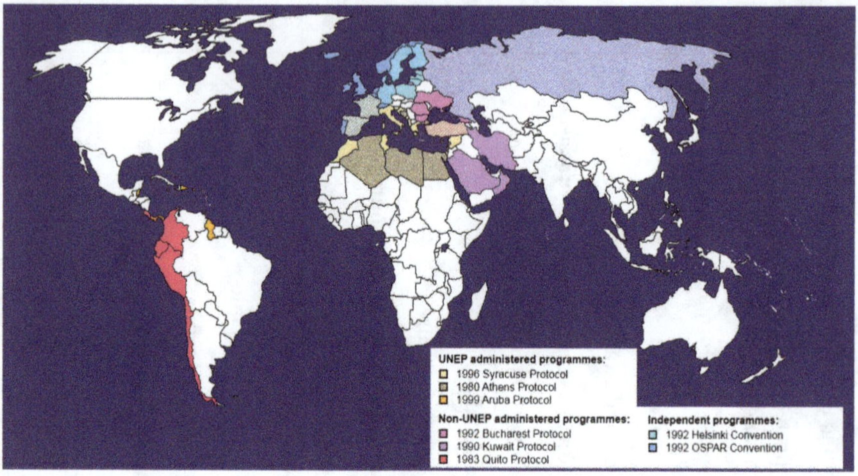

FIGURE 19 Parties to regional protocols (and conventions) on land-based sources currently in force
AUTHOR

the MAP, the Convention for the Protection of the Mediterranean Sea against Pollution (1976 Barcelona Convention) was adopted. Both the MAP and the convention were revised in 1995. The revision reflects a shift of emphasis from pollution control to a more integrated approach, including integrated coastal zone planning and management and the protection of biodiversity and ecosystems. MAP Phase II was adopted[1230] and the amended convention was renamed Convention for the Protection of the Marine Environment and the Coastal Region of the Mediterranean (1995 Barcelona Convention). The Barcelona Convention can be considered one of the forerunners for a number of later instruments concluded under the umbrella of UN Environment. It serves as a model type for a quite comprehensive legal instrument, touching on most of the issues as discussed above. Twenty-one states and the European Union are party to the convention.[1231] Eight states parties are also member of the European Union.

1230 Barcelona Convention, 'Report of the 9th Ordinary Meeting of the Contracting Parties' (1995) UNEP(OCA)/MED IG.5/16 Annex IX.

1231 Parties: Albania, Algeria, Bosnia and Herzegovina, Croatia, Cyprus, Egypt, European Union, France, Greece, Israel, Italy, Lebanon, Libya, Malta, Monaco, Montenegro, Morocco, Slovenia, Spain, Syria, Tunisia, Turkey. The convention's status of ratification is available at Barcelona Convention, 'Status of Signatures and Ratifications' <https://www.unep.org/unepmap/who-we-are/contracting-parties/barcelona-convention-and-amendments> accessed 19 February 2022.

The Barcelona Convention works as a framework convention and has been supplemented by seven protocols, including on dumping (from ships and aircraft), prevention and emergency (with regard to pollution from ships), land-based sources and activities, specially protected areas and biological diversity, pollution from exploration and exploitation of offshore resources, hazardous wastes, and integrated coastal zone management.

Core Obligations and Governing Principles

The territorial scope of application of the Barcelona Convention is, in principle, limited to 'maritime waters of the Mediterranean Sea proper', but can be extended by the parties to their coastal areas.[1232] Similar to UNCLOS, the core obligation as stipulated by the convention relates to the adoption of measures and environmental legislation in particular. Unlike UNCLOS, however, the regional convention requires parties to take all appropriate measures not only to prevent and control marine pollution, but also to 'abate, combat and to the fullest possible extent eliminate pollution of the Mediterranean Sea Area […] so as to contribute towards its sustainable development'.[1233] The principle of sustainable development is also reflected in a reference made to policy integration and intra- and intergenerational justice.[1234] In addition, the Barcelona Convention requires parties to apply the precautionary principle and the polluter pays principle, undertake environmental impact assessment, promote cooperation in the development of assessment procedures, and promote integrated coastal zone management.[1235] In 2008 and 2012, respectively, the parties adopted two decisions to apply and implement the ecosystem approach in their activities with potential effect on the Mediterranean Sea.[1236] Respective

1232 1995 Barcelona Convention art 1(1–2).

1233 ibid art 4(1).

1234 ibid art 4(2).

1235 ibid art 4(3).

1236 Barcelona Convention MoP Decision IG.17/6 (2008), 'Implementation of the Ecosystem Approach to the Management of Human Activities That May Affect the Mediterranean Marine and Coastal Environment' UNEP(DEPI)/MED IG.17/10 Annex V, 179; Barcelona Convention MoP Decision IG.20/4 (2012), 'Implementing MAP Ecosystem Approach Roadmap: Mediterranean Ecological and Operational Objectives, Indicators and Timetable for Implementing the Ecosystem Approach Roadmap' UNEP(DEPI)/MED IG.20/8 Annex II, 39. The documents refer to a CBD COP decision defining the ecosystem approach as a 'strategy for the integrated management of land, water and living resources that promotes conservation and sustainable use in an equitable way': CBD COP Decision V/6 (2000) (n 1088). At their Joint Ministerial Meeting in 2003, the OSPAR and Helsinki Commissions defined the ecosystem approach as the comprehensive integrated management of human activities based on the best available scientific knowledge about the ecosystem and its dynamics, in order to identify and take action on influences which are

implementation objectives include the prevention and control of marine and coastal litter.[1237] In 2013, the parties agreed on a list of good environmental status indicators and targets for the implementation of the ecosystem approach.[1238] As a further step in this direction, they launched the Integrated Monitoring and Assessment Programme (IMAP) in 2016. IMAP will monitor environmental concerns, including with regard to biodiversity, pollution and marine litter, in an integrated manner.[1239]

Implementation

In implementing the convention, parties shall adopt programmes and measures, define time limits for their completion, utilize best available techniques and the best environmental practices and 'promote the application of, access to and transfer of environmentally sound technology, including clean production technologies'.[1240] Parties further have to 'draw up and implement plans for the reduction and phasing out of substances that are toxic, persistent and liable to bioaccumulate arising from land-based sources'.[1241] The convention calls on states to establish a monitoring system and to participate in pollution monitoring in areas beyond national jurisdiction.[1242] Emphasis is also given to research on, access to and transfer of environmentally sound technology and to the provision of assistance in fields relating to marine pollution, with priority to be given to the special needs of developing countries.[1243]

The convention provides that parties have to give the public access to information on the state of the marine environment, on activities with potential adverse impact in this regard and on measures taken in implementing the convention. The public should be given the opportunity to participate

---

critical to the health of marine ecosystems, thereby achieving sustainable use of ecosystem goods and services and maintenance of ecosystem integrity:

> OSPAR-HELCOM Joint Ministerial Meeting, 'Statement on the Ecosystem Approach to the Management of Human Activities "Towards an Ecosystem Approach to the Management of Human Activities"' (2003).

1237 Barcelona Convention MoP Decision IG.20/4 (2012) (n 1236) 59.

1238 Barcelona Convention MoP Decision IG.21/3 (2013), 'Decision IG.21/3 on the Ecosystems Approach Including Adopting Definitions of Good Environmental Status (GES) and Targets' UNEP(DEPI)/MED IG.21/9 Annex II, 33.

1239 Barcelona Convention MoP Decision IG.22/7 (2016), 'Integrated Monitoring and Assessment Programme of the Mediterranean Sea and Coast and Related Assessment Criteria' UNEP(DEPI)/MED IG.22/28, 419.

1240 1995 Barcelona Convention art 4(4).

1241 ibid art 8.

1242 ibid art 12.

1243 ibid art 13.

in decision-making processes related to the implementation of the convention.[1244] A broad participation and the involvement of major actors are also envisaged in the MAP II. In 2009, parties adopted a formal procedure for the involvement of NGOs and other civil society representatives.[1245] In general, the secretariat is responsible for maintaining relations and coordinating activities with international organizations and NGOs.

More specific provisions can be found in the corresponding protocols, including the one on land-based sources. The Protocol for the Protection of the Mediterranean Sea against Pollution from Land-Based Sources (Athens Protocol) was adopted in 1980. It was revised in 1996 in Syracuse (Syracuse Protocol).

The territorial scope of application of the Syracuse Protocol is considerably wider than the scope of the Barcelona Convention, as it includes the entire watershed area within the territories of the parties to the protocol, draining into the Mediterranean Sea.[1246] The protocol also applies to inputs of polluting substances transported through the atmosphere to the Mediterranean Sea Area from land-based sources or activities.[1247] The main focus of mitigation measures prescribed by the protocol lies on the phasing out of inputs of substances that are toxic, persistent and liable to bioaccumulate.[1248] To this end, states shall adopt and implement 'national and regional action plans and programmes, containing measures and timetables for their implementation'.[1249] Annex I of the protocol provides some guidance for the preparation of action plans, programmes and measures for the elimination of pollution from land-based sources and activities. It defines the sectors of activity and the groups of substances to be covered due to a number of specific characteristics.[1250] Binding short-term and medium-term regional action plans and programmes are adopted by the meetings of the parties. Such plans and

1244 ibid art 15(1–2).

1245 See Barcelona Convention MoP Decision IG.19/6 (2009), 'MAP/Civil Society Cooperation and Partnership' UNEP(DEPI)/MED IG.19/8 Annex II, 59. The Regional Cooperation Platform on Marine Litter in the Mediterranean, serving as a forum for consultation and exchange of good practices, involves private organizations and academic institutions along with the regional centres of the Barcelona Convention.

1246 Referred to in the protocol as the hydrologic basin: 1996 Syracuse Protocol art 3(b) in conjunction with art 2(d).

1247 ibid art 4(1)(b) in conjunction with Annex III.

1248 ibid art 1.

1249 ibid art 5(2).

1250 Various industry sectors involving the production, use and disposal of plastics are covered by the annex. Also, marine litter is mentioned explicitly as a category of substance of particular concern with regard to the implementation of the protocol.

programmes are to contain measures and timetables for their implementation, too. They are adopted by a two-third majority, with the possibility for parties to opt out.[1251]

According to the Syracuse Protocol, point source discharges and releases that may, directly or indirectly, reach the Mediterranean Sea have to be subject to authorization. Parties have to provide for systems of inspection and establish sanctions in the event of non-compliance.[1252] Further guidance in this respect is provided by Annex II of the protocol. Parties are also required to adopt common standards dealing, for instance, with the 'control and progressive replacement of products [...] causing significant pollution of the marine environment'.[1253] Different types of plastic goods, especially single-use items and non-recoverable microbeads, fall into this category of goods.

The European Union is party to the Barcelona Convention and its protocols. Within the MAP system, it plays an important role in policy coordination and the formulation of common standards and practices.[1254] The MAP uses concepts that have been developed in an EU context, such as that of good environmental status.[1255] The EU is also an important donor for MAP projects, including a project related to the prevention and management of marine litter (Marine litter MED 2016–2019).

A regional action plan on marine litter for the MAP region was adopted in 2013.[1256] The prevention, reduction and control of marine litter generation and environmental impact are also a major objective in the Barcelona Convention

1251 1996 Syracuse Protocol art 15.

1252 ibid art 6.

1253 ibid art 7(1)(d).

1254 According to Kütting, EU law and the Barcelona regime complement each other successfully: Gabriela Kütting, 'Mediterranean Pollution: International Cooperation and the Control of Pollution from Land-Based Sources' (1994) 18 Marine Policy 233, 245.

1255 Good environmental status is defined as 'the environmental status of marine waters where these provide ecologically diverse and dynamic oceans and seas which are clean, healthy and productive': European Parliament and Council Directive 2008/56/EC of 17 June 2008 establishing a framework for community action in the field of marine environmental policy (Marine Strategy Framework Directive) [2008] OJ L164/19 art 3(5).

1256 UNEP-MAP (n 1204). See also Barcelona Convention MoP Decision IG.22/10 (2016), 'Implementing the Marine Litter Regional Plan in the Mediterranean (Fishing for Litter Guidelines, Assessment Report, Baselines Values, and Reduction Targets)' UNEP(DEPI)/MED IG.22/28, 523. A currently planned update of the action plan aims to increase the focus on a circular economy: Barcelona Convention MoP Decision IG.24/10 (2019), 'Main Elements of the Six Regional Plans to Reduce/Prevent Marine Pollution from Land- Based Sources; Updating the Annexes to the LBS and Dumping Protocols of the Barcelona Convention' UNEP/MED IG.24/22, 492 Annex ch 7.

Mid-Term Strategy 2016–2021. Further focal areas include integrated coastal zone management, marine protected areas and sustainable production and consumption.

Liability and Compensation

In the implementation of Article 16 of the amended Barcelona Convention, the contracting parties adopted guidelines on liability and compensation in 2008[1257] and a uniform questionnaire to regularly evaluate the liability regime of each party in 2009.[1258] The guidelines play a merely coordinative role in the adoption of national liability and compensation schemes and are not binding in character. They do not provide for subsidiary liability by the state. Instead, they call on states to implement the polluter pays principle and to impose strict liability for damage on operators of activities covered by the Barcelona Convention or its protocols. For the purposes of the guidelines, *damage* includes both traditional damage (such as loss of life, injury or damage to property) and environmental damage.[1259] The guidelines also apply to damage caused by pollution of a diffuse character 'provided that it is possible to establish a causal link between the damage and the activities of individual operators'. The evaluation questionnaire assesses participation in and implementation of various instruments related to liability issues, including relevant EU legislation, as well as the application and implementation of the polluter pays principle by the contracting parties. The establishment of a compulsory insurance regime and of a Mediterranean Compensation Fund is envisaged in the guidelines but has not yet been realized.[1260]

1257 'Guidelines on Liability and Compensation for Damage Resulting from Pollution of the Marine Environment in the Mediterranean Sea Area' in Barcelona Convention, 'Report of the 15th Ordinary Meeting of the Contracting Parties' (2008) UNEP(DEPI)/MED IG.17/10 Annex V, 135.

1258 Barcelona Convention MoP Decision IG.19/3 (2009), 'Implementation of and Reporting on Guidelines for the Determination of Liability and Compensation for Damages Resulting from Pollution of the Marine Environment in the Mediterranean Sea Area' in Barcelona Convention, 'Report of the 16th Ordinary Meeting of the Contracting Parties' (2009) UNEP(DEPI)/MED IG.19/8 Annex II, 15.

1259 Environmental damage includes, among other things, costs related to the assessment of the damage, clean-up and restoration costs, as well as possible diminution in value of natural resources.

1260 For more information on the Mediterranean liability guidelines, see Scovazzi, 'The Mediterranean Guidelines for the Determination of Environmental Liability and Compensation' (n 1211).

Institutional Framework

Secretariat services are provided by UN Environment in line with Article 17 of the convention. UN Environment provides these services through the MAP Coordinating Unit (MEDU), which was established in 1979 and moved to its current location in Athens, Greece, in 1982. The MEDU is assisted by the different MAP components. One of these components is the Mediterranean Pollution Assessment and Control Programme (MED POL). Its main objective is the prevention and elimination of land-based pollution of the Mediterranean. MED POL assists the parties in the implementation of the Barcelona Convention and the dumping, land-based sources and hazardous wastes protocols. It plays an important role in the monitoring and assessment of marine pollution and the implementation of national action plans to address land-based pollution, including litter. Project and policy coordination, including with regard EU policies and law, is another important task of the MED POL.

In addition to the MEDU and the MAP components, the Barcelona system involves a complex institutional framework. The contracting parties to the Barcelona Convention hold ordinary meetings on a biennial basis. A rotating bureau consisting of six representatives of the contracting parties assists the Meeting of the Parties. The parties also cooperate among each other through a network of national focal points. In 1995, the Mediterranean Commission on Sustainable Development (MCSD) was established. The commission includes representatives from governments, local authorities, international organizations, NGOs and other actors. It serves as an advisory body to the parties and assists them in their efforts to integrate environmental concerns in their economic policies and development programmes. Also, the MCSD enhances cooperation between the different levels of governance, from local to global, and among various actors.

Dispute Settlement, Compliance and Reporting

With regard to dispute settlement, Annex A to the Barcelona Convention proposes an ad hoc arbitration procedure. The procedure includes a tribunal with three members. Decisions by the tribunal are binding on the parties to the dispute. At the request of one of the parties to the dispute, the tribunal may recommend essential interim measures of protection.

In 2008, the Meeting of the Parties established a compliance committee.[1261] The aim of the committee is to assist parties and to facilitate, promote, monitor

1261 See Barcelona Convention MoP Decision IG.17/2 (2008), 'Procedures and Mechanisms on Compliance under the Barcelona Convention and Its Protocols' UNEP(DEPI)/MED IG.17/10 Annex V, 21, as amended by Decisions IG.20/1, IG. 21/1 and IG.22/15; Barcelona

and secure compliance. To this purpose, it may require the submission of action plans or progress reports. The committee is the core element of a non-adversarial compliance procedure, complementing and supplementing the dispute settlement procedures as defined in the convention and its protocols. The compliance mechanism may be triggered by any party finding itself in a situation of non-compliance, any other state party to the convention and relevant protocols, the convention secretariat or the compliance committee itself. The role of the committee is mainly one of a facilitator. It does not apply sanctions but reports its findings to the contracting parties. The meetings of the parties can take further steps (such as capacity-building measures) and may publish cases of non-compliance. In serious, ongoing or repeated cases of non-compliance, the contracting parties may consider further action necessary to achieve the purposes of the convention and its protocols.[1262] Transboundary pollution originating from the territory of a contracting party of the Syracuse Protocol can be brought directly to the Meeting of the Parties by any of the parties concerned.[1263]

Every two years, parties have to report on the legal, administrative or other measures taken by them for the implementation of the convention, its protocols and recommendations adopted by the meeting of the contracting parties. They also have to report on the effectiveness of such measures.[1264] The Syracuse Protocol further requires reporting on authorizations, data resulting from monitoring and quantities of discharged pollutants.[1265] There is a uniform reporting format.[1266] Also, the parties adopted a number of indicators for measuring the effectiveness of implementing measures.[1267] The meetings of the parties assess compliance with the convention on the basis of the party reports.[1268] Reporting therefore plays a fundamental role in the compliance procedure. The failure by a number of parties to comply with their reporting

---

Convention MoP Decision IG.19/1 (2009), 'Rules of Procedure for the Compliance Committee and Its Work during 2010–2011 Biennium' UNEP(DEPI)/MED IG.19/8 Annex II, 1, as amended by Decision IG.21/1.

1262 Irini Papanicolopulu, 'Procedures and Mechanisms on Compliance under the 1976/1995 Barcelona Convention on the Protection of the Mediterranean Sea and Its Protocols' in Tullio Treves and others (eds), *Non-Compliance Procedures and Mechanisms and the Effectiveness of International Environmental Agreements* (TMC Asser Press 2009) 166.

1263 See 1996 Syracuse Protocol art 12.

1264 1995 Barcelona Convention art 26.

1265 1996 Syracuse Protocol art 13.

1266 Barcelona Convention MoP Decision IG.17/3 (2008), 'Format for the Implementation of the Barcelona Convention and Its Protocols' UNEP(DEPI)/MED IG.17/10 Annex V, 29.

1267 Barcelona Convention MoP Decision IG.19/4 (2009), 'Testing MAP Effectiveness Indicators' UNEP(DEPI)/MED IG.19/8 Annex II, 29.

1268 1995 Barcelona Convention art 27.

obligations thus not only puts these parties in a situation of non-compliance but also constitutes one of the main stumbling blocks to adequately evaluating implementation of the convention and related instruments and to identifying the main challenges.[1269]

Budget

The programme budget is prepared by the coordination unit and adopted by the Meeting of the Parties. It usually covers a period of two years. The programme is mainly funded by country contributions to the Mediterranean Trust Fund. Relative contribution levels derive from the United Nations assessment scale. In 2020–21, total expected ordinary country contributions (excluding in-kind contributions by countries hosting the secretariat or regional activity centres) amounted to about €11.5 million of the total budget, with France, Italy and Spain being the largest contributors.[1270] Further donors include the EU, the GEF, UN Environment and a number of international organizations. Major projects in the region include, for instance, the Strategic Partnership for the Mediterranean Sea Large Marine Ecosystem, aiming, among other things, at reducing pollution from land-based sources, and a project on marine litter (Marine litter MED 2016–2019).

b) East Asian Seas Region (EAS)

The East Asian Seas region is characterized by a number of sensible ecosystems and one of the highest degrees of biological diversity. It is especially rich in sea grass, mangroves and large coral reefs.[1271] The region, however, is also characterized by large population growth, particularly in coastal regions, and rapid economic development over the past decades. It is home to one-fifth of the world's population and comprises some of the world's most polluted cities. Much to the detriment of the coastal and marine environments of the region, environmental considerations have come up short.[1272] A lack of regional

1269 Barcelona Convention MoP Decision IG.22/15 (2016), 'Compliance Mechanisms and Procedures, Membership and Working Programme of the Compliance Committee for the Biennium 2016–2017' UNEP(DEPI)/MED IG.22/28, 629 Annex I.

1270 See Barcelona Convention MoP Decision IG.24/14 (2019), 'Programme of Work and Budget 2020–2021' UNEP/MED IG.24/22, 696 at 700.

1271 Joseph F DiMento and Alexis Jaclyn Hickman, *Environmental Governance of the Great Seas: Law and Effect* (Edward Elgar Publishing 2012) 70.

1272 Unsustainable practices include inadequate sewage systems, land reclamation, removal of mangrove belts and general deforestation, uncontrolled aquaculture and agriculture practices, littering, dumping, unsustainable tourism and industrial waste run off: see ibid 71.

cooperation has been considered one of the causes for the fact that environmental conditions of the East Asian Seas continue to rapidly deteriorate.[1273] The region also suffered severe impacts from the 2004 Indian Ocean tsunami.

As it is the case for the Arctic, South-West Atlantic, North-West Pacific and South Asian Seas regions, there is no regional convention covering on the protection of the marine environment in the East Asian Seas.[1274] Instead, the programme is based on non-binding documents. Compliance is voluntary. The Action Plan for the Protection and Development of the Marine Environment and Coastal Areas of the East Asian Seas Region was adopted by Indonesia, Malaysia, the Philippines, Singapore and Thailand in 1981. It was revised in 1994, when Australia, Cambodia, the People's Republic of China, the Republic of Korea and Vietnam joined in. Australia withdrew its commitment in 2011. In the action plan, the development of a regional database is envisaged, as well as long-term monitoring, environmental assessment and other scientific activities. Environmental management is another element that is addressed in the action plan, which for the purpose of the action plan includes, for instance, employing appropriate technologies for the prevention and management of pollution and capacity-building. The plan was complemented by a regional programme of action on land-based activities in 2000[1275] and a regional action plan on marine litter in 2008, which was revised in 2019.[1276] In 2018, the newest strategic directions were adopted for the period up to 2022. In the document, member countries acknowledge that their region generates as much as half the world's marine plastic litter, due to a change in economies and lifestyles.[1277] Respective commitments remain, however, extremely vague and solely focus on review and implementation of the existing action plan on marine litter.[1278]

The regional action plan is operated by the Coordinating Body on the Seas of East Asia (COBSEA). Supposedly, the nine member countries are represented at the biennial COBSEA meetings, at which decisions are taken by consensus. However, efficiency of the organization is hampered by limited decision-making authority of participants, frequent absences, limited

1273 See ibid 70; Hugh Kirkman, 'The East Asian Seas UNEP Regional Seas Programme' (2006) 6 International Environmental Agreements: Politics, Law and Economics 305, 306.

1274 What is more, only very few South East Asian countries are party to international environmental agreements, including the 1972 London Dumping Convention.

1275 UNEP-COBSEA, 'Regional Programme of Action for the Protection of the Marine Environment of the East Asian Seas from the Effects of Land-Based Activities' (2000).

1276 UNEP-COBSEA, *Marine Litter in the East Asian Seas Region* (n 1202); 'Regional Action Plan on Marine Litter' (n 1204).

1277 UNEP-COBSEA, 'COBSEA Strategic Directions 2018–2022' (2018) para 7.

1278 ibid para 23. See also DiMento and Hickman (n 1271) 74.

personal interest in the matter by individual participants, limited preparation and high fluctuations among state representatives, which results in a 'lack of understanding of the regional problems in the East Asian Seas and of COBSEA activities'.[1279] The work of the COBSEA Secretariat is often impeded by long ratification periods. Its tasks include the collection of data on the seas, the provision of guidance to the member states and the coordination of national policies and strategies.[1280]

Limited financial resources are one of the main challenges of the programme. Start-up funding from UN Environment ended in 2006. Staff costs and costs related to the tasks of the secretariat are now covered by voluntary contributions made by member states via the COBSEA Trust Fund.[1281] However, financial contributions from member countries are low and hardly suffice even to cover minimum staff costs. Implementing projects are usually funded by donor countries or regional or global funding institutions, including the GEF.[1282] COBSEA has not been successful in acquiring enough funding and competes for the scarce available financial resources with other regional agencies having a similar focus.[1283] At a domestic level, limited capacity is also a contributing factor to poor enforcement of implementing legislation.[1284]

Other constraining factors include the absence of leadership, the lack of a compliance mechanism, low commitment and low cooperative efforts.[1285] Moreover, a lack of coordination among regional actors leads to a duplication of activities and governance gaps. UN Environment headquarters in Nairobi has also been criticized for not showing the desired degree of leadership and

---

1279 Kirkman (n 1273) 311–12.

1280 See DiMento and Hickman (n 1271) 74–75.

1281 Gabino Gonzalez and Frédéric Hérbert, 'Conventions Relating to Pollution Incident Preparedness, Response, and Cooperation' in David Joseph Attard and others (eds), *The IMLI Manual on International Maritime Law Volume III: Marine Environmental Law and International Maritime Security Law* (Oxford University Press 2016) 215.

1282 The UNEP/GEF South China Sea Project is an example for a regionally coordinated programme of action funded by the GEF. The project aimed to reverse environmental degradation, including from land-based pollution.

1283 See, for instance, UNEP-COBSEA, 'Report of the Twenty-First Meeting of the Coordinating Body on the Seas of East Asia (COBSEA)' (2013) UNEP/DEPI/COBSEA IGM 21/6 paras 48–50. Such competing agencies include the Partnerships in Environmental Management for the Seas of East Asia (PEMSEA), the Association of Southeast Asian Nations (ASEAN), FAO, and IOC/WESTPAC.

1284 See DiMento and Hickman (n 1271) 82.

1285 See ibid 75–76; Kirkman (n 1273) 312.

interest in the regional activities 'apart from desiring a legally binding regional agreement'.[1286]

The region's high pollution potential (which is due to a combination of high coastal population and insufficient waste management) along with the absence of a functioning regional system effectively protecting the marine environment results in extremely high plastic input into the sea. The region could, therefore, benefit from integration into a global regime on plastic pollution providing for a strong capacity-building scheme. Moreover, control of plastic input from the East Asian Seas Region into the ocean would benefit the global marine environment. The international community as a whole has, therefore, an interest in an effective preventive system in the East Asian Seas.

B *Strengths and Deficiencies*

While marine plastic pollution is a global problem, regional and local impacts, such as the loss of local ecosystem services, are usually the most prompt, direct and visible. This direct impact and the common interest in preserving the regional marine environment suggest that states seek regional solutions tailored to their specific situation. States bordering the same sea basin or sharing a coastline also share the responsibility for its protection, as degradation of the respective marine environments affects them all. What is more, neighbouring states often have a tradition of information exchange, policy coordination and cooperation. They usually share a wide range of common interests and values. It naturally seems easier for a small group of states with similar interests to agree on how to address a specific problem than it is for a large and diverse one.[1287] Against this backdrop, regional cooperation schemes seem a suitable or even necessary response to the problem of marine pollution from land-based sources. In any case, they form an integral part of the current regime. This section examines the potential strengths and weaknesses of the regional approach with respect to the prevention of marine plastic pollution. It will show that while regional schemes have contributed significantly to the development of the law and policies on the protection of the marine environment, they do not by themselves provide a sufficient response to the problem of marine plastic pollution.

1286 Kirkman (n 1273) 312. According to Kirkman, the lack of a legally binding instrument on the protection of the marine environment in the East Asian Seas is a source of conflict between UNEP and the COBSEA member countries: ibid 307.

1287 cf Hassan (n 364) 104.

i General Effectiveness and Coverage of the Regional Programmes

Assessing the effectiveness of the regional conventions and their protocols in terms of physical impacts (that is, causal change in the conditions of the marine environment) is an extremely complex task and goes beyond the scope of this book. It has been asserted in this regard that while there are regional differences, general conditions of the marine environment are not improving.[1288] At the same time, it seems evident that the regional programmes and the related work of UN Environment and other institutions have had a major impact on policy development and the evolution of environmental law at different levels. They played an important role in the development of new governance structures and legal instruments. This, rather than the real and effective improvement of the state of the marine environment, is what is widely considered the regional programmes' major success.[1289] The programmes also provided for opportunities for synergies, joint initiatives and policy coordination.[1290] The degree to which such opportunities have been seized and corresponding potential has been harnessed is subject to major regional differences.

Overall, the design of the governing instruments, available resources, implementation and political commitment are very uneven. Some programmes, agreements and action plans are dense and comprehensive in character. They are periodically reviewed and adjusted, while others are not. Some instruments award their different bodies relatively wide competences, while the secretariats and bodies of other programmes have known long periods of inaction or still struggle with a lack of personnel and financial resources.

Such regional differences generally follow socio-economic and geographic factors: regional programmes mainly or partly involving developed countries are usually considered relatively successful. These programmes especially include the OSPAR, Baltic and Mediterranean programmes, all of which share a long history of cooperation.[1291] By contrast, programmes with mainly developing-country membership are deemed less successful. Owing to scarce resources and other hurdles, their institutions often lack the necessary capacity

1288 See DiMento and Hickman (n 1271) 156.

1289 See, for instance, Hassan (n 364) 126.

1290 Prominent examples of inter-regional cooperation include the Baltic2Black Project between the Black Sea Commission and the Helsinki Commission, as well as capacity building by the OSPAR Commission in the WACAF region.

1291 See DiMento and Hickman (n 1271) 166; Jon M van Dyke, 'Whither the z Regional Seas Programmes?' in Harry N Scheiber and Jin-Hyun Paik (eds), *Regions, Institutions, and Law of the Sea: Studies in Ocean Governance* (Martinus Nijhoff Publishers 2013) 92.

to act and authoritative power. The performance of Asian programmes has been especially subject to criticism, including for low commitment of the parties and the inexistence of binding agreements on the protection of the marine environment, in particular from land-based sources. In many developing country regions, cooperation for the protection of the marine environment and implementation are hampered by political conflicts, the prevalence of short-term economic policies and the lack of public awareness. In addition, the competent ministries and agencies often lack the political power in order to get the national support and resources needed for the adoption of a regional convention or a meaningful implementation of the action plans. These factors come along with a lack of inter-agency cooperation and a poor science–policy interface. In general, it seems that poorer regions are more reluctant or faced with more difficulties to adopting binding regulation or build up strong institutions. The lack of a common and firm regulatory framework, however, leaves them more vulnerable to marine pollution.[1292]

Another weakness of the regional approach relates to the fact that scientific criteria for ecosystem-based management played a limited role as a factor in the determination of the different regions under the Regional Seas Programme. Instead, the regions were established corresponding to political or practical considerations. They do not encompass the whole oceanic system but leave some regions uncovered and widely unregulated. Also, there is no uniform approach with regard to the geographic scope of corresponding instruments: only a few of them include internal waters and coastal areas, and inclusion of the watershed is exceptional. The seaward limit of the covered regions also varies, with only a few instruments that include parts of the high seas.

The overall coverage of the programmes is, thus, limited in two respects. On the one hand, some of the most polluting regions are not covered by a legal instrument or by any programme at all. On the other hand, areas beyond national jurisdiction are included but to a very limited extent. While land-based pollution sources are obviously located within areas under national jurisdiction and must be addressed and prevented in these areas, plastic debris also highly affects areas beyond national borders, and poses a threat to marine species and ecosystems in these areas. Such impacts have to be taken into account in an ecosystem-based approach, but fall out of scope of the regional conventions and programmes. It therefore seems that regional

1292 See Hassan (n 364) 147; DiMento and Hickman (n 1271) 169; van Dyke (n 1291) 108; VanderZwaag and Powers (n 462) 448–51.

schemes are not sufficient or appropriate to address pollution in the high seas and the deep seabed, including plastic accumulation in oceanic gyres and on the ocean floor.

ii Pollution Prevention Standards and Environmental Management

Regional programmes facilitate the formulation, adoption and implementation of common standards that reflect a common degree of commitment of the states involved. They allow groups of states to go beyond international standards, as far as they exist, and to contribute to the creation of a level playing field among neighbouring countries. Most regional instruments on land-based sources add some level of detail to the international framework, which is exactly in line with the concept of UNCLOS Part XII, as UNCLOS precisely refers to regional specificities and the possibility or the obligation to define regional standards, in particular with regard to land-based sources. Regional instruments are highly relevant for the implementation of UNCLOS Article 194 and related provisions when identifing specific groups of substances and activities or sectors that need to be addressed by national measures or when listing a number of substance characteristics that need to be taken into account in the adoption of measures. Several industry sectors and activities that are major sources of plastic pollution (including, for instance, the management of municipal solid waste) are covered by these instruments. Litter ranks among the priority substance categories. Moreover, a number of problematic characteristics of marine plastic debris are explicitly mentioned as substance characteristics that need to be given particular attention in the preparation of action plans, programmes and measures.

Some of the regional conventions and the newer generation of the regional protocols on land-based sources oblige their parties to apply environmental management principles such as the precautionary principle or approach, the polluter pays principle, the principle of sustainable development, or integrated coastal area management. The relevance of some of these principles to plastic pollution mitigation has been explained in previous sections.[1293] The principles provide for important guidance with regard to the implementation of the general duties and the commonly defined standards.

Through the use of BATS, BEPS, environmental management principles and other tools, regional instruments on land-based sources give more or less detailed guidance on how different land-based sources of pollution should

---

1293 See Sections 2.1.A.ii and 2.1.B.ii.3)c) above.

be addressed. Some of the criteria used for the determination of BATs and suggested measures for BEPs are highly relevant for the prevention and management of marine plastic pollution. Such criteria and suggested measures include: the focus on non-waste technology; the provision of information and education; the application of labels, economic instruments, restrictions and bans; the provision of collection and disposal systems; avoidance of the use of hazardous substances; and the emphasis on recycling, recovery and reuse. While states still have, of course, wide discretion with regard to the measures they adopt, the obligation to use BATs and BEPs may be helpful in specifying the standard of care and the required minimum level of protection on a regional basis.[1294] This being, regional conventions theoretically have great potential to address one of the major weaknesses of the UNCLOS regime. State and legal practice will show whether and to what extent this potential can actually be realized.

BATs and BEPs are not static and uniform, but rather vary according to time and space. They lose their clear shape when confronted with the different social, economic and political realities of countries across the globe. A specific technique or practice may be available in one country but not economically feasible in another. The economic feasibility of a technique is, however, one of the factors to be taken into account in the determination of a BAT or BEPs. The regional definition of BATs and BEPs therefore allows to better addess the economic, political and technological gaps between different countries and regions, especially between developed and developing countries.

Along with the use of BATs and BEPs, regional instruments require their parties to strictly regulate and control point sources of pollution through a system of waste and discharge permits, authorization and inspection. Industrial wastes or effluents containing (micro-)plastic particles and synthetic fibres should, thus, be subject to prior authorization. The system of discharge permits and authorization seems to contrast with the general aim of these instruments to phase out inputs of the substances that are toxic, persistent and liable to bioaccumulate. With the duty to adopt such a regulation system, emphasis is put on pollution control rather than pollution prevention. At least, increasing implementation of the ecosystem approach and integrated coastal zone and river basin management (for instance in the Barcelona regime) strengthens preventive approaches.[1295]

1294 See Tanaka, 'Regulation of Land-Based Marine Pollution' (n 363) 564.
1295 VanderZwaag and Powers (n 462) 446.

iii Institutional Considerations, Reporting and Compliance

Institutional advantages of the regional schemes include the more flexible reception and mainstreaming of new topics and challenges, their increased discussion in competent bodies and fora, the greater proximity of regional bodies to their parties, the network of national focal points, as well as reporting and compliance systems. Depending on the design and effectiveness of such systems, monitoring and reporting obligations allow the supervision and control of national implementation. As such, they provide the governing bodies with a limited means to react to cases of non-compliance, including cases of domestic pollution in which no direct interests of other states are at stake, and allow these bodies to provide assistance or push for more effective measures.[1296]

Potential disadvantages include institutional overlaps with other regional bodies, duplication of activities, and institutional competition for scarce funding.[1297] Severe financial constraints, along with low commitment and disadvantageous priority setting by the member countries, are among the main reasons for the institutional inefficiency of some of the regional seas bodies. In view of the low priority they are given by their members and the little impact they have on the ground, it has been questioned whether such weak institutions should be maintained at all, especially if their focus is limited to pollution control and does not include ecosystem-based management, resource exploitation and the protection of biodiversity.[1298] Moreover, the regional seas programmes have not, so far, drawn on their potential to influence action and decision-making under UNCLOS. Overall, there has been little cooperation between the two governance regimes.[1299]

iv Means of Implementation

One of the most obvious challenges of the regulation of land-based sources of pollution relates to the widespread lack of the necessary means for the implementation of corresponding instruments. In theory, this is true for both global and regional instruments. A purely regional approach would, however, potentially exacerbate the problem, as it accentuates regional differences, does not provide the legal and institutional basis for the necessary

1296 See Birnie, Boyle and Redgwell (n 488) 462.

1297 DiMento and Hickman (n 1271) 76; Jan PM van Tatenhove, 'How to Turn the Tide: Developing Legitimate Marine Governance Arrangements at the Level of the Regional Seas' (2013) 71 Ocean & Coastal Management 296, 296.

1298 See DiMento and Hickman (n 1271) 135; van Dyke (n 1291) 108.

1299 See DiMento and Hickman (n 1271) 173.

assistance between regions and may therefore serve as a legitimization of a pluri-standard regime in which poorer nations are less well protected. This assumption is evidenced in practice by the obvious differences with regard to the level of commitment and effectiveness of the programmes between developed- and developing-country regions and the correlation between the level of economic development and the standard of care even within the same region.

From a global point of view, strengthening the means of implementation is, therefore, key to a more effective and efficient regime. Both the 2030 Agenda for Sustainable Development and the Addis Ababa Action Agenda on Financing for Development acknowledge the importance of creating an 'enabling environment at all levels' in the spirit of global partnership and solidarity.[1300] SDG 17 is fully devoted to strengthening the means of implementation, including through: the mobilization of financial resources from public and private sources; investment in least developed countries; cooperation on and access to science, technology and innovation; the promotion of the development, transfer, dissemination and diffusion of environmentally sound technologies to developing countries; targeted capacity-building activities; equitable trade; enhanced policy coherence; public–private partnerships and private-sector engagement.

Capacity-building encompasses 'the country's human, scientific, technological, organisational, institutional and resource capabilities'.[1301] It may consist of a wide range of activities building abilities and creating conditions that will enable public and private actors to improve their performance with regard to their environmental and development objectives. Increased environmental performance will, in turn, allow countries to achieve their goals as defined in the respective instruments. Capacity-building includes strengthening processes, systems and rules, as well as 'people's technical ability and willingness to play new developmental roles'.[1302] Resource mobilization and capacity-building are important for industrialized and developing countries alike, but in order to allow developing-country regions to achieve the necessary level of protection for a sustainable development, they need assistance by others. Not

1300 See United Nations, 'Addis Ababa Action Agenda of the Third International Conference on Financing for Development' (2015) 1; UNGA Res 70/1 (2015) (n 515) paras 39–46 and 60–71. See also 'Washington Declaration on Protection of the Marine Environment from Land-Based Activities' (n 457) paras 4 and 6.

1301 Agenda 21 (n 450) para 37.1.

1302 UNEP (ed), *Capacity Building for Sustainable Development: An Overview of UNEP Environmental Capacity Development Initiatives* (2002) 11.

only is financial, scientific and technical assistance by richer nations essential but also the exchange of experiences and best practices among developing countries. The provision of financial, scientific and technical assistance to developing and least developed countries, the dissemination of best practices and granting access to environmentally more friendly technologies is essential for enabling these countries to effectively discharge their obligations and to achieve the environmental goals as set in the instruments on land-based pollution sources. It is also important with a view to the use of BATs and BETs. The duty to provide these forms of assistance is a corollary to the differentiated responsibilities and – ideally – a remedy to the problem of double-standards within and between regions.

With regard to the prevention and elimination of marine plastic pollution, financial, scientific and technical assistance is needed in the fields as listed in Table 11.

Almost all instruments on land-based sources require their parties to cooperate in the fields of scientific research, technology transfer, exchange of data and knowledge, technical assistance and capacity-building. Yet, inter-regional and inter-institutional cooperation in these fields is not generally regulated or coordinated and, thus, rather exceptional. It may be project-based or based on a memorandum of understanding (MoU) or other agreement on cooperation.[1303] Also, only a few instruments, most of which are not yet in force, address the provision and mobilization of additional funds and other resources for their implementation.[1304] They require states to raise sufficient domestic and external financial resources (e.g. assessed and voluntary contributions, grants, donations and loans) and encourage them to explore innovative methods for mobilizing and channelling resources[1305] (e.g. cost internalization through market-based instruments or consumption taxes). The private sector and public–private partnerships play an increasingly important role in resource mobilization.

1303 As an example of an inter-regional MoU see 'Memorandum of Understanding between the Secretariat of the OSPAR Convention and the Secretariat of the Abidjan Convention' (2013) <http://www.ospar.org/about/international-cooperation/memoranda-of-understanding> accessed 19 February 2022. See also BSC, HELCOM and EU, 'Environmental Monitoring of the Black Sea with Focus on Nutrient Pollution (Baltic2Black)' (2014) Final Report for the Grant Agreement No 07.0204/2010/580913/SUB/D2.

1304 See 2012 Abidjan Protocol art 21; 1999 Aruba Protocol art XVI; 2005 Jeddah Protocol art 15 para 3 and art 16; 2012 Moscow Protocol art 20; 2010 Nairobi Protocol art 20; 2009 Sofia Protocol art 18.

1305 See, for instance, 2010 Nairobi Protocol art 20 paras 3–4.

TABLE 11 Relevant fields for capacity-building as well as technology and knowledge transfer in the prevention and elimination of marine plastic pollution

1. Marine litter in the environment, including with regard to: – monitoring of the state of the marine environment, hotspots, rivers and disposal sites – assessment of marine litter quantities, distribution and impacts, as well as of sources and pathways
2. Waste and resource management, including with regard to: – waste reduction technologies and practices; reuse and recycling – waste collection strategies and technology – waste disposal strategies and technology, taking into account the region-specific waste composition
3. Production and consumption patterns, including with regard to: – the use of economic incentives and market-based instruments – the use of technical and other regulations – the quality and service life of consumer and other goods – the development of environmentally friendly product and packaging designs and materials
4. Clean-up and restoration strategies and technologies, including with regard to: – beach clean-up methods and technology – open water clean-up technology – waste catchment technology for point sources, rivers, etc.

C *Evaluation: Can Regional Programmes Close the Gaps?*

Table 12 gives an overview on different aspects to the question whether and to what extent the regional schemes may close the gaps of the global regime.

In view of the above, the regional schemes may be seen both as a mechanism of flexibility and a testing ground for new and innovative solutions. Their pioneering work is of crucial importance for the development of global standards and the evolution of a global regime. On the other hand, this implies that a regional system may bear the risk of regulatory fragmentation and a pluri-standard regime in which the regulatory density and/or effectiveness depends on legal traditions, political commitment, priority setting and geo-economic factors. In some regions, the lack of resources especially is a major stumbling block for the effective protection and preservation of the marine environment. In addition to these regional disparities and the absence of legally binding agreements in the main polluting regions, the geographic scope of the regional

TABLE 12 How regional programmes address the main challenges under the UNCLOS regime with regard to marine plastic pollution

Main challenges under the UNCLOS regime:	Responses by the regional programmes:
Pollution prevention standards and level of protection:	
– UNCLOS does not, by itself, define standards on pollution prevention. Its reference to international rules and standards has partly weaker language in relation to land-based sources than in relation to other pollution sources. There are hardly any binding global rules and standards for the adoption of national mitigation measures. The standard of care varies according to the level of economic development and capacities. All these factors contribute to the fact that the standard of care and the required level of protection are not clearly defined.	– Regional programmes facilitate the formulation, adoption and implementation of common standards. Most regional instruments on land-based sources request their parties to regulate several industry sectors and activities that are major sources of plastic pollution. Litter ranks among the priority substance categories that need to be taken into account for regulation. Many regional instruments on land-based sources define standards on how to regulate and control point and non-point sources of marine pollution. Most often, they require states to set up a national system of authorization, monitoring, and inspection (sometimes with the possibility of sanctions). Some instruments require their parties to commonly adopt timetables for the phase-out of products and the implementation of other agreed measures.

TABLE 12 How regional programmes address the main challenges under the UNCLOS regime with regard to marine plastic pollution (*cont.*)

Main challenges under the UNCLOS regime:	Responses by the regional programmes:
Environmental management principles:	
– In addition to the lack of standards, UNCLOS does not provide guidance on the required level of protection or how it should be achieved by reference to environmental management principles that are highly relevant in tackling the problem of marine plastic pollution. Such principles include, in particular, sustainable development, the precautionary approach, the polluter pays principle, integrated coastal zone management and clean production.	– Some of the regional instruments oblige their parties to apply environmental management principles such as the precautionary principle or approach, the polluter pays principle or the principle of sustainable development. These and other principles provide for valuable guidance with regard to the implementation of general duties and plastic pollution mitigation:
	– The *precautionary principle or approach* implies that scientific uncertainty with regard to the probability of plastics to reach the marine environment or with regard to their effects on the marine environment and human health may not serve as a justification for inaction. – The *polluter pays principle* implies the notion of cost internalization and promotes the use of economic incentives (market-based instruments). It further provides guidance on how to best define a suitable liability scheme and plays an important role in the shift towards more sustainable production and consumption patterns.

TABLE 12 How regional programmes address the main challenges under the UNCLOS regime with regard to marine plastic pollution (*cont.*)

Main challenges under the UNCLOS regime:	**Responses by the regional programmes:**
	– The *principle of sustainable development* requires states to take into account environmental and social impacts of plastic pollution in policy formulation. In order to do so, states need to assess and weigh up costs of action and inaction, including for poor country regions and future generations. Sustainable development thus demands a coherent, transparent and equitable formulation of policy and law.
Reference to plastic-specific tools providing for additional guidance:	
– As a framework convention dealing with a wide range of issues related to ocean governance, UNCLOS does not directly refer to plastic-specific or waste-specific tools. There is also no direct reference to relevant BATs and BEPs such as the gradual and continuous replacement of products and facilities by more environmentally sustainable ones. However, UNCLOS indirectly covers such tools by reference to internationally agreed rules and standards (such as the GPA). It requires states to take them into account when adopting measures for the protection and preservation of the marine environment.	– Some of the protocols on land-based sources specifically refer to the GPA and the principles or tools promoted therein. Moreover, reference to BATs and BEPs is very common, especially in the newer generation instruments. Some regional instruments also provide for the possibility of defining marine protected areas and require their parties to take account of hotspots and endangered species. None of the instruments has been specifically tailored to marine plastic pollution, but the different treaty bodies often make reference to topical and emerging plastic-specific issues within the scope of their respective competences.

TABLE 12 How regional programmes address the main challenges under the UNCLOS regime with regard to marine plastic pollution (*cont.*)

Main challenges under the UNCLOS regime:	Responses by the regional programmes:
Environmental impact assessment and monitoring:	
– Obligations under UNCLOS to undertake environmental impact assessment and monitor activities are not sufficiently applied to some point sources of plastic pollution, such as coastal dumpsites, and are not well tailored to non-point sources of plastic pollution. Alternative, complementary schemes, such as impact assessments of products, life-cycle analysis, consumer information and green procurement are needed. Also, impact assessment of policies seems essential, especially with regard to production and consumption patterns.	– Most regional instruments on the protection of the marine environment essentially reflect UNCLOS Article 206. Some of them, however, require their parties to commonly set up more detailed standards on environmental impact assessment and refer to public participation and information in assessment procedures. According provisions are usually complemented by reporting requirements on the measures taken in implementation of the convention or protocol. Only few among the regional protocols define a broader scope of application with regard to the duty to undertake environmental impact assessment. Under the Nairobi 2010 Protocol, once it enters into force, parties will have to 'ensure that new or existing activities, developments, programmes, plans, policies and processes that are likely to cause significant adverse impacts to the marine and/or coastal environment are subjected to environmental impact assessment, environmental audit or strategic environmental assessment, as appropriate, and prior authorization by a competent national authority or authorities as a matter of law'.

TABLE 12 How regional programmes address the main challenges under the UNCLOS regime with regard to marine plastic pollution (*cont.*)

Main challenges under the UNCLOS regime:	**Responses by the regional programmes:**
	The 1990 Kuwait Protocol defines the minimum content of environmental impact assessment reports (Article VIII). Reference to the progressive replacement of products that cause significant pollution to the marine environment (such as microbeads-containing cosmetics) can be found in most of the instruments dealing with land-based pollution sources. Reference to further complementary concepts such as life-cycle analysis or green procurement, that are relevant to diffuse sources of plastic pollution in particular, is much less common.
Means of implementation and capacity-building:	
– In UNCLOS, the concept of graduation and differentiated levels of obligation does not come with a sufficiently strong and clearly defined obligation for scientific and technical assistance and technology transfer. As a consequence, many low-income countries have difficulties in properly implementing the convention and apply very low standards. Capacity-building is crucial for the regime to be enhanced.	– Nearly all the regional instruments call for scientific and technical cooperation, including with regard to monitoring. Most of the protocols also cover technical assistance and capacity-building, and some also address resource mobilization and fundraising, including with regard to domestic and external funding sources as well as the private sector. However, a lack of means of implementation, along with high regional disparities in this regard, remains one of the major challenges of the regional seas programmes.

TABLE 12 How regional programmes address the main challenges under the UNCLOS regime with regard to marine plastic pollution (*cont.*)

Main challenges under the UNCLOS regime:	Responses by the regional programmes:
Compliance and enforcement:	
– In spite of the unique dispute settlement system established under UNCLOS, obligations of UNCLOS Part XII are hardly enforceable with regard to marine plastic pollution from land-based sources. Especially with regard to areas beyond national jurisdiction and domestic pollution, enforcement is particularly challenging. Reasons include: – the lack of binding standards and guidance on the required level of protection; – the fact that UNCLOS is not well tailored to the particular challenges related to sources of marine plastic pollution, including their continuous, dispersed and diffuse character; – the fact that UNCLOS does not include any form of compliance procedure as known by a number of multilateral environmental agreements. It lacks the necessary institutional setting with a supervisory body responsible for continuously assessing implementation and compliance of Part XII. Also, there are no reporting obligations under UNCLOS, and states are not required to assess their policies and implementing measures.	– Almost all of the regional conventions define a dispute settlement procedure which, as the case may be, complements UNCLOS dispute settlement. In some regions, judiciary bodies have played a role in the evolvement of the regime (for example in the OSPAR region); in others, however, resort to these bodies has been low. In addition to traditional dispute settlement procedures, some of the protocols on land-based sources provide (the development of) non-confrontational compliance procedures. These are closely related to reporting obligations. In most of the regions, parties need to report on a regularly basis to the governing body. Usually, they report on the regulatory measures they have adopted in implementation of the protocol or convention, as well as on the effectiveness of these measures, discharge permits, environmental conditions, data resulting from monitoring, and difficulties in implementing the instrument. On the basis of the reports, the governing bodies can review and evaluate compliance and make recommendations. For instance, the OSPAR Commission supervises the implementation of the OSPAR Convention and decides upon steps to bring about full compliance with it.

TABLE 12 How regional programmes address the main challenges under the UNCLOS regime with regard to marine plastic pollution (*cont.*)

Main challenges under the UNCLOS regime:	Responses by the regional programmes:
	In promotion of the implementation of its decisions or recommendations, the commission can decide on measures to assist a party to carry out its obligations. In general, compliance with regional instruments varies among regions and much depends on available resources, political commitment and institutional arrangements.
Institutional arrangements:	
– While concerns regarding the devastating impact of marine plastic debris and microplastics have been repeatedly expressed at the Meeting of the States Parties,[a] the issue has not been further addressed. UNCLOS does not provide for a suitable forum to do so, nor do the representatives participating in the Meeting of the States Parties necessarily have the right expertise (especially with regard to land-based pollution sources).	– The regional programmes provide for a network of national focal points and institutions specifically dealing with land-based pollution sources. Ideally, these institutions continuously review the state of the marine environment, the implementation of the legal agreements, cases of non-compliance, the effectiveness of measures taken in the past and the need of future actions at different levels of governance. The institutional strength of the different regimes is, however, highly variable. In some developing-country regions especially, the secretariat is poorly resourced and the governing body has little impact. Only very few regional instruments provide for advisory or technical bodies.

a UNCLOS, 'Report of the 25th Meeting of States Parties' (2015) SPLOS/287 para 90; 'Report of the 26th Meeting of States Parties' (2016) SPLOS/303 para 98; 'Report of the 27th Meeting of States Parties' (2017) SPLOS/316 paras 98 and 99; 'Report of the 28th Meeting of States Parties' (2018) SPLOS/324 paras 89 and 93.

seas programmes is further limited by the fact that internal waters, watersheds and areas beyond national jurisdiction are not covered well enough.

To put it in a nutshell, the regional schemes complement the global regime as under UNCLOS and other relevant conventions. They form an integral and essential part of the current framework and conceivably increase its effectiveness by defining clearer standards with respect to land-based pollution sources and plastics, thereby providing some guidance on how to implement the general duties in this respect. Their advantages and added value are, however, much limited to certain regions, which usually benefit from favourable geopolitical and economic conditions. Regional disparities and important gaps in their geographic scope prevent the regional programmes – at least in their current form – from giving a sufficient answer to the challenges related to marine plastic pollution.

3 Implementation at the Subregional and National Levels

The prevention and elimination of marine plastic pollution in implementation of the general and more specific obligations under UNCLOS and the regional schemes require targeted policies, well-designed laws and a range of complementary measures. They should be tailored to the specific situation of a country or a region. States can choose from a range of different strategies and need to design their own set of measures. Overall, they are still much at the beginning of a learning process, and effective, sustainable and viable solutions are still under development. Continuing assessment and evaluation of measures and strategies, as well as a meaningful exchange of information and knowhow, are, therefore, crucial for the regime to take the greatest possible effect. UNCLOS and the regional schemes require policy harmonization and common efforts, as appropriate.

A number of documents recently elaborated by international organizations and other bodies,[1306] as well as the GPA[1307] and the regional legal instruments

1306 See, among others, UNEP and NOAA (n 501); UNEP, 'Marine Litter Legislation: A Toolkit for Policymakers' (n 509); CBD Secretariat (n 375); ten Brink and others (n 354); UNEP, 'UNEA-2 Technical Report on Marine Plastic Debris' (n 509) chapters 8 and 9; UNGA Res 70/1 (2015) (n 515); A Arroyo Schnell and others, 'National Marine Plastic Litter Policies in EU Member States: An Overview' (IUCN 2017); European Commission, 'A European Strategy for Plastics in a Circular Economy' (2018) COM(2018) 28 final, with Annexes; UNEP, 'Stocktaking Rport' (n 509); *Single-Use Plastics: A Roadmap for Sustainability* (n 94); 'Legal Limits on Single-Use Plastics' (n 509).

1307 UNEP, 'GPA' (n 458) chs II and V.

and marine litter action plans[1308] provide valuable guidance to policymakers on how to prevent marine pollution from land-based sources, and marine plastic pollution in particular. Respective reports take stock of implementing strategies and measures as adopted in a number of countries around the world. This chapter gives an overview of different types and categories of measures that may be adopted, taking effect at different stages of the life cycle of plastic products (A). Specific attention will be given to the European approach, which is peculiar in that it is of a holistic nature. In a second part, the chapter analyses possible issues of consistency of measures with relevant WTO provisions (B).

A *A Typology of Implementing Strategies and Measures*

i General Overview

When implementing their duties with regard to marine plastic litter prevention, reduction and control, states should be guided by the relevant environmental management principles and thus

> apply preventive, precautionary and anticipatory approaches; ensure prior assessment of activities that may have significant adverse impacts upon the marine environment; integrate protection of the marine environment into relevant general environmental, social and economic development policies; develop economic incentives consistent with the internalization of environmental costs and the polluter pays principle; and take into account equity concerns.[1309]

Moreover, given the primordial importance of prevention, legislation and other measures should target marine plastic litter, including microplastics, at source. While litter removal is important, measures are deemed more successful when governing the production, use and disposal of products, following a life-cycle approach. Insights gained from the first part of this book suggest that main regulatory concerns in this respect include waste and resource management on the one hand, and sustainable production and consumption patterns on the other hand. Enhanced producer and consumer responsibility are among the targets of the measures to adopt. In this vein, some states and the European Union have resorted to holistic approaches and adopted comprehensive legislation based on models such as a circular economy. Many countries, however,

---

1308 See UNEP-NOWPAP (n 1204); HELCOM (n 1204); OSPAR Commission, 'Marine Litter Action Plan' (n 1204); UNEP-CAR/RCU (n 1204); UNEP-MAP (n 1204).

1309 Agenda 21 (n 450) para 17.22.

use a combination of separate measures, most of which form part of these countries' general waste management frameworks. Only a minor part of the measures is specifically designed to address marine plastic litter.[1310]

Measures can be regulatory in character but can also be of a non-regulatory nature. A specific category of measures is market-based instruments (MBI), which may be anchored in law or based on (voluntary) industry agreements. MBIs are not typical command and control measures but set economic incentives (or disincentives) in order to influence product demand and individual or corporate behaviour. MBIs allow for the internalization of environmental costs associated with the consumption of a product, and thus for an implementation in accordance with the polluter pays principle.[1311]

In 2018, UN Environment published a report on national laws and regulations addressing the manufacture, import, sale, use or disposal of selected single-use plastics and microplastics, finding that such regulation has great impact on the production of marine litter.[1312] The report took into account both product-specific regulation (such as plastic bag bans or bans of specific polystyrene products) and sector-specific regulation (such as packaging or waste management laws, investment laws and tax legislation). According to the report, 127 out of 192 countries reviewed had adopted some form of legislation to regulate plastic bags, including restrictions on the manufacture, distribution, use or trade of plastic bags, taxes and levies, and post-use disposal.[1313] The report identified restriction on free retail distribution as the most common form of plastic bag regulation. A growing number of countries have included elements of extended producer responsibility for plastic bags within legislation (43 countries) or enacted such measures for single-use plastics (63 countries). Extended producer responsibility measures may, for instance, consist of deposit and refund schemes, product take-back, or recycling targets. The report has moreover found that bans of microbeads[1314] in products through national laws or regulations are much less common, with only eight countries having adopted such bans, most of which only cover a subset of personal care products. New Zealand's law on microbeads is highlighted by the report, as it

1310 See UNEP, 'Marine Litter Legislation: A Toolkit for Policymakers' (n 509) 3.

1311 See Section 2.1.A.ii.2) above.

1312 UNEP, 'Legal Limits on Single-Use Plastics' (n 509).

1313 Regulation on sub-national level is excluded. The report notes, however, that some states in the US have adopted preemptive legislation preventing states from enacting plastic bag bans: ibid 12.

1314 For the purposes of the report, microbeads are defined as man-made plastic particles intentionally added to consumer products, typically less than or equal to 5 mm in size.

includes not only personal care wash-off products, but also abrasive household, car and industrial cleaning products.[1315]

Under the CleanSeas campaign as launched by the UN in 2017, and on the occasion of the World Environment Day on 5 June 2018, which was convened under the theme 'Beat Plastic Pollution', 57 nations covering over 60 per cent of the world's coastlines committed to take measures against marine plastic litter.[1316]

Table 13 lists a number of possible measures that states have taken in order to prevent marine plastic pollution at the stage of production, use or disposal, respectively, or eliminate it once it found its way into the environment.

ii Implementation at the Subregional Level: The Case of the European Union

The European Union is an interesting example for coordinated subregional implementation of the duty to prevent, reduce and control marine plastic pollution.[1317] European Union environmental policy is based on the precautionary principle, the preventive principle, the principle to address environmental damage at its source and the polluter-pays principle.[1318] These principles are of considerable relevance in plastic pollution mitigation strategies and are to be taken into account in the interpretation of relevant legislation. The strategic direction of European Union environmental policy is defined in the Environment Actions Programs, which since 2013 have included a target for marine litter reduction.[1319] The European Union's environmental policy is closely related to the circular economy action plan, which was first adopted in December 2015 and identifies plastics as a priority area of action.[1320] Circular economy tools can play an important role in marine plastic pollution mitigation from land-based sources. Useful tools include:

- Extended producer responsibility, especially with regard to single-use packaging items;

1315 UNEP, 'Legal Limits on Single-Use Plastics' (n 509) 3–4.

1316 UNEP, 'Annual Report 2018' (2019).

1317 For a comprehensive overview on EU regulation relevant to marine plastic pollution up to 2015, see Aleke Stöfen-O'Brien, *The International and European Legal Regime Regulating Marine Litter in the EU* (Nomos Verlag 2015) ch 4.

1318 See TFEU art 191(2).

1319 European Parliament and Council Decision No 1386/2013/EU of 20 November 2013 on a General Union Environment Action Programme to 2020 'Living well, within the limits of our planet' (7th EAP) [2013] OJ L354/171 Priority objective 1 para 28(iii).

1320 European Commission, 'Closing the Loop – an EU Action Plan for the Circular Economy' (2015) COM(2015) 614 final 13 ch 5.1.

TABLE 13 Non-exhaustive list of implementing measures according to different life-cycle stages

		Command and control measures	Market-based instruments	Other
life cycle	**Production and use**	**bans**,[a] such as: – bans of pre-production plastic – bans on oxo-degradable plastics or other types of plastic – bans and prohibitions of substitutable, unnecessary or unrecoverable products (e.g. microbeads in personal care products;[b] single-use products, including plastic bags[c] and disposable cups and cutlery[d]) – cigarette bans on beaches **technical regulations**, such as – minimal requirements with regard to the handling of pre-production plastic; obligation to use best practices[e]	– **taxes or levies** on products (such as plastic bags or single-use cups and cutlery) or materials (such as polystyrene) at the production or retail level (charged on producers, retailers or consumers).[g] Such taxes or levies set incentives with regard to individual and corporate behaviour and generate public revenues that might be invested in awareness-raising campaigns etc. – **standards and labels** informing consumers about material properties and environmental performance of a product (recyclability, degradability, expected lifespan)[h]	– awareness-raising campaigns – education programmes on sustainable production and consumption, including with respect to: consumption reduction, especially of single-use products; product substitution towards more environmentally friendly, long-living products; optimal lifespan of products; fight against planned and perceived obsolescence – reuse and recycling targets (proportion of produced or imported plastic materials to be reused or recycled) – stakeholder involvement; public–private partnerships[i] – research and development in the field of eco-friendly product and packaging design or product alternatives

TABLE 13 Non-exhaustive list of implementing measures according to different life-cycle stages (*cont.*)

	Command and control measures	Market-based instruments	Other
	– regulation of product and packaging design; quantitative and qualitative packaging regulations; regulation of the use of additives in plastics; thickness requirements with regard to plastic bags; material content requirements – obligatory use of markings and other information tools (for consumers or recyclers) **other:** – production volume limits – punitive law[f]	– **subsidization** of sustainable products or business models (production of alternative materials; plastic-free product substitutes; bulk markets and zero-waste stores) – **green public procurement** with a focus on marine litter prevention	
Disposal	– waste and wastewater management regulations, including landfill bans – penalties for littering and fly tipping/dumping[j]	– landfill taxes – waste disposal charges (may be an incentive for waste dumping if the dumping ban is not enforced)	– capacity-building and waste infrastructure investment – public–private partnerships with private waste management operators, the recycling and waste water

TABLE 13 Non-exhaustive list of implementing measures according to different life-cycle stages (*cont.*)

	Command and control measures	**Market-based instruments**	**Other**
	– reuse and recycling requirements for retailers and consumers	– extended producer responsibility (take-back obligation of products; cost internalization with regard to environmental costs, including clean-up costs) – deposit and refund schemes	treatment industries or the tyre industry; research and development of technical solutions (for washing machines, treatment plants etc.) – awareness-raising campaigns – education programmes on disposal – collection of data on plastic wastes
Coastal and marine litter	– clean-up requirements for beach tourism – obligatory tracking devices for fishing nets and other gear	– refund schemes for marine litter (e.g. fishing gear) – beach labels for litter-free beaches	– publicly organized coastal clean-ups – marine strategy in view to achieve or maintain good environmental status in the marine environment – collection of data on marine litter – impact research – research and development in the fields of monitoring and ocean and beach clean-up systems

a For a list of national bans, including impact assessment, see UNEP, *Single-Use Plastics: A Roadmap for Sustainability* (n 94) 27ff.

b See Microbead-Free Waters Act of 2015 (United States), 21 U.S.C. 331 (2015).

c As examples for bans of the manufacture and, as the case may be, import of plastic bags, see Bangladesh Environment Conservation Act of 1995, as amended 2002; Government Notice (GN) R625/2003 (South Africa); Law N°57/2008 of 10 September 2008, Law Relating to the Prohibition of Manufacturing, Importation, Use and Sale of Polythene Bags in Rwanda, Rwanda Management Authority; Notice of the Chinese General Office of State Council on Restricting the Production, Sale and Use of Plastic Shopping Bags (SC GO G [2008] No.72).

TABLE 13 Non-exhaustive list of implementing measures according to different life-cycle stages (*cont.*)

d A ban of several single-use plastic products, including cutlery, plates and stirrers, has been adopted in the EU: European Parliament and Council Directive 2019/904 of 5 June 2019 on the reduction of the impact of certain plastic products on the environment [2019] OJ L155/1 art 5.

e Without the required care in handling, pre-production plastics, such as nurdles, pellets and powders, easily leak into the environment from factories, trucks, trains and ships. Leakage happens during normal use, as well as because of accidental spills. Nurdles and pellets accumulate in the marine environment, especially on sandy beaches, in great quantities and with highly adverse impacts: see Gregory, 'Plastic Pellets on New Zealand Beaches' (n 328); Yukie Mato and others, 'Plastic Resin Pellets as a Transport Medium for Toxic Chemicals in the Marine Environment' (2001) 35 Environmental Science & Technology 318; Fabiana T Moreira and others, 'Revealing Accumulation Zones of Plastic Pellets in Sandy Beaches' (2016) 218 Environmental Pollution (Barking, Essex: 1987) 313; Alexander Turra and others, 'Three-Dimensional Distribution of Plastic Pellets in Sandy Beaches: Shifting Paradigms' (2014) 4 Scientific Reports. As an example for nurdle management regulation, see California Water Code (2007) § 13367(b)(1).

f In Kenya, for example, the making, selling and using of plastic bags is illegal and punishable by up to four years imprisonment: Gazette Notice No. 2334, Issued on March 14, 2007 under the Authority of Sections 3 and 86 of the Environmental Management and Coordination Act cap 387 on Plastic Bags 2017; Environment Management Coordination Act (EMCA) of 1999, as amended 2015.

g Similar to many other countries and municipalities, Scotland introduced a minimum 5p charge for single use carrier bags on 20 October 2014 through the Single Use Carrier Charge (Scotland) Regulations.

h See, for instance, European Commission Decision 2014/893/EU of 9 December 2014 establishing the ecological criteria for the award of the EU Ecolabel for rinse-off cosmetic products [2014] OJ L354/47.

i For a list of examples, see UNEP, *Single-Use Plastics: A Roadmap for Sustainability* (n 94) 21–22.

j The Scottish Government introduced a fixed penalty of £80 for anyone who drops litter: Environmental Protection Act 1990 Section 87. The fixed penalty notice for fly tipping is £200: ibid Section 33.

- eco-friendly product design to facilitate reuse, repair, remanufacture and recycling;
- bans for unnecessary and damaging products or activities where viable substitutes exist (e.g. microbeads in cosmetics);
- improved legislation;
- economic incentives targeting consumption in implementation of the polluter pays principle;
- transparency and labelling, especially with regard to toxic additives in plastics;
- enhanced waste management, including with regard to infrastructure and waste treatment; and
- awareness-raising among consumers, including with regard to sustainable product alternatives.[1321]

Relevant legal and policy responses at the European Union level involve both source-related and impact-related instruments. Extensive waste management legislation, including plastic-specific, belongs to the first category. In the context of the European Union's work on a circular economy, some of the relevant instruments have undergone significant adjustments in 2018. Impact-related regulation include instruments on freshwater quality, the marine environment or biodiversity protection.[1322]

The European Union's waste management legislation includes prevention measures and recycling targets for plastics. Most fundamentally, the Waste Framework Directive 'lays down measures to protect the environment and human health by preventing or reducing the generation of waste, the adverse impacts of the generation and management of waste and by reducing overall impacts of resource use'.[1323] It defines a priority order in waste prevention and management legislation and policy (waste hierarchy),[1324] as well as obligations in respect to waste prevention, recovery, reuse, recycling and disposal. It further promotes extended producer responsibility[1325] and obliges member states to adopt waste management plans and waste prevention programmes.

1321 ten Brink and others (n 354).

1322 Stöfen-O'Brien (n 1317) 270.

1323 Waste Framework Directive art 1.

1324 ibid art 4. The waste hierarchy includes: prevention; preparing for reuse; recycling; other recovery, e.g. energy recovery; and disposal; in this order of priority.

1325 In the European packaging industry, producer responsibility is widely outsourced to the Packaging Recovery Organisation (PRO) Europe, an umbrella organization for European packaging and packaging waste recovery and recycling schemes. The organization operates in most European countries through the Green Dot trademark of which PRO Europe is the general licensor. The Green Dot is used as a label on packaging of consumer goods

In 2018, the Waste Framework Directive was amended to strengthen its focus on waste prevention and resource efficiency. With the amendment, member states are called to 'facilitate innovative production, business and consumption models that reduce the presence of hazardous substances in materials and products, that encourage the increase of the lifespan of products and that promote re-use' including through re-use and repair networks, deposit-refund and return-refill schemes and sharing platforms.[1326] Minimum requirements for extended producer responsibility schemes are definded in a new Article 8a. Furthermore, member states are required to encourage environmentally friendly product designs allowing for multiple use and recycling. Quantitative targets were introduced with regard to the preparing for re-use and the recycling of municipal waste. One of the explicit aims of the amendments is to improve the protection of the oceans by reducing marine litter.

The Waste Framework Directive is complemented by the Packaging and Packaging Waste Directive, which 'aims to harmonize national measures concerning the management of packaging and packaging waste in order [...] to prevent any impact thereof on the environment'.[1327] To this end, it lays down measures aimed at preventing the production of packaging waste, reusing packaging and recovering packaging waste, thereby reducing the final disposal of such waste.[1328] Packaging may be placed on the market only if it complies with all essential requirements defined in the directive, including its Annex II. According to these requirements, packaging 'shall be so manufactured that the packaging volume and weight be limited to the minimum adequate amount to maintain the necessary level of safety, hygiene and acceptance for the packed product and for the consumer' (quantitative regulation). Moreover, 'packaging shall be designed, produced and commercialized in such a way as to permit its reuse or recovery, including recycling, and to minimize its impact on the

---

and informs consumers about the producers' contribution to the cost of recovery and recycling. Taking into account the cost of collection, sorting and recycling methods, the licence fee depends on the sort and amount of packaging materials and thus encourages producers to reduce packaging in order to save packaging costs. PRO Europe has concluded cooperation agreements with similar systems in the UK and North America in order to ensure that licensees of the Green Dot do not encounter problems when using labelled packaging in these regions. For more information, see PRO Europe, 'About Packaging Recovery Organisation Europe' <http://www.pro-e.org/about-us/who-we-are> accessed 19 February 2022.

1326 European Parliament and Council Directive 2018/851 of 30 May 2018 amending Directive 2008/98/EC on waste [2018] OJ L150/109 preambulatory para 29.

1327 Packaging and Packaging Waste Directive art 1(1).

1328 ibid art 1(2).

environment when packaging waste or residues from packaging waste management operations are disposed of' (qualitative regulation).[1329] For the purpose of monitoring and implementation assessment, member states are required to establish databases on packaging and packaging waste providing information on the magnitude, characteristics and evolution of respective waste flows (including information on the toxicity or danger of packaging materials and components used for their manufacture).[1330] The directive envisages the standardization of methods and methodologies concerning, among other things, the life-cycle analysis of packaging, measuring concentration levels of hazardous substances in packaging materials, and recycling. It also explicitly provides for the possibility for member states to adopt economic instruments in the implementation of the objectives set by the directive, to the extent that such action is not taken at the community level. Further provisions address the definition of a marking and identification system, as well as reporting.

Following a call by the European Parliament,[1331] the Packaging and Packaging Waste Directive was amended in 2015 to now include measures on reducing the consumption of lightweight plastic carrier bags.[1332] To promote the circular economy, a further amendment was adopted in 2018.[1333] It aims to minimize the generation of packaging waste, including through the use of quantitative and qualitative targets, extended producer responsibility schemes and ecomonic instruments, as well as an increase in the share of reusable packaging placed on the market and the reuse of packaging. States have

1329 On the compatibility of packaging and packaging waste regulations with WTO law, see subchapter 2.3.B.iii below. The essential requirements of the Packaging and Packaging Waste Directive have been transposed into national legislation of member states, for instance into UK law through The Packaging (Essential Requirements) Regulations 2015 (Statutory Instruments).

1330 Packaging and Packaging Waste Directive art 12.

1331 European Parliament, 'Resolution of 14 January 2014 on a European Strategy on Plastic Waste in the Environment' 2013/2113(INI) para 4.

1332 European Parliament and Council Directive 2015/720 of 29 April 2015 amending Directive 94/62/EC as regards reducing the consumption of lightweight plastic carrier bags [2015] OJ L115/11 art 1(2). The amendment requires member states to:

- adopt measures ensuring that the annual consumption level does not exceed 90 lightweight plastic carrier bags per person by 31 December 2019 and 40 lightweight plastic carrier bags per person by 31 December 2025, or equivalent targets set in weight; or
- adopt instruments ensuring that, by 31 December 2018, lightweight plastic carrier bags are not provided free of charge at the point of sale of goods or products, unless equally effective instruments are implemented.

1333 European Parliament and Council Directive 2018/852 of 30 May 2018 amending Directive 94/62/EC on packaging and packaging waste [2018] OJ L150/141.

to ensure that, by the end of 2024, extended producer responsibility schemes are established for all packaging. With the 2018 amendment, Article 6 of the Packaging and Packaging Waste Directive now includes quantitative recycling targets, including for plastic packaging.

The Landfill Directive of 1999 was also amended in 2018.[1334] It establishes operational and technical requirements for landfill operation in order to prevent negative effects on the environment, in particular the pollution of surface water, groundwater, soil and air.[1335] Since 2018, it also aims to 'ensure a progressive reduction of landfilling of waste, in particular of waste that is suitable for recycling or other recovery'. Member states shall endeavour to ensure that, as of 2030, waste suitable for recycling or other recovery, in particular contained in municipal waste, shall, in principle, not be accepted in a landfill.[1336] They moreover have to take the necessary measures to ensure that by 2035, the amount of municipal waste disposed of in landfills is reduced to 10 per cent or less of the total amount of municipal waste generated.[1337]

In January 2018, the European Commission adopted the European Strategy for Plastics in a Circular Economy. The strategy 'lays the foundations to a new plastics economy, where the design and production of plastics and plastic products fully respect reuse, repair and recycling needs and more sustainable materials are developed and promoted'.[1338] As a response to China's recent decision to restrict imports of certain types of plastic waste,[1339] the strategy defines the target that, by 2030, all plastics packaging placed on the European Union market will be either reusable or able to be recycled in a cost-effective manner. Moreover, it envisages the decoupling of plastic waste generation and economic growth, as well as the promotion of better design and new business models offering more sustainable consumption patterns. In this vein, the European Commission proposed new EU-wide rules banning some of the most common single-use plastic products, including plastic cotton buds, cutlery, plates, straws, drink stirrers, sticks for balloons and certain drinks containers. The ban was sealed by the European Parliament and the Council in March

1334 European Parliament and Council Directive 2018/850 of 30 May 2018 amending Directive 1999/31/EC on the landfill of waste [2018] OJ L150/100.

1335 Council Directive 1999/31/EC of 26 April 1999 on the landfill of waste (Landfill Directive) [1999] OJ L182/1 art 1.

1336 ibid art 5(3a).

1337 ibid art 5(5).

1338 European Commission, 'A European Strategy for Plastics in a Circular Economy' (n 1306) 1.

1339 See WTO Notification G/TBT/N/CHN/1211 of 18 July 2017.

2019.[1340] It also covers so-called oxo-plastics[1341] and is flanked by consumption reduction targets, obligations for producers and collection targets. According to the European Strategy for Plastics in a Circular Economy, an evaluation of the Urban Waste Water Treatment Directive[1342] as regards microplastics capture and removal is also envisaged. The intentional addition of microplastics to products is to be restricted under EU chemicals law.[1343] The 2019 plastic amendments to the Basel Convention have been implemented by new rules applying to shipments of plastic waste, banning the export of hazardous plastic waste and plastic waste that is hard to recycle from the European Union to non-OECD countries.[1344]

At an international level, the strategy envisages a project to reduce plastic waste and marine litter in East and South-East Asia.[1345] The planned project will promote a transition to sustainable consumption and production patterns and a significant reduction of marine litter in China, Indonesia, Japan, the Philippines, Singapore, Thailand and Vietnam, in particular. In addition, the European Union announced the allocation of EUR 100 million under its Horizon 2020 Research and Innovation programme 'to finance innovation on the development of smarter and more recyclable plastic materials, improving recycling chains as well as tracing and removing hazardous substances and contaminants from recycled plastics'.[1346] Owing to these and other measures, the European Commission expects the leakage of plastics and microplastics into the environment to decrease.

European Union regulation relevant to marine plastic pollution mitigation includes not only source-related instruments, but also impact-related

1340 European Parliament and Council Directive 2019/904 of 5 June 2019 on the reduction of the impact of certain plastic products on the environment [2019] OJ L155/1.

1341 Oxo-degradable plastics are conventional plastic materials with artificial additives allowing them to fragment more rapidly but not (necessarily) to biodegrade.

1342 Council Directive 19/271/EEC of 21 May 1991 concerning urban waste water treatment (Urban Waste Water Treatment Directive) [1991] OJ L135/40.

1343 Especially REACH.

1344 Commission Delegated Regulation (EU) 2020/2174 of 19 October 2020 amending Annexes IC, III, IIIA, IV, V, VII and VIII to Regulation (EC) No 1013/2006 of the European Parliament and of the Council on shipments of waste [2020] OJ L433/11. On the 2019 plastic amendments to the Basel Convention, see Section 2.1.D.ii.1) above.

1345 European Commission, 'A European Strategy for Plastics in a Circular Economy, Annexes' (2018) COM(2018) 28 final, Annexes.

1346 European Commission, 'Fact Sheet: European Union Commitments to Our Ocean 2018' (2018) MEMO/18/6210 <http://europa.eu/rapid/press-release_MEMO-18-6210_en.htm> accessed 19 February 2022.

instruments. These include notably the Water Framework Directive,[1347] the Marine Strategy Framework Directive (MSFD)[1348] and the Habitat Directive.[1349]

The purpose of the Water Framework Directive is to establish a framework for the protection of inland surface waters, transitional waters, coastal waters and groundwater, including through the progressive reduction of discharges, emissions and losses of specific substances and the phasing-out of discharges, emissions and losses of hazardous substances.[1350] The directive follows a river basin approach. A river basin is defined as 'the area of land from which all surface run-off flows through a sequence of streams, rivers and, possibly, lakes into the sea at a single river mouth, estuary or delta'.[1351] Member states have to adopt and periodically revise a programme of measures and establish management plans for each river basin within their territory, including measures addressing both point and non-point sources of pollution. They have to protect, enhance and restore all bodies of surface water, with the aim of achieving good surface water status in a defined period of time. Annex V contains an extensive list of quality elements for the classification and monitoring of the ecological and chemical status of surface waters and the quantitative and chemical status of groundwater.[1352]

The MSFD directive 'establishes a framework within which Member States shall take the necessary measures to achieve or maintain good environmental status in the marine environment by the year 2020 at the latest'.[1353] In order for an area to be considered as having good environmental status, it has to meet several criteria, including that 'properties and quantities of marine litter do not cause harm to the coastal and marine environment'.[1354] Each coastal Member State has to adopt a marine strategy, which is to be reviewed and updated every six years. In their marine strategies, states have to identify the measures that need to be taken in order to achieve or maintain good environmental status in

1347 European Parliament and Council Directive 2000/60/EC of 23 October 2000 establishing a framework for Community action in the field of water policy (Water Framework Directive) [2000] OJ L327/1.

1348 Marine Strategy Framework Directive.

1349 Council Directive 92/43/EEC of 21 May 1992 on the conservation of natural habitats and of wild fauna and flora (Habitats Directive) [1992] OJ L206/7.

1350 See Water Framework Directive art 1.

1351 ibid art 2(13).

1352 For a more detailed analysis of the role of the Water Framework Directive with regard to marine plastic pollution mitigation, see Stöfen-O'Brien (n 1317) 329–350.

1353 Marine Strategy Framework Directive art 1.

1354 ibid Annex I (Qualitative descriptors for determining good environmental status), Descriptor 10. See also Arroyo Schnell and others (n 1306) 4.

their marine waters.[1355] Some countries have adopted specific action plans or strategies for marine litter.[1356]

B *Consistency with WTO Law*

i Plastics and Trade

The value of global trade in plastics is over 1 trillion US dollars per year, or 5 per cent of total merchandise trade. This value is higher than previously thought, as it includes more products than are listed in the plastics chapter of the Harmonized Commodity Description and Coding System (HS), which is administered by the World Customs Organization (WCO). In particular, plastics embedded in products or used in pre-packaged products are not reported as such in the HS. Trade flows in such plastic goods is referred to as hidden flows, whose value and volume are not captured. Due to this lack of transparency, the total value of trade in plastics remains underestimated.[1357]

Trade in plastics concerns the entire life cycle from feedstock and additives to empty packaging materials and packaged products to consumer goods and plastic waste. Virtually all nations are involved in the global plastics trade, often on both the import and export side. Trade in plastic waste has grown strongly in recent decades and flows primarily from developed to developing countries, although the impact of the plastic amendments to the Basel Convention is not yet apparent in the figures. In implementation of the plastic amendments, an increasing number of OECD countries has banned or severely restricted the export of plastic waste to non-OECD countries.[1358] The number of developing countries that have severely restricted imports of plastic waste has also increased, spurred by China's far-reaching ban on most plastic waste imports in 2018. The starting drop-off of plastic waste streams from developed to developing countries is an important step in the global fight against marine plastic

1355 Marine Strategy Framework Directive art 13(1).

1356 Including, for instance, Scotland: In June 2010, the Scottish Government launched Scotland's Zero Waste Plan, which sets out a vision for a zero waste society. The plan is complemented by Scotland's Marine Litter Strategy and National Litter Strategy: Scottish Government, 'Scotland's Zero Waste Plan' (2010); 'Marine Scotland: A Marine Litter Strategy for Scotland' (2014); 'Towards a Litter-Free Scotland: A Strategic Approach to Higher Quality Local Environments' (2014). The two documents were adopted in 2014 in implementation of the MSFD and other commitments of the country, including under the OSPAR Convention. See UNEP, 'Marine Litter Legislation: A Toolkit for Policymakers' (n 509) 16–18; Arroyo Schnell and others (n 1306) 5. In their study, Schnell and others provide a broad overview on implementation policies in EU Member States.

1357 Barrowclough, Deere Birkbeck and Christen (n 91) 11.

1358 See Deere Birkbeck and others (n 134) 311–12.

pollution, as 'most recipient countries lack the capacity to recycle, incinerate or otherwise manage the scale of plastic waste they generate or import in an environmentally sound manner, resulting in extensive leakage of plastic waste into the environment'.[1359] This is an important example of the potential role of global trade in the present context.

The plastic amendments to the Basel Convention are currently still a rare example of a globally coordinated approach to trade in plastics. Apart from them, the states are largely left to their own devices. Many countries have taken trade measures that are related to plastics. Not all of these measures have an environmental objective. Such measures are also taken to ensure food safety, protect human health or protect or support domestic production, including of feedstocks. Subsidies to the fossil fuel industry contribute to virgin plastic and its feedstock being available at low prices. This gives the market little incentive to switch to recycled or alternative materials or to cut back on production.[1360] Subsidies along the value chain are thus also highly relevant and can have a positive or negative impact on the fight against global plastic pollution.

Since 2009, governments have implemented about 860 trade distorting or restricting interventions to key parts of the plastics sector, especially in the form of import tariffs and financial grants.[1361] The high number of such interventions suggests that by adjusting plastic trade policy, great incentives can be given for a more sustainable resource management, e.g. by promoting alternative materials. This potential is still being explored, with particular attention to the opportunities and risks for developing and least developed countries. For example, developing countries are among the main suppliers of natural packaging materials such as jute, abaca, coir, kenaf and sisal. They may have a comparative advantage in the production of such materials and benefit from new export opportunities.[1362]

According to the WTO's Environmental Database, WTO Members notified 128 measures affecting trade in plastics for environmental reasons from 2009 to 2018. Over 80 per cent of the measures were notified under the TBT Agreement, others under the SPS Agreement. Over 80 per cent of the measures were notified by developing countries, in particular from Africa and the

1359 Deere Birkbeck (n 952) 4.
1360 ibid 3.
1361 ibid 11.
1362 See UNCTAD (n 952). For more sustainable trade policy choices, the environmental footprint of alternative materials, whether in terms of deforestation, pesticide use in plantations or water consumption, must also be considered.

Middle East and Asia. Common trade-related measures with an environmental rationale include:

- *Import bans and restrictions*: including import licensing schemes and import bans or restrictions on plastic waste and certain plastic products, such as single-use products.
- *Export bans and restrictions*: especially in implememtation of the plastic amendments to the Basel Convention.
- *Behind-the-border measures*: including bans or restrictions, levies or taxes on the manufacture or use of certain kinds of plastics, such as single-use plastic products and materials.[1363]

Environment-related trade measures applied to the plastics sector have not yet been the subject of any formal dispute under the WTO. Hoewever, five measures have been raised as specific trade concerns in the TBT Committee.[1364] Discussions focused on the appropriateness of the standards rather than their environmental objective. The following subsections hence examine a number of issues related to the consistency of specific types of measures with WTO law.

ii Bans, Taxes and Levies

Import bans of products *per se*, such as pre-production plastics, oxo-degradable plastics or single-use plastic bags and other items, constitute the most restrictive form of a quantitative restriction and thus typically violate GATT Article XI. However, when such a ban comes along with a prohibition of domestic production, the measure may be assessed under the national treatment obligation of GATT Article III. Article III is also applicable to taxes and levies when imposed on both imported and like (or directly competitive or substitutable)

1363 Deere Birkbeck and others (n 134) 310–14. See also UNEP, 'Legal Limits on Single-Use Plastics' (n 509).

1364 These include measures implemented by Chinese Taipei ('Regulation on plastic trays and packaging'), Jamaica ('Ban on single-use plastic products'), Trinidad and Tobago ('Ban on plastic products of polystyrene'), Saudi Arabia ('Regulation on oxo–biodegrade able plastic products') and China ('Catalogue of solid wastes forbidden to import into China'): Deere Birkbeck and others (n 134) 307. France's ban on plastic cups and plates was also criticized by manufacturers and other stakeholders as a form of disguised protectionism infringing EU legislation on the free movement of goods. France was the first European country to ban plastic cups and plates. The measure forms part of France's Energy Transition for Green Growth Act. It stipulates that, by the year 2025, at least 60 per cent of the material used to produce targeted items will have to be produced from renewable sources. See, for instance, Simon Lester, 'Legitimate Regulation or Disguised Protectionism: Plastic Bag Bans' (*International Economic Law and Policy Blog*, April 2016) <http://worldtradelaw.typepad.com/ielpblog/2016/04/legitimate-regulation-or-hidden-protectionism-plastic-bag-bans.html> accessed 19 February 2022.

domestic products, provided that they accrue due to an internal event, such as the distribution, sale, use or transportation of the imported product. Sales taxes imposed on single-use plastic carrier bags typically fall into this category. Finally, GATT Article III has to be observed with regard to internal regulation, such as a regulation on pellet management.

In the context of GATT Article III, the nature and extent of the competitive relationship between imported and domestic products is crucial. In view of the border tax criteria, goods made from plastics and similar goods made from other materials (such as paper, wood, metal, porcelain, glass or natural fibres), may or may not be considered to be like products, depending on the specific circumstances of a case. For example, an argument can be made that single-use plastic cups, cutlery or dishes and single-use paper cups, cutlery or dishes are like products if they serve the same end use and different ecological impacts are not taken into account. By contrast, single-use plastic cups, cutlery or dishes and their conventional, reusable counterparts would probably not be considered like products when the differences in the products' properties are complemented by different end-uses and consumer habits (such as takeaway food versus dine in). A ban on the production and import of such single-use plastic products would therefore hardly be considered a discriminatory measure only because porcelain dishes etc. are not equally banned. The case may be different again if a state bans the import of single-use goods made from petroleum-based plastics but does not similarly regulate domestic production of corn-based plastic goods with similar end uses. The measure might be identified as one applied to imported products so as to afford protection to domestic production by the domestic corn-based plastic industry.

In the event of a tax on the import of targeted goods, GATT-consistency of the measure would be examined under Article III:2, in the event of a ban on both production and import, or a regulation affecting sale, use or distribution of these products, the case would fall under Article III:4. A mere import ban that is not complemented by a regulation of domestic products would fall under GATT Article XI.

Whenever a measure is considered to be inconsistent with GATT Article III, Article XI or any other provision under GATT, it must fulfil the requirements of Article XX in order to be compatible with the agreement. The state will have to prove that the measure serves a legitimate policy objective, with a sufficiently strong link to that objective. With regard to the measures considered in this chapter, states will probably argue that the measure either is necessary to protect human, animal or plant life or health, or is relating to the conservation of exhaustible natural resources. In the former case, the requirement that the measure must be *necessary* to reach the policy objective seems particularly challenging, especially with regard to bans. If the same effect can be produced through the use of a different, less trade-distorting measure (e.g. a tax or a label), a ban will not be justifiable. In the latter case, the measure is to be made effective in conjunction with restrictions on domestic production or consumption.

In the *US Shrimp* case, the Appellate Body accepted the protection and conservation of a species, such as marine turtles, as a legitimate policy objective even when that species does not spend all of its time or every life-cycle stage on the territory of the state invoking the exception. This does not mean, however, that the protection and conservation of exhaustible natural resources with no sufficient nexus to the territory of a state would equally be accepted as a legitimate policy objective under GATT Article XX. In this respect, a landlocked country may have a difficult position before a WTO dispute settlement body to justify a measure infringing GATT Articles III or XI in order to protect and conserve albatrosses of Midway Island (even if the items at stake can be found in the stomach of these albatrosses). Yet, plastic wastes and microplastics in the marine environment is an issue of global concern in that it negatively affects the environment and biodiversity in common areas, including the high seas and the deep seabed, the latter of which has been defined as the common heritage of mankind. Preventive measures that effectively reduce the risk of plastic accumulation in the marine environment should thus be admissible whether or not a state has access to the sea, if such measures are designed in the least trade-distorting way.[1365]

Once a sufficient link to a legitimate policy objective is demonstrated, the measure needs to pass the *chapeau* test. A ban corresponds to a halt in trade of a specific product and is therefore considered a rather harsh measure. In order to pass the *chapeau* test, facilitating factors include prior consultation, coordination and cooperation, or, if possible, an international agreement for the implementation of which the measure is taken.

iii Packaging Regulations and Other Technical Barriers to Trade

In order to curb plastic pollution, countries must be able to regulate a product over its entire life cycle, including its packaging. Packaging regulations are essential not only because 40 per cent of plastics are processed into packaging and the share of packaging in marine debris is particularly high, but also because packaging serves as a carrier of product information and advertising. Packaging regulations can thus refer to mandatory information on a product or

1365 cf Cottier, 'The Principle of Common Concern' (n 1064).

the limitation of visual purchase incentives. Qualitative regulations promote the use of less harmful materials and packaging designs, better recyclability or degradability of packaging materials, as well as lower rates of chemical contamination. Quantitative regulations aim to limit the use of plastic packaging where this is compatible with sanitary standards.

Regulations on obligatory consumer information on packaging and the mandatory use of labels, as well as regulations on PPMs (both product and non-product-related) are potential technical barriers to trade. They fall under the scope of the TBT. Mandatory packaging regulations have to meet the restrictive requirements of Article 2.2 TBT and shall not be more trade-restrictive than necessary to fulfil a legitimate objective, such as the protection of the environment.

In *Australia – Plain Packaging*, a number of states opposed a set of regulatory measures in Australia that included strict requirements on the packaging of cigarettes and cigars. The set of measures included requirements on the shape, material and colour of the packaging, uniform and unobtrusive labelling with the product brand, and the use of graphics and warnings that drew attention to the health consequences and risks of tobacco consumption, whereby these graphics and warnings had to cover significant parts of the front and back of the packaging.[1366] The objective of the Australian measures was to improve public health by reducing the use of, and exposure to, tobacco products. In its report, the panel confirmed that the regulations were technical regulations within the meaning of Article 1.1 of the TBT Agreement, in that they applied to an identifiable product or group of products (tobacco); laid down one or more characteristics of those products (including with respect to their marking, packaging or labelling); and mandated compliance with those characteristics.

After thorough analysis of the measures, the panel concluded that the complainants had not demonstrated that the measures were more trade-restrictive than necessary to fulfil a legitimate objective, within the meaning of Article 2.2 of the TBT Agreement. In its analysis, the panel referred to the broader regulatory context of the measure, which included a number of other wide-ranging tobacco control measures, such as restrictions on advertisement and promotion, taxation measures, restrictions on the sale and consumption of tobacco products, social marketing campaigns, and measures to address illicit tobacco trade. The disputed measures were therefore to be seen as part of a

---

1366 *Australia – Certain Measures Concerning Trademarks, Geographical Indications and Other Plain Packaging Requirements Applicable to Tobacco Products and Packaging* (*Australia Plain Packaging*) [2018] Panel Report WT/DS467/R, WT/DS467/R/Add.1 and WT/DS467/R/Suppl.1 para 2.32.

comprehensive suite of reforms to reduce smoking and its harmful effects.[1367] The complainants had not demonstrated that there were less trade-restrictive measures that could have achieved the same effect in this policy context. *Australia – Plain Packaging* shows that comprehensive and stringent regulation on packaging can be compatible with the TBT Agreement if it makes a meaningful contribution to a legitimate policy objective and is consistent with a country's broader policy.

Similar to other agreements covered by the WTO, international standards play an important role in the TBT Agreement. The TBT Agreement demands the use of relevant international standards as a basis for the regulations if such standards exist, unless their use is ineffective or inappropriate.[1368] If regulations are in accordance with relevant international standards, they are presumed not to create an unnecessary obstacle to international trade.[1369] The use of standards can thus play a decisive role in the implementation of UNLCOS Part XII and related provisions. Specifically, ISO and other standardisation bodies can make an important contribution to improving the sustainability of plastic production, packaging, product design and trade.[1370] ISO/TC 323 and its Circular Economy series seem promising in this respect. Yet, especially in the field of packaging regulation, additional work seems necessary. It is noteworthy in this context, however, that in *Australia – Plain Packaging*, Australia had not demonstrated its measures to be in accordance with relevant international standards, but they nevertheless withstood before the panel.

To the extent that there is no conflict of rules, the GATT remains applicable in parallel. Under the national treatment obligation of both the TBT Agreement and the GATT, the question arises whether differentiation according to packaging is allowed. To the extent that the competitive relationship between packaging materials as such (e.g. plastic bottles *vs.* glass bottles) is at stake in a dispute concerning the packaging industry, the (empty) package will be considered as a product itself. By contrast, packaged goods (such as orange juice in plastic bottles versus orange juice in glass bottles) are considered as products including their packaging when it is the competitive relationship between these products, or their market access, that is at stake. To the extent that packaging has a significant impact on the product's properties, nature and quality or consumer's tastes and habits, differentiation between products based on packaging is allowed. The potential likeness of two differently packaged but

1367 ibid paras 7.1724–32.

1368 TBT art 2.4.

1369 ibid art 2.5 second sentance.

1370 See Deere Birkbeck and others (n 134) 315–17. See also Sections 1.1.B.i.4) and 1.1.C.i above.

otherwise identical products has thus to be considered on a case-by-case basis. If it is affirmed, discriminatory treatment between the two products is only compatible with the GATT if the conditions of the exceptions clause are met.

While so far, packaging regulations have been a minor issue in WTO law, they are a topical matter in EU law, including with respect to thorough balancing of environmental and market concerns. Under the Packaging and Packaging Waste Directive, EU member states are bound to recovery and recycling targets, which are to be substantially increased in a process cycle of five years. They may strive for more ambitious targets than the ones defined in the directive, as long as the respective measures do not distort the internal market.[1371] The European Commission is to verify that the measure do not constitute an arbitrary means of discrimination or a disguised restriction on trade between member states.[1372] In addition, member states are required to set up systems for the return, collection, reuse or recovery, including recycling, of packaging and packaging wastes. These measures shall also apply to imported products under non-discriminatory conditions, including the detailed arrangements and any tariffs imposed for access to the systems, and shall be designed so as to avoid barriers to trade or distortions of competition in conformity with EU Law.[1373]

In general, packaging regulations, including marking requirements and obligatory take-back schemes, are essential features of extended producer responsibility policies, as requested under the Waste Framework Directive.[1374] Redycling targets can only be realized if the necessary infrastructure is available (including with regard to waste collection, sorting, recycling or take-back schemes) and packaging is designed in a way that allows reuse or recycling. The Court of Justice decided in this respect that a EU Member State fails to fulfil its obligations related to the free movement of goods when it replaces a global packaging-collection system with a deposit and return system without affording producers and distributors a transitional period sufficient to enable them to adapt to the requirements of the new system. According to the Court, national rules capable of hindering trade within the EU may be justified by

1371 See *Commission v Federal Republic of Germany* [2004] European Court of Justice C-463/01, 2004 I-11705 Rep Cases; *Radlberger and Spitz v Land Baden-Württemberg* [2004] European Court of Justice C-309/02, 2004 I-11763 Rep Cases.

1372 Packaging and Packaging Waste Directive art 6(10).

1373 ibid art 7 para 1.

1374 Waste Framework Directive art 8. See also European Parliament and Council Directive 2019/904 of 5 June 2019 on the reduction of the impact of certain plastic products on the environment [2019] OJ L155/1 art 8.

overriding environmental provisions only if the means which they employ are suitable for the purpose of attaining the desired objectives and do not go beyond what is necessary for that purpose.[1375] Market considerations, at least with regard to the internal market, thus form an integral part of EU packaging regulation and explicitly limits the policy space of member states in this regard.

EU obligations related to the free movement of goods go beyond obligations related to non-discrimination under the auspices of the WTO regime. The findings by the Court of Justice may nevertheless be relevant even under WTO law.[1376] Packaging regulations and deposit and return schemes can induce additional information costs, compliance costs and costs related to low volume or non-standard packaging. In particular, foreign small and medium-sized enterprises and companies from developing countries may *de facto* bear a higher burden when compared to local companies and thus be penalized by labelling and other packaging requirements.[1377] Recycled content requirements for packaging may also be problematic for foreign enterprises if such requirements do not reflect their local environmental circumstances. Consultation with trading partners, transparency of the measures, adequate transition periods and consistency with international standards (where existing) seem thus crucial in this respect. Furthermore, packaging requirements are to be notified to the countries concerned and relevant international bodies.

C *Evaluation: Implementation and the Role of Trade Law*

In order to address marine plastic pollution from land-based sources, a broad range of measures have been adopted at different levels of governance, from subregional to local. They address different life-cycle stages of plastic products and include regulatory measures, market-based instruments and other

1375 See *Commission v Federal Republic of Germany* (n 1371); *Radlberger and Spitz v Land Baden-Württemberg* (n 1371).

1376 In a case decided by a GATT Panel in 1992, a number of Canadian provinces levied a charge on all alcoholic beverage containers that were not part of a deposit and return system, or on non-refillable containers, both domestic and imported. The US argued that importers were not accorded national treatment because unlike local producers, they were not allowed to use private delivery systems to distribute their product. Because of this difference in treatment, it was cheaper for locals to establish container collection schemes. The panel found that the restrictions on the private delivery of imported beer were inconsistent with GATT Article III:4. It did not, however, address the environmental tax itself: *Canada – Import, Distribution and Sale of Certain Alcoholic Drinks by Provincial Marketing Agencies* [1992] GATT Panel Report DS17/R, BISD 39S/27.

1377 See OECD, *Extended Producer Responsibility* (n 557) 67.

measures. Overall, implementation is very uneven, both with regard to the types of measures applied as well as with regard to political priority setting and the level of protection achieved. While total or partial bans on products are common in many African countries, economic instruments and public–private partnerships typically conform to Western European policy traditions.[1378] Plastic bag bans have also been introduced in Asian countries more than a decade ago, such as in Bangladesh. Owing to poor enforcement, however, single-use plastic bags and other single-use products continue to be widely used and mismanaged in several Asian countries.[1379]

With its holistic approach to marine litter, the European Union is playing a vanguard role with regard to subregional implementation. Apart from internal regulation on sustainable waste and resource management towards a circular economy, plastic consumption reduction, especially of single-use products, and good environmental status of the marine environment, the European Union's strategy on the combat against marine litter includes extraterritorial aspects. It envisages plastic waste and marine litter reduction in several main contributing countries in East and South East Asia through technology and knowledge transfer and infrastructure projects. It moreover includes major research and innovation programmes contributing to the combat against marine plastic pollution. The effectiveness of the EU strategy very much depends on national implementation and enforcement within member states.

The US announced a more unilateral approach in 2018, but has never implemented it in this way. When he signed a bipartisan bill on marine debris in November 2018,[1380] former President Trump announced trade measures against Asian countries, which he claimed bear the primary responsibility for the US 'being inundated by debris from other countries'.[1381] The former president notably held that the US 'will be responding and very strongly' in order to hold the 'abusers' of the oceans accountable for their global impact.[1382] The then US Trade Representative, Robert Lighthizer, held in this respect that he thought of a 'more novel trade remedy', without however unsealing its character or content.[1383] However, the bill and a follow-up bill signed in 2020

1378 See UNEP, *Single-Use Plastics: A Roadmap for Sustainability* (n 94) 25.
1379 ibid 24.
1380 Save Our Seas Act.
1381 'Remarks by President Trump at Signing of S. 3508, the "Save Our Seas Act of 2018"' (n 9).
1382 ibid.
1383 'U.S. Trade Representative Lighthizer Testifies Before the Senate Finance Committee on the Administration's Trade Strategy and the United States-Mexico-Canada Ageement' (18 June 2019) <http://archive.org/details/CSPAN_20190618_141600_U.S._Trade_Representative_Lighthizer_Testifies_Before_Senate_Finance> accessed 19 February 2022.

rather provide for cooperation with affected states, as well as US support and increased US engagement in relevant international fora. The 2020 bill also provides for consideration of an international agreement dealing with land-based sources of marine debris, as well as for the consideration of marine debris in other agreements, including free-trade and investment agreements.[1384]

The policy space of states with regard to marine litter management is partially framed by international trade regulation in general, and WTO law in particular. WTO law disciplines states in the adoption of measures, particularly with regard to arbitrariness and discriminatory treatment. Yet, the potential of conflict is limited when measures are formulated in a non-discriminatory way and equally affect domestic production and imported goods. This being the case, there have been little conflicts in international trade on measures addressing marine plastic pollution to date. While the virtual absence of such conflicts may be due to the fact that awareness of the size and significance of the problem has only arisen in recent years, the wide and fast proliferation of measures in combat against marine litter at regional, national and local levels does not bear witness to widespread concerns with respect to international trade law.

An intrdisciplinary research project on *Transforming the Global Plastics Economy* is currently investigating the impact of trade policy choices on plastic pollution. Experts involved are trying to better understand trade flows and how a transition to a more sustainable use of resources can be achieved. The WTO can play an important role in this context, as a multilateral forum for trade cooperation and policy coherence. It could:

- promote transparency and monitoring of plastic trade flows, global supply chains and plastic-related trade interventions;
- serve as a forum for information sharing in this context; or
- promote policy coherence, including with regard to the reduction of tariff and non-tariff barriers to trade in plastic substitutes or technologies and services for waste disposal, recycling and cleaning.[1385]

The WTO could also envisage reform with regard to:

- *The likeness test and the role of non-product-related PPMs:* States should be able to differentiate between plastic products that, while exhibiting the same physical characteristics, have different marine plastic pollution

1384 US, Save Our Seas 2.0 Act of 2020, S.1982, 116th Cong. Sections 201-05. As an example of a free-trade agreement addressing marine debris, see: Agreement between the United States of America, the United Mexican States, and Canada (USMCA) (signed on 30 November 2018, entered into force on 1 July 2020) art 24.12.

1385 Deere Birkbeck (n 952) 13–14.

footprints, for instance due to different pellet and waste management during production or due the use of different technologies and chemicals in the production process. Acceptance of non-product-related PPMs as part of or along with the border tax criteria would allow a state to differentiate between plastic feedstock produced by the use of best practices against pellet loss, such as promoted under the Operation Clean Sweep, and other feedstock. Also, PPM-based measures regulating both import and domestic products should be dealt with under the national treatment obligation rather than as a form of a quantitative restriction, as the prohibition of quantitative restrictions does not base upon the competitive relationship among products, so that no likeness test is applied.

– *Environmental exceptions and the link requirement:* in view of the global scope of marine plastic pollution, its transboundary dispersal behaviour and the threat it poses to the global commons, the requirement of a sufficient nexus between an exhaustible natural resource to be protected by a specific measure and the territory of the state enacting the measure should be reconsidered.[1386]

After all, the analysis of the role of trade law in the implementation of UNCLOS Article 192 and related obligations shows that international trade regulation can play a restraining role with regard to the adoption of measures with (negative) extraterritorial trade effects, especially with regard to measures aiming at influencing the behaviour of actors abroad and enforcing self-set standards in other countries, including in protection of the global commons. Whether with regard to packaging requirements or producer responsibility policies, transparency of the measures, consultation, notification and adherence to international standards seem key. As outlined above, WTO law clearly gives preference to concerted action over unilateral actions.[1387] This preference is in line with the core principles under UNCLOS and general international law.

The implicit requirement under the *chapeau* of the exceptions clause that states have to make full use of diplomatic means prior to the adoption of a measure, including through, as the case may be, international negotiations, may be partially satisfied by ongoing international negotiations in the field of plastics. Given that such negotiations may take several years or decades and do not necessarily yield to a result, the *chapeau* requirement cannot hinder states from taking immediate action. Immediate action by states first and foremost focuses on the domestic level. However, marine plastic pollution is a shared

1386 The same applies to other matters deemed to be of common concern of humankind: see Cottier, 'The Principle of Common Concern' (n 1064) 67.

1387 See Section 2.1.C.iv above.

responsibility. Hence, not only should states be allowed to deal with input sources abroad but it's their responsibility to do so, in accordance with their capabilities. Input sources by foreign countries can be addressed either in a supportive way (by the use of technology and knowledge transfer, the dissemination of legal concepts and strategies, the provision of financial means, infrastructure projects etc.) or by trade remedies with the aim to exert pressure.[1388]

1388 The author argues that 'economic sanctions arguably have limited or undesirable effects with regard to environmental problems that are not caused by a lack of commitment and willingness in the first place, but to a lack of necessary means and capacities. As main contributors to marine plastic pollution mostly include lower-middle income countries, awareness-raising activities and capacity building seems the more effective means to encourage global commitment': Schäli (n 20).

Conclusion and Outlook

The legacy of the plastic age is persistent, potentially toxic and pervasive. If humankind would disappear from the world in this very moment, it would remain one of our long-lasting traces. Plastics would outlive our crop fields and gardens, and endure in the ruins of our houses, streets and towns, bridges and magnificent buildings, but also in the soil, rivers and seas. Even if we manage to stop plastic input into the ocean, existing plastic debris would continue to break down into fragments in the form of microplastics and nanoplastic particles for hundreds of years to come.[1389] These fragments and particles accumulate ecotoxic substances on their surface and are susceptible to transferring them to animal tissues when entering the food chain. Owing to the high and potentially irreversible impacts on the environment and human health, the economic impacts on the shipping and fishing industries and tourism in particular, and the costs related to these impacts, plastics have come into focus of regulatory efforts at all levels of governance. Today, plastic pollution, especially of the oceans, is high on the policy agenda of numerous international bodies and organisations. Negotiations for an international agreement are practically on the doorstep.

The process related to the reception of the topic in the political and legal agenda of individual states and the international community is exemplary. It shows how general obligations, as stipulated in UNCLOS, must be filled with specific content at different levels of governance in order to be fully effective for the problem at stake. The framework provided by UNCLOS is tested and strained by specific challenges related to marine plastic pollution from land-based sources. Various barriers have been pointed out in this regard. Some of them are related to the materials themselves, social behaviour patterns, or economic circumstances and inequalities; others are legal in nature. Legal and other barriers are inherently interrelated. The main findings with regard to these barriers shall be brought to the point once again in this concluding chapter. This chapter also looks ahead, as there are various ways on the horizon in which the identified challenges can be dealt with.

1389 See UNEP, *UNEP Year Book 2014: Emerging Issues in Our Global Environment* (n 292) 52.

© JUDITH SCHÄLI, 2022 | DOI:10.1163/9789004508613_005
This is an open access chapter distributed under the terms of the CC BY-NC 4.0 license.

1 Challenges Related to Plastic Materials, Social Behaviour and Economic Capacities

Their high degree of biological inertness, the toxic or ecotoxic effects of some of their components or additives, and their abundance constitute some of the most challenging features of plastic wastes. Moreover, plastic debris spreads easily and widely, so that macro- and microplastics, and most likely nano-plastics, occur in all compartments of the sea, from the surface to the seabed. Owing to the wide dispersal and constant fragmentation, open-ocean clean-up projects have had little success, and no technology has yet been created that would allow large-scale deplasticization of the ocean without endangering the life that occurs there.[1390]

Yet, while there is growing awareness with regard to the size, invasiveness and structural nature of the problem and increasing public outcry, plastic production continues to grow. This typical contradiction between people's ecological ideas and their actual behaviour may partially be explained by the sluggishness of the regulatory framework conditions in the sudden event of environmental problems. In the case of plastic pollution, challenging factors in this regard include the cumulative and indirect nature of the risk associated with the production, use and disposal of plastics, the diffuseness of this form of pollution and its global scale. As a typical collective action problem, most people contribute to (marine) plastic pollution in one way or the other, but no one is held responsible for it. The protection of the oceans against plastic pollution from land-based sources inherently is a shared responsibility, involving all actors within the life cycle of plastic products, and all levels of governance.

Marine plastic pollution from land-based sources is closely related to inadequate waste management infrastructure, especially in densely populated coastal areas of low and lower-middle-income countries. Illegal dumping sites, often situated close to rivers or shores, are particularly widespread in such areas, where rapid urban expansion comes along with poor waste management services. Poor waste management in developing countries is partially due to inadequate financing and insufficient administrative capacities, and

1390 A number of models of marine garbage collectors are currently under development or in early testing phases. They mainly target surface plastics but miss plastics below a certain benchmark size, as well as submerged plastics or benthic plastics. Researchers disagree on the environmental impact of large-scale marine garbage collectors, but promotion campaigns are being carried out to their benefit, nourishing the public misconception that new technologies are making marine plastic pollution easy to manage.

the high costs related to waste management infrastructure and activity. Low capacities often come along with information barriers, including a lack of data on products and wastes, low transparency and a lack of public awareness and good sanitary practices.[1391] Developing countries moreover face a couple of technological barriers: owing to the different waste composition, waste management practices from high-income countries, such as waste incineration, are not necessarily a valid disposal option for some regions. Plastic products are also often designed with no regard for the prevailing conditions in the receiving countries, including a number of East Asian countries. Finally, financial and economic barriers are often complemented by regulatory deficits and limited enforcement.[1392]

On the other hand, marine plastic pollution is related to social behaviour, consumption and production patterns and the economic system as a whole. While waste collection and disposal systems in high-income countries often are more sophisticated and benefit form high-level technologies, the conclusion that these countries do not contribute to marine plastic pollution seems erroneous. As high-income countries have the highest per capita waste generation rates, their so-called grey footprint may be considerable when taking into account production wastes from goods consumed domestically but produced abroad and shipped globally.[1393] A grey plastic footprint also includes plastic wastes generated by inhabitants during their holidays abroad. Packaging and disposable goods make up a large proportion of the wastes encountered in marine environments, along with primary and secondary microplastic particles from tyre wear, laundering, cosmetics, plastic production and abrasives. The wide and improvident use of disposable or non-recoverable plastic items is a contributing factor to what seems an avoidable part of the environmental, social and economic costs related to marine plastic pollution. With regard to microplastics such as from laundering and tyre wear, even high-income countries have not yet been able to master many technological challenges and are dependent on innovation from academia and the private sector.

In the absence of effective clean-up technologies, prevention and input reduction appear to be the key to any successful mitigation strategy.[1394] Moreover, such mitigation strategies need to be based on a life-cycle approach, cost internalization and the polluter pays principle, and transnational support and solidarity. They need to address all relevant actors and take into account different

1391 See UNEP, 'AHEG Background Paper on Marine Litter' (n 21) para 19.
1392 See ibid para 19.
1393 On plastic footprint methodologies, see Boucher and others (n 229).
1394 See Jambeck and others (n 291) 768.

regulatory areas in a holistic manner. Enhanced consumer and producer responsibilities and a sustainable resource management are key elements, as is the regulation of packaging, disposables and non-recoverable microplastics.

2 Legal Framework and Regulatory Challenges

UNLCOS provides a relatively strong general framework on the protection of the marine environment and the regulation of marine pollution – a framework that essentially builds on global and regional cooperation. When interpreted in the light of contemporary international environmental law, then the obligations as contained in UNCLOS are based on the core elements of due diligence, environmental impact assessment and precaution. UNCLOS and relevant case law moreover suggest that in the adoption of national mitigation measures, due regard has to be given to the conservation and the preservation of ecosystems. The general obligations of states under UNCLOS and related instruments are given even more weight by acknowledgement by the international community of the severity and global scope of the problem, amounting to a common concern of humankind.

Yet, as a framework instrument, UNCLOS does not by itself give a sufficient response to the problem of marine plastic pollution. The general duty to protect and preserve the marine environment, as stipulated in UNCLOS, needs to be substantiated by internationally agreed legally binding standards on land-based sources of pollution. Challenges in this regard include deficiencies in the implementation and enforcement of existing standards and regulations, regulatory *lacunae*, including with regard to the geographical scope of application of legally binding commitments, and a need for coordination and coherence at the global and regional levels.[1395]

A *Implementation and Enforcement*

Difficulties in the implementation and enforcement of UNCLOS Part XII are related to the dispersed nature of marine plastic pollution, its diffuse sources and cumulative effects, as well as the weak link between a potential polluter and such negative impacts. The traditional, interstate enforcement mechanisms, which UNCLOS widely relies on, do not seem to provide an effective means to appropriately address these challenges. Uncertainties remain with regard to due diligence obligations and the standard of care, especially in a

1395 See UNEP, *Marine Litter* (n 284) 7.

developing-country context (is existing regulation of plastic production, use and disposal in a given country sufficient to conform to UNCLOS obligations?), the threshold of environmental damage (is there an acceptable level of plastic input into the seas? What would that level be? How can environmental damage be adequately quantified?) or the burden of proof (in order to bring a case under UNCLOS against a specific country, is it enough to show that beached plastics stem from a factory of that country?). Further uncertainties relate to the protection of domestic areas, including highly sensible coastal ecosystems, and the global commons, such as the high seas and the deep seabed.

Guidance for implementation can be provided by various political commitments by the international community and several international and regional bodies, as well as by regional schemes on the protection and conservation of the marine environment, especially the regional seas conventions and protocols addressing land-based sources of pollution. The analysis of the regional schemes has shown that they complement the global framework and form an integral and essential part of the current regime, as they define clear standards with respect to land-based pollution sources and plastics. The effectiveness of the regional frameworks, however, depends heavily on political willingness, as well as geopolitical and economic conditions. The regional system thus bears a risk of regulatory fragmentation and a pluri-standard regime, in which especially developing countries, and among them some of the most polluting countries, do not commit or benefit. Nonetheless, the experience that has been gained through the regional programmes allows the identification of important building blocks for a functioning system in terms of implementation and enforcement. These include the creation of a compliance facilitation procedure with reporting obligations by states on national implementation, as well as global implementation review and a strong capacity-building scheme.

At the national level, implementation is uneven and reflects much the same patterns as identified at the regional level. Poor implementation and enforcement, including in Asian countries, is due to low capacities, but also to a lack of clear targets and firm numerical limits in regulations.[1396] Poor waste management services are particularly typical in rural areas, in which little disposal options are available. Improvements in waste management practices depend on available funding and capacity-building, including through technology and knowledge transfer.[1397] On the other hand, national experiences show how

1396 See UNEP, 'AHEG Background Paper on Marine Litter' (n 21) para 14.

1397 According to the concept of common concern of humankind as developed by Cottier and others, the recognition of a problem as a common concern of humankind entails the obligation of states to make contributions commensurate with their level of GDP to

states can set an enabling environment and stimulate behavioural changes and innovation in product design and technologies through the adoption of mitigation policies, regulatory measures and a broad range of market-based instruments. Behavioural changes include consumption reduction of disposable items, packaging, non-recoverable microplastics and hardly recyclable products, including compounds, but also littering reduction, increased recycling, and disposal control. Industry involvement seems key, including through public–private partnerships, green public procurement, and the promotion of best practices and technologies. National implementation moreover shows that the measures' effectiveness much depend on information, education and public awareness.[1398]

Due to the large trade flows in plastics, trade policies also play an essential role. In particular, coherent and coordinated trade policy responses have great potential to induce a shift towards more sustainable resource management. International standards can serve a unified approach to plastics in this context and also play a role with regard to WTO consistency, especially under the TBT Agreement.

B *Regulatory* Lacunae

The absence of legally binding standards in the main polluting regions (including East Asia and South East Asia) is one of the most evident gaps of the regime.[1399] Apart from the Basel Convention as amended in May 2019, which regulates transboundary movements of plastic wastes in particular, there are no global legally binding standards on land-based sources of plastic pollution, nor is the Regional Seas Programme sufficiently effective in these regions. The geographical scope of the regional seas programmes is further limited by the fact that internal waters, watersheds and areas beyond national jurisdiction are usually not covered. There are also geographical gaps in the coverage of relevant global agreements, as, for instance, the US is not a member of UNCLOS, the CBD or the Basel Convention.

Since UNCLOS Part XII gives clear priority to national regulation in the field of land-based pollution sources, there is little international control with regard

the global effort in solving the identified problem. Financial contributions are complemented by contributions in kind relevant to the issue of common concern, inclduing in the fields of trade, investment and technology transfer: see Cottier, 'The Principle of Common Concern' (n 1064) 62.

1398 See Kershaw and others (n 96) 28.

1399 There are no regional legal instruments on the protection of the marine environment applying to the South Asian Seas, South-East Asian Seas, North-West Pacific and South-West Atlantic regions.

to the most problematic type of pollution sources. Although UNCLOS stipulates that international standards, including non-legally binding standards such as the GPA, SDG 14 or the Honolulu Strategy, must be taken into account in the adoption of national measures, the weakened incorporation mechanism is not effective enough in this area to give sufficient normative content to the general due diligence obligations under Part XII.

Instead, guidance for implementation can be drawn from the regional conventions. Most relevant instruments request their parties to regulate several industry sectors and activities that are major sources of plastic pollution, and to formulate action plans, programmes and measures in this regard, including the phase-out of products. They define standards on how to regulate and control point and non-point sources of marine pollution and require states to set up a national system of authorization, monitoring, and inspection. Environmental management principles, such as the precautionary principle or approach, the polluter pays principle, the principle of sustainable development, and the ecosystem approach, play an important role in some of the regional instruments on land-based sources, including from the newer generation. The use of BATs and BEPs, as well as reference to the GPA, is also highly common among these instruments. Some regional instruments provide for the possibility of defining marine protected areas, require their parties to take account of hotspots and endangered species, or set up more detailed standards on environmental impact assessment. Such specific standards, as stipulated in some regional instruments, can serve as a basis for reporting obligations and compliance assessment procedures.[1400]

In order to close the significant geographical gap in the scope of the regime and to especially include developing countries with high levels of mismanaged plastics, harmonized mitigation standards must be anchored at the international level. Yet, in order for these states to be effectively integrated into a system of detailed binding standards in the field of land-based plastic pollution, a much stronger and more effective capacity-building system is needed. Without the pledge of financial resources and the necessary technology and knowledge transfer, the integration is likely to have little impact and does not seem politically realistic. With regard to plastics, technology and knowledge transfer is important with respect to waste collection and disposal systems, sewage and wastewater treatment, chemical safety, green design, recycling, biodegradable materials, monitoring methods and methodology, and valuable clean-up technologies. Financial assistance is needed for covering administrative

1400 See Section 2.2.B.ii above.

and institutional costs related to plastic pollution mitigation and prevention (including for regional seas offices), as well as the costs related to waste infrastructure, waste management, education and awareness campaigns, and coastal cleanups. Information exchange at both national and regional levels, and legal formation are also highly important.

C *Coherence*

As marine litter affects many different regulatory areas, coherence is an issue of concern at all levels of governance. At the national level, these regulatory areas are usually managed by different ministries or political entities. The regulation of packaging or products, for example, often falls within the competence of the economic authorities, which sometimes lack of the necessary environmental background knowledge and may have a more powerful position in internal decision-making processes when compared to environmental offices. As a consequence, other interests, including industrial or health-related (e.g. hygiene standards in packaging) may be placed above the interest in reducing marine litter. Internal fragmentation is a hindering factor in the adoption of integral plastic waste mitigation strategies and life-cycle management of plastics.

At the international level, several legal instruments are relevant to marine plastic pollution, some of which have been ratified almost universally. The member states and bodies of the Basel and Stockholm Conventions, as well as the CBD, CMS and other biodiversity-related conventions have included the plastic issue in their focus and addressed it within their scope of application. They have commissioned studies, drafted policy guidelines, promoted awareness-raising and adopted measures in their specific field of activity. The Basel Convention has adjusted its scope of application to now include plastic wastes and to better address them throughout their life cycle. As marine plastic pollution is a cross-cutting concern involving different fields of law, none of these instruments covers all relevant aspects in a holistic way. In order to reduce the risk of fragmentation, the bodies to these conventions work in a mutually supportive way, with increasing cooperation and information exchange.

With its reference mechanism, UNCLOS has the potential to play a bridging role and strengthen coherence. In accordance with UNCLOS Article 237 and the principle of systemic integration, the obligation to protect and preserve the marine environment includes an obligation to take other relevant instruments into account and implement corresponding duties to the extent that they are applicable and compatible with UNCLOS Part XII.

The coherence issue is potentially more complex with respect to instruments that do not serve congruent policy objectives, such as international trade regulation agreements. There have so far been no formal disputes specifically related to plastic pollution mitigation measures under WTO dispute settlement. The WTO dispute settlement system currently bears the risk of complete paralysis as the re-election of Appellate Body members is blocked.[1401] In view of the recent proliferation of national (or local) measures specifically designed to reduce marine plastic pollution, concrete reform options for WTO obligations have nevertheless been identified. On the one hand, states should be allowed to treat products with different ecological footprints (and different marine pollution footprints) differently, regardless of whether they differ in physical properties. This demand has already been formulated on several occasions in the context of the long-running debate on non-product-related PPMs. With respect to plastic products, typical non-product-related PPMs include, for instance, pellet and waste management during production and transportation. On the other hand, the nexus requirement should be reconsidered. With regard to (the trading of) a specific plastic product, preventive measures that effectively reduce the risk of plastic accumulation in the marine environment should be admissible whether or not a state has access to the sea (or any other type of territorial link), if such measures are designed in the least trade-distorting way. The WTO's role in the fight against plastic pollution can go beyond such legal adjustments, e.g. by serving as a platform to promote transparency in plastic trade flows or trade policy coherence.

In general, WTO obligations are geared towards cooperation instead of coercion, the avoidance of discrimination and protectionism, joint negotiations, harmonized internationally agreed standards and the creation of a level playing field.[1402] If these objectives are adequately taken into account in the adoption of measures, compatibility with WTO law is usually unproblematic. In this sense, promotion of internationally agreed standards on plastic pollution mitigation from land-based sources goes in line with the strategic thrust of the WTO regime. Such standards would potentially alleviate conflicts, enhance policy harmonization and rise the minimal level of protection in support of a level playing field. Measures such as bans of non-recoverable microplastics in products, which often end up in waterways and the sea, could be more easily justified before a WTO panel when required by an internationally agreed instrument. The same is true for technical regulations, such as quantitative or qualitative packaging regulations. The formulation of internationally agreed standards would thus promote coherence between the two regimes and their

1401 Tom Miles, 'U.S. Blocks WTO Judge Reappointment as Dispute Settlement Crisis Looms' *Reuters* (27 August 2018) <https://www.reuters.com/article/us-usa-trade-wto-idUSKCN1LC19O> accessed 19 February 2022.

1402 See *US Shrimp* (n 677) 63–76 paras 161–86. cf *Tuna II* (*Mexico*) (n 965) 324–31 paras 124–28.

mutual supportiveness. It would moreover strengthen the member states' regulatory authority to enact environmental legislation under the WTO regime.

3 Successes and Way Forward

To support the decision-making process, the UN Environment Executive Director was requested by the UNEA to present reports on both short- and long-term approaches to the problem of marine plastic debris and microplastics, as well as on assessment results with regard to the effectiveness of relevant international, regional and subregional governance strategies and approaches.[1403] The studies are part of a dynamic process towards a common response to the challenge of marine plastic pollution by the international community. The outcome of the process is currently open, even if the call for an international agreement is loud.[1404] The central fora of discussion in this context are the UNEA and the Ad Hoc Open-Ended Expert Group on Marine Litter and Microplastics that has been established at UNEA-3.[1405] The extert group could occasionally be replaced by an intergovernmental negotiation committee, e.g. at UNEA-5 in February 2022. At the beginning of this process is the recognition of the fundamental effects and severe impacts of plastic pollution and their global scale, which are of concern to the international community as a whole. A thorough review of the legal framework in this area constitutes an essential part of the process. The clarifications in this book contributed to this review and have been fed into the process.

The UN Environment reports present various options for further action, including the option of creating an international legally binding instrument on (marine) plastic pollution and microplastics.[1406] Since then, the possible content of such an agreement has been widely discussed. Possible building blocks include the following pillars:

- *monitoring and reporting*: including harmonisation of definitions and methodologies; national inventories on plastic production and use, plastic waste

---

1403 UNEP, 'UNEA-2 Technical Report on Marine Plastic Debris' (n 509); 'UNEA-3 Legal Report' (n 414). The author of this book has participated in the preparation of the two studies behind the executive director's reports as a member of the Advisory Group.

1404 See Environmental Investigation Agency and others, 'Convention on Plastic Pollution: Toward a New Global Agreement to Address Plastic Pollution' (2020).

1405 UNEA Resolution 3/7 (2017) (n 523) para 10.

1406 UNEP, 'UNEA-3 Legal Report' (n 414) 124–142. See also UNEP, 'UNEA-3 Legal Report – Summary for Policy Makers' (n 509).

management and trade; periodic reporting on national action; implementation assessment;
- *plastic pollution prevention*: including global objectives; national action plans; labelling and product design standards and certification schemes;
- *coordination*: including through reference to different international instruments and bodies; definition of their role;
- *technical and financial support*: including scientific and socio-economic assessment panels; implementing agencies; financial mechamisms; monitoring and reporting; and a compliance facilitation mechanism.[1407]

The present analysis confirms the need for such a plastics-specific, binding global instrument and identifies similar possible building blocks of such an agreement: with the overriding goal of minimizing global plastic waste generation and eliminating input into the marine environment, indispensable elements include *harmonized pollution prevention standards* with regard to the whole life-cycle of plastics and both point and non-point sources, and a *strong capacity-building scheme*. A global instrument on plastics would inform the obligation to protect and preserve the marine environment with regard to plastics and could provide a platform for states to formulate national commitments towards a sustainable future in implementation of plastic-related targets under SDG 14.

National implementation of global standards can take place through nationally determined implementation targets[1408] relating to different areas (such as waste collection, recycling or consumption rates) depending on the situation of a specific country. Implementation takes place in accordance with environmental principles such as the polluter pays principle and sustainable development, and through various tools, including regulatory measures and MBIs, green public procurement and educational measures. With regard to substantive obligations, the role of environmental management principles and institutional arrangements, the instrument could build upon the experiences gained under the regional instruments on marine pollution and the GPA.

In order to strive for harmonized standards, capacity needs, especially of developing countries and small island states, must be identified and taken into account. An effective and efficient funding scheme is essential to provide for

1407 See Environmental Investigation Agency and others (n 1404) 7. See also UNEP, 'Report of the First Meeting of the Ad Hoc Open-Ended Expert Group on Marine Litter and Microplastics' (n 524) paras 62 and 65; 'Progress in the Work of the Ad Hoc Open-Ended Expert Group on Marine Litter and Microplastics Established by Resolution 3/7 – Report of the Executive Director' (n 525) para 11(c). cf Simon and Schulte (n 1137).

1408 cf 2015 Paris Agreement art 4.

the necessary means of implementation, including through the mobilization of financial resources from public and private sources. The scheme should also build on the cooperation on and access to science, technology and innovation, as well as the development, transfer and dissemination of environmentally sound technologies to developing countries. Assistance should be provided to governments in accessing available resources for marine litter activities.[1409]

Enforceability of agreed standards depends on flanking procedural obligations related to monitoring and reporting, compliance facilitation, implementation review, and the institutional set-up.[1410] A compliance facilitation procedure would complement and supplement the UNCLOS dispute settlement regime. A special instrument on marine plastic pollution in furtherance of the principles as set forth in UNCLOS would inform the more general provisions of UNCLOS Part XII. On the other hand, UNCLOS would strengthen the effect of international standards on marine plastic pollution mitigation adopted by a competent international organization or a diplomatic conference.

While UNCLOS basically provides an optimal basis for a coherent framework in normative terms, UNCLOS has not been seriously considered the institutional home for any kind of platform instrument promoting cooperation among relevant conventions in the field of marine plastic pollution. UN Environment seems perhaps a more appropriate candidate in this regard. It administers several of the mentioned treaties, as well as the Regional Seas Programme, several regional seas conventions, the GPA and the GPML. It is a driver in the promotion of public awareness, research, data collection and policy formulation. At the UNEA, possible options for future action are discussed in terms of both content and institutions, and new processes are initiated. The UNEA is a political body capable of taking action and making binding decisions. In the legal assessment for UNEA-3, UN Environment has therefore been identified as a strong candidate for the institutional home of a new global architecture on marine plastic litter and microplastics.[1411]

Shortly after UNEA-4, five Northern European countries[1412] adopted a ministerial declaration calling for a global agreement to combat marine plastic litter and microplastics. In the declaration, they held that the issue 'by its global

1409 See UNEP, 'Progress in the Work of the Ad Hoc Open-Ended Expert Group on Marine Litter and Microplastics Established by Resolution 3/7 – Report of the Executive Director' (n 525) para 11(c).

1410 See UNEP, 'AHEG Background Paper on Marine Litter' (n 21).

1411 UNEP, 'UNEA-3 Legal Report – Summary for Policy Makers' (n 509) 11.

1412 Nordic Cooperation, including Denmark, Finland, Iceland, Norway and Sweden (along with the Faroe Islands, Greenland and the Åland Islands).

nature cannot be solved by any one country alone and that effective, dedicated global governance is needed to address existing gaps and promote coherence, coordination and effective prioritization of our efforts'. They underlined 'the need for a stronger global response for the effective implementation of measures to reach [SDG 14]' and called 'for the development of a global agreement to more effectively and comprehensively deal with the issue of marine plastic litter and microplastics on a global level in an integrated manner'.[1413]

Also, in April 2019, the Basel Convention was amended to better include plastic wastes in its legally binding framework. Also, since the Ban Amendment came into force, transboundary movements of hazardous wastes from OECD countries to developing countries are generally no longer permitted under the Basel Convention. The combined effect of the plastic amendments to the Basel Convention, the Ban Amendment and unilateral import restrictions by several Asian countries might attenuate the phenomenon of plastic scraps dumped on international markets – a phenomenon that undercuts recycling efforts in importing developing countries. The trade flow of plastic wastes from industrialised countries to developing countries with limited disposal options will hopefully be interrupted to a large extent and OECD countries will increasingly have to dispose of their plastic waste domestically. With the Plastic Waste Partnership, a platform has moreover been created under the Basel Convention to mobilize business, government, academic and civil society actors and to identify national, regional and international initiatives and actors that can provide capacity-building, technical advice and technology transfer.[1414]

In addition to international efforts and negotiations within the framework of the UNEA and multilateral environmental agreements such as the Basel Convention, various positive developments can be observed at the subregional and national levels. Particularly noteworthy in this respect are the unilateral commitments and pledges of high-income countries and the EU to provide financial assistance to Asian countries for marine litter prevention and

1413 Nordic Cooperation, 'Nordic Ministerial Declaration on the Call for a Global Agreement to Combat Marine Plastic Litter and Microplastics' (*Nordic Cooperation*, 10 April 2019) <https://www.norden.org/en/declaration/nordic-ministerial-declaration-call-global-agreement-combat-marine-plastic-litter-and> accessed 19 February 2022. The Nordic Council of Ministers also agreed to provide financial support for a Nordic Report to inform decision-making and explore possible elements and approaches of such a new global agreement.

1414 Basel Convention, 'Plastic Waste Partnership: Overview' (2019) <http://www.basel.int/Implementation/Plasticwastes/PlasticWastePartnership/tabid/8096/Default.aspx> accessed 19 February 2022.

mitigation programmes. Norway, for instance, established a multidonor trust fund in the World Bank to improve waste management and prevent marine litter, and allocated US$13 million to the fund in 2018.[1415]

Another important source of funding and capacity-building measures with potentially great leverage and impact is the private sector. A growing number of industry initiatives (e.g. the Global Plastics Alliance; Circulate Capital; Operation Clean Sweep) focus on marine debris mitigation projects or invest in such projects or sound waste management practices and infrastructure. Private-sector engagement also plays an important role in research and development, innovation and the dissemination of best environmental practices and environmentally friendly technologies.[1416]

A look at the ongoing process and proliferating activities concerning marine plastic litter and microplastics at all levels of governance shows the complexity and dynamics of our response to global man-made challenges. The creation of a convention, as proposed in this book and currently being considered in relevant fora, is only one element of this response. It is a response that must include pioneers and free riders, developing and developed nations, polluters and sufferers. It encompasses every individual and the international community as a whole. It encompasses all the regulatory areas concerned and must be designed in a coherent way. It is based on our vision of our planet, our environment and our lives, all of which depend on a healthy, living and life-sustaining ocean. The ocean reflects us and our society. It mercilessly shows the limits of our one-way economy. Thus, our response must also include a change in thinking and action towards sustainability and circularity.

1415 UNEP, 'Report of the First Meeting of the Ad Hoc Open-Ended Expert Group on Marine Litter and Microplastics' (n 524) para 67.

1416 See UNEP, 'AHEG Background Paper on Marine Litter' (n 21) para 23.

Bibliography

Adede AO, *The System for Settlement of Disputes Under the United Nations Convention on the Law of the Sea: A Drafting History and a Commentary* (BRILL 1987).

Adibi JJ and others, 'Prenatal Exposures to Phthalates among Women in New York City and Krakow, Poland' (2003) 111 Environmental Health PerspC.

Aguado J and Serrano DP, *Feedstock Recycling of Plastic Wastes* (Royal Society of Chemistry 1999).

Alexander S, 'Planned Economic Contraction: The Emerging Case for Degrowth' (2012) 21 Environmental Politics 349.

Aliani S and Molcard A, 'Hitch-Hiking on Floating Marine Debris: Macrobenthic Species in the Western Mediterranean Sea' (2003) 503 Hydrobiologia 59.

Allsopp M and others, *World Watch Report 174: Oceans in Peril: Protecting Marine Biodiversity* (Worldwatch Institute 2007).

Anastas PT and Warner JC, *Green Chemistry: Theory and Practice* (Oxford University Press 1998).

Anastas PT and Zimmerman JB, 'Design through the 12 Principles of Green Engineering' (2003) 37 Environmental Science & Technology 94A.

Anderson D, 'Freedoms of the High Seas in the Modern Law of the Sea' in David Freestone, Richard Barnes and David Ong (eds), *The Law of the Sea: Progress and Prospects* (Oxford University Press 2006).

Andrade AJM and others, 'A Dose-Response Study Following in Utero and Lactational Exposure to Di-(2-Ethylhexyl)-Phthalate (DEHP): Non-Monotonic Dose-Response and Low Dose Effects on Rat Brain Aromatase Activity' (2006) 227 Toxicology 185.

Andrady AL, 'Microplastics in the Marine Environment' (2011) 62 Marine Pollution Bulletin 1596.

Andrady AL, and Neal MA, 'Applications and Societal Benefits of Plastics' (2009) 364 Philosophical Transactions of the Royal Society B: Biological Sciences 1977.

Andrews ES and others, *Guidelines for Social Life Cycle Assessment of Products: Social and Socio-Economic LCA Guidelines Complementing Environmental LCA and Life Cycle Costing, Contributing to the Full Assessment of Goods and Services within the Context of Sustainable Development* (Catherine Benoît and Bernard Mazijn eds, UNEP 2009).

Ankley G and others, 'Overview of a Workshop on Screening Methods for Detecting Potential (Anti-) Estrogenic/Androgenic Chemicals in Wildlife' (1998) 17 Environmental Toxicology and Chemistry 68.

Arcuri A, 'Food Safety at the WTO After "Continued Suspension": A Paradigm Shift?' in Antonis Antoniadis, Robert Schütze and Eleanor Spaventa (eds), The European Union and Global Emergencies: A Law and Policy Analysis (Hart Publishing 2010).

Arroyo Schnell A and others, 'National Marine Plastic Litter Policies in EU Member States: An Overview' (IUCN 2017).

Atapattu SA, *Emerging Principles of International Environmental Law* (Transnational Publishers 2006).

Attard DJ and others (eds), *The IMLI Manual on International Maritime Law Volume III: Marine Environmental Law and International Maritime Security Law* (Oxford University Press 2016).

Backer H and others, 'HELCOM Baltic Sea Action Plan – A Regional Programme of Measures for the Marine Environment Based on the Ecosystem Approach' (2010) 60 Marine Pollution Bulletin 642.

Baekeland LH, 'Method of Making Insoluble Products of Phenol and Formaldehyde', U.S. Patent No. 942699 (1907).

Bagwell LS and Bernheim BD, 'Veblen Effects in a Theory of Conspicuous Consumption' (1996) 86 The American Economic Review 349.

Barcena A, 'An Overview of the Oceans in Agenda 21 of the 1992 United Nations Conference on Environment and Development' (1992) 25 Marine Pollution Bulletin 107.

Barnes DKA, 'Biodiversity: Invasions by Marine Life on Plastic Debris' (2002) 416 Nature 808.

Barnes DKA, 'Remote Islands Reveal Rapid Rise of Southern Hemisphere Sea Debris' (2005) 5 Scientific World Journal 915.

Barnes DKA, and others, 'Accumulation and Fragmentation of Plastic Debris in Global Environments' (2009) 364 Philosophical Transactions of the Royal Society B: Biological Sciences 1985.

Barnes DKA, and Milner P, 'Drifting Plastic and Its Consequences for Sessile Organism Dispersal in the Atlantic Ocean' (2005) 146 Marine Biology 815.

Barnett RC, Bhattacharya J and Bunzel H, 'Choosing to Keep Up with the Joneses and Income Inequality' (2009) 45 Economic Theory 469.

Barrowclough D, Deere Birkbeck C and Christen J, 'Global Trade in Plastics: Insights from the First Life-Cycle Trade Database' UNCTAD Research Paper No 53 UNCTAD/SER.RP/2020/12.

Basel Convention, 'Basel Convention Technical Guidelines on Wastes Collected from Households (Y46)' (1994).

Basel Convention, 'Basel Convention Technical Guidelines on Incineration on Land (D10)' (1995).

Basel Convention, 'Basel Convention Technical Guidelines on Specially Engineered Landfill (D5)' (1995).

Basel Convention, 'Technical Guidelines for the Identification and Environmentally Sound Management of Plastic Wastes and for Their Disposal' (2002) UNEP/CHW.6/21.

Basel Convention, 'Interim Guidelines on the Hazardous Characteristics H12-Ecotoxic' (2003).

Basel Convention, 'Approach to Basel Convention Hazard Characteristic H11: Characterization of Chronic or Delayed Toxicity' (2004) UNEP/CHW. 7/11/Add.2/ Rev. 1.

Basel Convention, 'The Basel Convention Mechanism for Promoting Implementation and Compliance' (2006).

Basel Convention, 'Revised Technical Guidelines for the Environmentally Sound Management of Used and Waste Pneumatic Tyres' (2011) UNEP/CHW.10/6/Add.1/ Rev.1.

Basel Convention, 'The Basel Convention Mechanism for Promoting Implementation and Compliance: Celebrating a Decade of Assistance to Parties' (2011).

Basel Convention, 'General Technical Guidelines on the Environmentally Sound Management of Wastes of Wastes Consisting of, Containing or Contaminated with Persistent Organic Pollutants' (2015) UNEP/CHW.12/5/Add.2/Rev.1.

Basel Convention Secretariat, 'Report on Possible Options Available under the Basel Convention to Further Address Marine Plastic Litter and Microplastics' (2018) UNEP/CHW/OEWG.11/INF/22.

Basel Convention, 'Basel Convention Regional and Coordinating Centres' (2019) UNEP/CHW.14/17.

Basel Convention, 'Marine Plastic Litter and Microplastics' (2019) UNEP/CHW.14/11.

Becker R, 'MARPOL 73/78: An Overview in International Environmental Enforcement' (1998) 10 Georgetown International Environmental Law Review 625.

Bergmann M, Gutow L and Klages M, 'Preface' in Melanie Bergmann, Lars Gutow and Michael Klages (eds), *Marine Anthropogenic Litter* (Springer 2015).

Beyerlin U, 'New Developments in the Protection of the Marine Environment: Potential Effects of the Rio Process' (1995) 55 Zeitschrift für ausländisches öffentliches Recht und Völkerrecht 544.

Birnie P, Boyle A and Redgwell C, *International Law and the Environment* (3rd edn, OUP Oxford 2009).

Blumenthal K, 'Generation and Treatment of Municipal Waste' (Eurostats 2011) 31/2011.

Boisson de Chazournes L, *Fresh Water in International Law* (Oxford University Press 2013).

Boisson de Chazournes L, and Tignino M, 'Introduction' in Laurence Boisson de Chazournes and Mara Tignino (eds), *International Water Law* (Edward Elgar 2015).

Bolt HM, 'Vinyl Chloride – a Classical Industrial Toxicant of New Interest' (2005) 35 Critical Reviews in Toxicology 307.

Bossche P van den and Zdouc W, *The Law and Policy of the World Trade Organization: Text, Cases, and Materials* (3rd edn, Cambridge University Press 2013).

Boucher J and Billard G, 'The Challenges of Measuring Plastic Pollution' [2019] Field Actions Science Reports 68.

Boucher J and others, *Review of Plastic Footprint Methodologies: Laying the Foundation for the Development of a Standardised Plastic Footprint Measurement Tool* (IUCN 2019).

Boucher J and Friot D, 'Primary Microplastics in the Oceans: A Global Evaluation of Sources' (IUCN 2017).

Bowman M and Boyle AE (eds), *Environmental Damage in International and Comparative Law: Problems of Definition and Valuation* (Oxford University Press 2002).

Boyle AE, 'Marine Pollution under the Law of the Sea Convention' (1985) 79 The American Journal of International Law 347.

Boyle AE, 'Land-Based Sources of Marine Pollution: Current Legal Regime' (1992) 16 Marine Policy 20.

Boyle AE, 'Dispute Settlement and the Law of the Sea Convention: Problems of Fragmentation and Jurisdiction' (1997) 46 International and Comparative Law Quarterly 37.

Boyle AE, 'Codification of International Environmental Law and the International Law Commission: Injurious Consequences Revisited' in Alan Boyle and David Freestone (eds), *International Law and Sustainable Development: Past Achievements and Future Challenges* (Oxford University Press 1999).

Boyle AE, 'Globalising Environmental Liability: The Interplay of National and International Law' (2005) 17 Journal of Environmental Law 3.

Boyle AE, 'Further Development of the 1982 Convention on the Law of the Sea: Mechanisms for Change' in David Freestone, Richard Barnes and David Ong (eds), *The Law of the Sea: Progress and Prospects* (Oxford University Press 2006).

Boyle AE, 'Relationship between International Environmental Law and Other Branches of International Law' in Daniel Bodansky, Jutta Brunnée and Ellen Hey (eds), *The Oxford Handbook of International Environmental Law* (Oxford University Press 2007).

Boyle AE, 'The Environmental Jurisprudence of the International Tribunal for the Law of the Sea' (2007) 22 The international journal of marine and coastal law 369.

Boyle AE, 'Liability for Injurious Consequences of Acts Not Prohibited by International Law' in James Crawford, Alain Pellet and Simon Olleson (eds), *The Law of International Responsibility* (Oxford University Press 2010).

Boyle AE, and Chinkin C, *The Making of International Law* (OUP Oxford 2007).

Boyle AE, and Freestone D, 'Introduction' in Alan Boyle and David Freestone (eds), *International Law and Sustainable Development: Past Achievements and Future Challenges* (Oxford University Press 1999).

Brans E, *Liability for Damage to Public Natural Resources: Standing, Damage and Damage Assessment* (Kluwer Law International 2001).

Braun D, *Kleine Geschichte der Kunststoffe* (Carl Hanser Verlag 2013).

Brooks AL, Wang S and Jambeck JR, 'The Chinese Import Ban and Its Impact on Global Plastic Waste Trade' (2018) 4 Science Advances eaat0131.

Brown Weiss E, *In Fairness to Future Generations: International Law, Common Patrimony, and Intergenerational Equity* (Transnational Pub/United Nations University 1989).

Brown Weiss E, 'Environment and Trade as Partners in Sustainable Development: A Commentary' [1992] American Journal of International Law 728.

Browne MA and others, 'Ingested Microscopic Plastic Translocates to the Circulatory System of the Mussel, Mytilus Edulis (L)' (2008) 42 Environmental Science & Technology 5026.

Browne MA and others, 'Microplastic Moves Pollutants and Additives to Worms, Reducing Functions Linked to Health and Biodiversity' (2013) 23 Current Biology 2388.

Brunnée J, 'Of Sense and Sensibility: Reflections on International Liability Regimes as Tools for Environmental Protection' (2004) 53 The International and Comparative Law Quarterly 351.

Brydson JA, *Plastics Materials* (7th edn, Butterworth-Heinemann 1999).

BSC, *Marine Litter in the Black Sea Region: A Review of the Problem* (2007).

BSC, HELCOM and EU, 'Environmental Monitoring of the Black Sea with Focus on Nutrient Pollution (Baltic2Black)' (2014) Final Report for the Grant Agreement No 07.0204/2010/580913/SUB/D2.

Bucci K and others, 'Impacts to Larval Fathead Minnows Vary between Preconsumer and Environmental Microplastics' (2021) Environmental Toxicology and Chemistry <https://onlinelibrary.wiley.com/doi/abs/10.1002/etc.5036> accessed 19 February 2022.

Buchanan JB, 'Pollution by Synthetic Fibres' (1971) 2 Marine Pollution Bulletin 23.

Bulow J, 'An Economic Theory of Planned Obsolescence' (1986) 101 The Quarterly Journal of Economics 729.

Burdick DL and Leffler WL, *Petrochemicals in Nontechnical Language* (4th edn, Pennwell Books 2010).

Bürgi Bonanomi E, *Sustainable Development in International Law Making and Trade: International Food Governance and Trade in Agriculture* (Edward Elgar Publishing 2015).

Bush J and others, 'Synthetic Polyisoprene (IR)', *The Vanderbilt Rubber Handbook* (14th edn, RT Vanderbilt 2010).

Brown Weiss E and others, *International Environmental Law and Policy* (2nd edn, Aspen Publishers 2007).

Bylinsky G, 'Manufacturing for Reuse' (1995) 131 Fortune 102.

Calafat AM and others, 'Exposure to Bisphenol A and Other Phenols in Neonatal Intensive Care Unit Premature Infants' (2009) 117 Environmental Health Perspectives 639.

Carpenter EJ and others, 'Polystyrene Spherules in Coastal Waters' (1972) 178 Science 749.

Carpenter EJ and Smith KL, 'Plastics on the Sargasso Sea Surface' (1972) 175 Science 1240.

Carson HS and others, 'Small Plastic Debris Changes Water Movement and Heat Transfer through Beach Sediments' (2011) 62 Marine Pollution Bulletin 1708.

Cassese A, *International Law* (OUP Oxford 2005).

Cavaré L, 'Les problèmes juridiques posés par la pollution des eaux maritimes au point de vue interne et international' [1964] Revue Generale de Droit International Public 617.

CBD, 'Synthesis Document on the Impacts of Marine Debris on Marine and Coastal Biodiversity: Note by the Executive Secretary' (2012) UNEP/CBD/SBSTTA/16/INF/15.

CBD, 'Report of the Expert Workshop to Prepare Practical Guidance on Preventing and Mitigating the Significant Adverse Impacts of Marine Debris on Marine and Coastal Biodiversity and Habitats' (2014) UNEP/CBD/MCB/EM/2014/3/2.

CBD Secretariat, 'Marine Debris: Understanding, Preventing and Mitigating the Significant Adverse Impacts on Marine and Coastal Biodiversity' (McGraw-Hill Education, 2016) CBD Technical Series No 83.

CBD, and STAP, Impacts of Marine Debris on Biodiversity: Current Status and Potential Solutions' (2012) CBD Technical Series 67.

CEP, *Marine Litter in the Caspian Region: Review and Framework Strategy* (2009).

Chandra R and Rustgi R, 'Biodegradable Polymers' (1998) 23 Progress in Polymer Science 1273.

Chandrasekhara Rao P, 'Law of the Sea, Settlement of Disputes', *Max Planck Encyclopedia of Public International Law* (2011).

Charney JI, 'Third State Remedies for Environmental Damage to the World's Common Spaces' in Fancesco Francioni and Tullio Scovazzi (eds), *International Responsibility for Environmental Harm* (Graham & Trotman/Martinus Nijhoff 1991).

Charney JI, 'The Marine Environment and the 1982 United Nations Conventions on the Law of the Sea' (1994) 28 International Lawyer 879.

Charney JI, 'The Implications of Expanding International Dispute Settlement Systems: The 1982 Convention on the Law of the Sea' (1996) 90 The American Journal of International Law 69.

Cherrier H and Ponnor T, 'A Study of Hoarding Behavior and Attachment to Material Possessions' (2010) 13 Qualitative Market Research: An International Journal 8.

Cheshire A and others, *UNEP/IOC Guidelines on Survey and Monitoring of Marine Litter* (UNEP/IOC 2009).

Chircop A, 'Marine Pollution from Land-Based Activities: Legal Regimes and Management Frameworks' in Davor Vidas and Willy Østreng (eds), *Order for the Oceans at the Turn of the Century* (Kluwer Law International 1999).

Cho S, 'United States-Continued Suspension of Obligations in the EC-Hormones Dispute' (2009) 103 Am. J. Int'l L. 299.

Choi W-M, *'Like Products' in International Trade Law: Towards a Consistent GATT/WTO Jurisprudence* (Oxford University Press 2003).

Christen M and Morgan RM, 'Keeping Up With the Joneses: Analyzing the Effect of Income Inequality on Consumer Borrowing' (2005) 3 Quantitative Marketing and Economics 145.

Churchill RR and Lowe AV, *The Law of the Sea* (3rd edn, Manchester University Press 1999).

Cicin-Sain B, 'Earth Summit Implementation: Progress since Rio' (1996) 20 Marine Policy 123.

CIEL, 'Fueling Plastics: Fossils, Plastics, & Petrochemical Feedstocks' (2017).

CIEL, 'Fueling Plastics: How Fracked Gas, Cheap Oil, and Unburnable Coal Are Driving the Plastics Boom' (2017).

CIEL, 'Fueling Plastics: Untested Assumptions and Unanswered Questions in the Plastics Boom' (2017).

CIEL, 'Plastic & Health: The Hidden Costs of a Plastic Planet' (2019).

Ciroth A and others, *Towards a Life Cycle Sustainablity Assessment: Making Informed Choices on Products* (Sonia Valdivia and others eds, UNEP/SETAC Life Cycle Initiative 2011).

Claessens M and others, 'Occurrence and Distribution of Microplastics in Marine Sediments along the Belgian Coast' (2011) 62 Marine Pollution Bulletin 2199.

Cliff G and others, 'Large Sharks and Plastic Debris in KwaZulu-Natal, South Africa' (2002) 53 Marine and Freshwater Research 575.

CMS, 'Report I: Migratory Species, Marine Debris and Its Management' (2014) UNEP/CMS/COP11/Inf.27.

CMS, 'Report II: Marine Debris and Commercial Marine Vessel Best Practice' (2014) UNEP/CMS/COP11/Inf.28.

CMS, 'Report III: Marine Debris Public Awareness and Education Campaigns' (2014) UNEP/CMS/COP11/Inf.29.

CMS, and UNEP, *Impacts of Plastic Pollution on Freshwater Aquatic, Terrestrial and Avian Migratory Species in the Asia and Pacific Region* (2021).

Colborn T, 'Neurodevelopment and Endocrine Disruption' (2004) 112 Environmental Health Perspectives 944.

Colborn T, and Clement C, 'Chemically-Induced Alterations in Sexual and Functional Development: The Wildlife/Human Connection' [1992] Advances in Modern Environmental Toxicology (USA).

Colborn T, vom Saal FS and Soto AM, 'Developmental Effects of Endocrine-Disrupting Chemicals in Wildlife and Humans'. (1993) 101 Environmental Health Perspectives 378.

Cole M and others, 'Microplastics as Contaminants in the Marine Environment: A Review' (2011) 62 Marine Pollution Bulletin 2588.

Collier JG and Lowe AV, 'Dispute Settlement in the Law of the Sea' in John G Collier and Alan Vaughan Lowe (eds), *The Settlement of Disputes in International Law: Institutions and Procedures* (Oxford University Press 1999).

Colton JB, Burns BR and Knapp FD, 'Plastic Particles in Surface Waters of the Northwestern Atlantic' (1974) 185 Science 491.

Conrad CR, *Processes and Production Methods (PPMs) in WTO Law: Interfacing Trade and Social Goals* (Cambridge University Press 2011).

Cooper T, 'Slower Consumption Reflections on Product Life Spans and the "Throwaway Society"' (2005) 9 Journal of Industrial Ecology 51.

Cooper T, and Mayers CK, *Prospects for Household Appliances* (Urban mines 2000).

Cordonier Segger M-C and Khalfan A, *Sustainable Development Law: Principles, Practices and Prospects* (Oxford University Press 2004).

Cottier T, 'Multilayered Governance, Pluralism, and Moral Conflict' (2009) 16 Indiana Journal of Global Legal Studies 647.

Cottier T, 'Towards a Five Storey House' in Christian Joerges and Ernst-Ulrich Petersmann (eds), *Constitutionalism, Multilevel Trade Governance and International Economic Law* (Hart 2011).

Cottier T, 'International Economic Law in Transition from Trade Liberalization to Trade Regulation' (2014) 17 Journal of International Economic Law 671.

Cottier T, *Equitable Principles of Maritime Boundary Delimitation: The Quest for Distributive Justice in International Law* (Cambridge University Press 2015).

Cottier T, 'The Common Law of International Trade and the Future of the World Trade Organization' (2015) 18 Journal of International Economic Law 3.

Cottier T, 'Technology and the Law of International Trade Regulation' in Roger Brownsword, Eloise Scotford and Karen Yeung (eds), The Oxford Handbook of Law, Regulation and Technology (Oxford University Press 2017).

Cottier T, 'The Changing Structure of International Trade Law' (2018) 21 Zeitschrift für europarechtliche Studien 421.

Cottier T, 'The Implications of EC – Seal Products for the Protection of Core Labour Standards in WTO Law' in Henner Gött (ed), Labour Standards in International Economic Law (Springer International Publishing 2018).

Cottier T, 'The Principle of Common Concern of Humankind' in Thomas Cottier and Zaker Ahmad (eds), *The Prospects of Common Concern of Humankind in International Law* (Cambridge University Press 2021).

Cottier T, and Ahmad Z (eds), *The Prospects of Common Concern of Humankind in International Law* (Cambridge University Press 2021).

Cottier T, and Hertig M, 'The Prospects of 21st Century Constitutionalism' (2003) 7 Max Planck Yearbook of United Nations Law 261.

Cottier T, and Matteotti-Berkutova S, 'International Environmental Law and the Evolving Concept of "Common Concern of Mankind"' in Thomas Cottier, Olga Nartova and Sadeq Z Bigdeli (eds), *International Trade Regulation and the Mitigation of Climate Change* (Cambridge University Press 2009).

Cottier T, and Oesch M, *International Trade Regulation: Law and Policy in the WTO, the European Union and Switzerland: Cases, Materials and Comments* (Staempfli Publishers 2005).

Cottier T, Tuerk E and Panizzon M, 'Handel und Umwelt im Recht der WTO: Auf dem Wege zur praktischen Konkordanz' [2003] Zeitschrift für Umweltrecht 155.

Cózar A and others, 'Plastic Debris in the Open Ocean' (2014) 111 Proceedings of the National Academy of Sciences 10239.

Cózar A and others, 'The Arctic Ocean as a Dead End for Floating Plastics in the North Atlantic Branch of the Thermohaline Circulation' (2017) 3 Science Advances e1600582.

CPPS, *Marine Litter in the Southeast Pacific Region: A Review of the Problem* (2007).

Craik N, *The International Law of Environmental Impact Assessment: Process, Substance and Integration* (Cambridge University Press 2008).

Craik N 'Principle 17: Environmental Impact Assessment' in Jorge E Viñuales (ed), *The Rio Declaration on Environment and Development: A Commentary* (Oxford University Press 2015).

Crain DA and others, 'An Ecological Assessment of Bisphenol-A: Evidence from Comparative Biology' (2007) 24 Reproductive Toxicology (Elmsford, N.Y.) 225.

Crawford J, 'Overview of Part Three of the Articles on State Responsibility' in James Crawford, Alain Pellet and Simon Olleson (eds), *The Law of International Responsibility* (Oxford University Press 2010).

CSD, 'Report of the Expert Group Meeting on Identification of Principles of International Law for Sustainable Development, Background Paper (CSD Report on Principles for Sustainable Development)' (1995).

Cullet P, 'Differential Treatment in International Law: Towards a New Paradigm of Inter-State Relations' (1999) 10 European Journal of International Law 549.

Cullet P, 'Common but Differentiated Responsibilities' in Malgosia Fitzmaurice, David M Ong and Panos Merkouris (eds), *Research Handbook on International Environmental Law* (Edward Elgar Publishing 2010).

Cundell AM, 'Plastic Materials Accumulating in Narragansett Bay' (1973) 4 Marine Pollution Bulletin 187.

Curran MA, 'Life Cycle Assessment: A Review of the Methodology and Its Application to Sustainability' (2013) 2 Current Opinion in Chemical Engineering 273.

Curtis JB, 'Vessel-Source Oil Pollution and MARPOL 73/78: An International Success Story' (1984) 15 Envtl. L. 679.

Danson T, *Oceana: Our Endangered Oceans and What We Can Do to Save Them* (Rodale Books 2011).

Davies A, 'Interpreting the Chapeau of GATT Article XX in Light of the "New" Approach in Brazil – Tyres' (2009) 43 Journal of World Trade Law 507.

Day RH and Shaw DG, 'Patterns in the Abundance of Pelagic Plastic and Tar in the North Pacific Ocean, 1976–1985' (1987) 18 Marine Pollution Bulletin 311.

de La Fayette LA, 'The OSPAR Convention Comes into Force: Continuity and Progress' (1999) 14 The International Journal of Marine and Coastal Law 247.

Degli Innocenti F, 'Biodegradability and Compostability' in Emo Chiellini and Roberto Solaro (eds), *Biodegradable Polymers and Plastics* (Springer Science & Business Media 2003).

Delimatsis P, '"Relevant International Standards" and "Recognised Standardisation Bodies" Under the TBT Agreement' in Panagiotis Delimatsis (ed), *The Law, Economics and Politics of International Standardisation* (Cambridge University Press 2015).

Deere Birkbeck C, 'Strengthening International Cooperation to Tackle Plastic Pollution: Options for the WTO' (2020) Global Governance Brief 1.

Deere Birkbeck C, and others, 'A Review of Trade Policies and Measures Relevant to Trade in Plastics and Plastic Pollution' (2021) 16 Global Trade and Customs Journal 303.

Derraik JGB, 'The Pollution of the Marine Environment by Plastic Debris: A Review' (2002) 44 Marine Pollution Bulletin 842.

DiMento JF and Hickman AJ, *Environmental Governance of the Great Seas: Law and Effect* (Edward Elgar Publishing 2012).

Dixon TR and Cooke AJ, 'Discarded Containers on a Kent Beach' (1977) 8 Marine Pollution Bulletin 105.

Dixon TR and Dixon TJ, 'Marine Litter Surveillance' (1981) 12 Marine Pollution Bulletin 4.

Domininghaus H, *Die Kunststoffe und ihre Eigenschaften* (Peter Elsner, Peter Eyerer and Thomas Hirth eds, Springer 2005).

Doorn MR, Barlaz MA and Thorneloe SA, *Estimate of Global Methane Emissions from Landfills and Open Dumps* (US Environmental Protection Agency EPA 1995).

Dormer A and others, 'Carbon Footprint Analysis in Plastics Manufacturing' (2013) 51 Journal of Cleaner Production 133.

Duffus J, 'Glossary for Chemists of Terms Used in Toxicology (IUPAC Recommendations 1993)' (1993) 65 Pure and Applied Chemistry 2003.

Dumitriu S, 'Preface' in Severian Dumitriu (ed), *Polymeric Biomaterials* (2nd edn, CRC Press 2001).

Dupuy P-M and Viñuales JE, *International Environmental Law* (Cambridge University Press 2015).

Earle SA, *The World Is Blue: How Our Fate and the Ocean's Are One* (Reprint, National Geographic 2010).

Ebbesmeyer CC and Ingraham W James, 'Shoe Spill in the North Pacific' (1992) 73 Eos, Transactions American Geophysical Union 361.

Ebbesmeyer CC and Ingraham W James, 'Pacific Toy Spill Fuels Ocean Current Pathways Research' (1994) 75 Eos, Transactions American Geophysical Union 425.

Ehlers P, 'The Baltic Sea Area: Convention on the Protection of the Marine Environment of the Baltic Sea Area (Helsinki Convention) of 1974 and the Revised Convention of 1992' (1994) 29 Marine Pollution Bulletin 617.

Elferink AGO, 'Environmental Impact Assessment in Areas beyond National Jurisdiction' (2012) 27 The International Journal of Marine and Coastal Law 449.

Elias H-G, *Makromoleküle: Band 4: Anwendungen von Polymeren* (4th edn, John Wiley & Sons 2003).

Enders H-J and others, 'Biopolymers as a Source of Energy' (2010) 8 Kunststoffe 83.

Environmental Investigation Agency and others, 'Convention on Plastic Pollution: Toward a New Global Agreement to Address Plastic Pollution' (2020).

Eriksen M and others, 'Plastic Pollution in the South Pacific Subtropical Gyre' (2013) 68 Marine Pollution Bulletin 71.

Eriksen M and others, 'Plastic Pollution in the World's Oceans: More than 5 Trillion Plastic Pieces Weighing over 250,000 Tons Afloat at Sea' (2014) 9 PLoS ONE e111913.

Eriksson C and Burton H, 'Origins and Biological Accumulation of Small Plastic Particles in Fur Seals from Macquarie Island' (2003) 32 Ambio 380.

Eubeler JP and others, 'Environmental Biodegradation of Synthetic Polymers I. Test Methodologies and Procedures' (2009) 28 TrAC Trends in Analytical Chemistry 1057.

Eubeler JP, Bernhard M and Knepper TP, 'Environmental Biodegradation of Synthetic Polymers II. Biodegradation of Different Polymer Groups' (2010) 29 TrAC Trends in Analytical Chemistry 84.

European Commission, 'Green Paper on a European Strategy on Plastic Waste in the Environment' (2013) COM(2013) 123 final.

European Commission 'Closing the Loop – an EU Action Plan for the Circular Economy' (2015) COM(2015) 614 final.

European Commission 'A European Strategy for Plastics in a Circular Economy' (2018) COM(2018) 28 final.

European Commission 'A European Strategy for Plastics in a Circular Economy, Annexes' (2018) COM(2018) 28 final, Annexes.

European Commission 'Fact Sheet: European Union Commitments to Our Ocean 2018' (2018) MEMO/18/6210 <http://europa.eu/rapid/press-release_MEMO-18-6210_en.htm> accessed 19 February 2022.

Fahim MA, Al-Sahhaf TA and Elkilani A, *Fundamentals of Petroleum Refining* (Elsevier 2009).

FAO, 'Code of Conduct for Responsible Fisheries' (1995).

FAO *International Guidelines on Bycatch Management and Reduction of Discards* (2011).

FAO 'Abandoned, Lost or Otherwise Discarded Gillnets and Trammel Nets: Methods to Estimate Ghost Fishing Mortality, and the Status of Regional Monitoring and Management' (2016) FAO Fisheries and Aquaculture Technical Paper 600.

FAO 'Report of the Expert Consultation on the Marking of Fishing Gear, Rome, Italy, 4–7 April 2016' (2016) FAO Fisheries and Aquaculture Report R1157.

FAO and UNEP, 'Abandoned, Lost or Otherwise Discarded Fishing Gear' (2009) FAO Fisheries and Aquaculture Technical Paper 523 UNEP Regional Seas Reports and Studies 185.

Fava J and others (eds), *Conceptual Framework for Life-Cycle Impact Assessment* (SETAC 1993).

Fawcett EW, Gibson RO and Perrin MW, 'Polymerization of Olefins'.

Fisher HL, *Rubber and Its Use* (Chemical Publishing 1941).

Fisher MM, 'Plastics Recycling' in AL Andrady (ed), *Plastics and the Environment* (Wiley Interscience 2003).

Fodella A, 'Mechanism for Promoting Implementation and Compliance with the 1989 Basel Convention on the Transboundary Movements of Hazardous Wastes and Their Disposal' in Tullio Treves and others (eds), *Non-Compliance Procedures and Mechanisms and the Effectiveness of International Environmental Agreements* (TMC Asser Press 2009).

Foltea M, *International Organizations in WTO Dispute Settlement: How Much Institutional Sensitivity?* (Cambridge University Press 2012).

Foster CE, 'Precaution, Scientific Development and Scientific Uncertainty under the WTO Agreement on Sanitary and Phytosanitary Measures' (2009) 18 Review of European Community & International Environmental Law 50.

Franck A and others, *Kunststoff-Kompendium: Herstellung, Aufbau, Verarbeitung, Anwendung, Umweltverhalten und Eigenschaften der Thermoplaste, Polymerlegierungen, Elastomere und Duroplaste* (7th edn, Vogel 2011).

Freestone D, 'The Road from Rio: International Environmental Law After the Earth Summit' (1994) 6 Journal of Environmental Law 193.

Freestone D, Barnes R and Ong D (eds), *The Law of the Sea: Progress and Prospects* (Oxford University Press 2006).

French D, 'Developing States and International Environmental Law: The Importance of Differentiated Responsibilities' (2000) 49 International and Comparative Law Quarterly 35.

GA Circular, 'The Role of Gender in Waste Management: Gender Perspectives on Waste in India, Indonesia, the Philippines and Vietnam' (Report commissioned by Ocean Conservancy 2019).

Galgani F and others, 'Litter on the Sea Floor Along European Coasts' (2000) 40 Marine Pollution Bulletin 516.

Galgani F and others, 'Chapter 12: Changes in Inputs and Distribution of Solid Waste, Other Than Dredged Material, in the Marine Environment', *Second World Ocean Assessment* (United Nations 2021).

Galgani F, Hanke G and Maes T, 'Global Distribution, Composition and Abundance of Marine Litter' in Melanie Bergmann, Lars Gutow and Michael Klages (eds), *Marine Anthropogenic Litter* (Springer 2015).

Galí J, 'Keeping up with the Joneses: Consumption Externalities, Portfolio Choice, and Asset Prices' (1994) 26 Journal of Money, Credit and Banking 1.

Gallo F and others, 'Marine Litter Plastics and Microplastics and Their Toxic Chemicals Components: The Need for Urgent Preventive Measures' (2018) 30 Environmental Sciences Europe <https://www.ncbi.nlm.nih.gov/pmc/articles/PMC5918521> accessed 19 February 2022.

Gary JH and Handwerk GE, *Petroleum Refining* (CRC Press 2001).

Gautier P, 'Environmental Damage and the United Nations Claims Commission: New Directions for Future International Environmental Cases?' in Tafsir Malick Ndiaye and Rüdiger Wolfrum (eds), *Law of the Sea, Environmental Law and Settlement of Disputes* (Martinus Nijhoff Publishers 2007).

GEF, 'Operational Strategy' (1995) GEF/C.6/3.

Gehne K, *Nachhaltige Entwicklung als Rechtsprinzip: normativer Aussagegehalt, rechtstheoretische Einordnung, Funktionen im Recht* (Mohr Siebeck 2011).

Gehring MW and Segger M-CC, *Precaution in World Trade Law: The Precautionary Principle and Its Implications for the World Trade Organization* (CISDL 2002).

Gerigny O and others, 'Déchets en mer et sur le fond', *Plan d'action pour le milieu marin: Sous-région marine Méditerranée Occidentale: Évaluation initiale des eaux marines* <http://www.dirm.mediterranee.developpement-durable.gouv.fr/IMG/pdf/Evaluation_initiale_des_eaux_marines_web.pdf> accessed 19 February 2022.

GESAMP, 'The Review of the Health of the Oceans' (UNESCO 1982) Reports and Studies No 15.

GESAMP 'The State of the Marine Environment' (UNEP 1990) Reports and Studies No 39.

GESAMP 'Protecting the Oceans from Land-Based Activities: Land-Based Sources and Activities Affecting the Quality and Uses of the Marine, Coastal and Associated Freshwater Environment' (UNEP 2001) Reports and Studies No 71.

GESAMP 'Guidelines for the Monitoring and Assessment of Plastic Litter in the Ocean' (2019) 99 Reports and Studies.

Geyer R, Jambeck JR and Law KL, 'Production, Use, and Fate of All Plastics Ever Made' (2017) 3 Science Advances e1700782.

Gilek M and Kern K (eds), *Governing Europe's Marine Environment: Europeanization of Regional Seas Or Regionalization of EU Policies?* (Ashgate 2015).

Gilg A, Barr S and Ford N, 'Green Consumption or Sustainable Lifestyles? Identifying the Sustainable Consumer' (2005) 37 Futures 481.

Gill K, *Of Poverty and Plastic: Scavenging and Scrap Trading Entrepreneurs in India's Urban Informal Economy* (Paperback edn, Oxford University Press 2012).

Gómez EF and Michel FC, 'Biodegradability of Conventional and Bio-Based Plastics and Natural Fiber Composites during Composting, Anaerobic Digestion and Long-Term Soil Incubation' (2013) 98 Polymer Degradation and Stability 2583.

Gonzalez G and Hérbert F, 'Conventions Relating to Pollution Incident Preparedness, Response, and Cooperation' in David Joseph Attard and others (eds), *The IMLI Manual on International Maritime Law Volume III: Marine Environmental Law and International Maritime Security Law* (Oxford University Press 2016).

Gooch JW (ed), *Encyclopedic Dictionary of Polymers* (Springer New York 2011).

Gratzer W, *Giant Molecules: From Nylon to Nanotubes* (Oxford University Press 2009).

Green R and others, 'Use of Di(2-Ethylhexyl) Phthalate-Containing Medical Products and Urinary Levels of Mono(2-Ethylhexyl) Phthalate in Neonatal Intensive Care Unit Infants' (2005) 113 Environmental Health Perspectives 1222.

Greene JP, *Sustainable Plastics: Environmental Assessments of Biobased, Biodegradable, and Recycled Plastics* (John Wiley & Sons 2014).

Gregory MR, 'Plastic Pellets on New Zealand Beaches' (1977) 8 Marine Pollution Bulletin 82.

Gregory MR, 'Accumulation and Distribution of Virgin Plastic Granules on New Zealand Beaches' (1978) 12 New Zealand Journal of Marine and Freshwater Research 399.

Gregory MR, 'Virgin Plastic Granules on Some Beaches of Eastern Canada and Bermuda' (1983) 10 Marine Environmental Research 73.

Gregory MR, 'Plastics and Other Seaborne Litter on the Shores of New Zealand's Sub-Antarctic Island' (1987) 7 New Zealand Antarctic Record 32.

Gregory MR, 'Environmental Implications of Plastic Debris in Marine Settings – Entanglement, Ingestion, Smothering, Hangers-on, Hitch-Hiking and Alien Invasions' (2009) 364 Philosophical Transactions of the Royal Society B: Biological Sciences 2013.

Gregory MR, and Andrady AL, 'Plastics in the Marine Environment' in AL Andrady (ed), *Plastics and the Environment* (Wiley-Interscience 2003).

Gregory MR, and Ryan PG, 'Pelagic Plastics and Other Seaborne Persistent Synthetic Debris: A Review of Southern Hemisphere Perspectives' in James M Coe and Donald B Rogers (eds), *Marine Debris: Sources, Impacts and Solutions* (Springer New York 1997).

Griffin A, 'MARPOL 73/78 and Vessel Pollution: A Glass Half Full or Half Empty?' (1994) 1 Indiana Journal of Global Legal Studies 489.

Guiltinan J, 'Creative Destruction and Destructive Creations: Environmental Ethics and Planned Obsolescence' (2008) 89 Journal of Business Ethics 19.

Guinée JB and others, *Handbook on Life Cycle Assessment: Operational Guide to the ISO Standards,* vol 7 (Jeroen B Guinée ed, Kluwer Academic Publishers 2004).

Gupta AK, 'Thermal Destruction of Wastes and Plastics' in AL Andrady (ed), *Plastics and the Environment* (Wiley Interscience 2003).

Guttinger P, 'Allocation of Responsibility for Harmful Consequences of Acts Not Prohibited by International Law' in James Crawford, Alain Pellet and Simon Olleson (eds), *The Law of International Responsibility* (Oxford University Press 2010).

Hagen PE, 'International Community Confronts Plastics Polluting from Ships: MARPOL Annex V and the Problem That Won't Go Away' (1990) 5 Am. UJ Int'l L. & Pol'y 425.

Häkkinen T and Vares S, 'Environmental Impacts of Disposable Cups with Special Focus on the Effect of Material Choices and End of Life' (2010) 18 Journal of Cleaner Production 1458.

Halpern BS and others, 'A Global Map of Human Impact on Marine Ecosystems' (2008) 319 Science 948.

Hammer J, Kraak MHS and Parsons JR, 'Plastics in the Marine Environment: The Dark Side of a Modern Gift' in David M Whitacre (ed), *Reviews of Environmental Contamination and Toxicology,* vol 220 (Springer New York 2012).

Handl G, 'Environmental Security and Global Change: The Challenge to International Law' (1990) 1 Yearbook of International Environmental Law 3.

Handl G, 'Transboundary Impacts' in Daniel Bodansky, Jutta Brunnée and Ellen Hey (eds), *The Oxford Handbook of International Environmental Law* (Oxford University Press 2007).

Hardy M, 'International Control of Marine Pollution' (1971) 11 Nat. Resources J. 296.

Harper CA, *Handbook of Plastic Processes* (John Wiley & Sons 2006).

Harrison J, 'Pollution of the Marine Envrionment from or Through the Atmosphere' in David Joseph Attard and others (eds), *The IMLI Manual on International Maritime Law Volume III: Marine Environmental Law and International Maritime Security Law* (Oxford University Press 2016).

Hassan D, *Protecting the Marine Environment from Land-Based Sources of Pollution: Towards Effective International Cooperation* (Ashgate 2006).

Hayashi M, 'The 1995 UN Fish Stocks Agreement and the Law of the Sea' in Davor Vidas and Willy Østreng (eds), *Order for the Oceans at the Turn of the Century* (Kluwer Law International 1999).

Hays H and Cormons G, 'Plastic Particles Found in Tern Pellets, on Coastal Beaches and at Factory Sites' (1974) 5 Marine Pollution Bulletin 44.

Heim JJ, 'Consumer Demand for Durable Goods, Nondurable Goods and Services' (2009) 2 Proceedings of the New York State Economics Association 22.

Heindel JJ and vom Saal FS, 'Role of Nutrition and Environmental Endocrine Disrupting Chemicals during the Perinatal Period on the Aetiology of Obesity' (2009) 304 Molecular and Cellular Endocrinology 90.

HELCOM, 'Regional Action Plan for Marine Litter in the Baltic Sea' (2015).

HELCOM-MARLIN, 'Final Report of Baltic Marine Litter Project Marlin: Litter Monitoring and Raising Awareness 2011–2013' (2014).

Henderson JR, 'A Pre- and Post-MARPOL Annex V Summary of Hawaiian Monk Seal Entanglements and Marine Debris Accumulation in the Northwestern Hawaiian Islands, 1982–1998' (2001) 42 Marine Pollution Bulletin 584.

Hernandez E, Nowack B and Mitrano DM, 'Polyester Textiles as a Source of Microplastics from Households: A Mechanistic Study to Understand Microfiber Release During Washing' (2017) 51 Environmental Science & Technology 7036.

Heslenfeld P and Enserink EL, 'OSPAR Ecological Quality Objectives: The Utility of Health Indicators for the North Sea' (2008) 65 ICES Journal of Marine Science: Journal du Conseil 1392.

Heudorf U, Mersch-Sundermann V and Angerer J, 'Phthalates: Toxicology and Exposure' (2007) 210 International Journal of Hygiene and Environmental Health 623.

Holt R, 'The Carpet Sea Squirt Didemnum Vexillum: Eradication from Holyhead Marina – Progress to October 2009' (Presentation to the Scottish Natural Heritage Conference 'Marine Non-native Species: Responding to the threat', Battleby, UK, 27 October 2009).

Holzer K, *Carbon-Related Border Adjustment and WTO Law* (Edward Elgar Publishing 2014).

Honkonen T, *The Common but Differentiated Responsibility Principle in Multilateral Environmental Agreements: Regulatory and Policy Aspects* (Kluwer Law International 2009).

Honkonen T, 'The Principle of Common but Differentiated Responsibility in Post-2012 Climate Negotiations' (2009) 18 Review of European Community & International Environmental Law 257.

Hoornweg D and Bhada-Tata P, 'What a Waste: A Global Review of Solid Waste Management' (World Bank 2012) No. 15.

Horvat P and Kržan A, 'Certification of Bioplastics' (Innovative Value Chain Development for Sustainable Plastics in Central Europe (PLASTiCE) 2012).

Hottle TA, Bilec MM and Landis AE, 'Sustainability Assessments of Bio-Based Polymers' (2013) 98 Polymer Degradation and Stability 1898.

Howse R, Langille J and Sykes K, 'Pluralism in Practice: Moral Legislation and the Law of the WTO after Seal Products' (2015) 48 Geo. Wash. Int'l L. Rev. 81.

Hudec RE, '"Like Product": The Differences in Meaning in GATT Articles I and III' in Thomas Cottier and Petros Mavroidis (eds), *Regulatory Barriers and the Principle of Non-Discrimination in World Trade Law* (University of Michigan Press 2000).

Humbert S and others, 'Life Cycle Assessment of Two Baby Food Packaging Alternatives: Glass Jars vs. Plastic Pots' (2009) 14 The International Journal of Life Cycle Assessment 95.

Humes E, *Garbology: Our Dirty Love Affair with Trash* (Reprint, Avery 2012).
Hunkeler D and others (eds), *Environmental Life Cycle Costing* (SETAC; CRC Press 2008).
Hunter S, Helling R and Shiang D, 'Integration of LCA and Life-Cycle Thinking within the Themes of Sustainable Chemistry & Engineering' in Mary Ann Curran (ed), *Life Cycle Assessment Handbook: A Guide for Environmentally Sustainable Products* (John Wiley & Sons 2012).
Huppes G and Curran MA, 'Environmental Life Cycle Assessment: Background and Perspective' in Mary Ann Curran (ed), *Life Cycle Assessment Handbook: A Guide for Environmentally Sustainable Products* (John Wiley & Sons 2012).
Idris A, Inanc B and Hassan MN, 'Overview of Waste Disposal and Landfills/Dumps in Asian Countries' (2004) 6 Journal of Material Cycles and Waste Management 104.
IISD, 'Summary of the Seventeenth Meeting of the United Nations Open-Ended Informal Consultative Process on Oceans and the Law of the Sea: 13-17 June 2016' (2016) 25 Earth Negotiations Bulletin: ICP-17 Final <https://enb.iisd.org/events/icp-17/summary-report-13-17-june-2016 > accessed 19 February 2022.
IISD, 'Summary of the Ocean Conference: 5-9 June 2017' (2017) 32 Earth Negotiations Bulletin: Ocean Conference Final.
IISD, 'Summary of the Fourth Session of the United Nations Environment Assembly: 11–15 March 2019' (2019) 16 Earth Negotiations Bulletin: UNEA-4 FINAL <http://enb.iisd.org/download/pdf/enb16153e.pdf> accessed 19 February 2022.
IISD, 'Summary of the Meetings of the Conferences of the Parties to the Basel, Rotterdam and Stockholm Conventions: 29 April – 10 May 2019' (2019) 15 Earth Negotiations Bulletin: COPs FINAL <http://enb.iisd.org/download/pdf/enb15269e.pdf> accessed 19 February 2022.
IISD, 'Ministerial Conference on Marine Litter and Plastic Pollution: 1–2 September 2021' [2021] Marine Litter & Plastic Pollution Bulletin <https://enb.iisd.org/sites/default/files/2021-09/ministerial_conference_on_marine_litter_and_plastic_pollution_summary.pdf> accessed 19 February 2022.
IISD and UNEP, *Environment and Trade: A Handbook* (IISD 2005).
ILC, 'Draft Articles on Prevention of Transboundary Harm from Hazardous Activities', *Report of the International Law Commission 53th session* (UN Doc A/56/10 ch VE1 2001).
ILC, 'Draft Articles on Responsibility of States for Internationally Wrongful Acts', *Report of the International Law Commission 53th session* (UN Doc A/56/10 ch IVE1 2001).
ILC, 'Draft Principles on the Allocation of Loss in the Case of Transboundary Harm Arising Out of Hazardous Activities', *Report of the ILC 60th session* (UN doc A/61/10 ch VE1 2006).
ILC, 'Fragmentation of International Law: Difficulties Arising From the Diversification and Expansion of International Law (Fragmentation Report)' (Study Group of the International Law Commission 2006) A/CN.4/L.682.

ILC, 'Draft Articles on the Responsibility of International Organizations', *Report of the ILC 63th session* (UN doc A/66/10 ch VE1 2011).

ILO, 'Chapter 55 – Environmental Pollution Control', *Encyclopaedia of Occupational Health and Safety* (4th edn, ILO 2016) Part VII <http://www.ilocis.org/documents/chpt55e.htm#JD_Ch55_1> accessed 19 February 2022.

IMO, 'Implications of the United Nations Convention on the Law of the Sea for the International Maritime Organization' (1987) LEG/MISC/1.

IMO, 'Implications of the United Nations Convention on the Law of the Sea for the International Maritime Organization' (2014) LEG/MISC/8.

IMO, 'Guidelines for the Reduction of Underwater Noise from Commercial Shipping to Address Adverse Impacts on Marine Life' (2014) MEPC.1/Circ.833.

International Solid Waste Association ISWA, 'Closing of Open Dumps: Key Issue Paper' (2007).

International Union of Pure and Applied Chemistry, *Compendium of Polymer Terminology and Nomenclature: IUPAC Recommendations, 2008* (RSC Pub: IUPAC 2009).

Ioakeimidis C and others, 'A Comparative Study of Marine Litter on the Seafloor of Coastal Areas in the Eastern Mediterranean and Black Seas' (2014) 89 Marine Pollution Bulletin 296.

IPCC, 'Climate Change 2013: The Physical Science Basis. Contribution of Working Group I to the Fifth Assessment Report of the Intergovernmental Panel on Climate Change' (Cambridge University Press 2013).

IPRC (International Pacific Research Center), 'Tracking Ocean Debris' (2008) 8 IPRC Cimate 14.

Jaeger RJ and Rubin RJ, 'Plasticizers from Plastic Devices: Extraction, Metabolism, and Accumulation by Biological Systems' (1970) 170 Science 460.

Jaeger RJ and Rubin RJ, 'Migration of a Phthalate Ester Plasticizer from Polyvinyl Chloride Blood Bags into Stored Human Blood and Its Localization in Human Tissues' (1972) 287 New England Journal of Medicine 1114.

Jambeck JR and others, 'Plastic Waste Inputs from Land into the Ocean' (2015) 347 Science 768.

Jamieson AJ and others, 'Microplastics and Synthetic Particles Ingested by Deep-Sea Amphipods in Six of the Deepest Marine Ecosystems on Earth' (2019) 6 Royal Society Open Science 180667.

Jang YC and others, 'Estimation of Lost Tourism Revenue in Geoje Island from the 2011 Marine Debris Pollution Event in South Korea' (2014) 81 Marine Pollution Bulletin 49.

Johnson A and others, 'Fishing Gear Involved in Entanglements of Right and Humpback Whales' (2006) 21 Marine Mammal Science 635.

Johnson D, 'Environmental Indicators: Their Utility in Meeting the OSPAR Convention's Regulatory Needs' (2008) 65 ICES Journal of Marine Science: Journal du Conseil 1387.

Johnson D, 'Can Competent Authorities Cooperate for the Common Good: Towards a Collective Arrangement in the North-East Atlantic' in Paul Arthur Berkman and Alexander N Vylegzhanin (eds), *Environmental Security in the Arctic Ocean* (Springer Netherlands 2013).

Kahneman D and others, 'Would You Be Happier If You Were Richer? A Focusing Illusion' (2006) 312 Science 1908.

Kallis G, 'In Defence of Degrowth' (2011) 70 Ecological Economics 873.

Kallis G, Kerschner C and Martinez-Alier J, 'The Economics of Degrowth' (2012) 84 Ecological Economics 172.

Karau J, 'The Control of Land-Based Sources of Marine Pollution' (1992) 25 Marine Pollution Bulletin 80.

Kartar S, Abou-Seedou F and Sainsbury M, 'Polystyrene Spherules in the Severn Estuary – A Progress Report' (1976) 7 Marine Pollution Bulletin 52.

Kartar S, Milne RA and Sainsbury M, 'Polystyrene Waste in the Severn Estuary' (1973) 4 Marine Pollution Bulletin 144.

Kathuria V, 'Pollution: Prevention vs Control: Is EOP Treatment the Solution?' (2001) 36 Economic and Political Weekly 2745.

Kaza S and others, What a Waste 2.0: A Global Snapshot of Solid Waste Management to 2050 (World Bank Group 2018).

Kazazi M, 'The UNCC Follow-up Programme for Environmental Awards' in Tafsir Malick Ndiaye and Rüdiger Wolfrum (eds), *Law of the Sea, Environmental Law and Settlement of Disputes* (Martinus Nijhoff Publishers 2007).

Kemp AR and Malm FS, 'Hard Rubber (Ebonite)' (1935) 27 Industrial & Engineering Chemistry 141.

Kenyon KW and Kridler E, 'Laysan Albatrosses Swallow Indigestible Matter' (1969) 86 Auk 339.

Kern K, 'Governance For Sustainable Development in the Baltic Sea Region' (2011) 42 Journal of Baltic Studies 21.

Kerschner C, 'Economic De-Growth vs. Steady-State Economy' (2010) 18 Journal of Cleaner Production 544.

Kershaw P and others, 'Plastic Debris in the Ocean', *UNEP Year Book 2011: Emerging Issues in Our Global Environment* (UNEP 2011).

Khan SR, 'Trade Liberalization and the Environment: Northern and Southern Perspectives' in Shahrukh Rafi Khan (ed), *Trade and Environment: Difficult Policy Choices at the Interface* (Zed Books 2002).

Kiessling T, Gutow L and Thiel M, 'Biodiversity: Invasions by Marine Life on Plastic Debris' in Melanie Bergmann, Lars Gutow and Michael Klages (eds), *Marine Anthropogenic Litter* (Springer 2015).

Kim E-J, Kim J-W and Lee S-K, 'Inhibition of Oocyte Development in Japanese Medaka (Oryzias Latipes) Exposed to Di-2-Ethylhexyl Phthalate' (2002) 28 Environment International 359.

Kirkman H, 'The East Asian Seas UNEP Regional Seas Programme' (2006) 6 International Environmental Agreements: Politics, Law and Economics 305.

Kiss A and Shelton D, *International Environmental Law* (2nd edn, Transnational Publishers 2000).

Kiss A and Shelton D, 'Strict Liability in International Environmental Law' in Tafsir Malick Ndiaye and Rüdiger Wolfrum (eds), *Law of the Sea, Environmental Law and Settlement of Disputes* (Martinus Nijhoff Publishers 2007).

Klabbers J, 'Compliance Procedures' in Daniel Bodansky, Jutta Brunnée and Ellen Hey (eds), *The Oxford Handbook of International Environmental Law* (Oxford University Press 2007).

Klein N, *Dispute Settlement in the UN Convention on the Law of the Sea* (Cambridge University Press 2005).

Klemm D and others, 'Cellulose: Fascinating Biopolymer and Sustainable Raw Material' (2005) 44 Angewandte Chemie International Edition 3358.

Knight J and Gunatilaka R, 'Income, Aspirations and the Hedonic Treadmill in a Poor Society' (2012) 82 Journal of Economic Behavior & Organization 67.

Koellner T and Scholz R, 'Assessment of Land Use Impacts on the Natural Environment. Part 1: An Analytical Framework for Pure Land Occupation and Land Use Change' (2007) 12 The International Journal of Life Cycle Assessment 16.

Kostecki M (ed), *The Durable Use of Consumer Products: New Options for Business and Consumption* (Springer US 1998).

Koutsodendris A and others, 'Benthic Marine Litter in Four Gulfs in Greece, Eastern Mediterranean; Abundance, Composition and Source Identification' (2008) 77 Estuarine, Coastal and Shelf Science 501.

Krzan A and others, 'Standardization and Certification in the Area of Environmentally Degradable Plastics' (2006) 91 Polymer Degradation and Stability 2819.

Kühn S, Bravo Rebolledo EL and van Franeker JA, 'Deleterious Effects of Litter on Marine Life' in Melanie Bergmann, Lars Gutow and Michael Klages (eds), *Marine Anthropogenic Litter* (Springer 2015).

Kütting G, 'Mediterranean Pollution: International Cooperation and the Control of Pollution from Land-Based Sources' (1994) 18 Marine Policy 233.

Kuyper PJ, 'The Law of GATT as a Special Field of International Law: Ignorance, Further Refinement or Self-Contained System of International Law?' (1994) 25 Netherlands Yearbook of International Law 227.

Laffoley D d'A and others, 'The Protection and Management of the Sargasso Sea: The Golden Floating Rainforest of the Atlantic Ocean: Summary Science and Supporting Evidence Case' (Sargasso Sea Alliance 2011).

Laist DW, 'Impacts of Marine Debris: Entanglement of Marine Life in Marine Debris Including a Comprehensive List of Species with Entanglement and Ingestion Records' in James M Coe and Donald B Rogers (eds), *Marine Debris* (Springer New York 1997).

Lang I and others, 'Association of Urinary Bisphenol a Concentration with Medical Disorders and Laboratory Abnormalities in Adults' (2008) 300 JAMA 1303.

Latouche S, *Le pari de la décroissance* (Fayard 2006).

Latouche S, *Vers une société d'abondance frugale: Contresens et controverses de la décroissance* (Fayard/Mille et une nuits 2011).

Lavers JL and Bond AL, 'Exceptional and Rapid Accumulation of Anthropogenic Debris on One of the World's Most Remote and Pristine Islands' (2017) 114 Proceedings of the National Academy of Sciences 6052.

Law KL and others, 'Plastic Accumulation in the North Atlantic Subtropical Gyre' (2010) 329 Science 1185.

Law KL and others, 'Distribution of Surface Plastic Debris in the Eastern Pacific Ocean from an 11-Year Data Set' (2014) 48 Environmental Science & Technology 4732.

Lawrence WH and others, 'A Toxicological Investigation of Some Acute, Short-Term, and Chronic Effects of Administering Di-2-Ethylhexyl Phthalate (DEHP) and Other Phthalate Esters' (1975) 9 Environmental Research 1.

Lebow V, 'Price Competition in 1955' (1955) 31 Journal of Retailing 5.

Lebreton L and others, 'Evidence That the Great Pacific Garbage Patch Is Rapidly Accumulating Plastic' (2018) 8 Scientific Reports <http://www.nature.com/articles/s41598-018-22939-w> accessed 19 February 2022.

Lebreton LC-M, Greer SD and Borrero JC, 'Numerical Modelling of Floating Debris in the World's Oceans' (2012) 64 Marine Pollution Bulletin 653.

Lee DI, Cho HS and Jeong SB, 'Distribution Characteristics of Marine Litter on the Sea Bed of the East China Sea and the South Sea of Korea' (2006) 70 Estuarine, Coastal and Shelf Science 187.

Lefeber R, *Transboundary Environmental Interference and the Origin of State Liability* (Martinus Nijhoff Publishers 1996).

Lefeber R 'The Liability Provisions of Regional Sea Conventions: Dead Letters in the Sea?' in Davor Vidas and Willy Østreng (eds), *Order for the Oceans at the Turn of the Century* (Kluwer Law International 1999).

Lemann MF, *Waste Management* (Peter Lang 2008).

Lendlein A and Kelch S, 'Shape-Memory Polymers' (2002) 41 Angewandte Chemie International Edition 2034.

Leonas KK and Gorden RW, 'An Accelerated Laboratory Study Evaluating the Disintegration Rates of Plastic Films in Simulated Aquatic Environments' (1993) 1 Journal of Environmental Polymer Degradation 45.

Liffmann M and Boogaerts L, 'Linkages Between Land-Based Sources of Pollution and Marine Debris' in James M Coe and Donald B Rogers (eds), *Marine Debris: Sources, Impacts and Solutions* (Springer New York 1997).

Lindroos A and Mehling M, 'Dispelling the Chimera of "Self-Contained Regimes" International Law and the WTO' (2005) 16 European Journal of International Law 857.

Linzner R and Salhofer S, 'Municipal Solid Waste Recycling and the Significance of Informal Sector in Urban China' (2014) 32 Waste Management & Research 896.

Liu T-K, Wang M-W and Chen P, 'Influence of Waste Management Policy on the Characteristics of Beach Litter in Kaohsiung, Taiwan' (2013) 72 Marine Pollution Bulletin 99.

Lowe V, 'Sustainable Development and Unsustainable Arguments' in Alan Boyle and David Freestone (eds), *International Law and Sustainable Development: Past Achievements and Future Challenges* (Oxford University Press 1999).

Lucas N and others, 'Polymer Biodegradation: Mechanisms and Estimation Techniques – A Review' (2008) 73 Chemosphere 429.

Lyubomirsky S, 'Hedonic Adaptation to Positive and Negative Experiences' in Susan Folkman (ed), *The Oxford Handbook of Stress, Health, and Coping* (Oxford University Press, USA 2010).

Macfadyen G, Huntington T and Cappell R, *Abandoned, Lost or Otherwise Discarded Fishing Gear* (UNEP/FAO 2009).

Mackenzie R and Khalastchi R, 'Liability and Compensation for Environmental Damage in the Context of the Work of the United Nations Compensation Commission' (1996) 5 Review of European Community & International Environmental Law 281.

Maheim Jr BS, 'Annex V of the MARPOL Convention: Will It Stop Marine Plastic Pollution?' (1988) 1 Georgetown International Environmental Law Review 71.

Martin M and Parsapour A, 'Upcycling Wastes with Biogas Production: An Exergy and Economic Analysis', *Venice 2012: International Symposium on Energy from Biomass and Waste* (2012).

Martínez-Alier J, 'Environmental Justice and Economic Degrowth: An Alliance between Two Movements' (2012) 23 Capitalism Nature Socialism 51.

Martínez-Alier J, 'Sustainable De-Growth: Mapping the Context, Criticisms and Future Prospects of an Emergent Paradigm' (2010) 69 Ecological Economics 1741.

Mato Y and others, 'Plastic Resin Pellets as a Transport Medium for Toxic Chemicals in the Marine Environment' (2001) 35 Environmental Science & Technology 318.

Maximenko N, Hafner J and Niiler P, 'Pathways of Marine Debris Derived from Trajectories of Lagrangian Drifters' (2012) 65 Marine Pollution Bulletin 51.

McCarthy SP, 'Biodegradable Polymers' in AL Andrady (ed), *Plastics and the Environment* (Wiley-Interscience 2003).

McIlgorm A, Campbell HF and Rule MJ, 'The Economic Cost and Control of Marine Debris Damage in the Asia-Pacific Region' (2011) 54 Ocean & Coastal Management 643.

McIntyre O, *Environmental Protection of International Watercourses Under International Law* (Routledge 2016).

McLachlan C, 'The Principle of Systemic Integration and Article 31(3)(c) of the Vienna Convention' (2005) 54 International and Comparative Law Quarterly 279.

McNair AD, *The Law of Treaties* (2nd edn, Clarendon Press 1961).

Mead L, 'The "Crown Jewels" of Environmental Diplomacy: Assessing the UNEP Regional Seas Programme' (IISD Earth Negotiation Bulletin 2021) Still only one Earth: Lessons from 50 years of UN sustainable development policy Brief#17.

Meeker JD, Sathyanarayana S and Swan SH, 'Phthalates and Other Additives in Plastics: Human Exposure and Associated Health Outcomes' (2009) 364 Philosophical Transactions of the Royal Society B: Biological Sciences 2097.

Meier-Wehren B, 'The Global Programme of Action for the Protection of the Marine Environment from Land-Based Activities' (2013) 17 NZJ Envtl. L. 1.

Meijer LJJ and others, 'More Than 1000 Rivers Account for 80% of Global Riverine Plastic Emissions into the Ocean' (2021) 7 Science Advances eaaz5803.

Meikle JL, *American Plastic: A Cultural History* (Rutgers University Press 1995).

Mensah TA, 'The Dispute Settlement Regime of the 1982 United Nations Convention on the Law of the Sea' (1998) 2 Max Planck Yearbook of United Nations Law 307.

Mensah TA, 'The International Legal Regime for the Protection and Preservation of the Marine Environment from Land-Based Sources of Pollution' in Alan E Boyle and David Freestone (eds), *International Law and Sustainable Development: Past Achievements and Future Challenges* (Oxford University Press 1999).

Merrell TR, 'Accumulation of Plastic Litter on Beaches of Amchitka Island, Alaska' (1980) 3 Marine Environmental Research 171.

Merrills JG, *International Dispute Settlement* (Cambridge University Press 2011).

Miles EL, 'The Approaches of UNCLOS and Agenda 21 – A Synthesis' in Mochtar Kusuma-Atmadja, Thomas A Mensah and Bernard H Oxman (eds), *Sustainable Development and Preservation of the Oceans: The Challenges of UNCLOS and Agenda 21 – Proceedings the Law of the Sea Institute Twenty-Ninth Annual Conference (Despansar, Bali, Indonesia, 1995)* (Law of the Sea Institute 1997).

Mohee R and others, 'Biodegradability of Biodegradable/Degradable Plastic Materials under Aerobic and Anaerobic Conditions' (2008) 28 Waste Management 1624.

Molenaar EJ and Oude Elferink AG, 'Marine Protected Areas in Areas beyond National Jurisdiction: The Pioneering Efforts under the OSPAR Convention' (2009) 5 Utrecht Law Review.

Montjoie M, 'The Concept of Liability in the Absence of an Internationally Wrongful Act' in James Crawford, Alain Pellet and Simon Olleson (eds), *The Law of International Responsibility* (Oxford University Press 2010).

Mooibroek H and Cornish K, 'Alternative Sources of Natural Rubber' (2000) 53 Applied Microbiology and Biotechnology 355.

Moore C and Phillips C, *Plastic Ocean: How a Sea Captain's Chance Discovery Launched a Determined Quest to Save the Oceans* (Avery Trade 2011).

Moore CJ and others, 'A Comparison of Plastic and Plankton in the North Pacific Central Gyre' (2001) 42 Marine Pollution Bulletin 1297.

Moore CJ, Lattin GL and Zellers AF, 'Density of Plastic Particles Found in Zooplankton Trawls from Coastal Waters of California to the North Pacific Central Gyre', *The Plastic Debris Rivers to Sea Conference, Redondo Beach, california, USA* (2005).

Moreira FT and others, 'Revealing Accumulation Zones of Plastic Pellets in Sandy Beaches' (2016) 218 Environmental Pollution (Barking, Essex: 1987) 313.

Morishige C and others, 'Factors Affecting Marine Debris Deposition at French Frigate Shoals, Northwestern Hawaiian Islands Marine National Monument, 1990–2006' (2007) 54 Marine Pollution Bulletin 1162.

Morosini F, 'Trade and Climate Change: Unveiling the Principle of Common but Differentiated Responsibilities from the WTO Agreements' (2010) 42 George Washington International Law Review 713.

Morris AW and Hamilton EI, 'Polystyrene Spherules in the Bristol Channel' (1974) 5 Marine Pollution Bulletin 26.

Mouat J, Lopez Lozano R and Bateson H, 'Economic Impacts of Marine Litter' (KIMO International 2010).

Muthu SS and others, 'Carbon Footprint of Shopping (Grocery) Bags in China, Hong Kong and India' (2011) 45 Atmospheric Environment 469.

Myers BK, 'Trade Measures and the Environment: Can the WTO and UNCLOS Be Reconciled?' (2005) 23 UCLA J. Envtl. L. & Pol'y 37.

Netherlands Institute for the Law of the Sea, *International Organizations and the Law of the Sea: Documentary Yearbook*, vol 7 (1991).

Netherlands Institute for the Law of the Sea, *International Organizations and the Law of the Sea: Documentary Yearbook*, vol 8 (1992).

Newman S and others, 'The Economics of Marine Litter' in Melanie Bergmann, Lars Gutow and Michael Klages (eds), *Marine Anthropogenic Litter* (Springer 2015).

NOAA Physical Oceanography Division, 'Project Report 2017' (NOAA 2018) <http://www.aoml.noaa.gov/phod/docs/PhOD_programs.pdf> accessed 19 February 2022.

Nordquist MH and Nandan SN, *United Nations Convention on the Law of the Sea 1982: A Commentary, Vol VI: Articles 133 to 191* (Center for Oceans Law and Policy and Kluwer Law International 1985).

Nordquist MH, Nandan SN and Rosenne S, *United Nations Convention on the Law of the Sea 1982: A Commentary, Vol II: Articles 1 to 85* (Center for Oceans Law and Policy and Kluwer Law International 2002).

Nordquist MH, Nandan SN and Rosenne S, *United Nations Convention on the Law of the Sea 1982: A Commentary, Vol III: Articles 86 to 132* (Center for Oceans Law and Policy and Kluwer Law International 2002).

Nordquist MH, Rosenne S and Sohn LB (eds), *United Nations Convention on the Law of the Sea 1982: A Commentary, Vol V: Articles 279 to 320* (Center for Oceans Law and Policy and Kluwer Law International 1989).

Nordquist MH, Rosenne S and Yankov A (eds), *United Nations Convention on the Law of the Sea 1982: A Commentary, Vol IV: Articles 192 to 278* (Center for Oceans Law and Policy and Kluwer Law International 2002).

Nordsletten AE and Mataix-Cols D, 'Hoarding versus Collecting: Where Does Pathology Diverge from Play?' (2012) 32 Clinical Psychology Review 165.

Nzeadibe TC and Madu IA, 'Open Dump' in Carl Zimring and William Rathje, *Encyclopedia of Consumption and Waste: The Social Science of Garbage* (SAGE Publications, Inc 2012).

O'Cass A and McEwen H, 'Exploring Consumer Status and Conspicuous Consumption' (2004) 4 Journal of Consumer Behaviour 25.

Ocean Conservancy, 'International Coastal Cleanup 2017 Report' (2017) <https://oceanconservancy.org/wp-content/uploads/2017/04/2017-Ocean-Conservancy-ICC-Report.pdf> accessed 19 February 2022.

O'Connell DP, *The International Law of the Sea*, vol 1 (Ivan Anthony Shearer ed, Clarendon Press 1983).

O'Connell DP, *The International Law of the Sea*, vol 2 (Ivan Anthony Shearer ed, Clarendon Press 1984).

OECD, 'Recommendation of the Council on Guiding Principles Concerning International Economic Aspects of Environmental Policies' (1972) C(72)128.

OECD, 'Recommendation of the Council on the Implementation of the Polluter-Pays Principle' (1974) C(74)223.

OECD, 'Recommendation of the Council Concerning the Application of the Polluter-Pays Principle to Accidental Pollution' (1989) C(89)88.

OECD, 'Processes and Production Methods (PPMs): Conceptual Framework and Considerations on Use of PPM-Based Trade Measures' (OECD 1997) OCDE/GD(97)137.

OECD, *Extended Producer Responsibility: A Guidance Manual for Governments* (OECD Publishing 2001).

OECD, 'Revised Introduction to the OECD Guidelines for Testing of Chemicals, Section 3', *OECD Guidelines for the Testing of Chemicals, Section 3: Degradation and Accumulation* (OECD Publishing 2006).

OECD, *The Polluter Pays Principle: Definition, Analysis, Implementation* (OECD Publishing 2008).

Orós J and others, 'Diseases and Causes of Mortality among Sea Turtles Stranded in the Canary Islands, Spain (1998–2001)' (2005) 63 Diseases of Aquatic Organisms 13.

OSPAR Commission, *Background Document for the EcoQO on Plastic Particles in Stomachs of Seabirds* (2008).

OSPAR Commission, *Marine Litter in the North-East Atlantic Region: Assessment and Priorities for Response* (2009).

OSPAR Commission 'Regional Action Plan for Prevention and Management of Marine Litter in the North-East Atlantic' (2014).

OSPAR-HELCOM Joint Ministerial Meeting, 'Statement on the Ecosystem Approach to the Management of Human Activities "Towards an Ecosystem Approach to the Management of Human Activities"' (2003).

Ostromislenski I and Obstchestvo Proizv & Torgovli, 'A Process for Obtaining Rubber or Similar Substances from Polymerised Vinyl-Bromide or Polymerised Vinyl-Chloride or Their Methyl Homologues' Oude Elferink AG and Molenaar EJ (eds), *The International Legal Regime of Areas beyond National Jurisdiction: Current and Future Developments* (Martinus Nijhoff Publishers 2010).

Oxman BH, 'The Territorial Temptation: A Siren Song at Sea' (2006) 100 The American Journal of International Law 830.

Packard V, *The Waste Makers* (Reprint edn, Ig Publishing 1960).

Pagga U, 'Biodegradability and Compostability of Polymeric Materials in the Context of the European Packaging Regulation' (1998) 59 Polymer Degradation and Stability 371.

Panizzon M, Arnold L and Cottier T, 'Handel und Umwelt in der WTO: Entwicklungen und Perspektiven' [2010] Umweltrecht in der Praxis.

Papanicolopulu I, 'Procedures and Mechanisms on Compliance under the 1976/1995 Barcelona Convention on the Protection of the Mediterranean Sea and Its Protocols' in Tullio Treves and others (eds), *Non-Compliance Procedures and Mechanisms and the Effectiveness of International Environmental Agreements* (TMC Asser Press 2009).

Parkes A, Burt TS and Hall E, 'On the Properties of Parkesine, and Its Application to the Arts and Manufactures' (1865) 14 The Journal of the Society of Arts 81.

Pauwelyn J, 'The Role of Public International Law in the WTO: How Far Can We Go?' (2001) 95 American Journal of International Law 535.

Pauwelyn J, *Conflict of Norms in Public International Law: How WTO Law Relates to Other Rules of International Law* (Cambridge University Press 2003).

Pavasovic A, 'The Mediterranean Action Plan Phase II and the Revised Barcelona Convention: New Prospective for Integrated Coastal Management in the Mediterranean Region' (1996) 31 Ocean & Coastal Management 133.

Peck JD and others, 'Intra- and Inter-Individual Variability of Urinary Phthalate Metabolite Concentrations in Hmong Women of Reproductive Age' (2009) 20 Journal of Exposure Science and Environmental Epidemiology 90.

Peeken I and others, 'Arctic Sea Ice Is an Important Temporal Sink and Means of Transport for Microplastic' (2018) 9 Nature Communications 1505.

Peel J, *Science and Risk Regulation in International Law* (Cambridge University Press 2010).

Peet G, 'The MARPOL Convention: Implementation and Effectiveness' (1992) 7 Int'l J. Estuarine & Coastal L. 277.

Peeters JR and others, 'Closed Loop Recycling of Plastics Containing Flame Retardants' (2014) 84 Resources, Conservation and Recycling 35.

Pelouze TJ and Frémy E, *Notions générales de chimie avec un Atlas de 24 planches en coleur* (V Masson 1853).

Percival RV, 'International Responsibility and Liability for Environmental Harm' in Shawkat Alam and others (eds), *Routledge Handbook of International Environmental Law* (Routledge 2015).

Perrez FX, Cooperative Sovereignty: From Independence to Interdependence in the Structure of International Environmental Law (Kluwer Law International 2000).

Perrez FX, 'The Mutual Supportiveness of Trade and Environment' (2006) 100 ASIL Proceedings 26.

PERSGA, *Marine Litter in the PERSGA Region* (2008).

PlasticsEurope, 'Plastics – the Facts 2020: An Analysis of European Plastics Production, Demand and Waste Data' (2020).

Pol VG, 'Upcycling: Converting Waste Plastics into Paramagnetic, Conducting, Solid, Pure Carbon Microspheres' (2010) 44 Environmental Science & Technology 4753.

Pontavice E, 'Pollution' in Leo J Bouchez and L Kaijen (eds), *The Future of the Law of the Sea: Proceedings of the Symposium on the Future of the Sea organized at Den Helder by the Royal Netherlands Naval College and the International Law Institute of Utrecht State University 26 and 27 June 1972* (Martinus Nijhoff 1973).

Preston SD, 'Toward an Interdisciplinary Science of Consumption' (2011) 1236 Annals of the New York Academy of Sciences 1.

Puth S, *WTO und Umwelt: Die Produkt-Prozess-Doktrin* (Duncker & Humblot 2003).

Qing-Nan M, *Land Based Marine Pollution: International Law Development* (Graham & Trotman/Martinus Nijhoff 1987).

Raakjaer J and others, 'Ecosystem-Based Marine Management in European Regional Seas Calls for Nested Governance Structures and Coordination – a Policy Brief' (2014) 50, Part B Marine Policy 373.

Rajamani L, 'The Principle of Common but Differentiated Responsibility and the Balance of Commitments under the Climate Regime' (2000) 9 Review of European Community & International Environmental Law 120.

Rakestraw A, 'Open Oceans and Marine Debris: Solutions for the Ineffective Enforcement of MARPOL Annex V' (2012) 35 Hastings Int'l & Comp. L. Rev. 383.

Rauscher M, 'Keeping up with the Joneses: Chaotic Patterns in a Status Game' (1992) 40 Economics Letters 287.

Rayfuse R, 'Future of Compulsory Dispute Settlement under the Law of the Sea Convention' (2005) 36 Victoria University of Wellington Law Review 683.

Read R, 'Process and Production Methods and the Regulation of International Trade' in Nicolas Perdikis and Robert Read (eds), *The WTO and the Regulation of International*

Trade: Recent Trade Disputes Between the European Union and the United States (Edward Elgar 2005).

Redgwell C, 'From Permission to Prohibition: The 1982 Convention on the Law of the Sea and Protection of the Marine Environment' in David Freestone, Richard Barnes and David Ong (eds), *The Law of the Sea: Progress and Prospects* (Oxford University Press 2006).

Reyne M, *Plastic Forming Processes* (John Wiley & Sons 2013).

Roach JA, 'Today's Customary International Law of the Sea' (2014) 45 Ocean Development & International Law 239.

Robertson GL, *Food Packaging: Principles and Practice* (3rd edn, CRC Press 2013).

Robinson PR, 'Petroleum Processing Overview' in Chang S Hsu and Paul R Robinson (eds), *Practical Advances in Petroleum Processing* (Springer New York 2006).

Rochette J and others, 'Regional Oceans Governance Mechanisms: A Review' (2015) 60 Marine Policy 9.

Rochman CM, 'The Complex Mixture, Fate and Toxicity of Chemicals Associated with Plastic Debris in the Marine Environment' in Melanie Bergmann, Lars Gutow and Michael Klages (eds), *Marine Anthropogenic Litter* (Springer 2015).

Rochman CM, 'Ingested Plastic Transfers Hazardous Chemicals to Fish and Induces Hepatic Stress' (2013) 3 Scientific Reports 3263.

Rochman CM, 'Early Warning Signs of Endocrine Disruption in Adult Fish from the Ingestion of Polyethylene with and without Sorbed Chemical Pollutants from the Marine Environment' (2014) 493 The Science of the Total Environment 656.

Rochman CM, 'The Ecological Impacts of Marine Debris: Unraveling the Demonstrated Evidence from What Is Perceived' (2016) 97 Ecology 302.

Rosato DV, Rosato M and Rosato DV (eds), *Concise Encyclopedia of Plastics* (Springer Science & Business Media 2000).

Rosato DV, Rosato MG and Schott NR, *Plastics Technology Handbook Volume 1* (Momentum Press 2010).

Rosevelt C and others, 'Marine Debris in Central California: Quantifying Type and Abundance of Beach Litter in Monterey Bay, CA' (2013) 71 Marine Pollution Bulletin 299.

Rothwell DR and Stephens T, *The International Law of the Sea* (2nd edn, Hart Publishing 2016).

Roy A, 'Open Burning' in Carl Zimring and William Rathje, *Encyclopedia of Consumption and Waste: The Social Science of Garbage* (SAGE Publications, Inc 2012).

Rudel RA and others, 'Correlations Between Urinary Phthalate Metabolites and Phthalates, Estrogenic Compounds 4-Butyl Phenol and o-Phenyl Phenol, and Some Pesticides in Home Indoor Air and House Dust' (2008) 19 Epidemiology ISEE 2008 Conference Abstracts Supplement.

Rudnik E, *Compostable Polymer Materials* (Elsevier 2008).

Rushbrook P, *Solid Waste Landfills in Middle- and Lower-Income Countries: A Technical Guide to Planning, Design, and Operation* (The World Bank 1999).

Ryan PG, 'The Characteristics and Distribution of Plastic Particles at the Sea-Surface off the Southwestern Cape Province, South Africa' (1988) 25 Marine Environmental Research 249.

Ryan PG, 'A Simple Technique for Counting Marine Debris at Sea Reveals Steep Litter Gradients between the Straits of Malacca and the Bay of Bengal' (2013) 69 Marine Pollution Bulletin 128.

Ryan PG, 'Litter Survey Detects the South Atlantic "Garbage Patch"' (2014) 79 Marine Pollution Bulletin 220.

Ryan PG, 'A Brief History of Marine Litter Research' in Melanie Bergmann, Lars Gutow and Michael Klages (eds), *Marine Anthropogenic Litter* (Springer 2015).

Ryan PG, 'Monitoring the Abundance of Plastic Debris in the Marine Environment' (2009) 364 Philosophical Transactions of the Royal Society of London B: Biological Sciences 1999.

Ryan PG, 'Rapid Increase in Asian Bottles in the South Atlantic Ocean Indicates Major Debris Inputs from Ships' [2019] Proceedings of the National Academy of Sciences 201909816.

SACEP, *Marine Litter in the South Asian Seas Region* (2007).

SACEP, 'Towards Litter Free Indian Ocean: Summary of the Regional Marine Litter Action Plan for South Asian Seas Region' (2018).

Sadeleer N de, *Environmental Principles: From Political Slogans to Legal Rules* (Oxford University Press 2002).

Salman SMA, 'The Helsinki Rules, the UN Watercourses Convention and the Berlin Rules: Perspectives on International Water Law' (2007) 23 International Journal of Water Resources Development 625.

Sands P, 'Sustainable Development: Treaty, Custom, and the Cross-Fertilization of International Law' in Alan Boyle and David Freestone (eds), *International Law and Sustainable Development: Past Achievements and Future Challenges* (Oxford University Press 1999).

Sands P, and Peel J, *Principles of International Environmental Law* (3rd edn, Cambridge University Press 2012).

Sathyanarayana S and others, 'Baby Care Products: Possible Sources of Infant Phthalate Exposure' (2008) 121 Pediatrics e260.

Schäli J, 'Marine Plastic Pollution as a Common Concern of Humankind' in Thomas Cottier (ed), *The Prospects of Common Concern of Humankind in International Law* (Cambridge University Press 2021).

Schäli J, 'Intergenerational Justice and the Concept of Common Concern in Marine Resource Allocation and Ocean Governance' in Thomas Cottier, Shaheeza Lalani and Clarence Sibiza (eds), *Intergenerational Equity: Environmental and Cultural Concerns* (Brill Nijhoff 2019).

Scheinberg A, Wilson DC and Rodic L, *Solid Waste Management in the World's Cities: Water and Sanitation in the World's Cities 2010* (Earthscan for UN-HABITAT 2010).

Schneider F, Kallis G and Martinez-Alier J, 'Crisis or Opportunity? Economic Degrowth for Social Equity and Ecological Sustainability' (2010) 18 Journal of Cleaner Production 511.

Schoenbaum TJ, 'WTO Dispute Settlement: Praise and Suggestions for Reform' (1998) 47 The International and Comparative Law Quarterly 647.

Schrijver N, *Sovereignty over Natural Resources: Balancing Rights and Duties* (Cambridge University Press 1997).

Schrijver N, *The Evolution of Sustainable Development in International Law: Inception, Meaning and Status* (Martinus Nijhoff Publishers 2008).

Schwarz AE and others, 'Sources, Transport, and Accumulation of Different Types of Plastic Litter in Aquatic Environments: A Review Study' (2019) 143 Marine Pollution Bulletin 92.

Scott G, 'Plastics Packaging and Coastal Pollution' (1972) 3 International Journal of Environmental Studies 35.

Scott G, 'Science and Standards' in Emo Chiellini and Roberto Solaro (eds), *Biodegradable Polymers and Plastics* (Springer Science & Business Media 2003).

Scott SV, 'The LOS Convention as a Constitutional Regime for the Oceans' in Alex G Oude Elferink (ed), *Stability And Change in the Law of the Sea: The Role of the LOS Convention* (Martinus Nijhoff Publishers 2005).

Scottish Government, 'Scotland's Zero Waste Plan' (2010).

Scottish Government, 'Marine Scotland: A Marine Litter Strategy for Scotland' (2014).

Scottish Government, 'Towards a Litter-Free Scotland: A Strategic Approach to Higher Quality Local Environments' (2014).

Scovazzi T, 'The Mediterranean Guidelines for the Determination of Environmental Liability and Compensation: The Negotiations for the Instrument and the Question of Damage That Can Be Compensated' (2009) 13 Max Planck Yearbook of United Nations Law 183.

Scovazzi T, 'The Seabed beyond the Limits of National Jurisdiction: General and Institutional Aspects' in AG Oude Elferink and EJ Molenaar (eds), *The International Legal Regime of Areas beyond National Jurisdiction: Current and Future Developments* (Koninklijke Brill NV 2010).

Scovazzi T, 'The Governance of the Mediterranean Sea' in Joseph F DiMento and Alexis Jaclyn Hickman (eds), *Environmental Governance of the Great Seas: Law and Effect* (Edward Elgar Publishing 2012).

Selke SEM, 'Plastics in Packaging' in AL Andrady (ed), *Plastics and the Environment* (Wiley Interscience 2003).

Semon WL, 'Synthetic Rubber-like Composition and Method of Making Same'.

Semon WL, 'Method of Preparing Polyvinyl Halide Products'.

Serpin P, 'The Public Morals Exception after the WTO Seal Products Dispute: Has the Exception Swallowed the Rules' [2016] Colum. Bus. L. Rev. 217.

Sershen S and West J, 'Implantable, Polymeric Systems for Modulated Drug Delivery' (2002) 54 Advanced Drug Delivery Reviews 1225.

Seyfang G, *The New Economics of Sustainable Consumption: Seeds of Change* (1st edn, Palgrave Macmillan 2009).

Shah AA and others, 'Biological Degradation of Plastics: A Comprehensive Review' (2008) 26 Biotechnology Advances 246.

Shelton D, 'Common Concern of Humanity' (2009) 5 Iustum Aequum Salutare 33.

Simcock A, 'OSPAR Convention on the Protection of the Marine Environment of the North-East Atlantic' in Ulrich Beyerlin, Peter-Tobias Stoll and Rüdiger Wolfrum (eds), *Ensuring Compliance with Multilateral Environmental Agreements: A Dialogue between Practitioners and Academics* (Martinus Nijhoff Publishers 2006).

Simma B, 'Doctrinal Expressions of Community Interest in International Law', *Collected Courses of the Hague Academy of International Law*, vol 250 (The Hague Academy of International Law/Brill Online 1994).

Simma B, 'Of Planets and the Universe: Self-Contained Regimes in International Law' (2006) 17 European Journal of International Law 483.

Simma B, 'Universality of International Law from the Perspective of a Practitioner' (2009) 20 European Journal of International Law 265.

Simon N and Schulte ML, 'Stopping Global Plastic Pollution: The Case for an International Convention' (Heinrich Böll Stiftung 2017) Ecology Publication Series 43.

Singh J and others, 'Progress and Challenges to the Global Waste Management System' (2014) 32 Waste Management & Research 800.

Slade G, *Made to Break: Technology and Obsolescence in America* (Harvard University Press 2007).

Slat B and others, *How the Oceans Can Clean Themselves: A Feasibility Study* (2.0, The Ocean Cleanup 2014).

Smith SDA, 'Marine Debris: A Proximate Threat to Marine Sustainability in Bootless Bay, Papua New Guinea' (2012) 64 Marine Pollution Bulletin 1880.

Song JH and others, 'Biodegradable and Compostable Alternatives to Conventional Plastics' (2009) 364 Philosophical Transactions of the Royal Society B: Biological Sciences 2127.

Spaargaren G, 'Sustainable Consumption: A Theoretical and Environmental Policy Perspective' (2003) 16 Society & Natural Resources 687.

SPREP, 'Cleaner Pacific 2025: Pacific Regional Waste and Pollution Management Strategy 2016–2025' (2016).

STAP, 'Marine Debris as a Global Environmental Problem: Introducing a Solutions Based Framework on Plastic' (GEF 2011).

Stephens T, 'The Settlement of Disputes in International Environmental Law' in Shawkat Alam and others (eds), *Routledge Handbook of International Environmental Law* (Routledge 2015).

Sterngass J and Kachur M, *Great Inventions: Plastics* (World Almanac Library 2006).

Stockholm Convention, 'Guidelines on Best Available Techniques and Provisional Guidance on Best Environmental Practices Relevant to Article 5 and Annex C of the Stockholm Convention on Persistent Organic Pollutants: Open Burning of Waste, Including Burning of Landfill Sites' (2008).

Stockholm Convention, 'Guidance on Best Available Techniques and Best Environmental Practices for the Recycling and Disposal of Articles Containing Polybrominated Diphenyl Ethers (PBDEs) Listed under the Stockholm Convention on Persistent Organic Pollutants'.

Stockmann R, 'Understanding Sustainability Evaluation and Its Contributions to Policy-Making' in Anneke von Raggamby and Frieder Rubik (eds), *Sustainable development, evaluation and policy making: theory, practise and quality assurance* (Edward Elgar 2012).

Stöfen-O'Brien A, *The International and European Legal Regime Regulating Marine Litter in the EU* (Nomos Verlag 2015).

Stoll P-T and Vöneky S, 'The Swordfish Case: Law of the Sea v. Trade' (2002) 62 ZAÖRV 21.

Stone CD, 'Common but Differentiated Responsibilities in International Law' (2004) 98 The American Journal of International Law 276.

Stutzer A, 'The Role of Income Aspirations in Individual Happiness' (2004) 54 Journal of Economic Behavior & Organization 89.

Sun R-D and others, 'Suppressing Effect of CaCO3 on the Dioxins Emission from Poly(Vinyl Chloride) (PVC) Incineration' (2003) 79 Polymer Degradation and Stability 253.

Sundt P, Schulze P-E and Syversen F, 'Sources of Microplastics-Pollution to the Marine Environment' (Norwegian Environment Agency 2015) M-321|2015.

Swan PL, 'Optimum Durability, Second-Hand Markets, and Planned Obsolescence' (1972) 80 Journal of Political Economy 575.

Swan SH, 'Environmental Phthalate Exposure in Relation to Reproductive Outcomes and Other Health Endpoints in Humans' (2008) 108 Environmental Research 177.

Swan SH, 'Decrease in Anogenital Distance among Male Infants with Prenatal Phthalate Exposure' (2005) 113 Environmental Health Perspectives 1056.

Sykes P, Jones K and Wildsmith JohnD, 'Managing the Potential Public Health Risks from Bioaerosol Liberation at Commercial Composting Sites in the UK: An Analysis of the Evidence Base' (2007) 52 Resources, Conservation and Recycling 410.

Tabone MD and others, 'Sustainability Metrics: Life Cycle Assessment and Green Design in Polymers' (2010) 44 Environmental Science & Technology 8264.

Taha MPM and others, 'Bioaerosol Releases from Compost Facilities: Evaluating Passive and Active Source Terms at a Green Waste Facility for Improved Risk Assessments' (2006) 40 Atmospheric Environment 1159.

Tams CJ, 'Individual States as Guardians of Community Interests' in Ulrich Fastenrath and others (eds), *From Bilateralism to Community Interest: Essays in Honour of Judge Bruno Simma* (Oxford University Press 2011).

Tanaka Y, 'Regulation of Land-Based Marine Pollution in International Law: A Comparative Analysis between Global and Regional Legal Frameworks' (2006) 66 Zeitschrift fuer Ausländisches Öffentliches Recht und Völkerrecht [Heidelberg Journal of International Law] 535.

Tanaka Y, *The International Law of the Sea* (2nd edn, Cambridge University Press 2015).

Tanzi A and Arcari M, *The United Nations Convention on the Law of International Watercourses: A Framework for Sharing* (Kluwer Law International 2001).

ten Brink P and others, *Guidelines on the Use of Market-Based Instruments to Address the Problem of Marine Litter* (UNEP 2009).

ten Brink P and others, 'Plastics Marine Litter and the Circular Economy: A Briefing by IEEP for the MAVA Foundation' (IEEP 2016).

ter Halle A and others, 'Understanding the Fragmentation Pattern of Marine Plastic Debris' (2016) 50 Environmental Science & Technology 5668.

Teuten EL and others, 'Transport and Release of Chemicals from Plastics to the Environment and to Wildlife' (2009) 364 Philosophical Transactions of the Royal Society B: Biological Sciences 2027.

The Law of the Sea: Official Text of the United Nations Convention on the Law of the Sea (United Nations 1983).

Thiel M and others, 'Spatio-Temporal Distribution of Floating Objects in the German Bight (North Sea)' (2011) 65 Journal of Sea Research 368.

Thiel M and others, 'Anthropogenic Marine Debris in the Coastal Environment: A Multi-Year Comparison between Coastal Waters and Local Shores' (2013) 71 Marine Pollution Bulletin 307.

Thompson RC, 'Plastic Debris in the Marine Environment: Consequences and Solutions' in Jochen C Krause, Henning von Nordheim and Stefan Bräger (eds), *Marine Nature Conservation in Europe 2006: Proceedings of the Symposium held in Stralsund, Germany, 8th–12th May 2006* (German Federal Agency for Nature Conservation 2007).

Thompson RC, 'Microplastics in the Marine Environment: Sources, Consequences and Solutions' in Melanie Bergmann, Lars Gutow and Michael Klages (eds), *Marine Anthropogenic Litter* (Springer 2015).

Thompson RC, and others, 'Plastics, the Environment and Human Health: Current Consensus and Future Trends' (2009) 364 Philosophical Transactions of the Royal Society B: Biological Sciences 2153.

'Throwaway Living: Disposable Items Cut Down Household Chores' [1955] *LIFE* 49.

Titow WV, *PVC Technology* (4th edn, Elsevier Applied Science Publishers 1984).

Tolinski M, *Plastics and Sustainability: Towards a Peaceful Coexistence between Bio-Based and Fossil Fuel-Based Plastics* (John Wiley & Sons 2011).

Tomczak M, 'Defining Marine Pollution: A Comparison of Definitions Used by International Conventions' (1984) 8 Marine Policy 311.

Topçu EN and others, 'Origin and Abundance of Marine Litter along Sandy Beaches of the Turkish Western Black Sea Coast' (2013) 85 Marine Environmental Research 21.

Torrens DL, 'Protection of the Marine Environment in International Law: Toward an Effective Regime of the Law of the Sea' (1994) 19 Queens Law Journal 613.

Treves T, 'A System for the Law of the Sea Dispute Settlement' in David Freestone, Richard Barnes and David Ong (eds), *The Law of the Sea: Progress and Prospects* (Oxford University Press 2006).

Treves T, 'Principles and Objectives of the Legal Regime Governing Areas Beyond National Jurisdiction' in AG Oude Elferink and EJ Molenaar (eds), *The International Legal Regime of Areas beyond National Jurisdiction: Current and Future Developments* (Koninklijke Brill NV 2010).

Trigg AB, 'Veblen, Bourdieu, and Conspicuous Consumption' (2001) 35 Journal of Economic Issues 99.

Truman HS, 'Presidential Proclamation No. 2667 – Policy of the United States With Respect to the Natural Resources of the Subsoil and Sea Bed of the Continental Shelf' (1945) 10 Fed. Reg. 12,303.

Tuerk H, 'The Work of the International Tribunal for the Law of the Sea' (2012) 26 Ocean Yearbook Online 181.

Turra A and others, 'Three-Dimensional Distribution of Plastic Pellets in Sandy Beaches: Shifting Paradigms' (2014) 4 Scientific Reports.

UNCTAD, 'Material Substitutes to Address Marine Plastic Pollution and Support a Circular Economy: Issues and Options for Trade Policymakers' (2021) UNCTAD/DITC/TED/INF/2021/5.

UNDP and GEF, 'Plastics and Circular Economy Community Solutions' (2019).

UNECE Watercourse Convention, 'Guide to Implementing The Water Convention' (United Nations 2013) ECE/MP.WAT/39.

UNECE Watercourse Convention, 'The Global Opening of the 1992 Water Convention' (United Nations 2016) ECE/MP.WAT/43/Rev.1.

UNEP, 'Goals and Principles of Environmental Impact Assessment (UNEP 1987 EIA Principles)' (1987) Governing Council Res 14/25 (1987), endorsed by UN General Assembly Res 42/184 (1987).

UNEP, *Marine Litter – Trash That Kills* (2001).

UNEP, (ed), *Capacity Building for Sustainable Development: An Overview of UNEP Environmental Capacity Development Initiatives* (2002).

UNEP, *Marine Litter: An Analytical Overview* (UNEP 2005).

UNEP, *Marine Litter: A Global Challenge* (UNEP 2009).

UNEP, *UNEP Year Book 2014: Emerging Issues in Our Global Environment* (UNEP 2014).

UNEP, 'Valuing Plastic: The Business Case for Measuring, Managing and Disclosing Plastic Use in the Consumer Goods Industry' (UNEP 2014).

UNEP, *Biodegradable Plastics & Marine Litter: Misconceptions, Concerns and Impacts on Marine Environments* (UNEP 2015).

UNEP, *Plastic in Cosmetics: Are We Polluting the Environment through Our Personal Care?* (2015).

UNEP, *Marine Litter Legislation: A Toolkit for Policymakers* (UNEP 2016).

UNEP, 'Marine Plastic Debris and Microplastics: Global Lessons and Research to Inspire Action and Guide Policy Change' (2016) (UNEA-2 Technical Report on Marine Plastic Debris).

UNEP, 'Regional Oceans Governance: Making Regional Seas Programmes, Regional Fishery Bodies and Large Marine Ecosystem Mechanisms Work Better Together' (UNEP 2016) UNEP Regional Seas Reports and Studies No 197.

UNEP, 'Combating Marine Plastic Litter and Microplastics: An Assessment of the Effectiveness of Relevant International, Regional and Subregional Governance Strategies and Approaches' (2017) (UNEA-3 Legal Report) UNEP/EA.3/INF/5.

UNEP, 'Addressing Marine Plastics: A Systemic Approach – Stocktaking Report' (2018).

UNEP, 'Mapping of Global Plastics Value Chain and and Plastics Losses to the Environment (with a Particular Focus on Marine Environment)' (2018).

UNEP, *Single-Use Plastics: A Roadmap for Sustainability* (2018).

UNEP, 'Combating Marine Plastic Litter and Microplastics: An Assessment of the Effectiveness of Relevant International, Regional and Subregional Governance Strategies and Approaches – Summary for Policy Makers' (2018) UNEP/AHEG/2018/1/INF/3.

UNEP, 'Legal Limits on Single-Use Plastics and Microplastics: A Global Review of National Laws and Regulations' (2018).

UNEP, 'Analysis of Voluntary Commitments Targeting Marine Litter and Microplastics Pursuant to Resolution 3/7 – Report of the Executive Director' (2018) UNEP/EA.4/11.

UNEP, 'Annual Report 2018' (2019).

UNEP, 'Plastics and Shallow Water Coral Reefs: Synthesis of the Science for Policy-Makers' (2019).

UNEP, 'Addressing Single-Use Plastic Products Pollution Using a Life Cycle Approach (2021).

UNEP, 'Review of Development Activities Since 1985 – Note by the Secretariat' UNEP/MG/IG/1/2 of 29 April 1994.

UNEP, and GPA, *The State of the Marine Environment: Trends and Processes* (UNEP/GPA Coordination Office 2006).

UNEP, and GRID-Arendal, *Marine Litter: Vital Graphics* (2016).

UNEP, and NOAA, 'Summary Proceedings of the 5th International Marine Debris Conference, Held on 20–25 March 2011 in Honolulu, HI, USA' (2011).

UNEP, and NOAA, 'The Honolulu Strategy: A Global Framework for Prevention and Management of Marine Debris' (2011).

UNEP, and WIOMSA, *Marine Litter in the Eastern Africa Region: An Overview Assessment* (2008).

UNEP-CAR/RCU, 'Regional Action Plan on Marine Litter Management (RAPMali) for the Wider Caribbean Region 2014' (2014).

UNEP-CEP, *Marine Litter in the Wider Caribbean: A Regional Overview and Action Plan* (2008).

UNEP-COBSEA, 'Regional Programme of Action for the Protection of the Marine Environment of the East Asian Seas from the Effects of Land-Based Activities' (2000).

UNEP-COBSEA, *Marine Litter in the East Asian Seas Region* (2008).

UNEP-COBSEA, *Regional Action Plan on Marine Litter* (2019).

UNEP-COBSEA, 'Report of the Twenty-First Meeting of the Coordinating Body on the Seas of East Asia (COBSEA)' (2013) UNEP/DEPI/COBSEA IGM 21/6.

UNEP-COBSEA, 'COBSEA Strategic Directions 2018–2022' (2018).

UNEP-MAP, 'Regional Plan for the Marine Litter Management in the Mediterranean' (2013) UNEP (DEPI)/MED WG.379/5.

UNEP-MAP, *Marine Litter Assessment in the Mediterranean* (2015).

UNEP-NOWPAP, *Marine Litter in the Northwest Pacific Region* (2008).

UNEP-NOWPAP, 'NOWPAP Regional Action Plan on Marine Litter' (2008).

UNGA, 'Our Ocean, Our Future: Call for Action' (A/CONF230/11, Annex 2017).

United Nations, 'Glossary of Environment Statistics' (United Nations 1997) Series F, No. 67 (UN Doc. ST/ESA/STAT/SER.F/67).

United Nations, 'UNCLOS at 30' (United Nations 2012) <http://www.un.org/depts/los/convention_agreements/pamphlet_unclos_at_30.pdf> accessed 19 February 2022.

United Nations, 'Addis Ababa Action Agenda of the Third International Conference on Financing for Development' (2015).

University of Chicago (ed), *Encyclopaedia Britannica*, vol 14 (15th edn, 1977).

US Environmental Protection Agency, *Municipal Solid Waste Generation, Recycling, and Disposal in the United States: Tables and Figures for 2012* (2014).

US Environmental Protection Agency, Curlee TR and Das S, *Plastic Wastes: Management, Control, Recycling, and Disposal – Pollution Technology Review No. 201* (Noyes Data Corp 1991).

Utaka A, 'Planned Obsolescence and Marketing Strategy' (2000) 21 Managerial and Decision Economics 339.

Van Cauwenberghe L and others, 'Microplastic Pollution in Deep-Sea Sediments' (2013) 182 Environmental Pollution 495.

van Dyke JM, 'Whither the UNEP Regional Seas Programmes?' in Harry N Scheiber and Jin-Hyun Paik (eds), *Regions, Institutions, and Law of the Sea: Studies in Ocean Governance* (Martinus Nijhoff Publishers 2013).

van Leeuwen J, van Hoof L and van Tatenhove J, 'Institutional Ambiguity in Implementing the European Union Marine Strategy Framework Directive' (2012) 36 Marine Policy 636.

van Sebille E, England MH and Froyland G, 'Origin, Dynamics and Evolution of Ocean Garbage Patches from Observed Surface Drifters' (2012) 7 Environmental Research Letters 044040.

van Sebille E and others, 'A Global Inventory of Small Floating Plastic Debris' (2015) 10 Environmental Research Letters 124006.

van Tatenhove JPM, 'How to Turn the Tide: Developing Legitimate Marine Governance Arrangements at the Level of the Regional Seas' (2013) 71 Ocean & Coastal Management 296.

Vandenberg LN and others, 'Human Exposure to Bisphenol A (BPA)' (2007) 24 Reproductive Toxicology 139.

Vandenberg LN and others, 'Hormones and Endocrine-Disrupting Chemicals: Low-Dose Effects and Nonmonotonic Dose Responses' (2012) 33 Endocrine Reviews 378.

VanderZwaag D and Powers A, 'The Protection of the Marine Environment from Land-Based Pollution and Activities: Gauging the Tides of Global and Regional Governance' (2008) 23 The International Journal of Marine and Coastal Law 423.

Vaurs-Chaumette A-L, 'The International Community as a Whole' in James Crawford, Alain Pellet and Simon Olleson (eds), *The Law of International Responsibility* (Oxford University Press 2010).

Veblen T, 'The Theory of the Leisure Class' [1899] New York: The New American Library.

Victor PA, 'Growth, Degrowth and Climate Change: A Scenario Analysis' (2012) 84 Ecological Economics 206.

Vidas D (ed), *Law, Technology and Science for Oceans in Globalisation: IUU Fishing, Oil Pollution, Bioprospecting, Outer Continental Shelf* (Brill 2010).

Vidas D, 'Responsibility for the Seas' in Davor Vidas (ed), *Law, Technology and Science for Oceans in Globalisation: IUU Fishing, Oil Pollution, Bioprospecting, Outer Continental Shelf* (Brill 2010).

Vidas D, and Schei PJ (eds), *The World Ocean in Globalisation: Climate Change, Sustainable Fisheries, Biodiversity, Shipping, Regional Issues* (Brill 2011).

Viñuales JE (ed), *The Rio Declaration on Environment and Development: A Commentary* (Oxford University Press 2015).

Voigt C, *Sustainable Development as a Principle of International Law: Resolving Conflicts between Climate Measures and WTO Law* (Martinus Nijhoff Publishers 2009).

vom Saal FS and Welshons WV, 'Large Effects from Small Exposures. II. The Importance of Positive Controls in Low-Dose Research on Bisphenol A' (2006) 100 Environmental Research 50.

Vranes E, *Trade and the Environment: Fundamental Issues in International Law, WTO Law, and Legal Theory* (Oxford University Press 2009).

Wagner M and Oehlmann J, 'Endocrine Disruptors in Bottled Mineral Water: Total Estrogenic Burden and Migration from Plastic Bottles' (2009) 16 Environmental Science and Pollution Research 278.

Waldman M, 'A New Perspective on Planned Obsolescence' (1993) 108 The Quarterly Journal of Economics 273.

Wang J and others, 'Chapter 25: Marine Debris' in UN (ed), *First World Ocean Assessment* (United Nations 2016).

Watkins E and others, 'Marine Litter: Socio-Economic Study – Scoping Report' (IEEP 2015).

WCED, *Our Common Future (Brundtland Report)* (Oxford University Press 1987).

Weber H, 'Landfills, Modern' in Carl Zimring and William Rathje, *Encyclopedia of Consumption and Waste: The Social Science of Garbage* (SAGE Publications, Inc 2012).

Weiler JHH, 'The Rule of Lawyers and the Ethos of Diplomats Reflections on the Internal and External Legitimacy of WTO Dispute Settlement' (2001) 35 Journal of World Trade 191.

Weilgart LS, 'The Impacts of Anthropogenic Ocean Noise on Cetaceans and Implications for Management' (2007) 85 Canadian Journal of Zoology 1091.

Weisslitz M, 'Rethinking the Equitable Principle of Common but Differentiated Responsibility: Differential versus Absolute Norms of Compliance and Contribution in the Global Climate Change Context' (2002) 13 Colorado Journal of International Environmental Law and Policy 473.

Welshons WV and others, 'Large Effects from Small Exposures. I. Mechanisms for Endocrine-Disrupting Chemicals with Estrogenic Activity'. (2003) 111 Environmental Health Perspectives 994.

Wendel B and others, 'Additive Processing of Polymers' (2008) 293 Macromolecular Materials and Engineering 799.

Whinfield JR and Dickson JT, 'Verfahren zur Herstellung hochpolymerer Polyester'.

WHO, *Microplastics in Drinking-Water* (2019).

Wiener JB, 'Precaution' in Daniel Bodansky, Jutta Brunnée and Ellen Hey (eds), *The Oxford Handbook of International Environmental Law* (Oxford University Press 2007).

Wiers J, 'WTO Rules and Environmental Production and Processing Methods (PPMs)' (2001) 2 ERA-Forum 101.

Williams JA and others, 'Synthetic, Implantable Polymers for Local Delivery of IUdR to Experimental Human Malignant Glioma' (1998) 42 International Journal of Radiation Oncology*Biology*Physics 631.

Williams PT, *Waste Treatment and Disposal* (2nd edn, John Wiley & Sons 2005).

Wolfrum R, 'The Settlement of Disputes Before the International Tribunal for the Law of the Sea – A Progressive Development of International Law or Relying on Traditional Mechanisms?' (2008) 51 Japanese Yearbook of International Law.

Wolfrum R, and Matz N, *Conflicts in International Environmental Law* (Springer 2003).

Woodall LC and others, 'The Deep Sea Is a Major Sink for Microplastic Debris' (2014) 1 Royal Society Open Science 140317.

Wormuth M and others, 'What Are the Sources of Exposure to Eight Frequently Used Phthalic Acid Esters in Europeans?' (2006) 26 Risk Analysis 803.

Wyeth NC and Roseveare RN, 'Biaxially Oriented Poly(Ethylene Terephthalate)Bottle'.

Xue H, *Transboundary Damage in International Law* (Cambridge University Press 2003).

Yamashita R and Tanimura A, 'Floating Plastic in the Kuroshio Current Area, Western North Pacific Ocean' (2007) 54 Marine Pollution Bulletin 485.

Yang CZ and others, 'Most Plastic Products Release Estrogenic Chemicals: A Potential Health Problem That Can Be Solved' (2011) 119 Environmental Health Perspectives 989.

Yankov A, 'The Law of the Sea Convention and Agenda 21: Marine Environmental Implications' in Alan Boyle and David Freestone (eds), *International Law and Sustainable Development: Past Achievements and Future Challenges* (Oxford University Press 1999).

Yates MR and Barlow CY, 'Life Cycle Assessments of Biodegradable, Commercial Biopolymers – A Critical Review' (2013) 78 Resources, Conservation and Recycling 54.

Young LC and others, 'Bringing Home the Trash: Do Colony-Based Differences in Foraging Distribution Lead to Increased Plastic Ingestion in Laysan Albatrosses?' (2009) 4 PLOS one e7623.

Young W and others, 'Sustainable Consumption: Green Consumer Behaviour When Purchasing Products' (2010) 18 Sustainable Development 20.

Zhou P and others, 'The Abundance, Composition and Sources of Marine Debris in Coastal Seawaters or Beaches around the Northern South China Sea (China)' (2011) 62 Marine Pollution Bulletin 1998.

Zhuo C and Levendis YA, 'Upcycling Waste Plastics into Carbon Nanomaterials: A Review' (2014) 131 Journal of Applied Polymer Science 39931 (1).

Decisions and Meeting Reports of International Bodies

AHEG, 'Chair's Summary of the Work of the Ad Hoc Open-Ended Expert Group on Marine Litter and Microplastics for Consideration by the United Nations

Environment Assembly at Its Fifth Session' (November 2020) <https://wedocs.unep.org/bitstream/handle/20.500.11822/34635/K2100061.pdf?sequence=11&isAllowed=y> accessed 19 February 2022.

Barcelona Convention MoP Decision IG.17/2 (2008), 'Procedures and Mechanisms on Compliance under the Barcelona Convention and Its Protocols' UNEP(DEPI)/MED IG.17/10 Annex V, 21, as amended by Decisions IG.20/1, IG. 21/1 and IG.22/15.

Barcelona Convention MoP Decision IG.17/3 (2008), 'Format for the Implementation of the Barcelona Convention and Its Protocols' UNEP(DEPI)/MED IG.17/10 Annex V, 29.

Barcelona Convention MoP Decision IG.17/6 (2008), 'Implementation of the Ecosystem Approach to the Management of Human Activities That May Affect the Mediterranean Marine and Coastal Environment' UNEP(DEPI)/MED IG.17/10 Annex V, 179.

Barcelona Convention MoP Decision IG.19/1 (2009), 'Rules of Procedure for the Compliance Committee and Its Work during 2010–2011 Biennium' UNEP(DEPI)/MED IG.19/8 Annex II, 1, as amended by Decision IG.21/1.

Barcelona Convention MoP Decision IG.19/4 (2009), 'Testing MAP Effectiveness Indicators' UNEP(DEPI)/MED IG.19/8 Annex II, 29.

Barcelona Convention MoP Decision IG.19/6 (2009), 'MAP/Civil Society Cooperation and Partnership' UNEP(DEPI)/MED IG.19/8 Annex II, 59.

Barcelona Convention MoP Decision IG.20/4 (2012), 'Implementing MAP Ecosystem Approach Roadmap: Mediterranean Ecological and Operational Objectives, Indicators and Timetable for Implementing the Ecosystem Approach Roadmap' UNEP(DEPI)/MED IG.20/8 Annex II, 39.

Barcelona Convention MoP Decision IG.21/3 (2013), 'Decision IG.21/3 on the Ecosystems Approach Including Adopting Definitions of Good Environmental Status (GES) and Targets' UNEP(DEPI)/MED IG.21/9 Annex II, 33.

Barcelona Convention MoP Decision IG.22/7 (2016), 'Integrated Monitoring and Assessment Programme of the Mediterranean Sea and Coast and Related Assessment Criteria' UNEP(DEPI)/MED IG.22/28, 419.

Barcelona Convention MoP Decision IG.22/10 (2016), 'Implementing the Marine Litter Regional Plan in the Mediterranean (Fishing for Litter Guidelines, Assessment Report, Baselines Values, and Reduction Targets)' UNEP(DEPI)/MED IG.22/28, 523.

Barcelona Convention MoP Decision IG.22/15 (2016), 'Compliance Mechanisms and Procedures, Membership and Working Programme of the Compliance Committee for the Biennium 2016–2017' UNEP(DEPI)/MED IG.22/28, 629.

Barcelona Convention MoP Decision IG.24/10 (2019), 'Main Elements of the Six Regional Plans to Reduce/Prevent Marine Pollution from Land- Based Sources; Updating the Annexes to the LBS and Dumping Protocols of the Barcelona Convention' UNEP/MED IG.24/22, 492.

Barcelona Convention MoP Decision IG.24/14 (2019), 'Programme of Work and Budget 2020–2021' UNEP/MED IG.24/22, 696.

Barcelona Convention 'Report of the 9th Ordinary Meeting of the Contracting Parties' (1995) UNEP(OCA)/MED IG.5/16.

Barcelona Convention 'Report of the 15th Ordinary Meeting of the Contracting Parties' (2008) UNEP(DEPI)/MED IG.17/10.

Barcelona Convention 'Report of the 16th Ordinary Meeting of the Contracting Parties' (2009) UNEP(DEPI)/MED IG.19/8.

Basel Convention COP decision BC 10/2 (2011), 'Strategic Framework for the Implementation of the Basel Convention for 2012–2021'.

Basel Convention COP decision BC 13/11 (2017), 'Technical Assistance' UNEP/CHW.13/11.

Basel Convention COP decision BC 13/14 (2017), 'Partnership on Household Waste' UNEP/CHW.13/14.

Basel Convention COP decision BC 13/17 (2017), 'Work Programme and Operations of the Open-Ended Working Group for the Biennium 2018–2019' UNEP/CHW.13/17.

Basel Convention COP decision BC 14/12 (2019), 'Amendments to Annexes II, VIII and IX to the Basel Convention' UNEP/CHW.14/12.

Basel Convention OEWG decision 11/8, 'Draft Elements as a Basis for a Decision on Marine Plastic Litter' Annex.

Basel Convention 'Report of COP to the Basel Convention on the Work of Its 13th Meeting' (2017) UNEP/CHW.13/28.

CBD COP Decision V/6 (2000), 'Ecosystem Approach' UNEP/CBD/COP/5/23, 103.

CBD COP Decision X/2 (2010), 'The Strategic Plan for Biodiversity 2011–2020 and the Aichi Biodiversity Targets' UNEP/CBD/COP/DEC/X/2.

CBD COP Decision XI/18 (2012), 'Marine and Coastal Biodiversity: Sustainable Fisheries and Addressing Adverse Impacts of Human Activities, Voluntary Guidelines for Environmental Assessment, and Marine Spatial Planning' UNEP/CBD/COP/DEC/XI/18.

CBD COP Decision XIII/10 (2016), 'Addressing Impacts of Marine Debris and Anthropogenic Underwater Noise on Marine and Coastal Biodiversity' CBD/COP/DEC/XIII/10.

CBD COP Decision 14/10 (2018), 'Other Matters Related to Marine and Coastal Biodiversity' CBD/COP/DEC/14/10.

CBD 'Report of the Open-Ended Working Group on the Post-2020 Global Biodiversity Framework on Its Third Meeting (Part I)' (2021) CBD/W2020/3/4.

CMS COP Resolution 10.4 (2011), 'Marine Debris' UNEP/CMS/Resolution 10.4.

CMS COP Resolution 11.30 (2014), 'Management of Marine Debris' UNEP/CMS/Resolution 11.30.

CMS COP Resolution 12.20 (2017), 'Management of Marine Debris' UNEP/CMS/Resolution 12.20.

CMS COP Decisions 13.122 to 13.125 (2020), 'Impacts of Plastic Pollution on Aquatic, Terrestrial and Avian Species'.

COP to the Basel and Stockhom conventions, 'Report on the Activities of the Basel and Stockholm Conventions Regional Centres (Joint Document)' (2017) UNEP/CHW.13/INF/29/Rev.1 and UNEP/POPS/COP8/INF26/Rev.1.

CSD, 'Report of the Expert Group Meeting on Identification of Principles of International Law for Sustainable Development' (1996) Prepared by the Division for Sustainable Development for the CSD 4th session.

CSD, Decision 7/1, 'Ocean and Sea' (1999) E/1999/25.

GATT, 'Report of the Working Party on Border Tax Adjustments (Adopted on 2 December 1970)' (1972) BISD 18th Supp. 97.

GESAMP, 'Report of the First Session' (1969) UN Doc GESAMP I/11.

IMO, 'Report of the 13th Consultative Meeting of the Contracting Parties to the 1972 London Dumping Convention' (1990) UN Doc IMO/LDC.13/15.

IMO, Marine Environment Protection Committee Resolution MEPC.310(73), 'Action Plan to Address Marine Plastic Litter from Ships' (2018) MEPC 73/19/Add.1 Annex 10.

IWC, 'Report of the Workshop on Welfare Issues Associated with the Entanglement of Large Whales' (2010) IWC/62/15.

IWC, 'Report of Second IWC Workshop on Welfare Issues Associated with the Entanglement of Large Whales With a Focus on Entanglement Response' (2011) IWC/64/WKM & AWI REP1.

IWC, 'Report of the 2013 IWC Scientific Committee Workshop on Marine Debris' (2013) SC/65a/Rep06.

IWC, 'Report of the IWC Workshop on Mitigation and Management of the Threats Posed by Marine Debris to Cetaceans' (2014) IWC/65/CCRep04.

IWC, 'Report of the Third Workshop on Large Whale Entanglement Issues, Provincetown, MA, USA, 21–23 April 2015' (2015) IWC/66/WK-I-Rep01.

IWC, Res 2018-3, 'Resolution on Ghost Gear Entanglement Among Cetaceans'.

IWC, 'Report of IWC Workshop on Marine Debris: The Way Forward' (2019) SC/68B/REP/03.

UN Doc A/CONF.62/C.3/SR.19, '19th Meeting of the Third Committee' in United Nations (ed), *Official Records of the Third United Nations Conference on the Law of the Sea*, vol IV (2009).

UN Doc A/CONF.62/C.3/SR.33, '33rd Meeting of the Third Committee' in United Nations (ed), *Official Records of the Third United Nations Conference on the Law of the Sea*, vol VI (2009).

UNCC, 'Report and Recommendations Made by the Panel of Commissioners Concerning the Fifth Instalment of "F4" Claims' (2005) S/AC.26/2005/10.

UNCLOS, 'Report of the 25th Meeting of States Parties' (2015) SPLOS/287.

UNCLOS, 'Report of the 26th Meeting of States Parties' (2016) SPLOS/303.

UNCLOS, 'Report of the 27th Meeting of States Parties' (2017) SPLOS/316.

UNCLOS, 'Report of the 28th Meeting of States Parties' (2018) SPLOS/324.

UNEA Resolution 1/6 (2014), 'Marine Plastic Debris and Microplastics' UNEP/EA.1/Res.6.

UNEA Resolution 2/11 (2016), 'Marine Plastic Litter and Microplastics' UNEP/EA.2/Res.11.

UNEA Resolution 3/7 (2017), 'Marine Litter and Microplastics' UNEP/EA.3/Res.7.

UNEA Resolution 4/6 (2019), 'Marine Plastic Litter and Microplastics' UNEP/EA.4/L.7.

UNEA Resolution 4/9 (2019), 'Addressing Single-Use Plastic Products Pollution' UNEP/EA.4/L.10.

UNEP, 'Development of an International Legally Binding Instrument for the Application of the Prior Informed Consent Procedure for Certain Hazardous Chemicals in International Trade, and Consideration of Further Measures to Reduce the Risks from Hazardous Chemicals' (1995) UNEP/GC.18/12.

UNEP, 'Persistent Organic Pollutants' (1995) UNEP/GC.18/32.

UNEP, 'Implementation of the Global Programme of Action for the Protection of the Marine Environment from Land-Based Activities' (1997) UNEP/GC.19/14A.

UNEP, 'Report of the First Intergovernmental Review Meeting on the Implementation of the Global Programme of Action for the Protection of the Marine Environment from Land-Based Activities' (2001) UNEP/GPA/IGR.1/9.

UNEP, 'Report of the Second Session of the Intergovernmental Review Meeting on the Implementation of the Global Programme of Action for the Protection of the Marine Environment from Land-Based Activities' (2006) UNEP/GPA/IGR.2/7.

UNEP, 'Resolution 1/6: Marine Plastic Debris and Microplastics – Report of the Executive Director' (2016) UNEP/EA.2/5.

UNEP, 'Report of the First Meeting of the Ad Hoc Open-Ended Expert Group on Marine Litter and Microplastics' (2018) UNEP/AHEG/2018/1/6.

UNEP, 'Consolidated Background Paper of the Discussion Papers Presented at the First Meeting of the Ad Hoc Open-Ended Expert Group on Marine Litter and Microplastics, Held in Nairobi from 29 to 31 May 2018' (2018) UNEP/AHEG/2018/2/2.

UNEP, 'Progress in the Work of the Ad Hoc Open-Ended Expert Group on Marine Litter and Microplastics Established by Resolution 3/7 – Report of the Executive Director' (2018) UNEP/EA.4/12.

UNEP, 'Draft Report of the Third Meeting of the Ad Hoc Open-Ended Expert Group on Marine Litter and Microplastics' (2019) UNEP/AHEG/2019/3/L.1.

UNGA annual Res 'Oceans and the Law of the Sea' (Res 57/141 [2002], Res 59/24 [2004], Res 60/30 [2005], Res 63/111 [2008]; Res 64/71 [2009]; Res 65/37 [2010]; Res 66/

231 [2011], Res 67/78 [2012], Res 68/70 [2013], Res 69/245 [2014], Res 70/235 [2015], Res 71/257 [2016], Res 72/73 [2017], Res 73/124 [2018], Res 74/19 [2019], Res 75/239 [2021]).

UNGA annual Res 'Report of the Secretary-General: Oceans and the Law of the Sea' (2004) UN Doc A/59/62/Add.1.

UNGA annual Res 'Report on the Work of the United Nations Open-Ended Informal Consultative Process on Oceans and the Law of the Sea at Its Sixth Meeting' (2005) UN Doc A/60/99.

UNGA annual Res 'Report on the Work of the United Nations Open-Ended Informal Consultative Process on Oceans and the Law of the Sea at Its Seventeenth Meeting' (2016).

UNGA Res 2574 (XXIV) (1969), 'Question of the Reservation Exclusively for Peaceful Purposes of the Sea-Bed and the Ocean Floor, and the Subsoil Thereof, Underlying the High Seas beyond the Limits of Present National Jurisdiction, and the Use of Their Resources in the Interests of Mankind'.

UNGA Res 2749 (XXV) (1970), 'Declaration of Principles Governing the Sea-Bed and the Ocean Floor, and the Subsoil Thereof, beyond the Limits of National Jurisdiction'.

UNGA Res 2750 C (XXV) (1970).

UNGA Res 2994 (XXVII) (1972), 'United Nations Conference on the Human Environment'.

UNGA Res 2995 (XXVII) (1972), 'Co-Operation between States in the Field of the Environment'.

UNGA Res 3281 (XXIX) (1974), 'Charter of Economic Rights and Duties of States'.

UNGA Res 38/161 (1983), 'Process of Preparation of the Environmental Perspective to the Year 2000 and Beyond'.

UNGA Res 42/187 (1987), 'Report of the World Commission on Environment and Development'.

UNGA Res 44/228 (1989), 'United Nations Conference on Environment and Development'.

UNGA Res 51/189 (1996), 'Institutional Arrangements for the Implementation of the Global Programme of Action for the Protection of the Marine Environment from Land-Based Activities'.

UNGA Res. 66/288 (2012), annex, 'The Future We Want'.

UNGA Res 69/292 (2015), 'Development of an International Legally Binding Instrument under the United Nations Convention on the Law of the Sea on the Conservation and Sustainable Use of Marine Biological Diversity of Areas beyond National Jurisdiction'.

UNGA Res 70/1 (2015), 'Transforming Our World: The 2030 Agenda for Sustainable Development'.

UNGA Res 72/249 (2017), 'International Legally Binding Instrument under the United Nations Convention on the Law of the Sea on the Conservation and Sustainable Use of Marine Biological Diversity of Areas beyond National Jurisdiction'.

UNGA Res 74/4 (2019), 'Political Declaration of the High-Level Political Forum on Sustainable Development Convened under the Auspices of the General Assembly'.

UNGA 'Twenty-Second Session Official Records: First Committee, 1515th Meeting' (1967) UN Doc A/C.1/PV.1515.

UNGA 'Twenty-Second Session Official Records: First Committee, 1516th Meeting' (1967) UN Doc A/C.1/PV.1516 (1967).

United Nations, 'Report of the Intergovernmental Working Group on Marine Pollution on Its Second Session' (1971) UN doc A/CONF.48/IWGMP.II/5.

United Nations, 'Report of the United Nations Conference on the Human Environment' (1972) UN Doc A/CONF.48/14/Rev. 1 (1972).

United Nations, 'Report of the Secretary-General of the Conference on the Protection of the Oceans, All Kinds of Seas Including Enclosed and Semi-Enclosed Seas, Coastal Areas and the Protection Rational Use and Development of Their Living Resources' (1991) UN Doc A/CONF.151/PC/30 and Corr. 1.

UNSC (1991) S/RES/687.

WTO, 'Ministerial Decision on Trade and Environment' (1994).

WTO, Notification G/TBT/N/CHN/1211 of 18 July 2017.

WTO, Notification G/TBT/N/CHN/1228 of 15 November 2017.

WTO Committee on Trade and Environment, 'Communication on Trade in Plastics, Sustainability and Development by the United Nations Conference on Trade and Development (UNCTAD)' (2020) JOB/TE/63.

European Union Decisions and Law

Council Directive 78/142/EEC of 30 January 1978 on the approximation of the laws of the Member States relating to materials and articles which contain vinyl chloride monomer and are intended to come into contact with foodstuffs [1978] OJ L44/15.

Council Directive 19/271/EEC of 21 May 1991 concerning urban waste water treatment [1991] OJ L135/40.

Council Directive 92/43/EEC of 21 May 1992 on the conservation of natural habitats and of wild fauna and flora (Habitats Directive) [1992] OJ L206/7.

Council Directive 1999/31/EC of 26 April 1999 on the landfill of waste (Landfill Directive) [1999] OJ L182/1.

European Commission Decision 2014/893/EU of 9 December 2014 establishing the ecological criteria for the award of the EU Ecolabel for rinse-off cosmetic products [2014] OJ L354/47.

European Commission Delegated Regulation (EU) 2020/2174 of 19 October 2020 amending Annexes IC, III, IIIA, IV, V, VII and VIII to Regulation (EC) No 1013/2006 of the European Parliament and of the Council on shipments of waste [2020] OJ L433/11.

European Commission Proposal for a Council Directive on the Landfill of Waste 1997 [COM (97) 105 final [1997] OJ C156/10].

European Parliament and Council Decision No 1386/2013/EU of 20 November 2013 on a General Union Environment Action Programme to 2020 'Living well, within the limits of our planet' (7th EAP) [2013] OJ L354/171.

European Parliament and Council Directive 94/62/EC of 20 December 1994 on packaging and packaging waste (Packaging and Packaging Waste Directive) [1994] OJ L365/10.

European Parliament and Council Directive 2000/60/EC of 23 October 2000 establishing a framework for Community action in the field of water policy (Water Framework Directive) [2000] OJ L327/1.

European Parliament and Council Directive 2008/56/EC of 17 June 2008 establishing a framework for community action in the field of marine environmental policy (Marine Strategy Framework Directive) [2008] OJ L164/19.

European Parliament and Council Directive 2008/98/EC of 19 November 2008 on Waste and Repealing Certain Directives (Waste Framework Directive) [2008] OJ L312/3.

European Parliament and Council Directive 2008/105/EC of 16 December 2008 on environmental quality standards in the field of water policy [2008] OJ L348/84.

European Parliament and Council Directive 2015/720 of 29 April 2015 amending Directive 94/62/EC as regards reducing the consumption of lightweight plastic carrier bags [2015] OJ L115/11.

European Parliament and Council Directive 2018/850 of 30 May 2018 amending Directive 1999/31/EC on the landfill of waste [2018] OJ L150/100.

European Parliament and Council Directive 2018/851 of 30 May 2018 amending Directive 2008/98/EC on waste [2018] OJ L150/109.

European Parliament and Council Directive 2018/852 of 30 May 2018 amending Directive 94/62/EC on packaging and packaging waste [2018] OJ L150/141.

European Parliament and Council Directive 2019/904 of 5 June 2019 on the reduction of the impact of certain plastic products on the environment [2019] OJ L155/1.

European Parliament and Council Regulation (EC) No 1907/2006 of 18 December 2006 concerning the Registration, Evaluation, Authorisation and Restriction of Chemicals (REACH) [2006] OJ L396/1.

European Parliament, 'Resolution of 14 January 2014 on a European Strategy on Plastic Waste in the Environment' 2013/2113(INI).

Table of Soft Law

Agenda 21, *Report of the United Nations Conference on Environment and Development, Rio de Janeiro, 3–14 June 1992, Vol I, Resolutions Adopted by the Conference* (United Nations publication, Sales No E93I8 and corrigendum).

'Beijing Declaration on Furthering the Implementation of the Global Programme of Action for the Protection of the Marine Environment from Land-Based Activities' (2006).

Declaration of the United Nations Conference on the Human Environment (1972 Stockholm Declaration) in Report of the Stockholm Conference, UN Doc. A/CONF.48/14/Rev. 1 (1972) 3, reprinted in 11 ILM 1416 (1972).

Global Ministerial Environment Forum, 'Malmö Ministerial Declaration' (Sixth Special Session of the UNEP Governing Council 2000) UNEP/GC/DEC/SS.VI/1.

'Honolulu Commitment' (2011) <https://5imdc.files.wordpress.com/2011/03/honolulu commitment.pdf> accessed 19 February 2022.

'ILA New Delhi Declaration of Principles of International Law Relating to Sustainable Development' 2 International Environmental Agreements 209.

Johannesburg Plan of Implementation in Report of the World Summit on Sustainable Development (2002), UN Doc A/CONF.199/20.

'Manila Declaration on Furthering the Implementation of the Global Programme of Action for the Protection of the Marine Environment from Land-Based Activities' (2012) UNEP/GCSS.XII/INF/10, Annex.

'Montreal Declaration on the Protection of the Marine Environment from Land-Based Activities' (2001).

Non-Legally Binding Authoritative Statement of Principles for a Global Consensus on the Management, Conservation and Sustainable Development of All Types of Forests (Forest Principles) (adopted on 14 June 1992) UN Doc A/CONF.151/26 (Vol. III).

Nordic Cooperation, 'Nordic Ministerial Declaration on the Call for a Global Agreement to Combat Marine Plastic Litter and Microplastics' (*Nordic cooperation*, 10 April 2019) <https://www.norden.org/en/declaration/nordic-ministerial-declaration-call-global-agreement-combat-marine-plastic-litter-and> accessed 19 February 2022.

Rio Declaration on Environment and Development (1992 Rio Declaration) in Report of the United Nations Conference on Environment and Development (1992), UN Doc A/CONF.151/26 (Vol. I).

UN Conference on Sustainable Development, 'A 10-Year Framework of Programmes on Sustainable Consumption and Production Patterns' (2012) A/CONF.216/5.

UNEP, 'Montevideo Programme for the Development and Periodic Review of Environmental Law (1981)' (UNEP Governing Council Decision 10/21 of 31 May 1982).

UNEP, 'Montreal Guidelines for the Protection of the Marine Environment Against Pollution from Land-Based Sources' (Decision 13/18/II of the Governing Council of UNEP, of 24 May 1985).

UNEP, 'Global Programme of Action for the Protection of the Marine Environment from Land-Based Activities' (1995) UN Doc UNEP(OCA)/LBA/IG.2/7.

UNEP, 'Washington Declaration on Protection of the Marine Environment from Land-Based Activities' (UNEP 1995).

Table of National and State Law

Bangladesh Environment Conservation Act of 1995, as amended 2002.

California Water Code (2007) § 13367(b)(1).

China, Notice of the Chinese General Office of State Council on Restricting the Production, Sale and Use of Plastic Shopping Bags (SC GO G [2008] No.72).

France, Décret N° 2016-1170 Du 30 Août 2016 Relatif Aux Modalités de Mise En Œuvre de La Limitation Des Gobelets, Verres et Assiettes Jetables En Matière Plastique.

Kenya, Environment Management Coordination Act (EMCA) of 1999, as amended 2015.

Kenya, Gazette Notice No. 2334, Issued on March 14, 2007 under the Authority of Sections 3 and 86 of the Environmental Management and Coordination Act cap 387 on Plastic Bags 2017.

Rwanda, Law N°57/2008 of 10 September 2008, Law Relating to the Prohibition of Manufacturing, Importation, Use and Sale of Polythene Bags in Rwanda.

South Africa, Government Notice (GN) R625/2003.

UK, Environmental Protection Act 1990.

UK, The Packaging (Essential Requirements) Regulations 2015 (Statutory Instruments).

US, Microbead-Free Waters Act of 2015, 21 U.S.C. 331 (2015).

US, Save Our Seas Act of 2018, S.3508, 115th Cong.

US, Save Our Seas 2.0 Act of 2020, S.1982, 116th Cong.

Websites

Barcelona Convention, 'Status of Signatures and Ratifications' <http://web.unep.org/unepmap/who-we-are/legal-framework/status-signatures-and-ratifications> accessed 19 February 2022.

Basel Convention, 'Plastic Waste Partnership: Overview' (2019) <http://www.basel.int/Implementation/Plasticwastes/PlasticWastePartnership/tabid/8096/Default.aspx> accessed 19 February 2022.

BIR, 'BIR – Bureau of International Recycling: Plastics' <https://archive.bir.org/industry/plastics> accessed 19 February 2022.

Center for Oceans Law and Policy, University of Virginia, 'PART XII – Protection and Preservation of the Marine Environment (IV)', *United Nations Convention on the Law of the Sea* (Brill Online 2016) <http://referenceworks.brillonline.com/entries/united-nations-convention-on-the-law-of-the-sea/part-xii-LAOS_Part12> accessed 19 February 2022.

European Environment Agency, 'Total Waste Generation by Sector, 2004' (2009) <http://www.eea.europa.eu/data-and-maps/figures/total-waste-generation-by-sector-2004> accessed 19 February 2022.

Eurostat, 'Archive: Waste Statistics' (*Statistics Explained*, 2011) <http://ec.europa.eu/eurostat/statistics-explained/index.php/Archive:Waste_statistics> accessed 19 February 2022.

'Fifth Our Ocean Conference 2018' <https://ourocean2018.org/?l=our-ocean-commitments> accessed 19 February 2022.

Food Packaging Forum, 'UV-328 Qualifies for Screening as POP' (22 January 2021) <https://www.foodpackagingforum.org/news/uv-328-qualifies-for-screening-as-pop> accessed 19 February 2022.

G7, 'G-7 Action Plan to Combat Marine Litter' (White House Press Release 2015) Annex to the G-7 Leaders' Declaration <https://www.whitehouse.gov/the-press-office/2015/06/08/annex-g-7-leaders-declaration> accessed 19 February 2022.

G7, 'Ocean Plastics Charter' (2018) <https://www.consilium.europa.eu/media/40516/charlevoix_oceans_plastic_charter_en.pdf> accessed 19 February 2022.

G20, 'Annex to G20 Leaders Declaration: G20 Action Plan on Marine Litter' (2017) <https://www.g20germany.de/Content/DE/_Anlagen/G7_G20/2017-g20-marine-litter-en___blob=publicationFile&v=4.pdf> accessed 19 February 2022.

G20, 'G20 Implementation Framework for Actions on Marine Plastic Litter' <https://www.g20karuizawa.go.jp/assets/pdf/G20%20Implementation%20Framework%20for%20Actions%20on%20Marine%20Plastic%20Litter.pdf> accessed 19 February 2022.

GPML Secretariat, 'GPML Framework Document' <https://marinelitternetwork.engr.uga.edu/wp-content/uploads/2018/03/gpml_framework_document.pdf> accessed 19 February 2022.

GRID-Arendal, 'The Trade in Plastic Waste' (April 2017) <https://grid-arendal.maps.arcgis.com/apps/Cascade/index.html?appid=002738ffb18548818a61cc88161ac464> accessed 19 February 2022.

IISD's SDG Knowledge Hub, 'Our Ocean Conference Participants Pledge USD 64 Billion to Protect Oceans' (29 October 2019) <http://sdg.iisd.org/news/our-ocean-conference-participants-pledge-usd-64-billion-to-protect-oceans/> accessed 19 February 2022.

IWC, 'Understanding the Threat to Cetaceans from Microplastics and PAHs – Pollution 2020' <https://iwc.int/understanding-the-threat-to-cetaceans-from-micropl> accessed 19 February 2022.

Lester S, 'Legitimate Regulation or Disguised Protectionism: Plastic Bag Bans' (*International Economic Law and Policy Blog*, April 2016) <http://worldtradelaw.typepad.com/ielpblog/2016/04/legitimate-regulation-or-hidden-protectionism-plastic-bag-bans.html> accessed 19 February 2022.

'Memorandum of Understanding between the Secretariat of the OSPAR Convention and the Secretariat of the Abidjan Convention' <http://www.ospar.org/about/international-cooperation/memoranda-of-understanding> accessed 19 February 2022.

Merriam-Webster Online Encyclopaedia, 'Resin' (2019) <http://www.merriam-webster.com/dictionary/resin> accessed 19 February 2022.

Miles T, 'U.S. Blocks WTO Judge Reappointment as Dispute Settlement Crisis Looms' *Reuters* (27 August 2018) <https://www.reuters.com/article/us-usa-trade-wto-idUSKCN1LC19O> accessed 19 February 2022.

Mosbergen D, 'How America Is Sabotaging The Global War On Plastic Waste' (*HuffPost*, 54:41 400AD) <https://www.huffpost.com/entry/plastic-regulation-us-obstruction-basel-convention_n_5cde76f0e4b00e035b8da236> accessed 19 February 2022.

OECD, 'Generation of Primary Waste by Sector' (2018) <https://stats.oecd.org/Index.aspx?DataSetCode=WSECTOR> accessed 19 February 2022.

OECD, 'Municipal Waste (Indicator)' (2022) <https://data.oecd.org/waste/municipal-waste.htm> accessed 19 February 2022.

PRO Europe, 'About Packaging Recovery Organisation Europe' <http://www.pro-e.org/about-us/who-we-are> accessed 19 February 2022.

'Regular Process' <https://www.un.org/regularprocess/> accessed 19 February 2022.

'Remarks by President Trump at Signing of S. 3508, the "Save Our Seas Act of 2018"' (*The White House*) <https://trumpwhitehouse.archives.gov/briefings-statements/remarks-president-trump-signing-s-3508-save-seas-act-2018/> accessed 19 February 2022.

UNEP, 'SAICM: Overview' (*International Chemicals Management*) <http://www.saicm.org/About/SAICMOverview/tabid/5522/language/en-US/Default.aspx> accessed 19 February 2022.

United Nations, 'United Nations Convention on the Law of the Sea' (UN Treaty Collection, 2021) <https://treaties.un.org/Pages/ViewDetailsIII.aspx?src=TREATY&mtdsg_no=XXI-6&chapter=21&Temp=mtdsg3&clang=_en#1> accessed 19 February 2022.

University of Rhode Island, 'Subseafloor Sediment In South Pacific Gyre One Of Least Inhabited Places On Earth' (*ScienceDaily*, 1 July 2009) <http://www.sciencedaily.com/releases/2009/06/090622171408.htm> accessed 19 February 2022.

'U.S. Trade Representative Lighthizer Testifies Before the Senate Finance Committee on the Administration's Trade Strategy and the United States-Mexico-Canada Ageement' (18 June 2019) <http://archive.org/details/CSPAN_20190618_141600_U.S._Trade_Representative_Lighthizer_Testifies_Before_Senate_Finance> accessed 19 February 2022.

'Waste Atlas – Interactive Map with Visualized Waste Management Data' <http://www.atlas.d-waste.com> accessed 19 February 2022.

World Bank, 'World Bank Country and Lending Groups – Data' (2021) <https://datahelpdesk.worldbank.org/knowledgebase/articles/906519-world-bank-country-and-lending-groups> accessed 10 October 2021.

World Economic Forum, 'The New Plastics Economy: Rethinking the Future of Plastics' (2016) <http://www3.weforum.org/docs/WEF_The_New_Plastics_Economy.pdf> accessed 19 February 2022.

WTO, 'Plastics Pollution Dialogue Advances Discussions, Eyeing MC12 Outcome' (*Informal Dialogue on Plastics Pollution and Environmentally Sustainable Plastics Trade*, 21 June 2021) <https://www.wto.org/english/news_e/news21_e/ega_21jun21_e.htm> accessed 19 February 2022.

Index

www.ingramcontent.com/pod-product-compliance
Lightning Source LLC
LaVergne TN
LVHW010638300926
849161LV00005B/974
9789004508606